T0325201

Statistical Techniques for Network Security:
Modern Statistically-Based Intrusion Detection and Protection

Yun Wang
Center for Outcomes Research and Evaluation, Yale University and Yale New Haven Health, USA

INFORMATION SCIENCE REFERENCE

Hershey · New York

Director of Editorial Content:	Kristin Klinger
Director of Production:	Jennifer Neidig
Managing Editor:	Jamie Snavely
Assistant Managing Editor:	Carole Coulson
Typesetter:	Carole Coulson
Cover Design:	Lisa Tosheff
Printed at:	Yurchak Printing Inc.

Published in the United States of America by
Information Science Reference (an imprint of IGI Global)
701 E. Chocolate Avenue, Suite 200
Hershey PA 17033
Tel: 717-533-8845
Fax: 717-533-8661
E-mail: cust@igi-global.com
Web site: http://www.igi-global.com/reference

and in the United Kingdom by
Information Science Reference (an imprint of IGI Global)
3 Henrietta Street
Covent Garden
London WC2E 8LU
Tel: 44 20 7240 0856
Fax: 44 20 7379 0609
Web site: http://www.eurospanbookstore.com

Library of Congress Cataloging-in-Publication Data

Wang, Yun.
  Statistical techniques for network security : modern statistically-based intrusion detection and protection / by Yun Wang.
    p. cm.
  Includes bibliographical references and index.
  Summary: "This book aims to provide a guide for applying modern statistical techniques for intrusion detection and prevention, and serve as a reference for individuals such as network administrators, information and network security specialists, IT professionals, IT-related risk analysis and management professionals, and students and researchers who are interested in the use of statistical techniques for network security"--Provided by publisher.
  ISBN 978-1-59904-708-9 (hbk.) -- ISBN 978-1-59904-710-2 (ebook)
  1. Computer networks--Security measures 2. Computer security. I. Title.
  TK5105.59.W36 2008
  005.8--dc22
                    2008023192

British Cataloguing in Publication Data
A Cataloguing in Publication record for this book is available from the British Library.

All work contributed to this book is original material. The views expressed in this publication are those of the authors, but not necessarily of the publisher.

To My Parents and My Family

Table of Contents

Preface viii

Acknowledgment xi

Section I:
Foundations

Chapter I
Statistical Opportunities, Roles, and Challenges in Network Security 1
Introduction 1
Overview 2
Statistical Approaches in Practice 14
Fundamental Statistical Roles and Challenges in Network Security 22
Summary 27
References 27
Endnotes 34

Chapter II
Statistical Analysis Software 35
Introduction 35
The SAS System 37
STATA 45
R 48
Other Packages 54
Summary 58
References 59
Endnotes 59

Chapter III
Network Traffic and Data...**60**
Introduction...60
System-Specific Traffic...60
User-Specific Data..65
Publicly Available Data..70
Summary...91
References...92
Endnotes...94
Appendix...95

Chapter IV
Network Data Characteristics...**104**
Introduction...104
Random Variables...105
Variable Distributions..109
Network Data Modules..116
Summary...121
References...121

Section II:
Data Mining and Modeling

Chapter V
Exploring Network Data..**124**
Introduction...124
Descriptive Analysis...125
Visualizing Analysis...134
Data Transformation...144
Summary...155
References...156
Appendix...157

Chapter VI
Data Reduction...**172**
Introduction...172
Data Structure Detection..173
Sampling Network Traffic...188
Sample Size...199
Summary...206
References...206
Appendix...210

Chapter VII

Models Network Data for Association and Prediction **220**

Introduction..220

Bivariate Analysis 221

Linear Regression Modeling...232

Robustness Association...249

Summary 257

References..257

Appendix 260

Chapter VIII

Measuring User Behavior..**261**

Introduction..261

User Behavior Pattern...262

Scoring Methods 276

Profiling Models..286

Summary 297

References..297

Appendix 301

Section III:
Classifications, Profiles, and Making Better Decisions

Chapter IX

Classification Based on Supervised Learning.. **305**

Introduction..305

Generalized Linear Methods 306

Nonparametric Methods 316

Other Linear and Nonlinear Methods..333

Summary 342

References..343

Endnote 347

Chapter X

Classification Based on Unsupervised Learning **348**

Introduction..348

Probability Models..349

Similarity Models..365

Multidimensional Models...379

Summary 390

References 392

Appendix 395

Chapter XI

Decision Analysis in Network Security **396**

Introduction 396

Analysis of Uncertainty 398

Statistical Control Chart 411

Ranking 415

Summary 422

References 423

Appendix 425

Chapter XII

Evaluation **427**

Introduction 427

Data Reliability, Validity, and Quality 428

Goodness of Classification 435

Assess Model Performance 447

Summary 455

References 456

About the Author **458**

Index **459**

Preface

This book describes modern statistical techniques for intrusion detection and prevention from an applied perspective. The use of statistical techniques in network security has attracted a lot of attention by researchers and professionals from the information system, computer science, and statistics fields over the last three decades. The idea behind intrusion detection and prevention seems simple: use legitimate user behavior patterns to identify anomalous user behavior patterns. Unfortunately, intrusion detection and prevention are difficult tasks to implement, and each has its own set of unique challenges. This discipline is still in development and there are many complicated topics that future research still needs to address. Any IP addresses mentioned or used in the book are synthetic and they do not reflect IP addresses in the real world

This book aims to provide a guide for applying modern statistical techniques for intrusion detection and prevention, and serve as a reference for individuals such as network administrators, information and network security specialists, IT professionals, IT-related risk analysis and management professionals, and students and researchers who are interested in the use of statistical techniques for network security. Since the topics coved in this book are interdisciplinary (network security, risk management, and statistics), how to present materials from these different fields effectively and efficiently has proven to be a great challenge. As a result, this book attempts to focus on the application perspective with minimal statistical theoretical statements. Each section generally begins with a limited number of necessary statistical concepts that are related to the topic being presented, and is then followed by examples to help readers better understand specific topics. References are provided at the end of each chapter to help readers gain a more detailed and topic-specific understanding of the materials. There are over 80 examples in this book, nearly all of which are accompanied by corresponding programming codes. These examples can benefit readers by motivating and enhancing the understanding of the discussed concepts and topics. Although there is no prerequisite for readers to have taken an elementary statistics course before using this book, familiarity with basic statistical concepts and statistical analytic tools will be helpful in better utilizing the materials introduced in this book.

The book contains 12 chapters and appendices. The chapters are divided into three sections: Foundations (Chapter I through Chapter IV), Data Mining and Modeling (Chapter V through Chapter VIII), and Classifications, Profiles, and Making Better Decisions (Chapter IX through Chapter XII). Topics are introduced hierarchically. Chapter I starts with an introduction to the history of network security in intrusion detection and prevention, is followed by an overview of the statistical approaches in practice, and ends with discussions of fundamental statistical roles and challenges in the network security field. Chapter II provides a quick review of statistical analytic packages, mainly focusing on SAS, Stata, and R, but also discussing S-Plus, WinBugs, and MATLAB. Essential features and attributes of each of these software applications are reviewed and discussed with examples. Chapter III covers network traffic and data (both system-specific data and user-specific data). This chapter also introduces some popular and publicly available datasets: (1) the Defense Advanced Research Projects Agency (DARPA) Intrusion Detection Evaluation Offline Data developed by the Lincoln Laboratory at the Massachusetts Institute of Technology (MIT), (2) the Third International Knowledge Discovery and Data Mining Tools Competition's (KDD-Cup) 1999 data that was created based on the MIT-DARPA data, (3) the spam-email data created by Mark Hopkins, Erik Reeber, George Forman, and Jaap Suermondt at the Hewlett-Packard Labs, (4) the web visit sequence data donated by Jack S. Breese, David Heckerman, and Carl M. Kadie at Microsoft Research, and (5) the masquerading user data created by Matt Schonlau from RAND. All of these datasets were available to be downloaded off the web for free during the time this book was written. The programming codes used to process these datasets are also included (except for the masquerading user data).

Despite the fact that the MIT-DARPA data has contributed tremendously to research progress in the field of intrusion detection during the past decade, it has been criticized and considered by many researchers. More specifically, critiques focus on the data being outdated and unable to accommodate the latest trend in attacks. However, this data is still the largest publicly available data for researchers today, and is still the most widely used public benchmark for testing intrusion detection systems. One of the important values of this data is to be a proxy for developing, testing and evaluating detecting algorithms, rather than to be a solid data source for a real time system. If a detection and prevention system has a high performance based on the MIT-DARPA data, this system is more likely to have a good performance in real time data, which is why the MIT-DARPA data was chosen, used and adapted within many examples in this book.

Chapter IV examines the characteristics of network traffic and data. Limited and essential concepts, including variables, distributions and data types, are reviewed to provide readers with a statistical background. Chapter V reviews the methods for exploring network data. It covers both descriptive and visualizing analyses, which aim to detect data structures and data attributes. Approaches for normalized, centralized and standardized data are also provided in this chapter. Materials introduced in this chapter are important for gaining necessary techniques and tools to understand the unique characteristics of network traffic data. Chapter VI covers the topic of data reduction. Factor analysis and statistical sampling approaches are introduced for eliminating unnecessary and redundant variables and reducing the size of network traffic data.

Chapters VII and VIII cover the topics of modeling network traffic for association and prediction and measuring and profiling user behavior. Chapter VII introduces various approaches to modeling for association and prediction, including bivariate analysis, linear regression, and the time-to-event modeling, which is important when tracking site or system behavior patterns change over time. Chapter VII also examines several approaches for selecting robust predictors, such as bootstrapping simulation and stepwise procedures. Chapter VIII reviews the characteristics and attributes of user behavior patterns and presents score modeling approaches to measure user and system behavior. Chapter VIII also introduces the methods for profiling user behavior, including use of the item response modeling and hierarchical generalized linear modeling techniques for the network security area.

Classification is the key task in network security. Profiling user or system behavior is only meaningful when a robust classifier exists. In general, classification in network security aims to achieve three goals: (1) determine what the classes or categories of the entire network traffic should be (e.g., normal connections, attacks, anomaly connections), (2) develop an algorithm to classify data into these classes, and (3) validate this algorithm. Chapters IX through XII are designed to address these three goals. Chapters IX and X focus more specifically on the first and second goals, and cover various modern supervised and unsupervised statistical learning topics with examples and programming codes for most of the topics discussed. Chapter IX examines both parametric- and nonparametric-based classification techniques, including logistic, Poisson, probit regressions, linear discriminant analysis, k-nearest neighbor, Naïve Bayesian approach, regression trees, and support vector machines. Chapter X discusses unsupervised learning techniques for network traffic classification. Topics cover probability models, measure of similarity, and multidimensional analyses. Various techniques, such as latent class model, hidden Markov model, k-means clustering, principal component analysis, multidimensional scaling, and self-organizing maps are discussed.

Finally, Chapters XI and XII provide discussions on decision analysis and evaluation of classification results. Statistical simulation techniques, along with the interval estimates, are introduced to address uncertainty in network security at the beginning of Chapter XI. Statistical control charts and ranking methods are discussed to support the ability to make better network security-related decisions. Chapter XII covers various methods and techniques used to assess the reliability, validity and quality in network traffic data, as well as the procedures used for evaluate the goodness of classification and model performance. Covered topics include sensitivity, specificity, receiver operating characteristic curve, misclassification, goodness-of-fit, predictive ability, and residual analysis. The appendices include supplementary materials, such as large tables, long programming codes, programming macros, and analysis results that are useful, but not necessary to present in formal chapters or sections of this book.

Acknowledgment

This book has benefited greatly from the assistance of many people. First, I would like to express my sincere appreciation to Dr. Harlan Krumholz (Yale University) for the help, understanding, interest, advice, and support that he has given me during the 15 years that I have been working with him. Without him, this project would not have been possible. I am extremely grateful to Dr. Sharon-Lise Normand (Harvard University), who has provided invaluable help, advice, and guidance in both advanced statistical theory and applied statistics for many years. I would like to thank my colleagues and friends, including Drs. Martha Radford (New York University), JoAnne Foody (Harvard University), Jonathan Fine (Norwalk Health), Jennifer Mattera, Judy Lichtman (Yale University), and Thomas Meehan (Qualidigm) for many useful and insightful discussions. Although many of these discussions were restricted to the classification and profiling tasks in the healthcare area, they provided the roots for me to expand basic principles into the network security area. Special appreciation goes to Jane Yoon (Harvard University), who provided many helpful suggestions and a thorough, line-by-line critique of the manuscript. I would also like to acknowledge Emi Watanabe (Yale University) for her great work in producing many of the figures in this book. Assistance was also provided by Tierney Giannotti and Lynda Grayson (both at Qualidigm), and Mian Wang (Massachusetts Institute of Technology). I am grateful to Dr. Inyoung Kim (Virginia Tech) for an early discussion of the content of this book, Nate Melby (Trane Inc.), my editor at IGI Global, and the anonymous reviewers for their reading and detailed comments, which have substantially improved the presentation of the research provided in this book. Finally, I am deeply appreciative to Marcia Petrillo, CEO of Qualidigm, who provided me the opportunity to work with her 15 years ago after I had graduated. Without her influences, I would not have been able to conduct this project.

I have worked on this book for many nights and weekends over the past years. I would like to thank my family members for their understanding, assistance and patience, and thank Lhong Dxj for her encouragements. It was their support, love, and help that allowed me to complete this project. I have tried to eliminate any and all foreseeable errors in this book, but I am sure that there may still be some errors, ambiguities or oversights that have not been revised, for which I take full responsibility. I would greatly appreciate any feedback and suggestions. They can be emailed to me at yun.wang.yw38@yale.edu.

    The content of this publication does not necessarily reflect the views or policies of
Yale University or Yale New Haven Health; nor does mention of trade names, commercial
products, or organizations imply endorsement by Yale University or Yale New Haven
Health. The author assumes full responsibility for the accuracy and completeness of the
ideas represented.

Yun Wang
New Haven, CT
April 2008

Section I
Foundations

Chapter I
Statistical Opportunities, Roles, and Challenges in Network Security

To me, a personal computer should be small, reliable, convenient to use and inexpensive.
-The Apple-II, Stephen Wozniak

INTRODUCTION

In this chapter, we will provide a brief overview of network security and introduce essential concepts of intrusion detection and prevention and review their basic principles and guidelines. Then, we will discuss statistical approaches in practice as well as statistical opportunities, roles, and challenges in network security.

Network security has become a very popular topic. A simple Google search based on the keyword "network security" showed 2.2 million items on February 29, 2008. Network security aims to protect the entire infrastructure of a computer network and its corresponding services from unauthorized access. The two key elements of network security are risk assessment and risk management. There are several fundamental components in network security: (1) security-specific infrastructures, such as hardware- and software-based firewalls and physical security approaches, (2) security polices, which include security protocols, users' authentications, authorizations, access controls, information integrity and confidentiality, (3) detection of malicious programs, including anti-viruses, worms, or Trojan horses, and spyware or malware, and (4) intrusion detection and prevention, which encompasses network traffic surveillance and analyzing and profiling user behavior. Since the topic of network security links a great number of research areas and disciplines, we will focus on the component of intrusion detection and prevention in this book. Readers who are interested in other components or want to gain more detailed information on the entire topic may refer to Smedinghoff (1996), Curtin (1997), Garfinkel and Spafford (1997), McClure, Scambray, and Kurtz, (1999), Strebe and Perkins (2000), Bishop (2003), Maiwald (2003), Stallings (2003), Lazarevic, Ertoz, Kumar, Ozgur, & Srivastava, (2003), Bragg, Rhodes-Ousley, Strassberg (2004), McNab (2007), and Dasarathy (2008). For wireless network security, Vacca (2006) provides an essential step-by-step guide that explains the wireless-specific security challenges and tasks, and for mobile phone related intrusion detection refer to Isohara, Takemori & Sasase (2008). Finally, for an overall introduction on network security, including key tools and technologies used to secure network access, refer to *Network Security Principles and Practices* by Malik (2003) and *Network Security Fundamentals* by Laet & Schauwers (2005).

The use of statistical techniques in network security for intrusion detection and prevention has attracted great attention by researchers from both statistical and computer science fields. The idea behind intrusion detection and prevention is to use normal (anomaly-free) patterns of legitimate user behavior to identify and distinguish the behavior patterns of anomalous users (Anderson, 1972; Anderson, 1980; Stallings, 2003), and although this idea seems simple, intrusion detection and prevention are difficult tasks to implement and each have their own set of unique challenges. This discipline is in development and many difficult topics for research need to be addressed (INFOSEC Research Council, 1999; McHugh, 2000b; Taylor & Alves-Foss, 2002). Ideally, a perfect detection system needs four essential characteristics: (1) the ability to detect a wide variety of intrusions, (2) the ability to detect intrusions in a timely fashion, (3) the ability to present the analysis in a simple format, and (4) the ability to perform these tasks accurately (Bishop, 2003). Although statistical methods have been adapted to achieve these goals over the past decades (Anderson, 1980; Vaccaro & Liepins, 1989; Lunt & Jagannathan, 1988; Smaha, 1988; Teng, Chen & Lu, 1990; Anderson, Frivold & Valdes, 1995; Forrest, Hofmeyr, Somayaji & Longstaff, 1996; Qu, Vetter & Jou, 1997; Neumann & Prras, 1999; Masum, Ye, Chen & Noh, 2000; Valdes & Skinner, 2000; Barbard, Wu & Jajodia, 2001; Jha, Tan & Maxion, 2001; Taylor & Alves-Foss, 2001; Zhang, Li, Manikopoulos, Jorgenson & Ucles, 2001; Ye, Emran, Chen & Vilbert, 2002; Shyu, Chen, Sarinnapakorn, & Chang, 2003; Zhou & Lang, 2003; Qin & Hwang, 2004; Leung & Leckie, 2005; Wang 2005; Wang & Cannady 2005, Wang & Seidman, 2006; Wang & Normand, 2006; Gharibian & Ghorbani, 2007; Khan, Awad & Thuraisingham, 2007; Wang 2007; Herrero, al. et, 2007; Nayyar & Ghorbani, 2008), the gap between the performance of what we expect and what is currently available in both intrusion detection and intrusion prevention systems is still remarkable. With rapid advancements being made in computer and network technology, as well as increasing information and national security threats, the demand for reducing this gap has increased significantly; regardless, there are great challenges and technical difficulties in overcoming such a gap. In the following sections, we will briefly review previous studies and discuss some basic challenges. More historical information and trends on this topic also can be found from McHugh (2000b) and Patcha & Park (2007).

OVERVIEW

Although the idea behind intrusion detection is simple—using normal patterns of legitimate user behavior to identify and distinguish the behavior of an anomalous user, intrusion detection is a difficult task to implement. In the below sections, we will briefly review the history of network security, outline some basic concepts of intrusion detection and prevention and present some principles and guidelines for developing a robust security system.

Brief History of Network Security

Since James P. Anderson (1972) outlined the increasing awareness of computer security problems and presented a project plan to address computer security challenges in 1972 for the United States Air Force (USAF), interest in intrusion detection research has been growing. For more than three decades, this issue has evolved from its embryonic stage, through early development, to today's modern era as briefly summarized below.

Embryonic Stage (1970-1979) During this period, almost all research was performed under United States Government contracts and limited to providing security solutions for sharing classified information on the same network without compromising security. The report of the *Defense Science Board Task Force (DSBTF) on Computer Security* written by Willis H. Ware (1970), a researcher from the RAND Corporation, raised for the first time the broader issue of using computers to store and process classified information in a multi-user, multi-access, multi-job environment regardless of the configuration. Later, the USAF published two reports: *Computer Security Technology Planning Study Volumes I and II* – authored by James P. Anderson (1972) that presented a detailed plan for USAF computer security requirements and outlined the USAF's increasing awareness of computer security problems. The Volume II report described an advanced development and engineering program with a multi-level secure computing capability to address computer security problems, and also addressed the related development of communication security products and the interim solution to computer security challenges during the early 1970s. These reports established an important milestone in the computer security field during its early development. Anderson has been an independent contractor since the 1960s, and his work has centered on research and development activities for United States Government agencies that needed to make computer security a reality. He contributed to the Trusted Computer System Evaluation Criteria (TCSEC) and the draft of the Network Interpretation of the TCSEC (Department of Defense, 1985). Anderson received the National Computer System Security Award given jointly by the National Computer Security Center and NIST in 1990.

Other important studies conducted during the 1970s included the USAF report, *Multics Security Evaluation: Vulnerability Analysis* by Karger and Schell (1974), the U.S. Department of Commerce's report, *Operating System Structures to Support Security and Reliable Software* by Linden (1976) and the Stanford Research Institute's study, *Provably Secure Operating System*, conducted by Neumann and his colleagues (1975). Nevertheless, after more than 30 years, not only does the initial security challenge of how to share classified information on the same network without compromising security still remain, but new challenges, such as wireless network security, Internet security, are also emergening.

During this period, one remarkable milestone in the discipline of computer science is the birth of the Apple[1]-I and Apple-II computer designed by Stephen Wozniak, which started the Macintosh[2] and Personal Computer era. The Apple-I was designed late in 1975 and later sold nationwide through retail computer stores with a price below $700. It was the first microprocessor system product on the market to completely integrate the display generation circuitry, microprocessor, memory and power supply on the same board, which allowed the users to run the Apple BASIC interpreter with no additional electronics other than a keyboard and video monitor (Wozniak, 1977). The Apple II was released on April 1977 with 48K RAM, 4k ROM, 1.0 MHz CPU, and a generic cassette drive with a price of US $2638. Figure 1.1 shows a revised mode of Apple II, the Apple II plus released on 1979 with an external 143K floppy drive.

Nevertheless, while researchers and consumers were intoxicated with the capabilities demonstrated by Apple computers, a new era of computer and network security, the anti-computer's virus or simple anti-virus had been initializing. Five years later, a 15-year-old high school freshman, Richard Skrenta, wrote the world's first computer virus, Elk Cloner, on an Apple II computer. The virus started as a teenage prank ended up infecting floppy disks where the machines operating system resided.

Early Period (1980-1989) James P. Anderson (1980) conducted the USAF computer security plan and published the results in 1980. In the 142-page report entitled *Computer Security Threat Monitoring and Surveillance*, he described the fact that network audit data collected daily from all computers can play an important role in the security program for a network system and that these data should be used to monitor threats. However, at that time, the importance of such data had not been realized, and all available security efforts were focused on denying access to sensitive data from an unauthorized source. The conclusions of the report did not suggest the elimination of any existing security audit data collection and distribution; rather, it recommended using the data for detecting intrusion, which was an initial effort to provide an opportunity for applying statistical science in network security. This report is considered the most important article that initiated the original intrusion detection concept and established the notion of intrusion detection.

In 1983, Dorothy Denning, a researcher from SRI International, led a project that focused on analyzing audit trail data from government mainframe computers and created profiles of user activities. Between 1984 and 1986, Denning (1984) and her team researched and developed the first model for intrusion detection known as the Intrusion Detection Expert System (IDES), which was initially a rule-based expert system trained to detect known misuse activity. In 1987, Denning published the decisive work entitled *An Intrusion-Detection Model*, which revealed the necessary information for commercial intrusion detection system development. In this paper, Denning proposed the first comprehensive model of intrusion detection systems based on the hypothesis that a computer system's vulnerabilities involve abnormal use of the system. Therefore, security violations could be

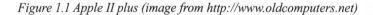

Figure 1.1 Apple II plus (image from http://www.oldcomputers.net)

detected from abnormal patterns of system usage. The article demonstrated that to detect abnormal patterns, one could construct a model based on six main components: subjects, objects, audit records, profiles, anomaly records, and activity rules. This paper was another important milestone in the history of intrusion detection. Although the idea was proposed in 1987, it remains true today, and the six components have become individual research topics for modern intrusion detection.

The birth of TCSEC is a remarkable event during this period. TCSEC, as defined in the Department of Defense (DoD) TCSEC 5200.28-STD, December 1985, is a DoD's standard that establishes basic requirements for assessing the effectiveness of computer security controls built into a computer system. This standard finally led to the birth of Air Force Systems Security Instructions 5024 (AFSSI 5024) on September 1997.

Another remarkable milestone in this period is the birth of the World Wide Web (WWW) in 1989, which was delivered by Tim Berners-Lee from the United Kingdom and Robert Cailliau from Belgium who was working in Switzerland. The Web is a collection of interconnected documents and other resources through the Internet that is subsequently, a collection of interconnected computer networks. Since the creation of the Web, network security has encountered a series of new generational challenges including anti-attacks from the Web.

During the late 1980s, there were other significant advanced developments. In 1988, the Haystack system was developed by S. Smaha (1988), a researcher at Lawrence Livermore Laboratories at the University of California at Davis, to assist USAF security officers in detecting misuse of the mainframes at USAF bases. This project created an intrusion detection system that analyzed audit data by comparing them with defined patterns. In 1989, members from the original Haystack project formed a commercial company called Haystack Labs and released the newest version of the technology, Stalker, which was a host-based, pattern-matching detection system with robust search capabilities to either manually or automatically query the audit data.

Also in 1988, the Morris worm caused the Internet to be unavailable for several days. This incident highlighted the need for computer security. Since 1980, the Institute of Electrical and Electronics Engineers (IEEE) Symposium on Security and Privacy has been the premier forum for the presentation of developments in computer security and electronic privacy. In 1998 the Journal of Cryptology established and issued its first volume. As an official journal of the International Association for Cryptologic Research, the journal provides a forum for publication of original results in all areas of modern information security and brings together researchers and practitioners in the field.

Development and Commercial Period (1990-1999) The theme of network security on intrusion detection research entered a new phase in the 1990's. Unlike the previous decade in which the U.S. Government founded most studies and the scope of work was limited directly to governmental priorities, two significant changes occurred. First, the increasing threat and need for network security had attracted the attention of researchers from many academic institutions, and new ideas and studies were introduced and conducted at academic levels. 1990 was another important milestone year in the history of intrusion detection; a year in which Heberlein (1990) and his colleagues from the University of California at Davis published their article entitled *A Network Security Monitor*. This article introduced a new concept to the intrusion detection research area; instead of examining audit trail data on a host computer system, network traffic could be used for monitoring suspicious behavior. As a result, two intrusion detection system's research branches were formed:

host-based intrusion detection (HID), which looks for attack signatures in log files, and network-based intrusion detection (NID), which looks for these patterns in network traffic. The Distributed Intrusion Detection System (DIDS) concept was introduced by a group of researchers from the Computer Security Laboratory, Division of Computer Science, at the University of California at Davis and was led by Snapp (1991). DIDS is designed to detect coordinated attacks against a set of hosts based on integrated and merged audit data from multiple hosts. In 1993, Paul Helman and Gunar Liepins published a paper entitled *Statistical Foundations of Audit Trail Analysis for the Detection of Computer Misuse*, which provided the fundamental concepts of using statistical methods to detect computer misuse. In 1994, Mark Crosbie and Gene Spafford, researchers from the Department of Computer Sciences at Purdue University, introduced the autonomous agent—a new concept and prototype for intrusion detection to improve the scalability, maintainability, efficiency, and fault tolerance of intrusion detection systems. In 1995, SRI International released its new version of the IDES, known today as the Next-Generation Intrusion Detection Expert System (NIDES), a classic intrusion detection system that has been cited in many studies and reports. NIDES performs real-time monitoring of user activity on multiple target systems via two complementary detection components: a rule-based signature analysis unit and a statistical profile-based anomaly detection unit. NIDES is a host-based agent that runs on its own workstation, analyzes audit data collected from networks, and searches for activity that may indicate unusual or malicious user behavior (Anderson, Frivold, & Valdes, 1995). Researchers also sought to apply newer solutions other than the statistically-based solutions for intrusion detection. The Artificial Intelligence (AI) neural network-based approach was employed for detecting misuse. The data mining approach was also introduced to the intrusion detection area during the same period. Lee (1999) and his co-workers presented *A Data Mining Framework for Building Intrusion Detection Models* at the IEEE Symposium on Security and Privacy Conference.

In addition, since 1998, the Information Systems Technology Group (ISTG) of the Lincoln Laboratory at the Massachusetts Institute of Technology (MIT) has collected and distributed audit data for evaluating probabilities of detection and false alarms for each system under the Defense Advanced Research Projects Agency (DARPA) test. The MIT-DARPA datasets are public domain intrusion detection audit records that are extremely valuable to the intrusion detection research field; they provide a gold-standard likely benchmark and a direction for research efforts addressing the general problem of workstation and network intrusion detection. Many studies have been conducted based on the DARPA data. Results of the 1998 and 1999 DARPA off-line intrusion detection evaluations were summarized in three papers: *Evaluating Intrusion Detection Systems: The 1998 DARPA Off-line Intrusion Detection Evaluation*, *The 1999 DARPA Off-line Intrusion Detection Evaluation*, and *Analysis and Results of the 1999 DARPA Off-line Intrusion Detection Evaluation* by the ISTG team (Cunningham, Lippmann, Fried, Garfinkle, Graf, Kendall, et al., 1999; Lippmann, Haines, Fried, Korba, & Das, 2000). These reports described the data collection methods, attack types, and performance measures used by authors. They included a ratio of attack detection to false positives, the ability to detect new and stealthy attacks, a comparison of host-based systems versus network-based systems to detect different types of attacks, the ability of anomaly detection techniques to identify new attacks, improvements during 1999, and the ability of systems to accurately identify attacks. This research also attempted to identify reasons for why each intrusion detection system failed to detect an attack or generated a false positive result.

The second remarkable change in the intrusion detection development during this period was that intrusion detection system-related research migrated from academic labs to the commercial market. Many privately funded, commerce-oriented projects were developed beginning in the early 1990s. Haystack Labs was the first commercial vendor of intrusion detection system tools, with its Stalker line of host-based products. In 1994, the Wheel Group developed the NetRanger, the first commercially viable network intrusion detection device. In 1997, the security market leader, ISS, developed a network-based intrusion detection system called RealSecure, and then Cisco[3] purchased the Wheel Group to gain a security solution for its customers. Thus, the commercial intrusion detection systems' market expanded and many start-up companies, mergers, and acquisitions ensued.

Another remarkable milestone during this period was the emergence of wireless computer network systems. Although the idea of a wireless system can be traced back to the late 1880s with the experiments conducted by D. E. Hughes, T.A. Edison, H. R. Hertz, and N. Tesla, the original wireless computer network, operating at a carrier frequency of around 400MHz bandwidth, was built at the University of Hawaii in 1971 by N. Abramson who received the 2007 IEEE Alexander Graham Bell Medal. In 1990, AT & T released WaveLan, operating at 1.5 Mbit/s, half-duplex, in a carrier-sense multiple-access environment. Since then, various wireless network techniques have been rapidly developed and the speed of data transformation has increased significantly. In 1997 the IEEE LAN/WAN Standards Committee released the IEEE 802.11 that included a set of protocols for wireless local area network computer communication. The 802.11a protocol operates in a 5 GHz band with a maximum data transfer rate of 54 Mbit/s, while the 802.11b protocol operates at 2.4 GHz with a 54 Mbit/s maximum data transfer rate. Both of these protocols were released on October 1999.

Compared to a wired network system, a wireless network system is more vulnerable and many traditional security methods and approaches are either useless or ineffective when applied to wireless networks. For example, wireless access to networks cannot be monitored easily, or controlled with firewalls and proxy servers. As a result, the discipline of network security has a new and rapidly growing area of research: wireless network security.

Modern Era (2000 – Present) Despite the fact that Anderson's computer intrusion detection system has been around for more than thirty years and there has been a dramatic rise since the year 2000 in the incorporation of intrusion detection into the overall information security infrastructure, the ability to make timely and accurate intrusion detection has become increasingly more difficult. This can be attributed to the rapid increase in network bandwidth from megabits to gigabits per second, and growing ad hoc wireless network access. Today, research in intrusion detection and prevention has four notable characteristics representing the trends in this area. First, with respect to techniques, more complex statistical approaches, including Bayesian models (e.g., Barbard, Wu & Jajodia, 2001; Jha, Tan, & Maxion, 2001; Liu, Scott, 2004; Comaniciu & Man, 2006; Wang & Kim 2006), HMMs (e.g., Gao, Ma & Yang, 2002; Cho & Park, 2003; Wright, Monrose & Masson, 2004; Joshi & Phoha, 2005), data mining (Hossain & Bridges, 2001; Qin & Hwang, 2004; Marinova-Boncheva, 2007; Christodorescu, Jha & Kruegel, 2008), and more complex neural networks and fuzzy logic techniques (Bridges & Vaughn, 2000; Cannady, 2000; Krishnapuram, Joshi, Nasraoui, 2001; Zhang, Li, Manikopoulos, Jorgenson & Ucles, 2001; Gomez & Dasgupta, 2002; Mukkamala, Janoski & Sung, 2002; Goss, Botha & von Solms, 2007; Khan, Awad & Thuraisingham, 2007) have been introduced and applied. The target has also moved from the traditional statically wired networks to ad hoc wireless network environments (e.g.,

Brutch & Ko, 2003; Robertson, Siegel, Miller, & Stolfo, 2003; Zhang, Lee & Huang, 2003; Boukerche & Ren, 2007; Jahnke et al. 2007; Mano et al., 2008). Agent-based approaches have become a promising direction for developing collaborative intrusion detection systems (e.g., Pikoulas, Buchanan, Mammion, & Triantafyliopoulos, 2002; Gowadia, Farkasl, & Valtorta, 2003; Shyu, Quirino, Xie, Chen & Chang, 2007).

Second, computer and network security has become one of the most important topics for many organizations. Almost every organization has been attacked. The 2002 computer security survey conducted by the Computer Security Institute and the Federal Bureau of Investigation shows that among 503 computer security practitioners in the U.S. primarily large corporations, government agencies, financial institutions, medical institutions and universities: (1) 90% of respondents detected computer security breaches within the last 12 months; (2) 80% acknowledged financial losses due to computer breaches, and 44% reported about $456 million in financial losses; (3) 74% cited their Internet connection as a frequent point of attack, while 33% mentioned their internal systems; (4) a wide range of attacks and abuses have been detected – 40% reported system penetration from the outside, 40% detected denial of service attacks, 78% detected employee abuse of Internet access privileges, and 85% detected computer viruses; and (5) among respondents that conduct electronic commerce via the Internet, 38% suffered unauthorized access or misuse on their Web sites within the last 12 months (Power, 2002, Spring).

Third, Statistical roles have been emphasized. Marchette (2003) has identified denial of service attacks, passive fingerprinting, and user profiling as the basic three areas in which statistics can play an important role in network security. He also specified the areas that require much work to be done including anomaly detection, network tomography, worm and virus propagation, fraud detection and user profiling by keystroke timing or application usage. Additional information can be found in Vardi (1996), Marchette (2001), Schonlau et al (2001), Bolton and Hand (2002), Wang (2005, 2006), Chouchane, Walenstein, & Lakhotia (2007).

Moreover, Certification and Accreditation (C&A) models have been developed since the late 1990s and early 2000s. There are four primary C&A models, the National Information Assurance Certification and Accreditation Process (NIACAP), the National Institute of Standards and Technology (NIST), the Defense Information Technology Systems Certi-fication and Accreditation Process (DITSCAP), and the Director of Central Intelligence Directive 6/3 (DCID 6/3) model, which are being used by various government agencies. Many private and public businesses also develop their own C&A guidelines or adopt one of the four C&A models used by the government to create their own security auditing program.

Finally, various wireless network techniques have been rapidly developed and the speed of data transformation has increased significantly. While such techniques are bringing the benefits of knowledge, trade, and communication to more people in more ways than ever before, the security challenges from wireless network are still prevalent in the computer security area. Networks are at risk to anyone who gains access merely by moving around an area in search of a wireless network signal to gain unauthorized access. Brutch and Ko (2003) addressed this challenge in their article, *Challenges in Intrusion Detection for Wire-less ad hoc Networks* where they presented a brief survey of current research in intrusion detection systems for wireless ad hoc networks, reviewed current research efforts to detect attacks against the ad hoc routing infrastructure, and illustrated the challenges to intrusion detection. The authors also examined several intrusion detection architectures that may be used for different wireless ad hoc network infrastructures and proposed methods of intrusion response. From the statistically-based intrusion detection perspective, the difficulty is that there is not enough audit data that can be collected to profile normal user behavior. Zhang, Lee and Huang (2003) argued that the traditional way of protecting networks with firewalls and encryption software is no longer sufficient or effective in wireless networks and a mobile environment. The need to search for new architecture and mechanisms to protect wireless networks and mobile computing applications has increased significantly. They examined the major differences between fixed networks and mobile ad hoc networks and identified three research issues in developing various intrusion detection systems for mobile ad hoc networks: 1) system architecture, 2) audit data sources, and 3) models. The authors also presented a new architecture, followed by an experimental study to evaluate its feasibility.

In March 2007, the 802.11-2007 standard, which is the most modern 802.11 document available and has merged previous protocols/amendments (802.11a to 802.11j) together, was released (*IEEE 802.11 Working Group, 2007*). In the near future, the 802.11n, which includes multiple-input multiple-output functions and many other newer features, is expected to be released in June 2009. It is clear that with these new protocols in place, we will face new security challenges. How we employ statistical approaches to address these challenges will become an essential task in the network security area.

Intrusion Detection and Prevention

We have briefly introduced some fundamental concepts of network security in the previous section, and will give a more detailed discussion in this section. Some of the statistical terminologies and concepts mentioned in this section will be explained in the corresponding chapters in the rest of this book. The subjects of intrusion detection, intrusion prevention and network protection are related to each other each with their own focus. An intrusion detection system functions as a "Radar" to monitor network traffic for detecting and identifying any signal that could be considered an attack or anomalous event. It carries out the detection task through its classification and determination rules that are composed of two main parts: a pre-existing knowledgebase and a set of classification algorithms. The pre-existing knowledgebase mainly includes (1) a set of estimated parameters based on the previous network traffic, (2) a set of known and labeled attacks or anomaly events, and (3) a group of data sources. The classification algorithms are mainly constructed based on either statistical modeling, AI, or a hybrid of both. Depending upon the quality of the pre-existing knowledgebase, the robustness of the classification algorithms, and the uniqueness of attacks or anomalous events, the performance of intrusion detection systems, which are usually measured by sensitivity, specificity, and correctly classified rates, could vary a great deal. The pre-existing knowledgebase should be updated regularly so that any newly discovered attacks or malicious codes can be labeled and the classification parameters revised accordingly.

The main function of intrusion detection systems is to classify network traffic. Based on classification rules, we generally can have two types of these systems, misuse detection based on "signature" and anomaly detection based on "pattern." A misuse detection system looks at the packets in network traffic and compares the data sources for a "signature" that correspond to attack data, and issues an alert if any suspicious activity has been identified. Although the idea of using a signature for detection is simple, it is understood that the development of such a system is labor and time intensive, and is consequently one-step behind the attacks. Detecting new attacks require new rules and such a system generally performs poorly and has high false positive and false negative rates.

Anomaly detection identities behavior deviations from the normal or anomaly-free behavior patterns. Theoretically, such a system may be able to detect some new attacks but it is difficult in practice because it is hard to define an anomaly-free behavior pattern. In general, statistical anomaly detection can be categorized into two aspects: threshold-based detection and profile-based detection. The threshold method evaluates the frequency of anomalous events occurring over a specified interval and, by itself, has higher false positive and false negative rates (Stallings, 2003). By contrast, the profile-based method focuses on analyzing current or historical user behavior and detects any outlier values based on a series of measures such as mean, median, standard deviation, or interval estimates of various user activity-related parameters and variables (e.g., login time zone, length of connections, types of protocol, connection statuses).

Regardless of which type of system is used, having a good history of data, as well as a robust pre-existing knowledge is necessary. Statistical methods can be applied for both types of systems but it is more widely used for pattern detection whereas signature detection is more commonly implemented through a set of rules that function as a switch to grant or reject access from a particular site, group or user.

An intrusion prevention system aims to take actions to protect a network system in real time. Such actions could be, for example, to block any suspicious traffic that may potentially hurt the entire network system. It achieves such actions by utilizing the evidence generated from an intrusion detection system. An ideal intrusion prevention system could include three essential components: (1) a set of action items that represent the available incidence responses for a particular network system, (2) a set of rules that represent of the system security policies, and (3) a set of parameters that describe the user, group, site, or system behavior patterns to be "normal" or "anomaly-free", "abnormal", or "unable to be determined." Of these components, the first does not involve using any statistical algorithms. Rather, it requires a sequence of actions that range from issuing warning messages and blocking the index traffic, to disconnecting the suspicious workstation or system from the network. The second component translates the security policies, regulations and historical information into action, but does not require any statistical activities. A traditional rule-based system could be an example of such a component in an intrusion prevention system. The third component is a profiling device that essentially depends on statistical analyses and the classification results from a detection system. Unlike intrusion detection, which mainly focuses on the individual network traffic level, intrusion prevention also focuses on behavior patterns at the levels of user, sub-network system, or entire system. Accordingly, intrusion prevention may not restrict its data source to network traffic and also obtains information on users or systems by profiling data. For example, we can link users' working schedules with their network traffic patterns. When a particular IP address, which could represent a site, group, or a user, in the network suddenly generates a large volume of traffic at an inappropriate time, an intrusion prevention system can take action to block all the traffic to and from this IP address due to the traffic pattern does not match with the corresponding its normal pattern, regardless of whether or not these traffic pass through the intrusion detection system.

A network protection system has a wider range of protecting the entire network system. An ideal of such a prevention system has at least four key domains including: (1) hardware,

(2) software, (3) security policies and regulations, and (4) knowledgebase. The main elements in the hardware domain include firewalls, secure devices for physically accessing the network systems, and backup systems. Intrusion detection and prevention systems are two key components for the software domain in addition to other secure software applications such as anti-virus and anti-spyware programs. Spam email detection is also a particular component in this domain. The secure policies and regulations category mainly includes access rights, password guidelines, policies for using email and the Internet, and network traffic surveillance. Finally, a knowledgebase should include as much historical traffic data as possible, and all the known and labeled attacks and anomalous patterns. The historical data can be sampling data. Other data that describe the infrastructure of network systems, as well as individual site, group, and user, also need to be included to support the intrusion detection and prevention systems.

Basic Principles and Guidelines

Although the initial security challenges raised by the DSBTF and USAF in the early 1970's remains unchanged, it has been uncovered over the past few decades that data, modeling, and system infrastructure are the three essential domains used to create robust intrusion detection and prevention systems. Despite the fact that each of these domains has its unique characteristics and particular concerns that need to be addressed and to be treated individually, together they can lead us to develop a great system that aims to meet the following goals: (1) to reduce the statistical uncertainty on profiling user behavior, (2) to increase sensitivity and specificity in anomaly detection, and (3) to provide real time evidence-based decision support. To achieve these goals, we present the following basic principles and guidelines corresponding to each domain. Addition information can be found from the classic paper *Information Systems Security Design Methods: Implications for Information Systems Development* by Baskerville (1993). Readers who are interested in principles and practices related to network hardware and infrastructures should refer to Malik (2003).

Data. In general, data mainly include three sources: (1) network traffic at the network system level, (2) user profiling data at the individual user, site or group level, and (3) network configuration information. Data-related concerns are mainly related to collections, sampling, sample size analysis, and reliability and validity tests. Being able to collect good data is a necessity in developing a robust model. Any sampling has to be randomly drawn from the population. Sample size and power have to be carefully calculated to meet the minimum requirements for constructing models.

It is important to detect an attack or anomalous event at the earliest possible stage. This requires quickly processing incoming data and comparing them to the historical data to locate any abnormalities. Because network traffic data are usually huge in size (74 hours of logged traffic data from a large enclave network could include 344 million observations in 24 GB, for example), it is clear that analyses conducted directly from such raw data may not be necessary and may also be inefficient. Consequently, not only does statistical sampling play a key role in the analyses, but also different sampling approaches may affect the final classification results. Scanning a randomly selected small sample of traffic data with human eyes may also provide a great opportunity to understand the quality of data being collected and may even help to identify any new attacks or anomalous events.

Unlike in other research areas, statistical analysis in network security faces unique challenges because of the rapid changes in computer and network hardware and software provide that provided great challenges in both the data collection process and data analysis. There is no gold-standard approach for data collection and there is no gold-standard benchmark data for testing various algorithms. Each network system has its unique characteristics and requires developing a particular algorithm to collect its data. Despite this, there are a few principles that may serve as guidelines for collecting data in practice.

First, good data have to meet several basic criteria, including (1) adequate sample size for fitting statistical models, (2) stability for profiling user behavior, (3) reliability for lowering false alarm rates, (4) detectability, predictability, and discrimate power, and (5) associability.

Second, efforts should be made to ensure that the data in which the profiling is based on are accurate and reliable across the different users or groups that are being evaluated and, when appropriate, across time. This includes standardizing the definitions of the predicting variables and where possible disclosing the quality of the data with regard to accuracy and reliability. Such information should be clearly described and substantiated. When the quality of data is variable, an effort should be made to determine its impact on the profiling results.

Third, data should also be timely. Old data may not represent the current patterns of the user or group being profiled. In many cases, practical considerations limit the ability to acquire and analyze the data soon after an actual event encounter. Also, in some cases, data from earlier time periods may be pooled with more recent data to improve the precision of the estimates, which may compromise the ability to determine whether behavior patterns are changing over time.

Modeling. Classification algorithms include supervised learning and unsupervised learning, linear and nonlinear models, parametric methods and non-parametric methods, and simple hypothesis tests (e.g., χ^2 test to compare categorical variables, t-test to compare continuous variables) and complex approaches (e.g., probability models, Markov models, and the Bayesian approach). A robust classification system must have good sensitivity and specificity, a low false alarm rate, a high positive alarm rate, and the ability to detect new incidents, of which are fundamental goals in network security. There are great challenges in reach such goals. Although the potential benefits of applying the statistical technique in network security are countless, many intrusion detection and prevention systems continually suffer high false alarm rates and have difficultly in identifying new attacks. Nevertheless, some basic principles and guidelines for classification and modeling are given below.

First, statistical models, particularly those intended for classification and profiling purposes, should account for particular features of the organization of the data. An important aspect of data used for profiling users relates to the "clustering" of network traffics within a group (or sub-network system), and statistical models used for profiling should take into account the group effect, which is known as intra-group correlation. In addition to the clustered nature of the data, the classification model ought to be able to account for the differential amounts of information across groups, measured in terms of the number of observations per group. If two groups have the same anomaly-free rate, there would be greater confidence in the estimate for the group having large volume traffic than for the one with small volume traffic. Credible statistical models must be designed to accommodate groups with widely varying sample sizes. Groups with less traffic may have observed rates at the extreme ends of the range, but such rates may not accurately reflect their "true" behavior. Although some methodologies specifically exclude groups with fewer observations than a minimum threshold, it is almost impossible to remove all of the variability in sample sizes across groups.

Second, hierarchical regression models can address the design issues that typically occur in profiling efforts, in that clustered data and differential information can be addressed by hierarchical generalized linear models. These models are used commonly in education and healthcare, where students or patients are clustered within classrooms or hospitals and classroom or hospitals sizes vary. Hierarchical models explicitly quantify intra-group variation and produce better group-specific estimates for small groups. This particular approach avoids "regression to the mean," a statistical concept describing the tendency for groups who have been identified as outliers in the past to become less extreme in the future. This approach also affords a more realistic assessment of the role of chance in the observed variation between groups.

Third, with regard to these model performance measures, classification models should be evaluated by measures of discrimination, calibration, and goodness-of-fit. The decision about what constitutes a "good" or "good enough" model will be based more on subjective considerations than on predefined criteria, but the model performance will depend on the degree to which traffic characteristics contribute to the outcome and the availability of variables that reflect variables associated with the outcome. Also, these models should be developed and validated in different samples to assess robustness, and such evaluations should be conducted repeatedly. If validation has not been performed, then that should also be reported. In addition, models developed from traffic data from one network system should be validated against data from a different network system as possible. This validation should include a comparison of how much agreement in classification exists between two systems' models.

Fourth, all models are not good and there is no one "gold-standard" model that can be used to compare the model performances. A stream of network traffic data with many positive predictor variables might not represent a true attack, and a look-alike normal stream could present a novel attack due to uncertain factors and users changing their behavior. In general, increasing the sensitivity could reduce the false positive alarm rate, and increasing the specificity could reduce the false negative alarm rate. The objective of a good statistical model is to demonstrate high values in sensitivity, specificity, and correctly classified rate. To achieve this goal, the process of selecting predictive variables must consider the issues of sampling variability and stability of variables' statistical significance.

Fifth, we may be able to develop a robust attack-specific model to detect a particular type of attack or abnormal event but we cannot develop a model that can cover all types of attacks. Such a model may not exist. Finally, model parameters should be updated frequently to take into account new attacks and user behavior changes in over time.

System infrastructure. Both intrusion and prevention systems needs to be constructed with a hybrid approach. Use of a hybrid modeling approach means that a final classification decision on real time traffic, such as anomaly-free or anomalous, should be made based on a vote of multi-classification algorithms; the assignment of a membership of user behavior patterns for any new user or group should also be voted by multi-profiling algorithms. A hybrid model that integrates and combines more than one classification of models and algorithms has shown potential for reducing false positive and false negative alarms rates that could maximize the strengths and minimize the weaknesses of each individual classification and profiling approaches.

Uncertainty should be treated carefully and rationally. Statistics is concerned with how data change people beliefs (Woodworth, 2004). A confidence level is the desired "certainty" we wish to have in making a conclusion about the population. Both the probability and the confidence interval provide measurements for the uncertainty. Probability tells us how likely the observed traffic belong to a particular pattern and the confidence interval tells us the error margin for the estimate of interest. Statistical simulation techniques, such as bootstrap (Efron & Tibshirani, 1994) and Monte Carlo (Berg, 2004) can be used to acquire a probability of the outcome in which we are interested. Standard error can be utilized to the calculate confidence interval that depends on the confidence level selected.

The decision of whether we should use a statistical modeling approach or an alternative approach depends on many known and unknown factors, and should be gauged by the accuracy of predicting results. Although in many situations, an empirical historical data-based statistical modeling approach is used as a principal tool for intrusion detection and prevention, it can also be used as an alternative tool to benefit both researchers and network administrators for making better evidence-based decisions.

STATISTICAL APPROACHES IN PRACTICE

In this section we will briefly review some previous works and literatures with various statistical approaches. In general, the benefit of using a statistical methodology in network security is that it offers a wide variety of methods and approaches ranging from simple significance tests to complex modeling analyses, such as multidimensional scaling, multiple regression, cluster analysis, factor analysis, decision tree, and AI-based techniques, to meet the challenges from the discipline of network security. Readers who like to gain additional information on this frame shall refer to *Statistical Methods in Computer Security* by Chen (2005).

Linear and Nonlinear Modeling Methods

Significance test. A significance test can be achieved by using either linear or nonlinear approach. The simplest statistical test-based intrusion detection approaches are the χ^2 (chi-square) test and t-test. The former examines the frequency difference between two categorical variables, while the latter tests the difference between two continuous variables. Masum, Ye, Chen & Noh (2000) presented a study, *Chi-square Statistical Profiling for Anomaly Detection*, in the annual technical conference of the 2000 IEEE Workshop on Information Assurance and Security, which described a multivariate statistical approach based on the χ^2 test of goodness-of-fit to detect intrusions. That approach used long-term profile data of normal activities acquired from a computer and network system to train the classifier. The training data included 250 auditable events, where each of these events was represented by the event type. The system then sent a signal if an observed event deviated from the norm profile. The authors computed the false alarm rate and the detection rate based on the χ^2 test, and the results showed a low false alarm rate and a high detection rate. Recently, Goonatilake, Herath, Herath, and Herath (2007) also developed a course module that aims to help computer security students understand a use of the χ^2 test and goodness-of-fit test to detect possible intrusions.

$\chi2$ is a nonparametric test of statistical significance. It is a mathematical basis for examining how well observed data fit or differ from predicted or expected data. Statistically, the $\chi2$ test alone may not provide enough evidence for supporting decision making. With a large sample size, $\chi2$ more likely tends to be statistically significant, even if there is a minor difference between the data; with a small sample size, the test tends to deny everything for significance. In intrusion detection, the sample size of historical data usually is much larger than the sample size obtained from the real-time monitoring system. Developing a detection system based on simple $\chi2$ could yield high false positive and false negative response rates.

Linear methods. The common linear methods are multiple analysis and multivariate analysis. The use of multivariate and multiple analyses, which attempt to employ complex statistical modeling techniques to examine user behavior based on traffic data, has increasing interest in the intrusion detection research area. Studies based on regression model, factor analysis, principal component analysis, and cluster analysis have been reported in various technical conferences over the past few decades.

Logistic Model: The logistic regression model has become, in many fields, the standard method of data analysis concerned with describing the relationship between a response variable and one or more predictor variables where the response variable follows a binomial distribution. Logistic regression is used to model the probability p of occurrences of a binary or dichotomous outcome. Binary-valued covariates are usually given arbitrary numerical coding such as 0 for one possible response and 1 for the other possible response. Linear regression models may not be used when the response variable is binary valued because the probability of being modeled must lie between 0 and 1 where ordinary linear regression does not guarantee these limits. Dichotomous data may be analyzed using a logistic function where the logit transformation of p is used as the predictor variable.

Moreover, a logistic regression model with a binary response variable is a particular case of the general multinomial logistic regression model that its dependent variable can have more than two choices that are coded categorically, and one of the categories is taken as the reference category. Wang (2005) published a study using the bootstrap simulation method to fit 3,000 multinomial logistic regression models with a 5-level of categorical variable, *normal, probe, DoS, U2R, and R2L*, as an unordered response variable. Wang identified 13 predictors that are statistically significantly associated with the response variable and reported that compares with the KDD-cup 1999 winning results (Elkan, 2000) conducted by the *c4.5* decision tree algorithm. The multinomial logistic model-based classification results had similar sensitivity values in detecting *normal* (98.3% vs. 99.5%), *probe* (85.6% vs. 83.3%), and *DoS* (97.2% vs. 97.1%); remarkably high sensitivity in *U2R* (25.9% vs. 13.2%) and *R2L* (11.2% vs. 8.4%); and a significantly lower overall misclassification rate (18.9% vs. 35.7%).

Regression Model: Multivariate Adaptive Regression Splines (MARS) is a nonparametric regression procedure for solving regression-type problems and which aims to predict the value of a continuous response variable from a set of predictor variables. It makes no assumption about the underlying functional relationship between the response and predictor variables. Rather, it constructs this relationship from a set of coefficients and basic functions that are entirely driven from regression data. The MARS approach seems to become particularly useful in the area of data mining because it does not assume or impose any particular type or class of relationship (i.e., linear, logistic, etc.) between the predictors and the response variable of interest. At the 6th International Conference on

Enterprise Information Systems, Mukkamala and Sung (2004) presented a study entitled, *Intrusion Detection Systems Using Adaptive Regression Splines,* which demonstrates a performance analysis between the MARS, neural networks, and support vector machines based on the 1998 MIT-DARPA data. They found that the MARS approach can correctly classify and detect 96.1% of normal behavior, 92.3% of Prob, 94.7% of DoS, 99.7% of U2Su, and 99.5% of R2L attacks.

Principal component analysis: Shyu, Chen, Sarinnapakorn and Chang (2003) presented a study entitled *A Novel Anomaly Detection Scheme Based on Principal Component Classifier* in the 3rd IEEE International Conference on Data Mining, which proposed a new classification approach based on principal component analysis. Assuming that anomalies can be treated as outliers, the authors constructed an intrusion predictive model that measures the difference between an anomaly and the normal instance as the distance in the principal component space. The authors reported that the distance based on major components accounted for 50% of the total variation and that the minor components accounted for less than 20% of the variance. Experiments based on the KDD-cup 1999 data demonstrated that the principal component-based classifier achieved 98.9% in sensitivity and 97.9% in specificity, with a false alarm rate of 0.9%.

Principal component analysis is the oldest and most widely used multivariate approach, and one of the advantages of this method is that it reduces the dimensions of the original data. The basic idea of principal component analysis is to present the variation of a set of multivariate data in terms of a set of uncorrelated latent factors, each of which is a particular linear combination of the original variables. The new variables are sorted in decreasing order as much as possible in the original data to see whether the first few components account for the most variation in the original data. In modern statistics, the principal component analysis becomes a fundamental branch of multivariate analysis that considers a fairly large variety of procedures, all of which have the aim of determining where the interrelations between a large number of observed variables are explicable in terms of a small number of underlying, unobservable components.

Cluster analysis: Cluster analysis attempts to accomplish the task of partitioning a set of objects into relatively homogeneous subsets based on inter-object similarities. With this in mind, we can cluster the network traffic stream based on TCP/IP sessions. Ye, Emran, Li and Chen (2001), researchers from the Information and Systems Assurance Laboratory at Arizona State University, presented a cluster-based prototype of a distributed and host-based intrusion detection system at the DARPA Information Survivability Conference and Exposition. They first used the χ^2 test to detect anomalous user behavior, and then used cluster analysis to detect misuse. They reported that each technique determines an intrusion warning (IW) level for each audit event. The IW levels from different intrusion detection techniques are then combined, using a fusion technique, into a composite IW level: 0 for normal, 1 for intrusive, and any value in between to signify the intrusiveness.

Nonlinear methods. The widely used nonlinear methods in network security include artificial intelligence (AI) methods (e.g., neural network, fuzzy logic), support vector machines (SVM), k-nearest neighbors (KNN), Naive Bayes, and decision tree. AI relies on science and engineering theories and methods to make intelligent machines and computer programs. Since normal and abnormal user behavior patterns are difficult to profile due to the fact that the boundaries are not well defined, and traditional statistically based algorithms usually generate high false alarms, researchers have tried to gain success from AI in the intrusion detection area. Neural networks and fuzzy logic are two of the most frequently used AI approaches to cover the weaknesses of statistical methods.

Artificial neural networks: Artificial neural networks use a pattern recognition approach to solve problems and has been employed successfully in many research areas. Cannady (1998) published a study based on multi-level perceptron (MLP) and self-organizing maps for misuse detection based on a feed forward network with a back-propagation learning neural networks approach at the 1st *International Workshop on the Recent Advances in Intrusion Detection.* The article entitled *The Application of Artificial Neural Networks to Misuse Detection: Initial Results* presented detailed analyses of the advantages and disadvantages of a neural network-based approach in intrusion detection and its potential implementation.

The neural networks approach has attracted research interest by its strength and advantage for intrusion detection, especially for detecting misuse patterns. Lately, Lippmann and Cunningham (1999) of the MIT Lincoln Laboratory demonstrated another neural networks-based model for misuse detection that searches for attack-specific keywords in network traffic. The model also used the MLP prototype to detect Unix-host attacks and attacks to obtain root-privilege on a server. They reported that the neural network approach reduced false alarms, increasing the detection rate to roughly 80% with the MIT-DARPA 1999 data. Mukkamala, Janoski and Sung (2002) described another approach to intrusion detection using neural networks and SVMs. The key ideas presented in their article were the discovery of useful patterns or features that describe user behavior on a system, and then use relevant features to build classifiers that recognize anomalies and known intrusions. The authors, researchers from the Department of Computer Science at the New Mexico Institute of Mining and Technology, used the 1999 KDD-cup data to demonstrate that efficient and accurate classifiers can be built to detect intrusions. They also compared the performance of two approaches—neural network-based and SVM-based systems, and reported that both systems showed greater than 99% accuracy on the testing dataset. The SVM-based system had a shorter running time than the neural networks.

Fuzzy logic: Compared with the large volume of studies on applying neural networks in intrusion detection, there have been remarkably few published studies that focused on using fuzzy logic in intrusion detection. Fuzzy logic is a Boolean value-based approach developed by Dr. Lotfi Zadeh from the University of California at Berkeley in the 1960s to model the uncertainty of natural language. It aims to address the concept of partial truth, a value between absolutely true and absolutely false. Since then, fuzzy logic has been widely used in the AI and automatic control areas. In particular, in the late 1970s and early 1980s the Japanese had integrated this approach in many of their products (e.g., washing machines, elevator traffic control, subway traffic control). Gomez and Dasgupta (2002) published an interesting article that applies fuzzy logic to develop rule-based intrusion detection systems in the 3rd Annual IEEE Information Assurance Workshop. Based on experiments performed using the KDD-cup 1999 data with 41 variables and a total of 494,021 observations, they reported that by applying fuzzy logic and defining a set of fuzzy rules for normal and abnormal behavior, the false alarm rate in determining intrusive activities could be significantly reduced. Their results showed that the accuracy of the fuzzy classification approach is acceptable and comparable to those results from previous literature.

The principle of fuzzy logic is that everything is a matter of degrees. Some things are not fuzzy no matter how closely we look at them (e.g. $1 + 1 = 2$). However, most things in the real world are fuzzy. For example, neither traditional statistical approaches nor neural network methods could draw a clear line to distinguish "tall" men from the "not-tall." Fuzzy logic addresses this question by establishing the fuzzy sets and fuzzy membership functions for "tall" and "not-tall", which in most cases are in non-linear formats. There are no standard methods to develop fuzzy sets and membership functions; they all depend on real research questions and data. The challenge of using fuzzy logic in the intrusion detection area lies in how to establish membership functions. Bridges and Vaughn (2000) presented a prototype that uses genetic algorithms to construct fuzzy membership functions. This prototype combines both anomaly-based intrusion detection with fuzzy data mining techniques, and misuse detection with traditional rule-based expert system techniques. The authors tested the prototype with unknown network traffic; system audit data demonstrated that the new prototype supports both anomaly detection and misuse detection components at the individual workstation and network level, and that both fuzzy and non-fuzzy rules are supported within the system.

K-nearest neighbor: Yihua and Vemuri (2002) presented a study entitled *Use of K-Nearest Neighbor Classifier for Intrusion Detection*, which reported that the KNN method has some computational advantages in profiling use behavior. Their preliminary experiments with the 1998 MIT-DARPA BSM audit data showed that the KNN-based classifier can effectively detect intrusive attacks and achieve a low false positive rate.

Bayesian and Probability Approaches

Use of the Bayesian approach for developing statistically based intrusion detection systems has many advantages. The conventional statistical approach considers parameters as fixed, but unknown, constants to be estimated using sample data taken randomly from the population. Although we can calculate a confidence interval for an unknown parameter, it is really a frequency statement of the likelihood that numbers calculated from a sample captured the true parameter. We cannot make probability statements about the true parameter since it is fixed, not random. The Bayesian approach, on the other hand, treats these population-based parameters as random, rather than fixed, quantities. Before looking at the current data, we can use old information to construct a prior distribution model for these parameters. Thus, the Bayesian model starts with an assessment about how likely various values of the unknown parameters are, and then makes use of the current data to revise this starting assessment so that parameters can be considered random, not fixed. This attribute allows an intrusion detection system to make a more precise decision based on the probability approach.

Latent Class Model: Wang, Kim, Mbateng, and Ho (2006) present a latent class modeling approach to examine network traffic data when labeled abnormal events are absent in training data, or such events are insufficient to fit a conventional regression model. They used six anomaly-associated variables identified from previous studies to fit a latent class model, and report that the latent class model yields acceptable classification results compared with a logistic regression model (correctly classified: 0.95 vs. 0.98, sensitivity: 0.99 vs. 0.99, and specificity: 0.77 vs. 0.97). They concluded that the study demonstrates a great potency for using the latent class modeling technique to analyze network traffic data.

Bayes role: Barbard, Wu and Jajodia (2001) presented a study based on the Bayesian approach, *Detecting Novel Network Intrusions Using Bayes Estimators* in the first Society for Industrial and Applied Mathematic (SIAM) International Conference on Data Mining.

The study focused on reducing false alarm rates for intrusion detection. The authors applied Bayesian inference to enhance an intrusion detection system based on 1998 and 1999 MIT-DARPA data. They conducted two experiments: (1) given a training dataset, they created a Bayes classifier by removing one attack type at a time and then tested it against the removed attack, using the test dataset, and (2) given a training dataset and a test dataset, they created a Bayes classifier based on the training dataset and tested it against the test dataset. To evaluate the classifier's ability to detect new attacks, they chose the test dataset in such a way that it consisted of at least one attack that did not appear in the training data. Their results from the two experiments demonstrated low false alarm rates. The authors believed that since any attack will "do something" that is different from normal activities, if one has comprehensive knowledge about normal activities and the corresponding normal deviations, then any activities that are not normal should be suspicious. Although this belief has been the root of the anomaly detection for several decades, and there has been progress towards having "comprehensive knowledge about normal activities and the corresponding normal deviations," this goal has never been achieved. Bayesian statistics may provide a new solution.

Hidden Markov Model: Hidden Markov Model (HMM) is a sub-approach of the simulation method that provides a unifying framework for many complex statistical problems and general statistical modeling challenges to measure uncertainty. HMM was initially used in the speech recognition area, and it was a powerful modern statistical technique that has been applied to many subject areas. Recently, studies illustrated that HMM can be used for intrusion detection. Gao, Ma and Yang (2002) conducted an HMM-based study that includes four experiments to profile the normal and abnormal patterns for intrusion detection in the Unix environment. They reported that, compared with the non-HMM-based approach, HMMs could provide "stronger signals" of anomalies from the intrusion-traces.

Despite the fact that the HMM approach could lead to development of a detection system with good performance, there are still two major difficulties in applying this model to real intrusion detection systems: it requires large amounts of resources (i.e., time and computing power) to model normal behaviors, and the false positive error rate is relatively high. Cho and Park (2003), researchers from Yonsei University in Korea, proposed an approach to address the first issue. They used the extraction of privilege flows to reduce normal behaviors and combined multiple models to reduce the false positive error rate. The experimental results based on real audit data showed that this method could significantly reduce the time for training HMM without any loss in the detection rate, as well as in the false positive error rate. Jha, Tan and Maxion (2001) presented a statistical anomaly detection algorithm that categorized user behavior into normal or anomalous based on Markov chains in the 14th IEEE Computer Security Foundations Workshop. The study showed that the HMM *is potentially effective at* detecting some types of attacks. Nevertheless, in the real world, since user behavior cannot be simply treated as a binary outcome (1 or 0, or normal vs. anomaly), an alternative value between 1 and 0, or a gray buffer between normal or anomalous, is necessary in many cases when applying the HMM approach.

Other Methods

Data mining: Data mining is an information extraction approach used to discover hidden facts contained in data. It employs a combination of machine learning, statistical analysis, modeling techniques, and database technology to find patterns and subtle relationships in data and infers rules that allow the prediction of future results. Lee, Stolfo and Mok (1999) presented a framework for adaptively building intrusion detection models based on the data mining method. The essential idea of the framework was to utilize auditing programs to extract an extensive set of attributes for describing each network connection or host session, and then apply data mining to develop rules that accurately capture the behavior of intrusions and normal activities. The authors illustrated three types of algorithms that could be particularly useful for mining audit data: (1) classification–to map a data item into one of several predefined categories, (2) link analysis–to determine relationships between fields in the database records, and (3) sequence analysis–to discover what time-based sequences of audit events frequently occur together. The article also presented results obtained from data mining based on the 1998 MIT-DARPA data. The authors found that the data mining-based detection models performed as well as the best system built using manual knowledge engineering approaches.

Fourier Analysis: Fourier analysis is a mathematical technique that views real world signals as approximately a sum of sinusoids, each at a different frequency. The more sinusoids included in the sum, the better the approximation. The applications of Fourier analysis range from number theory, numerical analysis, control theory, and statistics to earth science, astronomy, and electrical engineering. Zhou and Lang (2003) presented a study that uses the Fourier analysis method to mine frequency content of network traffic for intrusion detection. Their study aims for detecting *DoS* and *Probe* attacks for rule-based intrusion detection systems in a practical way. The basic idea of the detection method is to analyze periodicity patterns in either packet streams or connection arrivals. The authors reported that by applying Fourier analysis to the time series created by network traffic signals, it is possible to identify whether periodicity patterns exist in the traffic. They demonstrated the effectiveness of this approach based on the 1999 MIT-DARPA data and other synthetic data captured by the network sniffer tool called *Ethertal*, which was installed on the authors' local networks. The experimental results based on 1999 MIT-DARPA data indicated that the new approach is effective in detecting anomalous traffic data from large-scale time series data that exhibit patterns over time and does not depend on prior knowledge of attack signatures.

Hybrid Model: Marin, Ragsdale and Surdu (2001) presented initial results of a hybrid intrusion detection model based on multiple approaches at the DARPA Information Survivability Conference & Exposition. They used a dataset that includes 50 users and more than 5,000 individual commands entered at a UNIX server. The authors applied expert rules and a genetic algorithm to reduce the dimensionality of the data, used cluster analysis to regroup the data, and refined the data using the learning vector quantization (LVQ) as a classifier to construct the final hybrid model. The authors reported that the advantage of using LVQ is that the model does not require anomalous records to be included in the training set because the LVQ is a nearest neighbor classifier. A new record presented to the network that lies outside a specified distance is classified as a masquerader. Moreover, the authors believed that their hybrid method could classify legitimate users into categories based on the percentage of commands that users employ in a specified period. Zhang, Li, Manikopoulos, Jorgenson and Ucles (2001) illustrated a hybrid intrusion detection system that combines both statistical modeling and neural network techniques. They also constructed five different types of neural network classifiers: Perceptron, Backpropagation (BP), Perceptron-backpropagation-hybrid (PBH), Fuzzy ARTMAP, and Radial-based Function. The system was tested with a network traffic dataset captured via a virtual network simulation tool with 6,000 records used for training and 4,000 records for testing. They reported that BP and PBH provide more efficient classifications based on their data than the alternatives, and that the system can reliably detect UDP flooding attacks with attack intensity as low as five to ten percent of background traffic. Recently Hooper (2007) proposed a hybrid detection strategy that employs ward hierarchical clustering analysis to enhance the accuracy of detection in real network infrastructures. It seems that the hybrid approach can provide a good solution for improving the performance of classification in intrusion detection.

Agent-Based Approach: The distributed autonomous agent-based approach has raised much attention in the intrusion detection area. This approach uses a collection of autonomous agents running on hosts within a mixed network and provides the foundation for real-time intrusion detection and response in which the agents monitor intrusive activity on their individual hosts. In addition, each agent can be configured to the operating environment in which it runs. Researchers on the intelligent agent-based approach come from a wide range of disciplines including distributed network systems technology, statistical modeling, artificial intelligence, data mining techniques, and software engineering. Studies show that this technology seems to be a promising direction for developing collaborative intrusion detection systems. Pikoulas, Buchanan, Mammion and Triantafyliopoulos (2002) developed a detection system that uses short-term prediction to identify user behavior, at which point the system advises the system administrator based on both intelligent agent software technology and a Bayesian statistical model. Short-term profile-based intrusion detection is a difficult and challenging task. It raises many questions in practice (how to determine the sample size of audit data, how to determine the alerting threshold, how to communicate between monitoring programs and software implementation, etc.). In this article, the authors found the results from their agent-based model to be consistent with actual user behavior. Gowadia, Farkasl and Valtorta (2003) presented another study supported by a research grant from the National Science Foundation, which proposed a framework called Probabilistic Agent-Based Intrusion Detection (PAID) in the 14th IRMA International Conference. PAID was developed based on using the agent-encapsulated Bayesian networks approach. The authors reported that the Bayesian agent-based solution is more economical than current non-Bayesian agent-based approaches, and it allows sharing of decisions among the agents as well as easy exploration of the trade-off between sensitivity and selectivity that affects the rate of false positive and false negative decisions.

Kernel approach: Kernel-level based intrusion detection systems have several advantages. For example, the kernel has the only reliable view of system status; it can avoid overhead due to extra context switching; and information is registered and processed at or near the place where it is produced, reducing the time and resources for transferring the information to the analysis engine. It is harder for an intruder to tamper with the intrusion detection system, as the attacker would have to modify the kernel. Warrender, Forrest and Pearlmutter (1999) used the kernel-level system calls data generated by nine different programs to compare the ability of different data modeling methods to distinguish between normal and abnormal behavior. They compared four methods—enumeration sequences, frequency-based sequences, data mining, and HMM, and reported that the HMM approach yielded the highest accuracy among those methods.

FUNDAMENTAL STATISTICAL ROLES AND CHALLENGES IN NETWORK SECURITY

Statistical science is concerned with the evidentiary value of observations (Woodworth, 2004) and it can play four basic roles in network security: (1) study design, (2) data exploration and dimension reduction, (3) outcome prediction and classification, and (4) user, site, or group profiling and decision-support. While these roles provide greatly opportunities for employing various statistical methods in network security, they also raise numbers of outstanding challenges. There are challenges in study design, in prediction and classification, in the uncertainty of decision-making, in the uncertainty of profiling user behavior, in determining within-user and between-user variances, and in tracking the changes of user behavior over time. We discuss these challenges in this section.

Study Design

Study design provides a fundamental step in the ultimate success of a project or study. It addresses three key questions: (1) what target(s) to measure and how to measure it (them), (2) what data to use, how to collect them and how large the data sample should be, and (3) what statistical methods to use and how to apply them with the data to be collected. A robust intrusion detection system demands a careful study design in action. However, unlike in other disciplines, such as market survey, healthcare, and the life sciences, where statisticians typically play a leading role in designing a study, statistical inputs have not gained enough attention in the design stage for most studies or projects in the network security area. Statisticians are usually asked to help during the analysis phase when the data have been collected. Given the complex and unique characteristics that network traffic has, it is important to involve a statistician in the study design phase and the beginning of a data collection procedure to ensure that target(s) can be measured correctly, data can be assembled in a statistically sound approach, and statistical methods will be applied properly. In network security, the challenges in study design are primarily from the data and data collection area and need to be emphasized. Generally,there are three types of network traffic log data: (1) network log (e.g., tcpdump, netflows), (2) host logs, and (3) security logs. Each type of log focuses on a different area: the network log focuses on the packets on the network, the host log focuses on the host activities, commands, logged in users, etc., and the security log focus specifically on the applications. As we discussed previously, while network traffic data have become increasingly utilized for training and testing various classification and profiling algorithms, statistical methods for analyzing such data have been studied and have grown substantially. But methods for the collection of such data are relatively limited and are insufficiently studied. Below we briefly discuss some of the outstanding challenges.

First, there is a need in determination of optimum sample size for collecting traffic. On one hand, the large size of network data raises challenges in analyzing and maintaining such data to both statisticians and network security engineers. For example, 74 hours of logged traffic data from a large enclave network could include as many as 344 million observations, and five hours of "tcpdump" packet traces may comprise 110 million observations. A middle size university usually has 35-40 megabytes of header information per minute and 50-60 gigabytes per day. McHugh (2001) reported that the total traffic into and out of the single building housing part of the Computer Science and Electrical Engineering departments at Portland State University averages about 500 Kb per second for about 100 workstations. Similarly, traffic for the Portland State Engineering School, which had about 1000 workstations and servers, is about 5 MB per second in each direction (into or out of the location). Although many statistical modeling approaches used in the network security area require accounting for sample size in order to meet a certain level of statistical power, sample size has not really been studied well in this field. One of the reasons could be that there is always a large among of data available, so the statistical power has never been an issue for network traffic data. However, large datasets usually require more resources and delay the system's response time.

On the other hand, as wireless networks become more popularly, we also face a new issue of too little traffic data in which many mobile and ad-hoc computing environments have only limited information that is available to be collected. This issue leads to inadequate sample size that increases both false positive and false negative rates. One of the statistical roles is to guide us on how to determine the optimum sample size required for modeling network traffic. We will discuss some possible solutions in Chapter VI.

Second, the type of data to be collected also poses a challenge. Ideally, we need three levels of data to better achieve the goals described in Section 1.1. We need: (1) the overall system-level traffic data (e.g., TCP/IP packs or flows), (2) user-level data that includes user-specific information, such as demographics, job-related data (e.g., working schedules, job functions, responsibilities, department or the section to which the user belongs), access privilege (e.g., login ID, authentications, authorizations), computer information (e.g., workstation configurations), and in some high security environments, users' keystroke and mouse dynamic data, and behavior patterns, and (3) system-specific information, which includes department information, (e.g., Research and Development, Financial, or Customer Services), the type of operating systems (e.g., Microsoft Windows XP, 2000, Linux, or UNIX), security-related policies and regulations, security-related hardware and software information (e.g., firewalls, secure sockets layer, virtual private network), and the range of IP addresses. These data do not all change dynamically and need to be collected in real time; some user-specific and system-specific information are fixed and can be located in different departments (e.g., Human Resource and Management of Information System). Moreover, not all data collections are purely technical tasks. Keystroke and mouse dynamic data could be a component of human biometric and could raise legal challenges that must be overcome before such data can be collected and analyzed. Nevertheless, with many data being linked and merged together, we can provide better security information. For example, if a user's work schedule is from 8:00 am to 5:00 pm, Monday to Friday, and we detected network traffic logged with this user ID or from this user's computer in a time zone that does not match with his/her specified working schedule, it would be reasonable to issue an alarm for verification (i.e. to send a message or make a phone call to the user to confirm). An intrusion prevention system can automatically conduct such verifications.

Despite the fact that each of the above three levels of data has strengths and weaknesses, they all contain unique information that represent one or more characteristics of the network traffic, users, and network infrastructure. Thus, having more data and developing a mixed database to bring all the strengths of each level of data together will lead to the reduction of the statistical uncertainty and increase in sensitivity and specificity in intrusion detection and prevention. We will continuously discuss these data types in Chapter III.

How do we collect the required system-level traffic data? This challenge is also associated with the task of how to sample data. Although both packet-based and flow-based data have pros and cons, both of them should be sampled randomly. Questions such as, what is the best sampling method and what is a reasonable sampling fraction and interval have to be addressed and we will examine them in Chapter VI.

Finally, use of user-specific data also raises challenges in data collection and analysis. For example, with keyboard and mouse data, the challenges are to determine which variables (e.g., the speed and the angles of mouse movements, or durations between two typed letters or words) should be collected and how they should be collected. To gather meaningful information from the sequence of commands or other types of information that have been retrieved from users, certain issues need to be addressed, such as how to extract these true commands from the data noise.

Data Exploration and Dimensional Reduction

Data exploration and dimensional reduction aim to examine data and to let the data tell us about the phenomena of the entity being studied without preconceived beliefs and represent data in a low-dimensional space. Data exploration provides a first picture about the data what which have been collected. During the data exploration, we can identify various issues related to data quality such as variable reliability and validity, outliers, missing values, mean and frequency. We can briefly understand the patterns of network traffic and even identify a particular pattern by assessing the distributions of key variables. Data dimensional reduction mainly employs methods and procedures from the multivariate analysis family. An appropriate dimension reduction analysis leads to represent high-dimensional information in a low-dimensional space without losing of significant information. For example, using factor analysis, we can retain more than 90% of information with a reduction of more than 80% of dimensions. Because of the large size of network traffic, the statistical principles of dimension reduction can make great contributions.

There are challenges in data exploration and in dimensional reduction. First, although data exploration always visualizes the information in data (William, 1997; Friendly, 2000; Unwin, Theus & Hofmann, 2006; Young, Valero-Mora & Friendly, 2006), but because of the large size of network traffic, we are not always able to analyze network data graphically. Often, the visualizing results may not be meaningful. Second, because the collectable information is limited, comparing to the analysis of dimensional reduction in other areas, such as healthcare and life sciences where rich information at the patient-level are acquirable by reviewing medical charts, dimensional reduction in network security is difficult on balancing between the benefits to be gained from reduced dimensions and the loss of information.

Third, we can reduce the number of variables by using a stepwise procedure that examines the impact of each variable to the model step by step. The variable that cannot contribute much to the variance explained would be removed. The challenge with the stepwise procedure is that such a procedure is only valid if all "independent" variables are in fact independent, and this requirement can often be difficult. Other ways to reduce the number of variables include factor analysis, principal component analysis and partial least squares (PLS). The philosophy behind these methods is very different from variable selection methods. In the former group of procedures "redundant" variables are not excluded, but rather they are retained and combined to form latent factors. It is believed that a construct should be an "open concept" that is triangulated by multiple indicators instead of a single measure (Salvucci, Walter, Conley, Fink, & Saba, 1997). In this sense, redundancy enhances reliability and yields a better model.

However, factor analysis and principal component analysis do not have the distinction between response and predictor variables and thus may not be applicable to research with the purpose of regression analysis. One way to reduce the number of variables in the context of regression is to use the PLS method, which is useful for constructing predictive models when the variables are highly collinear (Tobias, 1999). Besides collinearity, PLS is also robust against other data structural problems such as skew distributions (Cassel, Westlund, & Hackl, 1999).

Fourth, there is a challenge in the phenomena of "statistical significance." Because "statistical significance" is strongly associated with sample size, all differences could be "statistically significant" when dealing with a large sample size. However, when dealing with a small sample size, none may be. As a result, true abnormal behavior could be misidentified as "normal," and vice versa. Given the natural characteristics of attacks or anomalous activities that are difficult to model, some intrusion detection systems that try to determine the anomalous threshold based on measuring "statistically significant" differences (Anderson, Frivold, & Valdes, 1995; Goodman, 1999; Masum, Ye, Chen, & Noh, 2000; Sterne & Smith, 2001) can produce incorrect results. Overcoming the above mentioned issues and challenges could be a long-term task and will likely require many studies. Nevertheless, we will come back to discuss some possible solutions in Chapter VI.

Prediction and Classification

Prediction, classification, and profiling are three ultimate goals of modeling data. The aim of statistical prediction is to learn the patterns from historical data and to assign a value to each observation in new data where such a value usually is presented as a probability. Statistical classification, on the other hand, mainly focuses on placing individual items into groups. It aims to exploit the predicted probability for assigning a membership to observations with unknown memberships. Thus, the results of classification usually can be presented as a category with $k > 0$ of levels. Prediction requires heavy statistical modeling and classification, which may requires large-scale statistical simulations. Both supervised learning and unsupervised learning procedures directly affect the results of prediction and classification. Consequentially, results from both prediction and classification will support profiling, which focuses on capturing behavior patterns.

There are several fundamental challenges in prediction and classification in network security. First, reducing both false positive and false negative rates has been a constant challenge in the intrusion detection and prevention area. On one side, a stream of network traffic data with many positive risk factors might not represent a true attack, and a seemingly anomaly-free stream could represent a novel attack because of unknown factors and changing user behavior. On the other hand, network traffic data are usually high volume, and as a result of such large volumes of data, a 4% misclassification rate can yield approximately 300 alarms (excluding repeated connections) within one second. Validating every such case for human review is not practical.

Second, there is an increasing need for high performance unsupervised learning algorithms. In many real world scenarios, available network traffic data either may not include any anomalous event or such events are inadequate to fit a conventional regression model for establishing an association between the response variable and its predictors. For example, initial audit data are more likely to have all anomaly-free events in newly constructed network systems. Therefore a regression-based intrusion detection model cannot be activated until a certain percentage of abnormal events is acquired. While high-speed mobile wireless and ad-hoc network systems have became popular, the importance and need to develop new methods that allow the modeling of network traffic data to use attack-free training data have significantly increased.

Third, there is a challenge in modeling attack detection as opposed to profiling user behavior. For profiling user behavior we need more common variables that are statistically meaningful, but for detecting attacks we need to gather particular features that directly link to a particular attack. Such features may not have statistically predictive power (i.e., too low in frequencies) but they are strongly linked with a particular attack. For example, if we describe the characteristics for German shepherds as a whole, the criteria for select characteristics to describe them must have some basic common characteristics so we can distinguish the German shepherd group from others. However, suppose I want to identify my German shepherd, Jaime, from a group of German shepherds; I have to identify her with her unique characteristics that may not have any statistical meaning to the whole German shepherd group.

Fourth, detecting new types of attacks and anomaly in real time is a significant challenge. Anomaly-free and abnormal behavior in networked computers is hard to predict, as the boundaries cannot be well defined and no prior knowledge about novel attacks is available (Barbara, Wu & Jajodia, 2001). As we discussed earlier, the goals for current detection methods are to reduce false alarm rates and to detect new type of attacks. Rule-based detection has a low rate of false alarms, but it could be difficult to detect novel types of attacks. Anomaly detection, in principle, has the ability to detect new attacks, but also has the potential to generate too many false alarms. As new attacks emerge, the need for intrusion detection systems to detect novel attacks becomes critical. We will discuss these topics in more detail in Chapters VII, IX and X.

Profiling and Decision-Support

Profiling and decision-support is another main goal of modeling network traffic data. Unlike classification, which focuses on the level of individual observation and aims to assign a membership to each observation, profiling focuses on the level of the individual user, site, group, or sub-network system and the results are more subjective. Assume we have a set of network traffic data collected from one site and 10% of the data are classified as anomaly-free, 15% are classified as anomalous, and the remaining 75% are in a category of "unable to determined." With such classified results, the decision of profiling is: how can we appropriately categorize this site? Should we label it as an anomalous site because only 10% of traffic data are classified as anomaly-free? Or should we label it as an anomaly-free site because only 15% of traffic data are classified as anomalous? Or should we categorize it as an "unable to determine" site? It seems that a decision could be difficult to reach based on such data.

There is a challenge in measuring user behavior. Statistically, we can measure user behavior in four dimensions: (1) central tendency, (2) dispersion, (3) relative position, and (4) relationship. In Chapter V, we will briefly discuss the central tendency that is measured by mean, median and mode and dispersion (measured by range), deviation, variance, and standard deviation. The measure of relative positions are conversions of values to develop a standardized score and show where a given user stands in relation to others in the same score range. We will introduce scoring models in Chapter VIII. We will also discuss measuring relationship on user behavior in Chapter XI.

Statistical techniques have been used to build a profile of long-term normal user behavior and to detect significant anomalous behavior from the long-term profile. However, most long-term based detection techniques can be inaccurate in the short-term profile and could yield unacceptably high false positive or false negative rates (Pikoulas, Buchanan, Mannion, & Triantafyllopoulos, 2002; Foong, Yin, & Ng, 2003). One of the main barriers is that an intrusion detection system may not be able to correctly estimate the parameters to establish a baseline pattern that is close to the underlying "true" pattern of user behavior within a short time period or with limited traffic data being available to analyze.

The mapping of observed user behavior patterns to the underlying "true" user behavior patterns is a challenge in profiling user behavior. In general, by inference from the sample variability issue, observed user behavior might not represent the "true" pattern of a user, and the information could therefore result in misprofiling. Although the "true" pattern itself cannot be directly measured, it can be inferred via statistical modeling methods. The challenge lies in making such an inference. We will discuss some statistical simulation methods to address this challenge in Chapter XI.

SUMMARY

We have briefly discussed the overall statistical opportunities and challenges in network security in this chapter. National efforts have been undertaken to change information security strategies in the United States. Since early 2000s Congress has considered several proposals for improving information security across both the public and private sectors (U.S. Government, 2003). One of the proposals would require businesses to submit a cyber-security checklist in their filings with the U.S. Securities and Exchange Commission. By adapting various statistical methods and approaches and knowing opportunities and challenges, we would be able to significantly advance the area of network security and facilitate the development of robust intrusion detection and prevention systems particularly in the high-speed mobile wireless network environment.

REFERENCES

Anderson, P. J. (1972). Computer security technology planning study volume II, ESD-TR-73-51, Vol. II, Electronic Systems Division, Air Force Systems Command,   Hanscom Field, Bedford, MA.

Anderson, D., Frivold, T. & Valdes, A. (1995). Next-generation intrusion detection expert system (NIDES). Summary Report, SRI International.

Anderson, P. J. (1980). Computer security threat monitoring and surveillance. Fort Washington, PA: James P. Anderson Co.

Barbard, D., Wu, N., & Jajodia, S. (2001). Detecting novel network intrusions using Bayes estimators. In: Proceedings of the 1st SIAM International Conference on Data Mining, pp. 24-29.

Baskerville, R. (1993). Information systems security design methods: implications for information systems development, ACM Computing Surveys, 25(4), pp. 375-414.

Berg, B. A. (2004). *Markov Chain Monte Carlo simulations and their statistical analysis with Web-based Fortran code,* NJ: World Scientific.

Bishop, M. (2003). *Computer security: art and science.* Boston: Addison-Wesley.

Bolton, R. J. &D. J. Hand. D. J. (2002). Statistical fraud detection: A review (with discussion). *Statistical Science,* 17(3):235-255.

Boukerche, A. & Ren, Y. (2007). A novel solution based on mobile agent for anonymity in wireless and mobile ad hoc networks. In *Proceedings of the 3rd ACM Workshop on QoS and Security For Wireless and Mobile Networks* (Q2SWinet '07), pp. 86-94. ACM, New York, NY.

Bragg, R. Rhodes-Ousley, M. & Strassberg, K. (2004). *Network security: the complete reference.* California: McGraw-Hill

Bridges, S. M., Vaughn, R. B. (2000). Fuzzy data mining and genetic algorithms applied to intrusion detection. In: *Proceedings of the 23rd National Information Systems Security Conference,* 13-31.

Brutch, P. & Ko, C. (2003). Challenges in intrusion detection for wireless ad-hoc networks. In: *Proceedings of the Applications and the Internet Workshops,* 368-373.

Cannady, J. (1998). The application of artificial neural networks to misuse detection: Initial results. In: *Proceedings of the 1st International Workshop on the Recent Advances in Intrusion Detection (RAID),* 31-47.

Cannady, J. (2000). Next generation intrusion detection: autonomous reinforcement learning of network attacks. In: *Proceedings of the 23rd National Information Systems Security Conference,* 443-456.

Cassel, C., Hackl, P. & Westlund, A. H. (1999). Robustness of partial least-squares method for estimating latent variable quality structures, *Journal of Applied Statistics,* 26(4): pp. 435-446(12).

Chen, W.W.S. (2005). *Statistical methods in computer security,* Boca Raton, Florida: Chapman & Hall/CRC.

Cho, S. B. & Park, H. J. (2003). Efficient anomaly detection by modeling privilege flows using hidden Markov model. *Computer and Security 22*(1), 45-55.

Chouchane, M. R., Walenstein, A., and Lakhotia, A. (2007). Statistical signatures for fast filtering of instruction-substituting metamorphic malware. In *Proceedings of the 2007 ACM Workshop on Recurring Malcode* (WORM '07), pp. 31-37. ACM, New York, NY.

Christodorescu, M., Jha, S., and Kruegel, C. (2008). Mining specifications of malicious behavior. In *Proceedings of the 1st Conference on India Software Engineering Conference.* ACM, New York, NY, pp. 5-14.

Goonatilake, R., Herath, A., Herath, S., and Herath, J. (2007). Intrusion detection using the chi-square goodness-of-fit test for information assurance, network, forensics and software security. *J. Comput. Small Coll.* 23(1), pp. 255-263.

Goss, R., Botha, M. & von Solms, R. (2007). Utilizing fuzzy logic and neural networks for effective, preventative intrusion detection in a wireless environment. In *Proceedings of the 2007 Annual Research Conference of the South African institute of Computer Scientists and information Technologists on IT Research in Developing Countries* (SAICSIT '07), 226, pp. 29-35. ACM, New York, NY.

Cunningham, R. K., Lippmann, R. P., Fried, D. J., Garfinkle, S. L., Graf, I., Kendall, K. R., *et al.* (1999). Evaluating intrusion detection systems without attacking your friends: the 1998 DARPA intrusion detection evaluation. *SANS*.

Curtin, M. (1997). Introduction to network security. Retrieved Feb. 29, 2008 from http://www. interhack.net/pubs/network-security.pdf.

Denning, D. (1987). An intrusion-detection model. *IEEE Transaction on Software Engingeering, 13*(2), 222-232.

Department of Defense (1985). National security institute - 5200.28-STD: *Trusted Computer System Evaluation Criteria,* Retrieved on April 29, 2008 from http://nsi.org/Library/Compsec/orangebo. txt.

Efron, B. & Tibshirani, E. R. (1994). *An introduction to the bootstrap.* London: Chapman & Hall.

Elkan, C. (2000). Results of the KDD'99 classifier learning contest. *ACM Transactions on Information and System Security, 3*(4), 262-294.

Foong, H. W., Yin, N. A., & Ng, N. J. (2003). Intrusion detection in wireless ad-hoc networks. Retrieved January 20,2004, from http://www.comp.nus.edu.sg/~cs4274/termpapers/0304-I/group4/paper.pdf

Forrest, S., Hofmeyr, S., Somayaji, A., & Longstaff, T. (1996). A sense of self for UNIX processes. In: *Proceedings of the 1996 IEEE Symposium on Security and Privacy,* 120-128.

Friendly, M. (2000). *Visualizing categorical data.* Cary, NC: SAS Publishing.

Gao, B., Ma, H., & Yang, Y. (2002). HMMS (hidden markov models) based on anomaly intrusion detection method. In: *Proceedings of the First International Conference on Machine Learning and Cybernetics,* 381-385.

Garfinkel, S. & Spafford, G. (1997). *Web security & commerce.* California: O'Reilly & Associates, Inc.

Gharibian, F. & Ghorbani, A.A. (2007). Comparative study of supervised machine learning techniques for intrusion detection, In *Proceedings of the Fifth Annual Conference on Communication Networks and Services Research,* pp. 350-358.

Gomez, J. & Dasgupta, D. (2002). Evolving fuzzy classifiers for intrusion detection. In: *Proceedings of 3rd Annual IEEE Information Assurance Workshop,* 68-75.

Goodman, S. N. (1999). Toward evidence-based medical statistics 1: the p value fallacy. *Annals of Internal Medicine, 130,* 995-1004.

Gowadia, V., Farkasl, C., & Valtorta, M. (2003). Agent based intrusion detection with soft evidence. In: *Proceedings of the 14ᵗʰ IRMA International Conference.* 345-350.

Heberlein, L. T., Dias, G. V., Levitt, K. N., Mukherjee, B., Wood, J., & Wolber, D. (1990). A network security monitor. In: *Proceedings of the 1990 IEEE Symposium on Research in Security and Privacy,* 296-304.

Herrero, A., Corchado, E., Gastaldo, P., Leoncini, D., Picasso, F. & Zunino, R. (2007). Intrusion detection at packet level by unsupervised architectures, *Lecture Notes in Computer Science, 4881,* pp. 718-727.

Hooper, E. (2007).An intelligent intrusion detection and response system using hybrid ward hierarchical clustering analysis, In *Proceedings of 2007 International Conference on Multimedia and Ubiquitous Engineering (MUE'07),* pp. 1187-1192.

Hossain, M. & Bridges, S. M. (2001). A framework for an adaptive intrusion detection system with data mining. In: *Proceedings of the 13th Canadian information technology security symposium,* pp.279-284.

IEEE 802.11 Working Group (2007). IEEE 802.11-2007: *wireless LAN medium access control (MAC) and physical layer (PHY) specifications.* ISBN0-7381-5656-9.

INFOSEC Research Council (1999). National scale INFOSEC research hard problems list. Retrieved January 21, 2004, from http://www.infosec-research.org/

Isohara, T., Takemori, K. & Sasase, I. (2008). Anomaly detection on mobile phone based operational behavior, *IPSJ Digital Courier,* 4, pp. 9-17.

Jahnke, M., Toelle, J., Finkenbrink, A., Wenzel, A., Gerhards-Padilla, E., Aschenbruck, N. & Martini, P. (2007). Methodologies and frameworks for testing ids in ad-hoc networks. In *Proceedings of the 3rd ACM Workshop on QoS and Security For Wireless and Mobile Networks* (Q2SWinet '07), pp. 113-122. ACM, New York, NY.

Jha, S., Tan, K., & Maxion, R. A. (2001). Markov chains, classifiers, and intrusion detection. In: *Proceedings of the 14th IEEE Computer Security Foundations Workshop (CSFW),* pp.206-219.

Joshi, S. S. & Phoha, V. V. (2005). Investigating hidden Markov models capabilities in anomaly detection, In *Proceedings of the 43rd annual Southeast regional conference - Volume 1* ACM-SE 43. ACM, New York, NY, pp. 98-103.

Karger, A. P. & Schell, R. R. (1974). Multics security evaluation: Vulnerability analysis. *ESD-TR-74-193 Vol. II, ESD/AFSC,* Hanscom AFB, Bedford, MA.

KDD Cup (1999). Data available on the Web. Retrieved February 19, 2004, from http://kdd.ics.uci.edu/databases/kddcup99/kddcup99.html

Khan, L., Awad, M. & Thuraisingham, B. (2007).A new intrusion detection system using support vector machines and hierarchical clustering , *The International Journal on Very Large Data Bases* pp. 507-521.

Krishnapuram, R., Joshi, A., Nasraoui, O., Yi, L.(2001). Low-complexity fuzzy relational clustering algorithms for Web mining. *IEEE Transactions on Fuzzy Systems,* Vol. 9 (4), 595-608

Lazarevic, A., Ertoz, L., Kumar, V., Ozgur, A., & Srivastava, J. (2003). A comparative study of anomaly detection schemes in network intrusion detection, In *Proceedings of the Third SIAM International Conference on Data Mining,*

Laet, G. D., & Schauwers, G. (2005). *Network security fundamentals.* Cisco Press fundamentals series. Indianapolis, Ind: Cisco.

Lee, W., Stolfo, S., & Mok, K. (1999). A data mining framework for building intrusion detection models. In: *Proceedings of the IEEE Symposium on Security and Privacy,* 120-132.

Leung, K. & Leckie, C. (2005). Unsupervised anomaly detection in network intrusion detection using clusters. In *Proceedings of the Twenty-Eighth Australasian Conference on Computer Science - Volume 38* (Newcastle, Australia). V. Estivill-Castro, Ed. ACM International Conference Proceeding Series, vol. 102. Australian Computer Society, Darlinghurst, Australia, pp. 333-342.

Linden, T. (1976). Operating system structures to support security and reliable software. *NBS Technical Note 919,* Institute for Computer Sciences and Technology, National   Bureau of Standards, US Department of Commerce, Washington DC.

Lippmann, R., & Cunningham, S. (1999). Improving intrusion detection performance using keyword selection and neural networks. In *Proceedings of the Second International Workshop on Recent Advances in Intrusion Detection (RAID99)*. West Lafayette, Indiana.

Lippman, R. & Cunningham, S. (2000). Improving intrusion detection performance using keyword selection and neural networks. *Computer Networks, 34*(4), 594-603.

Lippmann, R., Haines, W. J., Fried, D. J., Korba, & Das, K. (2000). The 1999 DARPA off-line intrusion detection evaluation. *Computer Networks, 34*(4), 579-595.

Lunt, T. & Jagannathan, R. (1988). A prototype real-time intrusion-detection expert system. In: *Proceedings of the 1988 IEEE Symposium on Security and Privacy*, 2-10.

Marin, J., Ragsdale, D., & Surdu, J. (2001). A hybrid approach to the profile creation and intrusion detection. In: *Proceedings of the DARPA Information Survivability Conference & Exposition (DISCEX II)*, 69-76.

Maiwald, E. (2003). *Network security: a beginner's guide, 2nd Edition*. California: McGraw-Hill

Mano, C., Blaich, A., Liao, Q., Jiang, Y., Cieslak, D., Salyers, D., & Striegel, A. (2008). RIPPS: Rogue Identifying Packet Payload Slicer Detecting Unauthorized Wireless Hosts Through Network Traffic Conditioning. *ACM Trans. Inf. Syst. Secur.* 11(2), pp. 1-23.

Marchette, D. J. (2001). *Computer intrusion detection and network monitoring: a statistical viewpoint*, Springer.

Marchette, D. J. (2003). Statistical opportunities in network security,

Proceedings of the 35th Symposium on the Interface of Computing Science and Statistics, Computing Science and Statistics, Vol. 35, pp 28-38.

Marinova-Boncheva, V. (2007). Applying a data mining method for intrusion detection. In *Proceedings of the 2007 international Conference on Computer Systems and Technologies*. B. Rachev, A. Smrikarov, and D. Dimov, Eds. CompSysTech '07, 285, pp. 1-6. ACM, New York, NY.

Masum, S., Ye, E. M., Chen, Q., & Noh, K. (2000). Chi-square statistical profiling for anomaly detection. In: *Proceedings of the 2000 IEEE Workshop on Information Assurance and Security*, 182-188.

McClure, S., Scambray, J. & Kurtz, G. (1999). *Hacking exposed: network security secrets and solutions*. California: Osborne/McGraw-Hill.

McHugh, J. (2000a). Testing intrusion detection systems: a critique of the 1998 and 1999 DARPA intrusion detection system evaluations as performed by Lincoln Laboratory, *ACM Transactions on Information and System Security*, 3(4) pp. 262-294.

McHugh, J. (2000b). Intrusion and intrusion detection, *International Journal of Information Security*, 1(1). pp. 14-35.

McNab, C. (2007). *Network security assessment: know your network, 2nd Edition*. California: O'Reilly & Associates, Inc.

Malik, S. (2003). *Network security principles and practices*. Indianapolis, Ind: Cisco.

Mukkamala, S., Janoski, G., & Sung A. (2002). Intrusion detection using neural network and support vector machines. In: *Proceedings of the IEEE 2002 International Joint Conference on Neural Networks*, 1702-1707.

Mukkamala, S. & Sung A. (2004). Intrusion detection systems using adaptive regression splines. In: *Proceedings of the 6th International Conference on Enterprise Information Systems,* 26-33.

Nayyar, H. & Ghorbani, A.A.(2008). Approximate autoregressive modeling for network attack detection, *Journal of Computer Security,16(2)*, pp. 165-197.

Neumann, P. G., Robinson, L., Levitt, K, L., Boyer, R. S., & Saxena, A. R. (1975). A Provably secure operating system. *M79-225*, Stanford Research Institute, Menlo Park, CA.

Neumann, P. G. & Prras, P. A. (1999). Experiences with emerald to date. In: *Proceedings of 1st Usenix Workshop on Intrusion Detection and Network Monitoring,* 201-211.

Patcha, A. & Park, J-M. (2007). An overview of anomaly detection techniques: Existing solutions and latest technological trends, *Computer Networks*, 51(12). pp.3448-3470.

Pikoulas, J., Buchanan, W., Mammion, M., Triantafyliopoulos, K. (2002). An intelligent agent security intrusion system. In: *Proceedings of the 9th Annual IEEE Internation Conference and Workshop on the Engineering of Computer-Based Systems,* 94-102.

Qin, M. & Hwang, K. (2004). Frequent rules for intrusive anomaly detection with Internet data mining. In: *Proceedings of the 13th USENIX Security Symposium,* 456-462.

Qu, D., Vetter, B., M., & Jou, Y. F. (1997). Statistical anomaly detection for link-state routing protocols. In: *Proceedings of 1997 IEEE Symposium on Security and Privacy,* 62-70.

Robertson, S., Siegel, E. V., Miller, M., & Stolfo, S. J. (2003). Surveillance detection in high bandwidth environments. In: *Proceedings of the 2003 DARPA DISCEX III Conference,* 130-138.

Salvucci, S., Walter, E., Conley, V., Fink, S. & Saba, M. (1997). *Measurement error studies at the national center for education statistics,* National Center for Education Statistics (ED), Washington, DC.

Scott, S. L. (2004). A Bayesian paradigm for designing intrusion detection systems, *Computational Statistics & Data Analysis*, 45(1), pp. 69-83.

Schonlau, M., DuMouchel, W., Ju, W.H., Karr, A.F., Theus, M., & Vardi, Y. (2001). Computer intrusion: Detecting masquerades, *Statistical Science* 16:58: pp. 58-74.

Shyu, M., Chen, S., Sarinnapakorn, K., & Chang, L. (2003). A novel anomaly detection scheme based on principal component classifier. In: *Proceedings of the IEEE Foundations and New Directions of Data Mining Workshop, in conjunction with the 3rd IEEE International Conference on Data Mining (ICDM),* 172-179.

Shyu, M., Quirino, T., Xie, Z., Chen, S. & Chang, L. (2007). Network intrusion detection through Adaptive Sub-Eigenspace Modeling in multiagent systems. *ACM Trans. Auton. Adapt. Syst.* 2(3) No. 9.

Smaha, S. (1988). Haystack: An intrusion detection system. In: *Proceedings of the 1998 IEEE Symposium on Security and Privacy,* 37-44.

Smedinghoff, T. J. (1996). *Online Law: The SPA's Legal Guide to Doing Business on the Internet,* Boston: Addison-Wesley Developers Press.

Snapp, S. R., Brentano, J., Dias, G. V., Goan, T. L., Heberlein, L. T., Ho, C., Levitt, K. N., Mukherjee, B., Smaha, S. E., Grance, T., Teal, D. M., & Mansur, D. (1991). DIDS (Distributed Intrusion Detection system) - motivation, architecture and an early prototype. In: *Proceedings of the 14th National Security Conference,* 167-176.

Stallings, W. (2003). *Network security essentials, applications and standards. 2nd Ed.* New Jersey: Pearson Education.

Sterne, J., A. C. & Smith, G. D. (2001). Sifting the evidence-what's wrong with significance test? *British Medical Journal, 322,* 226-31.

Strebe, M. & Perkins, C. (2000). *Firewalls,* CA: SYBEX Network Press.

Taylor, C & Alves-Foss, J. (2001). "Low cost" network intrusion detection, (pp. 89-96). In *Proceeding of New Security Paradigms Workshop.*

Taylor, C & Alves-Foss, J. (2002). An empirical analysis of NATE: Network Analysis of Anomalous Traffic Events. In: *Proceedings of the 2002 workshop on new security Paradigms,* 18-26.

Teng, H., Chen, K., & Lu, S. (1990). Adaptive real-time anomaly detection using inductively generated sequential patterns. In: *Proceedings of the 1990 IEEE Symposium on Research in Security and Privacy,* 278-284.

Tobias, R. D. (1999). *An introduction to partial least squares regression.* Cary, NC: SAS Institute.

Unwin, A., Theus, M., Hofmann, H. (2006). *Graphics of large datasets: visualizing a million.* New York: Springer-Verlag.

U.S. Government. (2003, February). The national strategy to secure cyberspace. The White House, Washington. Retrieved January 18, 2004, from http://www.whitehouse.gov/pcipb/cyberspace_strategy.pdf

Vacca, J. R. (2006). *Guide to wireless network security.* New York: Springer-Verlag.

Vaccaro, H. S. & Liepins, G. E. (1989). Detection of anomalous computer session activity. In: *Proceedings of the 1989 IEEE Symposium on Security and Privacy,* 280-289.

Valdes, A. & Skinner, K. (2000). Adaptive, model-based monitoring for cyber attack detection. In: *Proceedings of the 3rd International workshop on Recent Advances in Intrusion Detection,* 281-290.

Vardi, Y. (1996). Network tomography: estimating source-destination traffic intensities from link data, *Journal of the American Statistical Association,* 91, pp. 365-377.

Wang, Y. & Cannady, J. (2005). Develop a composite risk score to detect anomalyintrusion. In: *Proceedings of the IEEE SoutheastCon 2005,* 445-449.

Wang Y. (2005). A multinomial logistic regression modeling approach for anomaly intrusion detection. *Computers & Security;*24(8):662-674

Wang Y. (2007). A bootstrap-based simple probability-based profiling model to profile user behavior, *Security Journal* (in press)

Wang Y., Kim, I., Mbateng, G., and Ho, H-Y. (2006). A latent class modeling approach for anomaly intrusion detection, *Computer communications,* 30(1),91-100.

Wang, Y., Normand, SL.T. (2006). Determining the minimum sample size of audit data required to profile user behavior and detect anomaly intrusion. *International Journal of Business Data Communications and Networking;* 2(3), pp 31-45.

Wang Y., Seidman, L. (2006). Risk factors to retrieve anomaly intrusion information and profile user behavior. *International Journal of Business Data Communications and Networking;*2(1), pp. 41-57.

Ware, W. (1970). Security controls for computer systems. *Report of Defense Science Board Task Force on Computer Security, RAND Report R609-1,* The RAND Corporation, Santa Monica, CA.

Warrender, C., Forrest, S., & Pearlmutter, B. (1999). Detecting intrusion using system calls: alternative data models. In: *Proceedings of the IEEE Symposium on Security and Privacy,* 133-145.

Woodworth, G. G. (2004) *Biostatistics a Bayesian introduction,* New Jersey, John Wiley & Sons, Inc.

Wozniak, S. (1977). The Apple-II, *Byte,* 2(5).

Wright, C., Monrose, F., and Masson, G. M. (2004). HMM profiles for network traffic classification. In *Proceedings of the 2004 ACM Workshop on Visualization and Data Mining For Computer Security.* ACM, New York, NY, pp 9-15.

Ye, N., Emran, S. M., Li, X., & Chen, Q. (2001). Statistical process control for computer intrusion detection. In: *Proceedings of the DARPA Information Survivability Conference & Exposition (DISCEX II),* 397-343.

Ye, N., Emran, S.M., Chen, Q., & Vilbert, S. (2002). Multivariate statistical analysis of audit trails for host-based intrusion detection. *IEEE Transaction on Computers,* 51(7): 810-820.

Yihua L. and Vemuri, V. R. (2002). Use of k-nearest neighbor classifier for intrusion detection, *Computers & Security,* 21(5), pp 439-448.

Young, F. W. Valero-Mora, P. M. & Friendly, M. (2006). *Visual statistics: seeing data with dynamic interactive graphics.* New Jersey, John Wiley & Sons, Inc.

William, G. J. (1997). *Statistical graphics for univariate and bivariate data,* California: SAGE Publications Inc.

Zhang, Y., Lee, W., & Huang, Y. (2003). Intrusion detection techniques for mobile wireless networks. *IEEE Wireless Networks Journal,* 9(5), 545-556.

Zhang, Z., Li, J., Manikopoulos, C. N., Jorgenson, J., & Ucles, J. (2001). HIDE: A hierarchical network intrusion detection system using statistical preprocessing and neural network classification. In: *Proceedings of the 2001 IEEE Workshop Information Assurance and Security,* 85-90.

Zhou, M. & Lang, S. D. (2003). Mining frequency content of network traffic for intrusion detection. In: *Proceedings of the IASTED International Conference on Communication, Network, and Information Security,* 101-107.

ENDNOTES

[1]   Apple is a registered trademark of Apple Computer, Inc.
[2]   Macintosh is a registered trademark of Apple Computer, Inc.
[3]   Cisco is the registered trademark of Cisco Systems, Inc

Chapter II
Statistical Analysis Software

You only live once - but if you work it right, once is enough.

- Joe E. Lewis

INTRODUCTION

Statistical software and their corresponding computing environments are essential factors that will lead to the achievement of efficient and better research. If we think of computing and classifying algorithms as the roadmap to arrive at our final destination, a statistical package is the vehicle that is used to reach this point. Figure 2.1 shows a basic roadmap of the roles that statistical software packages play in network security.

One of the advantages of using a statistical package in network security is that it provides a fairly easy and quick way to explore data, test algorithms and evaluate models. Unfortunately, not every package is suitable for analyzing network traffic. Given the natural characteristics of the network traffic data (i.e., large size and the ability to change dynamically), several fundamental attributes are necessary for specific packages. First, the package should have good data management capacities, which include the capacity to read large data and output/save resulting files in different formats, the capability to merge and link processed data with other data sources, and the ability to create, modify and delete variables within data. Second, it should be able to process large amounts of data efficiently because statistical analyses in network security are usually based on dynamic online data, which requires the application to conduct analyses timely; this differs from areas such as healthcare, life science, and epidemiology where statistical analyses are conducted based

Figure 2.1 Roles of statistical software in network security

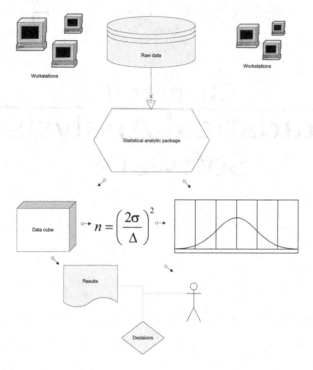

on static offline data. Third, it should support modern modeling procedures and methods, such as the Bayesian methods, hidden Markov model, hierarchical generalized linear model, etc. Finally, because usability is an important factor, we want the software to be both accessible and user-friendly. These attributes are particularly important during the development phase because they allow us to quickly test hypotheses and examine modeling strategies effectively.

Since many commercial and research-oriented software packages may not have all of the aforementioned attributes, we may need to implement multiple packages, such as packages for data management, for fitting a particular model, and for displaying results graphically. In the end, we may more likely use a general-purpose programming language, such as C, C++ or Java to create a customized application which we can later integrate with the other components of the intrusion detection or prevention system. The results obtained from the statistical software can be used as a gold-standard benchmark to validate the results from the customized application.

In this chapter, we will introduce several popular commercial and research-oriented packages that have been widely used in the statistical analysis, data mining, bioinformatics, and computer science communities. Specifically, we will discuss SAS[1], Stata[2] and R in Sections The SAS System, STATA and R, respectively; and briefly describe S-Plus[3], WinBUGS, and MATLAB[4] in Section Other Packages. The goal of this chapter is to provide a quick overview of these analytic software packages with some simple examples to help readers become familiar with the computing environments and statistical computing languages that will be referred to in the examples presented in the rest of these chapters. We have included some fundamental materials in the Reference section for further reading for those readers who would like to acquire more detailed information on using these software packages.

Before beginning our discussion on the statistical software programs, there are a few notes worth mentioning. First, all software that is discussed in this chapter are all the Professional Editions since we want to avoid any limitations that a student edition or standard edition may have. All software is running from the Microsoft Windows XP platform. We assume that we all know how to install and start software from the operating system that we are using. Second, all the examples present in this chapter are for demonstration proposes only and may need to be modified when applying them to any real conditions. Finally, throughout this chapter, and the rest of chapters, whenever we refer to any particular statistical language's commands, functions, or statements, we will use italicized font, for example, *PROC FREQ*.

THE SAS SYSTEM

SAS is a registered trademark or trademark of the SAS Institute Inc. The SAS system (http://www.sas.com) is an integrated software package that allows users to perform a wide range of tasks, including for example, data entry, data management, data warehousing, data mining, data reporting, data visualization, statistical analysis, business intelligence, decision support, etc. SAS is an acronym that stands for Statistical Analysis System, which was developed as a statistical software package in the 1970s. Since then, the SAS system has become very popular and many new features and products have been added to the system that make it more than just as a statistical analysis system. The SAS Institute decided to officially drop the name Statistical Analysis System, and simply refer to it by its acronym, SAS. The SAS system supports various platforms including Windows, UNIX, Linux, and Solaris. It also has a server-side version to support many large-scale database systems. In this book, we will use the Microsoft Windows platform with the SAS version of 9.1.3.

User Interface

SAS is not command-driven (i.e., enter a command to see the result), but rather uses a scripting language software application. The Graphic User Interface (GUI) of the SAS display screen includes three main components: (1) Program Editor, (2) Program Log, and (3) Result Output (Figure 2.2). The Program Editor window is where users develop and edit their SAS program statements. The log window contains information about the program execution after the program has been submitted, including error messages, and CPU and real times used by executing the program statements. The output window displays results of the analysis. Figures 2.2 through 2.4 show detailed information on how to fit a multiple logistic regression model, and we will discuss this model in more detail in Chapter VIII.

A SAS program consists of three main steps: LIBNAME, DATA, and PROC. A LIBNAME step assigns an alias, known as *libref,* to a directory of in a physical location where SAS will store or retrieve SAS datasets. The *libref* is then used in subsequent programs

Figure 2.2 SAS Interface: Program Editor (bottom), Log (middle), and Output (top)

to refer its specific directory name. If the LIBNAME step is missing, SAS will save and retrieve the data from its default directory, *saswork,* which is a temporary directory that will be destroyed after SAS is closed.

The DATA step creates and reads SAS datasets. Generally, a SAS dataset can be created in two ways: inputting it from an existing data source or creating it within the SAS DATA statement. SAS can input various types of data including Microsoft Excel, Access, and ASCII data. It can also access data from a variety of database systems, including Microsoft SQL Server, Assess, Oracle, MySQL, and MaxDB (formerly SAP) through the Open Database Connectivity (ODBC), or the corresponding SAS database component installed on the server-side.

Example 2.1→ Assess Data from SQL Server. Assume we have a SQL Server database either in the server or on a local machine, and a SAS client version is installed on the local machine. To access the database using SAS, we first create an ODBC connection (following the steps: Settings → Control Panel → Administrative Tools → Data Sources (ODBC) that bridges the database with SAS. Figures 2.3 through 2.6 illustrate the major steps used to create the ODBC source; SAS codes used to access the SQL Server database from the local machine are given in Display 2.1.

Display 2.1
SAS codes to assess SQLserver database

```
Proc sql noprint;
connect to odbc (datasrc="SQL_test" USER=dbo PASSWORD=sa);
create Table as sql select * from connection to ODBC
(select * from dbo.orders);
disconnect from odbc;
quit;
```

The *PROC* step includes programming statements that conduct specific data managements and statistical analyses of the data specified in the LIBNAME and/or DATA step sections. SAS has very thorough procedures for data management and statistical analyses.

Figure 2.3 Select System DSN for ODBC and click the Add button

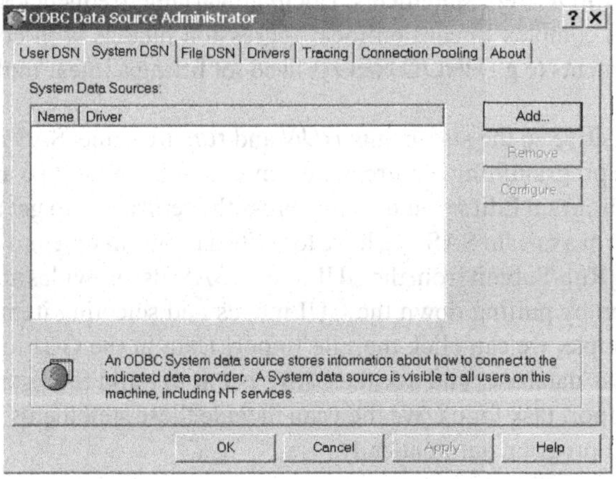

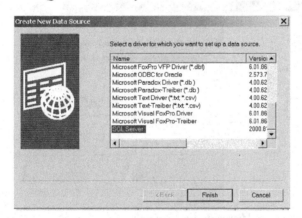

Figure 2.4 Select the SQL Server driver from the driver list and click Finish

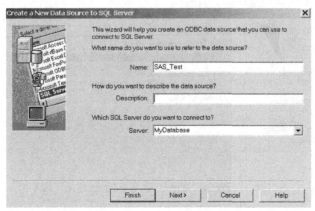

Figure 2.5 Create source name and select the SQL Server name (the SQL server has to be installed first)

For example, we can use *PROC SQL* to merge and link data from different sources, collapse or sort data with *PROC SQL* statements, calculate variable frequencies with *PROC FREQ* statements or fit complex linear/nonlinear regression models with corresponding *PROC* modeling statements (e.g., *PROC REG* is used for fitting a linear multiple regression model).

SAS is not case sensitive so the statements *RUN* and *run* are same. SAS also does not offer a command-drive programming feature, which means, we cannot type an expression (e.g., 50+100) into the Program Editor window and press the return key to get an output (in this case 150). To perform a task in SAS, we have to write a program first and then execute the program by clicking Run/Submit from the GUI screen. SAS also provides a user-friendly point-and-click function by pulling down the GUI menus and selecting items to conduct specific tasks. For example, we can click the File/Import Data in the GUI to import data from a Microsoft Access database, and ask the SAS system to build SAS statements that actually perform the import task for us. We then can include these statements in a program so that SAS can run the program automatically.

Figure 2.6 Select the appropriate authenticity method and click Next

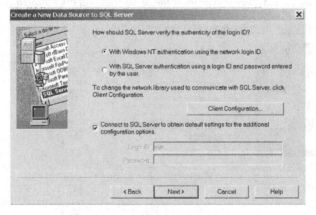

Figure 2.7 Import data from Microsoft Access database

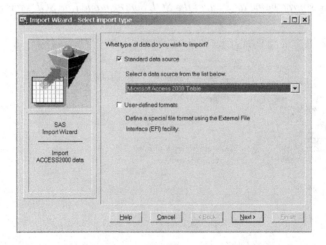

Running SAS

Let us use the KDD-Cup 1999 data to fit a multiple logistic regression model using SAS. We will discuss in detail about the KDD-Cup data in Chapter III but for now let us adapt it temporally. The SAS codes for this exercise are shown in Display 2.2. First, we assigned an alias named "temp" in the LIBNAME step, which refers to the data directory "Book/Chapter 2" in the F drive. We then created a temporary dataset in the DATA step named "IDS," which was stored in the SAS default directory, *saswork*. Finally, we fit the model in the PROC step by specifying the logistic procedure, *PROC LOGISTIC*, the model has "attack" (yes/no) as a response (dependent) variable and 16 predictor (independent) variables. To execute this program click the "RUN" button in the program window. Note that the *RUN* statement at the end of *DATA* and *PROC* steps tells SAS to process the preceding program statements. SAS requires a *RUN* statement for each *DATA* and *PROC* step to compile and execute the step independently from every other step. If this statement is missing in one step, this step will not be executed when the program is submitted.

Display 2.2
SAS codes to fit a logistic regression example

```
/*-------------------------------------------------
Libname step section
------------------------------------------------*/;
libname temp 'F:\Book\Chapter 2\';
/*-------------------------------------------------
   Data step section
------------------------------------------------*/;
data IDS;
set temp.var_16_val;
run;
/*-------------------------------------------------
   Procedure statement section
------------------------------------------------*/;
proc logistic data=IDS descending;
model attack=
Duration TCP UDP HTTP RST logged_I Num_comp is_guest Count Same_srv
Diff_srv Dst_host Dst_hos1 Dst_hos3 Dst_hos4 Dst_hos5/lackfit rsq stb;
run;
```

Once the program is executed, SAS displays detailed information on the program execution in the Log window (Display 2.3) and results in the Output window (Display 2.4), respectively.

Display 2.3
Log window of the logistic regression example

```
149  /*------------------------------------------------
150     Libname statement section
151  ----------------------------------------------*/;
152  libname temp 'F:\Book\Chapter 2\';
NOTE: Libref TEMP was successfully assigned as follows:
      Engine:         V8
      Physical Name: F:\Book\Chapter 2
153
154  /*------------------------------------------------
155     Data statement section
156  ----------------------------------------------*/;
157  data IDS;
158  set temp.var_16_val;
159  run;

NOTE: There were 311029 observations read from the dataset TEMP.VAR_16_VAL.
NOTE: The data set WORK.IDS has 311029 observations and 18 variables.
NOTE: DATA statement used:
      real time          47.05 seconds
      cpu time           0.75 seconds

160  /*------------------------------------------------
161     Procedure statement section
162  ----------------------------------------------*/;
163
164  proc logistic data=IDS descending;
165  model attack=
166  Duration TCP UDP HTTP RST logged_I Num_comp is_guest Count Same_srv
167  Diff_srv Dst_host Dst_hos1 Dst_hos3 Dst_hos4 Dst_hos5/lackfit rsq stb;
168  run;

NOTE: PROC LOGISTIC is modeling the probability that attack='Normal'.
NOTE: Convergence criterion (GCONV=1E-8) satisfied.
NOTE: There were 311029 observations read from the dataset WORK.IDS.
NOTE: PROCEDURE LOGISTIC used:
      real time          26.90 seconds
      cpu time           16.43 seconds
```

Display 2.4
Output from the logistic regression example

```
          The SAS System          09:58 Sunday, April 30, 2006    1

                                      The LOGISTIC Procedure
                                        Model Information

                     Data Set                        WORK.IDS
                     Response Variable               attack
                     Number of Response Levels        2
                     Number of Observations          311029
                     Link Function                   Logit
                     Optimization Technique          Fisher's scoring

                                      Response Profile
                             Ordered                           Total
                              Value       attack            Frequency

                                 1        Normal               60593
                                 2        Anomaly             250436

                            Model Convergence Status
```

continued on following page

Display 2.4 continued

```
        Convergence criterion (GCONV=1E-8) satisfied.

                                    Model Fit Statistics

                                               Intercept
                                   Intercept       and
                       Criterion      Only      Covariates

                       AIC          306757.09    60380.196
                       SC           306767.74    60561.206
                       -2 Log L     306755.09    60346.196

              R-Square   0.5472   Max-rescaled R-Square   0.8726

                   Testing Global Null Hypothesis: BETA=0

              Test              Chi-Square    DF    Pr > ChiSq

              Likelihood Ratio   246408.891   16      <.0001
              Score              242955.202   16      <.0001
              Wald                27331.6478   16      <.0001


   The SAS System        09:58 Sunday, April 30, 2006   2

                        The LOGISTIC Procedure

                 Analysis of Maximum Likelihood Estimates

                             Standard                         Standardized
    Parameter   DF   Estimate   Error   Chi-Square  Pr > ChiSq    Estimate
    Intercept    1    -6.5993   0.0731    8141.1634     <.0001
    Duration     1    -0.0217   0.00931      5.4382     0.0197     -0.0120
    TCP          1    -0.2249   0.0912       6.0781     0.0137     -0.0603
    UDP          1     6.9260   0.0846    6697.2573     <.0001      1.0697
    HTTP         1     5.6335   0.0487   13394.9079     <.0001      1.0533
    RST          1    -4.8991   0.1274    1479.4657     <.0001     -0.2298
    logged_i     1     3.7827   0.0640    3487.9346     <.0001      0.7879
    Num_comp     1    -0.0240   0.00756     10.0912     0.0015     -0.0132
    is_guest     1    -4.8729   0.1424    1171.5843     <.0001     -0.1321
    Count        1     1.0731   0.0400     719.3765     <.0001      0.5916
    Same_srv     1     3.3580   0.0802    1753.4538     <.0001      1.8514
    Diff_srv     1     0.4902   0.0164     896.4457     <.0001      0.2702
    Dst_host     1    -0.8369   0.0172    2353.9437     <.0001     -0.4614
    Dst_hos1     1    -2.4700   0.0383    4163.5453     <.0001     -1.3618
    Dst_hos3     1    -0.2114   0.0146     209.9105     <.0001     -0.1165
    Dst_hos4     1    -1.2129   0.0366    1100.3494     <.0001     -0.6687
    Dst_hos5     1    -0.1334   0.00983    184.2496     <.0001     -0.0735


        Odds Ratio Estimates

                              Point        95% Wald
              Effect        Estimate   Confidence Limits

              Duration       0.979      0.961      0.997
              TCP            0.799      0.668      0.955
              UDP         >999.999    862.745   >999.999
              HTTP         279.639    254.194    307.631
              RST            0.007      0.006      0.010
              logged_i      43.934     38.751     49.810
              Num_comp       0.976      0.962      0.991
              is_guest       0.008      0.006      0.010
              Count          2.924      2.704      3.163
              Same_srv      28.732     24.553     33.623
              Diff_srv       1.633      1.581      1.686
              Dst_host       0.433      0.419      0.448
              Dst_hos1       0.085      0.078      0.091
              Dst_hos3       0.809      0.787      0.833
              Dst_hos4       0.297      0.277      0.319
              Dst_hos5       0.875      0.858      0.892
```

continued on following page

Display 2.4 continued

```
          The SAS System        09:58 Sunday, April 30, 2006    3
                                The LOGISTIC Procedure

          Association of Predicted Probabilities and Observed Responses

               Percent Concordant            98.9    Somers' D    0.980
               Percent Discordant             0.8    Gamma        0.983
               Percent Tied                   0.3    Tau-a        0.308
               Pairs                   15174668548    c            0.990

                     Partition for the Hosmer and Lemeshow Test

                                      attack = Normal        attack = Anomaly
              Group      Total      Observed    Expected    Observed    Expected

                 1       10815         48           1.08     10767     10813.92
                 2       55905          5          11.24     55900     55893.76
                 3       24992         14           8.23     24978     24983.77
                 4       29351          0          38.76     29351     29312.24
                 5      101631          2         144.53    101629    101486.5
                 6       32528       9864       10648.29     22664     21879.71
                 7       31121      26194       25223.65      4927      5897.35
                 8       24686      24466       24506.95       220       179.05

                  Hosmer and Lemeshow Goodness-of-Fit Test

                     Chi-Square        DF      Pr > ChiSq
                     2515.0420          6        <.0001

     NOTE: In calculating the Expected values, predicted probabilities less than 0.0001 and
     greater than 0.9999 were changed to 0.0001 and 0.9999 respectively.
```

Attributions

One of the many great characteristics of the SAS system is that it has the capacity to handle very large data. For example, we can easily fit a multiple logistic regression model with more than 20 million observations and 20 variables using a Dell XEON machine equipped with a 2.00 GHz CPU and 2GB RAM. We could also fit a multiple logistic regression model with 98 million observations and about 200GB in data size with the same Dell machine. Since network traffic data are usually very large in size, this capacity is important in analyzing network traffic. The SAS system also allows users to run DOS or Windows' commands or execute programs written in general-purpose programming languages such as C++, Java, or Visual Basic through its X command. This attribute allows users to construct an optimum network traffic analysis system for real time applications. For example, we can first ask SAS to read raw data collected by sensors, and then estimate or update a statistical model's parameters. We can then ask SAS to output the parameters (e.g., in ASCII format) that can be used to redirect and change all or a part of the sensors behavior, so that the sensors get updated, etc. This loop can be run for many iterations until an optimum status is reached. On the other side, SAS can also be run in batch mode—programs run in the background of the Windows environment. When running in batch mode, the editor, log and output windows will not be displayed on the screen, and SAS writes the results directly to the log (*.log) and output (*.lst) files to be viewed at a later time. In batch mode, a SAS program can be started immediately or be left in queue behind other Windows tasks. Batch jobs can also be setup to run at specific times when the computer is not in use, or may run in the background while the user continues to work in other programs on the computer. Delwiche and Slaughter provide a useful guide, *The Little SAS Book*, for beginner SAS users.

For statistical analysis and SAS functions, Cody (1997, 2004), and Hatcher and Stepanski (1994) provide comprehensive introductions in their books.

STATA

Stata is a registered trademark of the StataCorp LP. Stata (http://www.Stata.com) is a widely used statistical analysis package with rich functions in statistics, graphics, and data management. Unlike SAS, Stata is a command-driven statistical application that users can use to issue a command and get a response from the system immediately. Stata is available for a variety of platforms, including Windows, UNIX, and Macintosh; it also supports multiprocessors. The Windows platform professional version of Stata (Stata/SE) supports a maximum of 32,766 variables with string variables up to 244 characters, matrices up to 11,000 x 11,000, and observations, which are only limited by the RAM size in a machine. The Stata version 9.0 and higher also supports the 64-bit Microsoft operating system, and its Stata/MP supports run on multiprocessor computers, up to 32 processors, for conducting parallel computations.

User Interface

The newest version of Stata that was made available during the publication of this book (April 2008) was version 10.0; however we are using the 9.02 version throughout in this book. Although the initial GUI includes four windows: Reviewer, Variable, Results, and Command (Figure 2.8), we recommend only using the Results and Command windows since the Reviewer window only shows past commands and the Variable window lists the variables in the current dataset. By using only two of the four windows, we can have a large viewable area for the Results window.

Stata has its own data format but users can import data in several different formats (Figure 2.9). Since Stata is a command-driven application, we can type the command *use mydata, replace* to load an existing dataset named "mydata." Stata supports the ODBC standard for accessing data through its *odbc* command to read any ODBC data sources. Once a dataset is loaded, we can issue the command *des* to describe variable information about the data, and use the *list* command to list the observations in the dataset. If the data size is too big to fit into the default memory setting, we can use the *set memory* command to increase the amount of memory allocated to Stata while it is running. For example, *set memory 400000k* will allocate approximate 390 MB of data space. Note that, unlike SAS, Stata is case sensitive, which means, *car*, *Car*, and *caR* all represent three different variables. All commands in Stata have to be typed in low-case. To recall the last command entered, we can simply press the up or down arrows.

In addition to typing commands into the Command window, Stata has two types of script files, **.do* and **.ado* Both file types are ASCII text files which are used to build up and keep a sequence of commands being used for conducting a typical analysis. The **.ado* is a macro program and **.do* is a simple command file that lets users submit several commands at the same time.

Figure 2.8 GUI of Stata (top-left: Review, bottom-left: Variables, tpp-right: Results, and bottom-right: Command windows)

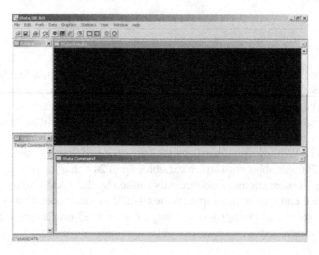

Figure 2.9 Importing data into Stata

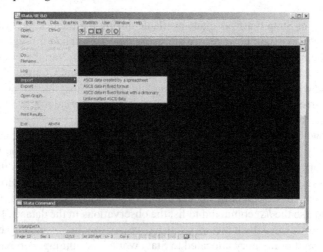

Running Stata

Let us fit a logistic model with the same dataset used in Section Running SAS. We first develop a Stata do-file that instructs Stata to read the data and fit the model with a response variable named attack (yes=1/no=0) and 16 predictor variables. Then, we save the do-file as *example_4_3_1.do* and execute it with the command *do example_4_3_1*. The codes are listed below in Display 2.6, and Figures 2.10 and 2.11 show the do-files and the final model, respectively.

Display 2.6
STAT codes to fit the logistic regression example presented in Section 2.2.2

```
#delimit;
/*----------------------------------------------------
 Clearing Stata's memory and allocate memory for loading the data
----------------------------------------------------*/;
clear;
set mem 400000k;
/*-------------------------------------------------
 Load data
-------------------------------------------------*/;
use var_16_val;
/*-------------------------------------------------
 display the variable information
-------------------------------------------------*/;
des;
/*-------------------------------------------------
 Fit the logistic model with attack as the response variable
-------------------------------------------------*/;
logistic attack
duration tcp udp http rst logged_i num_comp is_guest count same_srv
diff_srv dst_host dst_hos1 dst_hos3 dst_hos4 dst_hos5;
```

Attributes

Stata is very user-friendly statistical software that uses a convenient command-driven program language. We can explore and review data, discover relationships among variables, perform hypothesis tests, and fit numerous models just by typing the corresponding commands into the Command window. This feature sometimes allows us to examine our research ideas and questions more effectively. Similar to the SAS program, Stata also allows users to run DOS or Windows commands or execute programs written by general-purpose programming languages such as C++, Java, and Visual Basic. Since Stata allocates memory for data space, data size can be restricted by the physical memory capacity of the machine. To accommodate this limitation, Stata provides the *set virtual on* command to take advantage

Figure 2.10 Data window

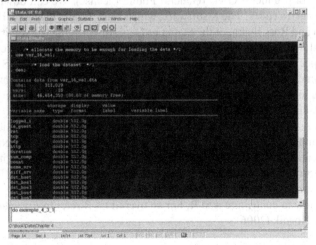

Figure 2.11 Result of the fitted multiple logistic regression model

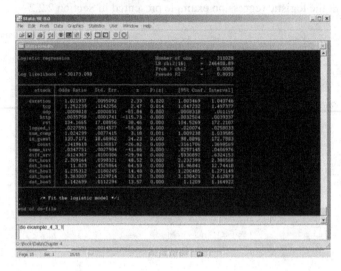

of the virtual memory feature provided by the operating system; however, since virtual memory is slow, we will most likely avoid using virtual memory to fit a large model.

One of advantages of using Stata is that it includes a great user manual with detailed examples that illustrate the usages of Stata commands and statistical procedures (StataCorp, 2007). Introductory information on the usage of Stata programs can also be found in the book, *Data Analysis Using Stata*, by Kohler and Kreuter (2005).

R

R is an open-source, free software environment that is used for statistical computing and graphics, and is widely used in the academic statistical community. R is similar to S-Plus (see the next section for more information) but it is free for downloading from the website: http://cran.r-project.org/ under a GNU (General Public License). We can download both raw sources and binaries codes. The R software, which was initially developed by R & R, Robert Gentleman and Ross Ihaka, of the Statistics Department at the University of Auckland, New Zealand, is the result of a collaborative effort with contributions from all over the world; more specifically, John Chambers, who principally developed the S language, graciously contributed advice and encouragement in the early days of development of R, and later became a member of the core team (http://www.r-project.org/). R supports various platforms including Windows, Linux, and Solaris. R is programmable and extensible. Because of its open-source attribute, many researchers, scientists, and professionals have contributed to R and have extended its capabilities to tailor many specialized fields. In addition to R currently having more than 100 contributed packages, we can write our own package(s) to perform specific tasks. The manual of Writing R Extensions (http://cran.r-project.org/doc/manuals/R-exts.pdf) provides detailed instructions on how to write a new package and how to contribute it to R. For an overall on R refer to *Frequently Asked Questions on R* by Hornik (2006).

Figure 2.12 Initial R GUI under Windows environment

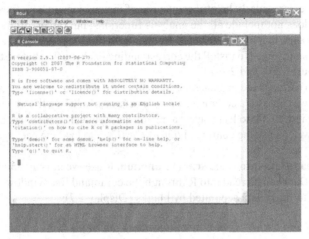

Figure 2.13 A simple calculation in R

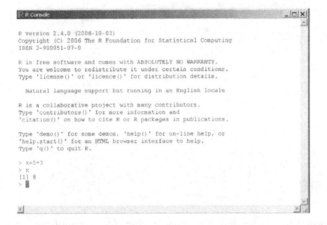

User Interface

During the production of this book, the most current version of R that is available is 2.7.0. When R is launched, the Console window will appear with the ">" prompt, which allows us to type commands (Figure 2.12). Similarly to Stata, R is an interactive program, so we can type commands individually or run multiple commands through a script. When we type commands and press the ENTER key, R will display the result(s) right on the screen.

Example 2.2 →Simple Calculation in R. Type in $x=5+3$ and then press "ENTER." When type in the new command x, and press "ENTER" again, we will get a return value of 8 (Figure 2.13).

The R programming language is an object-oriented language. This means that the script window of R allows us to create R programming scripts for complex analyses. We are able to save information on the screen by selecting the section of interest and choosing the "Save to file" option from the File menu. By default, R commands are saved in a session history, but we can also save particularly helpful sequences of instructions in ".R" files.

The GUI of R does not include all the analysis functions, but rather, offers a platform to accept new packages that are contributed frequently. Thus, depending on our analysis requirements, we usually need to install the corresponding package first before the analysis can be started (Figures 2.14 and 2.15).

R has an easy to use package management system. If we want to install a package called *e1071*, for example, we can issue a command, *install.packages("e1071"),* that R will display in the mirror screen (Figure 2.14) to let us select a mirror site from which we wish to download. After installation, we can use the command *library("e1071")* to load the package.

Example 2.3→ Read Data into R via scan() Function. R uses vectors and matrices as its basic data objects. Data can be read into R through the command line window. The *scan()* function allows us to input data separated by blanks (Display 2.7):

Figure 2.14 Choosing a CRAN mirror site to download packages

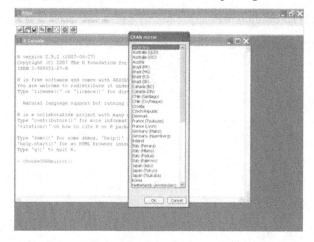

Figure 2.15 Selecting the corresponding package required for an analysis

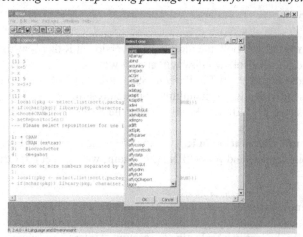

Display 2.7
Use *scan()* function to input data into R

```
> x=scan()
1: 1 2 3 4 5
6: 6 7 8 9
10:

Read 9 items
> x
[1] 1 2 3 4 5 6 7 8 9
```

In the above example, *scan()* prompts us to enter data, with a varying number of values in a line, until an entire blank line is entered, to signal the end of a data entry. A vector object only has one data type, numeric or string; a matrix object could have different data types for different columns. In this case, the data frame object is similar to a matrix object except that columns in the data frame can be mixed with numeric data, and string types can be employed. The *read.table()* function allows us to convert data available in an external text format directly into a data frame.

Example 2.4→ Read Data into R via read.table() Function. Suppose we have an ASCII dataset as shown in Table 2.1, in which the first two columns, Pattern and Response, are string variables, and the rest of the columns are in numeric format. This data can be entered into R via the following command given in Display 2.8:

Table 2.1 A portion of the test data to be read in R

Pattern	Response	Logged	Guest	RST	TCP	UDP	HTTP
000000	Anomaly	0	0	0	0	0	0
010000	Anomaly	0	0	0	0	1	0
100000	Anomaly	0	0	0	1	0	0
100010	Normal	1	0	0	1	0	0
100011	Anomaly	1	1	0	1	0	0
100100	Anomaly	0	0	1	1	0	0
100110	Normal	1	0	1	1	0	0
101000	Normal	0	0	0	1	0	1
101010	Normal	1	0	0	1	0	1
101110	Normal	1	0	1	1	0	1

Display 2.8
Using the *read.table()* function to read data into R

```
myData <-read.table("F:\\book\\chapter 2\\r-sample.txt",
            header=TRUE, as.is =TRUE, colClasses = "character")
```

Note the `as.is` option controls the conversion of columns that are not otherwise specified by `colClasses`. If the above data values are separated by a character, such as a comma, then the **sep=","** option can be added to the above command to indicate that the data are separated by ";".

Running R

Let us fit the same logistic model with the same dataset used in the Sections Runnin SAS and Running Stata. We first create R scripts that instruct R to read the data and fit the model with the response variable named attack (1/0), and 16 predictor variables. The codes are listed in Display 2.9 and the results of the fitted model are given in Display 2.10.

Display 2.9
R codes to fit the logistic regression model example presented in Section 2.2.2

```
require(Design)
# Read Ascii data to the data object KDD
KDD<-read.table("F:\\Book\\Chapter 2\\KDD_16_val_r.txt",header=TRUE,sep= ",")
#Fit the logistic model with attack as the response variable
fit <- lrm(formula =attack ~
Duration + TCP + UDP + HTTP + RST + logged_i + Num_comp + is_guest + Count +
Same_srv + Diff_srv + Dst_host + Dst_hos1 + Dst_hos3 + Dst_hos4 + Dst_hos5,

Data = KDD,
method="lrm.fit",
x=TRUE, y=TRUE)

#Obtain the fitted model
fit
anova(fit)
```

Display 2.10
R output of the fitted logistic regression model

```
Logistic Regression Model

lrm(formula = attack ~ Duration + TCP + UDP + HTTP + RST + logged_i +
    Num_comp + is_guest + Count + Same_srv + Diff_srv + Dst_host +
    Dst_hos1 + Dst_hos3 + Dst_hos4 + Dst_hos5, data = KDD, method = "lrm.fit",
    x = TRUE, y = TRUE)

Frequencies of Responses
Anomaly  Normal
 250436   60593

    Obs  Max Deriv  Model L.R.    d.f.       P       C      Dxy
 311029      3e-09    246408.9      16       0    0.99     0.98
  Gamma       Tau-a          R2   Brier
  0.983       0.308       0.873    0.03

              Coef      S.E.     Wald Z  P
Intercept  -6.59974  0.073153   -90.22  0.0000
Duration   -0.02170  0.009305    -2.33  0.0197
TCP        -0.22493  0.091217    -2.47  0.0137
UDP         6.92610  0.084633    81.84  0.0000
HTTP        5.63357  0.048676   115.73  0.0000
RST        -4.89908  0.127368   -38.46  0.0000
logged_i    3.78279  0.064051    59.06  0.0000
Num_comp   -0.02401  0.007558    -3.18  0.0015
is_guest   -4.87304  0.142366   -34.23  0.0000
Count       1.07306  0.040009    26.82  0.0000
Same_srv    3.35885  0.080240    41.86  0.0000
Diff_srv    0.49031  0.016378    29.94  0.0000
Dst_host   -0.83689  0.017250   -48.52  0.0000
Dst_hos1   -2.47005  0.038280   -64.53  0.0000
Dst_hos3   -0.21132  0.014591   -14.48  0.0000
Dst_hos4   -1.21284  0.036566   -33.17  0.0000
Dst_hos5   -0.13339  0.009827   -13.57  0.0000


> anova(fit)
                 Wald Statistics             Response: attack

  Factor    Chi-Square d.f.  P
  Duration        5.44    1  0.0197
  TCP             6.08    1  0.0137
  UDP          6697.28    1  <.0001
  HTTP        13394.57    1  <.0001
  RST          1479.47    1  <.0001
  logged_i     3487.94    1  <.0001
  Num_comp       10.09    1  0.0015
  is_guest     1171.63    1  <.0001
  Count         719.32    1  <.0001
  Same_srv     1752.26    1  <.0001
  Diff_srv      896.20    1  <.0001
  Dst_host     2353.83    1  <.0001
  Dst_hos1     4163.54    1  <.0001
  Dst_hos3      209.76    1  <.0001
  Dst_hos4     1100.15    1  <.0001
  Dst_hos5      184.25    1  <.0001
  TOTAL       27329.62   16  <.0001
```

Attributes

R is an interactive tool used for exploring datasets and generating a wide range of graphical representations of data properties. Although R is available in compiled form for many commonly used platforms, source codes are also available for compilation to other platforms.

With R's foreign package captivity we can exchange data files with many commonly used statistical software packages, including SAS, Stata, and SPSS.

The R user manual (*R Development Core Team,* 2007) and graphic package (Oehlsch-laegel-Akiyoshi, 2006) provide the most comprehensive material on R usage. Faraway (2005) provides a good introduction on linear modeling methods using R.

OTHER PACKAGES

In addition to SAS, Stata and R, there are many other commercial or non-commercial statistical packages that are available today. The following sections describe a few of the most popular applications.

S-Plus

S-Plus (http://www.insightful.com/) is a registered trademark of the Insightful Corporation. It is commercially available statistical software made by the Insightful Corporation. It was originally developed at the AT&T research labs during the 1980's. S-Plus provides a powerful environment and has many unique features for the statistical and graphical analysis of data. S-Plus is available for Windows, UNIX, and Linux. The most recent version of S-Plus available to date is version 8.0.

The initial S-Plus GUI contains an Object Explorer window (shown on the left in Figure 2.16) and a Commands window (shown on the right in Figure 2.16). Similarly to Stata, S-Plus supports both commands and script files. Commands can be typed into the Commands window following the ">" prompt and any results will appear in the same window. The Object window provides four types of objects: Data, Graphs, Reports, and Scripts. S-Plus can read data from a variety of sources, including statistical packages, such as SAS and Stata, spreadsheets and databases, such as Microsoft Excel, Access database, SQL server, Oracle, and of cause any ASCII files. S-Plus treats all data as vectors and matrices; for example, we can type *x<-rnorm(100)* to create a vector, **x**, which is composed of 100 random numbers.

Figure 2.16 S-Plus screens

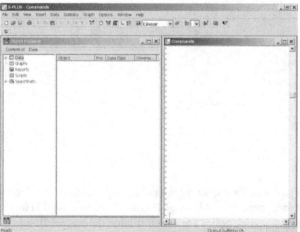

One of the strengths of S-Plus is its graphical capabilities. S-Plus has a rich set of graphical functions that support visualizing data analysis and data display. It has nearly 90 built-in two and three dimension plots that can be easily used. Moreover, S-Plus also allows us to create and customize our own graphic objects based on the existing built-in plots.

The S-Plus script window provides a place for us to create an S program to implement a sequence of commands that will conduct complex analysis and modeling. The S language is case sensitive and a variable or object name can be any length as long as it starts with a character. Similar to R, the S language is an object-oriented language. Tasks in S-Plus are accomplished by functions, which create new objects from existing ones. There are more than 3,000 functions in S-Plus and we can write our own objects using the S language or C++. More information on the use of S-Plus can be found from *A Handbook of Statistical Analysis Using S-Plus, 2nd edition* and *An R and S-PLUS Companion to Multivariate Analysis*, both authored by Everitt (2002, 2005).

MATLAB

MATLAB (http://www.mathworks.com/) is a registered trademark of the MathWorks, Inc. It is an interactive system developed by the MathWorks, Inc. for technical computing, data visualizing, and statistical and mathematical programming. Originally, it started as a Matrix Laboratory program that aimed to provide interactive access to the famous LINPACK and EISPACK libraries. The initial goal of MATLAB was to enable researchers and scientists to use matrix-based techniques for doing numerical computation with little to no efforts since this usually required writing complex program in the traditional languages such as C and FORTRAN. MATLAB supports Microsoft Windows, UNIX, Linux, and Macintosh operating systems.

The most current version of MATLAB to date is 7.4, which was released on March 2007; it supports the Windows 64-bit edition. The initial GUI of MATLAB has three components: (1) a directory window that illustrates all the files in the current directory, (2) a command window with the ">>" prompt, and (3) a command history window (Figure 2.17). After launching the software, the command window is the active window. Similar to Stata and S-Plus, we can type a MATLAB command and press enter to execute the command. Multiple commands can be entered on one line, as long as they are separated by commas.

Figure 2.17 MATLAB GUI

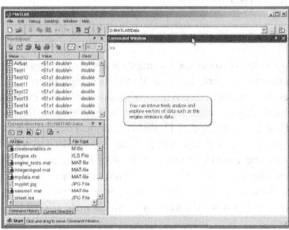

Separating commands using a semi-colon suppresses the output in the command window. As with Stata, to recall the last command entered, we simply press the up or down arrows, and are able edit them before executing them.

Because MATLAB works with matrices and vectors, it permits two types of variables: matrices and strings. It also provides many tools for accessing various sources, including ASCII, audio, video, and image files; MATLAB is also capable of accessing other applications, and databases. The software reads data interactively—information about data can be obtained by choosing and clicking them in the MATLAB environment. In addition to being able to read directly from external data sources, we are also able to enter data in a command window, or created in M-files.

Example 2.5→ Simple Matrix. The following command creates a 4×4 matrix and named it as "X":

Display 2.11
Creates a 4×4 matrix in MATLAB

```
X = [1 2 3 4; 4 3 2 1; 5 6 7 8; 8 7 6 5]
```

MATLAB has a separate command history window that logs each issued command issued and allows the user to recall previous commands. We can use this feature to test our ideas of data analysis via the command window and later retrieve the commands to generate a programming script. MATLAB saves its programming script files with filenames that end in ".m", which are text files and can be edited with the MATLAB Editor or any other text editors. For example, if we create a MATLAB programming file called myfile.m we can then simply type the command "myfile" from the command window, and it will run like any other MATLAB function. In addition, with MATLAB we are able to communicate with other applications, languages, and objects, such as C++, C, Visual Basic, Java, and DLLs to conduct complex analyses. Readers who are interested in finding additional information about using MATLAB can refer to *Exploratory data analysis with MatLAB* authored by Martinez and Martinez (2005).

WinBUGS

WinBUGS (http://www.mrc-bsu.cam.ac.uk/bugs/) is a statistical software package dedicated to Bayesian analysis of complex statistical models using Markov Chain Monte Carlo (MCMC) techniques. It is an interactive Windows version of the BUGS (Bayesian inference Using Gibbs Sampling) project that initially began in 1989 in the MRC Biostatistics Unit, Institute of Public Health, at Cambridge, United Kingdom. The BUGS project initially led to a Classic BUGS program, and then developed into the WinBUGS software, which was developed jointly with the Imperial College School of Medicine at St Mary's, London. WinBUGS can be downloaded for free from http://www.mrc-bsu.cam.ac.uk/bugs/winbugs/contents.shtml since the current license fee is zero dollars. However, users are required to submit a registration form to receive a key via email for unrestricted use—the same key

Figure 2.18 Initial WinBUGS screen

Figure 2.19 Script (top) and log results (bottom)

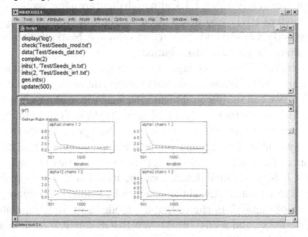

Figure 2.20 Model created by directed acyclic graph through Doodle

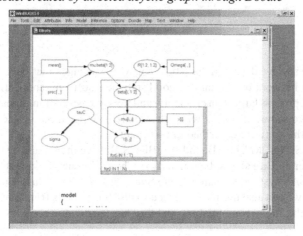

Table 2.2 Summary of statistical software for analyzing network traffics

Statistical Software	License Fee	Command-driven or command line	Case sensitive
SAS	Yes	No	No
Stata	Yes	Yes	Yes
S-Plus	Yes	Yes	Yes
MATLAB	Yes	Yes	Yes
R	None	Yes	Yes
WinBUGS	None	No	Yes

can be used for multiple installations. The lifetime of a key is usualy a year, and if it has expired, we need to require a new key.

The current version of WinBUGS is 1.4.3, although there are a few versions for different operating systems, such as UNIX and Linux. WinBUGS' programming language, called Bugs, allows us to specify a model and the starting values. A Markov chain simulation is then conducted to obtain the posterior distribution.

Like SAS, the WinBUGS Bugs language is not a command-driven language. We can use a standard point-and-click windows interface to control the analysis and develop a script (*.odc) for a model, or we can use the graphical interface, directed acyclic graph (DAG), also known as Doodle, to construct a model and generate the codes to run the model. We can write our codes using a common text editor (e.g., the Notepad program from Windows) or record the codes by double clicking the Doodle/Write Code option from the GUI menu (Spiegelhalter, Thomas, Best, & Lunn, 2003). Figures 2.18 to 2.20 are examples of the GUI. WinBUGS uses ASCII format. Small datasets can be included in the script file but large datasets can be saved in separated ASCII files and can be loaded into memory. The script file in the top section of Figure 2.19 shows that the model uses three separated datasets, seeds_data.txt, seeds_in.txt, and seeds_in1.txt. WinBUGS can also read data created by other software such as S-Plus or R.

SUMMARY

In this chapter we reviewed several statistical software packages that have been widely used for analyzing network traffic data. A good statistical software application has to be able to manage and process large data efficiently and timely, easily communicate with other network-specific programs, and work with other analytic applications. Table 2.2 shows a brief summary of the software described in this chapter.

SAS, Stata, R, S-Plus, MATLAB, and WinBUGS all have the capability to communicate with each other and are able to be remotely run by each other. Using the X command supported by the SAS system, we can execute Stata, MATLAB, S-Plus, R or WinBUGS in SAS. Similarly, we can also use remote execution SAS programs from Stata, R or other packages. With such a multi-commutable capability, we can divide a complex task into different components and use different software to accomplish individual tasks. For example, we can use SAS to process initial data that are usually very large in size, and then restrict the data into a relatively small sample and use R or WinBUGS to fit a statistical model.

REFERENCES

Cody, R. P. & Smith, J. K. (1997). *Applied statistics and the SAS programming language 4th Eds.* New Jersey: Prentice Hall.

Cody, R. (2004). *SAS functions by example*, North Carolina: SAS Institute Inc.

Dalgaard, P. (2002). *Introductory statistics with R*. New York: Springer-Verlag.

Delwiche, L. D., and Slaughter, S. J. (2003). *The little SAS Book: A primer, 3rd Edition*. North Carolina: SAS Institute Inc.

Everitt, S. B. (2002). *A handbook of statistical analysis using S-Plus, 2nd edition*. New York: Chapman & Hall/CRC.

Everitt, S. B. (2005). *An R and S-PLUS companion to multivariate analysis*. New York: Springer-Verlag.

Faraway, J. J. (2005). *Linear models with R*. New York: Chapman & Hall/CRC.

Hatcher, L. & Stepanski, E. J. (1994). *A step-by-step approach to using the SAS system for univariate and multivariate statistics*. North Carolina: SAS Institute Inc.

Hornik, K. (2006). *R FAQ, accessible form*. Retrieved from http://CRAN.R-project.org/doc/FAQ/

Kohler, U. & Kreuter, F. (2005). *Dada analysis using stata*. TX: Stata Press.

Martinez, W. L. & Martinez, A. R. (2005). *Exploratory data analysis with MatLAB*. New York: Chapman & Hall/CRC.

Oehlschlaegel-Akiyoshi, J. (2006). *The R graphics package*. Retrieved September 8, 2007 from http://astrostatistics.psu.edu/datasets/2006tutorial/html/graphics/html/pairs.html

R Development Core Team (2007). *The R manuals*. Retrieved May 6, 2006, from http://www.r-project.org/

Spiegelhalter, D., Thomas, A., Best, N., & Lunn, D. (2003). *WinBUGS user manual: Version 1.4*. Retrieved May 6, 2006, from http://www.mrc-bsu.cam.ac.uk/bugs/winbugs/manual14.pdf

StataCorp. (2007). *Stata statistical software: release 10*. College Station, TX: Stata Corporation.

ENDNOTES

[1]   SAS is a registered trademark or trademark of the SAS Institute Inc.
[2]   Stata is a registered trademark of the StataCorp LP.
[3]   S-Plus is a registered trademark of the Insightful Corporation.
[4]   MATLAB is a registered trademark of the MathWorks.

Chapter III
Network Traffic and Data

We cannot solve life's problems except by solving them.

–M. Scott Peck

INTRODUCTION

In this chapter we will focus on examining computer network traffic and data. A computer network combines a set of computers and physically and logically connects them together to exchange information. Network traffic acquired from a network system provides information on data communications within the network and between networks or individual computers. The most common data types are log data, such as Kerberos logs, transmission control protocol/Internet protocol (TCP/IP) logs, Central processing unit (CPU) usage data, event logs, user command data, Internet visit data, operating system audit trail data, intrusion detection and prevention service (IDS/IPS) logs, Netflow[1] data, and the simple network management protocol (SNMP) reporting data. Such information is unique and valuable for network security, specifically for intrusion detection and prevention. Although we have already presented some essential challenges in collecting such data in Chapter I, we will discuss traffic data, as well as other related data, in greater detail in this chapter. Specifically, we will describe system-specific and user-specific data types in Sections System-Specific Data and User-Specific Data, respectively, and provide detailed information on publicly available data in Section Publicly Available Data.

SYSTEM-SPECIFIC DATA

System-level data can provide important baseline information about user and system behaviors, traffic patterns, and provide warning information for any anomalous traffic that could harm the network system. These data types can also be collected with commercial products or data-specific programs. Log data can be drawn from three sources: network, host, and security. Data from each of such sources provide different components of the whole network behavior. The network log files that include TCPdump[2] and Netflows information focus on the packets of the network, and are the most important part of information that represents the network traffic. The host log files provide the host's activities, commands, and user log-in information, and the security log data, which includes firewall and other security-related information, specializes in the application activities. Most log data are easily acquired—the security log, application log, and event log files are automatically collected on both the server and workstation of the Microsoft windows system without specific hardware. TCP/IP data can be captured by various "sniffer" programs, which capture parts, if not all, TCP/IP packets that pass through a typical network point without modifying the packets. Such a program can be installed outside the firewall.

Packet, Flow and Session

Network traffic data is composed of packets, flows, and sessions. A packet is a unit of data that is routed between a source and a destination on the Internet or on any TCP/IP-based network. When we browse the Internet or send an email, we generate a series of packets. A network flow is a unidirectional sequence of packets between given source and destination endpoints. Session data represents the communication between computers, between hosts, or between a computer and a host. Usually such communication involves the exchange of many flows. Session information includes packet source and destination port information, IP addresses, and types of services. Typically, a session is defined by 6 elements: (1) destination IP address, (2) source IP address, (3) protocol type, (4) destination port, (5) source port, and (6) protocol type. A typical system capture flow data contains two components: a sensor that monitors the network and captures session data, and a collector connected to a hub, switch port or other device that observes network traffic and stores it somewhere for further analysis.

Communications between computers are carried out by the transmission of binary digits. In order for the sending and the receiving computers to know what these digits represent, the digits must be grouped together in some logical format. The naming of this grouping changes at various layers of the Department of Defense (DoD) model. At the Internet layer, the grouping is referred to as a datagram. Upper layers of the DoD model may refer to this grouping as a packet. Figure 3.1 shows an example of how a packet travels within a local subnet. If a server needs to communicate with a workstation, a packet would be generated and a destination address would be checked. Since the address is on the same subnet, the packet would be directed to the appropriate host system without the need of a router or a gateway.

Example 3.1→Flow Data. Each of the following lines given in Display 3.1 is a flow that records the source and destination IP addresses of assorted TCP/IP transactions. These flows represent two TCP/IP sessions. The first line indicates that traffic is coming from 172.16.30.247 (port number 80), to the host 216.98.200.250 (port number 63647). The next line shows traffic from the second host going to the first. This is one session. The third line shows traffic from 172.16.30.247 (port number 80) to 216.98.200.250 (port number 63648), and the last line shows the traffic flow back to the host, 172.16.30.247. This is another session.

Figure 3.1 An example of packet travels within a local subnet

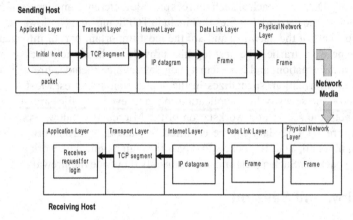

```
2005/04/28 19:14:01 172.16.30.247.80 -> 216.98.200.250.63647 6(SYN|ACK) 3 144
2005/04/28 19:14:01 216.98.200.250.63647 -> 172.16.30.247.80 6(SYN) 1 48
2005/04/28 19:14:01 172.16.30.247.80 -> 216.98.200.250.63648 6(SYN|ACK) 3 144
2005/04/28 19:14:01 216.98.200.250.63648 -> 172.16.30.247.80 6(SYN) 1 48
```

TCP/IP Data

Because we have mainly focused on TCP/IP data, we shall briefly describe some essential TCP/IP information in this section. TCP/IP is really comprised of a multitude of different protocols that are combined to provide communication between two computers. The types of communication that each of these protocols provides depends on the purpose of that communication. It was originally written by specifications laid out by the DoD; the special four-layer DoD model is compared to the current Open System Interconnect (OSI) seven-layer model, as shown in Figure 3.2. Knowing how the four layers of the DoD model map to the seven layers of the OSI model will help us understand the actual TCP/IP log data.

Currently we use an IP version 4.0 or Ipv4 address that includes a 32-bit long number divided into four 8-bit subgroups called "octets." Each octet is separated by a period and represents a decimal number in the range of 0 to 255. For example, 192.168.2.1 is the currently internal IP address on my computer that is being used to write this book, assigned by my route, within my house. In addition to the IP address, each computer can also be identified by several addresses. The first address is the Media Access Control (MAC) address, which is the network interface layer address. This address is specific to the network interface card (NIC) installed in the computer (i.e., computer's physical address) and does not divide into the host and network portions. A MAC address takes the format of 00-60-08-02-4D-D1, whereas an IP address takes the format of 207.98.156.52. Note that the format of the MAC address specifies the manufacturer of the hardware that the first 24 bits are registered to the company that made the interface card. The Address Resolution Protocol (ARP) resolves

Figure 3.2 Layer comparison between DoD and OSI models

DoD model			OSI model
System-level applications such as print, copy, FTP, DNS, and WINS	Application	→	Application
			Presentation
			Session
Transporting data from one computer to another	Transport	→	Transport
Addressing and delivery of packets from one computer to another	Internet	→	Network
This layer specifics how the computers will set signals on the physical network	Network Interface	→	Data link
		→	Physician

or equates the IP address (207.98.156.52) to the MAC address (00-60-08-02-4D-D1). To check a computer's IP and MAC addresses, open a command prompt by typing *cmd* in the RUN option, and then typing *ipconfig/all* for the Windows 2000 and XP systems, and we can use the same commands for the Windows Vista system as well.

The IP addressing scheme takes into account that some networks are very large (class A), some are medium sized (class B), and some are small (class C). Class A addresses can maximize 126 networks with 16,777,214 hosts per network, class B allows 16,384 networks with 65,534 hosts per network, and class C allows 2,097,152 networks with 254 hosts per network (Table 3.1).

Example 3.2→Information Included in an IP Address. An IP address of 207.46.130.17 indicates that it is a Class C address because the first network ID is greater than 191 and less than 224. The address also informs us that this host is on the network number 207.46.130.0, and the unique host number is 0.0.0.17. It is one host out of a possible 254.

IPv4 faces the challenge of the shortage of IP addresses. IP version 6 or IPv6, a new IP addressing scheme, has been developed to address this challenge. An Ipv6 address is a 128-bit address arranged as 8 groups of 16 bit numbers separated by colons; there are $3.4028236692093846337460743177 \times 10^{38}$ possible IP addresses available compared to the IPv4, which has approximately 4 billion. IPv6 will have a 128-bit source and destination address, which means it will be able to provide five IP addresses for every square meter on earth. An example of a new IP address is 1543:B24E:9853:574C:3336:43C7:4B3E:7C36.

TCP/IP is packet based. An IP packet, including source and destination addresses, packet description and option fields, checksums, and a data portion, can have a maximum of 165,535 bytes in length. An IP packet header considers of two parts: (1) the IP header that includes the source and destination IP addresses, versions, types, service information, options, and a data section, and (2) the TCP header, which includes several information fields including the source and destination host addresses. The generic structure of packet IP and TCP headers are showed in Tables 3.2 and 3.3, repetitively.

Table 3.1 Class ranges of network IDs

Address class	First network ID	Last network ID
Class A	1.0.0.0	126.0.0.0
Class B	128.0.0.0	191.255.0.0
Class C	192.0.0.0	223.255.255.0

Table 3.2 IP header format

00	01	02	03	04	05	06	07	08	09	10	11	12	13	14	15	16	17	18	19	20	21	22	23	24	25	26	27	28	29	30	31
Total 32- bits																														
Version (4-bits)				IHL (4-bits)				TOS (8-bits)								Total length (16-bits)															
Identification (16-bits)																Flag (3-bits)			Fragment offset (13-bits)												
TTL (8-bits)								Protocol (8-bits)								Header checksum (16-bits)															
Source IP address (32-bits)																															
Destination IP address (32-bits)																															
Options (variable length)																															
Padding* (variable length)																															

* To be used as a filler to guarantee that the data starts on a 32 bit boundary

Table 3.3 TCP header format

00	01	02	03	04	05	06	07	08	09	10	11	12	13	14	15	16	17	18	19	20	21	22	23	24	25	26	27	28	29	30	31
Total 32- bits																															
Source port (16-bits)																Destination port (16-bits)															
Sequence number (32-bits)																															
Acknowledgment number (32-bits)																															
Data offset (8-bits) |||||||| Reserved (12-bits) |||||||||||| U R G	A C K	P S H	P S Y T	S Y N	F I N	Window (16-bits)															
Checksum (16-bits)																Urgent pointer (16-bits)															
Options (24-bits)																								Padding (8-bits)							
Data (32-bits)																															

When we send a TCP/IP packet, we will know either that the packet will reach its destination, or that we will be informed of any problems with the transmission of the data. This task is carried out by encapsulating the packet transmission inside a network session. When we want to communicate with another computer using TCP/IP, we create a connection that allows us to send multiple packets. As we mentioned a series of packets together becomes a network session. Visualization of every transaction is a difficult task even in the IPv4 environment; however, statistical sampling methods can provide us an efficient technique to monitor these transactions. We will discuss some statistical sampling approaches to address this topic in Chapter VI.

Web Sequence Data

Sequence data are a particular type of time series data. Sequences are constructed by a limited number of events that are ordered in a specific way. Human Deoxyribonucleic acid (DNA) is a good example of sequence data, since each gene is ordered in a specific sequence. Music is another example of sequence data that is constructed by tones that appear in a specific order. My current activities of writing this book can be considered in terms of generating sequence data because each letter is organized in a way to be a word, and the words are organized specifically to form sentences, etc. When we browse the web, we also generate sequence data, which are logged by the web server. Such data includes information about the sites, the length of the visit to each site, and the sequence of sites visited by an individual visitor. The web visit sequence data provides rich information for market research to identify users' interests—collected data can be used to predict the next movement of a user and have the corresponding advertising ready, (Pazzani, Muramatsu, & Billsus, 1996; Pazzani, Billsus, 1997). Web visit sequence data is also valuable in network security for two main reasons. First, the data represents certain information on user behavior that can be modeled for establishing user-specific patterns. Users may conduct a sequence of visiting tasks every morning when they start their daily work, and such a sequence of ordering in tasks varies by persons. Users from a marketing department could be more likely to first visit the Wall Street Journal, followed by visits to consumer report websites, business news, etc., because they need the updated market-related information to start their work. Similarly, users from a human resources department may first review global news, career and job websites, educational sites, etc., since this may pertain to their specific job. Thus, the sequence of visiting the Internet contains certain information that reflects user characteristics (e.g., job responsibilities, interests), and such data can be further analyzed for potentially profiling user behavior.

Second, the web sequence data provides a source to track how malicious codes, the client side scripting attacks, are introduced to a system. When we are on the Internet, it is possible that we can become a victim of malicious programs from drive-by-download sites that automatically install malicious codes and Spyware without our knowledge. The drive-by-download has become an increasingly common threat to computers in that they infect the computer and network systems, and steal sensitive information. Researchers at Google found that 10% of web pages have the capability of launching drive-by-downloads (BBC News, 2007). Nevertheless, compared to TCP/IP data, studies based on web sequence data are limited and require much more attention (Joshi, Joshi & Krishnapuram, 2000).

USER-SPECIFIC DATA

System-level log data provides a portion, but not all, of the information on the user's side. To better understand user behavior patterns, we need to collect additional user-specific information, which includes but is not limited to: demographics, computer skills, working schedules, job responsibilities, sequence of computer commands, keyboard usage, mouse movements and click frequencies, historical behavior patterns, etc. User-level data is dedicated to the individual user level and it plays an important role in network security for two simple reasons. First, we have limited ability to track individual user activities with the system level data. When we observe a high volume of connections from a particular IP address at a particular time zone, it is difficult to determine whether such high volumes are normal or unusual based on the system-level data; this is due to the fact that the data provides no information on user job functions and working schedules. Although we may gather general knowledge about which region, department, or subgroup the IP address belongs to, this information seems inadequate to make a precautionary decision (e.g., issue an alarm or blackout the network connections).

Second, studies have suggested that it is necessary to profile users individually, but profiling is a dynamic process (Javitz & Valdes, 1994; Marchette, 2003). To achieve the maximum discriminatory power in profiling, we must take into account the fact that users may change behavior over time. Individual profiles may vary substantially from user to user, time to time, and the ability to constantly capture and update user profiles is an essential requirement for a robust profiling system. Because of such a requirement, very large amounts of data can be generated for each user daily, and the efficiency in analyzing such data and updating the corresponding user's profile is important.

Compared to system-level log data, user-level data could be relatively small in size and may not require a 24-hour time span record. Different information, however, may require different approaches and strategies to be acquired. For example, the keyboard and mouse click and movement data are user-related information and are more stable for analysis than job-related information, such as log-in schedule, and computer command sequences.

Keystroke and Mouse Dynamic Data

One of the measurements used to determine a user's computer skills is their typewriting style, which can be captured by the keystroke and mouse movement logs. Studies suggest that such data could be useful in preventing intrusion (Marchette, 2003; Ahmed, 2007). Keystroke and mouse dynamic data are not new to the computer science community; human-computer interaction (HCI) researchers have been using this data to model user behavior to design better user interfaces and software programs. Generally, HCI has used this data to develop applications such as mouse-driven text editors, workstations for directory-assistance telephone operators, space operations database systems, and CAD/CAM software (John & Kieras, 1996). For example, the data can be used to predict the time that will take a user to perform the tasks under analysis, as long as the developer can come up with time estimates for the operators involved in each model. The data has been used for description in the sense that it is a representation of the way a user performs tasks on a system. The data has also been used to serve as a guide for developing training programs and help systems.

The fundamental idea behind using keystroke dynamic data in HCI is to obtain personal identifiable information included in the data—such information could be further used to identify users based on their typing patterns (Spillane, 1975; Forsen, Nelson, and Staron, 1977), and to model user behavior (Card, Moran and Newell, 1980; John & Kieras, 1996; Kukreja, Stevenson, & Ritter, 2006).

Similar to forensic science, which uses footprints to describe individual walking styles and characteristics, the use of the computer mouse and keyboard can describe the unique styles and characteristics of two random users. This is the rationale that permits us to use keyboard, mouse movements, and mouse-click frequency data to describe different users. This data analysis has attracted much attention in the network and computer security area, (Umphress and Williams, 1985; Leggett & Williams, 1988; Joyce and Gupta, 1990; Leggett, Williams, Usnick, and Longnecker, 1991; Peacock, 2000; Cho, 2000; Zilberman, 2002; Marchette, 2003; Peacock, Ke, Wilkerson, 2004; Garg, Vidyaraman, Upadhyaya, & Kwiat, 2006), with hopes that such data will become a component of human biometric sources (keystroke biometrics) for computer security. US patents have also granted *the use of* a method *and apparatus for verification of users' identification* (e.g., Garcia, 1986; Brown & Rogers, 1996). Pilot tests were conducted to evaluate the possibility of replacing traditional passwords with keystroke data (Monrose, Reiter, & Wetzel, 1999; Monrose & Rubin, 2000; Ord & Furnell, 2000). Bill Gates also predicted that over time users would no longer need to use traditional passwords because they cannot meet the challenges of ensuring that information is secure (Kotadia, 2004). Nevertheless, the research in this area is very preliminary. On one hand, many technical and legal challenges must be overcome before this technique can be used in practice. On the other hand, studies have found that a small amount of keystroke data does not provide acceptable results. For example, studies found that typing names alone would not provide enough information to identify a user, and even typing approximately one page of text does not provide certainty for identification (Forsen, Nelson and Staron, 1977; Gaines, Lisowski, Press and Shapiro, 1980).

Keystroke and mouse data can be collected through hardware or software. In either case, the applications are usually small. For example, a hardware-based application could be a little device that is clipped onto the user's keyboard cable and records and saves each keystroke that the user types through the keyboard. One of the advantages of a hardware-based device is that it can be installed on a computer where the boot up or log in password is unknown. Although most of the software-based log programs do not require physical access to the user computer, it does require that the program must be downloaded and installed to the target machine.

Because keystroke data is easily collectable, the keystroke log applications themselves could present a serious risk to network security (Gillis, 2007). Many drive-by-download spyware programs have the capability to collect such data logs in order to obtain user ID, password, and other sensitive information. A hardware-based device could not only record user passwords, including the BIOS and Boot passwords, but could also be configured to allow data to be recorded on one computer and transferred to another. Because such a device does not use any system resources, it is difficult to be detected.

In the computer forensic field, criminal investigators also use the keystroke technique to collect evidence. In *United States of America v. Nicodemmo Scarfo*[3], the FBI collected the keystroke data from the defendant's computer in order to obtain the password of PGP encryption software that the defendant used to encode his confidential and incriminating business data.

Example 3.3→Sample of Mouse Movement Data. Table 3.6 shows a portion of mouse movement data from an unidentified user collected by a keystroke and mouse data collection software program. It seems that we can fit such data in a model for profiling individual users.

The followings are the measurements that have been recommended or used (or could be used) to model the user's typing patterns: interkey delays, digraphs latencies, key press delays, trigraph, keyhold timings, typing-error rates, and the use of specific keys and combined keys (e.g., Alt-Shift). Digraphs measure the time in milliseconds between the release

Table 3.6 An example of mouse movement data

Command	Time	Action	X-axis	Y-axis
Mouse	0	Move	170	24
Mouse	13	Move	172	24
Mouse	12	Move	168	15
Mouse	4	Move	176	14
Keyboard	0	Keydown	"G"	
Mouse	5	Move	168	15
Mouse	10	Move	169	16
Mouse	9	Move	157	4
Mouse	12	Move	157	10
Mouse	14	Move	170	20
Keyboard	0	Keyup	"D"	
Mouse	4	Move	155	10
Mouse		Move	167	15

of one key and the pressing of the next key. It is the most widely used measurement in the keystroke biometric field. Interkey delays are measured through Keyhold timing, which is the time between the press and the release of a key. Research literatures on keystroke dynamics have proven to be a reliable source of information on this type of data collection. The error rate is measured by counting the frequencies of the Backspace key used within a given key presses period (e.g., per 1000 keystrokes). Trigraphs measure the interkey timings between three consecutively typed letters.

Although keystroke applications as a surveillance approach have been used by companies to monitor their employees whereabouts in work progress, many privacy legal representatives also consider that because the potential risk of abusive use of such a technique is so high, legislation should be enacted to clearly make the unauthorized collection and use of such data a criminal offense. We must always remember that users are not the enemy (Adams & Sasse, 1999).

Demographic Data

Demographic data includes several components, of these job-related components including job title, reusability, work schedule, department or section in the organization, and years of employment. Depending on the required security level, demographic data may include physical and biometric information such as gender, height, eye color, face features, fingerprints, and other personally identifiable information. Such data provides supplemental information that may be used to validate the user in addition to the user name and password when high security is required. For example, an attacker may have gained access to an internal system by capturing an account password at another site. The attacker can then access an internal system and install backdoors on non-standard ports for later access.

This is also an insider threat. Even the currently popular PC-based backdoors (Netbus and BackOrifice) are "port agile", in that the attacker can choose the port to use for the backdoor. These backdoors can later be used to provide interactive access for chat channels or for file transfers. With demographic data, we may be able to prevent such unauthorized access. If the user account shows that this user only works during the daytime from 8:00 a.m. to 4:30 p.m. and has job responsibilities for the marketing department, and the attacker uses this account at night to try to access data from the finical department, it would be flagged as an anomalous event.

Similar to the use of keystroke data, the use of demographic data in network security should be careful to avoid any legal issues. Well developed and evaluated polices and procedures should be implemented.

Behavior Pattern Data

The user behavior pattern data includes the parameters derived from models and log data generated by individual users. The parameter data is usually small in size, but may be highly sensitive. For example, we may only use two parameters: the mean typing speed and its standard derivation, to describe a user's typewriting pattern and to accommodate for the large size of the raw data. Each time we gather more raw data from the user account, we compare the new data with the pre-established patterns to calculate the probability of the new data belonging to the user. We can also keep all of the initial raw data that trained the initial model to recalibrate the model when new data is available. This is an adaptive approach that updates the parameters regularly.

Example 3.4→Use Mean and Standard Derivation Describe User Behavior. Although a comprehensive intrusion detection scheme contains multiple data sources and measurements, the system-level traffic data provides important baseline information on anomalous traffic that could harm the network system. This information can be acquired from the training data. Wang and Kim (2007) proposed a simple probability model that aims to classify TCP/IP data into two groups (anomaly-free or anomaly) based on the bootstrap resampling method (Efron & Tibshirani, 1994) and the MIT-DARPA 1998 data. Table 3.7 shows parameters estimated from bootstrapping simulations for each site (user).

User behavior data also includes application related log data generated by individual users. The web visit sequence data is one example of such data that includes individual user web visit activities. For example, Cadez, et al. (2000) studied user navigation patterns on a web site and found patterns that consist of sequences of URL categories traversed by users. They employed cluster analysis to partition site users into clusters based on user navigation paths. The parameters obtained from cluster analysis were then used to classify user behavior during web navigations. Similar studies include Mobasher & Cooley, 2000; Nanopoulos, Katsaros & Manolopoulos, 2001).

Over the decades, user profile data has been used to detect deviations from anomaly-free activity. Some of the profile datasets are based on command-line instructions or directives executed by users on a system. With the advent and extensive use of GUIs, command-line data may no longer fully represent complete user behavior, which is essential for effectively detecting the anomalies in these GUI based systems. That is, although the methods for data collection, data formatting, and the variables in data could change over time, the natural characteristics of variables and data will remain the same, and the basic analysis approach will remain unchanged.

PUBLICLY AVAILABLE DATA

Although we need to collect network or system specific log data to develop anomaly detection and system profiles for a particular network system, it is greatly and heavily desired to have some publicly available data for researching, developing, and evaluating various algorithms. We will briefly describe four publicly available data: (1) the Defense Advanced Research Projects Agency (DARPA) Intrusion Detection Evaluation offline data developed by the Lincoln Laboratory at the Massachusetts Institute of Technology (MIT), (2) the Third International Knowledge Discovery and Data Mining Tools Competition's 1999 data (KDD-cup, 1999) that was created based on the 1998 MIT-DARPA, (3) the spam-email data that was created by Mark Hopkins, Erik Reeber, George Forman, and Jaap Suermondt at the Hewlett-Packard Labs, and (4) the web visit sequence data that was donated by Jack S. Breese, David Heckerman, and Carl M. Kadie at Microsoft Research. Throughout this book we use the *MIT-DARPA* to denote the 1998 MIT data, *KDD-cup* to denote the 1999 KDD-cup data, *SPAM-email* to denote the spam-email data, and *Web sequence visit* to denote the web sequence data. We will use these data to illustrate our analyses in the following chapters.

MIT-DARPA and 1999 KDD-Cup Data

From 1998 to 2001, the Lincoln Laboratory at MIT conducted several large simulations to create synthetic data, known as the Defense Advanced Research Projects Agency Intrusion Detection Evaluation Offline Data. MIT has made such data publicly available, which can be downloaded from the website, http://www.ll.mit.edu/IST/ideval/data/data_index.html. Despite the fact that the MIT-DARPA data has been criticized for having several downsides (McHugh, 2000), lacking some important variables (e.g., timestamp and user-level information) (Wang, Normand, 2006), out-of-date, and having an unrepresentative distribution of attack types to those of real populations that most researchers are aware of (e.g., 79.2% of DoS vs. 19.7% of normal, and only 1.0% of data split among other attack types), the data has been being the most widely used public benchmark for testing intrusion detection systems, and is still the most comprehensive data available today. Studies are still conducted based on MIT-DARPA data even after a decade (Gharibiani & Ghorbani, 2007; Minaei-Bidgoli, Analoui, Shahhoseini & Rezvani, 2007; Thomas, Sharma & Balakrishnan, 2008). We will use the 1998 data to conduct some analyses examples in this book.

The full 1998 MIT-DARPA data includes seven weeks of labeled training data that was processed into about five million TCP/IP connections and 24 different attack types, and two weeks of unlabeled testing data with 14 new attacks in addition to the 24 attacks included in the training data. The whole set of data was generated on a network that simulated 1,000 UNIX hosts and 100 users (Young and Hammon, 1989). The files were collected using Sun's Basic Security Monitoring software, and the raw packet data were collected using the tcpdump software. Each line in the file represents a separate session corresponding to an individual TCP/IP connection between two computers. A session is uniquely specified for User datagram protocol (UDP) and TCP protocols by the start time, by the source and destination IP addresses, and by the source and destination ports. Internet control message protocol (ICMP) sessions do not have assigned ports and are specified by the start time, by the packet type, and by the source and destination IP addresses.

Not all TCP/IP connections occurring in the MIT-DARPA study were included in the files; some services and sessions that were not involved in attacks have been ignored (Cunningham, Lippmann, Fried, Garfinkle, Graf, Kendall, et al, 2001). Each line in a file includes 11 columns: the session ID; start date (mm/dd/yyyy); start time (hh:mm:ss); session duration (hh:mm:ss); service type; source port; destination port; source IP address; destination IP address; attack score (anomaly-free = 0, anomaly = 1); and attack name. A list of ports and associated services can be found on http://www.isi.edu/in-notes/iana/assignments/port-numbers. The score and attack name columns are already filled in the training data, but not in the testing data.

Example 3.5→A Portion of MIT-DARPA Data. Shown below is a sample of the data from Thursday of the 4th week. Note that the lines with session IDs #628, #630 and #631 were attacks (warezclient).

Display 3.2
A section of traffic data from the Thursday of the 4th week on MIT-DARPA 1998 data

```
612 06/25/1998 08:13:34 00:00:01 snmp/u 2038 161 194.027.251.021 192.168.001.001 0 -
613 06/25/1998 08:13:39 00:00:01 snmp/u 161 2040 192.168.001.001 194.027.251.021 0 -
614 06/25/1998 08:13:39 00:00:01 snmp/u 2040 161 194.027.251.021 192.168.001.001 0 -
615 06/25/1998 08:13:43 00:00:01 http 5139 80 172.016.113.204 207.068.137.050 0 -
616 06/25/1998 08:13:44 00:00:01 snmp/u 161 2042 192.168.001.001 194.027.251.021 0 -
617 06/25/1998 08:13:44 00:00:01 snmp/u 2042 161 194.027.251.021 192.168.001.001 0 -
618 06/25/1998 08:13:46 00:00:01 http 5146 80 172.016.114.207 207.046.130.149 0 -
619 06/25/1998 08:13:46 00:00:01 http 5141 80 172.016.114.207 207.046.130.149 0 -
620 06/25/1998 08:13:46 00:00:01 http 5140 80 172.016.114.207 207.046.130.149 0 -
621 06/25/1998 08:13:46 00:00:01 http 5143 80 172.016.114.207 207.046.130.149 0 -
622 06/25/1998 08:13:46 00:00:01 http 5148 80 172.016.114.207 207.046.130.149 0 -
623 06/25/1998 08:13:46 00:00:01 http 5150 80 172.016.114.207 207.046.130.149 0 -
624 06/25/1998 08:13:46 00:00:02 http 5200 80 172.016.114.207 207.046.130.149 0 -
625 06/25/1998 08:13:46 00:00:01 http 5147 80 172.016.114.207 207.046.130.149 0 -
626 06/25/1998 08:13:46 00:00:01 http 5144 80 172.016.114.207 207.046.130.149 0 -
627 06/25/1998 08:13:46 00:00:01 http 5142 80 172.016.114.207 207.046.130.149 0 -
628 06/25/1998 08:13:47 00:00:03 ftp 2250 21 209.167.099.071 172.016.112.050 1
warezclient
629 06/25/1998 08:13:47 00:00:01 http 5201 80 172.016.114.207 207.046.130.149 0 -
630 06/25/1998 08:13:48 00:00:01 ftp-data 20 2253 172.016.112.050 209.167.099.071 1
warezclient
631 06/25/1998 08:13:48 00:00:01 ftp-data 20 2521 172.016.112.050 209.167.099.071 1
warezclient
632 06/25/1998 08:13:49 00:00:01 snmp/u 161 2046 192.168.001.001 194.027.251.021 0 -
633 06/25/1998 08:13:49 00:00:01 snmp/u 2046 161 194.027.251.021 192.168.001.001 0 -
634 06/25/1998 08:13:54 00:00:01 snmp/u 161 2048 192.168.001.001 194.027.251.021 0 -
635 06/25/1998 08:13:54 00:00:01 snmp/u 2048 161 194.027.251.021 192.168.001.001 0 -
636 06/25/1998 08:13:54 00:00:01 finger 2614 79 196.037.075.158 172.016.112.207 0 -
637 06/25/1998 08:13:57 00:00:01 smtp 2615 25 196.037.075.158 172.016.112.207 0 -
638 06/25/1998 08:13:59 00:00:01 snmp/u 161 1036 192.168.001.001 194.027.251.021 0 -
639 06/25/1998 08:13:59 00:00:01 snmp/u 1036 161 194.027.251.021 192.168.001.001 0 -
640 06/25/1998 08:14:04 00:00:01 snmp/u 161 1100 192.168.001.001 194.027.251.021 0 -
641 06/25/1998 08:14:04 00:00:01 snmp/u 1100 161 194.027.251.021 192.168.001.001 0 -
642 06/25/1998 08:14:05 00:00:01 http 5204 80 172.016.114.207 207.046.130.149 0 -
643 06/25/1998 08:14:05 00:00:01 http 5205 80 172.016.114.207 207.046.130.149 0 -
644 06/25/1998 08:14:05 00:00:01 http 5202 80 172.016.114.207 207.046.130.149 0 -
```

The full MIT-DARPA data includes a total of 35 files in ASCII format. Stata codes given in Display 3.3 read the ASCII format data each day for the first week over the 7-week

Table 3.7 Parameters estimated from bootstrapping (training sample)

Site (IP address)	Bootstrap parameters*				
	Sample size (#)	Mean	SD	1th percentile	99th percentile
135.008.060.182	2,185	0.3055	0.0629	0.2999	0.3121
135.013.216.191	3,073	0.3080	0.0592	0.3043	0.3116
172.016.112.020	5,563	0.3168	0.0721	0.3126	0.3199
172.016.112.050	1,124	0.2960	0.0627	0.2889	0.3002
172.016.112.149	16,564	0.2826	0.0542	0.2769	0.2865
172.016.112.194	19,127	0.2872	0.0541	0.2820	0.2910
172.016.112.207	20,848	0.2830	0.0518	0.2785	0.2865
172.016.113.050	377	0.2924	0.0772	0.2862	0.2980
172.016.113.084	15,368	0.2854	0.0541	0.2801	0.2883
172.016.113.105	9,964	0.2854	0.0552	0.2810	0.2887
172.016.113.204	14,551	0.2837	0.0540	0.2786	0.2878
172.016.114.050	1,612	0.2689	0.0791	0.2639	0.2733
172.016.114.148	22,715	0.2846	0.0538	0.2805	0.2880
172.016.114.168	12,804	0.2826	0.0565	0.2796	0.2854
172.016.114.169	18,885	0.2793	0.0503	0.2755	0.2827
172.016.114.207	17,975	0.2819	0.0543	0.2782	0.2863
172.016.115.005	14,953	0.3207	0.0600	0.3136	0.3226
172.016.115.087	16,215	0.3199	0.0578	0.3165	0.3207
172.016.115.234	15,315	0.3093	0.0552	0.3074	0.3105
172.016.116.044	14,802	0.3099	0.0544	0.3051	0.3105
172.016.116.194	16,468	0.3091	0.0529	0.3048	0.3183
172.016.116.201	17,125	0.3058	0.0590	0.3036	0.3110
172.016.117.052	17,310	0.3178	0.0573	0.3127	0.3226
172.016.117.103	13,001	0.3248	0.0620	0.3202	0.3315
172.016.117.111	18,740	0.3145	0.0570	0.3114	0.3185
172.016.117.132	12,532	0.2947	0.0462	0.2928	0.2951
192.168.001.001	2,395	0.3568	0.0642	0.3541	0.3585
192.168.001.005	788	0.4561	0.0440	0.4561	0.4561
192.168.001.010	737	0.3796	0.0624	0.3782	0.3806
192.168.001.020	5,177	0.3737	0.0422	0.3737	0.3737
192.168.001.090	1,044	0.3501	0.0565	0.3484	0.3522
194.007.248.153	2,717	0.2954	0.0608	0.2918	0.2985

continued on following page

Table 3.7 continued

194.027.251.021	2,306	0.3047	0.0614	0.2993	0.3094
195.073.151.050	2,142	0.3069	0.0611	0.3021	0.3113
195.115.218.108	1,976	0.3114	0.0608	0.3049	0.3161
196.037.075.158	1,929	0.3003	0.0619	0.2959	0.3059
196.227.033.189	1,841	0.3028	0.0607	0.2985	0.3081
197.182.091.233	2,521	0.3069	0.0625	0.3011	0.3110
197.218.177.069	1,776	0.2940	0.0601	0.2895	0.2982

* Unique connections

period of the MIT-DARPA list data, assigned an appropriate name to each variable, and saved the data in Stata format. Data from the other weeks can be read by the same codes by changing the file location in the code, *insheet using "F:\Book\Chapter 3\Week_1\Mon\ tcpdump.list"*, and the code of *index="week-1-Mon"* to correspond to each week.

Display 3.3
Stata codes to read ASCII format MIT-DARPA data and save in Stata format

```
#delimit;
/*-----------------------------------------------
    Week-1
-----------------------------------------------*/;
insheet using "F:\Book\Chapter 3\Week_1\Mon\tcpdump.list",delimiter(" ") clear;
do re_name_1_2;
gen str12 index="week-1-Mon";
save temp,replace;

insheet using "F:\Book\Chapter 3\Week_1\tue\tcpdump.list",delimiter(" ") clear;
do re_name_1_2;
gen str12 index="week-1-Tue";
append using temp;
save temp,replace;

insheet using "F:\Book\Chapter 3\Week_1\wed\tcpdump.list",delimiter(" ") clear;
do re_name_1_2;
gen str12 index="week-1-Wed";
append using temp;
save temp,replace;

insheet using "F:\Book\Chapter 3\Week_1\thr\tcpdump.list",delimiter(" ") clear;
do re_name_1_2;
gen str12 index="week-1-Thr";
append using temp;
save temp,replace;

insheet using "F:\Book\Chapter 3\Week_1\Fri\tcpdump.list",delimiter(" ") clear;
do re_name_1_2;
gen str12 index="week-1-Fri";
append using temp;
save temp,replace;

/*-------------------------------------------------
  Rename variables

-------------------------------------------------*/;
```

continued on following page

Display 3.3 continued

```
        gen long session=v1;
        drop v1 v2;
        drop if session==.;
        rename v3 date;
        rename v4 time_b;
        rename v5 duration;
        rename v6 service;
        rename v7 port_s;
        rename v8 port_d;
        rename v9 IP_s;
        rename v10 IP_d;
        rename v11 score;
        rename v12 attack;
        compress;

        replace v1="1" if v1=="1";
        gen long session=real(v1);
        drop v1 v2;
        drop if session==.;
        rename v3 date;
        rename v4 time_b;
        rename v5 duration;
        rename v6 service;
        rename v7 port_s;
        rename v8 port_d;
        rename v9 IP_s;
        rename v10 IP_d;
        rename v11 score;
        rename v12 attack;
        compress;
        save MIT_DARPA,replace;
```

After we read each week data and append them together, we will refer the full 7-week data as *MIT_DARPA* data throughout in the following chapters.

The 1998 MIT-DARPA data is the root for the KDD-cup 1999 data that is available to download from the Information and Computer Science website, at the University of California at Irvine (http://kdd.ics.uci.edu/databases/kddcup99/kddcup99.html). Similar to the 1998 MIT-DARPA data, the full KDD-cup 1999 dataset, includes seven weeks of TCP dump network traffic training data that was processed into approximately five million connection records, and two weeks of testing data, comprised of 38 different attack types that can be grouped into 5 categories (Table 3.8). The testing data does not have the same probability distribution as the training data, and includes additional specific attack types. The data unit is a connection consisting of 100 bytes of information representing a sequence of TCP packets starting and ending at a fixed time window. Data flow between a source IP address to a destination IP address under a pre-defined protocol occurred between each time frame. Each connection record is identified as either anomaly-free or as a specific attack type.

The KDD-cup 1999 data includes 41 variables that extended from the 11 variables of the raw 1998 MIT-DARPA data (Elkan, 2000). The following Stata codes (Display 3.4) read the KDD-cup 1999 data into Stata format, and Table 3.9 shows these variables and their corresponding labels.

Display 3.4
Stata codes to read ASCII format KDD-cup 1999 data and save in Stata format

```
#delimit;
/*-------------------------------------------------
This program can read both training and testing data
-----------------------------------------------------*/;
set more 1;
insheet
 duration
 protocol
 service
 flag
 src_byte
 dst_byte
 land
 wrong_fr
 urgent
 hot
 num_fail
 logged_i
 num_comp
 root_she
 su_attem
 num_root
 num_file
 num_shel
 num_acce
 num_outb
 is_host_
 is_guest
 count
 srv_coun
 serror_r
 srv_serr
 rerror_r
 srv_rerr
 same_srv
 diff_srv
 srv_diff
 dst_host
 dst_hos1
 dst_hos2
 dst_hos3
 dst_hos4
 dst_hos5
 dst_hos6
 dst_hos7
 dst_hos8
 dst_hos9
 y
using kdd_training.txt,c;



label variable duration "duration";
label variable  protocol    "protocol_type";
label variable  service     "service";
label variable  flag        "flag";
label variable  src_byte    "src_bytes";
label variable  dst_byte    "dst_bytes";
label variable  land        "Land";
label variable  wrong_fr    "wrong_fragment";
label variable  urgent      "Urgent";
```

continued on following page

Display 3.4 continued

```
label variable  hot        "hot";
label variable  num_fail   "num_failed_logins";
label variable  logged_i   "logged_in";
label variable  num_comp   "num_compromised";
label variable  root_she   "root_shell" ;
label variable  su_attem   "su_attempted";
label variable  num_root   "num_root";
label variable  num_file   "num_file_creations";
label variable  num_shel   "num_shells";
label variable  num_acce   "num_access_files";
label variable  num_outb   "num_outbound_cmds";
label variable  is_host_   "is_host_login";
label variable  is_guest   "is_guest_login";
label variable  count "count";
label variable  srv_coun   "srv_count";
label variable  serror_r   "serror_rate";
label variable  srv_serr   "srv_serror_rate";
label variable  rerror_r   "rerror_rate";
label variable  srv_rerr   "srv_rerror_rate";
label variable  same_srv   "same_srv_rate";
label variable  diff_srv   "diff_srv_rate";
label variable  srv_diff   "srv_diff_host_rate";
label variable  dst_host   "dst_host_count";
label variable  dst_hos1   "dst_host_srv_count";
label variable  dst_hos2   "dst_host_same_srv_rate";
label variable  dst_hos3   "dst_host_diff_srv_rate";
label variable  dst_hos4   "dst_host_same_src_port_rate";
label variable  dst_hos5   "dst_host_srv_diff_host_rate";
label variable  dst_hos6   "dst_host_serror_rate";
label variable  dst_hos7   "dst_host_srv_serror_rate";
label variable  dst_hos8   "dst_host_rerror_rate";
label variable  dst_hos9   "dst_host_srv_rerror_rate";

/*----------------------------------------
 Additional binary variables
-----------------------------------------*/;
gen byte REJ=(flag=="REJ");
gen byte S0=(flag=="S0");
gen byte SF=(flag=="SF");
gen byte RST=(substr(flag,1,3)=="RST");
gen byte ICMP=(prot=="icmp");
gen byte TCP=(prot=="tcp");
gen byte UDP=(prot=="udp");
gen HTTP=(service=="http");
gen Hot_0=(hot==0);

/*----------------------------------------
 Response variables
-----------------------------------------*/;
gen byte DOS=(y=="back.");
replace DOS=1 if y=="land.";
replace DOS=1 if y=="neptune.";
replace DOS=1 if y=="pod.";
replace DOS=1 if y=="smurf.";
replace DOS=1 if y=="teardrop.";

gen byte U2R=(y=="buffer_overflow.");
replace U2R=1 if y=="loadmodule.";
replace U2R=1 if y=="perl.";
replace U2R=1 if y=="rootkit.";
```

continued on following page

Display 3.4 continued

```
gen byte R2L=(y=="ftp_write.");
replace R2L=1 if y=="guess_passwd.";
replace R2L=1 if y=="imap.";
replace R2L=1 if y=="multihop.";
replace R2L=1 if y=="phf.";
replace R2L=1 if y=="spy.";
replace R2L=1 if y=="warezclient.";
replace R2L=1 if y=="warezmaster.";

gen byte PROB=(y=="ipsweep.");
replace PROB=1 if y=="nmap.";
replace PROB=1 if y=="portsweep.";
replace PROB=1 if y=="satan.";
gen byte NORMAL=(y=="normal.");

gen byte outcomes=0 if NORMAL==1;
replace outcomes=1 if PROB==1;
replace outcomes=2 if DOS==1;
replace outcomes=3 if U2R==1;
replace outcomes=4 if R2L==1;

label define outcomes 0 "normal" 3 "U2R" 4 "R2L" 1 "PROB" 2 "DOS";
label values outcomes outcomes;
save kdd_training,replace;
```

SPAM-Email Data

On May 3, 1978, Gary Thuerk, an over-enthusiastic sales and marketing representative, sent a massage to approximately 400 people, starting the era of spam-email—unsolicited commercial e-mails, although the message was not called spam at that time. Today, May 3, 2008, when I am revising this chapter, it is the 30th birthday of spam-email. Over these 30 years, spam-email has progressed from a minor nuisance to a significant problem of bandwidth, user time and disk storage, and millions of spam messages are sent from compromised computers everyday. They cause systems to slowdown and introduce malicious codes to both user computers and the network system. For a comprehensive introduction on spam-email, please refer to the article authored by Cranor, Lorrie, LaMacchia, and Brian (1998). The publicly available spam-email data was created by Mark Hopkins, Erik Reeber, George Forman, and Jaap Suermondt at the Hewlett-Packard Labs, and was donated by George Forman. The data was initially collected to determine whether a given email was spam or not. Currently, the data can still be downloaded in the ASCII format from the Machine Learning Repository Content Summary website at the University of California at Irvine (http://mlearn.ics.uci.edu/MLSummary.html). The Stata codes used to read this data are shown in Display 3.5.

Display 3.5
Stata codes used to read ASCII format spam-email data and saved in Stata format

```
#delimit;
insheet using "F:\Book\Chapter 3\spambase.data", clear;
des;
tab v58;
save spam_email,replace;
```

Table 3.8 Frequencies of major attacks from KDD-cup 1999 data

Attack Types	Training Data (N=494,021)		Testing Data (N=311,029)		P value
	#	%	#	%	
Legitimate users (normal)	97,278	19.7	60,593	19.5	0.021
Surveillance and other probing (probe)	4,107	0.8	4,166	1.3	<0.001
Denial of service (DoS)	391,458	79.2	229,853	73.9	<0.001
Unauthorized access to local super user (root) privileges (U2R)	52	0.0	228	0.1	<0.001
Unauthorized access from a remote machine (R2L)	1,126	0.2	16,189	5.2	<0.001

We will refer this data as *spam_email* data in the following chapters. The full data includes a total of 4601 observations (emails) with 39.4% labeled as spam, and with 57 continuous variables and one binary response variable (spam-email, yes/no). The 57 variables can be divided into three measures: (1) a particular word's frequency occurring in an email (variables 1 to 48), (2) a particular character frequency (variables 49 to 54), and (3) the length of sequences of consecutive capital letters (variables 55 to 57). Table 3.10 shows the descriptive information about the data.

Web Sequence Data

There are currently, only a few web sequence datasets available for researching purposes. One data was donated by Jack S. Breese, David Heckerman, and Carl M. Kadie at Microsoft Research and is publicly available to download from the website (http://kdd.ics.uci.edu/databases/msweb/msweb.html) of Information and Computer Science at the University of California at Irvine. The data was created by sampling and processing the www.microsoft.com log file. It includes 32711 anonymous and randomly selected users who visited the www.microsoft.com website during a week period in February of 1998. For each user, the data lists all the areas of the web site (named Vroots) that the user visited in that timeframe. Users are identified only by a sequential number (i.e., no personally identifiable information is available from the data). The data was constructed using three main components. The first is an attribute file that provides essential information about the sub-websites that users visited within the URL http://www.microsoft.com, a sequential order of the visits, and the number of sub-websites visited (the total number of attributes is 294). The second is a training dataset with a total of 32711 individual users. The third is a testing dataset with a total of 5000 individual users. The average Vroots of visits per user is 3 visits. Display 3.6 shows an example of a section of the raw attribute file:

Display 3.6

A section of the raw attribute file on the web sequence data

```
A,1287,1,"International AutoRoute","/autoroute"
A,1288,1,"library","/library"
A,1289,1,"Master Chef Product Information","/masterchef"
A,1297,1,"Central America","/centroam"
A,1215,1,"For Developers Only Info","/developer"
A,1279,1,"Multimedia Golf","/msgolf"
A,1239,1,"Microsoft Consulting","/msconsult"
A,1282,1,"home","/home"
```

Using the first row of Display 3.6 as an example, the first column *A* indicates that the line is an attribute line. The second column *1287* (called a Vroot) denotes the attribute ID number for an area of the website. The third column *1* can be ignored according to the original owner and donors. The fourth column *International AutoRoute* denotes the title of the attribute, and the last column */autoroute* denotes the URL relative to the website (http://www.microsoft.com). We can read the ASCII format raw data in SAS using the following SAS codes listed in Display 3.7. Table 3.11 illustrates the first 29 lines of the SAS data in which the third column of the raw data has been ignored. The full list of this attribute data is shown in the Appendix.

Display 3.7

SAS codes to read attribute data in ASCII format

```
PROC IMPORT OUT= WORK.attrib
     DATAFILE= "F:\Book\Chapter 3\msweb-train-Attrib.txt"
          DBMS=DLM REPLACE ;
     DELIMITER='2C'x;
     GETNAMES=YES;
     DATAROW=2;
RUN;
data attrib ;
set attrib (drop=dummy rename=(visited=site));
URL=substr(URL,2,length(trim(URL))-1);
visited='AAAA';
if _N_<10 then visited='AAA'|| put(_N_,1.);
if _N_<100 and _N_>9 then visited='AA'|| put(_N_,2.);
if _N_<1000 and _N_>99 then visited='A'|| put(_N_,3.);
vcode='V' || put(code,4.);
run;
```

The following lines derived from the training dataset show the web visits of seven users (Display 3.8). If the first column represents a new case, it is denoted by a value of *C*, and if it represents a visit, it is denoted by *V*. The second column shows either a user ID (when a *C* is in the first column) or an attribute or website (when a *V* is in the first column). The third column can be ignored for both *C* and *V*. Thus, for example, User *10002* has two visits with attributes of *1001* (Support Desktop) and *1003* (Knowledge Base), sequentially. User *10003* had three visits: *1001* (Support Desktop), *1003* (Knowledge Base), and *1004* (Microsoft.com Search) consecutively.

Display 3.8
An example of web visit data logged from seven users

```
C,"10002",10002
V,1001,1
V,1003,1
C,"10003",10003
V,1001,1
V,1003,1
V,1004,1
C,"10004",10004
V,1005,1
C,"10005",10005
V,1006,1
C,"10006",10006
V,1003,1
V,1004,1
C,"10007",10007
V,1007,1
C,"10008",10008
V,1004,1
```

While the raw ASCII data is row-based so that each visit starts with a new row, the data can also be reshaped into a column-based sequence structure, where each column would not just represent a visit event but also the order of a visit. This would convert the raw sequence data to a 32711×36 matrix, of which there are 32711 individual users and 35 possible visits (35 is the maximum number of visits in this dataset). The SAS codes for conducting the reshape task are shown in Display 3.9. The first column of the reshaped data is the user ID; the second column is the initial website where a user is on, and the remaining columns represent the sequence of websites visited for each user.

Display 3.9
SAS codes to reshape data from rows to columns (columns represent visits and the order in which they were visited)

```
PROC IMPORT OUT= WORK.attrib
    DATAFILE= "F:\Book\Chapter 3\msweb-train-Attrib.txt"
            DBMS=DLM REPLACE ;
    DELIMITER='2C'x;
    GETNAMES=YES;
    DATAROW=2;
RUN;
data attrib ;
set attrib (drop=dummy rename=(visited=site));
URL=substr(URL,2,length(trim(URL))-1);
visited='AAAA';
if _N_<10 then visited='AAA'|| put(_N_,1.);
if _N_<100 and _N_>9 then visited='AA'|| put(_N_,2.);
if _N_<1000 and _N_>99 then visited='A'|| put(_N_,3.);
vcode='V' || put(code,4.);
run;

PROC IMPORT OUT= WORK.TRAIN
     DATAFILE= "F:\Book\Chapter 3\msweb-train-case.txt"
            DBMS=DLM REPLACE;
    DELIMITER='2C'x;
    GETNAMES=YES;
    DATAROW=2;
RUN;
```

continued on following page

Display 3.9 continued

```
data temp_ (drop=dummy);
retain user_id ;
set train (rename=(user_id=code));
if index='C' then user_id=code;
if user_id=. then user_id=dif(user_id);
run;
data temp;
set temp_;
by user_id;
if first.user_id then cnt=1;
else cnt+1;
run;
proc sort data=temp;
by user_id cnt;
run;
/*------------------------------------------------------------
 Note data temp reshape the sequence data from raws to columns,
which the svisit1 denotes the 1st visit, svisit2 denotes the 2nd
visit, .....
The max number of sequence visits is 35 so svisit36-svisit50 can be removed
------------------------------------------------------------*/;
Data temp;
 array visit[50] svisit1-svisit50;
 retain svisit1-svisit50;
 set temp;
 by user_id;
 if first.user_id  then
    do i=1 to 50;
       visit[i]=0;
       end;
 if index~='C' then visit[cnt-1]=code;
 if last.user_id then output;
 keep user_id svisit1-svisit35 ;
run;
```

Moreover, we can also reshape the data to another format of column-based, a 32711 × 294 matrix, so that each column simply represents a visit event. The SAS codes for conducting such a task are shown in Display 3.10 below. The reshaped training data also includes 32711 individual users and 294 columns. The first column represents the user ID and the remaining columns represent the website ID (Vroot), where a value of 1 indicates that the visited event is present and a value of 0 indicates that the visited event is absent.

Display 3.10
SAS codes to reshape data from rows to columns (columns represent visits only)

```
PROC IMPORT OUT= WORK.TRAIN
      DATAFILE= "F:\book\Chapter 3\Microsoft-Web\msweb-train-case.txt"
           DBMS=DLM REPLACE;
      DELIMITER='2C'x;
      GETNAMES=YES;
      DATAROW=2;
RUN;

data temp_ (drop=dummy);
retain user_id ;
set train (rename=(user_id=code));
if index='C' then user_id=code;
if user_id=. then user_id=dif(user_id);
run;
/*------------------------------------------------------------
```

continued on following page

Display 3.10 continued

```
   Determine the most freq visited websites among 294 sites
-------------------------------------------------------------*/;
proc sql noprint;
create table temp as select temp_.*,visited,attrib.vcode from temp_ left join
attrib on temp_.code=put(attrib.code,4.);
quit;
data temp;
set temp;
if visited='' then visited='USER';
run;
proc sort data=temp;
by user_id index;
run;
proc freq data=temp;
table visited;
run;
data temp;
set temp;
by user_id;
if first.user_id then cnt=1;
else cnt+1;
run;
proc sort data=temp;
by user_id cnt;
run;
Data temp;
 array Dx[50] sDx1-sDx50;
 retain sDx1-sDx50;
 set temp;
 by user_id;
 if first.user_id  then
    do i=1 to 50;
       Dx[i]=0;
       end;
 if visited~='USER' then Dx[cnt-1]=code;
 if last.user_id then output;
 keep user_id sDx1-sDx50 ;
run;
/*-----------------------------------------------------------
 Temp data with 295 columns (294 attributes plus one index
-------------------------------------------------------------*/;
data tempV (keep=user_id vcode1000-vcode1294);
retain user_id ;
array vcode[294] vcode1000-vcode1294;

set train (rename=(user_id=code));
do j=1 to 294;
   vcode[j]=0;
end;
if index='C' then user_id=code;
if user_id=. then user_id=dif(user_id);
if index='C';
run;
/*-------------------------------------------------
 Merge two datasets
------------------------------------------------*/;
proc sql noprint;
create table tempw as select tempv.*, temp.* from tempv innor join temp on
tempv.user_id=temp.user_id;
quit;
```

```
data tempz (drop=j i sDx1-sDx50);
set tempw;
array vcode[294] vcode1000-vcode1294;
array Dx[50] sDx1-sDx50;
do j=1 to 294;
      do i=1 to 50;
         if (dx[i]-999)=j then vcode[j]=1;
         end;
      end;
run;
```

Table 3.9 Initial and additional variables in the KDD-cup 1999 data

Variable	Label
Basic features of individual TCP connections	
Duration	Length (number of seconds) of the connection
protocol_type	Type of the protocol
	ICMP (yes/no)
	TCP (yes/no)
	UDP (yes/no)
Service	Network service on the destination
	HTTP (yes/no)
src_bytes	Number of data bytes from source to destination
dst_bytes	Number of data bytes from destination to source
Flag	Normal or error status of the connection
	REJ (yes/no)
	S0 (yes/no)
	SF (yes/no)
	RSTO or RSTOS0 or RSTR (yes/no)
Land	Connection from/to the same host/port (yes/no)
Wrong_fragment	Number of WRONG fragments
Urgent	Number of urgent packets
Content features within a connection suggested by domain knowledge	
Hot	Number of HOT indicators
num_failed_logins	Number of failed login attempts
Logged_in	Log in successfully (yes/no)
num_compromised	Number of COMPROMISED conditions
root_shell	Root shell is obtained
su_attempted	SU ROOT command attempted (yes/no)
num_root	Number of ROOT accesses
num_file_creations	Number of file creation operations
num_shells	Number of shell prompts
num_access_files	Number of operations on access control files
num_outbound_cmds	Number of outbound commands in an ftp session

continued on following page

Table 3.9 continued

is_hot_login	HOT login (yes/no)
is_guest_login	GUEST login (yes/no)

Traffic features computed using a two-second time window

Count	Number of connections to the same host as the current connection in the past two seconds
Serror_rate	Percent of connections that have SYN errors
Rerror_rate	Precent of connections that have REJ errors
same_srv_rate	Precent of connections to the same service
diff_srv_rate	Precent of connections to different services
srv_count	Number of connections to the same service as the current connection in the past two seconds
srv_serror_rate	Percent of connections that have SYN errors
srv_rerror_rate	Percent of connections that have REJ errors
srv_diff_host_rate	Precent of connections to different hosts

Destination

dst_host_count	Number of connections having the same destination host
dst_host_srv_count	Number of connections having the same destination host and using the same service
dst_host_same_srv_rate	Percent of connections having the same destination host and using the same service
dst_host_diff_srv_rate	Percent of different services on the current host
dst_host_same_src_port_rate	Percent of connections to the current host having the same source port
dst_host_srv_diff_host_rate	Percent of connections to the same service coming from different hosts
dst_host_serror_rate	Percent of connections to the current host that have an S0 error
dst_host_srv_serror_rate	Percent of connections to the current host and specified service that have an S0 error
dst_host_rerror_rate	Percent of connections to the current host that have an RST error
dst_host_srv_rerror_rate	Percent of connections to the current host and specified service that have an RST error

Table 3.10 Descriptive information on spam-email data

Variable ID	Label	Range		Estimate		Coeff.Var (%)
		Min	**Max**	**Mean**	**Std**	
Word frequency (%)						
v1	word_freq_make	0	4.54	0.10455	0.30536	292
v2	word_freq_address	0	14.28	0.21301	1.2906	606
v3	word_freq_all	0	5.1	0.28066	0.50414	180
v4	word_freq_3d	0	42.81	0.065425	1.3952	2130
v5	word_freq_our	0	10	0.31222	0.67251	215
v6	word_freq_over	0	5.88	0.095901	0.27382	286
v7	word_freq_remove	0	7.27	0.11421	0.39144	343
v8	word_freq_internet	0	11.11	0.10529	0.40107	381
v9	word_freq_order	0	5.26	0.090067	0.27862	309
V10	word_freq_mail	0	18.18	0.23941	0.64476	269
V11	word_freq_receive	0	2.61	0.059824	0.20154	337
V12	word_freq_will	0	9.67	0.5417	0.8617	159
V13	word_freq_people	0	5.55	0.09393	0.30104	320
V14	word_freq_report	0	10	0.058626	0.33518	572
V15	word_freq_addresses	0	4.41	0.049205	0.25884	526
V16	word_freq_free	0	20	0.24885	0.82579	332
V17	word_freq_business	0	7.14	0.14259	0.44406	311
V18	word_freq_email	0	9.09	0.18474	0.53112	287
V19	word_freq_you	0	18.75	1.6621	1.7755	107
V20	word_freq_credit	0	18.18	0.085577	0.50977	596
V21	word_freq_your	0	11.11	0.80976	1.2008	148
V22	word_freq_font	0	17.1	0.1212	1.0258	846
V23	word_freq_000	0	5.45	0.10165	0.35029	345
V24	word_freq_money	0	12.5	0.094269	0.44264	470
V25	word_freq_hp	0	20.83	0.5495	1.6713	304
V26	word_freq_hpl	0	16.66	0.26538	0.88696	334
V27	word_freq_george	0	33.33	0.7673	3.3673	439
V28	word_freq_650	0	9.09	0.12484	0.53858	431

continued on following page

Table 3.10 continued

V29	word_freq_lab	0	14.28	0.098915	0.59333	600
V30	word_freq_labs	0	5.88	0.10285	0.45668	444
V31	word_freq_telnet	0	12.5	0.064753	0.40339	623
V32	word_freq_857	0	4.76	0.047048	0.32856	698
V33	word_freq_data	0	18.18	0.097229	0.55591	572
V34	word_freq_415	0	4.76	0.047835	0.32945	689
V35	word_freq_85	0	20	0.10541	0.53226	505
V36	word_freq_technology	0	7.69	0.097477	0.40262	413
V37	word_freq_1999	0	6.89	0.13695	0.42345	309
V38	word_freq_parts	0	8.33	0.013201	0.22065	1670
V39	word_freq_pm	0	11.11	0.078629	0.43467	553
V40	word_freq_direct	0	4.76	0.064834	0.34992	540
V41	word_freq_cs	0	7.14	0.043667	0.3612	827
V42	word_freq_meeting	0	14.28	0.13234	0.76682	579
V43	word_freq_original	0	3.57	0.046099	0.22381	486
V44	word_freq_project	0	20	0.079196	0.62198	785
V45	word_freq_re	0	21.42	0.30122	1.0117	336
V46	word_freq_edu	0	22.05	0.17982	0.91112	507
V47	word_freq_table	0	2.17	0.005445	0.076274	1400
V48	word_freq_conference	0	10	0.031869	0.28573	897
Character frequency (%)						
V49	char_freq_;	0	4.385	0.038575	0.24347	631
V50	char_freq_(	0	9.752	0.13903	0.27036	194
V51	char_freq_[	0	4.081	0.016976	0.10939	644
V52	char_freq_!	0	32.478	0.26907	0.81567	303
V53	char_freq_$	0	6.003	0.075811	0.24588	324
V54	char_freq_#	0	19.829	0.044238	0.42934	971
Run-length attributes						
V55	Capital_run_length_avera	1	1102.5	5.1915	31.729	611
V56	Capital_run_length_longe	1	9989	52.173	194.89	374
V57	Capital_run_length_total	1	15841	283.29	606.35	214
Outcome						
V58	Spam/non-spam (1/0)	0	1	0.39404	0.4887	124

Std denotes standard deviation; Coeff.Var denotes coefficient of variation (standard deviation divided by mean).

Table 3.11 First 29 records of the attribute file generated by SAS codes

Attribute	Code	Site	URL	Vcode
A	1287	International AutoRoute	autoroute	V1287
A	1288	Library	Library	V1288
A	1289	Master Chef Product Information	masterchef	V1289
A	1297	Central America	centroam	V1297
A	1215	For Developers Only Info	developer	V1215
A	1279	Multimedia Golf	Msgolf	V1279
A	1239	Microsoft Consulting	msconsult	V1239
A	1282	Home	Home	V1282
A	1251	Reference Support	referencesupport	V1251
A	1121	Microsoft Magazine	magazine	V1121
A	1083	MS Access Support	msaccesssupport	V1083
A	1145	Visual Fox Pro Support	vfoxprosupport	V1145
A	1276	Visual Test Support	vtestsupport	V1276
A	1200	Benelux Region	Benelux	V1200
A	1259	Controls	Controls	V1259
A	1155	Sidewalk	Sidewalk	V1155
A	1092	Visual FoxPro	Vfoxpro	V1092
A	1004	Microsoft.com Search	Search	V1004
A	1057	MS PowerPoint News	powerpoint	V1057
A	1140	Netherlands (Holland)	netherlands	V1140
A	1198	Picture It	Pictureit	V1198
A	1147	Microsoft Financial Forum	Msft	V1147
A	1005	Norway	Norge	V1005
A	1026	Internet Site Construction for Developers	sitebuilder	V1026
A	1119	Corporation Information	Corpinfo	V1119
A	1216	Virtual Reality Markup Language	Vrml	V1216
A	1218	MS Publisher Support	publishersupport	V1218
A	1205	Hardware Supprt	hardwaresupport	V1205
A	1269	Customer Guides	business	V1269

Table 3.12 First 25 observations with first 15 sequences of visits of the reshaped data

User	S1	S2	S3	S4	S5	S6	S7	S8	S9	S10	S11	S12	S13	S14	S15
10001	1000	1001	1002	0	0	0	0	0	0	0	0	0	0	0	0
10002	1001	1003	0	0	0	0	0	0	0	0	0	0	0	0	0
10003	1001	1003	1004	0	0	0	0	0	0	0	0	0	0	0	0
10004	1005	0	0	0	0	0	0	0	0	0	0	0	0	0	0
10005	1006	0	0	0	0	0	0	0	0	0	0	0	0	0	0
10006	1003	1004	0	0	0	0	0	0	0	0	0	0	0	0	0
10007	1007	0	0	0	0	0	0	0	0	0	0	0	0	0	0
10008	1004	0	0	0	0	0	0	0	0	0	0	0	0	0	0
10009	1008	1009	0	0	0	0	0	0	0	0	0	0	0	0	0
10010	1010	1000	1011	1012	1013	1014	0	0	0	0	0	0	0	0	0
10011	1015	1016	1017	1018	1019	0	0	0	0	0	0	0	0	0	0
10012	1020	1021	0	0	0	0	0	0	0	0	0	0	0	0	0
10013	1022	0	0	0	0	0	0	0	0	0	0	0	0	0	0
10014	1023	0	0	0	0	0	0	0	0	0	0	0	0	0	0
10015	1024	0	0	0	0	0	0	0	0	0	0	0	0	0	0
10016	1025	1026	0	0	0	0	0	0	0	0	0	0	0	0	0
10017	1027	1017	1026	1028	0	0	0	0	0	0	0	0	0	0	0
10018	1004	0	0	0	0	0	0	0	0	0	0	0	0	0	0
10019	1017	1004	1018	1029	1008	1030	1031	1032	1003	1033	1002	0	0	0	0
10020	1008	1001	1034	1002	0	0	0	0	0	0	0	0	0	0	0
10021	1017	1004	1018	1035	1036	1008	1037	1009	1038	1026	1039	1040	1032	1041	1042
10022	1008	1017	1004	0	0	0	0	0	0	0	0	0	0	0	0
10023	1008	0	0	0	0	0	0	0	0	0	0	0	0	0	0

Table 3.13 First 25 observations with first 5 variables of the reshaped data

User	vcode1000	Vcode1001	vcode1002	vcode1003	vcode1004	vcode1005
10001	1	1	1	0	0	0
10002	0	1	0	1	0	0
10003	0	1	0	1	1	0
10004	0	0	0	0	0	1
10005	0	0	0	0	0	0
10006	0	0	0	1	1	0
10007	0	0	0	0	0	0
10008	0	0	0	0	1	0
10009	0	0	0	0	0	0
10010	1	0	0	0	0	0
10011	0	0	0	0	0	0
10012	0	0	0	0	0	0
10013	0	0	0	0	0	0
10014	0	0	0	0	0	0
10015	0	0	0	0	0	0
10016	0	0	0	0	0	0
10017	0	0	0	0	0	0
10018	0	0	0	0	1	0
10019	0	0	1	1	1	0
10020	0	1	1	0	0	0
10021	0	0	0	0	1	0
10022	0	0	0	0	1	0
10023	0	0	0	0	0	0
10024	0	0	0	0	0	0
10025	0	0	0	0	0	0
10026	0	0	0	0	0	0

Another type of web sequence data that was donated by David Heckerman at Microsoft, is available on the Department of Information and Computer Science at the University of California at Irvine website, http://kdd.ics.uci.edu/databases/msnbc/msnbc.html. The data created by the Internet Information Server contains the websites visited by users who browsed www.msnbc.com on September 28, 1999 during a twenty-four hour period. Visits are recorded at the level of the URL category and were recorded in chronological order. Table 3.14 shows a total of 17 URL categories. The full data includes 989818 observations with an average number of 5.7 visits per user, and the number of URLs per category range from 10 to 5000 (Cadez, Heckerman, Meek, Smyth, & White, 2000).

Table 3.14 URL categories

URL
Frontpage
News
Tech
Local
Opinion
on-air
Misc
Weather
Health
Living
Business
Sports
Summary
(bulletin board service
Travel
msn-news
msn-sports

Masquerading User Data

Computer command line data has been used to conduct numerous analyses (Schonlau, DuMouchel, Ju, Karr, Theus, & Vardi, 2001; Maxion & Townsend, 2002; Yung, 2003; Wang and Stolfo, 2003). Matthias Schonlau from RAND donated a set of such data that can currently be downloaded from http://www.schonlau.net/. The full data consists of 50 individual files that each corresponds to one user. Each file includes 15000 observations, of which each observation corresponds to a command. The training data can be obtained from first 5000 observations that do not contain any masqueraders, and the remaining 10000 observations were divided into 100 blocks at 100 observations per block. These blocks can be used as test data that include masqueraders starting at a probability of 0.01. If the previous block is a masquerade, the next block will also be a masquerade with a probability of 0.8. Overall, approximately 5% of the testing data contains masquerades. Display 3.11 shows an example of commands issued by the 10th user. For additional information on how to use these datasets, please refer to Schonlau & Theus (2000), Theus & Schonlau (1998), and Schonlau, DuMouchel, Ju, Karr, Theus, & Vardi (2001).

Display 3.11
Commands issued by the 10th user (http://www.schonlau.net/)

```
Cat mail tcsh tcsh cat mail tcsh sh sendmail sendmail sh MediaMai
Sendmail sleep sh sh rm MediaMai ls ls pwd ls whereis unpack col
ul more sh man man ls ls pwd whereis whereis whereis ls
```

SUMMARY

In this chapter we focused on network traffic and user data, and discussed several essential concepts on these data types. In our discussions and throughout this book, the terms "network traffic," "traffic data," and "network data" are exchangeable and generally referred to as data that is collected for the purposes of resource utilization and between-network and within-network communications. In addition, the terms "site," "user", "group", and "IP address" are interchangeable as well. They denote a unique network identification that could represent either a signal user or a group of users who share the same IP address (for dynamic IP address, the range of IP numbers for an index site could be collapsed together to represent the site).

Data plays a fundamental role in network security and requires great attention. Data varies in scope and network environments, as well as in operating systems. System-level data are often very large in size and may include many repeated observations that have the exact the same values for every variable. In general, such raw data may not fit a model well and requires additional processes to make its analysis useful, especially when fitting data with a repeated model (Davis, 2002). Dummy variables are necessary to make the data become meaningful. Moreover, some important information for profiling may not be included in the existing traffic data, and additional data collecting efforts may be required.

A robust intrusion detection and prevention system requires three essential elements working together: (1) a sound research hypothesis, (2) a set of high quality data, and (3) a thorough analysis. To ensure data quality, reviewing data is very important since various data sources have their strengths and weaknesses. Prospectively collected data may be the highest in quality, but they are expensive and may include only selected samples of users because of the need for informed consent. Although statistical approaches can help to scan data and identify data issues in many situations, manually reviewing a part of collected data could add greater value to the entire data processes and could lead to increased sensitivity and specificity in further classification, regardless of such manual reviewing could be expensive and time-intensive. Experience suggests that a manually review data process could be the most effective method to identify a novel attack. If possible, we should determine whether classification results from a statistical model serve to be good proxies for the classification results from human review or abstract the network traffic data.

New benchmark data sources in additional to the introduced publicly available datasets are desired. Although MIT-DARPA datasets have been criticized, however, these data are still the largest publicly available data today for researchers, despite the fact that they are almost ten years old. We desire new data and more realistic characteristics with sampling in a statistically sound and clinically reasonable approach. Because wireless ad hoc traffic data have many unique characteristics, benchmark wireless network-based traffic data are also desired.

REFERENCES

Adams, A. & Sasse, M. A. (1999). Users are not the enemy. *Comm. ACM,* (42), 40-46.

Ahmed, A. A. (2007). A new biometric technology based on mouse dynamics. *IEEE Trans. Dependable Secur. Comput.* 4(3), 165-179.

BBC News (2007). *Google searches Web's dark side.* Retrieved June 20, 2007, from http://news.bbc.co.uk/2/hi/technology/6645895.stm

Brown. M. and Rogers, S. (1996). *Method and apparatus for verification of a computer user's identification, based on keystroke characteristics.* US patent number 5,557,686, Washington, DC.

Card, S, Moran, T. P., and Newell, A. (1980). The keystroke-level model for user performance with interactive systems. *Communications of the ACM,* 23, 396-210

Cadez, I., Heckerman, D., Meek, C., Smyth, P., & White, S. (2000). Visualization of navigation patterns on a Web site using model-based clustering, (pp.280-284). In *Proceedings of the sixth ACM SIGKDD international conference on Knowledge discovery and data mining.* Boston.

Cho, S. (2000). Web-based keystroke dynamics identity verification using neural network. *Journal of Organizational Computing and Electronic Commerce, 10,* 295-307.

Cunningham, R. K., Lippmann, R. P., Fried, D. J., Garfinkle, S. L., Graf, I., Kendall, K. R., *et al.* (1999). Evaluating intrusion detection systems without attacking your friends: The 1998 DARPA intrusion detection evaluation. *SANS.*

Cranor, Lorrie F., LaMacchia, Brian A. (1998). Spam! *Communications of the ACM, 41*(8), 74-83.

Davis, C. S. (2002). *Statistical methods for the analysis of repeated measurements.* New York: Springer-Verlag.

Efron, B. & Tibshirani, E. R. (1994) *An introduction to the bootstrap.* London: Chapman & Hall.

Elkan, C. (2000). Results of the KDD'99 classifier learning contest. *ACM Transactions on Information and System Security, 3*(4), 262-294.

Forsen, G., Nelson, M. and Staron, R. (1977). *Personal attributes authentication techniques.* Technical report RADC-TR-77-1033. Griffis Air Force Base.

Gaines, R.S. Lisowski, W., Press, S. J. & Shapiro, N. (1980). Authentication by keystroke timing: Some preliminary results. *RAND report R-2526-NSF.*

Garcia, J. (1986). *Personal identification \apparatus.* US patent number 4,621,334, Washington, DC.

Garg, A., Vidyaraman, S., Upadhyaya, S., Kwiat, S. (2006). USim: A user behavior simulation framework for training and testing IDSes in GUI based systems, *anss,* (pp. 196-203). In *Proceedings of 39th Annual Simulation Symposium (ANSS'06).*

Gharibian, F. & Ghorbani, A.A. (2007). Comparative study of supervised machine learning techniques for intrusion detection, (pp. 350-358). In *Proceedings of the Fifth Annual Conference on Communication Networks and Services Research.*

Gillis, T. (2007). *Upping the ANTI-in pursuit of the accountable Internet.* Message Media Press.

Javitz, H.S. & Valdes, A. (1994). The NIDES statistical component description and justification. Retrieved from http://wwwcsif.cs.ucdavis.edu/~zhangk1/papers/NIDES-STA-description.pdf

John, B and Kieras, D. E. (1996). The GOMS family of user interface analysis techniques: Comparison and contrast. *ACM Transactions on Computer-Human Interaction 3*(4), 320-351.

Joshi, A., Joshi, K., Krishnapuram, R. (2000). On mining Web access logs, (pp. 63-69). In *Proceedings of the ACM-SIGMOD Workshop on Research Issues in Data Mining and Knowledge Discovery*.

Joyce, R. and Gupta, G. (1990). Identity authentication based on keystroke latencies, *Comm. ACM, 33*(2), 168-176.

KDD Cup (1999), Data available on the Web. Retrieved February 19, 2006, from http://kdd.ics.uci.edu/databases/kddcup99/kddcup99.html

Kotadia, M. (2004, February). Gates predicts death of the password. *CNET News.com*, http://msn-cnet.com2100-1029_3-5164733.html

Kukreja, U., Stevenson, W. E. & Ritter, F. E. (2006). RUI—Recording user input from interfaces under Windows and Mac OS X. *Behavior Research Methods, 38*(4), 656-659.

Leggett, J. & Williams, G. (1988). Verifying identity via keystroke characteristics. *International Journal of Man-Machine Studies*, 67-76.

Leggett, J. Williams, G., Usnick, M. & Longnecker, M. (1991). Dynamic identity verification via keystroke characteristics. *International Journal of Man-Machine Studies, 35*(6), 859-870.

Marchette, D. J. (2003). Statistical opportunities in network security, ,(pp 28-38). In *Proceedings of the 35th Symposium on the Interface of Computing Science and Statistics, Computing Science and Statistics*, vol. 35.

Maxion, R. A. & Townsend, T. N. (2002). Masquerade detection using truncated command lines, (pp. 219-228). In *Proceedings of International Conference on Dependable Systems and Networks (DSN-02)*.

McHugh, J. (2000). Testing intrusion detection systems: a critique of the 1998 and 1999 DARPA intrusion detection system evaluations as performed by Lincoln Laboratory. *ACM Transactions on Information and System Security, 3*(4), 262-294.

Minaei-Bidgoli, B., Analoui, M., Shahhoseini, H.S. & Rezvani, M. H. (2007). Performance analysis of decision tree for intrusion detection with reduced DARPA offline feature sets. In *Proceedings of the 2007 International Multi-conference of Engineers and Computer Scientists (IMECS'07)*.

Mobasher, B., Cooley, R.(2000). Automatic personalization based on Web usage mining. *Communications of the ACM, 43*(8), 142-151.

Monrose, F. & Rubin, A. D. (2000). Keystroke dynamics as a biometric for authentication. *Future Generations Computing Systems, 16*(4), 351-359.

Monrose, F., Reiter, M.K. & Wetzel, S. (1999). Password hardening based on keystroke dynamics, (pp. 73-82). *In Proceedings of the 6th ACM Conf. Computer and Comm. Security*, ACM Press.

Nanopoulos, A., Katsaros, D., Manolopoulos, Y. (2001). Effective prediction of Web-user accesses: A data mining approach. In *Proceeding of the WEBKDD 2001 Workshop*, San Francisco.

Ord, T. and Furnell, S. M. (2000). User authentication for keypad-based devices using keystroke analysis, (pp. 263-272). *In Proceedings of the 2nd Int'l Network Conf. Inst. of Electrical Eng.*

Peacock, A. (2000). Learning user keystroke latency patterns. Retrieved Oct. 26, 2007, from http://pel.cs.byu.edu/~alen/personal/CourseWork/ cs572KeystrokePaper/

Peacock, A, Ke, X, Wilkerson, M. (2004). Typing patterns: A key to user identification. *IEEE Security & Privacy, 2*(5), 40-47.

Pazzani M., Billsus, D. (1997). Learning and revising user profiles: The identification of interesting Web sites. *Machine Learning, 27*, 313-331.

Pazzani, M., Muramatsu J., Billsus, D. (1996). Syskill & webert: Identifying interesting Web sites. In *Proceedings of the National Conference on Artificial Intelligence*, Portland, OR.

Schonlau, M., DuMouchel, W., Ju, W., Karr, A., Theus, M., Vardi, Y. (2001). Computer intrusion: Detecting masquerades. *Statistical Science, 16*(1), 58-74.

Schonlau, M., Theus, M. (2000). Detecting masquerades in intrusion detection based on unpopular commands. *Information Processing Letters, 76*, 33-38.

Spillane, R. (1975). Keyboard apparatus for personal identification. *IBM Technical Disclosure Bulletin, 17*(3346).

Theus, M., Schonlau, M., (1998). Intrusion detection based on structural zeroes'. *Statistical Computing & Graphics Newsletter, 9*(1), 12-17.

Thomas, C., Sharma, V. & Balakrishnan, N. (2008). Usefulness of DARPA dataset for intrusion detection system evaluation, (pp. 69730G-69738G). In *Proceedings of the 2008 Data Mining, Intrusion Detection, Information Assurance, and Data Networks Security (SPIE'08)*.

Umphress, D. & Williams, G. (1985). Identify verification through keyboard characteristics. *International Journal of Man-Machine Studies*, 263-273.

Wang Y., Kim, I. (2007). Profiling user behavior for intrusion detection using item response modeling. *Computer communications* (submitted).

Wang, Y., Normand, SL.T. (2006). Determining the minimum sample size of audit data required to profile user behavior and detect anomaly intrusion. *International Journal of Business Data Communications and Networking, 2*(3), 31-45.

Wang, K., Stolfo. S. J. (2003). One class training for masquerade Detection. *3rd IEEE Conference Data Mining Workshop on Data Mining for Computer Security*, Florida.

Young, J. and Hammon, R. (1989). *Method and apparatus for verifying an individual's identity*. US patent number 4,805,222, Washington, DC.

Zilberman, A.Z. (2002). *Security method and apparatus employing authentication by keystroke dynamics*. US patent number 6,442,692, Washington, DC.

ENDNOTES

[1] Netflow is an open but proprietary network protocol developed by Cisco Systems.
[2] Tcpdump is a tool for network monitoring, protocol debugging and data acquisition.
[3] 711 F. Supp. 1315; 1989 U.S. Dist. LEXIS 12972

APPENDIX

List of 294 Web Sites Included in the Web Sequence Data

Code	Site	URL	Vcode
1000	regwiz	regwiz	V1000
1001	Support Desktop	support	V1001
1002	End User Produced View	athome	V1002
1003	Knowledge Base	kb	V1003
1004	Microsoft.com Search	search	V1004
1005	Norway	norge	V1005
1006	misc	misc	V1006
1007	International IE content	ie_intl	V1007
1008	Free Downloads	msdownload	V1008
1009	Windows Family of OSs	windows	V1009
1010	Visual Basic	vbasic	V1010
1011	MS Office Development	officedev	V1011
1012	Outlook Development	outlookdev	V1012
1013	Visual Basic Support	vbasicsupport	V1013
1014	Office Free Stuff	officefreestuff	V1014
1015	Excel	msexcel	V1015
1016	MS Excel	excel	V1016
1017	Products	products	V1017
1018	isapi	isapi	V1018
1019	MS PowerPoint	mspowerpoint	V1019
1020	Developer Network	msdn	V1020
1021	Visual C	visualc	V1021
1022	Typography Site	truetype	V1022
1023	Spain	spain	V1023
1024	Internet Information Server	iis	V1024
1025	Web Site Builder's Gallery	gallery	V1025
1026	Internet Site Construction for Developers	sitebuilder	V1026
1027	Internet Development	intdev	V1027
1028	OLE Development	oledev	V1028
1029	Clip Gallery Live	clipgallerylive	V1029
1030	Windows NT Server	ntserver	V1030
1031	MS Office	msoffice	V1031
1032	Games	games	V1032
1033	MS Store Logo Merchandise	logostore	V1033
1034	Internet Explorer	ie	V1034

continued on following page

APPENDIX CONTINUED

1035	Windows95 Support	windowssup-port	V1035
1036	Corporate Desktop Evaluation	organizations	V1036
1037	Windows 95	windows95	V1037
1038	SiteBuilder Network Membership	sbnmember	V1038
1039	Internet Service Providers	isp	V1039
1040	MS Office Info	office	V1040
1041	Developer Workshop	workshop	V1041
1042	Visual Studio	vstudio	V1042
1043	Connecting Small Business	smallbiz	V1043
1044	Developer Media Development	mediadev	V1044
1045	NetMeeting	netmeeting	V1045
1046	IE Support	iesupport	V1046
1048	MS Publisher	publisher	V1048
1049	Support Network Program Information	supportnet	V1049
1050	Macintosh Office	macoffice	V1050
1051	MS Schedule+ News	scheduleplus	V1051
1052	MS Word News	word	V1052
1053	Jakarta	visualj	V1053
1054	Exchange	exchange	V1054
1055	MSHome Kids Stuff	kids	V1055
1056	sports	sports	V1056
1057	MS PowerPoint News	powerpoint	V1057
1058	SP Referral (ART)	referral	V1058
1059	Sweden	sverige	V1059
1060	MS Word	msword	V1060
1061	promo	promo	V1061
1062	MS Access News	msaccess	V1062
1063	Intranet Strategy	intranet	V1063
1064	MS Site Builder Workshop	activeplatform	V1064
1065	Java Strategy and Info	java	V1065
1066	Music Producer	musicpro-ducer	V1066
1067	FrontPage	frontpage	V1067
1068	VBScript Development	vbscript	V1068
1069	Windows CE	windowsce	V1069
1070	ActiveX Technology Development	activex	V1070
1071	N. American Automap	automap	V1071
1072	Visual InterDev	vinterdev	V1072

continued on following page

APPENDIX CONTINUED

1073	Taiwan	taiwan	V1073
1074	Windows NT Workstation	ntworkstation	V1074
1075	Job Openings	jobs	V1075
1076	NT Workstation Support	ntwkssupport	V1076
1077	MS Office Support	msofficesup-port	V1077
1078	NT Server Support	ntserversup-port	V1078
1079	Australia	australia	V1079
1080	Brazil	brasil	V1080
1081	Access Development	accessdev	V1081
1082	MS Access	access	V1082
1083	MS Access Support	msaccesssup-port	V1083
1084	UK	uk	V1084
1085	Exchange Support	exchangesup-port	V1085
1086	OEM	oem	V1086
1087	MS Proxy Server	proxy	V1087
1088	OutLook	outlook	V1088
1089	Office Reference	officereference	V1089
1090	Games Support	gamessupport	V1090
1091	Windows Hardware Development	hwdev	V1091
1092	Visual FoxPro	vfoxpro	V1092
1093	VBA Development	vba	V1093
1094	Microsoft Home	mshome	V1094
1095	Product Catalog	catalog	V1095
1096	Microsoft Press	mspress	V1096
1097	Latin America Region	latam	V1097
1098	For Developers Only	devonly	V1098
1099	Executive Computing	cio	V1099
1100	MS in Education	education	V1100
1101	Microsoft OLE DB	oledb	V1101
1102	Microsoft Home Essentials	homeessen-tials	V1102
1103	MS Works	works	V1103
1104	Hong Kong	hk	V1104
1105	France	france	V1105
1106	Czech Republic	cze	V1106
1107	Slovakia	slovakia	V1107

continued on following page

APPENDIX CONTINUED

1108	MS TeamManager	teammanager	V1108
1109	TechNet (World Wide Web Edition)	technet	V1109
1110	Mastering Series	mastering	V1110
1111	Visual Source Safe	ssafe	V1111
1112	Canada	canada	V1112
1113	Internet Security Framework	security	V1113
1114	Service Advantage	servad	V1114
1115	Hungary	hun	V1115
1116	Switzerland	switzerland	V1116
1117	Sidewinder	sidewinder	V1117
1118	SQL Server	sql	V1118
1119	Corporation Information	corpinfo	V1119
1120	Switching from Competitive Products	switch	V1120
1121	Microsoft Magazine	magazine	V1121
1122	Microsoft User Group Program	mindshare	V1122
1123	Germany	germany	V1123
1124	Industry Marketing Information (Vertical)	industry	V1124
1125	ImageComposer	imagecom-poser	V1125
1126	Media Manager	mediaman-ager	V1126
1127	NetShow	netshow	V1127
1128	MS Solutions Framework	msf	V1128
1129	ActiveX Data Objects	ado	V1129
1130	IT Technical Information	syspro	V1130
1131	MS Money Information	moneyzone	V1131
1132	MS Money Support	msmoneysup-port	V1132
1133	FrontPage Support	frontpagesup-port	V1133
1134	BackOffice	backoffice	V1134
1135	MS Word Support	mswordsup-port	V1135
1136	WorldWide Offices - US Districts	usa	V1136
1137	About Microsoft	mscorp	V1137
1138	Developer Magazine	mind	V1138
1139	MS in K-12 Education	k-12	V1139
1140	Netherlands (Holland)	netherlands	V1140
1141	Europe	europe	V1141
1142	South Africa	southafrica	V1142

continued on following page

APPENDIX CONTINUED

1143	Site Builder Workshop	workshoop	V1143
1144	For Developers Only News	devnews	V1144
1145	Visual Fox Pro Support	vfoxprosup-port	V1145
1146	Microsoft Solution Providers	msp	V1146
1147	Microsoft Financial Forum	msft	V1147
1148	Channel Resources	channel_re-sources	V1148
1149	Advanced Data Connector	adc	V1149
1150	Internet Information Server News	infoserv	V1150
1151	MS PowerPoint Support	mspowerpoint-support	V1151
1152	Russia	rus	V1152
1153	Venezuela	venezuela	V1153
1154	MS Project	project	V1154
1155	Sidewalk	sidewalk	V1155
1156	Powered by BackOffice	powered	V1156
1157	Windows 32 bit developer	win32dev	V1157
1158	Interactive Media Technologies	imedia	V1158
1159	Transaction Server	transaction	V1159
1160	Visual C Support	visualcsupport	V1160
1161	Works Support	workssupport	V1161
1162	IIS Support	infoservsup-port	V1162
1163	Open Type	opentype	V1163
1164	Systems Management Server	smsmgmt	V1164
1165	Poland	poland	V1165
1166	Mexico	mexico	V1166
1167	Windows Hardware Testing	hwtest	V1167
1168	Sales Information (infobase)	salesinfo	V1168
1169	MS Project	msproject	V1169
1170	Microsoft Mail	mail	V1170
1171	MS Merchant	merchant	V1171
1172	Belgium	belgium	V1172
1173	Microsoft OnLine Institute	moli	V1173
1174	New Zealand	nz	V1174
1175	MS Project Support	msprojectsup-port	V1175
1176	Java Script Development	jscript	V1176
1177	Master Marketing Calendar	events	V1177
1178	msdownload.	msdownload.	V1178

continued on following page

APPENDIX CONTINUED

1179	Colombia	colombia	V1179
1180	Slovenija	slovenija	V1180
1181	Kids Support	kidssupport	V1181
1182	Fortran	fortran	V1182
1183	Italy	italy	V1183
1184	MS Excel Support	msexcelsup-port	V1184
1185	SNA Server	sna	V1185
1186	Job Listings for Pre-Grads	college	V1186
1187	ODBC Development	odbc	V1187
1188	Korea	korea	V1188
1189	Internet News	internet	V1189
1190	Repository	repository	V1190
1191	Management	management	V1191
1192	Visual J++ Support	visualjsupport	V1192
1193	Office Developer Support	offdevsupport	V1193
1194	China	china	V1194
1195	Portugal	portugal	V1195
1196	ie40	ie40	V1196
1197	SQL Support	sqlsupport	V1197
1198	Picture It	pictureit	V1198
1199	feedback	feedback	V1199
1200	Benelux Region	benelux	V1200
1201	MS Hardware	hardware	V1201
1202	Advanced Technology	advtech	V1202
1203	Denmark	danmark	V1203
1204	MS Schedule+	msschedule-plus	V1204
1205	Hardware Supprt	hardwaresup-port	V1205
1206	Volume Purchasing Options	select	V1206
1207	Internet Control Pack	icp	V1207
1208	Israel	israel	V1208
1209	Turkey	turkey	V1209
1210	SNA Support	snasupport	V1210
1211	SMSMGT Support	smsmgmtsup-port	V1211
1212	World Wide Offices	worldwide	V1212
1213	Corporate Customers	corporate_so-lutions	V1213
1214	MS Financial Services	finserv	V1214

continued on following page

APPENDIX CONTINUED

1215	For Developers Only Info	developer	V1215
1216	Virtual Reality Markup Language	vrml	V1216
1217	Ireland	ireland	V1217
1218	MS Publisher Support	publishersup-port	V1218
1219	Corporate Advertising Content	ads	V1219
1220	Mac Office Support	macofficesup-port	V1220
1221	Microsoft TV Program Information	mstv	V1221
1222	MS Office News	msofc	V1222
1223	Finland	finland	V1223
1224	Authorized Technical Education Center Pro	atec	V1224
1225	Anti Piracy Information	piracy	V1225
1226	MS Schedule+ Support	msschedplus-support	V1226
1227	Argentina	argentina	V1227
1228	Visual Test	vtest	V1228
1229	Uruguay	uruguay	V1229
1230	Mail Support	mailsupport	V1230
1231	Windows NT Developer Support	win32devsup-port	V1231
1232	SiteBuilder Network Specs & Standards	standards	V1232
1233	vbscripts	vbscripts	V1233
1234	Office Free Stuff News	off97cat	V1234
1235	MS Training Evaluation	onlineeval	V1235
1236	Developing for Global Markets	globaldev	V1236
1237	Developer Days	devdays	V1237
1238	Excel Development	exceldev	V1238
1239	Microsoft Consulting	msconsult	V1239
1240	Thailand	thailand	V1240
1241	India	india	V1241
1242	MS Garden	msgarden	V1242
1243	MS Usability Group	usability	V1243
1244	Developer Newswire	devwire	V1244
1245	Open Financial Connectivity	ofc	V1245
1246	Developer Media Games	gamesdev	V1246
1247	Wine Guide	wineguide	V1247
1248	Softimage	softimage	V1248

continued on following page

APPENDIX CONTINUED

1249	Fortran Support	fortransup-port	V1249
1250	Middle East	middleeast	V1250
1251	Reference Support	referencesup-port	V1251
1252	Community Affairs	giving	V1252
1253	MS Word Development	worddev	V1253
1254	ie3	ie3	V1254
1255	Message Queue Server	msmq	V1255
1256	Solutions in Action	sia	V1256
1257	Professional Developers Series	devvideos	V1257
1258	Peru	peru	V1258
1259	controls	controls	V1259
1260	Exchange Trial	trial	V1260
1261	MS's Complete Do It Yourself Guide	diyguide	V1261
1262	Chile	chile	V1262
1263	Educational Services & Programs	services	V1263
1264	MS Partner Web	se_partners	V1264
1265	Source Safe Support	ssafesupport	V1265
1266	Licenses and Piracy	licenses	V1266
1267	Caribbean	caribbean	V1267
1268	javascript	javascript	V1268
1269	Customer Guides	business	V1269
1270	developr	developr	V1270
1271	mdsn	mdsn	V1271
1272	softlib	softlib	V1272
1273	mdn	mdn	V1273
1274	Professional Developer Conference	pdc	V1274
1275	security.	security.	V1275
1276	Visual Test Support	vtestsupport	V1276
1277	NetShow for PowerPoint	stream	V1277
1278	MS in Higer Education	hed	V1278
1279	Multimedia Golf	msgolf	V1279
1280	MS Interactive Music Control	music	V1280
1281	IntelliMouse	intellimouse	V1281
1282	home	home	V1282
1283	Cinemainia	cinemania	V1283
1284	partner	partner	V1284
1287	International AutoRoute	autoroute	V1287

continued on following page

APPENDIX CONTINUED

1288	library	library	V1288
1289	Master Chef Product Information	masterchef	V1289
1290	Activate the Internet Conference	devmovies	V1290
1291	news	news	V1291
1292	MS North Africa	northafrica	V1292
1293	Encarta	encarta	V1293
1294	Bookshelf	bookshelf	V1294
1295	Training	train_cert	V1295
1297	Central America	centroam	V1297

Chapter IV
Network Data Characteristics

When you know you are doing your very best within the circumstances of your existence, applaud yourself!

— Rusty Berkus

INTRODUCTION

Data represents the natural phenomena of our real world. Data is constructed by rows and columns; usually rows represent the observations and columns represent the variables. Observations, also called subjects, records, or data points, represent a phenomenon in the real world and variables, as also known as data elements or data fields, represent the characteristics of observations in data. Variables take different values for different observations, which can make observations independent of each other. Figure 4.1 illustrates a section of TCP/IP traffic data, in which the rows are individual network traffics, and the columns, separated by a space, are characteristics of the traffics. In this example, the first column is a session index of each connection and the second column is the date when the connection occurred.

In this chapter, we will discuss some fundamental key features of variables and network data. We will present detailed discussions on variable characteristics and distributions in Sections Random Variables and Variables Distributions, and describe network data modules in Section Network Data Modules. The material covered in this chapter will help readers who do not have a solid background in this area gain an understanding of the basic concepts of variables and data. Additional information can be found from *Introduction to the Practice of Statistics* by Moore and McCabe (1998).

Figure 4.1 A sample of TCP/IP traffic data

```
 1  06/24/1998 08:12:58 00:00:01 ntp/u 123 123 172.016.112.020 192.168.001.010 0 -
 2  06/24/1998 08:12:58 00:00:01 ntp/u 123 123 172.016.112.020 192.168.001.010 0 -
 3  06/24/1998 08:15:52 00:00:04 smtp 1024 25 172.016.114.169 195.115.218.108 0 -
 4  06/24/1998 08:15:55 00:00:01 domain/u 53 53 192.168.001.010 172.016.112.020 0 -
 5  06/24/1998 08:15:55 00:00:01 domain/u 53 53 192.168.001.010 172.016.112.020 0 -
 6  06/24/1998 08:15:55 00:00:02 smtp 1025 25 172.016.114.169 196.227.033.189 0 -
 7  06/24/1998 08:17:08 00:00:04 smtp 1026 25 172.016.113.084 195.115.218.108 0 -
 8  06/24/1998 08:17:11 00:00:02 smtp 1027 25 172.016.113.084 196.227.033.189 0 -
 9  06/24/1998 08:17:18 00:00:02 smtp 1028 25 172.016.112.149 195.115.218.108 0 -
10  06/24/1998 08:17:36 00:00:01 domain/u 53 53 192.168.001.010 192.168.001.020 0 -
11  06/24/1998 08:17:36 00:00:01 domain/u 53 53 192.168.001.010 192.168.001.020 0 -
12  06/24/1998 08:17:37 00:00:02 smtp 1029 25 172.016.114.169 194.027.251.021 0 -
13  06/24/1998 08:17:38 00:00:02 smtp 1048 25 172.016.114.169 194.007.248.153 0 -
14  06/24/1998 08:17:39 00:00:02 smtp 1049 25 172.016.114.169 197.182.091.233 0 -
15  06/24/1998 08:17:40 00:00:02 smtp 1051 25 172.016.114.169 195.115.218.108 0 -
16  06/24/1998 08:17:41 00:00:02 smtp 1052 25 172.016.114.169 196.227.033.189 0 -
17  06/24/1998 08:17:45 00:00:01 smtp 1104 25 172.016.114.169 135.008.060.182 0 -
19  06/24/1998 08:18:07 00:00:01 eco/i - - 192.168.001.005 192.168.001.001 0 -
20  06/24/1998 08:18:07 00:00:01 eco/i - - 192.168.001.005 192.168.001.001 0 -
21  06/24/1998 08:18:07 00:00:01 ecr/i - - 192.168.001.001 192.168.001.005 0 -
22  06/24/1998 08:18:20 00:00:04 smtp 1107 25 172.016.114.207 196.227.033.189 0 -
23  06/24/1998 08:18:29 00:00:04 http 1108 80 172.016.113.204 205.181.112.065 0 -
24  06/24/1998 08:18:29 00:00:04 smtp 1109 25 172.016.112.194 196.037.075.158 0 -
25  06/24/1998 08:18:32 00:00:02 smtp 1110 25 172.016.112.194 196.227.033.189 0 -
26  06/24/1998 08:18:33 00:00:01 http 1111 80 172.016.113.204 205.181.112.065 0 -
27  06/24/1998 08:18:33 00:00:01 http 1112 80 172.016.113.204 205.181.112.065 0 -
28  06/24/1998 08:18:33 00:00:01 http 1113 80 172.016.113.204 205.181.112.065 0 -
29  06/24/1998 08:18:33 00:00:01 http 1115 80 172.016.113.204 205.181.112.065 0 -
30  06/24/1998 08:18:33 00:00:01 http 1116 80 172.016.113.204 205.181.112.065 0 -
```

RANDOM VARIABLES

Understanding the concept of variables is important for developing and applying better statistical methods in network security. When we mention the word "variable", we usually mean "random variable"—its value is a real number determined by each element of a sample space, D (Stirzaker, 1999). A random variable can take on many possible values from the D, but only one of those values will actually occur. For example, if we toss a coin five times and record each time the head faces up (true or false), the number of heads could take a value of 0, 1, 2, 3, 4 and 5, therefore, it is a random variable that is determined by the toss. Throughout this book we will use an uppercase letter, X, to denote a random variable; its corresponding lowercase letter, x, will denote its values. Most data elements in the network traffic are random variables. For example, if D is constructed by all possible destination IP addresses within a network, then an actual destination IP address of a randomly selected connection (i.e., every connection has the same chance to be selected) could be any one of the addresses in that sample space. Therefore, the variable that is used to represent the destination IP address is a random variable, X. In Figure 4.1, however, the first column is not a random variable but an index to denote the order of sessions. For simplification, we will omit the term of "random" and only use the word "variable" throughout this book.

Variables have three essential attributes that warrant understanding: types, values, and distributions. A variable can be cataloged into different types, such as continuous, categorical or discrete based on the characteristic of its value. If the number of possible values in D is uncountable or infinite, a variable defined on such D is considered to be continuous, such as $D = \{1.01, 1.10, 3.00, ...\}$. If D has a finite or countable infinite value, a variable defined on such a space is known to be discrete, as in, $D = \{1, 2, 3, ...\}$. If a variable can only take two values, such as $D = \{0,1\}$, this variable is known as a binary or dichotomous variable. Figure 4.2 illustrates a simple diagram of the various categories of variables.

Figure 4.2 Variable types

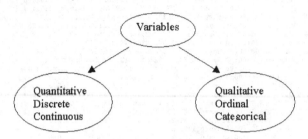

Quantitative and Qualitative Variables

Quantitative variables, which are also known as numeric variables, include continuous and discrete variables. Both continuous and discrete variables' values are numerical and they provide quantitative information about observations. A continuous variable describes data in qualitative means. For example, a variable that measures the "login time zone" can be considered as a continuous variable of 24:00 format with a range of 0.00 to 23.59. By contrast, a discrete variable only can take integral values such as $0,1,2,...n$, which include counts, dichotomous and ordinal variables. A count variable represents the frequency of an event occurred. For example, a network monitoring system can report the number of anomalous events that occurred within a particular window (e.g., 5 minutes); the variable to represent such anomalous connections is a count variable. A dichotomous variable is also known as binary variable that has only two values. Usually, we use 1 for an event that is present or an event that has a positive response and 0 for an absent or negative response (e.g., anomaly = 0 and anomaly-free = 1). A response variable is usually dichotomous. An ordinal variable can also fall under the scope of qualitative variables, and can have similar categories to the categorical variable except it has "ordered" values. We describe these attributes below.

Qualitative variables include categorical and ordinal variables. A categorical variable assigns group membership by categorizing data into one of several groups or categories and qualitatively describes data. For example, the "type of network" variable includes two categories: wireless and wired networks. The variable used to represent such information is a categorical variable. The possible values of a categorical variable are not numerical, but rather, descriptive; they have no ranking meaning between levels, regardless of the number of levels that the variable has. Thus, even though a categorical variable can be coded as $0,1,2,...n$, the numerical values are arbitrary in the sense that a lower value is not necessarily less than a higher value.

To include a categorical variable in statistical modeling, we can represent its values using dummy variable(s) that are usually binary or dichotomous. For example, user's gender is usually presented by a categorical variable, "Female" or "Male," or simply "F" or "M". We can have a dummy variable assigned for "Female" as 1 if a user is female, and 0 for a male user. The category of "type of services" in TCP/IP data can be extended by following dummy variables: UDP (yes/no), HTTP (yes/no), SMTP (yes/no), URP (yes/no), ECR (yes/no), ECO (yes/no), SNMP (yes/no), and FTP (yes/no), where "yes" has a value of 1 and "no" of 0.

An ordinal variable is similar to a categorical variable but its value has a clear ordering meaning. For example, the connecting time is a continual variable, but it can also be assigned a value of 1 if the time is less than 10, 2 if the time is between 10 and 20, and so on. Note that a high value will represent a longer connecting time. We can also create an ordinal variable with values 1, 2, and 3 to represent a network traffic volume in low, medium and high, respectively. We have to keep in mind that the interval between the values of an ordinal variable may not always be the same across the levels of the variable. If this occurs, either we can recode the variable to have the same interval or we can represent it using dummy variables. For example, we can have an ordinal variable as 1 when the volume of traffic per second is between 0 and less than 3000, 2 when the volume is between 3000 and less than 4000, and 3 for volumes greater than 4000 per second. Note that the actual volumes of this variable represented are not same across the three intervals.

$$x = \begin{cases} 1 & 0 \le V < 3000 \\ 2 & 3000 \le V < 4000 \\ 3 & 4000 \le V < \infty \end{cases}$$

Response, Predictor, and Latent Variables

From a functional perspective, variables can be categorized as either dependent or independent types. A dependent variable is also called a response variable or outcome variable, and its value depends on the value(s) of one or more independent variables, which known as predictor or explorative. Throughout of this book we will use the terms "response variable" to reflect a dependent variable and "predictor variable" to reflect an independent variable. Mathematically, a response variable is a function of the predictor variable(s): $y = f(x)$, where y and x represent the response variable and the predictor variable(s), respectively. In network security, the response variable is usually an outcome of a network connection (e.g., anomaly-free or abnormal connections); this outcome is usually binary. Rich literature is available on the selection of predictor variables for predicting attacks. Lee & Stolfo (2000), Guyon (2003), Kayacik & Zincir-Heywood (2005), Chebrolu, Abraham & Thomas (2005), and Wang & Seidman (2006) provide good discussions on this topic; many of these studies were based on the MIT-DARPA or KDD-cup data.

Although we may be able to directly measure most variable values, there are variables which have values that cannot be directed measured, but can be inferred and estimated. For example, the source and destination IP addresses, source and destination ports, and service types, are directly measurable variables for each connection; conversely, the outcome of a connection may not be directly measurable during the connecting period. Many factors are associated with why such an outcome cannot be directly measured. It could be that the current network secure agent cannot recognize a novel type of attacks, the classification algorithm provides a false result, or simply it is possible that we cannot measure the outcome in real time. A variable that cannot be directly measured, but is indirectly measurable, is called a latent variable. A latent variable also reflects a construct, or a factor that is measured by its respective variables. Either a response or a predictor variable, or both, can be latent.

Features, Variables, and Parameters

The term "feature," is commonly used in the forensic science field, where it is used to describe the characteristics of fingerprints, tool marks, footprints, and other identifiable evidences. This term has also been widely used in the computer science field in image, voice and signal processes. A feature represents a unique characteristic belonging to an observation in study, but may not be a random variable, which means that the probability of its occurrence is not the same across observations. Features can be grouped together if they are similar, but the location of each feature needs to be specific. For example, in forensic science, we classify fingerprints into three large groups of patterns: *Arch, Loop* and *Whorl*, of which each group has the same general characteristics. The patterns can be further classified into sub-groups based on the smaller differences existing between patterns in the same general group. For instance, *Loop* can be divided into *Radial loop* and *Ulnar loop* (U.S. Department of Justice Federal Bureau of Investigation, 1990). Also, a feature can be unique for a specified observation or event only. For example, *CORE* is a common feature in fingerprints but the probability of *CORE* locating at the left-bottom of a fingerprint is less 0.00001. Therefore, if we find a fingerprint with such a feature located in two crime scenes, we can be sure that the same person was involved in both locations. In this case, when we see the feature, we know exactly what the observation or event is.

A "variable" is a statistical term. A variable always associates with some levels of randomness and uncertainty. We present variable values as estimates and describe the uncertainty with the corresponding interval estimates. We actually do not focus on the uniqueness of a variable, and if a variable's frequency is too low, we may not want to use it in analysis. Alternatively, for a feature we usually do not consider its frequency but rather, its uniqueness that can be used to directly identify an event or a single phenomenon. If a feature only links to a single observation or event, it could be helpful to develop a rule-based, rather than statistics-based, introduction detection system. As we mentioned in Chapter I, to detect attacks, we need to gather robust features that link directly to a particular attack. Such features may have no statistically predictive power, but they have a one-to-one linkage with a particular attack. In general, we need more common variables that are statistically meaningful for profiling user behavior, and we need more attack-specific features for detecting attacks.

Parameters are numeric quantities that describe a certain population's characteristics, and are usually unknown. The relationship between parameters and variables is also important and may be easy to be confused. Unlike a variable, where values reflect characteristics of the data, the term "parameter" has a more mathematical meaning and its value(s) reflect some type of theoretical model. Variables are measurement-oriented in that their values depend on observations and vary from observation to observation. Parameters, on the other hand, are model-oriented. They define a theoretical model but are not associated with actual measurements. We select variables from data and analyze them by calculating means, medians, and standard deviations, or fitting a model, to get parameters for representing a theoretical model (Figure 4.3).

Figure 4.3 Data, variables, and parameters

Suppose we collect the legitimate users login time zone from a marketing department over a week-long period—the data could include more than 10 million observations. Now let us assume that the time zone variable has been converted into a continuous range between 0.00 and 23.59, and the mean of the login time is $\mu = 9.0$ with a standard deviation (SD) of $\sigma =2.0$. Note that μ and σ are the parameters that define a practical distribution of login time zone from the theoretical normal distribution family. In this case, they give the best estimate of the population distribution of legitimate user login time zones, assuming that the population login time follows a normal distribution. If we like to profile user behavior based on their login time zone, we can simply compare each of the user's actual login time zones with the estimated parameters, μ and σ, thereby, identifying any outliers. With such a comparison we do not need the original 10 million observations from the raw data, but rather, the two parameters, μ and σ, to describe the pattern of legitimate users in that marketing department.

In some situations parameters are values that can be altered to examine what happens to the performance of a network system. For example, the performance of a supervised learning algorithm will depend on aspects such as the sensitivity and specificity of classification. If we look to see how the performance would change if, say, sensitivity and specificity were improved, then we are treating these as parameters rather than using the values observed in a real set of data.

Example 4.1→Parameters. Table 4.1 shows an example of logistic regression model results (see Chapter VII for a more detailed discussion about this model). In this model, the response variable is an anomaly (yes/no) and the predictor variables are three binary variables, TCP (yes/no), UDP (yes/no) and HTTP (yes/no). The odds ratio, 95% confidence interval, and standardized estimate are parameters that define the typical logistic regression model. Again, the information hidden in the data have been retrieved and abstracted by the parameters, which define the model as: $\log[p_i/1 - p_i] = \beta_0 + \beta_1 x_{i1} + \beta_2 x_{i2} + \beta_3 x_{i3}$. They may have no meaning for individual observations, although they can be used to test if a connection is anomaly-free or anomalous.

VARIABLE DISTRIBUTIONS

The distribution of a variable represents its values and frequencies of the values that the variable takes. We define the distribution as the pattern of values obtained from measuring a quantity in a large number of observations (Altman & Bland, 1995). There are many

Table 4.1 Logistic regression model estimated parameters

Variables	Odds Ratio	95% Confidence Interval	Standardized Estimate
ICMP (reference)	1.00		
TCP	0.69	0.60 -0.79	-0.1001
UDP	0.08	0.07 -0.09	-0.2799
HTTP	1.63	1.47 -1.81	0.0907

different types of distribution families, each of which can be defined theoretically by a set of parameters. These types of distributions are known as theoretical distributions. Real data-driven distributions are called empirical distributions. Important distribution families in network security include normal (Gaussian distribution), binomial and Poisson distributions. We will briefly review these distribution types below, and readers who are interested in additional information should refer to Walpole & Myers (1978) and Moore & McCabe (1998).

Normal Distribution

Let μ be the mean and let σ be the SD of the mean. A continuous random variable, X, has a generalized univariate normal distribution: $X \sim N(\mu,\sigma)$. The probability density function is defined as

$$f(x) = \frac{1}{\sqrt{2\pi}\sigma} e^{-\frac{1}{2}(\frac{x-\mu}{\sigma})^2} \quad -\infty < x < \infty \qquad (4\text{-}1)$$

where σ^2 is known as the variance of the mean. The cumulative distribution function of the normal distribution is

$$F(x) = \int_{-\infty}^{\infty} f(x)dx = \frac{1}{\sqrt{2\pi}\sigma} \int_{-\infty}^{\infty} e^{-\frac{1}{2}(\frac{x-\mu}{\sigma})^2} dx \qquad (4\text{-}2)$$

A normal distribution, $N(\mu,\sigma)$ can be standardized to be the standard normal distribution $N(0,1)$ with $\mu = 0$ and $\sigma = 1$, through a standardized random variable

$$z = \frac{(x-\mu)}{\sigma}.$$

This transformation is common in use, and allows us to centralize continuous variable values with its mean. It also allows the results of a transformation to have a standard normal distribution.

With different values of μ and σ, the normal distribution $N(\mu,\sigma)$ is a large family, but they all have common properties. The most important attributes include the followings: (1) on the model, the point on the horizontal axis where the curve is a maximum occurs at $x =$

μ, (2) the curve has its points of inflection at x $= \mu \pm \sigma$, or is concave upward otherwise, (3) the normal curve approaches the horizontal axis asymptotically in either direction, away from μ, (4) the total area under the curve and above the horizontal axis is equal to 1, and (5) the rule of 68-95-99.7, which states that 68% of the observations fall within 1 SD of μ, or between $\mu - \sigma$ and $\mu + \sigma$; 95% of the observations fall within 2 SDs of μ, or between $\mu - 2\sigma$ and $\mu + 2\sigma$, and 99.7% of the observations fall within 3 SDs of μ, or between $\mu - 3\sigma$ and $\mu + 3\sigma$ (Figure 4.4). If we randomly select a value from a normal distribution, two thirds of the times we will have a value that is between $\mu - 2\sigma$ and $\mu + 2\sigma$.

Statistical modeling and testing methods have parametric and non-parametric differences. The parametric methods estimate parameters of some underlying theoretical distribution. The non-parametric methods do not assume any particular family for the distribution of the data; therefore, they do not estimate any parameters for such a distribution. Over the past several decades, parametric methods, such as regression models and the t-test, have been mainly employed in the network security area (Claffy, Braun & Polyzos, 1995), but non-parametric approaches have also been introduced recently (Marchette, 2003; Cho & Park, 2003; Scott, 2004; Kim & Kim, 2006). We will revisit the non-parametric methods again in Chapter XI.

The normal distribution is essential for many parametric statistical methods that will be discussed in the following Chapters. Such methods include linear regression, t-test, and factor analysis, which make assumptions about the normality. The normal distribution has been provided as a root of researching in the network security field. In Denning's (1987) decisive article entitled, *An Intrusion-Detection Model*, one of her proposed approaches was to measure the mean and standard derivation of certain key variables over a historical period to obtain a reflection of the average user behavior and the variability. Although Denning's paper was published in 1987 and such measures were considered by themselves too crude for intrusion detection purposes (Stallings, 2003), the idea remains true today.

Example 4.2→Distributions of a Risk Score. Figure 4.5 shows theoretical distributions of a risk score for a set of anomaly-free connections drawn from a training dataset, and a set of anomaly-free and anomalous connections drawn from a testing dataset, which were all based on the MIT-DARPA data. These distributions were generated based on simulations—they will be discussed in more detailed in Chapter X.

The curve of any continuous probability distribution or density function is constructed so that the area under the curve bounded by the two ordinates $x = a$ and $x = b$, equals the probability that the random variable X assumes a value between $x = a$ and $x = b$. Therefore, the probability that X falls within (a,b) can be calculated as

$$P(a < X < b) = \frac{1}{\sqrt{2\pi}\sigma} \int_a^b e^{-\frac{1}{2}(\frac{x-\mu}{\sigma})^2} dx. \tag{4-3}$$

Example 4.3→Probability of Being Anomalous. In Figure 4.5, the distribution of the risk score for anomalous connections has $\mu = 0.11$ and $\sigma = 0.06$. Suppose that a connection has a score of 0.15, the probability of this connection being an anomaly is

Figure 4.4 The 68-95-99.7 rule for normal distribution

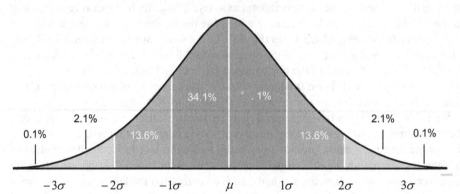

$$P(X \geq 0.15) = P(\frac{X - 0.11}{0.06} \geq \frac{0.15 - 0.11}{0.06}) = P(Z \geq 0.6667) = 1 - 0.7475 = 0.2525.$$

That is, the probability of a connection with a risk score of 0.15 being anomalous is greater than 0.25. Note that we employed the normalization factor,

$$z = \frac{(x - \mu)}{\sigma},$$

to transform the index distribution into a standardized normal distribution.

Binomial Distribution

We use a binomial function to describe the distribution of a dichotomous variable. Let each observation in a sample size of n be coded on 1 or 0; let p and q be the probability of being 1 and being 0 for any observation, respectively (note $p + q = 1$, since the variable can only take either 1 or 0). We use the terms of "trials" to reflect the total number of observations denoted by n in the sample, "success" to define a trial that has a value of 1, and "failure" to reflect a trial that has a value of 0. The distribution of the count of successes, X, in the binomial setting is called the binomial distribution, $X \sim B(n, p)$.

Binomial distribution is one of the most commonly used distributions for discrete or count data. The mean of the number of successes (e.g., normal connections) in n trials for X is given by

$$\mu_x = np \tag{4-4}$$

and the variance, σ_X^2, and SD, σ_X, are

$$\sigma_X^2 = npq = np(1 - p), \text{ and}$$
$$\sigma_X = \sqrt{npq} = \sqrt{np(1 - p)}, \tag{4-5}$$

respectively.

Figure 4.5 Distributions of a risk score based on MIT-DARPA data

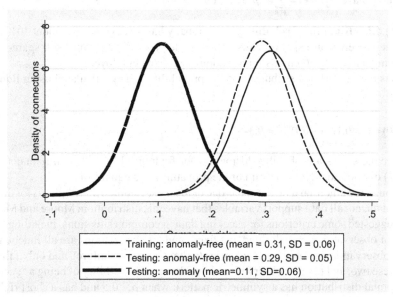

Training: anomaly-free (mean = 0.31, SD = 0.06)
Testing: anomaly-free (mean = 0.29, SD = 0.05)
Testing: anomaly (mean=0.11, SD=0.06)

Example 4.4→False Alarm Rate. Reducing both false positive and false negative rates has been an essential task in the intrusion detection field. Because of the large volume of data, a tiny misclassification rate can yield huge numbers of false alarms. Assuming a network system has a total network traffic volume of 4.78 million connections daily, what is the potential number of false alarms per hour with a misclassification rate of 0.4%?

Because the false alarm follows the distribution of $B(4.78 \times 10^6, 0.004)$, the mean of the number of false alarms can be calculated using Equation (4-4):

$$\mu_X = np = 4.78 \times 10^6 \times 0.004 = 1.91 \times 10^4.$$

As we can see, this number approximates 13.3 false alarms per minute or 795.8 false alarms per hour within a 24-hour window. Validating every such alarm for review is not practical. Thus, reducing both false positive and false negative rates is a constant challenge in network security, and in many situations a hybrid classification approach is required.

We can calculate a binomial probability as

$$f_X(k) = P_n(X = k) = C_k^n p^k q^{n-k}, \quad k = 0,1,\ldots,n, \qquad (4\text{-}6)$$

where $f_X(k) = P_n(X = k)$ is the probability of having exactly k successes (e.g., normal connections) in the n trials. The probability of getting at least m successes in n trials is given by

$$P = \sum_{k=m}^{n} P_n(k). \qquad (4\text{-}7)$$

Note that we have $\sum_{k=0}^{n} P_n(k) = \sum_{k=0}^{n} C_k^n p^k q^{n-k} = (p+q)^n = 1$.

Example 4.5→Binomial Probability. A company has discovered that about 10% of the emails they received are spam-emails. What is the probability of finding 0 spam-emails by randomly checking 10 emails for a randomly selected employee?

This is the *B(10, 0.1)* distribution, so the probability can be calculated using Equation (4-6)

$$p_{10}(X = 0) = C_0^{10}(0.1)^0(1-0.1)^{10-0} = 0.3487.$$

Figure 4.6 shows a probability histogram for finding 0,1,2,..., 10 spam-emails in the *B(10, 0.1)* distribution. Note the sum of the probabilities is equal to 1.

Although the binomial distribution is one of the most common distributions for discrete or count data, not all data support variables that have this distribution. Moore and McCabe (1998) suggested some criterions for checking data in common situations, including (1) the number of observations, *n*, is limited and fixed, and all observations are all independent; (2) each observation has only two categories (either success or failure), and only falls into one of these two, and (3) all *n* observations have the same probability of being a "success." The binomial distribution has a symmetric pattern when $\rho = 0.5$ and has a short right tail with a longer left tail when $\rho > 0.5$. By contrast, it has a longer right tail when $\rho < 0.5$. When *n* is large and ρ is either not too small or not too large, the binomial distribution can be approximated by a normal distribution. A workable rule of thumb is to assume that *n* is large if we have $np \geq 5$ and $n(1-p) \geq 5$.

The sample proportion of successes for a sample with a size of *n* is given by

$$\hat{\rho} = \frac{X}{n}, \tag{4-8}$$

and the mean and SD of $\hat{\rho}$ are

$$\mu_\rho = p \tag{4-9}$$

$$\sigma_\rho = \sqrt{\frac{pq}{n}}. \tag{4-10}$$

Be cautious not to mix the concepts in Equations (4-4) with (4-8). Equation (4-4) has a binomial distribution with a range of 0 to *n*, while equation (4-8) does not have a binomial distribution and always has a range of 0 to 1.

Poisson Distribution

Many variables that are counts of random events follow Poisson distributions, which is an approximation of a binomial distribution when the number of trials, *n*, is large and the probability of success, *p*, is small; specifically, when $n > 50$, $p < 0.05$, and $np < 5$. Let *k* be the number of successes occurring in a given time interval (i.e., $k = 0,1,2,...,K$), such as, and let λ be the average number of successes occurring in the given time interval or space.

The probability distribution of the Poisson random variable *k*, is given by

$$P(X = k) = \frac{e^{-\lambda}\lambda^k}{k!} \qquad (4\text{-}11)$$

where *e* is the base of the natural logarithm (*e* = 2.71828...) and $\lambda = np$ for the approximated binomial distribution when *n* is large and *p* is small.

The Poisson distribution has several important attributes in addition to serving as an approximation to the binomial distribution. These include (1) it has a single parameter λ its variance equals its mean: $\sigma^2 = \lambda$, so the SD equals the square root of the mean: $\sigma = \sqrt{\lambda}$, and (2) the number of successes occurring in one time interval or space are independent of those occurring in any other disjoint time interval or space. Walpole and Myers (1978) provided detailed discussions about the properties of the Poisson distribution for further reading. Figure 4.7 shows Poisson probability density functions with different values of λ, and the mean, and Display 4.1 illustrates the corresponding R codes to generate such distributions.

Display 4.1
Corresponding R codes for Figure 4.7

```
y<-0:50
fm5<-dpois(y,lambda=5)
fm10<-dpois(y,lambda=10)
fm20<-dpois(y,lambda=20)
fm30<-dpois(y,lambda=30)

plot(y,fm5,type="h",xlab="Variate value (k)",ylab="Probability mass function")
plot(y,fm10,type="h",xlab="Variate value (k)",ylab="Probability mass function")
plot(y,fm20,type="h",xlab="Variate value (k)",ylab="Probability mass function")
plot(y,fm30,type="h",xlab="Variate value (k)",ylab="Probability mass function")
```

Figure 4.6 Probability histogram for the B(10, 0.1) distribution

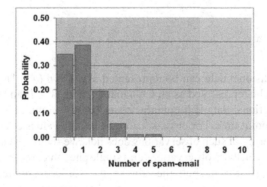

Figure 4.7 Poisson distribution function with different λ

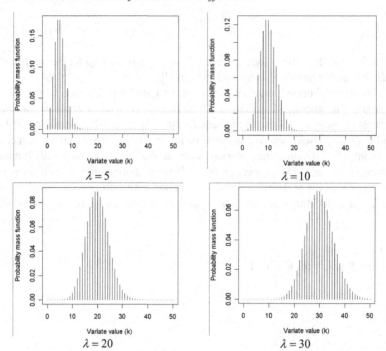

NETWORK DATA MODULES

Data are broadly classified according to their number of dimensions. Let us assume that we have k variables and n observations; we can then present the data shown in Figure 4.1 in a general format, as a two dimensional $k \times n$ matrix:

$$D_{k \times n} = \begin{matrix} x_{11} & x_{12} & \cdots & x_{1k} \\ x_{21} & x_{22} & \cdots & x_{2k} \\ \vdots & \vdots & \vdots & \vdots \\ x_{n1} & x_{n2} & \cdots & x_{nk} \end{matrix} \cdot$$

In general, one dimensional data can be represented as a $1 \times n$ $(n > 1)$ matrix, and two dimensional data can be represented as an $k \times n$ matrix, with $(k > 1)$ and $(n > 1)$. We refer a dataset as cross-sectional data if it contains observations on multiple phenomena and observed at a single-point time. For cross-sectional data, the values of observations have meaning, but the ordering of such observations does not. We refer a dataset as time series of longitudinal data if it includes observations on a single phenomenon observed over multi-time periods. For time series data, both the values and the ordering of the observations are meaninging. We refer a data as panel data if it has observations on multiple phenomena and observed over multi-time periods.

Figure 4.8 Data cube (variables, observations and occasions)

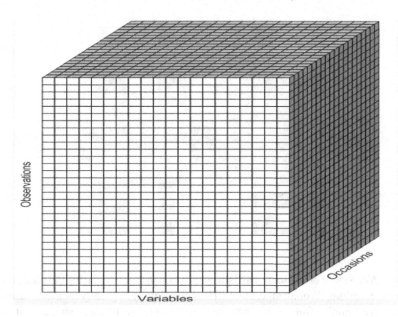

Expansion of the two dimensional $k \times n$ matrix can occur if data is collected over different time period where time is important for the analysis. We can have three dimensional data: an $k \times n \times t$ matrix, where the time dimension, t, is for all k and n. Any phenomenon can be described by data in three dimensions of which the first dimension defines the observations under study, the second dimension defines the variables to describe the various observations, and the third dimension shows the time-related occasions at which the phenomenon took place. Cattell (1952) used the term of "data cube" to illustrate such data dimensions in a simple and understandable mode (Figure 4.8).

As discussed in Chapter I, in network security, we face challenges in each of the three dimensions. The challenges in the dimension of observations include, for example, reducing the volume of observations and keeping observations independently. In the dimension of variables several challenges exist: detecting data structures, reducing the total number of variables, and identifying robust variables to classify and profile observations. For the dimension of occasions, handling longitudinal data, user change behavior over time, sequence of data, and time series data are all examples of typical challenges that need to be overcome. We will discuss these challenges in more detail in the following sections.

Cross-Sectional Data

Cross-sectional data is the data that is collected by analyzing observations at a given time or a fixed window period, assuming that the time window will have no impact on the collected observations. Such data is widely used in many social science research areas for conducting surveys and comparing quality of care in different hospitals, evaluating students'

Table 4.2 An example of cross-sectional data

Date	Time_b	Duration	Service	Port_d	Port_s	IP_s	IP_d	Date	Time_b	Duration	Service	Port_d	Port_s	IP_s	IP_d
7/17/1998	7:58:22	0:00:01		123	123		192.168.001.010	7/17/1998	7:58:22	0:00:01		123	123		192.168.001.010
7/17/1998	7:58:22	0:00:01		123	123		192.168.001.010	7/17/1998	7:58:22	0:00:01	ecol	123	123		192.168.001.010
7/17/1998	7:57:43	0:00:01	ecol			192.168.001.005	192.168.001.001	7/17/1998	7:57:43	0:00:01	ecol			192.168.001.005	192.168.001.001
7/17/1998	7:57:43	0:00:01	ecol			192.168.001.001	192.168.001.005	7/17/1998	7:57:43	0:00:01	ecol			192.168.001.001	192.168.001.005
7/17/1998	7:58:06	0:00:01	ecol			192.168.001.005	192.168.001.001	7/17/1998	7:58:06	0:00:01	ecol			192.168.001.005	192.160.001.001
7/17/1998	7:59:41	0:00:01		53	53		192.168.001.010	7/17/1998	7:59:41	0:00:01		53	53		192.168.001.010
7/17/1998	7:59:41	0:00:01		53	53		192.168.001.010	7/17/1998	7:59:41	0:00:01		53	53		192.168.001.010
7/17/1998	7:59:41	0:00:05	ntp	25	1024	172.016.113.105	194.007.251.021	7/17/1998	7:59:41	0:00:05	ntp	25	1024	172.016.113.105	194.007.251.021
7/17/1998	7:59:42	0:00:05	ntp	25	1026	172.016.112.194	194.007.251.021	7/17/1998	7:59:42	0:00:05	ntp	25	1026	172.016.112.194	194.007.251.021
7/17/1998	7:59:45	0:00:01	ntp	25	1025	172.016.113.105	135.008.060.182	7/17/1998	7:59:45	0:00:01	ntp	25	1025	172.016.113.105	135.008.060.182
7/17/1998	7:59:48	0:00:01	ntp	25	1027	172.016.112.194	135.073.161.060	7/17/1998	7:59:48	0:00:01	ntp	25	1027	172.016.112.194	135.073.161.060
7/17/1998	7:59:51	0:00:01	finger	79	1029	172.016.113.204	135.008.060.182	7/17/1998	7:59:51	0:00:01	finger	79	1029	172.016.113.204	135.008.060.182
7/17/1998	7:59:57	0:00:01	ntp	25	1028	172.016.112.194	197.182.091.233	7/17/1998	7:59:57	0:00:01	ntp	25	1028	172.016.112.194	197.182.091.233
7/17/1998	7:59:57	0:00:02	ntp	25	1048	172.016.112.194	198.087.075.158	7/17/1998	7:59:57	0:00:02	ntp	25	1048	172.016.112.194	198.087.075.158
7/17/1998	7:59:54	0:00:01	ntp	25	1051	172.016.112.194	135.008.060.182	7/17/1998	7:59:54	0:00:01	ntp	25	1051	172.016.112.194	135.008.060.182
7/17/1998	7:59:54	0:00:02	ntp	25	1052	172.016.113.204	135.008.060.182	7/17/1998	7:59:54	0:00:02	ntp	25	1052	172.016.113.204	135.008.060.182
7/17/1998	7:59:55	0:00:05	ntp	25	1104	172.016.112.207	195.073.161.060	7/17/1998	7:59:55	0:00:05	ntp	25	1104	172.016.112.207	195.073.161.060
7/17/1998	7:59:56	0:00:01		53	53		192.168.001.020	7/17/1998	7:59:56	0:00:01		53	53		192.168.001.020
7/17/1998	7:59:56	0:00:01		53	53		192.168.001.020	7/17/1998	7:59:56	0:00:01		53	53		192.168.001.020
7/17/1998	7:59:56	0:00:01		53	1080		172.016.112.020	7/17/1998	7:59:56	0:00:01		53	1080		172.016.112.020
7/17/1998	7:59:56	0:00:01		53	1080		172.016.112.020	7/17/1998	7:59:56	0:00:01		53	1080		172.016.112.020
7/17/1998	7:59:56	0:00:01		53	1146		172.016.112.020	7/17/1998	7:59:56	0:00:01		53	1146		172.016.112.020
7/17/1998	7:59:56	0:00:01		53	1146		172.016.112.020	7/17/1998	7:59:56	0:00:01		53	1146		172.016.112.020

performance. Analysis of cross-sectional data usually consists of comparing the differences among the observations (Wooldridge, 2002). Thus, this data type greatly facilitates a study of representative samples from whole populations (e.g., profile all user behavior within a given network system). Depending on the interest of an analysis, the observations in cross-sectional data can be data packets or connections made by a signal user or multiusers within a unique IP address or across various IP addresses. The given time or the fixed window period could be narrow or wide. For example, it could be from 8:00 a.m. to 9:00 a.m. in a single morning or from January 1st to January 30th for a given year.

The most important attribute of cross-sectional data is that each observation can be considered as conditionally independent. For cross-sectional data, the values of the data elements have meanings, but the ordering of the observations does not have any meaning. With modeling cross-sectional data, we can learn about the variation between observations and take into account the variance for classification.

Example 4.6→Cross-sectional Data. Table 4.2 shows a segment of cross-sectional data generated from the MIT-DARPA data. These observations are all normal connections made by eight individual sites (172.016.112.020, 192.168.001.005, 192.168.001.001, 172.016.113.105, 172.016.112.194, 172.016.113.204, 172.016.112.207, and 192.168.001.010). The data elements have the following order: session id (session), date (date), time (time_b), duration (duration), type of services (service), destination port (port_d), source port (port_s), source IP address (IP_s), destination IP address (IP_d) and an index field to indicate which sample group of the initial data were drawn from. As we can see although these are all normal connections, there are a few differences existing within a site and between sites. For example, the site, 172.016.112.020, had changed the service type from "ntp/u" to "domain/u," and between the sites 172.016.112.020 and 192.168.001.010, the source port was different. Thus, by having large real data and using appropriate modeling approach, we will be able to estimate site-specific patterns for each site we would like to profile.

Longitudinal Data

Longitudinal data provides a unique source to study user behavior changes over time. Such data represents a sequence of observations over a given period and follows the observations over the course of time. It provides hierarchical information about observations, for example, in life science, the weight changes of rats over time are longitudinal data that can be used to test whether these changes are treatment dependent. In epidemiology, longitudinal data is used to measure trends in treatments of a disease over time. Longitudinal data is sometime also used to describe repeated measurement data in healthcare or life science, in which multiple measurements of the response variable are obtained from each experimental unit (Davis, 2002). The most important attribute of longitudinal data is that the order of each observation provides additional information about a measurement (Diggle, Heagerty, Liang, & Zeger, 2002). Thus, the observations no longer need to be considered conditionally independent. For longitudinal data, the values of the data elements and the ordering of the observations both have meaning.

Longitudinal data is mainly used for three purposes in network security: (1) to predict future events based on known past events (e.g., to predict the next Web site to be visited based on a user's past and current visits), (2) to evaluate stability and reliability of observed patterns (e.g., user behavior, network system performance) and (3) to take into account the trend in pattern changes over time. We will discssus these purposes in greater detail in Chapter VIII.

Network traffic data has many attributes similar to longitudinal data, and can be converted to longitudinal data. Table 4.3 shows an example of a portion of longitudinal data drawn from the MIT-DARPA data for a particular site, 172.016.114.148, for a given time period (June 2, 1998 to July 17, 1998). The first column shows the date, the second shows

Table 4.3 Segment of longitudinal data set for site 172.016.114.148

Date	timeZone	Service	Port_d	Port_s	IP_s	IP_d
6/2/1998	3.656389	http	80	12815	172.016.114.148	167.008.029.015
6/2/1998	3.599722	http	80	12380	172.016.114.148	137.245.085.134
6/10/1998	17.24195	http	80	23252	172.016.114.148	205.181.112.065
6/10/1998	15.58056	http	80	24741	172.016.114.148	209.001.224.012
6/10/1998	16.62917	http	80	32350	172.016.114.148	207.068.137.064
6/11/1998	10.855	http	80	27970	172.016.114.148	209.121.083.008
6/11/1998	14.55722	http	80	16992	172.016.114.148	207.025.071.145
6/16/1998	17.69	ftp-data	30263	20	172.016.114.148	195.073.151.050
6/16/1998	11.03306	smtp	25	26673	172.016.114.148	197.218.177.069
6/16/1998	13.34056	ftp-data	4219	20	172.016.114.148	196.227.033.189
6/17/1998	12.36417	smtp	25	30518	172.016.114.148	194.007.248.153
6/18/1998	15.18444	ftp-data	8032	20	172.016.114.148	197.218.177.069
6/18/1998	10.67028	ftp-data	12664	20	172.016.114.148	194.027.251.021
6/18/1998	16.7425	smtp	25	10783	172.016.114.148	197.182.091.233
6/23/1998	15.92	ftp-data	15777	20	172.016.114.148	197.218.177.069
6/25/1998	21.22278	http	80	10830	172.016.114.148	207.087.027.037
6/26/1998	15.67972	ftp-data	9331	20	172.016.114.148	196.227.033.189
6/26/1998	13.95889	ftp-data	4175	20	172.016.114.148	196.227.033.189
6/26/1998	11.59389	ftp-data	30468	20	172.016.114.148	197.218.177.069
7/16/1998	10.095	http	80	13898	172.016.114.148	199.095.074.090
7/16/1998	9.953055	http	80	5692	172.016.114.148	199.095.074.090
7/16/1998	13.14194	ftp-data	8255	20	172.016.114.148	194.027.251.021
7/17/1998	14.16861	http	80	5435	172.016.114.148	199.095.074.090

the login time zone in a 24-hour format, and the other columns show service, destination port, source port, source IP address, and destination IP address, respectively. This data shows that there is a notable variance existing over the time period within sections (i.e., login time zone, ports, and services).

From modeling with longitudinal data we can learn about the variation within an observation across different occasions of an observation period. For example, we can simply test the null hypothesis that the means are equal for all occasions for a site, i, during occasions, 1,2,3,...,t:

$$H_0 : \mu_{i1} = \mu_{i2} = \mu_{i3} \cdots = \mu_{it} \tag{4-12}$$

$H_a : \mu_1$ has at least one occasion which is different and the between-occasion variance, $\sigma^2 > 0$ at an $\alpha = 0.05$ level of significance.

In longitudinal settings, each individual observation particularly has a vector Y of responses with a time ordering among the components. This attribute usually requires specific statistical attention, such as, employing the hieriarical and longitudinal modeling approach in data analysis (Verbeke & Molenberghs, 2000).

Panel Data

If the data include attributes of both cross-sectional and longitudinal, we refer to such data as panel data. Panel data provide information about observations on multiple phenomena observed over multiple time periods. A panel dataset may have data on n observations with k variables, over t time periods, in a $n \times k \times t$ space with a total of $n \times t$ rows. A simple example of panel data is the anomaly-free rates for each of 1000 randomly chosen workstations in a large worldwide company collected for each of 10 months in a given year. Such data can be represented as a set of double-indexed values, y_{ij} ($i = 1,2,\cdots,10$, $j = 1,2,\cdots,1000$). Generally, let D be a data space with X as a k dimensional vector ($k = 1,2,\cdots,K$), t occasions ($t = 1,2,\cdots,T$), and n observations ($n = 1,2,\cdots,N$). A general panel data regression model can be represented as

$$y_{it} = \mu_i + \sum_{k=1}^{K} \beta_{kt} x_{ikt} + u_t \tag{4-13}$$

$$\mu_i = \mu_0 + v_i \tag{4-14}$$

$$u_t = u_0 + \upsilon_t \tag{4-15}$$

where $v_i \sim N(0,\sigma_v^2)$, is at the individual observation level and $\upsilon_t \sim N(0,\sigma_\upsilon^2)$, is at the individual occasion level. They are independent from each other. Panel data is useful when we want to assess the improvement on security after a security-related intervention has been conducted. However, modeling panel data requires complx statistical modeling approaches that are beyond the scope of this book, but interested readers can find more information from Davies & Lahiri (2000), Cheng (2003), Frees (2004) and Shumway & Stoffer (2006).

SUMMARY

Variables and data are essential components in network security for developing robust intrusion detection and prevention systems. Variables should reflect the current understanding of the unique aspects of network infrastructures, user information, and the relationship between predictors and network security-related response variables. Clinical and experimental judgments and insights from the published literature should act as a guide for the selection of candidate predictive variables and the assessment of the model variables. Response variables should be meaningful and measured reliably. If a response variable cannot reasonably be considered important to network security or cannot be measured consistently, then it should not be used as a response variable. Any response variable should be measured similarly across sites and users. While advantages in network techniques, methods for data collection, and format of data could change over time, the basic concepts and attributes about variables and data discussed in this chapter will remain unchanged.

REFERENCES

Altman, D.G. and Bland, J. M. (1995). Statistics notes: The normal distribution. *BMJ, 310*, 298.

Cattell, R. B. (1952). *Factor analysis*. Harper, New York.

Chebrolu, S. Abraham, A., & Thomas, J. P. (2005). Feature deduction and ensemble design of intrusion detection systems. *Computer & Security, 24*(4), 295-307.

Cheng, H. (2003). *Analysis of panel data, 2ⁿᵈ Edition*. London: Cambridge University Press.

Cho, S. B. & Park, H. J. (2003). Efficient anomaly detection by modeling privilege flows using hidden Markov model. *Computer and Security, 22*(1), 45-55.

Claffy, K. C., Braun, H-W., and Polyzos, G. C. (1995). Parameterizable methodology for internet traffic flow profiling. *IEEE Journal on Selected Areas in Communications, 13*(8), 1481-1494.

Davis, C. S. (2002). *Statistical methods for the analysis of repeated measurements*. New York: Springer-Verlag.

Davies, A. and Lahiri, K. (2000). *Analysis of panels and limited dependent variable models*. London: Cambridge University Press.

Denning, D. (1987). An intrusion-detection model. *IEEE Transaction on Software Engineering, 13*(2), 222-232.

Diggle, P.J., Heagerty, P., Liang, KY, & Zeger, S.L. (2002). *Analysis of longitudinal data, 2ⁿᵈ Ed.* New York: Oxford University Press.

Frees, E. (2004). *Longitudinal and panel data*. London: Cambridge University Press.

Guyon, I. (2003). An introduction to variable and feature selection. *Journal of Machine Learning Research, 3*, 1157-1182.

Kayacik, G. H., Zincir-Heywood, A. N. (2005). Selecting features for intrusion detection: A feature relevance analysis on KDD 99 benchmark. In *Proceedings of the Third Annual Conference on Privacy, Security and Trust*.

Kim, E. & Kim, S. (2006). Anomaly detection in network security based on nonparametric techniques, (pp. 1-2). In *Proceedings of the 25th IEEE International Conference on Computer Communications (INFOCOM 2006).*

Lee, w. & Stolfo, S. J. (2000). A framework for constructing features and models for intrusion detection systems. *ACM Transactions on Information and System Security (TISSEC),* 3(4), 227-261.

Marchette, D. J. (2003). Statistical opportunities in network security, Vol. 35, (pp 28-38). In *Proceedings of the 35th Symposium on the Interface of Computing Science and Statistics, Computing Science and Statistics.*

Moore, D. S. & McCabe, G. P. (1998). *Introduction to the Practice of Statistics.* 3rd ed. New York: W. H. Freeman and Company.

Scott, S. L. (2004). A Bayesian paradigm for designing intrusion detection systems. *Computational Statistics & Data Analysis,* 45(1), 69-83.

Shumway, R. H. & Stoffer, D. S. (2006). *Time series analysis and its applications with R examples, 2nd Edition.* New York: Springer-Verlag.

Stallings, W. (2003). *Network security essentials, applications and standards, 2nd Ed.* New Jersey: Pearson Education.

Stirzaker, D. (1999). *Probability and random variables: A beginner's guide.* London: Cambridge University Press

U.S. Department of Justice Federal Bureau of Investigation (1990). *The science of fingerprints: Classification and uses.* U.S. Government Printing Office, Washington, D.C. 20402.

Verbeke, G. & Molenberghs, G. (2000). *Linear mixed models for longitudinal data.* New York: Springer-Verlag.

Wang Y., Seidman, L. (2006). Risk factors to retrieve anomaly intrusion information and profile user behavior. *International Journal of Business Data Communications and Networking,* 2(1), 41-57.

Walpole, R.H. & Myers, R.H. (1978). *Probability and statistics for engineers and scientists, 2nd Edition.* New York: Macmillan Publishing Co., Inc.

Wooldridge, J. M. (2002). *Econometric analysis of cross section and panel data.* London: Cambridge University Press.

Section II
Data Mining and Modeling

Chapter V
Exploring Network Data

You can't choose the ways in which you will be tested.

- Robert J. Sawyer

INTRODUCTION

In this chapter, we will review the basic concepts and procedures for data explanatory analysis, which provides the first step toward understanding and evaluating data. Data exploration is extremely important in network security because the volume of network traffic data is very large. We will discuss descriptive analysis, visualizing analysis and data transformation techniques in this chapter. The general idea behind explanatory analysis is to examine data without pre-conceived beliefs or notions and to let the data tell us about the phenomena of the subject(s) being studied. It not just focuses on displaying or extracting any "signal" from the data in the presence of noise, and discovers the type of information that the data holds (Everitt, 2005), but it also provides an essential direction for converting data from a high-dimensional space to a low-dimensional space. We may not know what the data looks like and we may not have specific questions in mind to analyze the data, but data exploration seeks patterns and variable relationships in the data, and provides paths for further data examinations. For example, outliers in traffic streams could represent important information about attacks (Petrovskiy, 2003; Angiulli & Fassetti, 2007; Kundur, Luh, Okorafor, & Zourntos, 2008; Nayyar & Ghorbani, 2008), but also could represent data errors. Data explanatory analysis provides a quickly and simply approach to discover such a paradox. Readers who like to obtain a comprehensive introduction to data exploration analysis should refer to Blaikie (2003).

Recently, with advances in computer hardware and software, visualizing large datasets has become possible, and more exploratory data analyses have been conducted based on the graphical method that visually conveys the information. Although the graphical method alone does not present rich convincing evidence for drawing robust conclusions, it does provide a road map for future analyses. It is also an important tool for illustrating data to those who have little to no statistical knowledge.

DESCRIPTIVE ANALYSIS

Descriptive analysis focuses on individual variables and presents its attributes by describing its frequency distribution, measuring its central tendency, spread, and range of values. We expect to gain a general overarching picture of the data from the descriptive analysis to support any further analysis. For example, by checking individual variables, we will know how well the sample data is, and whether or not we need to create new variables from the initial variables, check data reliability and validity (e.g., values outside oh the possible range), or to assess needs of any data transaction or normality. The main measurements for descriptive analysis are data structures, variables' mean, frequency, dispersion, and outliers, and we will discuss each of these individually in the following sections. Keep in mind that descriptive analysis alone is not robust enough to draw scientific conclusions because it does not have the capacity to handle a multivariate situation.

Data Contents

The first task to discover data is to understand the data structure by examining the variables, including total number of variables, names, labels, attributes, and any missing values. In a multi-dataset situation the relations among datasets, the primary keys, and the foreign keys are also necessary to determine. Both SAS and Stata provide procedures and commands to examine the data structure at the individual dataset level.

The *PROC CONTENTS* from SAS lists the data structure, including data size, variable names, labels, types (e.g., numeral or string), lengths, formats, positions, and the total number of variables and observations. The *PROC CONTENTS,* however, does not provide the data values that could be achieved by *PROC MEANS, PROC UNIVARIATE,* and *PROC FREQ,* which we will discuss later.

Example 5.1→Examine Data Structure. Let us use the following SAS codes given in Display 5.1 to examine the data structure of the 1999 KDD-cup training data.

Display 5.1
SAS codes to examine data structure of the 1999 KDD-cup training data

```
libname KDD 'F:\Book\Chapter 5\';
Proc contents data=KDD.KDD_trai position;
Run;
```

The SAS output is given in Display 5.2. As we can see, the 1999 KDD-cup training data includes a total of 494021 observations and 58 variables. The SAS output lists variables in both alphabetic and creation orders. Note the initial 1999 KDD-cup data includes 41 variable positions from #1 to #41, and one response variable, y (#42). Variables in positions from #43 to #58 are dummy variables derived from the initial variables.

Display 5.2
Output of the SAS Proc Contents procedure

```
                    The SAS System       12:18 Sunday, July 7, 2007   7

                              The CONTENTS Procedure

Data Set Name      KDD.KDD TRAI                    Observations         494021
Member Type        DATA                            Variables            58
Engine             V9                              Indexes              0

Created            Tuesday, January 28, 1997 02:00:00 AM  Observation Length   472
Last Modified      Tuesday, January 28, 1997 02:00:00 AM  Deleted Observations 0

Protection                                         Compressed           NO
Data Set Type                                      Sorted               NO
    Label
    Data Representation   WINDOWS_32
    Encoding              Default

                         Engine/Host Dependent Information

            Data Set Page Size           16384
            Number of Data Set Pages     14531
            First Data Page              1
            Max Obs per Page             34
            Obs in First Data Page       19
            Number of Data Set Repairs   0
            File Name                    D:\NOVA\KDD_BSP\kdd_trai.sas7bdat
            Release Created              7.00.00B
            Host Created                 WIN 95

                           The CONTENTS Procedure
                         Variables in Creation Order

        #    Variable    Type   Len    Format    Label

        1    duration    Num    8                duration
        2    protocol    Char   4                protocol_type
        3    service     Char   11               service
        4    flag        Char   6                flag
        5    src_byte    Num    8                src_bytes
        6    dst_byte    Num    8                dst_bytes
        7    land        Num    8                Land
        8    wrong_fr    Num    8                wrong_fragment
        9    urgent      Num    8                Urgent
       10    hot         Num    8                hot
       11    num_fail    Num    8                num_failed_logins
       12    logged_i    Num    8                logged_in
       13    num_comp    Num    8                num_compromised
       14    root_she    Num    8                root_shell
       15    su_attem    Num    8                su_attempted
       16    num_root    Num    8                num_root
```

```
17    num_file    Num     8              num_file_creations
18    num_shel    Num     8              num_shells
19    num_acce    Num     8              num_access_files
20    num_outb    Num     8              num_outbound_cmds
21    is_host_    Num     8              is_host_login
22    is_guest    Num     8              is_guest_login
23    count       Num     8              count
24    srv_coun    Num     8              srv_count
25    serror_r    Num     8              serror_rate
26    srv_serr    Num     8              srv_serror_rate
27    rerror_r    Num     8              rerror_rate
28    srv_rerr    Num     8              srv_rerror_rate
29    same_srv    Num     8              same_srv_rate
30    diff_srv    Num     8              diff_srv_rate
31    srv_diff    Num     8              srv_diff_host_rate
32    dst_host    Num     8              dst_host_count
33    dst_hos1    Num     8              dst_host_srv_count
34    dst_hos2    Num     8              dst_host_same_srv_rate
35    dst_hos3    Num     8              dst_host_diff_srv_rate
36    dst_hos4    Num     8              dst_host_same_src_port_rate
37    dst_hos5    Num     8              dst_host_srv_diff_host_rate
38    dst_hos6    Num     8              dst_host_serror_rate
39    dst_hos7    Num     8              dst_host_srv_serror_rate
40    dst_hos8    Num     8              dst_host_rerror_rate
41    dst_hos9    Num     8              dst_host_srv_rerror_rate
42    y           Char    16
43    REJ         Num     8
44    S0          Num     8
45    SF          Num     8
46    RST         Num     8
47    ICMP        Num     8
48    TCP         Num     8
49    UDP         Num     8
50    HTTP        Num     8
51    Hot_0       Num     8
52    DOS         Num     8
53    U2R         Num     8
54    R2L         Num     8
55    PROB        Num     8
56    NORMAL      Num     8
57    outcomes    Num     8     outcomes.
58    training    Num     8
```

Stata has a command called *codebook* to describe the contents of the data. Unlike the SAS *PROC CONTENTS*, the *codebook* command provides more detailed information on variable values. For variables that the *codebook* assumes to be categorical, it presents a range of values, frequency and any missing values. For variables that it deems continuous, it also presents the mean, standard deviation, and percentiles. When the *codebook* determines that neither a tabulation nor summary statistic is appropriate (e.g., string variables or numeric variables taking on many values, all of which are labeled), it presents a few examples of the data values (Stata 1997).

Example 5.2→Codebook. Let us use the Stata *codebook* command to examine the 1999 KDD-cup training data again. The codes and output are listed below in Displays 5.3 and 5.4, respectively. Note that in Display 5.3, the option *mv* specifies the codebook to report the pattern of missing values, and the option *tabulate(9)* specifics whether or not the number of unique values of a variable is greater than 9, which means that the variable is considered as a continuous variable.

Display 5.3
Stata codes to examine the 1999 KDD-cup training data

```
#delimit;
use kdd_tria,replace;
log using codelog,replace;
codebook, mv tabulate(9);
log close;
```

Display 5.4
Stata output of its codebook command
(Only shows two variables below. See Appendix for the full output)

```
. codebook, mv tabulate(9)

---------------------------------------------------------------------------
duration                                                           duration
---------------------------------------------------------------------------

                 type:  numeric (long)

                range:  [0,58329]                  units:  1
        unique values:  2495               missing .:  0/494021

                 mean:  47.9793
            std. dev:  707.746

          percentiles:        10%      25%      50%      75%      90%
                                 0        0        0        0        0

---------------------------------------------------------------------------
protocol                                                      protocol type
---------------------------------------------------------------------------

                 type:  string (str4)

        unique values:  3            missing "":  0/494021

           tabulation:  Freq.  Value
                        2.8e+05 "icmp"
                        1.9e+05 "tcp"
                          20354 "udp"

(output omitted see Appendix CH5 for a full list)
---------------------------------------------------------------------------
```

Mean and Frequency

The basic and most common statistics that are used to describe continuous data with normal distributions are the mean and its SD. For variables with a skewed distribution, we use the median with a pair of percentiles, such as the 10th and 90th, or the 25th and 75th, to describe them. The median is a useful summary statistic when some of the values are not actually measured—some values are outside of the measuring range(s) or are unknown (e.g., in time-to-event data, some of the failure times could be unknown). The common statistics used to describe a discrete variable are the frequency of its occurring values and the rate on each value. In general, regardless of how large a dataset is, we can describe and summarize it by a set of small statistics composed of means with corresponding SDs, a median with corresponding percentiles, and frequencies and rates.

As mentioned previously, a continuous variable can be categorized in statistical analyses. It can be grouped based on the quantile method that allows the same number of individuals in each group, or be categorized based on its clinical meaning. If we use the 00:00 as time zero and a minute as the unit, the range of login time is from 0 to 1440. We can code each time frame as its own categorical variable:

$$c = \begin{cases} middle-night & 0 \leq t < 180 \\ early-morning & 180 \leq t < 360 \\ morning & 360 \leq t < 480 \\ etc. \end{cases}$$

Categorizing discards information but may allow for simpler presentation, such as in a table. The fewer the number of groups created, the greater the loss of information will be.

Let $X = (x_1, x_2, \ldots, x_n)$ be a random variable from a random sample of size n. Then the sample mean, $\bar{x}$, variance, σ^2, and median, $\tilde{x}$, are defined as

$$\bar{x} = \frac{1}{n} \sum_{i=1}^{n} x_i, \tag{5-1}$$

$$\sigma^2 = \frac{\sum_{i=1}^{n} (x_i - \bar{x})^2}{n-1}, \tag{5-2}$$

$$\tilde{x} = \begin{cases} x_{(n+1)/2} & n = 1, 3, 5 \cdots \\ \dfrac{x_{n/2} + x_{(n/2)+1}}{2} & n = 2, 4, 6 \cdots \end{cases} \tag{5-3}$$

respectively. The SD, σ, is defined to be the positive square root of the variance.

Example 5.3→Calculate Mean, Median, and Frequency. Using the variables "ICMP" (Internet control message protocol) and "duration" (length of stay of a connection) from the KDD-cup 1999 training data, the following codes illustrate how to calculate the mean, median and frequency across different attack types by using the SAS procedures: *PROC MEANS, PROC UNIVARIATE,* and *PROC FREQ* (Display 5.5), and the Stata commands:

sum and *tab* (Display 5.6). Table 5.1 illustrates the results of the descriptive analysis performed to describe data characteristics by attack types based on the same data.

Display 5.5
SAS codes to calculate mean, median and frequency with 1999 KDD-cup training data

```
libname KDD "F:\Book\Chapter 5\";
data KDD_data;
set KDD.kdd_trai;
/*------------------------------------------------
 Create a categorical variable for holding attack's type
-----------------------------------------------------*/;
if normal=1 then Attack_type='Normal';
if DOS=1 then Attack_type='DoS';
if U2R=1 then Attack_type='U2R';
if R2L=1 then Attack_type='R2L';
if Prob=1 then Attack_type='Prob';

if normal=1 then Response=0;
if Prob=1 then Response=1;
if DOS=1 then Response=2;
if U2R=1 then Response=3;
if R2L=1 then Response=4;
/*------------------------------------------------
 Frequency of ICMP by attack's type
-----------------------------------------------------*/;
title Frequency of ICMP by attack type;
proc freq data=KDD_data;
table Attack_type*ICMP;
run;
/*------------------------------------------------
 Means connection's time by attack's type
-----------------------------------------------------*/;
title Length of connections by attack type;
proc means data=KDD_data;
class attack_type;
var duration;
run;
/*------------------------------------------------
 Examining the distribution of connection's time by attack's type
-----------------------------------------------------*/;
title Distribution of length of connections by attack type;
proc univariate data=KDD_data;
class attack_type;
var duration;
run;
```

Table 5.1. Characteristics of connections by attack types based on the KDD-cup training data

Variables	Normal (N = 97,278)		Probe (N = 4,107)		DoS (N = 391,458)		U2R (N = 52)		R2L (N = 1,126)	
	%*	#*	%	#	%	#	%	#	%	#
Basic features of connections										
Length (number of seconds) of the connection (mean, SD)	216.66	1359.21	485.03	3758.15	0.00	0.08	80.94	120.51	559.75	2108.34
Type of protocol										
ICMP (yes/no)	1.3%	1,288	30.7%	1,260	71.8%	281,054	0.0%	0	0.0%	0
TCP (yes/no)	79.0%	76,813	64.6%	2,652	28.0%	109,425	94.2%	49	100.0%	1,126
UDP (yes/no)	19.7%	19,177	4.7%	195	0.3%	979	5.8%	3	0.0%	0
Network service on the destination										
HTTP (yes/no)	63.6%	61,886	0.2%	8	0.6%	2,395	0.0%	0	0.4%	4
Number of data bytes from source to destination (per 1,000) (mean, SD)	1.16	34.23	168.83	10800.00	0.98	4.03	0.91	1.19	271.97	1146.29
Number of data bytes from destination to source (per 1,000) (mean, SD)	3.38	37.58	0.00	0.01	0.05	0.62	5.14	10.08	72.30	592.65
Normal or error status of the connection										
REJ (yes/no)	5.5%	5,341	37.3%	1,532	5.1%	20,002	0.0%	0	0.0%	0
S0 (yes/no)	0.1%	51	4.6%	190	22.2%	86,765	0.0%	0	0.1%	1
SF (yes/no)	94.3%	91,709	36.0%	1,477	72.6%	284,138	98.1%	51	94.6%	1,065
RSTO or RSTOS0 or RSTR (yes/no)	0.1%	98	19.4%	797	0.1%	546	1.9%	1	4.5%	51
Connection from/to the same host/port (yes/no)	0.0%	1	0.0%	0	0.0%	21	0.0%	0	0.0%	0
Number of WRONG fragments (mean, SD)	0.00	0.00	0.00	0.00	0.01	0.15	0.00	0.00	0.00	0.00
Number of urgent packets (mean, SD)	0.00	0.01	0.00	0.00	0.00	0.00	0.02	0.14	0.00	0.07
Content features within a connection suggested by domain knowledge										
Number of HOT indicators (mean, SD)	0.04	0.86	0.00	0.03	0.01	0.15	1.40	1.54	7.39	11.95
Number of failed login attempts (mean, SD)	0.00	0.02	0.00	0.00	0.00	0.00	0.02	0.14	0.05	0.26
Log in successfully (yes/no)	71.9%	69,939	0.2%	10	0.6%	2,203	88.5%	46	92.3%	1,039
Number of COMPROMISED conditions (mean, SD)	0.03	4.05	0.00	0.00	0.01	0.07	1.21	1.67	0.07	1.39
Root shell is obtained (mean, SD)	0.00	0.02	0.00	0.00	0.00	0.00	0.50	0.44	0.01	0.07
SU ROOT command attempted (yes/no)	0.0%	17	0.0%	0	0.0%	0	0.0%	0	0.1%	1
Number of ROOT accesses (mean, SD)	0.06	4.53	0.00	0.00	0.00	0.00	0.79	2.30	0.10	2.04
Number of file creation operations (mean, SD)	0.00	0.20	0.00	0.00	0.00	0.00	0.79	1.21	0.03	0.65
Number of shell prompts (mean, SD)	0.00	0.02	0.00	0.00	0.00	0.00	0.13	0.44	0.00	0.07
Number of operations on access control files (mean, SD)	0.01	0.08	0.00	0.00	0.00	0.00	0.02	0.14	0.01	0.10
Number of outbound commands in an FTP session (mean, SD)	0.00	0	0.00	0.00	0.00	0	0.00	0.00	0.00	0.00
HOT login (yes/no)	0.0%		0.0%		0.0%		0.0%		0.0%	0

continued on following page

Table 5.1. continued

Variables	Normal (N = 97,278)		Probe (N = 4,107)		DoS (N = 391,458)		U2R (N = 52)		R2L (N = 1,126)	
GUEST login (yes/no)	0.4%	371	0.0%	0	0.0%	0	0.0%	0	27.9%	314
Traffic features computed using a two-second time window										
Number of connections to the same host as the current connection in the past two seconds (mean, SD)	8.2	17.7	171.9	233.5	415.5	151.8	5.8	23.5	1.3	0.5
Percentage of connections that have SYN errors (mean, SD)	0.0	0.0	0.1	0.2	0.2	0.4	0.0	0.2	0.0	0.1
Percentage of connections that have REJ errors (mean, SD)	0.1	0.2	0.6	0.5	0.1	0.2	0.0	0.1	0.0	0.2
Percentage of connections to the same service (mean, SD) 1	.0	0.1	0.6	0.5	0.7	0.4	0.9	0.2	1.0	0.0
Percentage of connections to different services (mean, SD) 0	.0	0.1	0.4	0.5	0.0	0.0	0.1	0.2	0.0	0.1
Number of connections to the same service as the current connection in the past two seconds (mean, SD)	10.9	21.8	7.5	14.4	366.8	223.9	1.3	0.6	2.3	12.0
Percentage of connections that have SYN errors (mean, SD) 0	.0	0.0	0.1	0.3	0.2	0.4	0.0	0.0	0.0	0.1
Percentage of connections that have REJ errors (mean, SD) 0	.1	0.2	0.6	0.5	0.1	0.2	0.1	0.1	0.0	0.2
Percentage of connections to different hosts (mean, SD)	0.1	0.3	0.2	0.4	0.0	0.0	0.0	0.0	0.0	0.1
Destination										
Number of connections having the same destination host (mean, SD)	148.5	103.4	169.0	117.8	254.5	10.2	47.8	96.2	80.4	109.3
Number of connections having the same destination host and using the same service (mean, SD)	202.1	86.9	53.1	92.7	187.2	109.1	9.9	21.9	39.0	35.0
Percentage of connections having the same destination host and using the same service (mean, SD)	0.8	0.3	0.3	0.5	0.7	0.4	0.8	0.4	0.8	0.4
Percentage of different services on the current host (mean, SD)	0.1	0.2	0.6	0.6	0.0	0.0	0.0	0.1	0.0	0.1
Percentage of connections to the current host having the same source port (mean, SD)	0.1	0.3	0.6	0.6	0.7	0.4	0.6	0.4	0.6	0.5
Percentage of connections to the same service coming from different hosts (mean, SD)	0.0	0.0	0.2	0.3	0.0	0.0	0.1	0.2	0.1	0.1
Percentage of connections to the current host that have an S0 error (mean, SD)	0.0	0.0	0.1	0.2	0.2	0.4	0.0	0.0	0.0	0.1
Percentage of connections to the current host and specified service that have an S0 error (mean, SD)	0.0	0.0	0.1	0.3	0.2	0.4	0.0	0.0	0.0	0.1
Percentage of connections to the current host that have an RST error (mean, SD)	0.1	0.2	0.5	0.4	0.1	0.2	0.0	0.1	0.0	0.2
Percentage of connections to the current host and specified service that have an RST error (mean, SD)	0.1	0.2	0.6	0.5	0.1	0.2	0.0	0.1	0.0	0.2

SD denotes standard deviation

* Mean and SD for continuous variables

Figure 5.1 Theoretical distributions of composite behavior score for two groups with the same means

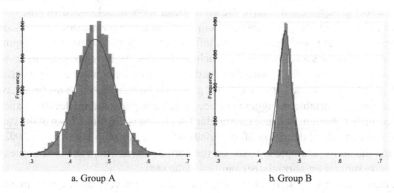

a. Group A   b. Group B

Display 5.6
Stata codes to calculate mean, median and frequency with 1999 KDD-cup data

```
#delimit;
clear;
set mem 454556;
use F:\Book\Chapter 5\kdd_trai,replace;
/*---------------------------------------------------------
 Create a categorical variable for holding attack's type
--------------------------------------------------------*/;
gen str6 Attack_type="Normal" if NORMAL==1;
replace Attack_type="DoS" if DOS==1;
replace Attack_type="U2R" if U2R==1;
replace Attack_type="R2L" if R2L==1;
replace Attack_type="Prob" if PROB==1;
/*---------------------------------------------------------
 Frequency of ICMP by attack's type
--------------------------------------------------------*/;
tab Attack_type ICMP,col row ;
/*---------------------------------------------------------
 Means connection's time by attack's type
--------------------------------------------------------*/;
tab Attack_type,sum(duration);
/*---------------------------------------------------------
 Examining the distribution of connection's time by attack's type
--------------------------------------------------------*/;
sort Attack_type;
by Attack_type: sum duration,d;
```

Dispersion and Outliers

Descriptive analysis describes the probability distribution of the population. Although various measurements can be calculated to describe the population, two measures: (1) central tendency, and (2) dispersion are the most often used measures. Central tendency describes the center of the distribution and the most used measures are mean and median. Dispersion describes the variation of the data, including variance, standard error, and standard deviation.

Let us consider two theoretical distributions of user behavior score for groups A and B, in which a network connection with a high score is more likely to be anomaly-free. Let us assume that groups A and B have the same mean score of 0.47 but different variances (Figure 5.1). As we can see, even though both distributions have the same mean score, the score inequality is greater in group A (the left half of the figure). If we only computed the mean of each of these scores, we might conclude that the two have the same behavior patterns. However Group A has a more dispersed distribution than group B. The variance for group A is $\sigma^2 \approx 0.02$ verses $\sigma^2 \approx 0.002$ for group B. The variance is a useful measure of the dispersion of a variable. A bigger variance means a larger standard deviation and wider dispersion in distribution. Because the standard deviation is the square root of the variance, group A has a standard deviation of $\sigma = \sqrt{0.02} \approx 0.14$ and group B has $\sigma = \sqrt{0.002} \approx 0.04$. Although the above example is based on the normal distribution, the idea of measuring dispersion in other than normal distributions is the same.

The mean can be very sensitive to observations that are very different from all of the other observations in the distribution. We refer to these very different observations as "outliers". Generally, we can label an observation as an outlier when the following conditions are satisfied:

$$x_i < x_{25th} - 1.5 \times (x_{75th} - x_{25th}), \text{ or} \tag{5-4}$$

$$x_i > x_{75th} + 1.5 \times (x_{75th} - x_{25th}), \tag{5-5}$$

where x_i is the value of the observation, and x_{25th} and x_{75th} are the 25th and 75th percentiles of the X in the sample, respectively (we will discuss the detailed concept of percentile in Chapter XI). As we mentioned early, outliers could represent attacks or data issues. If the latter is true, we can use several approaches to deal with outliers, including replacing them with the sample mean, re-estimating their values, or excluding them from the sample. Another approach to overcome outliers is to use measures that are not sensitive to outliers (e.g., use the median instead of the mean). Sometimes it will be obvious when an outlier is simply miscoded data and should be replaced by a correct value. For example, if a connection time is 100 hours, we know that it is an error on this value. Reviewing all of these approaches is beyond the scope of this book, but we want to be alert to the presence of outliers and to be aware of how they can influence our results.

VISUALIZING ANALYSIS

The needs of representing information from very large data have rapidly increased with fast computing systems that have become available, and network and database systems that have become larger. When data becomes very large with high-dimensional structure, the conventional descriptive analysis method may not be powerful enough to fully represent the data and therefore, graphically displaying data or visualizing the analysis has become a common approach for data explanation. Today, data visualization has become a very hot topic in analyzing large data. It is also useful in network security because it makes traffic patterns easy to detect and can convey a large amount of information concisely and quickly. In this section, we will briefly review some basic techniques for graphically displaying and visually analyzing data. Readers can find more detailed information about this topic from William (1997), Friendly (2000), Oehlschlaegel-Akiyoshi (2006), Unwin, Theus, & Hofmann (2006), Young, Valero-Mora & Friendly (2006), and Neuhaus & Bunke (2007).

Fitting and Graphing Discrete and Continuous Variables

As mentioned earlier, a continuous variable can be any value on the scale, including decimal points, while a discrete variable often involves counts of occurrences. For example, the occurrences of a typical symbol in an email and the total words in that email are two discrete variables. But the ratio of these two variables (defined as occurrences divided by the total number of words in the email), which is the rate of the symbol occurrences, is a continuous variable. Nevertheless, when the number of individual values for a discrete variable is large (e.g., greater than 20), it can be treated just as a continuous variable in a graphical model. In the following sections, the term "continuous" may also imply such a discrete variable.

We can assess information about a continuous variable with three fundamental characteristics: (1) the type of its distribution, (2) the range of its value, and (3) the location of its center. These questions represent the most important attributes for a majority of continuous variables that we will work with in the network security area. Although we can attain answers from the descriptive analysis methods discussed earlier, fitting the data through a graphical model provides more information about the variable and directs a way to visually understand the variable.

Let $X = (x_1, x_2, \cdots, x_n)$ be a random variable in D, where x_i can take any numerical value. The distribution of X can be found by obtaining the frequency tabulation of its values. We can then fit the frequency tabulation data into a histogram model, which is a typical type of bar chart that displays the information in relative frequency tabulation. The frequency information can be displayed based on individual values, or by grouping close values together. The role of the number to choose is a grouping number, g, which can be calculated by the following:

$$g = \min(\sqrt{N}, 10 \times \frac{\ln(N)}{\ln(10)}), \qquad (5\text{-}6)$$

where N is the total number of observations with no missing values in the data (Stata, 2003).

Example 5.4→Histogram. SAS, Stata and R all provide procedures and commands for fitting data into histogram models. Let us use the spam-email data to display the variable v19 (the frequency of the word "YOU" in an email). The SAS, Stata, and R codes to complete this task are shown in Displays 5.7, 5.8 and 5.9, respectively.

Display 5.7
SAS codes to create histogram image for variable v19 in the spam data

```
/*----------------------------------------------------------------
codes to fit a histogram model for variable v19
----------------------------------------------------------------*/;
libname spam "F:\Book\Chapter 5\";

title Histogram of variable v19;
proc univariate data=spam.spam noprint;
histogram v19;
run;
```

Display 5.8
Stata codes to create histogram image for variable v19 in the spam data

```
/*----------------------------------------------------------------
    Stata codes to fit a histogram model for variable v19
----------------------------------------------------------------*/;
#delimit;
use spam,replace;
histogram v19 , freq bin(400);  /*  bin(400) denotes g=400*/
histogram v19 if v19>0, freq bin(400);   /*   excluded v19=0  */
```

Display 5.9
R codes to create histogram image for variable v19 in the spam data

```
/*----------------------------------------------------------------  R
codes to fit a histogram model for variable v19
----------------------------------------------------------------*/;
require(gplots)
spam<-read.table("F:\\Book\\Chapter 5\\spam_r.txt",header = TRUE,sep=",")
x<-spam$v19
hist(x,col="blue",xlim=c(0,20),main="Histogram of v19 from the spam-email
data",xlab="v19")
```

Figure 5.2 shows the actual histogram of the variable v19. For the left panel of this figure, we can see that the range of v19 is from 0 to approximately 20 (the actual maximum value is 18.8), and the frequency of which v19 takes a zero value is much higher than the frequency of which it takes on other values. Knowing this, if we refit the data by excluding observations with zero values, we can have a good, approximate normal distribution for v19 as shown in the right panel of Figure 5.2.

The histogram model provides the most useful information for a single continuous variable on its distribution, its frequency of values, its range of values, and the location of its center. For instance, it seems the mean of Figure 5.2b is around 2.5 while the actual value is 2.4.

We are also interested to know the outliers and to determine the range in which the majority of the observations are filled. The box-plot graphic model provides such information. Figure 5.3 shows the plots fitted by variable v19 of the spam-email data. The outliers are represented by dots in the figures; the center line of the box is the median, and the

Figure 5.2 Histograms of variable 19

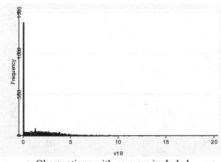

a. Observations with zero are included   b. Observations with zero are excluded

Figure 5.3 Outliers and ranges

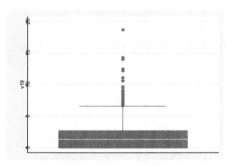

a. Observations with zero are included   b. Observations with zero are excluded

upper and lower hinges of the box are the 75th and 25th percentiles, respectively. Also, the upper and lower adjacent lines are the upper and lower adjacent values. All points further away from the adjacent values are marked as outliers by a single dot. It is clear that in both histograms and box-plot models, we can get enough information on an individual continuous variable.

By understanding the attributes of each individual variable, we may also be interested in seeking an association (or pattern) between two random variables. This task can be achieved by fitting the data into a scatter-plot model that constructs a two-dimensional space to display the association between two variables with one being the y-axis and another being at the x-axis. Figure 5.4 shows an example of a scatter-plot for variables v19 and v18 (frequency of the word of "EMAIL"). Both left and right panels of the figures suggest that there is a linear relationship between v19 and v18, but the pattern is clearer in the right panel since it excludes observations with zero values for both variables. The Stata and R codes used to generate Figure 5.4 are given in Displays 5.10 and 5.11, correspondingly.

Figure 5. 4 Scatter-plot to illustrate association between variables

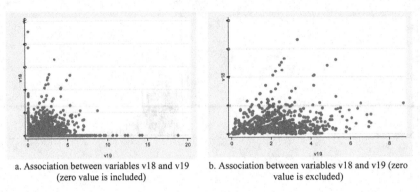

a. Association between variables v18 and v19
(zero value is included)

b. Association between variables v18 and v19 (zero
value is excluded)

Display 5.10
Stata codes to generate scatter-plots for illustrating association between variables

```
/*------------------------------------------------------------
  Stata codes for scatter-plots shown in Figure 5.4
------------------------------------------------------------*/;
#delimit;
use F:\Book\Chapter5\spam.dta,replace;
scatter v18 v19;
scatter v18 v19 if v18>0 & v19>0;
```

Display 5.11
R codes to generate scatter-plots for illustrating association between variables

```
#------------------------------------------------------------
#   R codes for scatter-plots shown in Figure 5.4
#------------------------------------------------------------
require(gplots)
spam<-read.table("F:\\Book\\Chapter 5\\spam_r.txt",header = TRUE,sep=",")
# example data, bivariate normal, no correlation
x<-spam$v19
y<-spam$v18
# Exclude observations with v18=0 or v19=0
x[x==0]<-NA
y[y==0]<-NA
# plot a 2-dimensional histogram
hist2d(x,y, same.scale=TRUE,nbins=100,col =c("white",heat.colors(16)))
box()
```

Moreover, if we want to know the association in a group of continuous variables (as opposed to only two variables), we can do so by fitting the data to a matrix-plot model in which each cell of the matrix shows an association of two variables. The matrix-plot is similar to a correlation matrix that shows the relationships among variables numerically, but it also shows such relationships graphically. Using the Stata or R codes listed in Displays 5.12 and 5.13 below, Figure 5.5 shows a matrix-plot for the first 10 variables of the spam-email data. Display 5.14 shows its corresponding correlation coefficient matrix. We will discuss the correlation coefficient in more detail in Chapter VI.

Display 5.12
Stata codes to generate matrix-plot for the first 10 variables of the spam-email data

```
#delimit;
use F:\Book\Chapter 5\spam,replace;
graph matrix v1-v10;
```

Display 5.13
R codes to generate matrix-plot for the first 10 variables of the spam-email data

```
require(graphics)
# Read Ascii data to the data object spam
spam<-read.table("F:\\Book\\Chapter 5\\spam_r.txt",header=TRUE,sep = ",")
pairs(spam[1:10])
```

Display 5.14
Correlation coefficient matrix corresponding to the matrix-plot shown in Figure 5.5

```
. corr v1-v10
(obs=4601)

     |     v1       v2       v3       v4       v5       v6       v7       v8       v9      v10
-----+----------------------------------------------------------------------------------------
  v1 |  1.0000
  v2 | -0.0168   1.0000
  v3 |  0.0656  -0.0335   1.0000
  v4 |  0.0133  -0.0069  -0.0202   1.0000
  v5 |  0.0231  -0.0238   0.0777   0.0032   1.0000
  v6 |  0.0597  -0.0248   0.0876  -0.0100   0.0541   1.0000
  v7 |  0.0077   0.0039   0.0367   0.0198   0.1473   0.0612   1.0000
  v8 | -0.0039  -0.0163   0.0120   0.0103   0.0296   0.0796   0.0445   1.0000
  v9 |  0.1063  -0.0038   0.0938  -0.0025   0.0208   0.1174   0.0508   0.1053   1.0000
 v10 |  0.0412   0.0330   0.0321  -0.0049   0.0345   0.0139   0.0568   0.0831   0.1306   1.0000
```

Fitting and Graphing Categorical Variables

The most common method to display categorical and binary variables is to fit them into a bar-plot model that provides information on the frequency of each categorical level. The left panel of Figure 5.6 shows a bar-plot of the variable of the type of attacks from the KDD-cup 1999 training data. The x-axis denotes the total number of connections by each attack, and the y-axis denotes the type of attacks.

In many situations, we may be interested in looking at the distributions of a subgroup of a categorical variable. For example, we may want to see the average connection time by different types of attacks and by different types of protocols. Here we have three variables,

Figure 5.5 Matrix-plot for the first 10 variables of the spam-email data

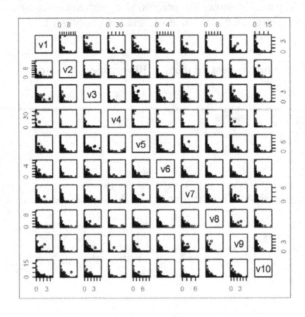

Figure 5.6 Graphically displayed categorical variables

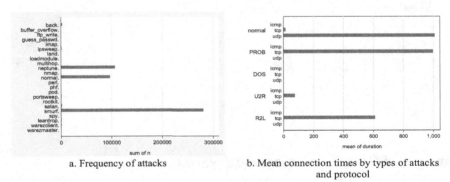

a. Frequency of attacks   b. Mean connection times by types of attacks and protocol

a continuous variable that represents the connection time, and two categorical variables that represent the attacks and the protocols. We can still fit such data with a bar-plot as shown in the right side of Figure 5.6. The Stata codes used to generate these figures are given in Display 5.15.

Display 5.15
Stata codes corresponding to Figure 5.6

```
#delimit;
use F:\book\Chapter 5\KDD_TRAI, clear;
gen byte n=1;
graph hbar (sum) n ,over(attacks);
graph hbar  (mean) duration  ,over(protocol) over(outcome);
```

In other situations, we may display categorical variables with mosaic plots, which were originally developed by Hartigan and Kleiner in the early 1980s (Hartigan and Kleiner, 1981; Hartigan and Kleiner, 1984). A mosaic plot represents a contingency table in which each cell corresponds to a portion of the plot, and the size is proportional to the cell entry. The goal of such a plot is to graphically illustrate the frequency counts of single or cross-classified variables. We use a mosaic plot to determine the overall structure between variables and to identify combinations of the variables that do not follow the overall structure. In general, mosaic plots are good to visualize the pattern of associations among variables in 2-way and larger tables. Because mosaic plots display the frequencies graphically, they are easier to understand than traditional cross-tabulations.

R has a great graphical package, *iPlots*, for fitting data to mosaic plots. *iPlots*, written in Java, provides high-interaction statistical graphics and offers a wide variety of plots, including histograms, bar charts, scatter-plots, box-plots, fluctuation diagrams, parallel coordinate plots, and spine-plots. To use *iPlots*, we have to install the Java Development Kit (JDK) version 1.4 or higher in the workstation running R. JDK can be downloaded from the Sun Microsystems Web site http://java.sun.com/j2se/1.4.2/download.html. In addition, the packages, *rJava* and *JGR*, also need to run the *iPlots* package. The R codes given in Display 5.16 illustrate how to create a mosaic plot with the KDD-cup data, and the corresponding frequency counts are also described in Display 5.17.

Display 5.16
R codes to create mosaic plots

```
library(MASS)
library(foreign)
require(JavaGD)
require(rJava)
require(JGR)
require(iplots)
library(iplots)
KDD <- read.dta("F:\\Book\\Chapter 5\\kdd_train_r.dta")
data(KDD)
attach(KDD)
iset.col(Species)
imosaic(data.frame(flag, Attack))
imosaic(data.frame(flag, Attack,protocol))
```

)

Figure 5.7 Example of mosaic plots based on KDD-cup data

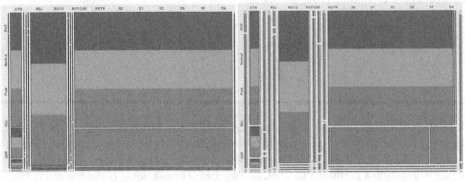

| a. Attacks vs. flag | b. Attacks, flag, and protocol |

Display 5.17
The frequency table corresponded to Figure 5.7

```
. tab  flag Attack
              |                         Attack
      flag |      DoS     Normal       Prob        R2L        U2R |     Total
-----------+---------------------------------------------------------+----------
       OTH |        0          1          7          0          0 |         8
       REJ |   20,002      5,341      1,532          0          0 |    26,875
      RSTO |      455         67         10         46          1 |       579
    RSTOS0 |        0          0         11          0          0 |        11
      RSTR |       91         31        776          5          0 |       903
        S0 |   86,765         51        190          1          0 |    87,007
        S1 |        2         54          0          1          0 |        57
        S2 |        5         17          1          1          0 |        24
        S3 |        0          7          0          3          0 |        10
        SF |  284,138     91,709      1,477      1,065         51 |   378,440
        SH |        0          0        103          4          0 |       107
-----------+---------------------------------------------------------+----------
     Total |  391,458     97,278      4,107      1,126         52 |   494,021
```

Fitting and Graphing Sequence Data

As discussed in Chapter III, Web sequence data provides unique information about network traffic as well as about user behavior. It could be a specific case of the longitudinal data, in which the measures on each stage are different. For example, we may measure the total number of connections created by each user or group over a period of one month, but use the day as a unit of measure. Thus, at the end of monitoring period, we have longitudinal data that includes a variable that denotes the daily volume of connections for each user. This variable is repeated 30 times (assuming the month has 30 days) for each user. In this dataset the measurement unit is the day, and the number of days is fixed for each user (i.e., all users are measured for a 30-day period. The volume measurement does not change, but its value changes daily, and the variable used to carry such information is continuous as shown below:

Measure unit (day)	Measurement (volume)
1	23000
2	13570
⋮	⋮
30	24312

Sequence data varies slightly from the above situation. Using Web visit data as an example, the measure unit is the sequence of visits, and the number of visits is not fixed for each user (i.e., some users may have a few visits and some users may have many visits). The measurement is taken of the Web site to be visited, and the value is the actually visited Webpage's attribute (e.g., Webpage A, C, A). A categorical variable can be used to carry such information as shown below:

Measure unit (visit)	Measurement (Webpage)
1	A
2	B
⋮	⋮
N	H

Let us illustrate how we can describe the sequence data graphically. The training dataset of the www.Microsoft.com Web visit sequence data includes 32711 individual users with a mean of 3.04 visits, a maximum to minimum range from 1 to 35, and the 25th and 75th percentiles from 1 to 4 (see the Stata outputs in Displays 5.18 and 5.19). Figure 5.8 shows the histograms of frequency of visits per user (left side) and the frequency of Web pages visited (right side). We can see that there are Web pages that have been visited more than 10000 times.

Display 5.18
Distribution of visits per user from Stata

```
                         cnt
-----------------------------------------------------------
        Percentiles      Smallest
 1%          1              1
 5%          1              1
10%          1              1          Obs              98654
25%          1              1          Sum of Wgt.      98654

50%          2                         Mean            3.041164
                         Largest       Std. Dev.        2.63083
75%          4             32
90%          6             33          Variance        6.921268
95%          8             34          Skewness        2.508593
99%         13             35          Kurtosis        13.36787
```

Figure 5.8 Frequencies of visits by users and Web pages visited

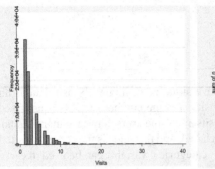

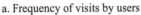

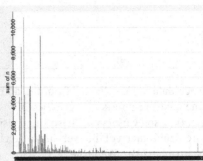

| a. Frequency of visits by users | b. Frequency of webpages visited (x-axis: webpage, y-axis: frequency) |

Display 5.19
Distribution of number of Web sites visited from Stata

```
                          (sum) n
-----------------------------------------------------------------
        Percentiles     Smallest
  1%         1              1
  5%         1              1
 10%         2              1      Obs                    285
 25%        10              1      Sum of Wgt.            285

 50%        46                     Mean              346.1544
                       Largest     Std. Dev.         1171.189
 75%       187           5330
 90%       636           8463      Variance           1371684
 95%      1160           9383      Skewness          6.274267
 99%      8463          10836      Kurtosis          46.96495
```

DATA TRANSFORMATION

Many statistical models and tests require data to meet the assumption of normality, which often leads to tests that are simple, mathematically tractable, and powerful compared to tests that do not make the normality assumption. Unfortunately, real data are usually not approximately normal. An appropriate transformation of data can often yield the data to be approximately followed by a normal distribution. This increases the applicability and usefulness of statistical techniques based on the normality assumption. In general, we can acquire three benefits form data transformations: (1) centering data, (2) standardizing data, and (3) normalizing data.

Assessing for Normality

Assessing for normality is the first step to determine if a data transformation is necessary. To assess normality assumptions, we measure the skewness and kurtosis values for a sample. Skewness, v, and kurtosis, υ, are defined below:

$$v = \frac{\sum_{i=1}^{n}(x_i - \overline{x})^3}{(n-1)s^3}, \quad \text{and} \tag{5-7}$$

$$\upsilon = \frac{\sum_{i=1}^{n}(x_i - \overline{x})^4}{(n-1)s^4}, \tag{5-8}$$

respectively.

Skewness measures the symmetry—a distribution is symmetric if it looks the same to the left and right of the center point. An ideal normal distribution has a skewness statistic value, $v = 0$. A positive value means long upper tails and heavy lower tails (skewed right); a negative value means heavy upper tails and long lower tails in the distribution charts (skewed left). Kurtosis is a measure of the sharpness or peak of the distribution. Positive kurtosis means a sharp distribution with a short tail, and negative kurtosis means a flat distribution

Figure 5.8 Different forms of distributions

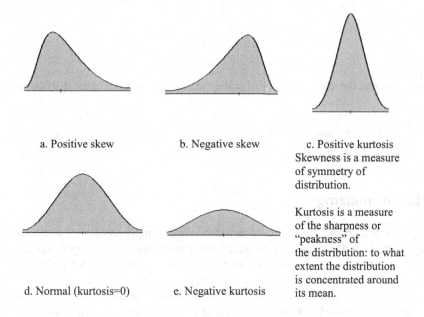

a. Positive skew   b. Negative skew   c. Positive kurtosis

d. Normal (kurtosis=0)   e. Negative kurtosis

Skewness is a measure of symmetry of distribution.

Kurtosis is a measure of the sharpness or "peakness" of the distribution: to what extent the distribution is concentrated around its mean.

with long tails. An ideal normal distribution sample has $\upsilon = 0$, and for a standard normal distribution, $N(0,1)$, $\upsilon = 3$. Figure 5.8 illustrates the possible shapes of a distribution.

In addition to measure skewness and kurtosis, we often use the Quantile-Quantile (QQ) plot to evaluate if a sample has normality. A QQ plot is a graphical display that compares the distributions of two datasets, A and B, to see if they come from populations with a common distribution. Usually, the vertical axis of the plot is the estimated quantile from dataset A, and the horizontal axis is the estimated quantile from dataset B. The normal QQ plot graphically compares the distribution of a given variable to the normal distribution as shown in Figure 5.9, where the 45 degree straight line represents what data would look like if they are perfectly normally distributed. The actual data is represented by the circle points along the straight line. The closer the circles are to the line, the more normally distributed the data looks.

QQ plots are available in SAS, Stata, R and other software applications described in Chapter II. The R codes used to create Figure 5.9 are listed in Display 5.20, and Stata codes given in Display 5.21 construct the QQ plots used to assess the normality distribution assumption of the variable v19, which measures the frequency of the word "you" in the spam-email data. Figure 5.10 shows the quantiles of v19 against the quantiles of the normal distribution, and the results show that the distributions are quite different.

Display 5.20
R codes construct a QQ plot for assessing normality distribution

```
# Generates a sample of 100 values from a standard normal distribution
  x = rnorm(n = 100)
  p = ((1:100)-0.5)/100
  q = qnorm(p)
# Computes the quantiles
  plot(q, sort(x))
  x = rnorm(n = 100, mean=10, sd=4)
  plot(q, sort(x))
  qqnorm(x)
  qqline(x)
```

Display 5.21
Stata codes plot the quantiles of v19 against the quantiles of the normal distribution

```
#delimit;
use F:\Book\Chapter 5\spam.dta;
qnorm v19, grid;
```

Data Normalizing

Many variables in the real world do not meet the assumptions of parametric statistical analyses and tests due to not being normally distributed, having inhomogeneous variances, or both. Data transformation can overcome such failures of normality. It can also correct for outliers, linearity, and homoscedasticity, although the scale of the data influences the utility of transformations, and increases the difficulty of interpretation of transformed variables. Normalized data provides two important results: (1) it reduces potentially misleading results

Figure 5.9 An example of Quantile-Quantile plot

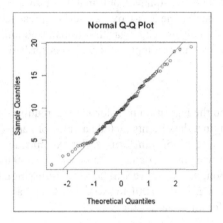

Figure 5.10 Compare the distribution of variable v19 with the normal distribution

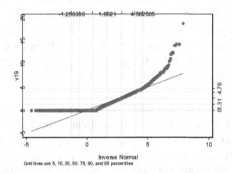

when fitting raw data with a parametric statistical test, and (2) in some situations, transforming a variable will make it fit the assumptions better. Figure 5.11 shows the distributions of the variable v56 (length of sequences of consecutive capital letters) in the spam-email data before and after data normalization through a log transform function.

The basic ideal of normalized data is to use a particular mathematical function, $Z = F$ (), to represent the raw data, X, so that the transformed data, $z = f(x)$, will be better fit a regression model or conduct a test that requires data to be normally distributed. The most popular data transforming functions are the Box-Cox transform (Box & Cox, 1964) and the logarithm transformation. The Box-Cox transform can be written as

$$z = \frac{x^\lambda - 1}{\lambda},$$
(5-9)

where the value of z ranges from 0 to 1. For $\lambda = 1$, we have $z = x - 1$. For $\lambda \to 0$, we have $z = \ln(x)$, when $\lambda = 0.5$ we have the square root transformation, $z = 2(\sqrt{x} - 1)$. For $\lambda = -1$, we have $z = 1 - 1/x$. We can see that the Box-Cox transform represents a family of popular transformations used in data analysis. The logarithm transformation, which is a specific case of the Box-Cox transform, can be simply achieved as described below

$$z = \log(x) \text{ or } z = \ln(x), \tag{5-10}$$

where both the Box-Cox and the logarithm transformations require that data is restricted to being positive. When original data points include a value of zero, Equation (5-10) will generate a missing value as a result of transformed. For example, let X_{ij} represents a difference in distance between two points, p_i and p_j, we may have $x = 0$ that indicates the two points are at the same position, $p_i = p_j$, so we will have $z = .$ (missing). In this case, we can add a small fractional to x, such as $x = 0.001$ to avoid a missing value of z. Note that this approach may not be good for all of the $x = 0$ cases.

Example 5.5→Data Transformation. The length of sequences of consecutive capital letters from an email could be associated with a spam-email. There are three variables, v55, v56, and v57, which measure the length of sequences in the spam-email data, and we are interested in examining their distributions and comparing the logistic model performance with and without transformation conducted on the data. We first apply the logarithm transformation function, $z = \log(x)$, for each of these three variables and then examine their distributions before and after using the transform. We know from Figure 5.11 that variable v56 is not normally distributed, and the distributions before and after transformation of the other two variables are shown in Figure 5.12.

We then fit two logistic regression models with the v58 (spam yes/no) as a response variable; one model uses the raw v55, v56 v57 variables as predictive variables, and the other model uses the transformed v55log, v56log, and v57log as the predictor variables. We will revisit the logistic regression model in greater detail in Chapter VII. The Stata codes used to conduct the transformations and analyses and the corresponding Stata outputs are shown in Displays 5.22 and 5.23, respectively.

Figure 5.11 Histograms of the length of sequences of consecutive capital letters (v56) from the spam-email data

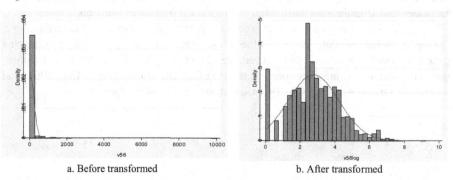

a. Before transformed   b. After transformed

Figure 5.12 Histograms of the length of sequences of consecutive capital letters (v55 [upper] and v57 [bottom])

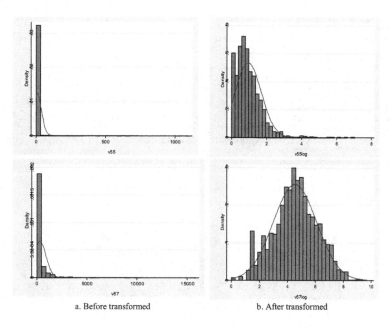

a. Before transformed b. After transformed

Display 5.22
Stata codes to conduct for logarithm transformations

```
#delimit;
use spam,replace;
log using log-tran,replace;
/*--------------------------------------
Use the log transformation function
----------------------------------*/;
gen v55log=log(v55);
gen v56log=log(v56);
gen v57log=log(v57);
/*--------------------------------------
Examine distributions of before and after log transformed
----------------------------------*/;
sum v55,d;
sum v55log,d;
sum v56,d;
sum v56log,d;
sum v57,d;
sum v57log,d;
/*--------------------------------------
Fit logistic regression models, calculate ROC and assess classification
results based on a cutoff point of p=0.6
----------------------------------*/;
logistic v58 v55 v56 v57;
lroc;
lstat,cut(0.6);

logistic v58 v55log v56log v57log;
lroc;
lstat,cut(0.6);
log close;
```

Display 5.23
Results of logarithm transformations from Stata

```
------------------------------------------------------------------
  log:  F:\Book\Chapter 5\log-tran.smcl
  log type:  smcl
  opened on:    7 Jul 2007, 12:40:53
. /*------------------------------------
>  Use the log transformation function
> ------------------------------------*/;
.  gen v55log=log(v55);
.  gen v56log=log(v56);
.  gen v57log=log(v57);
. /*------------------------------------
>  Examine distributions of before and
>  after log transformed
> ------------------------------------*/;
.  sum v55,d;
                              v55
------------------------------------------------------------------
        Percentiles     Smallest
  1%         1              1
  5%         1              1
 10%       1.148            1          Obs               4601
 25%       1.588            1          Sum of Wgt.       4601

 50%       2.276                       Mean          5.191515
                           Largest     Std. Dev.     31.72945
 75%       3.706           664
 90%       6.091           667         Variance      1006.758
 95%       8.851          1021.5       Skewness      23.75418
 99%      44.72           1102.5       Kurtosis      672.6391

.  sum v55log,d;
                            v55log
------------------------------------------------------------------
        Percentiles     Smallest
  1%         0              0
  5%         0              0
 10%      .1380213          0          Obs               4601
 25%      .4624754          0          Sum of Wgt.       4601

 50%      .8224195                     Mean          .9532786
                           Largest     Std. Dev.     .7501766
 75%     1.309953        6.498282
 90%     1.806812        6.50279       Variance      .562765
 95%     2.18053         6.929028      Skewness      2.025098
 99%     3.800421        7.005336      Kurtosis      11.70905

.  sum v56,d;
                              v56
------------------------------------------------------------------
        Percentiles     Smallest
  1%         1              1
  5%         1              1
 10%         3              1          Obs               4601
 25%         6              1          Sum of Wgt.       4601

 50%        15                         Mean          52.17279
                           Largest     Std. Dev.     194.8913
 75%        43            1505
 90%        99            2042         Variance      37982.62
 95%       181            2204         Skewness      30.75496
 99%       669            9989         Kurtosis      1482.032
```

continued on following page

Display 5.23 continued

```
.  sum v56log,d;
                              v56log
-------------------------------------------------------------------
         Percentiles     Smallest
  1%          0               0
  5%          0               0
 10%      1.098612            0        Obs                   4601
 25%      1.791759            0        Sum of Wgt.           4601

 50%      2.70805                      Mean              2.764966
                            Largest    Std. Dev.         1.459034
 75%      3.7612          7.316548
 90%      4.59512         7.621685     Variance          2.128779
 95%      5.198497        7.698029     Skewness           .2033583
 99%      6.505784        9.20924      Kurtosis          3.120103

.  sum v57,d;
                               v57
-------------------------------------------------------------------
         Percentiles     Smallest
  1%          3               1
  5%          6               1
 10%         10               1        Obs                   4601
 25%         35               1        Sum of Wgt.           4601

 50%         95                        Mean              283.2893
                            Largest    Std. Dev.         606.3479
 75%        266            9090
 90%        725            9163        Variance          367657.7
 95%       1223           10062        Skewness          8.707011
 99%       3027           15841        Kurtosis          148.6701

.  sum v57log,d;
                              v57log
-------------------------------------------------------------------
         Percentiles     Smallest
  1%      1.098612            0
  5%      1.791759            0
 10%      2.302585            0        Obs                   4601
 25%      3.555348            0        Sum of Wgt.           4601

 50%      4.553877                     Mean              4.532751
                            Largest    Std. Dev.         1.557179
 75%      5.583496        9.11493
 90%      6.586172        9.122929     Variance          2.424807
 95%      7.109062        9.216521     Skewness          -.0724366
 99%      8.015327        9.670357     Kurtosis          2.686816

.  /*---------------------------------------
>  Fit logistic regression models, calculate ROC and assess classification
results based on a cutoff point of p=0.6
>  ---------------------------------------*/;
.  logistic v58 v55 v56 v57;
```

continued on following page

Display 5.23 continued

```
Logistic regression                          Number of obs   =      4601
                                             LR chi2(3)      =   1089.90
                                             Prob > chi2     =    0.0000
Log likelihood = -2540.1264                  Pseudo R2       =    0.1766

------------------------------------------------------------------------
     v58 | Odds Ratio   Std. Err.      z    P>|z|    [95% Conf. Interval]
---------+--------------------------------------------------------------
     v55 |   1.113255   .0252443     4.73   0.000     1.06486    1.163849
     v56 |   1.019965   .0016523    12.20   0.000    1.016732    1.023209
     v57 |   1.000086   .0000797     1.08   0.282    .9999295    1.000242
------------------------------------------------------------------------

. lroc;
Logistic model for v58

number of observations =      4601
area under ROC curve   =    0.8059

. lstat,cut(0.6);

Logistic model for v58

              -------- True --------
Classified |         D            ~D  |      Total
-----------+----------------------------+-----------
     +     |        591           120  |        711
     -     |       1222          2668  |       3890
-----------+----------------------------+-----------
   Total   |       1813          2788  |       4601

Classified + if predicted Pr(D) >= .6
True D defined as v58 != 0
----------------------------------------------------
Sensitivity                     Pr( +| D)    32.60%
Specificity                     Pr( -|~D)    95.70%
Positive predictive value       Pr( D| +)    83.12%
Negative predictive value       Pr(~D| -)    68.59%
----------------------------------------------------
False + rate for true ~D        Pr( +|~D)     4.30%
False - rate for true D         Pr( -| D)    67.40%
False + rate for classified +   Pr(~D| +)    16.88%
False - rate for classified -   Pr( D| -)    31.41%
----------------------------------------------------
Correctly classified                         70.83%
----------------------------------------------------

. logistic v58 v55log v56log v57log;

Logistic regression                          Number of obs   =      4601
                                             LR chi2(3)      =   1438.51
                                             Prob > chi2     =    0.0000
Log likelihood = -2365.8213                  Pseudo R2       =    0.2331

------------------------------------------------------------------------
     v58 | Odds Ratio   Std. Err.      z    P>|z|    [95% Conf. Interval]
---------+--------------------------------------------------------------
  v55log |   1.985394   .2075288     6.56   0.000    1.617606    2.436806
  v56log |   1.918745   .1394728     8.97   0.000    1.663963    2.212538
  v57log |   1.082393   .0491614     1.74   0.081    .9902028    1.183166
------------------------------------------------------------------------
```

continued on following page

Display 5.23 continued

```
. lroc;
Logistic model for v58

number of observations =     4601
area under ROC curve   =   0.8092

. lstat,cut(0.6);
Logistic model for v58

                  -------- True --------
Classified |          D              ~D   |      Total
-----------+----------------------------+-----------
    +      |        879             244  |       1123
    -      |        934            2544  |       3478
-----------+----------------------------+-----------
  Total    |       1813            2788  |       4601

Classified + if predicted Pr(D) >= .6
True D defined as v58 != 0
----------------------------------------------------
Sensitivity                     Pr( +| D)    48.48%
Specificity                     Pr( -|~D)    91.25%
Positive predictive value       Pr( D| +)    78.27%
Negative predictive value       Pr(~D| -)    73.15%
----------------------------------------------------
False + rate for true ~D        Pr( +|~D)     8.75%
False - rate for true D         Pr( -| D)    51.52%
False + rate for classified +   Pr(~D| +)    21.73%
False - rate for classified -   Pr( D| -)    26.85%
----------------------------------------------------
Correctly classified                         74.40%
----------------------------------------------------

log closed on:    7 Jul 2007, 12:40:58
```

We found that the model improved remarkably after applying the log transformation: the R^2 value increased by nearly 32% from 0.1766 to 0.2331, and the correctly classified rate increased from 70.83% to 74.40%. Also, ROC values changed from 0.8059 to 0.8092, the association between the variable v57 and the response variable v58 changed from having no association to being nearly statistically significant, and the p value changed from 0.282 to 0.081. We will discuss the significance of the R^2, correctly classified rate, and ROC values in greater detail in Chapter XI.

Centralizing and Standardizing

In addition to normalized data, we can apply data transformations for centering and standardizing data. Centering data moves the sample mean, μ, to zero by subtracting each data values from μ:

$$x_i^c = x_i - \mu. \tag{5-11}$$

Thus, after centralizing, the mean of variable X^c is zero. Similarly, we can extend Equation (5-11) to a general formula that moves the sample mean to any particular location by adding or subtracting a constant c, $x_i^c = x_i - c$. The distribution of data does not change after being transformed by the centering method.

If we want to compare the results from different normal distributions, we will have to first arrange the results to the standard values that can be achieved by using data transformation approaches, of which the most widely used approach is the z-score. Let x be an observation from a sample with μ and σ. The standardization can be achieved by

$$z = \frac{x - \mu}{\sigma}, \qquad (5\text{-}12)$$

where the new variable z has attributes of $\mu = 0$ and $\sigma = 1$, which is the standard normal distribution, $N(0,1)$. A z-score represents how many SDs that the original observation, x, falls away from the mean, μ and in which direction. In other words, the value of a z-score represents the distance between the raw value and the population mean in units of the SD. If the raw value is less than the mean, $(x - \mu) < 0$, then the z-score is negative. If it is greater than the mean, $(x - \mu) > 0$, then the z-score is positive.

There are other useful standardizing approaches that are widely employed and practical. For example, if we do not want to center the data at zero by removing the sample mean, we can simply transform x by σ:

$$z = \frac{x}{\sigma}. \qquad (5\text{-}13)$$

If we want to rescale a variable to a range of 0 to 1, we can use the range of that variable as the divisor so the new variable can defined as:

$$z = \frac{x - \min(x)}{\max(x) - \min(x)}, \text{ or} \qquad (5\text{-}14)$$

$$z = \frac{x}{\max(x) - \min(x)}. \qquad (5\text{-}15)$$

Example 5.6→Standardized Spam-email Data. We learned previously that continuous variables in the spam-email data are in different measure scales that involve a bias on modeling. Let us use equation (5-12) to standardize these variables for further analyses. Display 5.24 lists the Stata codes used to conduct this example and save the standardized data as *spam_email_std*, which includes 57 new standardized variables, named sv_1 to sv_57.

Display 5.24
Stata codes to conduct standardization of continuous variables in spam-email data

```
#delimit;
*use F:\book\Chapter 5\spam_email,replace;
local i=1;
foreach var of varlist v1-v57 {;
sum `var';
gen sv_`i'=(`var'-_result(3))/sqrt(_result(4));
local i=`i'+1;
};
save F:\book\Chapter 5\spam_email_std,replace;
```

SUMMARY

Data exploration provides the first step toward understanding and evaluating data. In general, we have to compute the frequency, the mean with its standard deviation, and assess the distribution and normality for each key variable in network traffic. The central tendency and dispersion are the most frequently used measures that describe distributions of network traffic. Central tendency describes the center of the distribution, which are commonly represented by the mean and median values of the data. Dispersion describes the variation of the data, including variance, standard error, and standard deviation.

The normal distribution is the most widely used family of distributions in statistics, and many statistical tests are based on the assumption of normality. With the central limit theorem, we know that data can be approximated well by the normal distribution, or can be converted to the normal distribution through a transformation function. Sometimes, when we have a sample that the distribution of the population from which the sample is taken is not normal, we may still have the sampling distribution of the sample mean to be approximately normal. Therefore, although the normal distribution is required in many situations of analysis, this requirement is not difficult to be achieved.

Two procedures are widely used for conducting exploratory analysis: multivariate analysis and graphical analysis. Multivariate analysis includes a set of statistical analyses that are concerned with the simultaneous investigation of more than one variable in a dataset. For example, we may want to know the relationships among the variables: source IP address, destination IP address, user's job functions, and protocol types (e.g., HTTP, UDP, TCP). The multivariate analysis provides a robust solution that ensures that all the important variables are pooled together to construct a final set of predictors for a given response variable. We will discuss and review the multivariate analysis in next chapter. Graphical analysis focuses on visually representing data. The term of data visualization has become the most frequently used term to describe and graphically represent large data in network security. Modern data visualization methods can pick up where the conventional methods left off in helping to make rational inferences from large amounts of data and to provide an important step towards understanding data.

REFERENCES

Blaikie, N. W. H. (2003). *Analyzing quantitative data: from description to explanation.* London: Sage Publications Ltd.

Box, George, E. P. & Cox, D. R. (1964). An analysis of transformations. *Journal of Royal Statistical Society, Series, B 26,* 211-246.

Cuzick, J. (1985). A Wilcoxon-type test for trend. *Statistics in Medicine, 20*(4), 87-90.

Everitt, S. B. (2005). *An R and S-PLUS companion to multivariate analysis.* New York: Springer-Verlag.

Friendly, M. (2000). *Visualizing categorical data.* Cary, NC: SAS Publishing.

Hartigan, J. A., and Kleiner, B. (1981), Mosaics for contingency tables, (pp. 268-273). In W. F. Eddy (Ed.), *Computer Science and Statistics: Proceedings of the 13th Symposium on the Interface.*

Hartigan, J.A. & Kleiner, B. (1984). A mosaic of television ratings. *The American Statistician,* 38, 32-35.

Kundur, D. Luh, W. Okorafor, U.N. & Zourntos, T. (2008). Security and privacy for distributed multimedia sensor networks. In *Proceedings of the IEEE, 96*(1), 112-130.

Nayyar, H. & Ghorbani, A.A.(2008). Approximate autoregressive modeling for network attack detection. *Journal of Computer Security,16*(2), 165-197.

Neuhaus, M., & Bunke, H. (2007). *Bridging the gap between graph edit distance and kernel machines.* Series in machine perception and artificial intelligence, v. 68. Singapore: World Scientific.

Oehlschlaegel-Akiyoshi, J. (2006). *The R graphics package.* Retrieved September 8, 2007, from http://astrostatistics.psu.edu/datasets/2006tutorial/html/graphics/html/pairs.html

Petrovskiy, M. I. (2003). Outlier detection algorithms in data mining systems. *Programming and Computer Software. 29*(4), 228-237.

Stata (1997). *Stata reference.* Stata Corporation, TX: College Station.

Stata (2003). *Stata reference: Graphcs.* Stata Corporation, TX: College Station.

Unwin, A., Theus, M., Hofmann, H. (2006). *Graphics of large datasets: Visualizing a million.* New York: Springer-Verlag.

Young, F. W. Valero-Mora, P. M. & Friendly, M. (2006). *Visual statistics: Seeing data with dynamic interactive graphics.* New Jersey: John Wiley & Sons, Inc.

William, G. J. (1997). *Statistical graphics for univariate and bivariate data.* California: SAGE Publications Inc.

APPENDIX

Codebook of 1999 KDD-Cup Training Data

```
-------------------------------------------------------------------------------

  opened on:   8 Jul 2007, 14:20:09

 . codebook, mv tabulate(9)

-------------------------------------------------------------------------------
 duration                                                               durtion
-------------------------------------------------------------------------------

              type:  numeric (long)

             range:  [0,58329]                   units:  1
     unique values:  2495                     missing .:  0/494021

              mean:  47.9793
          std. dev:  707.746

       percentiles:       10%      25%      50%      75%      90%
                            0        0        0        0        0
-------------------------------------------------------------------------------
 protocol                                                         protocol_type
-------------------------------------------------------------------------------

              type:  string (str4)

     unique values:  3                        missing "":  0/494021

         tabulation:  Freq.  Value
                      2.8e+05 "icmp"
                      1.9e+05 "tcp"
                        20354 "udp"
-------------------------------------------------------------------------------
 service                                                                service
-------------------------------------------------------------------------------

              type:  string (str11)

     unique values:  66                       missing "":  0/494021

          examples:  "ecr_i"
                     "ecr_i"
                     "ftp_data"
                     "private"
-------------------------------------------------------------------------------
 flag                                                                      flag
-------------------------------------------------------------------------------

              type:  string (str6)

     unique values:  11                       missing "":  0/494021

          examples:  "S0"
                     "SF"
                     "SF"
                     "SF"


-------------------------------------------------------------------------------
 src_byte                                                             src_bytes
-------------------------------------------------------------------------------

              type:  numeric (long)

             range:  [0,6.934e+08]               units:  1
     unique values:  3300                     missing .:  0/494021

              mean:  3025.61
          std. dev:  988218

       percentiles:       10%      25%      50%      75%      90%
                            0       45      520     1032     1032
```

```
-----------------------------------------------------------------------------
dst_byte                                                            dst_bytes
-----------------------------------------------------------------------------

              type:  numeric (long)

             range:  [0,5155468]                 units:  1
     unique values:  10725                     missing .:  0/494021

              mean:  868.532
          std. dev:  33040

       percentiles:          10%      25%      50%      75%      90%
                               0        0        0        0      482
-----------------------------------------------------------------------------
land                                                                     Land
-----------------------------------------------------------------------------

              type:  numeric (byte)

             range:  [0,1]                        units:  1
     unique values:  2                         missing .:  0/494021

         tabulation:  Freq.  Value
                     4.9e+05  0
                        22    1
-----------------------------------------------------------------------------
wrong_fr                                                        wrong_fragment
-----------------------------------------------------------------------------

              type:  numeric (byte)

             range:  [0,3]                        units:  1
     unique values:  3                         missing .:  0/494021

         tabulation:  Freq.  Value
                     4.9e+05  0
                        268   1
                        970   3
-----------------------------------------------------------------------------
urgent                                                                 Urgent
-----------------------------------------------------------------------------

              type:  numeric (byte)

             range:  [0,3]                        units:  1
     unique values:  4                         missing .:  0/494021

         tabulation:  Freq.  Value
                     4.9e+05  0
                         2    1
                         1    2
                         1    3
-----------------------------------------------------------------------------
hot                                                                       hot
-----------------------------------------------------------------------------

              type:  numeric (byte)

             range:  [0,30]                       units:  1
     unique values:  22                        missing .:  0/494021

              mean:  .034519
          std. dev:  .782103

       percentiles:          10%      25%      50%      75%      90%
                               0        0        0        0        0
-----------------------------------------------------------------------------
num_fail                                                      num_failed_logins
-----------------------------------------------------------------------------

              type:  numeric (byte)

             range:  [0,5]                        units:  1
     unique values:  6                         missing .:  0/494021

         tabulation:  Freq.  Value
                     4.9e+05  0
                        57    1
                         3    2
                         1    3
                         1    4
                         1    5
```

```
--------------------------------------------------------------------------
logged_i                                                        logged_in
--------------------------------------------------------------------------

             type:  numeric (byte)

            range:  [0,1]                         units:  1
    unique values:  2                           missing .:  0/494021

        tabulation:  Freq.  Value
                    4.2e+05  0
                     73237  1
--------------------------------------------------------------------------
num_comp                                                   num_compromised
--------------------------------------------------------------------------

             type:  numeric (int)

            range:  [0,884]                       units:  1
    unique values:  23                          missing .:  0/494021

             mean:  .010212
         std. dev:  1.79833

      percentiles:        10%      25%      50%      75%      90%
                           0        0        0        0        0
--------------------------------------------------------------------------
root_she                                                        root_shell
--------------------------------------------------------------------------

             type:  numeric (byte)

            range:  [0,1]                         units:  1
    unique values:  2                           missing .:  0/494021

        tabulation:  Freq.  Value
                    4.9e+05  0
                       55  1
--------------------------------------------------------------------------
su_attem                                                        su_attempted
--------------------------------------------------------------------------

             type:  numeric (byte)

            range:  [0,2]                         units:  1
    unique values:  3                           missing .:  0/494021

        tabulation:  Freq.  Value
                    4.9e+05  0
                        6  1
                        6  2
--------------------------------------------------------------------------
num_root                                                          num_root
--------------------------------------------------------------------------

             type:  numeric (int)

            range:  [0,993]                       units:  1
    unique values:  20                          missing .:  0/494021

             mean:  .011352
         std. dev:  2.01272

      percentiles:        10%      25%      50%      75%      90%
                           0        0        0        0        0
--------------------------------------------------------------------------
num_file                                                  num_file_creations
--------------------------------------------------------------------------

             type:  numeric (byte)

            range:  [0,28]                        units:  1
    unique values:  18                          missing .:  0/494021

             mean:  .001083
         std. dev:  .096416

      percentiles:        10%      25%      50%      75%      90%
                           0        0        0        0        0
```

```
------------------------------------------------------------------------
num_shel                                                       num_shells
------------------------------------------------------------------------

              type:  numeric (byte)

             range:  [0,2]                      units:  1
     unique values:  3                    missing .:  0/494021

        tabulation:  Freq.  Value
                     4.9e+05  0
                        48  1
                         3  2
------------------------------------------------------------------------
num_acce                                                 num_access_files
------------------------------------------------------------------------

              type:  numeric (byte)

             range:  [0,8]                      units:  1
     unique values:  7                    missing .:  0/494021

        tabulation:  Freq.  Value
                     4.9e+05  0
                       424  1
                        25  2
                         2  3
                         1  4
                         1  6
                         1  8
------------------------------------------------------------------------
num_outb                                                 num_outbound_cmds
------------------------------------------------------------------------

              type:  numeric (byte)

             range:  [0,0]                      units:  1
     unique values:  1                    missing .:  0/494021

        tabulation:  Freq.  Value
                     4.9e+05  0
------------------------------------------------------------------------
is_host_                                                     is_host_login
------------------------------------------------------------------------

              type:  numeric (byte)

             range:  [0,0]                      units:  1
     unique values:  1                    missing .:  0/494021

        tabulation:  Freq.  Value
                     4.9e+05  0
------------------------------------------------------------------------
is_guest                                                    is_guest_login
------------------------------------------------------------------------

              type:  numeric (byte)

             range:  [0,1]                      units:  1
     unique values:  2                    missing .:  0/494021

        tabulation:  Freq.  Value
                     4.9e+05  0
                       685  1
------------------------------------------------------------------------
count                                                                count
------------------------------------------------------------------------

              type:  numeric (int)

             range:  [0,511]                    units:  1
     unique values:  490                  missing .:  0/494021

              mean:  332.286
          std. dev:  213.147

       percentiles:      10%     25%     50%     75%     90%
                           2     117     510     511     511
```

```
-------------------------------------------------------------------------------
srv_coun                                                              srv_count
-------------------------------------------------------------------------------

                type:  numeric (int)

               range:  [0,511]                    units:  1
       unique values:  470                     missing .:  0/494021

                mean:  292.907
            std. dev:  246.323

         percentiles:          10%       25%       50%       75%       90%
                                 2        10       510       511       511

-------------------------------------------------------------------------------
serror_r                                                             serror_rate
-------------------------------------------------------------------------------

                type:  numeric (float)

               range:  [0,1]                      units:  .01
       unique values:  92                      missing .:  0/494021

                mean:  .176687
            std. dev:  .380717

         percentiles:          10%       25%       50%       75%       90%
                                 0         0         0         0         1

-------------------------------------------------------------------------------
srv_serr                                                         srv_serror_rate
-------------------------------------------------------------------------------

                type:  numeric (float)

               range:  [0,1]                      units:  .01
       unique values:  51                      missing .:  0/494021

                mean:  .176609
            std. dev:  .381017

         percentiles:          10%       25%       50%       75%       90%
                                 0         0         0         0         1

-------------------------------------------------------------------------------
rerror_r                                                             rerror_rate
-------------------------------------------------------------------------------

                type:  numeric (float)

               range:  [0,1]                      units:  .01
       unique values:  77                      missing .:  0/494021

                mean:  .057433
            std. dev:  .231623

         percentiles:          10%       25%       50%       75%       90%
                                 0         0         0         0         0

-------------------------------------------------------------------------------
srv_rerr                                                         srv_rerror_rate
-------------------------------------------------------------------------------

                type:  numeric (float)

               range:  [0,1]                      units:  .01
       unique values:  51                      missing .:  0/494021

                mean:  .057719
            std. dev:  .232147

         percentiles:          10%       25%       50%       75%       90%
                                 0         0         0         0         0

-------------------------------------------------------------------------------
same_srv                                                           same_srv_rate
-------------------------------------------------------------------------------

                type:  numeric (float)

               range:  [0,1]                      units:  .01
       unique values:  99                      missing .:  0/494021

                mean:  .791547
            std. dev:  .388189

         percentiles:          10%       25%       50%       75%       90%
                               .05         1         1         1         1
```

```
--------------------------------------------------------------------------------
diff_srv                                                         diff_srv_rate
--------------------------------------------------------------------------------

                type:  numeric (float)

               range:  [0,1]                       units:  .01
       unique values:  78                   missing .:  0/494021

                mean:  .020982
            std. dev:  .082205

         percentiles:          10%      25%      50%      75%      90%
                                 0        0        0        0      .06

--------------------------------------------------------------------------------
srv_diff                                                      srv_diff_host_rate
--------------------------------------------------------------------------------

                type:  numeric (float)

               range:  [0,1]                       units:  .01
       unique values:  64                   missing .:  0/494021

                mean:  .028997
            std. dev:  .142397

         percentiles:          10%      25%      50%      75%      90%
                                 0        0        0        0        0

--------------------------------------------------------------------------------
dst_host                                                        dst_host_count
--------------------------------------------------------------------------------

                type:  numeric (int)

               range:  [0,255]                     units:  1
       unique values:  256                  missing .:  0/494021

                mean:  232.471
            std. dev:  64.7454

         percentiles:          10%      25%      50%      75%      90%
                               141      255      255      255      255

--------------------------------------------------------------------------------
dst_hos1                                                      dst_host_srv_count
--------------------------------------------------------------------------------

                type:  numeric (int)

               range:  [0,255]                     units:  1
       unique values:  256                  missing .:  0/494021

                mean:  188.666
            std. dev:  106.04

         percentiles:          10%      25%      50%      75%      90%
                                 8       46      255      255      255


--------------------------------------------------------------------------------
dst_hos2                                                   dst_host_same_srv_rate
--------------------------------------------------------------------------------

                type:  numeric (float)

               range:  [0,1]                       units:  .01
       unique values:  101                  missing .:  0/494021

                mean:  .75378
            std. dev:  .410781

         percentiles:          10%      25%      50%      75%      90%
                               .03      .41        1        1        1

--------------------------------------------------------------------------------
dst_hos3                                                   dst_host_diff_srv_rate
--------------------------------------------------------------------------------

                type:  numeric (float)

               range:  [0,1]                       units:  .01
       unique values:  101                  missing .:  0/494021

                mean:  .030906
            std. dev:  .109259

         percentiles:          10%      25%      50%      75%      90%
                                 0        0        0      .04      .07
```

```
-------------------------------------------------------------------------
dst_hos4                                      dst_host_same_src_port_rate
-------------------------------------------------------------------------

            type:   numeric (float)

           range:   [0,1]                    units:   .01
   unique values:   101                    missing .:   0/494021

            mean:   .601935
        std. dev:   .481309

     percentiles:         10%      25%      50%      75%      90%
                           0        0        1        1        1

-------------------------------------------------------------------------
dst_hos5                                      dst_host_srv_diff_host_rate
-------------------------------------------------------------------------

            type:   numeric (float)

           range:   [0,1]                    units:   .01
   unique values:   65                     missing .:   0/494021

            mean:   .006684
        std. dev:   .042133

     percentiles:         10%      25%      50%      75%      90%
                           0        0        0        0       .01

-------------------------------------------------------------------------
dst_hos6                                           dst_host_serror_rate
-------------------------------------------------------------------------

            type:   numeric (float)

           range:   [0,1]                    units:   .01
   unique values:   100                    missing .:   0/494021

            mean:   .176754
        std. dev:   .380593

     percentiles:         10%      25%      50%      75%      90%
                           0        0        0        0        1

-------------------------------------------------------------------------
dst_hos7                                        dst_host_srv_serror_rate
-------------------------------------------------------------------------

            type:   numeric (float)

           range:   [0,1]                    units:   .01
   unique values:   72                     missing .:   0/494021

            mean:   .176443
        std. dev:   .380919

     percentiles:         10%      25%      50%      75%      90%
                           0        0        0        0        1

-------------------------------------------------------------------------
dst_hos8                                            dst_host_rerror_rate
-------------------------------------------------------------------------

            type:   numeric (float)

           range:   [0,1]                    units:   .01
   unique values:   101                    missing .:   0/494021

            mean:   .058118
        std. dev:   .23059

     percentiles:         10%      25%      50%      75%      90%
                           0        0        0        0        0

-------------------------------------------------------------------------
dst_hos9                                        dst_host_srv_rerror_rate
-------------------------------------------------------------------------

            type:   numeric (float)

           range:   [0,1]                    units:   .01
   unique values:   101                    missing .:   0/494021

            mean:   .057412
        std. dev:   .23014

     percentiles:         10%      25%      50%      75%      90%
                           0        0        0        0        0
```

```
--------------------------------------------------------------------------
y                                                            (unlabeled)
--------------------------------------------------------------------------
              type:  string (str16)

    unique values:  23                      missing "":  0/494021

          examples:  "neptune."
                     "normal."
                     "smurf."
                     "smurf."
--------------------------------------------------------------------------
REJ                                                          (unlabeled)
--------------------------------------------------------------------------
              type:  numeric (byte)

             range:  [0,1]                       units:  1
    unique values:  2                      missing .:  0/494021

        tabulation:  Freq.  Value
                     4.7e+05  0
                     26875  1
--------------------------------------------------------------------------
S0                                                           (unlabeled)
--------------------------------------------------------------------------
              type:  numeric (byte)

             range:  [0,1]                       units:  1
    unique values:  2                      missing .:  0/494021

        tabulation:  Freq.  Value
                     4.1e+05  0
                     87007  1
--------------------------------------------------------------------------
SF                                                           (unlabeled)
--------------------------------------------------------------------------
              type:  numeric (byte)

             range:  [0,1]                       units:  1
    unique values:  2                      missing .:  0/494021

        tabulation:  Freq.  Value
                     1.2e+05  0
                     3.8e+05  1
--------------------------------------------------------------------------
RST                                                          (unlabeled)
--------------------------------------------------------------------------
              type:  numeric (byte)

             range:  [0,1]                       units:  1
    unique values:  2                      missing .:  0/494021

        tabulation:  Freq.  Value
                     4.9e+05  0
                     1493  1
--------------------------------------------------------------------------


--------------------------------------------------------------------------
ICMP                                                         (unlabeled)
--------------------------------------------------------------------------
              type:  numeric (byte)

             range:  [0,1]                       units:  1
    unique values:  2                      missing .:  0/494021

        tabulation:  Freq.  Value
                     2.1e+05  0
                     2.8e+05  1
--------------------------------------------------------------------------
```

```
-------------------------------------------------------------------------------
TCP                                                               (unlabeled)
-------------------------------------------------------------------------------

               type:  numeric (byte)

              range:  [0,1]                        units:  1
      unique values:  2                        missing .:  0/494021

          tabulation:  Freq.  Value
                       3.0e+05 0
                       1.9e+05 1
-------------------------------------------------------------------------------
UDP                                                               (unlabeled)
-------------------------------------------------------------------------------

               type:  numeric (byte)

              range:  [0,1]                        units:  1
      unique values:  2                        missing .:  0/494021

          tabulation:  Freq.  Value
                       4.7e+05 0
                       20354   1
-------------------------------------------------------------------------------
HTTP                                                              (unlabeled)
-------------------------------------------------------------------------------

               type:  numeric (float)

              range:  [0,1]                        units:  1
      unique values:  2                        missing .:  0/494021

          tabulation:  Freq.  Value
                       4.3e+05 0
                       64293   1
-------------------------------------------------------------------------------
Hot_0                                                             (unlabeled)
-------------------------------------------------------------------------------

               type:  numeric (float)

              range:  [0,1]                        units:  1
      unique values:  2                        missing .:  0/494021

          tabulation:  Freq.  Value
                       3192    0
                       4.9e+05 1
-------------------------------------------------------------------------------
DOS                                                               (unlabeled)
-------------------------------------------------------------------------------

               type:  numeric (byte)

              range:  [0,1]                        units:  1
      unique values:  2                        missing .:  0/494021

          tabulation:  Freq.  Value
                       1.0e+05 0
                       3.9e+05 1
-------------------------------------------------------------------------------
U2R                                                               (unlabeled)
-------------------------------------------------------------------------------

               type:  numeric (byte)

              range:  [0,1]                        units:  1
      unique values:  2                        missing .:  0/494021

          tabulation:  Freq.  Value
                       4.9e+05 0
                       52      1
-------------------------------------------------------------------------------
R2L                                                               (unlabeled)
-------------------------------------------------------------------------------

               type:  numeric (byte)

              range:  [0,1]                        units:  1
      unique values:  2                        missing .:  0/494021

          tabulation:  Freq.  Value
                       4.9e+05 0
                       1126    1
```

```
--------------------------------------------------------------------------------
PROB                                                                  (unlabeled)
--------------------------------------------------------------------------------
            type:  numeric (byte)

           range:  [0,1]                          units:  1
   unique values:  2                          missing .:  0/494021

      tabulation:  Freq.  Value
                   4.9e+05  0
                     4107  1

--------------------------------------------------------------------------------
NORMAL                                                                (unlabeled)
--------------------------------------------------------------------------------
            type:  numeric (byte)

           range:  [0,1]                          units:  1
   unique values:  2                          missing .:  0/494021

      tabulation:  Freq.  Value
                   4.0e+05  0
                    97278  1

--------------------------------------------------------------------------------
outcomes                                                              (unlabeled)
--------------------------------------------------------------------------------
            type:  numeric (byte)
           label:  outcomes

           range:  [0,4]                          units:  1
   unique values:  5                          missing .:  0/494021

      tabulation:  Freq.    Numeric  Label
                   97278        0    normal
                    4107        1    PROB
                   3.9e+05      2    DOS
                      52        3    U2R
                    1126        4    R2L

--------------------------------------------------------------------------------
training                                                              (unlabeled)
--------------------------------------------------------------------------------
            type:  numeric (byte)

           range:  [1,1]                          units:  1
   unique values:  1                          missing .:  0/494021

      tabulation:  Freq.  Value
                   4.9e+05  1

--------------------------------------------------------------------------------
Duration                                                              (unlabeled)
--------------------------------------------------------------------------------
            type:  numeric (float)

           range:  [-.06779165,82.347313]         units:  1.000e-12
   unique values:  2495                        missing .:  0/494021

            mean:  3.6e-09
        std. dev:  1

     percentiles:       10%       25%       50%       75%       90%
                   -.067792  -.067792  -.067792  -.067792  -.067792

--------------------------------------------------------------------------------
Src_byte                                                              (unlabeled)
--------------------------------------------------------------------------------
            type:  numeric (float)

           range:  [-.00306168,701.63928]         units:  1.000e-14
   unique values:  3300                        missing .:  0/494021

            mean:  9.0e-11
        std. dev:  1

     percentiles:       10%       25%       50%       75%       90%
                   -.003062  -.003016  -.002535  -.002017  -.002017
```

```
--------------------------------------------------------------------
Dst_byte                                              (unlabeled)
--------------------------------------------------------------------

              type:  numeric (float)

             range:  [-.0262873,156.01088]     units:  1.000e-12
     unique values:  10725                     missing .:  0/494021

              mean:  -3.8e-10
          std. dev:  1

       percentiles:        10%      25%      50%      75%      90%
                      -.026287  -.026287  -.026287  -.026287  -.011699

--------------------------------------------------------------------
Wrong_fr                                              (unlabeled)
--------------------------------------------------------------------

              type:  numeric (float)

             range:  [-.04772014,22.206606]    units:  1.000e-09
     unique values:  3                         missing .:  0/494021

         tabulation:  Freq.   Value
                      4.9e+05  -.04772014
                         268  7.3703885
                         970  22.206606

--------------------------------------------------------------------
Urgent                                                (unlabeled)
--------------------------------------------------------------------

              type:  numeric (float)

             range:  [-.00257147,544.43652]    units:  1.000e-10
     unique values:  4                         missing .:  0/494021

         tabulation:  Freq.   Value
                      4.9e+05  -.00257147
                           2  181.47714
                           1  362.95685
                           1  544.43652

--------------------------------------------------------------------
Hot                                                   (unlabeled)
--------------------------------------------------------------------

              type:  numeric (float)

             range:  [-.04413587,38.314003]    units:  1.000e-08
     unique values:  22                        missing .:  0/494021

              mean:  -1.7e-09
          std. dev:  1

       percentiles:        10%      25%      50%      75%      90%
                      -.044136  -.044136  -.044136  -.044136  -.044136


--------------------------------------------------------------------
Num_fail                                              (unlabeled)
--------------------------------------------------------------------

              type:  numeric (float)

             range:  [-.00978218,322.16354]    units:  1.000e-09
     unique values:  6                         missing .:  0/494021

         tabulation:  Freq.   Value
                      4.9e+05  -.00978217
                          57  64.424881
                           3  128.85954
                           1  193.2942
                           1  257.72888
                           1  322.16354

--------------------------------------------------------------------
Num_comp                                              (unlabeled)
--------------------------------------------------------------------

              type:  numeric (float)

             range:  [-.00567868,491.56253]    units:  1.000e-10
     unique values:  23                        missing .:  0/494021

              mean:  -2.6e-11
          std. dev:  1

       percentiles:        10%      25%      50%      75%      90%
                      -.005679  -.005679  -.005679  -.005679  -.005679
```

```
----------------------------------------------------------------------
Num_root                                                   (unlabeled)
----------------------------------------------------------------------

              type:  numeric (float)

             range:  [-.00564001,493.35699]     units:  1.000e-09
     unique values:  20                       missing .:  0/494021

              mean:  2.9e-10
          std. dev:  1

       percentiles:        10%       25%       50%       75%       90%
                        -.00564   -.00564   -.00564   -.00564   -.00564
----------------------------------------------------------------------
Num_file                                                   (unlabeled)
----------------------------------------------------------------------

              type:  numeric (float)

             range:  [-.01123207,290.39737]     units:  1.000e-09
     unique values:  18                       missing .:  0/494021

              mean:  -5.6e-10
          std. dev:  1

       percentiles:        10%       25%       50%       75%       90%
                       -.011232  -.011232  -.011232  -.011232  -.011232
----------------------------------------------------------------------
Num_shel                                                   (unlabeled)
----------------------------------------------------------------------

              type:  numeric (float)

             range:  [-.00991896,181.47812]     units:  1.000e-10
     unique values:  3                        missing .:  0/494021

         tabulation:  Freq.   Value
                      4.9e+05  -.00991896
                          48   90.7341
                           3   181.47812
----------------------------------------------------------------------
Num_acce                                                   (unlabeled)
----------------------------------------------------------------------

              type:  numeric (float)

             range:  [-.02763179,219.26045]     units:  1.000e-09
     unique values:  7                        missing .:  0/494021

         tabulation:  Freq.   Value
                      4.9e+05  -.02763179
                         424   27.383379
                          25   54.794392
                           2   82.205399
                           1   109.61641
                           1   164.43843
                           1   219.26045
----------------------------------------------------------------------


----------------------------------------------------------------------
Count                                                      (unlabeled)
----------------------------------------------------------------------

              type:  numeric (float)

             range:  [-1.5589478,.83845407]      units:  1.000e-10
     unique values:  490                      missing .:  0/494021

              mean:  1.3e-08
          std. dev:  1

       percentiles:        10%       25%       50%       75%       90%
                       -1.54956  -1.01003   .833762   .838454   .838454
```

```
--------------------------------------------------------------------------------
Srv_coun                                                          (unlabeled)
--------------------------------------------------------------------------------

            type:  numeric (float)

           range:  [-1.1891166,.88539684]      units:  1.000e-11
   unique values:  470                       missing .:  0/494021

            mean:  -1.6e-10
        std. dev:  1

     percentiles:        10%        25%        50%        75%        90%
                      -1.181   -1.14852    .881337    .885397    .885397

--------------------------------------------------------------------------------
Serror_r                                                          (unlabeled)
--------------------------------------------------------------------------------

            type:  numeric (float)

           range:  [-.46408927,2.162534]       units:  1.000e-09
   unique values:  92                        missing .:  0/494021

            mean:  1.6e-08
        std. dev:  1

     percentiles:        10%        25%        50%        75%        90%
                    -.464089   -.464089   -.464089   -.464089    2.16253

--------------------------------------------------------------------------------
Srv_serr                                                          (unlabeled)
--------------------------------------------------------------------------------

            type:  numeric (float)

           range:  [-.46351999,2.1610377]      units:  1.000e-09
   unique values:  51                        missing .:  0/494021

            mean:  1.2e-08
        std. dev:  1

     percentiles:        10%        25%        50%        75%        90%
                     -.46352    -.46352    -.46352    -.46352    2.16104

--------------------------------------------------------------------------------
Rerror_r                                                          (unlabeled)
--------------------------------------------------------------------------------

            type:  numeric (float)

           range:  [-.24796023,4.0693913]      units:  1.000e-09
   unique values:  77                        missing .:  0/494021

            mean:  -1.2e-08
        std. dev:  1

     percentiles:        10%        25%        50%        75%        90%
                     -.24796    -.24796    -.24796    -.24796    -.24796

--------------------------------------------------------------------------------
Srv_rerr                                                          (unlabeled)
--------------------------------------------------------------------------------

            type:  numeric (float)

           range:  [-.24863103,4.0589848]      units:  1.000e-09
   unique values:  51                        missing .:  0/494021

            mean:  3.0e-10
        std. dev:  1

     percentiles:        10%        25%        50%        75%        90%
                    -.248631   -.248631   -.248631   -.248631   -.248631

--------------------------------------------------------------------------------
Same_srv                                                          (unlabeled)
--------------------------------------------------------------------------------

            type:  numeric (float)

           range:  [-2.0390747,.53698689]      units:  1.000e-09
   unique values:  99                        missing .:  0/494021

            mean:  1.9e-08
        std. dev:  1

     percentiles:        10%        25%        50%        75%        90%
                    -1.91027    .536987    .536987    .536987    .536987
```

```
-------------------------------------------------------------------------------
Diff_srv                                                            (unlabeled)
-------------------------------------------------------------------------------

              type:  numeric (float)

             range:  [-.25524312,11.909394]     units:  1.000e-08
     unique values:  78                         missing .:  0/494021

              mean:  6.6e-09
          std. dev:  1

       percentiles:      10%       25%       50%       75%       90%
                     -.255243  -.255243  -.255243  -.255243   .474635
-------------------------------------------------------------------------------
Srv_diff                                                           (unlabeled)
-------------------------------------------------------------------------------

              type:  numeric (float)

             range:  [-.20363286,6.818964]      units:  1.000e-09
     unique values:  64                         missing .:  0/494021

              mean:  2.6e-09
          std. dev:  1

       percentiles:      10%       25%       50%       75%       90%
                     -.203633  -.203633  -.203633  -.203633  -.203633
-------------------------------------------------------------------------------
Dst_host                                                           (unlabeled)
-------------------------------------------------------------------------------

              type:  numeric (float)

             range:  [-3.5905385,.34796649]     units:  1.000e-10
     unique values:  256                        missing .:  0/494021

              mean:  5.9e-09
          std. dev:  1

       percentiles:      10%       25%       50%       75%       90%
                     -1.41278   .347966   .347966   .347966   .347966
-------------------------------------------------------------------------------
Dst_hos1                                                           (unlabeled)
-------------------------------------------------------------------------------

              type:  numeric (float)

             range:  [-1.7791861,.62555695]     units:  1.000e-09
     unique values:  256                        missing .:  0/494021

              mean:  1.4e-08
          std. dev:  1

       percentiles:      10%       25%       50%       75%       90%
                     -1.70374  -1.34539   .625557   .625557   .625557
-------------------------------------------------------------------------------
```

```
-------------------------------------------------------------------------------
Dst_hos2                                                           (unlabeled)
-------------------------------------------------------------------------------

              type:  numeric (float)

             range:  [-1.8349917,.59939557]     units:  1.000e-09
     unique values:  101                        missing .:  0/494021

              mean:  -5.8e-09
          std. dev:  1

       percentiles:      10%       25%       50%       75%       90%
                     -1.76196  -.836893   .599396   .599396   .599396
-------------------------------------------------------------------------------
Dst_hos3                                                           (unlabeled)
-------------------------------------------------------------------------------

              type:  numeric (float)

             range:  [-.28286639,8.869688]      units:  1.000e-09
     unique values:  101                        missing .:  0/494021

              mean:  -1.0e-09
          std. dev:  1

       percentiles:      10%       25%       50%       75%       90%
                     -.282866  -.282866  -.282866   .083236   .357812
-------------------------------------------------------------------------------
```

```
-------------------------------------------------------------------------
Dst_hos4                                                      (unlabeled)
-------------------------------------------------------------------------

                   type:  numeric (float)

                  range:  [-1.2506195,.82704675]      units:  1.000e-10
          unique values:  101                      missing .:  0/494021

                   mean:  1.3e-08
               std. dev:  1

            percentiles:        10%       25%       50%       75%       90%
                            -1.25062  -1.25062   .827047   .827047   .827047

-------------------------------------------------------------------------
Dst_hos5                                                      (unlabeled)
-------------------------------------------------------------------------

                   type:  numeric (float)

                  range:  [-.15862913,23.575806]      units:  1.000e-08
          unique values:  65                       missing .:  0/494021

                   mean:  -3.9e-09
               std. dev:  1

            percentiles:        10%       25%       50%       75%       90%
                            -.158629  -.158629  -.158629  -.158629   .078715

-------------------------------------------------------------------------
Dst_hos6                                                      (unlabeled)
-------------------------------------------------------------------------

                   type:  numeric (float)

                  range:  [-.46441716,2.1630609]      units:  1.000e-09
          unique values:  100                      missing .:  0/494021

                   mean:  3.1e-09
               std. dev:  1

            percentiles:        10%       25%       50%       75%       90%
                            -.464417  -.464417  -.464417  -.464417   2.16306

-------------------------------------------------------------------------
Dst_hos7                                                      (unlabeled)
-------------------------------------------------------------------------

                   type:  numeric (float)

                  range:  [-.46320191,2.162025]       units:  1.000e-09
          unique values:  72                       missing .:  0/494021

                   mean:  1.7e-09
               std. dev:  1

            percentiles:        10%       25%       50%       75%       90%
                            -.463202  -.463202  -.463202  -.463202   2.16202

-------------------------------------------------------------------------
Dst_hos8                                                      (unlabeled)
-------------------------------------------------------------------------

                   type:  numeric (float)

                  range:  [-.25203925,4.0846715]      units:  1.000e-09
          unique values:  101                      missing .:  0/494021

                   mean:  1.2e-08
               std. dev:  1

            percentiles:        10%       25%       50%       75%       90%
                            -.252039  -.252039  -.252039  -.252039  -.252039

-------------------------------------------------------------------------
Dst_hos9                                                      (unlabeled)
-------------------------------------------------------------------------

                   type:  numeric (float)

                  range:  [-.24946375,4.0957112]      units:  1.000e-09
          unique values:  101                      missing .:  0/494021

                   mean:  -4.5e-09
               std. dev:  1

            percentiles:        10%       25%       50%       75%       90%
                            -.249464  -.249464  -.249464  -.249464  -.249464
.
. log close
       log:  D:\Nova\KDD_BSP\codebook.smcl
  log type:  smcl
 closed on:  8 Jul 2007, 15:41:55
-------------------------------------------------------------------------
```

Chapter VI
Data Reduction

One must not lose desires. They are mighty stimulants to creativeness, to love, and to long life.

- Alexander A. Bogomoletz

INTRODUCTION

This chapter discusses several data reduction techniques that are important in intrusion detection and prevention. Network traffic data includes rich information about system and user behavior, but the raw data itself can be difficult to analyze due to its large size. Being able to efficiently reduce data size is one of the key challenges in network security and has been raised by many researchers over the past decade (Lam, Hui & Chung, 1996; Mukkamala, Tadiparthi, Tummala, & Janoski, 2003; Chebrolu, Abraham & Thomas, 2005; Khan, Awad & Thuraisingham, 2007).

Recall the concept of the data cube which was presented in Chapter IV; using various approaches, it is possible to reduce the size of data in all three cube dimensions (variables, observations, and occasions). More specifically, we can reduce the total number of observations by sampling network traffic, reduce the total number of variables by eliminating variables that are not robust and do not associate with the outcome of interest, and reduce the number of occasions by taking a sample of the time-related events. We will discuss these approaches in the following sections, including data structure detection, sampling, and sample size determination. In addition to statistical approaches for data reduction, we need to carefully select a data type for each variable to ensure that the final size of a given dataset does not increase due to any inappropriate data types. For example, we shall use the *byte* to store a binary variable.

Data reduction heavily involves multivariate analysis on which a great number of literatures are available on this topic. Readers who are interested in gaining a better understanding of detailed and advanced multivariate analysis can refer to Thomson (1951), Bartholomew (1987), Snook & Gorsuch (1989), Everitt & Dunn (1991), Kachigan (1991), Loehlin (1992), Hatcher & Stepanski (1994), Rencher (1995), Tabachnick (2000), and Everitt (2005).

DATA STRUCTURE DETECTION

As discussed in Chapter V, exploratory data analysis is essential in understanding raw traffic data and in seeking potential patterns and relationships within the data. It provides directions for further data examinations. If we believe that there is some redundancy in the observations and variables that are obtained from the exploratory data analysis, we can employ multivariate analysis to address such redundancies (Ye, Emran, Chen & Vilbert, 2002). In general, data structure detection employs various multivariate analysis approaches to aim on three basic tasks: (1) to identify variable(s) redundancy, (2) to identify underlying immeasurable but important variables and (3) to eliminate or minimize as much statistical noise as possible.

Factor Analysis

Factor analysis (Cattell, 1952; Kim & Mueller, 1978a & 1978b) is one of the common data reducing approaches, which removes redundant information from among a set of random variables. Studies have suggested that there are some benefits to employing factor analysis in network security (Wu & Zhang, 2003; Wat, Ngai & Cheng, 2005). The goal of factor analysis is to identify the internal relationship and patterns of such a relationship between a set of variables. This goal leads factor analysis to typically focus on a correlation matrix and aims to use a few factors to represent a large dimension of raw data. Factor analysis assumes that there are latent factors existing that represent the covariation for the observed variables. The latent factors, however, are unobservable, but have linear combinations of the directly measurable variables that represent similar attributes and characteristics of the data. If we believe that the data contain certain latent factors and exert causal influence on the observed variables on which we are focusing, we can use factor analysis to identify such latent factors.

To achieve the goal of factor analysis, we examine the relationship between the directly measurable variables, and classify variables into different groups where variables have similar structure and are highly correlated. Ideally, we would like each of these groups to represent one dimension of information, and the correlation between each dimension needs to be low. Thus, we create factors to represent each of these groups.

Factor analysis usually involves three steps: (1) extraction of factors; (2) rotation of factors for interpretation; and (3) name assignment and interpretation of each factor based on the estimated values for the factor loadings. A number of methods can be used for extracting factors, including the maximum-likelihood factor, the principal-components factor, the principal factor, and the iterated principal factor methods. The main advantage of using the maximum-likelihood factor method is that it provides a test of the hypothesis that m common factors are sufficient to describe the data against possible alternative hypotheses of $m + j$ common factors providing a better fit of the data.

Let X be a set of k observed random variables, $x_1, x_2, \ldots x_k$, and let F be a set of unobserved latent factors, $f_1, f_2, \ldots f_m$ $(m < k)$. A factor analysis model can be represented as

$$x_1 = \lambda_{11} f_1 + \lambda_{12} f_2 + \cdots + \lambda_{1m} f_m + \varepsilon_1$$

$$x_2 = \lambda_{21} f_1 + \lambda_{22} f_2 + \cdots + \lambda_{2m} f_m + \varepsilon_2$$

$$\vdots$$

$$x_k = \lambda_{k1} f_1 + \lambda_{k2} f_2 + \cdots + \lambda_{km} f_m + \varepsilon_k, \qquad (6\text{-}1)$$

where λ_{ij} $(i = 1, 2, \ldots, k$ and $j = 1, 2, \ldots, m)$ are factor loadings for x_i, and ε_i is a measurement error for x_i. Note that in Equation (6-1), the initial variable set, X, is represented by a linear function of a smaller number of factors, F, which are unobservable and used to predict the values of the observed variables, X. Because $m < k$, the dimensionality of data is reduced.

Factor analysis has two primary assumptions: (1) The measurement errors, ε_i, are normally distributed with mean 0 and a constant variance, $\varepsilon \sim N(0, \sigma^2)$, and (2) measurement errors are independent from the factors, F, and of each other; that is, $Cov(F, e_i) = 0$ and $Cov(e_j, e_i) = 0$.

Since the independent factors, F, in the above linear equations are latent variables, the traditional least squares technique cannot be used to estimate the factor loadings. Two main modeling approaches have been developed to address this issue: confirmatory factor analysis and exploratory factor analysis. In confirmatory factor analysis, we have to specify the exact number of factors there are in the model, and specify which observed variables depend on which factors. In exploratory factor analysis, we do not pre-determine the number of factors, but rather, let the algorithm select. However, the final factors vary by algorithms.

Figure 6.1 Diagrammatical representation of factors, variables, and measurement errors relationships

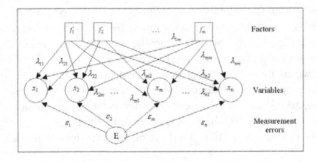

Because factor analysis can significantly reduce the number of data dimensions, it has a great role in network security. Assume the initial traffic data included k variables that can be represented by m factors—we can only keep the m factors in the final data. When m is much smaller than k, the amount of resources saved is remarkable.

Example 6.1→Fit Factor Analysis with Spam-email Data The spam-email data includes 57 continuous variables and one binary response variable (spam yes/no). Let us illustrate how to use factor analysis to reduce the total number of variables and compare the performances in classification between the full variable-based model and the factor-based model. We will illustrate the results by using both principal factor and the maximum-likelihood factor methods. First we fit the data with the principal factor method. The Stata codes to conduct this analysis are listed in Display 6.1.

Display 6.1
Stata codes to fit a factor analysis model with spam data

```
/* Conduct the factor analysis using principal factor method */
factor v1-v57,pf
/* Plots of eigenvalues */
screeplot,mean
```

Stata determines 30 factors from a total of 57 variables as shown in Display 6.2. The criterion of retaining the 30 factors is the eigenvalue ($E \geq 0$) that measures the variance in all of the variables, which is accounted for by a given factor. We then can use the score plot to plot the eigenvalues in decreasing order to further determine the number of factors to be retained (Figure 6.2). Although the model retained 30 factors, the plot shows that only the first 15 factors appear to be meaningful.

Display 6.2
30 factors retained from the factor analysis model with the eigenvalue value $E \geq 0$

```
. factor v1-v57,pf
(obs=4601)

Factor analysis/correlation                    Number of obs    =       4601
    Method: principal factors                  Retained factors =         30
    Rotation: (unrotated)                      Number of params =       1275

    --------------------------------------------------------------------------
        Factor  |   Eigenvalue   Difference        Proportion   Cumulative
    ------------+-------------------------------------------------------------
        Factor1  |      6.24146      3.72157           0.4643       0.4643
        Factor2  |      2.51989      1.18251           0.1875       0.6518
        Factor3  |      1.33738      0.49275           0.0995       0.7513
        Factor4  |      0.84463      0.04947           0.0628       0.8141
        Factor5  |      0.79516      0.12338           0.0592       0.8732
        Factor6  |      0.67178      0.02886           0.0500       0.9232
        Factor7  |      0.64292      0.00716           0.0478       0.9710
        Factor8  |      0.63577      0.14833           0.0473       1.0183
        Factor9  |      0.48744      0.04043           0.0363       1.0546
        Factor10 |      0.44701      0.01861           0.0333       1.0879
        Factor11 |      0.42840      0.12576           0.0319       1.1197
        Factor12 |      0.30264      0.00169           0.0225       1.1422
        Factor13 |      0.30094      0.07600           0.0224       1.1646
        Factor14 |      0.22495      0.01241           0.0167       1.1814
```

continued on following page

Display 6.2 continued

```
Factor15  |    0.21254      0.01741          0.0158      1.1972
Factor16  |    0.19513      0.01605          0.0145      1.2117
Factor17  |    0.17908      0.02086          0.0133      1.2250
Factor18  |    0.15822      0.01907          0.0118      1.2368
Factor19  |    0.13915      0.01936          0.0104      1.2471
Factor20  |    0.11979      0.01270          0.0089      1.2560
Factor21  |    0.10708      0.00901          0.0080      1.2640
Factor22  |    0.09807      0.01877          0.0073      1.2713
Factor23  |    0.07930      0.01823          0.0059      1.2772
Factor24  |    0.06107      0.01464          0.0045      1.2817
Factor25  |    0.04643      0.00471          0.0035      1.2852
Factor26  |    0.04172      0.00844          0.0031      1.2883
Factor27  |    0.03327      0.00466          0.0025      1.2908
Factor28  |    0.02862      0.01490          0.0021      1.2929
Factor29  |    0.01372      0.01280          0.0010      1.2939
Factor30  |    0.00092      0.00470          0.0001      1.2940
Factor31  |   -0.00378      0.00896         -0.0003      1.2937
Factor32  |   -0.01274      0.01181         -0.0009      1.2928
Factor33  |   -0.02455      0.01361         -0.0018      1.2909
Factor34  |   -0.03816      0.00827         -0.0028      1.2881
Factor35  |   -0.04644      0.01384         -0.0035      1.2847
Factor36  |   -0.06028      0.00742         -0.0045      1.2802
Factor37  |   -0.06770      0.00610         -0.0050      1.2751
Factor38  |   -0.07379      0.01165         -0.0055      1.2696
Factor39  |   -0.08544      0.01563         -0.0064      1.2633
Factor40  |   -0.10107      0.01159         -0.0075      1.2558
Factor41  |   -0.11265      0.00782         -0.0084      1.2474
Factor42  |   -0.12047      0.01240         -0.0090      1.2384
Factor43  |   -0.13287      0.00357         -0.0099      1.2285
Factor44  |   -0.13644      0.01164         -0.0101      1.2184
Factor45  |   -0.14807      0.00267         -0.0110      1.2074
Factor46  |   -0.15074      0.01951         -0.0112      1.1962
Factor47  |   -0.17025      0.01618         -0.0127      1.1835
Factor48  |   -0.18643      0.01327         -0.0139      1.1696
Factor49  |   -0.19970      0.00672         -0.0149      1.1548
Factor50  |   -0.20643      0.01525         -0.0154      1.1394
Factor51  |   -0.22167      0.01130         -0.0165      1.1229
Factor52  |   -0.23297      0.01707         -0.0173      1.1056
Factor53  |   -0.25004      0.01225         -0.0186      1.0870
Factor54  |   -0.26229      0.03083         -0.0195      1.0675
Factor55  |   -0.29313      0.00424         -0.0218      1.0457
Factor56  |   -0.29737      0.01924         -0.0221      1.0236
Factor57  |   -0.31660         .            -0.0236      1.0000
-------------------------------------------------------------------------
LR test: independent vs. saturated: chi2(1596) = 7.0e+04 Prob>chi2 = 0.0000
Factor loadings (pattern matrix) and unique variances
```

Figure 6.2 Eigenvalue plot based on principal factor analysis

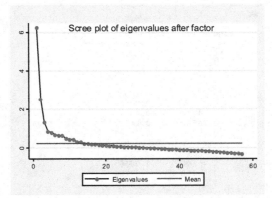

Next we show the factor loadings or pattern matrix and the unique variances represented by the column of *uniqueness*, which is the percentage of variance for the variable that is not explained by the factors (Display 6.3). A high uniqueness indicates that the variable is not well explained by the factors. Usually, values over 0.6 are considered high.

Display 6.3
Factor loading and unique variances (see Appendix CH VI for a full output)

```
Factor loadings (pattern matrix) and unique variances
-------------------------------------------------------------------------------------------
    Variable |  Factor1   Factor2   Factor3   Factor4   Factor5   Factor6   Factor7   Factor8
-------------+-----------------------------------------------------------------------------
          v1 |  -0.0939    0.2575   -0.0834    0.0162    0.0624   -0.0495    0.0438    0.0437
          v2 |  -0.0249   -0.0218   -0.0095    0.0132   -0.0559    0.0066   -0.0404   -0.0232
          v3 |  -0.1023    0.2507   -0.0324   -0.0286    0.0725    0.0127   -0.0475   -0.0119
          v4 |  -0.0135    0.0174    0.0104   -0.0009   -0.0343    0.0116    0.0053   -0.0026
          v5 |  -0.0791    0.1827   -0.1299   -0.2047    0.0663   -0.0098    0.0566    0.0200
          v6 |  -0.0985    0.2545   -0.0242    0.0703    0.0316    0.1317   -0.0758    0.0377
          v7 |  -0.0999    0.2179   -0.1338   -0.0026   -0.0221   -0.0616    0.1076   -0.0405
          v8 |  -0.0728    0.1971   -0.0659    0.0599    0.0608   -0.0388    0.1181   -0.0338
       output omitted (see Appendix for Chapter 6)
-------------------------------------------------------------------------------------------
```

Both SAS and Stata have an option that allows us to select the number of factors. We can also rotate the loading matrix both orthogonally and obliquely rotations in Stata and SAS. The following Stata codes given in Display 6.4 retain 15 factors and then rotate the loading matrix orthogonally (output ignored).

Display 6.4
Stata codes for restricting 15 factors and rotating the loading matrix orthogonally

```
/* Limit factor analysis to 15 factors */
factor v1-v57,pf  factor(15)
/*  Rotate the loading matrix orthogonally */
Rotate
```

Performing the maximum-likelihood factor method using the same data retrieved 19 factors for a total of 57 variables. The corresponding Stata codes and results are shown in Displays 6.5, 6.6 and 6.7, respectively. Figure 6.3 shows the eigenvalue plot corresponding to the results.

Display 6.5
Stata codes to fit a maximum-likelihood factor analysis model

```
/* Conduct the factor analysis using maximum-likelihood method */
factor v1-v57,ml
/* Plots of eigenvalues */
Screeplot
```

Display 6.6
Results of the maximum-likelihood factor analysis model

```
. factor v1-v57,ml
(obs=4601)
Factor analysis/correlation                    Number of obs    =    4601
   Method: maximum likelihood                  Retained factors =      19
   Rotation: (unrotated)                       Number of params =     912
                                               Schwarz's BIC    = 9186.13
   Log likelihood = -747.1462                  (Akaike's) AIC   = 3318.29
   Beware: solution is a Heywood case
   (i.e., invalid or boundary values of uniqueness)
   -----------------------------------------------------------------------
       Factor  |  Eigenvalue   Difference        Proportion   Cumulative
   -----------+-----------------------------------------------------------
       Factor1  |    1.30060     -0.56764           0.0607       0.0607
       Factor2  |    1.86823      0.62655           0.0872       0.1479
       Factor3  |    1.24168     -3.64719           0.0580       0.2059
       Factor4  |    4.88888      3.15605           0.2282       0.4341
       Factor5  |    1.73283      0.55729           0.0809       0.5150
       Factor6  |    1.17553     -0.02855           0.0549       0.5699
       Factor7  |    1.20408     -0.27498           0.0562       0.6261
       Factor8  |    1.47906      0.09988           0.0690       0.6951
       Factor9  |    1.37918      0.65283           0.0644       0.7595
      Factor10  |    0.72635     -0.16232           0.0339       0.7934
      Factor11  |    0.88867      0.09973           0.0415       0.8349
      Factor12  |    0.78894      0.16918           0.0368       0.8717
      Factor13  |    0.61976      0.09346           0.0289       0.9007
      Factor14  |    0.52631      0.07321           0.0246       0.9252
      Factor15  |    0.45310      0.18412           0.0212       0.9464
      Factor16  |    0.26898     -0.04989           0.0126       0.9589
      Factor17  |    0.31887      0.00123           0.0149       0.9738
      Factor18  |    0.31763      0.07473           0.0148       0.9887
      Factor19  |    0.24291          .             0.0113       1.0000
   -----------------------------------------------------------------------
LR test: independent vs. saturated: chi2(1596)= 7.0e+04 Prob>chi2 = 0.0000
LR test:  19 factors vs. saturated: chi2(684) = 1483.74 Prob>chi2 = 0.0000
(tests formally not valid because a Heywood case was encountered)
```

Figure 6.3 Eigenvalues loading based on maximum-likelihood factor analysis

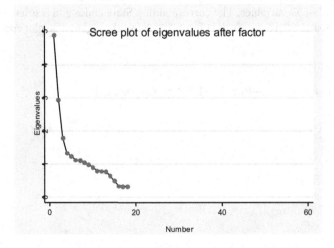

In the above results, the "Eigenvalue" column shows the initial variance of the corresponding factor, and the "Difference" column represents the difference of eigenvalues between the first factor and the second factor (e.g., 1.30060 - 1.86823 = -0.56764). This column provides information about the changes in eigenvalues. The "Proportion" column provides information about the proportion of the total variance accounted by each factor, and the last column illustrates the sum of the proportion variance column.

Display 6.7
Factor loadings of the maximum-likelihood factor analysis model

Factor loadings (pattern matrix) and unique variances

Variable	Factor1	Factor2	Factor3	Factor4	Factor5	Factor6	Factor7	Factor8	Factor9	Factor10
v1	-0.0256	-0.0209	-0.0269	-0.0275	0.0830	-0.0467	-0.0717	0.1375	0.2342	0.0072
v2	-0.0244	-0.0500	-0.0138	0.0113	0.0230	-0.0359		-0.0214	-0.0554	0.0148
v3	-0.0054	-0.0152	-0.0373	-0.0610	0.1608	0.0024	-0.0798	0.0941	0.1357	0.0945
v4	-0.0081	-0.0137	0.0268	-0.0033	0.0108	-0.0087	-0.0178	0.0207	-0.0078	-0.0042
v5	0.1158	-0.0425	-0.0209	-0.0143	0.1041	-0.0342	-0.1005	0.0451	0.1859	0.1055
v6	-0.0547	-0.0104	0.0057	-0.0378	0.2049	0.0220	-0.0444	0.0556	0.1512	-0.0231
v7	-0.0489	-0.0530	-0.0080	-0.0276	0.0916	-0.0514	-0.0831	0.0391	0.2069	0.1172
v8	-0.0430	-0.0329	-0.0202	-0.0267	0.0977	0.0003	-0.0545	0.0544	0.1407	0.0171
v9	-0.0476	-0.0314	-0.0237	-0.0275	0.2701	0.0767	-0.0846	0.2437	0.0761	-0.0162
v10	-0.0546	0.0022	0.0070	-0.0177	0.1674	0.0612	-0.0400	0.0858	0.0886	0.0520
v11	-0.0423	-0.0557	-0.0164	-0.0224	0.1192	-0.0266	-0.0945	0.1603	0.2856	0.0147
v12	0.1120	-0.0262	-0.0446	-0.0485	0.0362	0.0137	-0.0924	0.0372	0.1650	0.0006
v13	-0.0378	-0.0508	-0.0355	-0.0184	0.1133	-0.0045	-0.0409	0.1021	0.1307	-0.0782
v14	0.0054	-0.0049	-0.0198	-0.0183	0.0187	-0.0336	-0.0495	0.1641	0.0121	-0.1227
v15	-0.0318	-0.0032	-0.0054	-0.0249	0.8497	0.4615	0.0621	-0.0897	-0.0181	0.0050
v16	-0.0366	-0.0472	-0.0119	-0.0279	0.0518	-0.0752	-0.0722	0.0326	0.1480	0.0536
v17	-0.0400	-0.0360	-0.0253	-0.0339	0.0643	-0.0271	-0.1023	0.1299	0.2805	0.0595
v18	-0.0467	-0.0360	-0.0309	-0.0334	0.2394	0.1181	-0.0344	-0.0054	0.0849	0.0249
v19	-0.0860	-0.1299	-0.0373	-0.0411	0.1463	-0.1579	-0.0530	0.0439	0.4984	0.0580
v20	-0.0287	-0.0235	0.0312	-0.0188	0.0540	-0.0276	-0.0609	0.1292	0.1243	0.0589
v21	-0.0799	-0.0862	-0.0310	-0.0286	0.1704	-0.0991	-0.1381	0.1289	0.4493	0.0985
v22	-0.0260	-0.0861	0.9959	0.0000	-0.0000	0.0000	0.0000	-0.0000	0.0000	0.0000
v23	-0.0495	-0.0353	0.0189	-0.0349	0.3852	0.1286	-0.0560	0.0976	0.1844	-0.0575
v24	-0.0336	-0.0335	-0.0147	-0.0221	0.0807	-0.0394	-0.0614	0.1040	0.2113	-0.0189
v25	0.0178	0.1387	-0.0264	0.3520	-0.4604	0.7689	0.0183	0.0401	0.0547	0.0072
v26	0.0562	0.1474	-0.0210	0.3404	-0.2291	0.3663	0.0111	-0.0429	-0.1112	-0.0099
v27	-0.0049	-0.0277	-0.0296	0.0923	-0.0335	-0.0545	-0.0191	-0.1152	-0.2060	0.0036
v28	-0.0003	0.3143	-0.0003	0.4915	-0.1054	0.1254	0.0207	-0.0953	-0.1931	0.0121
v29	0.4313	0.1703	0.0062	0.4836	-0.0123	0.0169	-0.0045	-0.0138	-0.0238	0.0021
v30	-0.0190	0.2244	-0.0078	0.6264	-0.1325	0.1967	0.0208	-0.0335	-0.0999	0.0160
v31	-0.0139	0.2334	0.0008	0.7031	-0.0508	0.0750	-0.0033	-0.0243	-0.1119	0.0037
v32	-0.0120	0.3046	0.0090	0.9514	0.0070	-0.0097	0.0001	0.0000	0.0019	-0.0015
v33	0.0102	0.0296	-0.0166	-0.0268	-0.0283	0.0051	-0.0090	-0.0373	-0.1373	-0.0549
v34	-0.0124	0.3035	0.0087	0.9494	0.0073	-0.0105	-0.0009	0.0054	-0.0001	0.0046
v35	0.0290	0.2021	-0.0052	0.5243	-0.0777	0.1125	0.0121	-0.0446	-0.1652	0.0026
v36	-0.0263	0.2455	-0.0068	0.6914	-0.0836	0.1137	-0.0101	-0.0345	-0.1390	-0.0132
v37	0.0116	0.1090	-0.0235	0.0011	-0.1096	0.0958	0.1651	-0.0205	-0.1657	-0.0711
v38	0.1676	-0.0059	-0.0011	-0.0041	0.0085	0.0038	-0.0080	-0.0009	0.0068	0.0075
v39	0.0346	0.1093	-0.0086	0.0127	-0.0430	0.0250	0.0230	-0.0848	-0.0885	-0.0154
v40	-0.0206	0.2686	0.0011	0.8058	0.0550	0.0457	-0.0078	-0.0064	-0.0125	0.0092
v41	-0.0137	0.0177	-0.0131	-0.0163	-0.0317	-0.0170	0.3715	0.0286	-0.0440	-0.0062
v42	0.9999	0.0136	0.0068	0.0000	0.0000	-0.0000	0.0000	0.0000	0.0000	-0.0000
v43	0.0165	0.0617	-0.0159	0.1057	-0.0044	0.0979	0.0562	-0.0674	-0.1162	-0.0265
v44	0.0105	-0.0025	-0.0119	0.0060	-0.0229	-0.0098	-0.0066	-0.0545	-0.0875	-0.0015
v45	0.0079	0.0029	-0.0317	0.0162	-0.0672	0.0113	0.0629	-0.0833	0.0249	0.0306
v46	-0.0196	0.0150	-0.0201	-0.0259	-0.0293	-0.0997	0.9296	0.1267	0.0458	0.0068
v47	0.0132	-0.0024	-0.0083	0.0020	-0.0110	-0.0020	-0.0114	0.0006	-0.0129	-0.0174
v48	-0.0003	-0.0123	-0.0143	-0.0082	-0.0264	-0.0052	-0.0099	-0.0250	-0.0817	-0.0196
v49	-0.0111	0.0323	0.4208	-0.0235	-0.0399	0.0324	0.0316	0.0096	-0.0240	-0.0191
v50	-0.0270	0.9989	0.0392	-0.0003	-0.0000	-0.0000	-0.0000	-0.0000	0.0000	-0.0000
v51	0.0108	0.0226	0.0011	0.0079	-0.0253	0.0366	0.0105	-0.0167	-0.0930	-0.0368
v52	-0.0376	-0.0311	-0.0085	-0.0349	0.0726	-0.0662	-0.0562	0.0848	0.1605	0.0722
v53	-0.0442	0.0439	-0.0084	-0.0611	0.1872	-0.0013	-0.0960	0.2373	0.2015	-0.0268
v54	-0.0054	0.0159	0.1864	-0.0172	-0.0330	0.0644	-0.0159	0.0420	0.0340	0.0185
v55	-0.0185	0.0330	0.0240	-0.0210	0.0629	0.0047	-0.0733	0.4669	-0.2052	0.6425
v56	-0.0400	0.3680	0.0587	-0.1491	0.2702	0.0755	-0.1039	0.5676	-0.0854	0.2645
v57	-0.0587	0.1063	0.1120	-0.0861	0.2201	0.0770	-0.1303	0.7418	-0.1127	-0.3708

continued on following page

Display 6.7 continued

Variable	Factor11	Factor12	Factor13	Factor14	Factor15	Factor16	Factor17	Factor18	Factor19	Uniqueness
v1	0.0803	0.0781	-0.0310	-0.0203	0.1250	-0.1351	-0.1937	0.2088	0.0046	0.7805
v2	-0.0578	-0.0451	0.0339	0.0073	-0.0184	-0.0178	-0.0041	0.0538	-0.0775	0.9744
v3	0.1012	0.0194	-0.0859	-0.0194	0.0393	0.0316	0.0657	0.0957	0.1420	0.8717
v4	-0.0016	-0.0167	0.0113	0.0229	-0.0095	0.0050	-0.0072	0.0382	-0.0323	0.9946
v5	0.0351	-0.0171	0.0998	-0.0123	-0.0666	0.0722	0.2602	0.0658	0.1469	0.7994
v6	0.0275	-0.0350	0.0209	0.0772	0.0586	0.0108	0.0255	-0.0091	0.0412	0.9102
v7	0.0640	0.0027	0.1813	0.0768	-0.1224	0.0911	0.2484	0.0779	-0.1722	0.7544
v8	0.0495	0.0608	0.2549	0.0845	-0.0612	-0.0288	-0.0681	-0.1756	0.0346	0.8409
v9	0.0496	0.0449	0.1424	0.0243	-0.0178	-0.0899	-0.1068	-0.0110	0.0451	0.7967
v10	0.0828	0.1022	0.0305	-0.0166	-0.0070	-0.0836	0.0253	-0.0584	-0.0730	0.9105
v11	0.1253	0.1355	0.2006	-0.0633	-0.0739	-0.0813	-0.0806	0.0848	-0.0655	0.7547
v12	0.1423	0.1788	0.0127	-0.4865	0.2695	-0.0686	0.0974	-0.0285	-0.0057	0.5671
v13	0.0276	-0.0155	-0.0841	0.1284	0.1589	0.0274	0.0247	-0.0143	-0.0268	0.8941
v14	0.0266	-0.0108	-0.0138	0.0258	0.0306	-0.0194	-0.0544	-0.0291	0.0316	0.9453
v15	-0.0123	-0.0026	-0.0029	-0.0091	-0.0069	-0.0016	-0.0023	-0.0015	0.0002	0.0507
v16	0.0279	-0.0374	0.0515	0.0836	-0.0629	0.0441	0.0540	0.1554	-0.0942	0.9025
v17	0.1204	0.0624	0.3701	0.0628	-0.0656	0.0140	0.0312	-0.1684	0.0358	0.6865
v18	0.2192	0.0212	0.0068	0.0456	-0.0857	0.0881	0.0392	0.2003	-0.0444	0.8048
v19	0.1394	0.1016	-0.3934	-0.0158	-0.1405	0.0809	0.0097	-0.0956	-0.0089	0.4494
v20	0.0518	0.0344	0.2121	0.0108	-0.0959	-0.0364	-0.0997	-0.1037	0.0530	0.8713
v21	0.1519	0.1167	0.0797	-0.0176	-0.0930	-0.0618	-0.1176	0.0570	0.0423	0.6236
v22	0.0000	0.0000	0.0000	0.0000	0.0000	-0.0000	-0.0000	-0.0000	0.0000	0.0000
v23	0.0577	-0.0453	0.0033	0.2050	0.2396	-0.0262	0.0448	-0.0309	0.0326	0.6703
v24	0.0768	0.0228	-0.0921	0.0452	-0.0031	-0.0348	-0.1747	0.1459	-0.0588	0.8560
v25	-0.0281	-0.0120	-0.0021	-0.0001	-0.0019	0.0012	-0.0021	-0.0000	-0.0004	0.0467
v26	0.0928	0.1076	-0.0095	-0.0038	0.0155	-0.0842	0.0254	0.0222	0.0248	0.6284
v27	-0.1178	-0.1229	0.0477	0.0503	-0.0150	-0.0158	-0.1110	0.0102	-0.1202	0.8685
v28	-0.4470	0.0137	-0.0658	0.0719	-0.0662	-0.2121	0.0501	-0.0215	0.0058	0.3240
v29	0.1058	0.0020	0.0110	-0.1003	0.0753	0.0206	-0.0008	-0.0933	-0.1179	0.4998
v30	0.2926	0.0137	-0.0033	-0.0042	0.0042	0.0349	0.0283	0.0107	-0.0339	0.3997
v31	0.2732	0.0202	0.0216	-0.0008	0.0423	0.2377	-0.0979	0.0268	0.0331	0.2844
v32	-0.0038	-0.0004	0.0003	-0.0007	-0.0011	-0.0004	0.0006	-0.0001	0.0000	0.0017
v33	-0.0602	0.0266	0.0255	-0.0221	-0.0099	-0.0124	0.0081	0.0061	0.0785	0.9619
v34	-0.0059	0.0003	-0.0019	0.0018	0.0027	-0.0036	-0.0003	0.0016	0.0004	0.0060
v35	0.3681	0.0003	-0.0530	0.0749	-0.0580	-0.1015	0.0179	-0.0114	-0.0010	0.4772
v36	0.2688	0.0234	0.0343	-0.0222	0.0488	0.1195	-0.0064	-0.0021	0.0139	0.3289
v37	-0.1403	0.5165	0.0573	0.1128	0.0376	0.0477	0.0459	0.0449	-0.0305	0.5949
v38	-0.0237	-0.0254	0.0328	0.0493	-0.0676	0.0267	0.0831	0.1443	0.2384	0.8770
v39	-0.0825	0.3465	-0.0540	0.0570	0.0338	0.0508	0.0034	0.0022	0.0449	0.8295
v40	0.1262	0.0032	0.0493	0.0034	0.0178	0.1068	-0.0421	-0.0482	-0.0107	0.2384
v41	0.0096	0.0914	0.0188	0.0211	0.0115	-0.0506	0.0224	0.0164	-0.0119	0.8441
v42	-0.0000	-0.0000	-0.0000	0.0000	-0.0000	0.0000	-0.0000	0.0000	0.0000	0.0000
v43	-0.1294	0.4736	-0.0385	0.1223	-0.0214	0.0049	-0.0034	-0.0070	-0.0372	0.6936
v44	-0.0081	-0.0048	0.0299	-0.0567	0.0464	0.0945	-0.0289	0.0114	0.0804	0.9657
v45	-0.1119	0.0859	-0.2044	0.0919	-0.1106	0.0591	-0.0384	-0.1630	0.0352	0.8664
v46	0.0250	-0.0152	0.0096	-0.0059	0.0030	0.0015	0.0004	0.0018	0.0019	0.1040
v47	0.0078	0.0047	-0.0228	-0.0177	-0.0225	-0.0251	-0.0326	0.0134	0.0425	0.9939
v48	-0.0145	0.0320	-0.0090	-0.0599	0.0305	-0.0237	0.0238	-0.0004	0.0064	0.9841
v49	-0.0712	0.0451	-0.0162	0.0073	0.0362	0.0058	0.0152	0.0081	0.0071	0.8074
v50	-0.0000	-0.0000	0.0000	-0.0000	-0.0000	0.0000	-0.0000	0.0000	0.0000	0.0000
v51	-0.0428	0.1093	0.0071	0.0702	-0.0251	-0.0524	0.0030	-0.0022	0.0385	0.9633
v52	0.0311	-0.0076	-0.0927	0.1002	0.0461	0.0500	0.0441	-0.0569	-0.0070	0.9159
v53	0.0704	-0.0604	-0.0203	0.3140	0.3776	-0.0301	0.0396	-0.0228	-0.0189	0.5969
v54	0.0310	-0.0437	0.0086	0.0278	-0.0221	0.0753	0.0542	0.0398	-0.1143	0.9284
v55	-0.0428	0.0287	-0.0333	0.0044	0.0312	-0.0290	-0.0146	-0.0081	0.0250	0.3088
v56	-0.0221	-0.0145	-0.0281	-0.0233	-0.0289	0.0530	0.0076	-0.0007	-0.0504	0.3401
v57	0.0127	0.0041	-0.0261	-0.0238	-0.0500	0.0047	0.0183	-0.0041	0.0056	0.1891

Example 6.2→Use Factor Analysis to Identify Patterns of User Interests in the Internet
The web sequence data provide important information on user's interests in addition to the order of webpages visited. For example, let A, B, and C represent three different webpages, and let the sequence of visits be ABC, CAB, and BAC for three individual users, we can consider all three users have a similar interest pattern regardless of the order that these pages visited. That is, because of users A, B, and C share a similar interest, we can categorize them into one group. In practical, being able to profile users based on their interests is an important step to protect the system from malicious codes downloadable from the web, and we can use factor analysis to conduct such an interest-based profiling analysis.

Using SAS codes given in Display 3.8 we can reshape the web sequence data from the initial row-based format to the column-based format as shown in Table 3.13. The reshaped data includes 32711 individual users (rows), a user ID variable and 294 binary variables that each represents a particular website visiting status where a variable that has a value of 1 indicates that the website has been visited by the corresponding user, and 0 otherwise. Remember that our goal is to detect the data structure by classifying these 294 websites into *m* groups (*m* < 294), of which each represents one dimension of the interests of 32711 users, regardless of the order of their visits.

Unlike in Example 6.1, where there were only continuous variables, here we have all binary variables from our reshaped data. Although both SAS and Stata support factor analysis with binary data, we have to involve additional procedures. Stata provides a *tetrachoric* command to create a matrix of tetrachoric correlation coefficients of the binary variables to be analyzed. We can then use the *factormat* command to conduct a factor analysis based on this matrix (Display 6.8). Note the Stata's *tetrachoric* procedure computes pairwise estimates of the tetrachoric correlations following Edwards & Edwards (1984), and requires the resulting correlation matrix to be positive semidefinite. The *posdef* option in Display 6.8 aims to modify the correlation matrix to be positive definite or positive semidefinite. However, even with the *posdef* option we may not be guaranteed that the matrix is positive definite or positive semidefinite, and the Stata's *factormat* command will return an error message of "matrix not positive definite."

Display 6.8
Stata codes for conduct factor analysis of binary data

```
#delimit;
clear;
set mem 232431;
use "F:\Book\Chapter 6\SQ_row.dta", clear;

tetrachoric
vcode1000-vcode1046 vcode1048-vcode1284 vcode1295,notable posdef available;
matrix C = r(corr);
matrix symeigen eigenvectors eigenvalues=C;
matrix list eigenvalues;
factormat C,n(32711) ipf;
```

Similarly, SAS performs factor analysis of binary data through the latent trait modeling approach. SAS provides a macro called *Polychor* that can be downloaded from the SAS technical support web site, http://support.sas.com/ctx/samples/index.jsp?sid=512, and it creates a matrix of tetrachoric correlations for binary variables. With this matrix, we can then employ *PROC CALIS* or *PROC FACTOR* to conduct exploratory analysis. Display 6.9 presents SAS codes to conduct factor analysis of binary data based on web sequence data.

Display 6.9
SAS codes to conduct factor analysis of binary data based on web sequence data

```
%include "F:\Book\Chapter 6\polychor.sas";
%let infile1="F:\Book\Chapter 6\msweb-train-Attrib.txt";
%let infile2= "F:\Book\Chapter 6\msweb-train-case.txt";
%InputData(&infile1, &infile2, attrib, TEMPz);
/*-----------------------------------------------
 The most visited websites:
  0.01=47 websites
  0.1 = 7 websites
----------------------------------------------*/;
%let OutVar;
%FREQ_Cutoff(TEMPz, vcode1000-vcode1295,0.01)
proc means data=tempz;
var &outvar;
run;
data tempz1 (keep=user_ID vcode1000-vcode1046 vcode1048-vcode1284 vcode1295);
set tempz;
run;
%polychor(data=tempz1, var=_numeric_, type=corr,out=corrx,maxiter=100);
proc print noobs;
run;

proc factor data=corrx(TYPE='CORR') rotate=varimax score outstat=fact;
var vcode1000-vcode1046 vcode1048-vcode1284 vcode1295;
run;
/*-----------------------------------------------
 Output results of the retrieved factors
----------------------------------------------*/;
data group;
set fact;
if _TYPE_='PATTERN';
run;
proc transpose data=group out=long_group;
by _TYPE_;
run;

data long_group (drop=j);
array group[16] g1-g16;
set long_group;
max=max(of Factor1 - factor16);
group[1]=factor1; group[2]=factor2; group[3]=factor3; group[4]=factor4;
group[5]=factor5; group[6]=factor6; group[7]=factor7; group[8]=factor8;
group[9]=factor9; group[10]=factor10; group[11]=factor11; group[12]=factor12;
group[13]=factor13; group[14]=factor14;
group[15]=factor15; group[16]=factor16;
do j=1 to 16;
   if group[j]=max then Factor_gp=j;
end;
run;
data gp (keep=_NAME_ Factor_gp);
set long_group;
run;
proc sort data=gp;
by Factor_gp;
run;
```

Among the total of 294 binary variables, 285 have at least one visit and were included in the factor analysis. The results of the factor analysis are illustrated in Display 6.10, in which 16 factors are retrieved based on the principal-components factor method. The second part of Display 6.10 lists the rotated factor pattern for the first 6 factors and the 25 variables.

Display 6.10
Stata output of factor analysis of binary data

```
                        The FACTOR Procedure
                Initial Factor Method: Principal Components

                  Prior Communality Estimates: ONE


     Eigenvalues of the Correlation Matrix: Total = 285  Average = 1

              Eigenvalue    Difference    Proportion    Cumulative

         1    48.852185     23.858626       0.1714        0.1714
         2    24.993558      0.485767       0.0877        0.2591
         3    24.507791      4.176016       0.0860        0.3451
         4    20.331775      1.455398       0.0713        0.4164
         Output omitted (see Appendix CH6 for a full list)

     16 factors will be retained by the PROPORTION criterion.


                        The FACTOR Procedure
                     Rotation Method: Varimax

                       Rotated Factor Pattern

              Factor1     Factor2     Factor3     Factor4     Factor5     Factor6
vcode1000    0.29028184  -0.4170722   0.48959839  0.14449275  0.30723029  -0.3839571
vcode1001    0.59799452  -0.0829008   0.06310615  0.07666938  0.96339622  -0.2374128
vcode1002    0.43337541  -0.3622487  -0.108287   -0.4009233   0.12162139  -0.2541972
vcode1003    0.52142303  -0.2249713   0.08632207  0.12339422  0.63022495   0.70639794
vcode1004    0.22538698  -0.1482475  -0.1089298   0.07153502  0.15615845   0.5994879
vcode1005    0.05921365   0.35906725  0.04177892  0.22722969  -0.0903178  -0.0653921
vcode1006    0.52715942  -0.1066312   0.02024513 -0.0821561   0.08920071  -0.240753
vcode1007    0.02967682  -0.0817342  -0.144611   -0.1641886  -0.1554468  -0.2563858
vcode1008    0.21036504  -0.1026657   0.04271665 -0.0992985   0.14908234  -0.4569285
vcode1009    0.62828593  -0.081704   -0.1151818   0.04339597  0.22918468  -0.2153845
vcode1010    0.37505323  -0.6293515   0.06687647  0.29118165  -0.1656178  -0.0821946
vcode1011    0.58210756  -0.4087405   0.7503233   0.24082122  -0.5067897  -0.128836
vcode1012    0.41586158  -0.031693    0.65652191  0.55099729  -0.5066823  -0.1437531
vcode1013    0.20974149  -0.2926418   0.13422563  0.71992292  0.46683993  -0.1550077
vcode1014    0.36683102  -0.3451469   0.72515821 -0.0230961  -0.0993997  -0.2981008
vcode1015    0.02699034  -0.2816997   0.98290651 -0.2118993   0.05941777   0.12124898
vcode1016    0.38629099  -0.2778496   0.76997836 -0.1364697  -0.169191   -0.072559
vcode1017    0.44192007  -0.2727542   0.07607309 -0.1084647   0.27233577  -0.3465888
vcode1018    0.45078351  -0.035215   -0.0049947  -0.086405    0.57168207  -0.4093773
vcode1019    0.26401214  -0.1423222   0.31031062 -0.5593727  -0.0485029   0.16140668
vcode1020    0.58270848  -0.4311838   0.05005537  0.26517856  -0.1519301   0.83964138
vcode1021    0.6668649   -0.2332533   0.03793021  0.14740052  -0.2533241   0.90741389
vcode1022    0.32244719  -0.4800808  -0.0197385  -0.1307596  -0.2949417   0.06145172
vcode1023    0.09158584  -0.2014934  -0.2924102  -0.1275424   0.03469409  -0.1655896
vcode1024    0.72700865  -0.1965649  -0.468752    0.17715632  -0.1961442  -0.1167628
vcode1025    0.16397523  -0.2687981   0.06943191  0.17806272  -0.322881   -0.2724832
```

Table 6.1 shows how the 285 variables can be grouped into the 16 factors based on the maximum the factor loadings. Using the detailed website labels listed in Appendix A of Chapter III, we notice, for example, that Factor 4 (F4) groups 10 websites together: OLE Development (v1028), Microsoft OLE DB (v1101), ActiveX Data Objects (v1129), Site Builder Workshop (v1143), For Developers Only News (v1144), Advanced Data Connector (v1149), ODBC Development (v1187), Repository (v1190), Internet Control Pack (v1207), and Windows NT Developer Support (v1231). Therefore, it is clear that Factor 4 represents users with interests in database-related computer programming developments.

Principal Component Analysis

Principal component analysis, which was introduced by Pearson (1901), is a powerful multivariate data analysis procedure that examines data structure and aims to represent a complex structure by a small set of latent factors, known as principal components, which are linear functions of the observed variables and account for most of their variance. Principal

Table 6.1 Groups of websites based on factor loadings

F16	F15	F14	F13	F12	F11	F10	F9	F8	F7	F6	F5	F4	F3	F2	F1
v1007	v1023	v1048	v1029	v1086	v1010	v1033	v1008	v1044	v1082	v1003	v1001	V1028	v1000	v1005	v1002
v1022	v1032	v1120	v1051	v1124	v1013	v1055	v1025	v1091	v1083	v1004	v1018	V1101	v1011	v1094	v1006
v1059	v1045	v1121	v1064	v1134	v1019	v1061	v1026	v1098	v1084	v1020	v1049	V1129	v1012	v1106	v1009
v1073	v1056	v1132	v1069	v1140	v1042	v1090	v1027	v1105	v1100	v1021	v1077	V1143	v1014	v1107	v1017
v1080	v1066	v1139	v1071	v1164	v1053	v1095	v1034	v1138	v1118	v1128	v1085	V1144	v1015	v1115	v1024
v1104	v1097	v1145	v1108	v1185	v1057	v1102	v1038	v1157	v1146	v1173	v1117	V1149	v1016	v1152	v1030
v1116	v1109	v1174	v1122	v1191	v1092	v1103	v1041	v1158	v1148	v1214	v1133	V1187	v1036	v1161	v1031
v1123	v1127	v1183	v1142	v1198	v1093	v1125	v1068	v1167	v1159	v1233	v1151	V1190	v1040	v1165	v1035
v1141	v1153	v1217	v1154	v1206	v1096	v1131	v1070	v1203	v1168	v1248	v1160	V1207	v1050	v1170	v1037
v1172	v1156	v1218	v1169	v1225	v1110	v1137	v1126	v1215	v1180	v1259	v1163	v1231	v1052	v1175	v1039
v1194	v1166	v1222	v1177	v1239	v1111	v1147	v1176	v1246	v1197	v1265	v1181		v1081	v1178	v1043
v1200	v1179	v1223	v1188	v1252	v1182	v1155	v1202		v1221	v1270	v1196		v1088	v1186	v1046
v1212	v1209	v1236	v1204	v1256	v1192	v1201	v1208		v1224	v1271	v1199		v1089	v1195	v1054
v1216	v1227	v1237			v1213	v1219	v1232		v1235	v1272	v1205		v1135	v1210	v1058
v1241	v1258	v1260			v1228	v1243	v1247		v1295	v1273	v1220		v1184	v1211	v1060
					v1244	v1279	v1254			v1274	v1230		v1193	v1226	v1062
							v1255			v1276	v1251		v1234	v1229	v1063
							v1263			v1281			v1238	v1240	v1065
							v1268			v1283			v1253	v1242	v1067
							v1275							v1245	v1072
							v1277							v1249	v1074
							v1284							v1250	v1075
														v1257	v1076
														v1261	v1078
														v1262	v1079

continued on following page

Table 6.1 continued

F1	F2	F3	F4	F5	F6	F7	F8	F9	F10	F11	F12	F13	F14	F15	F16
v1002	v1005	v1000	V1028	v1001	v1003	v1082	v1044	v1008	v1033	v1010	v1086	v1029	v1048	v1023	v1007
v1006	v1094	v1011	V1101	v1018	v1004	v1083	v1091	v1025	v1055	v1013	v1124	v1051	v1120	v1032	v1022
v1009	v1106	v1012	V1129	v1049	v1020	v1084	v1098	v1026	v1061	v1019	v1134	v1064	v1121	v1045	v1059
v1017	v1107	v1014	V1143	v1077	v1021	v1100	v1105	v1027	v1090	v1042	v1140	v1069	v1132	v1056	v1073
v1024	v1115	v1015	V1144	v1085	v1128	v1118	v1138	v1034	v1095	v1053	v1164	v1071	v1139	v1066	v1080
v1030	v1152	v1016	V1149	v1117	v1173	v1146	v1157	v1038	v1102	v1057	v1185	v1108	v1145	v1097	v1104
v1031	v1161	v1036	V1187	v1133	v1214	v1148	v1158	v1041	v1103	v1092	v1191	v1122	v1174	v1109	v1116
v1035	v1165	v1040	V1190	v1151	v1233	v1159	v1167	v1068	v1125	v1093	v1198	v1142	v1183	v1127	v1123
v1037	v1170	v1050	V1207	v1160	v1248	v1168	v1203	v1070	v1131	v1096	v1206	v1154	v1217	v1153	v1141
v1039	v1175	v1052	v1231	v1163	v1259	v1180	v1215	v1126	v1137	v1110	v1225	v1169	v1218	v1156	v1172

component analysis is different from factor analysis. Unlike factor analysis, which assumes there are latent factors existing, principal component analysis makes no assumption about an underlying causal model. The fundamental difference between principal component analysis and factor analysis is that principal component analysis determines the factors that account for maximum variance of all observed variables, while factor analysis determines the factors to account maximally for the inter-correlations of the variables (Snook & Gorsuch, 1989; Gorsuch, 1990). Although principal component analysis could be considered one of the oldest multivariate methods, its applications have been significantly increased over the last two decades due to the widespread accessibility of high-speed computers.

Let $X = (x_1, x_2, \cdots x_k)$ be a set of k observed random variables, and let Y be a set of un-correlated variables $y_1, y_2, \cdots y_k$, each of which is a linear combination of the k variables. We have

$$y_1 = b_{11}x_1 + b_{12}x_2 + \cdots + b_{1k}x_k$$
$$y_2 = b_{21}x_1 + b_{22}x_2 + \cdots + b_{2k}x_k$$

$$\vdots \qquad\qquad\qquad\qquad\qquad\qquad\qquad (6\text{-}2)$$

$$y_k = b_{k1}x_1 + b_{k2}x_2 + \cdots + b_{nk}x_k,$$

where $y_j (j = 1,2,\ldots,k)$ is the jth principal component of the variable set X, and $b_{ij} (i = 1,2,\cdots,k)$ is the coefficient for x_i. Note in Equation (6-2) that the order of y_j is in decreasing order of "loading", which means y_1 is designed to account for the maximal amount of total variance in the linear combination of the observed variables, $X_1, X_2, \ldots X_n$. The second component, y_2 is designed to have two important characteristics: (1) it should be uncorrelated with y_1, and (2) it needs to account for a maximal amount of variance that was not accounted for by the first component, y_1. We can repeat this process until y_k. Ideally the aim of principal components analysis is to have the first few components represent most of the variation carried by the original observed variable set X so that the data dimension can be reduced.

Both SAS and Stata support principal component analysis. We can use SAS procedures of *PROC CORRESP* or *PROC PRINCOMP* to conduct principal component analysis with binary data. Whether to use *CORRESP* or *PRINCOMP* depends on whether we are interested in Euclidean or χ^2 distance. We can also use *PROC PRINQUAL*, but if data points are all binary, *PRINQUAL* will give the same results as *PRINCOMP*. We can use the *pca* command in Stata to fit a principal component model (Example 6.3).

Example 6.3→Fit Principal Component Analysis with Spam-email Data Let us use the spam-email data to conduct the principal component analysis with the Stata codes shown in Display 6.10.

Display 6.10
Stata codes for principal component analysis

```
/* Conduct principal component analysis */
pca v1-v57
/* Plots of eigenvalues */
screeplot, mean
loadingplot,comp(14) combined
```

Display 6.11
Results of principal component analysis

```
. pca v1-v57

Principal components/correlation                 Number of obs    =      4601
                                                 Number of comp.  =        57
                                                 Trace            =        57
        Rotation: (unrotated = principal)        Rho              =    1.0000
```

Component	Eigenvalue	Difference	Proportion	Cumulative
Comp1	6.59193	3.32451	0.1156	0.1156
Comp2	3.26742	1.26427	0.0573	0.1730
Comp3	2.00315	.389992	0.0351	0.2081
Comp4	1.61316	.0669516	0.0283	0.2364
Comp5	1.54621	.0836681	0.0271	0.2635
Comp6	1.46254	.048557	0.0257	0.2892
Comp7	1.41398	.039064	0.0248	0.3140
Comp8	1.37492	.0796334	0.0241	0.3381
Comp9	1.29529	.0183416	0.0227	0.3609
Comp10	1.27694	.0600172	0.0224	0.3833
Comp11	1.21693	.0868248	0.0213	0.4046
Comp12	1.1301	.0183196	0.0198	0.4244
Comp13	1.11178	.0166829	0.0195	0.4439
Comp14	1.0951	.00806673	0.0192	0.4631
Comp15	1.08703	.0235637	0.0191	0.4822
Comp16	1.06347	.014826	0.0187	0.5009
Comp17	1.04864	.0252632	0.0184	0.5193
Comp18	1.02338	.010716	0.0180	0.5372
Comp19	1.01266	.00984883	0.0178	0.5550
Comp20	1.00281	.0069013	0.0176	0.5726
Comp21	.995914	.0176494	0.0175	0.5901
Comp22	.978264	.0137314	0.0172	0.6072
Comp23	.964533	.023188	0.0169	0.6241
Comp24	.941345	.00475639	0.0165	0.6407
Comp25	.936588	.0122511	0.0164	0.6571
Comp26	.924337	.00898042	0.0162	0.6733
Comp27	.915357	.0107166	0.0161	0.6894
Comp28	.90464	.0312195	0.0159	0.7052
Comp29	.873421	.00742131	0.0153	0.7206
Comp30	.865999	.0295048	0.0152	0.7358
Comp31	.836495	.00976312	0.0147	0.7504
Comp32	.826731	.0290598	0.0145	0.7649
Comp33	.797672	.0159671	0.0140	0.7789
Comp34	.781705	.00508492	0.0137	0.7926
Comp35	.77662	.0210924	0.0136	0.8063
Comp36	.755527	.0214473	0.0133	0.8195
Comp37	.73408	.011021	0.0129	0.8324
Comp38	.723059	.0184683	0.0127	0.8451
Comp39	.704591	.0147352	0.0124	0.8574
Comp40	.689855	.0152508	0.0121	0.8695
Comp41	.674605	.00860997	0.0118	0.8814
Comp42	.665995	.0468784	0.0117	0.8931
Comp43	.619116	.0106649	0.0109	0.9039
Comp44	.608451	.026584	0.0107	0.9146

continued on following page

Display 6.11 continued

Comp45	.581867	.00478406	0.0102	0.9248
Comp46	.577083	.0526302	0.0101	0.9349
Comp47	.524453	.0357357	0.0092	0.9441
Comp48	.488717	.0383886	0.0086	0.9527
Comp49	.450329	.0412282	0.0079	0.9606
Comp50	.4091	.0334957	0.0072	0.9678
Comp51	.375605	.00989186	0.0066	0.9744
Comp52	.365713	.0308579	0.0064	0.9808
Comp53	.334855	.0294731	0.0059	0.9867
Comp54	.305382	.0449614	0.0054	0.9920
Comp55	.26042	.0701571	0.0046	0.9966
Comp56	.190263	.186408	0.0033	0.9999
Comp57	.00385485	.	0.0001	1.0000

We can determine how many components to keep as the result of the analysis by setting a percentage of variance that we wish to account for. In other words, we would like to retain components to account for a majority of the variance. For example, in the spam-email data, if we want to account for 80% of the variance we need to keep about 35 components. This is still a lot of components, but is substantially smaller than the initial 57-dimensional space. We also can use the scree-plot of eigenvalues to decide the number of components to be retained. Because we are analyzing a correlation matrix, the mean eigenvalue is 1. We can retain all the components with eigenvalues greater than the mean and drop all the components with eigenvalues less than the mean. Figure 6.4 shows that we can retain about 14 such components, of which the loading plots are shown in Figure 6.5.

In addition to data reduction, principal component analysis can also be used to detect intrusion, which we will discuss in Chapter X.

SAMPLING NETWORK TRAFFIC

The principle behind a statistical sampling is that a copious amount of information may be learned about a population by taking and analyzing a representative sample from it. A sample-based estimate represents observed values of a random variable that aims to approximate the true value of the population (e.g., actual quantity of anomaly-free traffic in a system). These observed values may change from sample to sample, which is known as sample variability. In general, there are three fundamental tasks in sampling: (1) specification, (2) design, and (3) evaluation (Deming, 1950). Although these tasks were initially major theoretical problems in survey design, they also need to be considered when sampling network traffic data.

Statistical sampling approaches have also been used in forensic accounts for financial and internal audits (Adams, & Johnson, 1988; Bright, Kadane, & Nagin, 1988; Fournier, & Raabe, 1983; Gavenda, 2001; Leib, 1985; McGoff, 2001; Mulrow, 1998; Naghavi, Mulrow, & Falk, 2002), and have also been accepted in courts against waste, fraud, and abuse of federal and state welfare programs such as Medicare, Medicaid, Food Stamps, and other similar programs (Health Care Financing Administration, 1986). The courts recognize that auditing every welfare claim is impossible, and the use of a sampling approach is admissible. In the *State of Georgia (Department of Human Services) v. Califano* (1977), the judge stated that an "audit on an individual claim-by-claim basis of the many thousands of claims submitted each month by each state (under Medicaid) would be a practical impossibility as well as unnecessary." In network security, use of sampling methods for data collection has been recommended (Kimberly, Claffy, George, Polyzos, & Braun, 1993; Choi, Park & Zhang, 2002; Duffield, Lund, & Thorup, 2002; Mori, Uchida, Kawahara, Pan, & Goto, 2004; Zhao, Zhang, Yang, & Hu, 2007) and has also been implemented in hardware (Cisco System, 2005).

Statistical sampling is based on probability, and many of its applications are in survey methodology. The most widely used statistical sampling methods include: (1) the simple random sample (SRS) method, (2) the stratified sample method, and (3) the cluster sample method. Although other sampling approaches, such as adaptive sampling, two-phase or double sampling, capture-recapture sampling, and line-intercept sampling, have been developed over decades, many of these approaches address the specific needs and demands of the survey research area. Thus, in the following sections, we only focus on the SRS, stratified sample and cluster sample methods. Readers who are interested in obtaining more comprehensive information on this topic should refer to Lohr (1999) and Thompson (2002).

What and How to Sample

In the network security field we have two essential sampling aims: (1) to draw a sample of traffic such as packets, flows, or connections, from existing collected data or directly from online traffic, and (2) to select a set of sample of network sites to be monitored, such as users, workstations, or sub-system from a network system. For the first task, there should be a clear, reproducible, and appropriate method of identifying the traffic that will be included in the final sample. This process must balance the interest of including all types of traffic that represent a typical condition with the need to avoid all types of traffic that do not have the condition. For example, assessments of the anomaly behavior of users accessing the system only at night should use valid criteria for the identification of these users while avoiding the inclusion of daytime users. Available information should be used to confirm the selection and standardize the sample.

As we discussed in Chapter III, network traffic is composed of packets, flows and sessions. We can sample traffic by individual packets at the packet-level. Many commercial products have the capability of taking a sampling of data. For example, NetFlow software, a Cisco IOS application that provides statistics on packets flowing through a Cisco router, provides two sampling options to allow us to collect data from either the entire network, or specific subsets of traffic. The first option is the random sampling approach that collects only one randomly selected packet from the n sequential packets, where n, ranging from 1 to 65535, is a sampling parameter determined by users. The other option is the deterministic sampling approach, which selects every n^{th} packet for Netflow processing on a pre-interface basis. The deterministic approach is less statistically accurate than the random sampling approach (Cisco, 2005).

The sample at the network site-level is important because the groups or individuals that are included, as well as the linkage between sites and their corresponding traffic, must be clearly defined. When profiling users that are usually represented by sites, it is straightforward to link a stream of traffic to a site unless the traffic issued by one user is linked to more than one site (e.g., a user logs in on more than one machine). In this case, these sites, as well as their corresponding traffic, need to be combined. The approach to combine sites and traffic must be justified. Often times, without detailed user-level information we may not be able to confirm that the traffic from two different sites was actually issued by the same user. Choices about sample specification need to be clearly stated and justified because they may have important implications on the results of the analysis; particularly, with regard to the comparability of sites and users.

Example 6.4→Per-packet Sampling Let $n = 100$, which corresponds to a sampling portion of 1-in-100 or 1%. NetFlow might sample the 5th packet, the 110th packet, 210th, 350th, and so on packets when the random sampling option is selected. Or it will sample the 1st, 201st, 301st, and so on packets with the deterministic sampling approach.

In addition to the above per-packet sampling approach, we can sample packets at the byte-level; that is, sample packets in proportion to the packet length. Traffic can also be sampled at the flow-level—an application layer sampling approach. Similar to the packet-level approach, we can select n sequential flows (1-in-n). Note that in the flow-level sampling, we no longer have the packet-level random sampling approach. For packets belonging to a particular flow, they will either be collected as a whole, if the flow is selected or they will not be collected at all if the flow is not selected. Finally, we can sample at the TCP/IP session-level, which includes sampling the IP source, destination addresses and port numbers. The publicly available tcpdump application is easy to use and widely utilized to collect such data.

Simple Random Sampling

Simple random sampling (SRS) is the simplest form of a probability sampling method. The SRS of size n is taken when every possible subset of the n units in the population has the same chance of being in the sample. Thus, at the packet-level, the probability of an HTTP-based packet to be sampled is same as the probability of a UDP-based packet to be sampled. One way of obtaining an SRS is to assign a random number to each observation in the population and then sort the random numbers in either ascending or descending order to draw n observations (e.g., the first 10000 observations), or to use a pre-determined threshold to draw the required sample. Most statistical software programs provide a seed function and a random number generating function, so the random number approach is easy to achieve with software.

Theoretically, SRS has a large sample space for all possible combinations of different samples for a given population and a fixed sample size. Let n be an SRS size, and N be the size of a finite population, we then have $k = C_N^n$ samples each with size n being obtained from N without replacement. k is given by

$$k = \frac{N!}{(N-n)!n!}$$

Given $N = 100$ and $n = 10$, the total combinations would be

$$k = \frac{100!}{(100-10)!10!} = 17,310,309,456,440.$$

Since all the observations have the same probability of being selected into a sample, SRS not only avoids bias in the choice of individual observations, but also gives every possible sample an equal chance. With SRS, both the sample mean and sample variance are unbiased estimators of a finite population mean and the population variance.

Let X be a continuous random variable and N be the size of a finite population. The population mean, μ, is given by

$$\mu = \frac{1}{N}\sum_{i=1}^{N} x_i, \tag{6-3}$$

and the population variance, σ^2, is defined as

$$\sigma^2 = \frac{1}{N-1}\sum_{i=1}^{N}(x_i - \mu)^2. \tag{6-4}$$

The sample mean, $\hat{\mu}$, which is an unbiased estimator of the finite population mean μ, is defined as

$$\hat{\mu} = \frac{1}{n}\sum_{i=1}^{n} x_i, \tag{6-5}$$

and the sample variance and unbiased estimator of the variance of $\hat{\mu}$ are defined as

$$\hat{\sigma}^2 = \frac{1}{n-1}\sum_{i=1}^{n}(x_i - \hat{\mu})^2, \tag{6-6}$$

and

$$\hat{\sigma}_{\hat{\mu}}^2 = \left(1 - \frac{n}{N}\right)\frac{\sigma^2}{n}, \tag{6-7}$$

respectively. The term $(1 - n/N)$ is called the finite population correction. If the population is large relative to the sample size and the sampling fraction n/N is small, the finite popula-

Figure 6.4 Eigenvalues loading based on principal component analysis

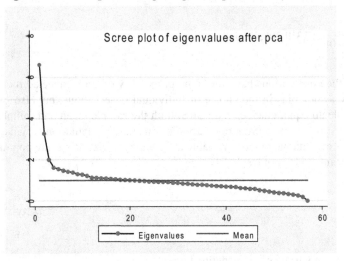

Figure 6.5 Eigenvalues loading plot of the 14 components

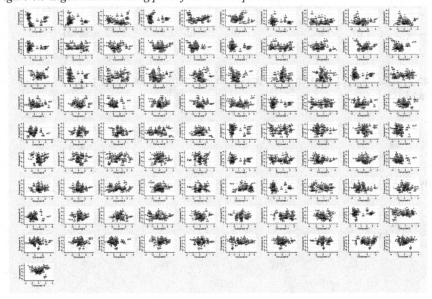

tion correction tends to be 1. Therefore, in the case where the finite population correction is 1, we can rewrite Equation (6-7) as

$$\hat{\sigma}_\mu^2 = \frac{\sigma^2}{n}.$$
(6-8)

Because in network security we more likely have $N \gg n$ as a result, Equation (6-8) is used more frequently than Equation (6-7).

Similarly, when X is a binary random variable, we can define the proportion, $\hat{p}$, and the sample variance, $\hat{\sigma}^2$, as

$$\hat{p} = \frac{1}{n}\sum_{i=1}^{n}x_i, \qquad\qquad (6\text{-}9)$$

and

$$\hat{\sigma}^2 = \frac{1}{n-1}\hat{p}(1-\hat{p})' \qquad\qquad (6\text{-}10)$$

respectively.

Example 6.5→SRS Approach to Select Network Sites for Sampling A corporation-level network system including 1,024 workstations (each with a unique IP address), assumes that all users' working schedules are equally distributed within a 10-hour window between 8:00 am to 6:00 pm. Save all the data traffic generated by the 1,024 workstations within the allotted time zone could result a huge dataset. Accordingly, we can use an SRS approach that randomly select 25 workstations from the system in a 5-minute interval. Thus, each workstation has a 0.29 ($60 / 5 \times 25 / 1024$) probability of being audited each hour and has near 3 time chances to be selected for auditing during the 10-hour period (Figure 6.6).

Example 6.6→SRS on Traffic Data Many statistical software packages provide sampling functions to draw an SRS. Let us first use the *sample* command in Stata to randomly draw 10% of the observations from the entire KDD-cup 1999 training data, and then check the frequency of the attack variable between the full and 10% datasets. The *sample* command draws random samples of the data in memory. We can use the *set seed* command followed

Figure 6.6. Randomly selected workstations by SRS (n = 25)

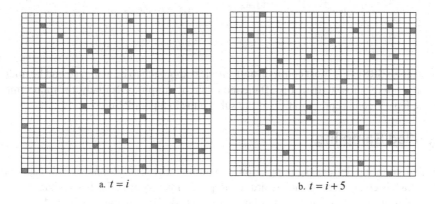

a. $t = i$ b. $t = i + 5$

by a number in Stata so we can draw a random sample that is reproducible (i.e., generate the same sample every time if we want to). Almost all versions of statistical software have a "seed" function, which utilizes an inputted number (the "seed") with which an application (e.g., Stata) starts its algorithm to generate the pseudo-random numbers. A particular Stata command for seeding is *set seed 345657*. Note the default number in Stata is *123456789*, but we can use any number we like and the number can be very large, including 30 or more digits. Display 6.12 shows the Stata codes to draw a 10% sample with a seed number of 345657 from the KDD-cup training data.

Display 6.11
Raw KDD-cup 1999 training data

```
use "F:\Book\Chapter 6\VAR-16-Trin.DTA", clear
tab attack

. tab attack
attack |      Freq.     Percent        Cum.
-----------+-----------------------------------
        0 |     97,278       19.69       19.69
        1 |    396,743       80.31      100.00
-----------+-----------------------------------
    Total |    494,021      100.00
```

Taking a different sample size, we see that the frequencies between the full data and the 10% sample are close (80.31% vs. 80.37%).

Display 6.12
Sampling 10% from KDD-cup 1999 training data

```
use "F:\ Book\Chapter 6\VAR-16-Trin.DTA", clear
Set seed 345657
Sample 10
. sample 10
(444619 observations deleted)

. tab attack
    attack |      Freq.     Percent        Cum.
-----------+-----------------------------------
        0 |      9,700       19.63       19.63
        1 |     39,702       80.37      100.00
-----------+-----------------------------------
    Total |     49,402      100.00
```

Although SRS is the most common and simplest approach to be achieved and be understood, it is not the most statistically efficient method of sampling. Namely, the final sample may not have a good representation of the subgroups in a population.

Stratified Sampling

Stratified sampling divides the population into non-overlapping groups, called strata, and then an SRS is conducted for each stratum independently (Figure 6.7). The strata represent open subgroups of interest to a particular sampling task. For instance, the flow-level sam-

Figure 6.7 Stratified sampling (The idea of this figure is credited to Lohr's [1999] book, Sampling: Design and Analysis)

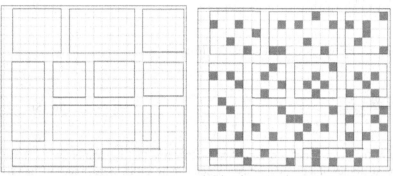

a. Divided population to H strata, stratum h has n_h observations

b. Select observations from each stratum based on SRS

pling approach is an example of the stratified sampling method. Additionally, for a large corporation, the strata can be divided by geographic locations, divisions, departments, servers, etc. In stratified sampling, the probability of an HTTP-based packet to be sampled is not the same as the probability of a UDP-based packet to be sampled.

Let h denote the ith stratum, H denote the total number of strata, n_h be an SRS size in the stratum, and N_h be the size of a finite population for the stratum. Assume that a sample is selected by SRS without replacement in each stratum. We can then estimate the sample mean, $\hat{\mu}_h$, and variance, $\hat{\sigma}_h^2$, for the stratum h as

$$\hat{\mu}_h = \frac{1}{n_h}\sum_{k=1}^{n_h} x_{hk} \tag{6-11}$$

and

$$\hat{\sigma}_h^2 = \frac{1}{n_h - 1}\sum_{k=1}^{n_h}(x_{hk} - \hat{\mu}_h)^2, \tag{6-12}$$

respectively. The total sample size is $n = \sum_{h=1}^{H} n_h$. The unbiased population mean is the stratified sample mean, $\hat{\mu}$:

$$\hat{\mu} = \frac{1}{N}\sum_{h=1}^{H} N_h \hat{\mu}_h, \tag{6-13}$$

and the unbiased estimator of the variance is given by:

$$\hat{\sigma}^2 = \sum_{h=1}^{H} \left(\frac{N_h}{N} \right)^2 \left(1 - \frac{n_h}{N_h} \right) \frac{\hat{\sigma}_h^2}{n_h}. \tag{6-14}$$

For $N_h >> n_h$, we can rewrite Equation (6-14) to

$$\hat{\sigma}^2 = \sum_{h=1}^{H} \left(\frac{N_h}{N} \right)^2 \frac{\hat{\sigma}_h^2}{n_h}. \tag{6-15}$$

One of the great benefits of stratified sampling is that it permits us to choose strata based on attributes of a particular task, which may result in more precision than from using an SRS. Generally, larger differences among each stratum, signify a greater amount of precision that can be achieved. With stratified sampling, we can apply different sampling fractions for different strata and over samples of the small group.

On the other hand, stratified sampling has several limitations to consider. It could be difficult to identify appropriate strata and their corresponding sampling fraction(s) in some complex situations. With sampling fractions that are different by strata, the within-stratum estimates have to be properly weighted with their corresponding sampling fraction to obtain the correct overall population estimates. Finally, although the use of stratified sampling could potentially lead to improve the precision of estimates, it will only be true if the strata or groups are homogeneous. If it is true, we can expect that the within-stratum variance will be smaller than the variance for the population as a whole.

Example 6.7→Stratified Sampling to Select Sites A large corporation network includes 1,000 workstations across three divisions: Marking, Accounting, and Research and development (R&D), of which each performs different functions. Let us assume both the Accounting and R&D divisions have relatively low volumes of workstations of 50 and 100, respectively. The sampling plan is to collect and monitor 100 workstations every minute. If we just conducted an SRS of n = 100 with a sampling fraction of 0.1, we would expect, by chance alone, that we would only get 5 and 10 workstations from each of the two smaller divisions. Consequently, by using the SRS method, we may obtain even less workstations. With stratification, we can gain a better result. We need to determine how many workstations we would like to have from each division. Let us assume that we would still like to draw a sample of 100 workstations from the population of 1,000 workstations per minute. In order to obtain robust information about these divisions, we will need at least 25 workstations from each division. Thus, we can sample 50 from Marking, 25 from Accounting, and 25 from R&D. Since the R&D represents 10% of the population (100 of total 1000 workstations), randomly sampling 25 of 100 will give us a sampling fraction of 25/100 or 0.25 within the stratum. Similarly, since there are 5%, or 50 workstations, in Accounting, the within-stratum sampling fraction will be 25/50 or 0.5. Finally, by subtraction we know that there are 850 workstations in Marketing, which means that the within-stratum sampling fraction for this division is about 0.059 (or 50/850). Because the divisions are more homogeneous within divisions than across the population as a whole, we can expect greater statistical precision

Figure 6.8 One-stage cluster sampling(The idea of this figure is credited to Lohr's [1999] book, Sampling: Design and Analysis)

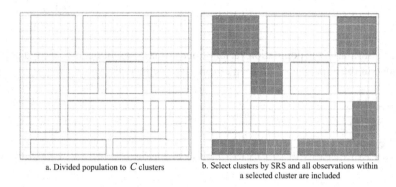

a. Divided population to *C* clusters   b. Select clusters by SRS and all observations within a selected cluster are included

(less variance). Also since we used stratified sampling, we will have enough workstations from each division to make meaningful division-oriented inferences.

Cluster Sampling

While SRS and stratified sampling select individual observations from the population, cluster sampling selects observations based on clusters (or groups). This approach first divides the population into clusters, and then applies the SRS method to each of these clusters. In cluster sampling, the sampling units are clusters, and the elements to be observed are the observations within the clusters. There are two modes of cluster sampling: (1) one-stage cluster sampling, in which all the observations within a selected cluster are included in the sample, and (2) the two-stage cluster sampling, in which only a part of the observations within a selected cluster are included in the sample. Ideally, each cluster should be chosen by being dissimilar to the others so that the sample is as representative of the population as possible. We only focus on the one-stage mode. Figure 6.8 illustrates the cluster sampling approach graphically.

Let N_c be the number of primary sampling units (the clusters) of a population ($i = 1, 2, \ldots, N_c$) and M_i be the total number of secondary sampling units in the ith primary sampling unit ($j = 1, 2, \ldots, M_i$). Also define n_c as the number of primary sampling units in the sample and m_i as the number of observations in the sample from the ith primary sampling unit. The population mean, μ, and the population mean in the ith primary sampling unit, μ_i, are defined as:

$$\mu = \sum_{i=1}^{N_c} \sum_{j=1}^{M_i} \frac{x_{ij}}{\sum_{i=1}^{N_c} M_i}, \tag{6-16}$$

and

$$\mu_i = \sum_{j=1}^{M_i} \frac{x_{ij}}{M_i},$$
(6-17)

respectively. Similarly, the population variance per primary sampling unit, σ^2, and population variance in the ith primary sampling unit, σ_i^2, are defined as:

$$\sigma^2 = \sum_{i=1}^{N} \sum_{j=1}^{M_i} \frac{(x_{ij} - \mu)^2}{\sum_{i=1}^{N} M_i - 1},$$
(6-18)

and

$$\sigma_i^2 = \sum_{j=1}^{M_i} \frac{(x_{ij} - \mu_i)^2}{M_i - 1},$$
(6-19)

respectively. The sample mean, $\hat{\mu}_i$, and variance for i^{th} primary sampling unit, $\hat{\sigma}_i^2$, are defined as

$$\hat{\mu}_i = \sum_{j=1}^{m_i} \frac{x_{ij}}{m_i}$$
(6-20)

and

$$\hat{\sigma}_i^2 = \sum_{j=1}^{m_i} \frac{(x_{ij} - \hat{\mu}_i)^2}{m_i - 1},$$
(6-21)

respectively.

Cluster sampling is useful when we cannot get all of the information of an entire population we wish to study, but can get a complete set of information from groups or clusters of the population. It is also useful when an SRS produces a pool of observations so widely scattered that auditing or surveying them would prove to be far too expensive. However, cluster sampling is considered to have less precision for estimates of population measures, because units close to each other may be very similar and so less likely to represent the whole population.

Example 6.8→Cluster Sampling Assume we develop a plan to monitor network traffic within a network including 1,000 workstations across many divisions and departments.

Because of the size of the network, we cannot monitor traffic for every workstation every minute from 8:00am to 4:00pm. Consequently, we have to randomly collect data across the workstations dynamically. If we consider the 1,000 workstations to be clusters, we can develop a cluster sampling approach that first selects workstations (clusters) based on SRS, and then collects all the traffics from the selected workstations. If we use a 6-minute interval as a time window for changing the clusters, then we can select 10 different sets of clusters every hour. Assuming we use a sampling fraction of 0.1 for selecting clusters (i.e., 100 workstations per 6-minute without replacement), the probability of a workstation to be sampled at least one time within an hour is 1.00 ($p = 100/1000 \times 10$), and every workstation has equal probability to be monitored 8 times per day from 8:00am to 4:00pm, which transfers a totally cumulative time of 48 minutes.

SAMPLE SIZE

Sample size plays an important role in network security. It impacts sampling variability, bias and precision on estimates, and the performances of classification and profiling. Although statistical methods for the analyses of network traffic data have been studied and have grown substantially, methods for the collection of such data are relatively limited. The determination of an appropriate sample size for monitoring network traffic remains a challenge. Statistically, large samples are good because they bring more information and give us more statistical power. Realistically, smaller samples require less computing resources and provide quick responses, which is important for ad hoc network security.

Statistical simulation also plays a great role in determining sample size to monitor network traffic. Repeatedly, we have to determine the sample size for each user or site in profiling user behavior. One question to address is how large the sample size should be for each site or group in order to achieve desired false negative and false positive detection thresholds in profiling user behavior. Being able to determine the minimum sample size for network traffic data that meets the desired detection thresholds is important in intrusion detection, especially in the mobile computing environment where limited information is available to be analyzed.

In the following sections, we will briefly review a few essential concepts on sampling variability and bias, and discuss the power and alpha for calculating sample size. We will also discuss an approach that uses the bootstrapping simulation method to determine the minimum sample size of audit data required to profile user behavior.

Sampling Variability and Bias

Sampling variability measures how the value of a statistic varies in repeated random sampling. If we sample 1% of the sites from a network system composed of 10,000 workstations, we want to estimate the proportion of specific packets (e.g., FTP), p, traversing the link in the entire network system. Let us assume that the sampled data included a total of 106 packets, of which 50 were FTP packets, so we may have a statistic of $\hat{p} = 0.47$ and use it to estimate the unknown population parameter p. But can $\hat{p}$, based on only 100 of the 10,000 total workstations, be an accurate estimate of p? If we draw a second sample from the same network at the same time, we may have an estimate of $\hat{p} = 0.49$. If we repeat this procedure, the third sample could have $\hat{\rho} = 0.51$. In general, the true underlying population parameter, ρ, can be presented as $\rho = \hat{\rho} + \varepsilon$, where $\hat{\rho}$ is the estimate derived from a sample, and ε represents error introduced by chance during sampling. We refer to such a chance as sampling variability, which represents the value of a statistic and varies in repeated random sampling.

Sampling variability impacts the accuracy of an estimate. The smaller the sampling variability is, the more accurate the estimate will be. If we have all possible samples of the same size from the same population, we can calculate the statistics and have the sampling distribution. Figure 6.9 shows two sampling distributions based on 10,000 draws from the 10,000 workstations with sample sizes of 100 and 1,000. Small sample size always associates with large sampling variability.

We use standard error (SE) to measure sampling variability. SE is defined as

$$S_E = \frac{\hat{\sigma}}{\sqrt{n}},$$

where $\hat{\sigma}$ is an estimate of the standard deviation of the population and n is the sample size. In general, for a fixed sample size, the more alike or homogeneous a population is with regard to a particular characteristic, the smaller the S_E will be on the estimate for the characteristic. Conversely, the more heterogeneous it is, the larger the S_E value will be.

Example 6.9→Sample Variability. Suppose that we take a 1-in-100 TCP/IP session sample for a network within a one-hour window between 8:00am to 4:00pm. We create 5 separate samples named #1 through #5, of which the #1 sample includes the 1st connection of every 100 connections, #2 includes the 20th connection of every 100 connections, #3 includes the 30th, #4 includes the 40th, and #5 includes the 50th connection of every 100 connections. We identify a total of 24, 23, 20, 25, and 20 anomalous connections in each sample within the one-hour window. The corresponding estimates for the total amount of anomalous connections for the entire TCP/IP sessions within the network during the 8 hours period for can be estimated as 192 (24 × 8), 184, 160, 200 and 160, respectively. We can see that the sampling variability impacts on the estimate of anomalous connections range from 160 to 200.

Figure 6.9 Sample size and sampling variability

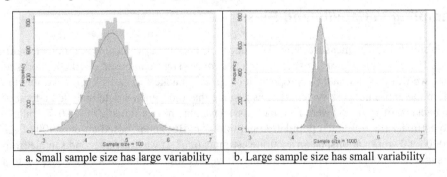

| a. Small sample size has large variability | b. Large sample size has small variability |

Figure 6.10 Bias and precision

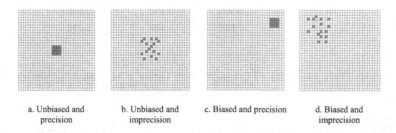

| a. Unbiased and precision | b. Unbiased and imprecision | c. Biased and precision | d. Biased and imprecision |

Sampling bias and precision both measure the quality of the sampling data. Bias measures how far the center of an estimator, $\hat{\theta}$, diverges from the parameter, θ, of a population, and precision measures how close an estimator, $\hat{\theta}$, is to the true value of the parameter, θ. As we mentioned, the smaller the S_E, the higher the precision will be. Figure 6.10 graphically illustrates the relationship between bias and precision. Variability, bias, and precision also associate with the uncertainty that will be examined detailed in Chapter XI.

Example 6.10→Sample Bias and Precision A large nationwide corporation wants to assess the volume of spam-email sent to their employees. Assuming the corporation's mail server is located in New York City. The initial plan is to take a 1-in-10 sampling fraction (i.e., select one in every ten emails) with a time window between 8:00am to 5:00pm (EST), to obtain a poll of selected emails from each receiver, and then to ask receivers to label their emails for spam (yes/no). Note that each employee will have different amounts of emails to be labeled; someone may have a longer list than others depending on their daily email volume. This plan is likely to produce a biased result because the time zone difference between the west and east locations, which will result in three less hours of emails for employees who work in the western most areas. The plan also is imprecise because each receiver may have different definitions of "spam." The revised plan should keep the same time window from 8:00am to 5:00pm but use the employees' local time zone instead of EST, and should also provide a standardized definition of spam-email to instruct receivers when labeling. The revised plan is an unbiased method of assessing spam-email and is also more precise compared to the initial self-report labeling approach.

Estimating Sample Size

A sample size of n is a function of both cost (such as manpower, examination times, and other integral resource needs) and precision (such as misclassification of user behavior and missing information). From a cost perspective, smaller samples require fewer resources, but have a higher risk of losing important information. From a precision perspective, the larger the sample, the higher the precision. The goal of choosing a better sample size is to have

$$P(|\theta - \hat{\theta}| \le e) = 1 - \alpha, \tag{6-22}$$

where e is the maximum allowable margin of error and α is the probability that the difference between θ and $\hat{\theta}$ may exceed the margin of error. Because SRS has its sample mean,

Table 6.1 Common used α and its corresponding z values

$1 - \alpha$	0.900	0.950	0.990
z	1.645	1.960	2.576

$\hat{\mu}$, being an unbiased estimator of the population mean, μ, we can write the margin of error, e, as:

$$e = z\sqrt{\left(\frac{N-n}{N}\right)\frac{\sigma^2}{n}}, \tag{6-23}$$

where z represents $1 - \alpha$ in the (6-22), and Table 6.1 shows the most widely used α values with its corresponding z values.

When the population size N becomes large, the term $(N-n)/N$ tends toward 1, so we can calculate the sample size as

$$n = \left(\frac{z \cdot \sigma}{e}\right)^2. \tag{6-24}$$

Equation (6-24) can be used for estimating the sample size on continuous and normally distributed variables. If we are interested in preparation, the sample size, n, can be estimated as

$$n = \left(\frac{z}{e}\right)^2 \times \hat{p}(1-\hat{p}), \tag{6-25}$$

where $\hat{p}$ has been defined in Chapter IV, Equation (4-9).

Example 6.11→Sample Size In a random sample of $n = 5000$ emails received by a marketing research company during a one-week period, it was found that 1000 of those emails were spam emails. How large of a sample is required if we want to calculate the probability that our estimate of the spam-email rate is off by less than 0.02 to be less than 0.05? Because we have $\hat{p} = 1000 / 5000 = 0.2$, $e = 0.02$, $\alpha = 0.05$ and $z = 1.96$ from Table 6.1, we can estimate the sample size, n, based on the Equation (6-25) as:

$$n = \left(\frac{z}{e}\right)^2 \times \hat{p}(1-\hat{p}) = \left(\frac{1.96}{0.02}\right)^2 \times 0.2(1-0.2) \approx 1537.$$

While estimating sample size, we also need to be sure that the final sample has the statistical power to detect reasonable departures from the null hypothesis. A sample is often used to make inferences about the population from which it was drawn. We may have to decide how likely it is that two samples came from the same population. For example, we may want to know that the traffic patterns from sites A and B are the same and from the anomaly-free population. Statistical tests start with the null hypothesis (H_0) of no difference in traffic patterns between sites A and B, and based on testing results, we may accept or reject the null hypothesis. As shown in Table 6.2 below, there are two ways we can make the wrong conclusion.

If we reject the null hypothesis when in reality it is true, we have made a Type I error. Conversely if we accept the null hypothesis when the alternative hypothesis (H_A) is true, we have made a Type II error. The probability of making these errors is denoted by α and β. Power, $1 - \beta$, is how likely we are to detect an effect if it is there. The goal is usually to obtain the most power we can afford, given a certain α-level. Power is considered moderate when it is 0.50 and high when it is at least 0.80. In general, the larger the sample size is, the higher the power will be. However, a sample size usually is restricted by computing resources, available budget, or some system limitations, such as ad hoc wireless network environments.

Simulation on Sample Size

As we mentioned, although a large dataset provides more statistical power, it could also be too sensitive and increase the false positive rate. Collecting and analyzing such data requires more resources. Inadequate sample sizes decrease both positive and negative predictive rates. Being able to determine the minimum sample size of network traffic required to profile each user or site is an essential challenge in network security.

Let us consider a network system with k IP addresses, that denote a unique network identification to represent k individual sites or a group of users who share the same IP address. Let i be the ith site $(i = 1, 2, \cdots, k)$, n_i be the total number of network traffic connections from the ith site, j be the jth connection $(j = 1, 2, \cdots, n_i)$, and s_{ij} be an anomaly-free score for the jth connection in i^{th} site. We will revisit such a score in more detail in Chapter IX, but for now, let us assume that we have the score already and it ranges from 0 to 1, where a connection with a high score is more likely to be anomaly-free. Recalling the binomial function discussed in Chapter III, each connection in a sample with a size of n connections can be classified either 1 (anomaly-free) or 0 (abnormal), therefore s_{ij} represents the probability of being 1 for the jth connection on the ith site.

From the central limit theorem we know that for a large number of network trials, the proportion of the number of anomaly-free connections in total connections

Table 6.2 Sample power

Decision based on sample	Truth about the population	
	H_0 True	H_A True
Reject H_0	Type I error (α)	Correct decision
Accept H_0	Correct decision	Type II error (β)

$$N = \sum_{i=1}^{k} n_i$$

independent Bernoulli trials can be approximated by a normal distribution, $N(\mu, \sigma^2)$. The μ term is represented by s (overall anomaly-free score) and is the probability of an anomaly-free connection for all sites, and σ^2 is the variance of the overall score. When we have enough connections we can think that the underlying "true" user behavior pattern can be represented by such a distribution. When only a limited number of connections are available for each site, data correspond to an "observed" behavior pattern, and can be represented by a binomial distribution, $B\ (n_i, \rho_i)$, at the individual site-level. This is what we observe in practice; the ρ_i can be represented by the mean of s_{ij}, and n_i denotes the site-specific sample size. Therefore, even though the "true" pattern of user behavior cannot be accessed, it can be inferred by linking these two distributions together in the following model (Normand, personal communication, Mar. 21, 2003):

$$\log it(\rho_i) \sim Normal(\ \mu, \sigma\ ) \qquad\qquad (6\text{-}26)$$

$$(Y_i \mid n_i, \rho_i) \sim Binomial(n_i,\ \rho_i) \qquad\qquad (6\text{-}27)$$

where Y_i is the total number of normal connections for the ith site. By assigning a "true" pattern of μ with a variance of σ as an aggregate behavior for all the sites in the network system, a "true" pattern of behavior for each site, $n_i(\mu_i, \sigma_i)$, can be drawn from Equation (6-26), and the $\log it(\rho_i)$ can be calculated for each site. Then, by linking ρ_i with Equation (6-27), the "observed" pattern of each site in a binomial distribution with the site-specific sample size can be calculated based on the Maximum Likelihood Estimation method. Sites can then be ranked into three groups: anomaly-free, abnormal, and unable to determine based on percentiles of their s score. For the ith site, when the sample size n_i is big enough, the ranking results derived from the "observed" pattern will have a high matched rate with those derived from the "true" pattern. When n_i is small, the two ranking results will have a low matching rate. Thus, the minimum sample size can be determined by varying n_i to reach a desired matched rate. Accordingly, simulations can be employed to run the "true" and "observed" distribution models, starting with a large sample size for each site and systematically reducing the sample size to compare the accuracy of ranking results between the models. If the accuracy reaches a pre-defined threshold, the minimum sample size per site can be determined.

Example 6.12→Determine Minimum Sample Size Wang and Normand (2006) presented a simulation study to assess how to determine the minimum sample size required to profile user behavior based on equations (6-26) and (6-27). They drew a dataset from the 1998 MIT-DARPA data, restricted to sites having at least 500 connections. They used bivariate analysis to identify potential variables that are statistically significantly associated with the response variable (anomaly-free). They selected variables with a frequency > 0.5% and a p value of 0.05 or less in the bivariate analysis to construct the anomaly-free score, s. Variables with a negative association with the response variable were recoded in the opposite way. They then used the Markov Chain Monte Carlo method (Gilks, Richardson and Spiegelhalter, 1996) to conduct the simulations with varying sample sizes: 10, 50, 100, and then every 500 increments in the range from 100 to 4,000. They conducted

Table 6.3 Simulation results on determining the minimum sample size

Minimum Sample Size Per Site	Median sample per site (#)	Classification between "True" and "Observed" Patterns		
		Specificity	Sensitivity	Kappa statistic
10	96	0.7302	0.4860	0.2059
50	477	0.8053	0.6425	0.4351
100	846	0.8447	0.7183	0.5516
500	4,230	0.9192	0.8545	0.7672
1,000	8,460	0.9407	0.8934	0.8294
1,500	12,690	0.9517	0.9131	0.8609
2,000	16,920	0.9577	0.9239	0.8782
2,500	21,150	0.9620	0.9317	0.8906
3,000	25,380	0.9649	0.9369	0.8990
3,500	29,610	0.9685	0.9433	0.9093
4,000	33,840	0.9700	0.9462	0.9139

Figure 6.11 Relationship between sample size and accuracy of classification

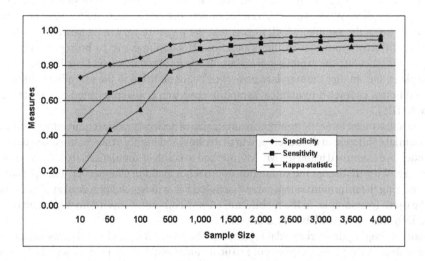

10000 iterations for each sample size and ranked the site into three groups based on the percentile of the score: top (greater than 75th), middle (25th to 75th), and low (less than 25th), for the simulated "true" and "observed" patterns during each iteration. Thus, each set of simulations contained 10000 pairs of ranking results, which were used for calculating the sensitivity, specificity, and accuracy of the two patterns. Table 6.3 and Figure 6.11 show the results of the simulations and the study recommends that a sample size of 500 per site can provide acceptable classification results.

SUMMARY

Network traffic data can be reduced in several approaches, such as sampling data, eliminating unnecessary variables, collapsing repeated observations, and fitting models with the minimum sample size. We have briefly discussed some of these approaches in this chapter. While traffic data has been utilized increasingly for profiling user behavior, methods for reducing data size are relatively limited. In many situations we need to utilize explanatory data analysis to provide the multiple relationships among variables and to provide evidence for eliminating duplicated information. In this chapter we have also discussed how to reduce the size of data on the variable side by detecting the data structure based on factor analysis and principle component analysis. The basic idea of factor analysis as well as principle component analysis is to see if we can use a small number of factors or components that count most of the variation from the initial variables to provide a highly condensed summary of the data that might be useful in later analyses. Moreover, while a number of variables represent similar information, we can combine these variables as one composite variable that will still carry the sufficient information that the initial variables carried. This idea is analogous to what we will discuss in Chapter VIII about the concept of scoring model that allows information carried by a large number of variables to be finally represented by a score.

   We also discussed how to reduce the data through the observation side of taking a sampling of the data. When we take a sample of network traffic there will always be some sampling error in the sample, which means that the measure we are interested in will be somewhat different from that in the population. If samplings are to be repeated many times, we can calculate the sampling distribution and its standard error. Usually, the larger the sample is, the smaller the standard error will be. In addition to the sampling examples discussed in this chapter, a dynamical sampling approach is also presented in Chapter XI (Example 11.5).

   Being able to determine the minimum sample size of network traffic required for profiling is an essential challenge in the development of a robust and highly efficient intrusion detection model. We examined using the MCMC method to conduct simulations to determine the sample size. We will discuss the simulation approaches again in Chapter XI. The approach of determining the minimum sample size discussed has widespread practical applications. It can be used, for example, in the mobile and ad-hoc computing environment, where only limited information is available for analysis.

   Finally, changing the variable data type could be an efficient and simple way to reduce the size of data. Assume that one hour of traffic includes one million records with 10 binary variables and has been initially formatted as the data type of *long* (64 bits). Because their values are all in the range of 0 or 1, therefore we can change their data type from *long* to *byte* (8 bits), and if we do so, we can theoretically reduce the data by more than 85%.

REFERENCES

Adams, V. N., & Johnson, K. (1988). Increasing auditor productivity through automated statistical sampling of taxpayer records. *Federation of Tax Administrators Workshop on Revenue Administration*, Washington, DC.

Bartholomew, D. 1987. *Latent Variable Models and Factor Analysis*. London: Charles Griffin & Company Limited.

Bright, J. C., Kadane, J. B., & Nagin, D. S. (1988) Statistical sampling in tax audits. *Law & Social Inquiry, 13,* 305.

Cattell, R. B. (1952). *Factor analysis*, Harper, New York.

Chebrolu, S.,Abraham, A., & Thomas J.P. (2005). Feature deduction and ensemble design of intrusion detection systems, *Computers & Security,* 24(4) pp. 295-307

Choi, B. Y., Park, J. & Zhang, Z-L. (2002). Adaptive random sampling for load change detection, *Proceedings of the 2002 ACM SIGMETRICS international conference on Measurement and modeling of computer systems*, pp. 34-36.

Cisco System (2005). *Using NetFlow filtering or sampling to select the network traffic to track.* Cisco Systems, Inc., CA, USA.

Deming, W. E. (1950). *Some theory of sampling.* Nee York: Dover Publications, Inc.

Duffield, N., Lund, C. & Thorup, M. (2001). Charging from sampled network usage, *Proceedings of the First ACM SIGCOMM Workshop on Internet Measurement,* San Francisco, California.

Duffield, N., Lund, C. & Thorup, M. (2002). Properties and prediction of flow statistics from sampled packet streams, *Proceedings of the second ACM SIGCOMM Workshop on Internet measurment,* Marseille, France

Everitt, B.S. and Dunn, G. (1991). *Applied multivariate data analysis,* London: Edward Aronld

Everitt, B.S. (2005). *An R and S-PLUS companion to multivariate analysis.* New York: Springer.

Fournier, L., & Raabe, W. (1983) Statistical sampling methods in state tax audits. *Journal of State Taxation, 2,* 115.

Gavenda, M. (2001). Statistical versus non-statistical sampling in sales and use tax audits. *Journal of State Taxation, 20,* 65.

Gilks, W. R., Richardson, S., & Spiegelhalter, D. J. (1996). *Markov Chain Monte Carlo in practice.* London: Chapman & Hall.

Gorsuch, R.L. (1990). Common factor analysis versus component analysis: Some well and little known facts. *Multivariate Behavioral Research, 25,* 33-39.

Hatcher, L. & Stepanski, E. J. (1994). *A step-by-step approach to using the SAS system for univariate and multivariate statistics.* North Carolina: SAS Institute Inc.

Health Care Financing Administration, (1986). HCFA Ruling 86-1: Use of statistical sampling to project overpayments to Medicare providers and suppliers.

Kachigan, S. K. (1991). *Multivariate statistical analysis: a conceptual introduction, 2nd Edition.* New York: Radius Press.

Khattree, R. and Naik, D. N. (2000). *Multivariate data reduction and discrimination with SAS software.* North Carolina: SAS Institute Inc.

Khan, L., Awad, M. & Thuraisingham, B. (2007).A new intrusion detection system using support vector machines and hierarchical clustering , *The International Journal on Very Large Data Bases* pp. 507-521.

Kim, J.-O., & Mueller, C.W. (1978a). *Introduction to factor analysis: What it is and how to do it.* Newbury Park: Sage.

Kim, J.-O., & Mueller, C.W. (1978b). *Factor analysis: Statistical methods and practical issues.* Newbury Park: Sage.

Kimberly C. Claffy , George C. Polyzos , & Braun, HW.(1993). Application of sampling methodologies to network traffic characterization, *Proceedings on Communications architectures, protocols and applications,* pp.194-203.

Lam, K., Hui, L., and Chung, S. (1996). A data reduction method for intrusion detection. *Journal of Systems and Software*, 33(1). pp.101-108.

Leib, H. (1985). Using sampling techniques to assess state taxes. *Journal of State Taxation , 3.*

Lohr, S. L. (1999). *Sampling: Design and analysis.* California: Duxbury Press.

Loehlin, J. C. (1992). *Latent variable models: An introduction to factor, path, and structural analysis.* Hillsdale, NJ: Lawrence Erlbaum. Second edition 1992.

McGoff, P. (2001). Sampling: influencing the outcome of an audit. *Sales and Use Tax Alert, (11)8,* pp. 1-4.

Mori, T., Uchida, M., Kawahara, R., & Pan, J., Goto, J. (2004). Identifying elephant flows through periodically sampled packets, In *Proceedings of the 4th ACM SIGCOMM conference on Internet measurement.* Pp. 45-48.

Mukkamala, S., Tadiparthi, G. R., Tummala, N., & Janoski, G. (2003). Audit data reduction for intrusion detection. In: *Proceedings of the IEEE 2003 International Joint Conference on Neural Networks,* pp. 456-460.

Mulrow, J. M. (1998). Statistical sampling as a win-win in tax audits. *State Tax Notes, 15,* 1491.

Naghavi, F., Mulrow, J., & Falk, E. (2002). Reverse sales and use tax audits and statistical sampling: a double benefit. *Journal of Multistate Taxation and Incentives, 11(10),* 18.Rencher, A.C. (1995). *Methods of multivariate analysis.* New York: Wiley.

Snook, S.C., & Gorsuch, R.L. (1989). Principal component analysis versus common factor analysis: A Monte Carlo study. *Psychological Bulletin, 106,* 148-154.

State of Georgia v. Califano (1977). 446 F.supp. 404 (N.D. Georgia).

Tabachnick, B.G., & Fidell, L.S. (2000). *Using multivariate statistics* (4th Ed.). New York: Harper-Collins.

Thomson, G.H. (1951). *The factor analysis of human ability.* London: London University Press.

Thompson, S. K. (2002). *Sampling.* 2nd ed. Wiley Series in Probability and Statistics, New York: John Wiley & Sons, Inc.

Wat, F.K.T., Ngai, E.W.T. & Cheng, T.C.E. (2005). Potential risks to e-commerce development using exploratory factor analysis, *International Journal of Services Technology and Management,* 6(1), pp. 55-71.

Wang, Y., Normand, SL.T. (2006). Determining the minimum sample size of audit data required to profile user behavior and detect anomaly intrusion. *International Journal of Business Data Communications and Networking;* 2(3), pp 31-45.

Wu, N., Zhang, J. (2003). Factor analysis based anomaly detection. In *Proceedings of the 2003 IEEE, Workshop on Information Assurance*, 108-115.

Ye, N., Emran, S.M., Chen, Q., & Vilbert, S. (2002). Multivariate statistical analysis of audit trails for host-based intrusion detection. *IEEE Transaction on Computers*, 51(7): 810-820.

Zhao, K., Zhang, M., Yang, K., & Hu, L. (2007). Data collection for intrusion detection system based on stratified random sampling, In *proceedings of Networking, Sensing and Control, 2007 IEEE International Conference*, pp. 852-855.

APPENDIX

Full Output of Factor Loading and Unique Variances in Display 6.3

```
Factor loadings (pattern matrix) and unique variances
-----------------------------------------------------------------------------------------------
    Variable |  Factor1    Factor2    Factor3    Factor4    Factor5    Factor6    Factor7    Factor8
-------------+---------------------------------------------------------------------------------------
          v1 |  -0.0939     0.2575    -0.0834     0.0162     0.0624    -0.0495     0.0438     0.0437
          v2 |  -0.0249    -0.0218    -0.0095     0.0132    -0.0559     0.0066    -0.0404    -0.0232
          v3 |  -0.1023     0.2507    -0.0324    -0.0286     0.0725     0.0127    -0.0475    -0.0119
          v4 |  -0.0135     0.0174     0.0104    -0.0009    -0.0343     0.0116     0.0053    -0.0026
          v5 |  -0.0791     0.1827    -0.1299    -0.2047     0.0663    -0.0098     0.0566     0.0200
          v6 |  -0.0985     0.2545    -0.0242     0.0703     0.0316     0.1317     0.0377
          v7 |  -0.0999     0.2179    -0.1338    -0.0026    -0.0221    -0.0616     0.1076    -0.0405
          v8 |  -0.0728     0.1971    -0.0659     0.0599     0.0608    -0.0388     0.1181    -0.0338
          v9 |  -0.0980     0.3690     0.0987     0.0300     0.0890     0.0479     0.0233    -0.0552
         v10 |  -0.0416     0.2294     0.0350     0.0580     0.0769     0.0291     0.0880    -0.0157
         v11 |  -0.1084     0.3371    -0.1297     0.0133     0.0800    -0.1016     0.2091    -0.0298
         v12 |  -0.0489     0.1112    -0.0869    -0.1811     0.1808    -0.0025     0.0971    -0.0060
         v13 |  -0.0809     0.1886    -0.0377     0.0603     0.0390     0.0902    -0.1071     0.0665
         v14 |  -0.0386     0.1045     0.0473    -0.0307    -0.0076    -0.0089    -0.0288     0.0061
         v15 |  -0.0664     0.3565     0.1188     0.1240     0.2009     0.3060    -0.1757     0.0258
         v16 |  -0.0925     0.1514    -0.1233    -0.0042    -0.0629    -0.0565     0.0338    -0.0039
         v17 |  -0.0969     0.3048    -0.1310    -0.0086     0.0419    -0.1104     0.2060    -0.0676
         v18 |  -0.0401     0.2530    -0.0678     0.0973     0.1074     0.1180    -0.0398    -0.0950
         v19 |  -0.1860     0.2910    -0.2955     0.0856     0.0001    -0.0873     0.0261     0.1443
         v20 |  -0.0654     0.2016    -0.0178    -0.0219    -0.0169    -0.0976     0.1572    -0.0437
         v21 |  -0.1662     0.4354    -0.2533     0.0264     0.0538    -0.1368     0.1654     0.0213
         v22 |  -0.0339    -0.0022     0.1417    -0.0100    -0.3329     0.2959     0.3269     0.1443
         v23 |  -0.1165     0.3999     0.0125     0.1068     0.1078     0.2912    -0.1517     0.0704
         v24 |  -0.0854     0.2225    -0.0976     0.0445     0.0002    -0.0270     0.0163     0.0331
         v25 |   0.5007    -0.1223     0.1171     0.0430     0.1546     0.0953     0.1635    -0.2505
         v26 |   0.4898    -0.1144     0.1065     0.0265     0.2093     0.0878     0.1454    -0.2212
         v27 |   0.0854    -0.1750    -0.0019    -0.0085    -0.1300    -0.0064    -0.1415    -0.0407
         v28 |   0.6789     0.0322     0.0239     0.0395     0.0342     0.0056    -0.0023    -0.1495
         v29 |   0.5342     0.0250    -0.0760    -0.4284     0.1406     0.0813    -0.0035     0.1927
         v30 |   0.7501     0.0671    -0.0184     0.0548     0.0147     0.0393     0.0608    -0.1339
         v31 |   0.7800     0.1228    -0.0606     0.0321    -0.0491     0.0002    -0.0141    -0.0118
         v32 |   0.9268     0.1846    -0.0956     0.0242    -0.1197    -0.0621    -0.0465     0.1897
         v33 |   0.0089    -0.1210     0.0846    -0.0136     0.0402     0.0036    -0.0260    -0.0202
         v34 |   0.9245     0.1869    -0.0916     0.0226    -0.1216    -0.0667    -0.0474     0.1905
         v35 |   0.6503     0.0526    -0.0147     0.0229     0.0120     0.0288    -0.0055    -0.1195
         v36 |   0.7915     0.0918    -0.0338     0.0346    -0.0234     0.0103     0.0029    -0.0679
         v37 |   0.1007    -0.2026     0.2250     0.1840     0.3006    -0.0707     0.1614     0.1483
         v38 |  -0.0051    -0.0281    -0.0126    -0.1576     0.0644     0.0332     0.0222     0.0148
         v39 |   0.0805    -0.1281     0.1164     0.0994     0.2116    -0.0631     0.0862     0.1466
         v40 |   0.8199     0.2214    -0.0870     0.0293    -0.0650    -0.0100    -0.0419     0.1055
         v41 |   0.0167    -0.1292     0.0998     0.1683     0.0782    -0.0775     0.0261     0.1998
         v42 |   0.0532    -0.1280    -0.0253    -0.5365     0.2439     0.1133     0.0160     0.1636
         v43 |   0.1468    -0.1134     0.1397     0.1746     0.2903    -0.0369     0.1157     0.1775
         v44 |   0.0244    -0.0835     0.0073    -0.0329    -0.0055     0.0011    -0.0214    -0.0241
         v45 |   0.0176    -0.1364    -0.0199     0.0891     0.0489    -0.0986    -0.0258     0.1195
         v46 |  -0.0099    -0.1607     0.0796     0.1709     0.0253    -0.1084    -0.0408     0.2357
         v47 |   0.0062    -0.0126     0.0013    -0.0095     0.0149     0.0063    -0.0003    -0.0285
         v48 |   0.0060    -0.0765     0.0257    -0.0125     0.0208    -0.0007    -0.0060    -0.0335
         v49 |  -0.0062    -0.0571     0.1957     0.0209    -0.2344     0.2367     0.3114     0.1765
         v50 |   0.3355     0.1002     0.3723    -0.0223     0.0066    -0.1597    -0.0618     0.0501
         v51 |   0.0388    -0.0742     0.0926     0.0543     0.0999     0.0254     0.0303     0.0180
         v52 |  -0.0965     0.1838    -0.0553     0.0197    -0.0508    -0.0435    -0.0025     0.0722
         v53 |  -0.1112     0.3734     0.0694     0.0396     0.0181     0.1074    -0.1109     0.0617
         v54 |   0.0026     0.0422     0.0734    -0.0135    -0.1272     0.1203     0.1483    -0.0109
         v55 |  -0.0356     0.2388     0.3477    -0.1572    -0.0871    -0.2401     0.0120    -0.0640
         v56 |  -0.0665     0.4754     0.6026    -0.1506    -0.0628    -0.1897    -0.0628    -0.0231
         v57 |  -0.0975     0.3885     0.4052    -0.0387    -0.0464     0.0534    -0.0026    -0.0024
-----------------------------------------------------------------------------------------------
```

continued on following page

```
Factor loadings (pattern matrix) and unique variances
----------------------------------------------------------------------------------------------
    Variable |  Factor9  Factor10  Factor11  Factor12  Factor13  Factor14  Factor15  Factor16
-------------+--------------------------------------------------------------------------------
         v1  |  0.1359   -0.1313   -0.1285   -0.0344   -0.0784    0.1003   -0.0162   -0.0683
         v2  | -0.0657    0.0217    0.0223   -0.0107   -0.0928    0.0279    0.0259   -0.0616
         v3  |  0.1435    0.0166    0.1274    0.0139   -0.0635   -0.0280   -0.0614    0.1003
         v4  | -0.0061   -0.0016   -0.0041   -0.0076   -0.0032    0.0668    0.0299   -0.0102
         v5  | -0.0369    0.0985    0.1574    0.0283    0.0782    0.0824   -0.1100    0.0836
         v6  | -0.0269    0.0325    0.0190   -0.0045    0.0696   -0.0535   -0.0367    0.0324
         v7  | -0.0776    0.1300    0.1574    0.0018    0.0842    0.1036   -0.0334   -0.0724
         v8  | -0.1784    0.0771   -0.0603    0.0262    0.1071   -0.0993    0.0769    0.0102
         v9  | -0.1299    0.0187   -0.1263   -0.0036   -0.1117   -0.0254    0.0615    0.0836
        v10  | -0.0197    0.0215    0.0086   -0.0153   -0.0712   -0.0777    0.0360   -0.0873
        v11  | -0.0634    0.0079   -0.1019   -0.0795   -0.0414    0.0346   -0.0167   -0.0694
        v12  |  0.1111   -0.0642   -0.0724   -0.0893   -0.0833   -0.1150   -0.1636   -0.0798
        v13  |  0.0684   -0.0991   -0.0738    0.0789    0.0775    0.0658   -0.0154   -0.0218
        v14  |  0.0086   -0.1229   -0.1802    0.0090    0.0348    0.0460    0.0425    0.0989
        v15  | -0.1084    0.1324    0.1077   -0.0399   -0.1169   -0.0673   -0.0042   -0.0190
        v16  |  0.0057    0.0291    0.1090    0.0199    0.0466    0.1764    0.0455   -0.0628
        v17  | -0.1720    0.0827   -0.0560    0.0311    0.1598   -0.0407   -0.0015    0.0040
        v18  |  0.0623    0.1304    0.1520   -0.1091   -0.0957    0.1050    0.0278    0.0143
        v19  |  0.2385   -0.0810    0.0967    0.0222   -0.0331   -0.0859    0.0266    0.0422
        v20  | -0.1331    0.0528   -0.0869    0.0061    0.0351   -0.0585    0.0635    0.0654
        v21  |  0.0421   -0.0250   -0.0088   -0.0496   -0.0481   -0.0169    0.0148    0.0296
        v22  |  0.0279    0.0047    0.0396   -0.0342   -0.0342   -0.0149    0.0282    0.0147
        v23  | -0.0400    0.0058   -0.0003    0.0643    0.0989   -0.0226   -0.0158   -0.0487
        v24  |  0.1292   -0.1053   -0.0775   -0.0212   -0.0682    0.1346    0.0847   -0.0202
        v25  |  0.0641   -0.0608   -0.0096    0.2084    0.0325   -0.0008   -0.0589   -0.0172
        v26  |  0.0709   -0.0497   -0.0160    0.1507   -0.0059    0.0070   -0.0483   -0.0152
        v27  | -0.1744   -0.0168   -0.0103    0.0152   -0.0441    0.0638    0.1135   -0.1213
        v28  |  0.1567    0.0796   -0.0022   -0.1451    0.0688   -0.0197    0.1297    0.0087
        v29  |  0.0064    0.0405   -0.0687   -0.0007   -0.0043   -0.0487    0.0902   -0.0913
        v30  |  0.1127    0.0798   -0.0065    0.0324    0.0040    0.0034    0.0103   -0.0142
        v31  |  0.0025    0.0084    0.0103   -0.0331   -0.0337    0.0280   -0.0227    0.0317
        v32  | -0.1172   -0.0635    0.0070    0.0517   -0.0448    0.0114   -0.0668    0.0179
        v33  | -0.0845   -0.0451   -0.0053   -0.1111    0.0074    0.0261   -0.0206    0.1221
        v34  | -0.1158   -0.0662    0.0074    0.0600   -0.0482    0.0141   -0.0664    0.0153
        v35  |  0.1228    0.0905   -0.0254   -0.0735    0.0219    0.0077    0.1439    0.0487
        v36  |  0.0151   -0.0061   -0.0003   -0.0487    0.0062    0.0071   -0.0252    0.0174
        v37  | -0.0716   -0.0443    0.0328    0.0021    0.0093    0.0777   -0.0152   -0.0351
        v38  | -0.0146    0.0497    0.0680    0.0353    0.0298    0.1418   -0.0384    0.1710
        v39  | -0.0282   -0.1434    0.1375   -0.0805    0.0185    0.0093    0.0263   -0.0023
        v40  | -0.1047    0.0099    0.0110    0.0079   -0.0230   -0.0197   -0.0211    0.0021
        v41  |  0.1142    0.3009   -0.1614    0.0522   -0.0072    0.0410   -0.0345    0.0045
        v42  |  0.0202    0.0555   -0.0184    0.0188    0.0177    0.0316    0.0842    0.0110
        v43  | -0.0935   -0.0938    0.1046    0.0012   -0.0564    0.0430    0.0730   -0.0115
        v44  | -0.0435   -0.0178    0.0043   -0.0446   -0.0057   -0.0100   -0.1024    0.0189
        v45  |  0.0547   -0.0838    0.1331    0.1065    0.0370   -0.1307    0.1234    0.0680
        v46  |  0.1299    0.3081   -0.1673    0.0553   -0.0038    0.0092   -0.0383    0.0100
        v47  |  0.0266   -0.0328   -0.0251   -0.0212   -0.0454   -0.0105    0.0136    0.0814
        v48  | -0.0025   -0.0330   -0.0168   -0.0200   -0.0361   -0.0183   -0.0482   -0.0243
        v49  |  0.0614   -0.0113    0.0317   -0.0306   -0.0032   -0.0176   -0.0180    0.0074
        v50  |  0.0788   -0.0340    0.0626   -0.2194    0.2350   -0.0343   -0.0572   -0.0535
        v51  | -0.0716   -0.0247    0.0079   -0.0338   -0.0096    0.0412    0.0584    0.1018
        v52  |  0.1158   -0.0394    0.1107    0.1204    0.0836   -0.0543    0.0728    0.0121
        v53  |  0.0605   -0.1004   -0.0707    0.1116    0.1765    0.0622    0.0242   -0.0480
        v54  |  0.0522    0.0344    0.0697    0.0184    0.0385    0.0389    0.0208   -0.0523
        v55  |  0.0141    0.0682    0.1112    0.1827   -0.1703   -0.0079    0.0415   -0.0126
        v56  |  0.0405    0.0336    0.0895    0.0010   -0.0188   -0.0170   -0.0067   -0.0341
        v57  | -0.0072   -0.1007   -0.1884   -0.0122   -0.0099    0.0575   -0.0077    0.0824
----------------------------------------------------------------------------------------------
```

continued on following page

```
Factor loadings (pattern matrix) and unique variances
-------------------------------------------------------------------------------
  Variable | Factor17  Factor18  Factor19  Factor20  Factor21  Factor22  Factor23  Factor24
-------------+-----------------------------------------------------------------------------
```

Variable	Factor17	Factor18	Factor19	Factor20	Factor21	Factor22	Factor23	Factor24
v1	-0.0601	0.1052	-0.0160	0.0387	0.0485	0.0376	0.0234	-0.0334
v2	0.0187	-0.1006	-0.0479	-0.0574	-0.0898	0.0271	0.0775	-0.1027
v3	0.0118	0.0739	0.0694	-0.0194	-0.0299	-0.1183	0.0363	-0.0236
v4	-0.0035	-0.0151	0.0148	0.0121	-0.0236	0.0561	-0.0404	0.0107
v5	0.0287	-0.0103	-0.0546	-0.0531	0.0449	0.0334	-0.0133	-0.0067
v6	-0.0477	0.0367	0.0554	0.0732	0.0043	-0.0354	-0.0311	-0.0446
v7	0.0359	-0.0740	-0.0515	0.0163	-0.0272	-0.0380	-0.0600	0.0352
v8	-0.0079	0.0046	0.0483	-0.0267	-0.0287	0.0330	0.0126	-0.0150
v9	-0.0277	0.0012	0.0150	0.0244	-0.0488	0.0005	0.0637	0.0092
v10	0.0297	-0.0858	-0.1295	-0.0543	0.0198	0.0207	0.0892	0.0023
v11	-0.0162	-0.0068	-0.0307	-0.0223	0.0995	-0.0191	-0.0105	0.0357
v12	0.0556	0.0272	-0.0107	0.0064	-0.0108	-0.0334	0.0179	0.0186
v13	0.1079	-0.0413	-0.0226	-0.0641	-0.0449	0.0189	-0.0419	0.0056
v14	0.0807	-0.1084	0.0319	-0.0556	0.0687	-0.0436	-0.0151	-0.0165
v15	-0.0516	-0.0172	0.0164	-0.0099	0.0266	0.0399	-0.0010	0.0222
v16	-0.0373	0.0121	0.0263	0.0328	-0.0005	-0.0481	0.0333	0.0341
v17	0.0444	0.0244	0.0144	-0.0015	-0.0482	0.0205	0.0002	-0.0049
v18	0.0066	-0.0607	0.0830	-0.0064	-0.0688	0.0245	-0.0234	0.0205
v19	-0.0131	-0.0670	-0.0232	0.0025	0.0299	0.0236	-0.0445	0.0373
v20	-0.0230	0.0529	0.0665	0.0339	0.0045	0.0062	0.0144	-0.0125
v21	-0.0633	0.0155	0.0098	-0.0226	0.0253	-0.0008	-0.0423	-0.0323
v22	0.0111	0.0258	-0.0013	-0.0071	0.0174	0.0050	-0.0220	-0.0010
v23	-0.0027	0.0862	-0.0467	0.0172	0.0866	-0.0143	-0.0089	-0.0190
v24	-0.0812	0.0066	0.0358	0.0644	-0.0695	0.0913	0.0163	-0.0101
v25	-0.0847	-0.0528	0.0215	0.0326	0.0091	0.0266	-0.0184	-0.0017
v26	-0.1100	0.0183	-0.0080	-0.0351	-0.0400	0.0125	-0.0395	0.0151
v27	-0.0389	0.0908	0.0736	-0.0383	0.0883	-0.0296	-0.0165	0.0353
v28	-0.0015	0.0478	-0.0774	-0.0722	0.0114	-0.0041	0.0033	-0.0100
v29	0.0112	-0.0403	0.0132	0.0564	-0.0408	-0.0182	-0.0318	0.0088
v30	0.0425	-0.0328	0.0246	0.0577	0.0587	-0.0352	0.0583	-0.0176
v31	0.1271	0.0372	0.0565	0.0535	0.0104	0.0754	-0.0223	-0.0066
v32	-0.0836	-0.0232	-0.0299	-0.0227	-0.0052	-0.0284	0.0146	-0.0116
v33	-0.0023	0.0105	-0.1205	0.1341	-0.0224	-0.0154	0.0115	0.0330
v34	-0.0820	-0.0155	-0.0369	-0.0219	-0.0053	-0.0309	0.0175	-0.0141
v35	0.0306	0.0624	-0.0702	-0.0434	0.0172	-0.0099	-0.0313	-0.0018
v36	0.1391	0.0023	0.0660	0.0111	-0.0053	-0.0053	0.0361	0.0294
v37	0.0564	0.0132	0.0365	-0.0046	-0.0258	-0.0247	0.0125	0.0134
v38	-0.0577	0.0322	0.0076	-0.0820	0.0652	0.0590	0.0966	0.0078
v39	0.0726	0.0509	0.0404	0.0053	0.0199	-0.0052	0.0359	-0.0132
v40	0.0134	-0.0004	0.0175	0.0070	-0.0346	0.0305	-0.0303	0.0373
v41	-0.0052	0.0224	-0.0075	0.0070	0.0064	-0.0112	0.0001	-0.0030
v42	-0.0209	-0.0045	0.0225	-0.0041	0.0037	0.0149	0.0084	-0.0070
v43	0.0446	-0.0079	0.0062	-0.0264	0.0203	-0.0208	-0.0411	-0.0407
v44	0.0904	0.0445	-0.0091	0.0593	0.0349	0.1373	-0.0255	-0.0585
v45	-0.0179	-0.0702	0.0114	0.0107	0.0738	0.0794	0.0116	0.0365
v46	-0.0069	-0.0227	0.0102	0.0116	0.0089	0.0136	0.0038	0.0090
v47	-0.0120	-0.0293	0.0621	-0.0551	-0.0183	-0.0806	-0.0697	-0.0635
v48	0.0231	0.0349	0.0122	-0.0353	-0.0004	-0.0014	0.0477	0.1085
v49	-0.0160	0.0659	-0.0004	-0.0656	-0.0525	0.0218	-0.0057	0.0163
v50	-0.1284	-0.0209	0.0268	-0.0161	-0.0155	0.0146	0.0180	-0.0219
v51	-0.0405	0.0136	-0.1555	0.0949	-0.0280	-0.0467	-0.0418	0.0120
v52	0.0233	0.0478	0.0175	0.0509	-0.0771	-0.0263	0.0749	0.0364
v53	0.0676	0.0612	-0.0560	-0.0247	-0.0419	-0.0002	0.0198	-0.0178
v54	0.0171	-0.1211	0.0254	0.1219	0.0917	-0.0460	0.0513	-0.0538
v55	0.0875	0.1037	-0.0630	0.0080	0.0022	-0.0050	-0.0230	-0.0287
v56	-0.0270	-0.0292	0.0250	0.0027	0.0205	0.0288	-0.0359	0.0092
v57	0.0341	-0.0934	0.0233	0.0005	0.0089	-0.0168	-0.0045	0.0573

continued on following page

```
Factor loadings (pattern matrix) and unique variances
------------------------------------------------------------------------
  Variable | Factor25  Factor26  Factor27  Factor28  Factor29  Factor30 |  Uniqueness
-----------+------------------------------------------------------------+------------
       v1 |   0.0095    0.0359   -0.0222    0.0154    0.0166   -0.0000 |    0.8087
       v2 |   0.0191    0.0539   -0.0537   -0.0201   -0.0235    0.0025 |    0.9255
       v3 |   0.0138   -0.0160    0.0035    0.0092   -0.0111   -0.0020 |    0.8328
       v4 |  -0.0248    0.0885    0.0684    0.0631   -0.0090   -0.0045 |    0.9692
       v5 |  -0.0275   -0.0079    0.0172    0.0020    0.0026   -0.0051 |    0.8136
       v6 |  -0.0693    0.0140   -0.0015   -0.0454   -0.0207   -0.0044 |    0.8584
       v7 |   0.0076    0.0284    0.0066   -0.0181    0.0281   -0.0002 |    0.8165
       v8 |  -0.0071    0.0007    0.0185    0.0299   -0.0305    0.0013 |    0.8506
       v9 |  -0.0017   -0.0188    0.0183   -0.0130    0.0415   -0.0033 |    0.7620
      v10 |   0.0136   -0.0577    0.0493    0.0207   -0.0054   -0.0027 |    0.8620
      v11 |   0.0452    0.0198   -0.0522   -0.0267   -0.0040    0.0009 |    0.7482
      v12 |   0.0019    0.0007    0.0170    0.0047    0.0011   -0.0017 |    0.8136
      v13 |  -0.0596   -0.0612   -0.0342   -0.0097    0.0077    0.0020 |    0.8593
      v14 |   0.0328    0.0165    0.0240    0.0061   -0.0059   -0.0035 |    0.8893
      v15 |   0.0153   -0.0015    0.0079    0.0057    0.0092   -0.0010 |    0.6059
      v16 |   0.0687   -0.0132    0.0422   -0.0096   -0.0267   -0.0028 |    0.8772
      v17 |  -0.0185   -0.0001    0.0006    0.0186    0.0292    0.0007 |    0.7446
      v18 |   0.0014    0.0157   -0.0321   -0.0043    0.0194    0.0037 |    0.7886
      v19 |  -0.0243   -0.0245    0.0096   -0.0109   -0.0024   -0.0002 |    0.6613
      v20 |  -0.0132   -0.0013   -0.0088   -0.0397   -0.0084    0.0028 |    0.8656
      v21 |  -0.0023   -0.0051   -0.0222    0.0266   -0.0119    0.0033 |    0.6502
      v22 |  -0.0099    0.0098   -0.0021    0.0003   -0.0035    0.0005 |    0.6448
      v23 |   0.0226    0.0458    0.0027    0.0166   -0.0141    0.0020 |    0.6508
      v24 |  -0.0448   -0.0254    0.0324    0.0075   -0.0061   -0.0008 |    0.8356
      v25 |   0.0072    0.0043   -0.0255    0.0078    0.0050   -0.0024 |    0.5268
      v26 |   0.0301   -0.0057    0.0173   -0.0126   -0.0053    0.0012 |    0.5616
      v27 |  -0.0067   -0.0537   -0.0051    0.0071    0.0220   -0.0023 |    0.8284
      v28 |  -0.0104    0.0089    0.0181   -0.0143    0.0042   -0.0019 |    0.4239
      v29 |   0.0007    0.0022   -0.0047   -0.0019   -0.0034   -0.0005 |    0.4277
      v30 |  -0.0475   -0.0202   -0.0077    0.0170    0.0115    0.0001 |    0.3673
      v31 |   0.0559   -0.0206   -0.0126   -0.0180   -0.0174    0.0005 |    0.3300
      v32 |  -0.0159    0.0191    0.0175   -0.0191    0.0096   -0.0008 |    0.0019
      v33 |   0.0042    0.0037   -0.0269    0.0331    0.0148    0.0019 |    0.9009
      v34 |  -0.0149    0.0253    0.0194   -0.0194    0.0201    0.0012 |    0.0028
      v35 |  -0.0157    0.0204    0.0137   -0.0390    0.0024    0.0030 |    0.4899
      v36 |  -0.0043    0.0333   -0.0177    0.0337   -0.0098   -0.0077 |    0.3250
      v37 |  -0.0184    0.0056    0.0101   -0.0206   -0.0082    0.0008 |    0.6978
      v38 |  -0.0105   -0.0197   -0.0153    0.0106   -0.0108    0.0031 |    0.8787
      v39 |  -0.0136    0.0166   -0.0099    0.0177    0.0263   -0.0014 |    0.8152
      v40 |   0.0277   -0.0520   -0.0234    0.0516   -0.0232    0.0061 |    0.2282
      v41 |   0.0128   -0.0029    0.0048    0.0093    0.0037    0.0002 |    0.7556
      v42 |   0.0070    0.0047   -0.0068   -0.0055    0.0052    0.0014 |    0.5788
      v43 |  -0.0112   -0.0179    0.0164   -0.0152   -0.0163   -0.0002 |    0.7379
      v44 |   0.0466   -0.0210    0.0588   -0.0467    0.0147    0.0043 |    0.9287
      v45 |   0.0270    0.0440   -0.0277    0.0036    0.0173    0.0004 |    0.8458
      v46 |   0.0105    0.0029   -0.0027    0.0040    0.0043    0.0001 |    0.7230
      v47 |   0.0535   -0.0001    0.0361    0.0374    0.0281    0.0114 |    0.9567
      v48 |  -0.0539    0.0438    0.0301   -0.0134   -0.0169    0.0181 |    0.9617
      v49 |   0.0186   -0.0103   -0.0148    0.0047    0.0110   -0.0033 |    0.6991
      v50 |   0.0116   -0.0205   -0.0029    0.0122    0.0016    0.0006 |    0.5645
      v51 |   0.0102   -0.0257   -0.0111    0.0095   -0.0238    0.0010 |    0.9057
      v52 |   0.0632    0.0080    0.0148   -0.0310    0.0066   -0.0001 |    0.8621
      v53 |   0.0160    0.0001   -0.0142    0.0145    0.0139    0.0054 |    0.7294
      v54 |  -0.0241   -0.0205    0.0169    0.0089    0.0043    0.0096 |    0.8766
      v55 |  -0.0259    0.0104   -0.0043    0.0202   -0.0004    0.0005 |    0.6200
      v56 |  -0.0048   -0.0015   -0.0095   -0.0051   -0.0070    0.0011 |    0.3216
      v57 |   0.0084    0.0116    0.0059   -0.0275   -0.0061   -0.0025 |    0.5976
------------------------------------------------------------------------
```

SAS Macro Codes Used for Display 6.9

```
%MACRO FREQ_Cutoff(INFILE, INVAR, CUTOFF,Condition);
  PROC SUMMARY DATA=&INFILE;
    VAR &INVAR;
      &condition;
    OUTPUT OUT=TEMP_1 MEAN=;
  PROC TRANSPOSE DATA=TEMP_1(DROP=_TYPE_ _FREQ_) OUT=TEMP_1(DROP=_LABEL_)
    NAME=VARN PREFIX=VARM;
  DATA TEMP_1;
    SET TEMP_1;
    IF VARM1>=&CUTOFF;
  PROC IML;
    USE TEMP_1;
    READ ALL VAR _CHAR_ INTO X;
    N=NROW(X);
    CLOSE;
    VARK="";
    VARKN=0;
    DO I=1 TO N;
      VARKN=VARKN+1;
      VARK=VARK + ' ' + X[I];
    END;
    NAMES={VARK};
    CREATE TEMP_1 FROM VARK[C=NAMES];
    APPEND FROM VARK;
    CLOSE;
    NAMES={VARKN};
    CREATE TEMP_2 FROM VARKN[C=NAMES];
    APPEND FROM VARKN;
    CLOSE;
  PROC SQL NOPRINT;
    SELECT VARK INTO:VARK FROM TEMP_1;
    SELECT VARKN INTO:VARKN FROM TEMP_2;
  quit;
    %let outvar=&vark;
  RUN;
%MEND;

%Macro InputData(infile1, infile2, outfile1, outfile2);
PROC IMPORT OUT= attrib
      DATAFILE= &infile1
          DBMS=DLM REPLACE ;
    DELIMITER='2C'x;
    GETNAMES=YES;
    DATAROW=2;
RUN;
```

```
data &outfile1 ;
set attrib (drop=dummy rename=(visited=site));
URL=substr(URL,2,length(trim(URL))-1);
visited='AAAA';
if _N_<10 then visited='AAA'|| put(_N_,1.);
if _N_<100 and _N_>9 then visited='AA'|| put(_N_,2.);
if _N_<1000 and _N_>99 then visited='A'|| put(_N_,3.);
vcode='V' || put(code,4.);
run;
PROC IMPORT OUT= TRAIN
      DATAFILE= &infile2
      DBMS=DLM REPLACE;
    DELIMITER='2C'x;
    GETNAMES=YES;
    DATAROW=2;
RUN;
data temp_ (drop=dummy);
retain user_id ;
set train (rename=(user_id=code));
if index='C' then user_id=code;
if user_id=. then user_id=dif(user_id);
run;
```

continued on following page

```
/*--------------------------------------------------------------
   Determine the most freq visited websites among 294 sites
   -----------------------------------------------------------*/;
proc sql noprint;
create table temp as select temp_.*,visited,attrib.vcode from temp_ left join
attrib on temp_.code=put(attrib.code,4.);
quit;

data temp;
set temp;
if visited='' then visited='USER';
run;
proc sort data=temp;
by user_id index;
run;
proc freq data=temp;
table visited;
run;
data temp;
set temp;
by user_id;
if first.user_id then cnt=1;
else cnt+1;
run;
proc sort data=temp;
by user_id cnt;
run;
Data temp;
 array Dx[50] sDx1-sDx50;
 retain sDx1-sDx50;
 set temp;
 by user_id;
 if first.user_id  then
    do i=1 to 50;
       Dx[i]=0;
       end;
 if visited~='USER' then Dx[cnt-1]=code;
 if last.user_id then output;
 keep user_id sDx1-sDx50 ;
run;
```

```
/*---------------------------------------------
 Temp data with 300 columns
 -------------------------------------------*/;
data tempV (keep=user_id vcode1000-vcode1299);
retain user_id ;
array vcode[300] vcode1000-vcode1299;

set train (rename=(user_id=code));
do j=1 to 300;
   vcode[j]=0;
end;
if index='C' then user_id=code;
if user_id=. then user_id=dif(user_id);
if index='C';
run;
/*--------------------------------------------------
 Merge two datasets
 --------------------------------------------------*/;
proc sql noprint;
create table tempw as select tempv.*, temp.* from tempv innor join temp on
tempv.user_id=temp.user_id;
quit;

data &outfile2 (drop=j i sDx1-sDx50);
set tempw;
array vcode[300] vcode1000-vcode1299;
array Dx[50] sDx1-sDx50;
do j=1 to 300;
      do i=1 to 50;
          if (dx[i]-999)=j then vcode[j]=1;
          end;
      end;
run;
%mend;
```

Output of Factor Analysis of Binary Data (Display 6.10)

```
                        The FACTOR Procedure
               Initial Factor Method: Principal Components

                   Prior Communality Estimates: ONE

       Eigenvalues of the Correlation Matrix: Total = 285   Average = 1

                 Eigenvalue    Difference    Proportion    Cumulative

            1     48.852185     23.858626       0.1714        0.1714
            2     24.993558      0.485767       0.0877        0.2591
            3     24.507791      4.176016       0.0860        0.3451
            4     20.331775      1.455398       0.0713        0.4164
            5     18.876377      2.299199       0.0662        0.4827
            6     16.577178      1.376676       0.0582        0.5408
            7     15.200502      0.637479       0.0533        0.5942
            8     14.563023      0.382294       0.0511        0.6453
            9     14.180729      0.200934       0.0498        0.6950
           10     13.979795      0.760586       0.0491        0.7441
           11     13.219209      0.288029       0.0464        0.7905
           12     12.931180      0.573225       0.0454        0.8358
           13     12.357956      0.096795       0.0434        0.8792
           14     12.261161      0.382856       0.0430        0.9222
           15     11.878305      0.184809       0.0417        0.9639
           16     11.693496      0.170976       0.0410        1.0049
           17     11.522520      0.229115       0.0404        1.0454
           18     11.293405      0.270432       0.0396        1.0850
           19     11.022973      0.220015       0.0387        1.1237
           20     10.802958      0.055043       0.0379        1.1616
           21     10.747915      0.087616       0.0377        1.1993
           22     10.660299      0.342395       0.0374        1.2367
           23     10.317903      0.141323       0.0362        1.2729
           24     10.176580      0.262931       0.0357        1.3086
           25      9.913649      0.065632       0.0348        1.3434
           26      9.848017      0.335981       0.0346        1.3779
           27      9.512037      0.091784       0.0334        1.4113
           28      9.420253      0.359855       0.0331        1.4444
           29      9.060398      0.092776       0.0318        1.4762
           30      8.967622      0.106453       0.0315        1.5076
           31      8.861169      0.033015       0.0311        1.5387
           32      8.828154      0.008820       0.0310        1.5697
           33      8.819333      0.373664       0.0309        1.6006
           34      8.445669      0.074154       0.0296        1.6303

           35      8.371515      0.031504       0.0294        1.6596
           36      8.340012      0.126829       0.0293        1.6889
           37      8.213183      0.251535       0.0288        1.7177
           38      7.961648      0.048341       0.0279        1.7457
           39      7.913307      0.055586       0.0278        1.7734
           40      7.857721      0.106911       0.0276        1.8010
           41      7.750810      0.067612       0.0272        1.8282
           42      7.683198      0.137290       0.0270        1.8551
           43      7.545909      0.090264       0.0265        1.8816
           44      7.455645      0.080305       0.0262        1.9078
           45      7.375340      0.056880       0.0259        1.9337
           46      7.318460      0.081669       0.0257        1.9593
           47      7.236791      0.055268       0.0254        1.9847
           48      7.181523      0.106673       0.0252        2.0099
           49      7.074850      0.179907       0.0248        2.0348
           50      6.894943      0.054124       0.0242        2.0589
           51      6.840819      0.074654       0.0240        2.0829
           52      6.766165      0.110926       0.0237        2.1067
           53      6.655239      0.156960       0.0234        2.1300
           54      6.498279      0.085387       0.0228        2.1528
           55      6.412892      0.080403       0.0225        2.1753
           56      6.332489      0.019400       0.0222        2.1976
           57      6.313089      0.088106       0.0222        2.2197
           58      6.224983      0.047466       0.0218        2.2416
           59      6.177517      0.104829       0.0217        2.2632
           60      6.072688      0.205431       0.0213        2.2845
           61      5.867258      0.096381       0.0206        2.3051
           62      5.770877      0.023211       0.0202        2.3254
           63      5.747665      0.112561       0.0202        2.3455
           64      5.635104      0.027848       0.0198        2.3653
           65      5.607256      0.070907       0.0197        2.3850
           66      5.536349      0.118761       0.0194        2.4044
           67      5.417588      0.073060       0.0190        2.4234
```

68	5.344529	0.041301	0.0188	2.4422
69	5.303227	0.137139	0.0186	2.4608
70	5.166089	0.025234	0.0181	2.4789
71	5.140854	0.025196	0.0180	2.4970
72	5.115658	0.116856	0.0179	2.5149
73	4.998802	0.043337	0.0175	2.5324
74	4.955464	0.116868	0.0174	2.5498
75	4.838597	0.056802	0.0170	2.5668
76	4.781794	0.052826	0.0168	2.5836
77	4.728968	0.115630	0.0166	2.6002
78	4.613338	0.067197	0.0162	2.6164
79	4.546141	0.103644	0.0160	2.6323
80	4.442497	0.023417	0.0156	2.6479
81	4.419080	0.085615	0.0155	2.6634
82	4.333465	0.071456	0.0152	2.6786
83	4.262009	0.044871	0.0150	2.6936
84	4.217138	0.130294	0.0148	2.7084
85	4.086844	0.016289	0.0143	2.7227
86	4.070555	0.057253	0.0143	2.7370
87	4.013302	0.157387	0.0141	2.7511
88	3.855916	0.037748	0.0135	2.7646
89	3.818168	0.095294	0.0134	2.7780
90	3.722874	0.038022	0.0131	2.7911
91	3.684852	0.067633	0.0129	2.8040
92	3.617219	0.044340	0.0127	2.8167
93	3.572879	0.037030	0.0125	2.8292
94	3.535849	0.073560	0.0124	2.8416
95	3.462289	0.064604	0.0121	2.8538
96	3.397685	0.050748	0.0119	2.8657
97	3.346937	0.074004	0.0117	2.8774
98	3.272933	0.031756	0.0115	2.8889
99	3.241176	0.027084	0.0114	2.9003
100	3.214092	0.130505	0.0113	2.9116
101	3.083587	0.080436	0.0108	2.9224
102	3.003151	0.067982	0.0105	2.9329
103	2.935169	0.031437	0.0103	2.9432
104	2.903732	0.006767	0.0102	2.9534
105	2.896966	0.098267	0.0102	2.9636
106	2.798698	0.058827	0.0098	2.9734
107	2.739871	0.034097	0.0096	2.9830
108	2.705775	0.047043	0.0095	2.9925
109	2.658731	0.134779	0.0093	3.0018
110	2.523952	0.034848	0.0089	3.0107
111	2.489104	0.019598	0.0087	3.0194
112	2.469505	0.058945	0.0087	3.0281
113	2.410560	0.036559	0.0085	3.0365
114	2.374001	0.069159	0.0083	3.0449
115	2.304842	0.027302	0.0081	3.0530
116	2.277540	0.025708	0.0080	3.0610
117	2.251832	0.084259	0.0079	3.0689
118	2.167572	0.028672	0.0076	3.0765
119	2.138901	0.046902	0.0075	3.0840
120	2.091999	0.079357	0.0073	3.0913
121	2.012642	0.060284	0.0071	3.0984
122	1.952358	0.023795	0.0069	3.1052
123	1.928563	0.047385	0.0068	3.1120
124	1.881179	0.039558	0.0066	3.1186
125	1.841621	0.054188	0.0065	3.1251
126	1.787433	0.074442	0.0063	3.1313
127	1.712991	0.007955	0.0060	3.1373
128	1.705036	0.034826	0.0060	3.1433
129	1.670210	0.024569	0.0059	3.1492
130	1.645641	0.031127	0.0058	3.1549
131	1.614514	0.043529	0.0057	3.1606
132	1.570985	0.009313	0.0055	3.1661
133	1.561672	0.027006	0.0055	3.1716
134	1.534666	0.065771	0.0054	3.1770
135	1.468895	0.037977	0.0052	3.1821
136	1.430919	0.013097	0.0050	3.1872
137	1.417821	0.010869	0.0050	3.1921
138	1.406952	0.054643	0.0049	3.1971
139	1.352309	0.038765	0.0047	3.2018
140	1.313544	0.049726	0.0046	3.2064
141	1.263818	0.022999	0.0044	3.2109
142	1.240819	0.084080	0.0044	3.2152
143	1.156739	0.023682	0.0041	3.2193
144	1.133056	0.047952	0.0040	3.2233
145	1.085104	0.038848	0.0038	3.2271
146	1.046257	0.028672	0.0037	3.2307
147	1.017585	0.137635	0.0036	3.2343
148	0.879950	0.059804	0.0031	3.2374
149	0.820146	0.010524	0.0029	3.2403

150	0.809622	0.071964	0.0028	3.2431
151	0.737658	0.036813	0.0026	3.2457
152	0.700845	0.017451	0.0025	3.2482
153	0.683394	0.060071	0.0024	3.2506
154	0.623323	0.097688	0.0022	3.2527
155	0.525634	0.078485	0.0018	3.2546
156	0.447149	0.005612	0.0016	3.2562
157	0.441537	0.078514	0.0015	3.2577
158	0.363023	0.070393	0.0013	3.2590
159	0.292630	0.012371	0.0010	3.2600
160	0.280259	0.055490	0.0010	3.2610
161	0.224770	0.054849	0.0008	3.2618
162	0.169920	0.069413	0.0006	3.2624
163	0.100507	0.050530	0.0004	3.2627
164	0.049977	0.049976	0.0002	3.2629
165	0.000001	0.000000	0.0000	3.2629
166	0.000001	0.000000	0.0000	3.2629
167	0.000001	0.000000	0.0000	3.2629
168	0.000001	0.037748	0.0000	3.2629
169	-0.037747	0.056737	-0.0001	3.2628
170	-0.094484	0.044962	-0.0003	3.2624
171	-0.139445	0.036796	-0.0005	3.2619
172	-0.176241	0.021805	-0.0006	3.2613
173	-0.198047	0.126118	-0.0007	3.2606
174	-0.324164	0.031477	-0.0011	3.2595
175	-0.355641	0.038587	-0.0012	3.2582
176	-0.394228	0.089556	-0.0014	3.2569
177	-0.483785	0.044317	-0.0017	3.2552
178	-0.528101	0.094354	-0.0019	3.2533
179	-0.622456	0.067800	-0.0022	3.2511
180	-0.690256	0.056952	-0.0024	3.2487
181	-0.747208	0.019183	-0.0026	3.2461
182	-0.766392	0.093343	-0.0027	3.2434
183	-0.859734	0.056307	-0.0030	3.2404
184	-0.916041	0.031174	-0.0032	3.2372
185	-0.947215	0.065510	-0.0033	3.2338
186	-1.012725	0.011714	-0.0036	3.2303
187	-1.024439	0.154335	-0.0036	3.2267
188	-1.178774	0.019958	-0.0041	3.2226
189	-1.198732	0.083753	-0.0042	3.2184
190	-1.282485	0.071143	-0.0045	3.2139
191	-1.353628	0.060119	-0.0047	3.2091
192	-1.413747	0.065709	-0.0050	3.2041
193	-1.479455	0.039536	-0.0052	3.1990
194	-1.518992	0.127464	-0.0053	3.1936
195	-1.646456	0.030885	-0.0058	3.1878
196	-1.677341	0.027632	-0.0059	3.1820
197	-1.704973	0.089384	-0.0060	3.1760
198	-1.794357	0.062974	-0.0063	3.1697
199	-1.857331	0.057549	-0.0065	3.1632
200	-1.914881	0.034279	-0.0067	3.1564
201	-1.949160	0.100553	-0.0068	3.1496
202	-2.049712	0.063494	-0.0072	3.1424
203	-2.113207	0.041296	-0.0074	3.1350
204	-2.154503	0.052280	-0.0076	3.1274
205	-2.206783	0.099601	-0.0077	3.1197
206	-2.306384	0.030424	-0.0081	3.1116
207	-2.336808	0.071739	-0.0082	3.1034
208	-2.408547	0.049147	-0.0085	3.0950
209	-2.457694	0.034058	-0.0086	3.0863
210	-2.491751	0.082210	-0.0087	3.0776
211	-2.573962	0.051139	-0.0090	3.0686
212	-2.625100	0.135600	-0.0092	3.0593
213	-2.760701	0.087001	-0.0097	3.0497
214	-2.847702	0.074859	-0.0100	3.0397
215	-2.922560	0.065984	-0.0103	3.0294
216	-2.988544	0.023259	-0.0105	3.0189
217	-3.011804	0.089908	-0.0106	3.0084
218	-3.101711	0.067202	-0.0109	2.9975
219	-3.168914	0.065768	-0.0111	2.9864
220	-3.234681	0.048351	-0.0113	2.9750
221	-3.283032	0.016201	-0.0115	2.9635
222	-3.299233	0.169242	-0.0116	2.9519
223	-3.468475	0.071157	-0.0122	2.9397
224	-3.539633	0.062537	-0.0124	2.9273
225	-3.602170	0.033316	-0.0126	2.9147

226	-3.635486	0.117054	-0.0128	2.9019
227	-3.752540	0.033724	-0.0132	2.8888
228	-3.786264	0.135234	-0.0133	2.8755
229	-3.921497	0.015337	-0.0138	2.8617
230	-3.936835	0.074830	-0.0138	2.8479
231	-4.011665	0.034151	-0.0141	2.8338
232	-4.045815	0.138035	-0.0142	2.8196
233	-4.183850	0.026784	-0.0147	2.8049
234	-4.210634	0.119102	-0.0148	2.7902
235	-4.329736	0.043404	-0.0152	2.7750
236	-4.373140	0.039711	-0.0153	2.7596
237	-4.412851	0.016140	-0.0155	2.7442
238	-4.428991	0.125706	-0.0155	2.7286
239	-4.554697	0.096682	-0.0160	2.7126
240	-4.651379	0.028889	-0.0163	2.6963
241	-4.680268	0.163244	-0.0164	2.6799
242	-4.843512	0.063195	-0.0170	2.6629
243	-4.906707	0.060810	-0.0172	2.6457
244	-4.967516	0.036567	-0.0174	2.6282
245	-5.004083	0.101734	-0.0176	2.6107
246	-5.105818	0.036394	-0.0179	2.5928
247	-5.142212	0.122907	-0.0180	2.5747
248	-5.265118	0.126169	-0.0185	2.5563
249	-5.391287	0.022186	-0.0189	2.5373
250	-5.413473	0.083628	-0.0190	2.5183
251	-5.497101	0.097362	-0.0193	2.4991
252	-5.594463	0.158346	-0.0196	2.4794
253	-5.752809	0.053060	-0.0202	2.4592
254	-5.805869	0.048237	-0.0204	2.4389
255	-5.854105	0.135393	-0.0205	2.4183
256	-5.989499	0.042832	-0.0210	2.3973
257	-6.032330	0.077561	-0.0212	2.3761
258	-6.109891	0.168157	-0.0214	2.3547
259	-6.278049	0.078058	-0.0220	2.3327
260	-6.356107	0.073652	-0.0223	2.3104
261	-6.429759	0.125507	-0.0226	2.2878
262	-6.555266	0.040980	-0.0230	2.2648
263	-6.596246	0.090790	-0.0231	2.2417
264	-6.687036	0.091941	-0.0235	2.2182
265	-6.778977	0.269758	-0.0238	2.1944
266	-7.048735	0.070055	-0.0247	2.1697
267	-7.118789	0.054875	-0.0250	2.1447
268	-7.173664	0.224932	-0.0252	2.1195
269	-7.398596	0.116941	-0.0260	2.0936
270	-7.515538	0.017775	-0.0264	2.0672
271	-7.533312	0.141806	-0.0264	2.0408
272	-7.675118	0.315169	-0.0269	2.0139
273	-7.990287	0.034935	-0.0280	1.9858
274	-8.025222	0.132372	-0.0282	1.9577
275	-8.157594	0.286744	-0.0286	1.9290
276	-8.444338	0.160423	-0.0296	1.8994
277	-8.604761	0.164918	-0.0302	1.8692
278	-8.769679	0.352909	-0.0308	1.8384
279	-9.122588	0.516204	-0.0320	1.8064
280	-9.638792	0.285632	-0.0338	1.7726
281	-9.924424	0.089635	-0.0348	1.7378
282	-10.014059	3.211905	-0.0351	1.7027
283	-13.225963	6.771238	-0.0464	1.6562
284	-19.997201	147.035554	-0.0702	1.5861
285	-167.03276		-0.5861	1.0000

16 factors will be retained by the PROPORTION criterion.

Chapter VII
Models Network Data for Association and Prediction

Whatever you are by nature, keep to it; never desert your line of talent. Be what nature intended you for and you will succeed.

- Sydney Smith

INTRODUCTION

Data exploratory analysis discovers data structures and patterns with all variables as a whole, but this analysis does not particularly focus on seeking associations between response variables and predictor variables. In this chapter, we will discuss how to identify and measure this response-prediction relationship, which is an essential element in intrusion detection and prevention. Even though the expression for models for association and prediction can have a broad range, in general the goals of modeling for association and prediction in network security are two-fold: (1) to identify variables that are significantly associated with the response variable and (2) to assess the robustness of these variables, if any, in predicting the response.

Although the term, model, is perhaps confusing to many people, a model is just a simplified representation of some aspect of the real world, whether an object or observation, or a situation or process. Models are of particular importance for network security because of the size of data and the complex relationship among variables and the desired outcomes. Statistical modeling procedures available for analyzing the response-predictor phenomenon mainly include bivariate analysis and multiple regression-based analysis. Bivariate analysis focuses on the relationship between two variables (e.g., a response and a predictor) without taking into account any impact from other predictor variables on the response variable. The multiple regression modeling approach, on the other hand, requires establishing a regression relationship between a response variable and a set of potential predictor variables, and the predictive power of each of the predictors as adjusted by others. Therefore, a variable associates with the response significantly in the bivariate analysis may no longer hold such an association in the regression analysis after adjusting from other variables. In the following sections, we will review and discuss these two main approaches in detail. For readers who would like to attain a more general knowledge on modeling associations should refer to Mandel (1964), Press & Wilson (1978), Cohen & Cohen (1983), Berry & Feldman (1985), Cox & Snell (1989), McCullagh & Nelder (1989), Agresti (1996), Ryan (1997), Long (1997), Burnham & Anderson (1998), Pampel (2000), Tabachnick & Fidell (2001), Agresti (2002), Myers, Montgomery & Vining (2002), Menard (2002), and O'Connell (2006). Comprehensive reviews on data mining and statistical learning can be found from Vapnik (1998, 1999), Hastie, Tibshirani & Friedman (2001), Bozdogan (2003).

BIVARIATE ANALYSIS

Bivariate analysis measures the association between two variables (Y, X) in a pair mutually. It answers fundamental questions of whether two variables are associated, and if such an association exists whether it is statistically significant or not. Bivariate analysis differs from descriptive analysis that we discussed in Chapter V because descriptive analysis aims to present information on describing the data attributes, while bivariate analysis aims to present information about the association. It is the most widely used statistical procedure in social science, medicine and healthcare. A large number of statistical procedures are available to investigate such relationships and to measure the association and test the statistical significance of these relationships. In the following sections we will discuss the basic concepts and methods to conduct bivariate analysis.

Measure of Bivariate Association

Let Y be a response variable of interest; we want to assess its relationship with the other variables, $X_1, X_2, ..., X_n$. We can make n pairs of measurements, $(Y \sim X_1), (Y \sim X_2), \cdots, (Y \sim X_n)$, to assess the relationship of each of the pairs. Using this measure of association helps us to understand the relationship between variables: for example, the impact of a change in X_i from a corresponding change in Y. Although a large number of statistical procedures are available to investigate such a relationship, measures of association vary by the level of the measurement of the variables analyzed. When Y and X_i, or both, are combinations of binary, categorical, or limited-scale ordinal variables, a contingency table is a common method to summarize the relationship giving the frequencies of observations that are cross-classified by such variables. Table 7.1 shows an example of an $i \times j$ contingency table. We know that when $i = j = 2$, we have a 2×2 cross-table, which is the most widely used statistical tool for bivariate analysis with binary variables.

When there is a Y and X_i pair and one is a non-continuous (e.g., binary, categorical or scale ordinal with limited scale), and the other is continuous, we can assess the relationship between variables by comparing the difference in distribution of the continuous variable according to the measurement level of the other variable. In doing so, we can measure the difference in means, medians, percentiles, and ranges of the continuous variable across the category of the non-continuous variable. Table 7.2 shows an example of such a comparison. When Y and X_i are both continuous, we use the correlation to measure the relationship; this measure will be discussed in detail in next section.

Example 7.1→Bivariate Analysis. A statistical model with a large number of predictor variables may not guarantee a high predicting power, and unnecessary variables could cause biases that lead the model to either overestimate or underestimate the predicted values. Identifying a small set of variables that are robust, statistically significant, and stable to use in detecting intrusion from a pool of all possible variables is desired. Bivariate analysis can be used to accomplish such a task by eliminating variables that are not associated with the outcome of interest so that we can construct a parsimonious model and present results in a simple format.

Let us use the 1999 KDD-cup data that has a response variable coded as attack (yes/no) and 41 predictor variables (Stolfo, 2000) to conduct a bivariate analysis. Our goal is to assess the associations between the predictor variables and the response variable. Before we can start the bivariate analysis, we decode the "type of the protocol," which is a categorical variable, into 3 dummy variables: ICMP (yes/no), TCP (yes/no), and UDP (yes/no) and divide the "normal or error status of the connection" categorical variable into 4 dummy variables: REJ (yes/no), S0 (yes/no), SF (yes/no), and RSTO/RSTOS0/RSTR (yes/no). The continuous variables, "number of data bytes from source to destination" and "number of data bytes from destination to source" are condensed by dividing the original values by 1,000 to match in scale with the other variables. The final total number of variables is therefore, 46. We also examine the frequency of each variable and remove variables with extraordinary low frequencies from the bivariate analysis. Table 7.3 shows the results of the

Table 7.1 An $i \times j$ contingency table to analyze binary, categorical or limited scale ordinal variables

Category (variable Y)	Category (variable X)				Total
	c_1	c_2	$\ldots$	c_j	
c_1	n_{11}	n_{12}	$\ldots$	n_{1j}	$\sum_{k=1}^{j} n_{1k}$
c_2	n_{21}	n_{22}	$\ldots$	n_{2j}	$\sum_{k=1}^{j} n_{2k}$
$\vdots$	$\vdots$	$\vdots$	$\ldots$	$\vdots$	$\vdots$
c_i	n_{i1}	n_{i2}	$\ldots$	n_{ij}	$\sum_{k=1}^{j} n_{ik}$
Total	$\sum_{k=1}^{i} n_{k1}$	$\sum_{k=1}^{i} n_{k2}$	$\ldots$	$\sum_{k=1}^{i} n_{kj}$	N

Table 7.2 Compare difference in distributions between a continuous variable and a non-continuous (e.g., binary, categorical or limited scale ordinal) variable

Non-continuous (variable Y)	Continuous (variable x)				Total
	Mean (SD)	Median	Max – min	25th – 75th	
c_1	$\mu_1(\sigma_1)$	η_1	x_1^{max}, x_1^{min}	x_1^{25th}, x_1^{75th}	n_1
c_2	$\mu_2(\sigma_2)$	η_2	x_2^{max}, x_2^{min}	x_2^{25th}, x_2^{75th}	n_2
$\vdots$	$\vdots$	$\vdots$	$\vdots$	$\vdots$	$\vdots$
c_i	$\mu_i(\sigma_i)$	η_i	x_i^{max}, x_i^{min}	x_i^{25th}, x_i^{75th}	n_i
Total	$\mu(\sigma)$	η	x^{max}, x^{min}	x^{25th}, x^{75th}	N

analysis; variables are organized into four groups: (1) basic features of individual TCP/IP connections, (2) content features within a connection suggested by domain knowledge, (3) traffic features computed using a two-second time window, and (4) destination features. Note that 10 variables have been eliminated due to extraordinarily low frequency values.

Correlation Analysis

When both Y and X are continuous and follow a normal distribution we can measure the correlation between Y and X by calculating the correlation coefficient, $\rho_{X,Y}$

$$\rho_{X,Y} = \frac{\sum_{i=1}^{n}(x_i - \overline{x})(y_i - \overline{y})}{\sqrt{\sum_{i=1}^{n}(x_i - \overline{x})^2}\sqrt{\sum_{i=1}^{n}(y_i - \overline{y})^2}} \tag{7-1}$$

to assess the relationship, where $\overline{y}$ and $\overline{x}$ are the means values of the variables, Y and X, respectively. If Y and X are totally independent then $\rho_{X,Y} = 0$, if $Y = X$ then $|\rho_{X,Y}| = 1$, if $\rho_{X,Y} < 0$ then Y and X have a negative linear relationship, and if $\rho_{X,Y} > 0$ then Y and X have a positive linear relationship. The closer the coefficient is to either -1 or 1, the stronger the correlation between Y and X will be. Figure 7.1 illustrates an example adopted from Wikipedia (http://en.wikipedia.org/wiki/Correlation), which shows different ranges of correlation coefficients. Displays 7.1 and 7.2 illustrate R codes to calculate the correlation coefficients of variables v1 to v57 for the spam-email data and the results of the first 5 variables, respectively.

Table 7.3 Bivariate analysis based on the 10% of the training data

ID	Variables	Anomaly		Anomaly-free	
	Basic features of individual TCP connections				
1	Length (number of seconds) of the connection (mean, SD)	6.62	402.56	216.66	1359.21
	Type of protocol				
2	ICMP (yes/no [%, #])	71.16	282,314	1.32	1,288
3	TCP (yes/no [%, #])	28.55	113,252	78.96	76,813
4	UDP (yes/no [%, #])	0.30	1,177	19.71	19,177
5	Network service on the destination, HTTP (yes/no [%, #])	0.61	2,407	63.62	61,886
6	Number of data bytes from source to destination (per 1,000) (mean, SD)	3.48	1102.60	1.16	34.23
7	Number of data bytes from destination to source (per 1,000) (mean, SD)	0.25	31.80	3.38	37.58
	Normal or error status of the connection				
8	REJ (yes/no [%, #])	5.43	21,534	5.49	5,341
9	S0 (yes/no [%, #])	21.92	86,956	0.05	51
10	SF (yes/no [%, #])	72.27	286,731	94.28	91,709
11	RSTO or RSTOS0 or RSTR (yes/no [%, #])	0.35	1,395	0.10	98
	Content features within a connection suggested by domain knowledge				
12	Login successfully (yes/no [%,#])	0.83	3,298	71.9	69,939
13	Number of compromised conditions (mean, SD)	0.01	0.11	0.03	4.05
14	Number of root accesses (mean, SD)	0.00	0.11	0.06	4.53
15	Number of file creation operations (mean, SD)	0.00	0.04	0.00	0.20
16	Number of operations on access control files (mean, SD)	0.00	0.01	0.01	0.08
17	Guest login (yes/no, [%, #])	0.08	314	0.38	371
	Traffic features computed using a two-second time window				
18	Connections to the same host as the current connection (mean, SD)	411.76	156.27	8.16	17.71

continued on following page

Table 7.3 continued

#	Description				
19	Rate of connections that have SYN errors (mean, SD)	0.22	0.41	0	0.03
20	Rate of connections that have REJ errors (mean, SD)	0.06	0.23	0.06	0.23
21	Rate of connections to the same service (mean, SD)	0.74	0.42	0.99	0.09
22	Rate of connections to different services (mean, SD)	0.02	0.71	0.02	0.12
23	Connections to the same service as the current connection (mean, SD)	362.04	226.19	10.94	21.80
24	Rate of connections that have SYN errors (mean, SD)	0.22	0.41	0	0.03
25	Rate of connections that have REJ errors (mean, SD)	0.06	0.23	0.06	0.23
26	Rate of connections to different hosts (mean, SD)	0	0.05	0.13	0.28
	Destination				
27	Connections having the same destination host (mean, SD)	253.06	21.13	148.51	103.40
28	Connections having the same destination host and using the same service (mean, SD)	185.38	109.98	202.06	86.91
29	Rate of connections having the same destination host and using the same service (mean, SD)	0.73	0.43	0.84	0.31
30	Rate of different services on the current host (mean, SD)	0.02	0.08	0.06	0.18
31	Rate of connections to the current host having the same source port (mean, SD)	0.72	0.45	0.13	0.28
32	Rate of connections to the same service coming from different hosts (mean, SD)	0.00	0.04	0.02	0.05
33	Rate of connections to the current host with S0 errors (mean, SD)	0.22	0.41	0.00	0.03
34	Rate of connections to the current host and specified service with S0 errors (mean, SD)	0.22	0.41	0.00	0.02
35	Rate of connections to the current host with RST errors (mean, SD)	0.06	0.23	0.06	0.22
36	Rate of connections to the current host and specified service with RST errors (mean, SD)	0.06	0.23	0.06	0.22

Figure 7.1 Example of linear correlation: 1000 pairs of normally distributed numbers are plotted against one another in each panel (bottom left), and the corresponding correlation coefficients shown (top right). This image is adapted from Wikipedia, the free encyclopedia (http://en.wikipedia.org/wiki/Correlation)

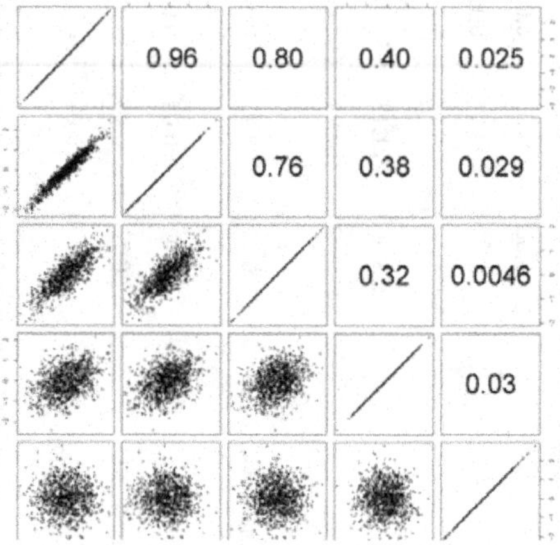

Display 7.1
R codes to calculate correlation coefficients of variables v1 to v57 of spam-email data

```
# Read Ascii data to the data object spam
spam<-read.table("F:\\Book\\Chapter 7\\spam_r.txt",header = TRUE, sep = ",")
attach(spam)
cor(cbind(v1,v2,v3,v4,v5,v6,v7,v8,v9,v10,v11,v12,v13,v14,v15,v16,v17,v18,v19,
v20,v21,v22,v23,v24,v25,v26,v27,v28,v29,v30,v31,v32,v33,v34,v35,v36,v37,v38,
v39,v40,v41,v42,v43,v44,v45,v46,v47,v48,v49,v50,v51,v52,v53,v54,v55,v56,v57))
```

Display 7.2
Correlation coefficients of the first 5 variables (v1 to v5)

	v1	v2	v3	v4	v5
v1	1.000000000	-0.0167594660	0.065626767	0.0132732322	2.311863e-02
v2	-0.016759466	1.0000000000	-0.033525680	-0.0069232125	-2.375991e-02
v3	0.065626767	-0.0335256801	1.000000000	-0.0202462310	7.773450e-02
v4	0.013273232	-0.0069232125	-0.020246231	1.0000000000	3.238151e-03
v5	0.023118631	-0.0237599118	0.077734499	0.0032381509	1.000000e+00

Equation (7-1) is also known as Pearson linear correlation coefficient because Pearson (1896, 1898) was the key person to popularize its use. However, the Pearson linear correlation coefficient could be greatly affected by even one single outlier. This is because the calculation is based on the mean, and a single extreme value can greatly increase or

Figure 7.2 Nonlinear association with a correlation coefficient equal to zero

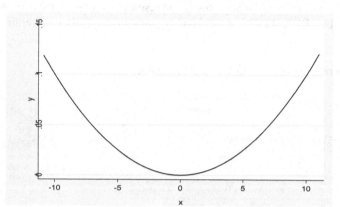

decrease the mean as we discussed previously. To overcome this issue, we can calculate the correlation based on the median of the rank, where extreme values have very little influence. Thus, as an alternate method to avoid the weakness of being sensitivity to a single point on the Pearson correlation coefficient, we can use the Spearman's rank correlation, a non-parametric measure of correlation, which is based on the median. To calculate such a correlation coefficient, we first rank variables Y and X from the highest to the lowest individual, and then calculate the difference between each pair of ranks. The Spearman's rank correlation coefficient can be calculated as

$$\rho_{X,Y} = 1 - 6\frac{\sum_{i=1}^{k} d_i^2}{n(n^2 - 1)}, \qquad (7\text{-}2)$$

where d_i is the difference between each rank of corresponding values of Y and X, and n is the number of ranks. Although Equation (7-2) is much less affected by a single influential value than the Pearson correlation coefficient, it is only good when tied ranks (i.e., two data points have the same value) do not exist. If any tied ranks exist, we have to use the Pearson's correlation coefficient.

When two variables are associated nonlinearly we cannot directly assess the relationship through either Equations (7-1) or (7-2). But we can divide the nonlinear values into several linear parts and measure each part within its linear range. For example, Figure 7.2 shows a U shape relationship of (Y, X), and we have $\rho_{X,Y} \to 0$ when directly applying (7-1). But if we divide X into X_1, where $x < 0$ and X_2, where $x \ge 0$, we will have $\rho_{X_1,Y} < 0$ and $\rho_{X_2,Y} > 0$; both show a considerable linear relationship.

If we want to obtain the correlation coefficient of two binary variables, we can calculate the Tetrachoric correlations that assumes a latent bivariate normal distribution (Y, X) for each pair of binary variables, (y, x), with a threshold model for the manifest variables ($y = 1$ if and only if $Y > 0$ or $x = 1$ if and only if $X > 0$). The means and variances of the latent variables are not identified, but the correlation $\rho_{X,Y}$ of Y and X can be estimated from the joint distribution of y and x —that is defined as the tetrachoric correlation coefficient (Stata 2006). Display 7.3 illustrates the Stata codes and result of the tetrachoric correlation coefficient for variables RST, HTTP logged_i and is_guest of the KDD-cup training data.

Display 7.3
Tetrachoric correlation coefficient for binary variables

```
tetrachoric RST  HTTP logged_i is_guest
(obs=494021)

matrix with tetrachoric correlations is not positive (semi-)definite;
  it has 1 negative eigenvalue
  maxdiff(corr,adj-corr) =  0.4958
  (adj-corr: tetrachoric correlations adjusted to be positive (semi)-definite)

             |      RST     HTTP logged_i is_guest
-------------+---------------------------------------
        RST  |   1.0000
       HTTP  |  -0.0727   1.0000
    logged_i |  -0.0618   0.9770   1.0000
    is_guest |  -0.0684  -1.0000   1.0000   1.0000
```

Statistical Tests of Association

A statistical test of an association between two variables may provide baseline information for alarming potential intrusion. For example, studies have illustrated that use of the χ^2 test alone can detect some attacks (Masum, Ye, Chen, & Noh, 2000; Kayacik & Zincir-Heywood, 2005; Goonatilake & Herath, 2007). The primary purpose of statistical tests of association is to assess the probability that the strength of a relationship is not occurring randomly or by chance. We use a pre-selected significance level value, usually $\alpha = 0.05$, to judge our decision. Although a great number of procedures are available for conducting statistical tests of an association, the selection of an appropriate method depends on the variable types. Table 7.4 illustrates some common combinations of variable types and their corresponding test procedures.

As we can see if Y and X are binomial proportions, then the simple tool to assess the significance level of association is the χ^2 test method. In the analysis of network traffic data, Y typically presents an incidence, such as an anomaly-free, attack event, and X could be, for example, a TCP/IP rate, UDP rate, or the proportion of network traffic from a typical department.

Let us assume that we have a total of $N = n_1 + n_2$ traffics from a network system and X represents a sub system with n_1 traffics. Let Y represent an outcome, anomaly-free traffic (yes/no), of which there are a total of $M = m_1 + m_2$ anomaly-free traffics. Table 7.5 summarizes these data in a 2×2 contingency table. Assuming that the normal approximation to be a binomial distribution is applicable, and each of the n_i ($i = 1,2$) traffics issued from X or issued from other than X have the same probability of ρ_i to be an anomaly, then

$$\rho_1 = \frac{m_1}{m_1 + m_2}$$

Table 7.4 Methods for accessing bivariate relationship

		Predictor Variable level (X)				
		Nominal	**Ordinal**	**Interval**	**Ratio**	**Binary**
Response Variable level (Y)	**Nominal**	χ^2 test				
	Ordinal	χ^2, Wilcoxon ranksum, or Kruskal-Wallis test	Spearman correlation			
	Interval	ANOVA	Spearman correlation	Pearson correlation or Spearman correlation		
	Ratio	ANOVA	Spearman correlation	Pearson correlation or Spearman correlation	Pearson correlation or Spearman correlation	
	Binary	t-test or Wicoxon ranksum				χ^2, Tetrachoric or Phi-correlation

Table 7.5 A 2×2 contingency table of sources of network traffic and outcome

Sources of network traffic	Anomaly-free $(Y = 1)$	Anomaly $(Y = 0)$	Total
Network traffic from X $(X = 1)$	m_1	$n_1 - m_1$	n_1
Network traffic not from X $(X = 0)$	m_2	$n_2 - m_2$	n_2
Total	$m_1 + m_2$	$(n_1 + n_2) - (m_1 + m_2)$	$n_1 + n_2$

and

$$\rho_2 = \frac{m_2}{m_1 + m_2}.$$

We want to know if network traffics from X are more likely to be anomaly-free. In other words, we want to test if X is statistically significantly associated with Y. Thus, we have our null and alternative hypotheses

$H_0 : \rho_1 = \rho_2$ and
$H_A : \rho_1 \neq \rho_2,$

respectively. The χ^2 of Table 7.4 is defined as

$$\chi^2 = \frac{(m_1 n_2 - m_2 n_1)^2 (n_1 + n_2)}{n_1 n_2 (m_1 + m_2)(n_1 + n_2 - m_1 - m_2)} \tag{7-3}$$

If we have $\chi^2 > \chi_1^2(\alpha)$, where χ_1^2 represents the one-degree of freedom and α is the significant level, we can reject H_0. When $\alpha = 0.05$, then $\chi_1^2(0.05) = 3.841$, which can be found from a critical values of the χ^2 distribution table that is usually supplied in any statistic textbook. Although the χ^2 test is an approximate test that requires the normal approximation to the binomial distribution to be valid, this assumption is easily met when analyzing the network traffic data because the sample size is always large. The χ^2 test can also be applied when either Y or X, or both, are categorical variables.

Example 7.2→ χ^2 Test. Let us assess the association between the protocol type as TCP (yes/no) and the attack (yes/no) using the 1999 KDD-cup training data. The following Stata results given in Display 7.2 show that TCP is statistically significantly associated as attack-free (59.6% vs. 93.3%, p<0.0001).

Display 7.2
An example of bivariate analysis by a 2×2 contingency table

```
.tab attack TCP ,col row chi

             |         TCP
   attack |       0         1 |    Total
-----------+----------------------+----------
        0 |    20,465    76,813 |   97,278
           |     21.04     78.96 |   100.00
           |      6.73     40.41 |    19.69
-----------+----------------------+----------
        1 |   283,491   113,252 |  396,743
           |     71.45     28.55 |   100.00
           |     93.27     59.59 |    80.31
-----------+----------------------+----------
    Total |   303,956   190,065 |  494,021
           |     61.53     38.47 |   100.00
           |    100.00    100.00 |   100.00

   Pearson chi2(1) =  8.4e+04   Pr = 0.000
```

Sometimes we also want to compare the means of two continuous variables, Y and X, assuming they are randomly drawn from two independent populations that are normally distributed and have the same variance. Examples of such circumstances might include the comparison of mean numbers of UDP connections between two groups of users having different working schedules, or mean times of accessing an application between two days. Let μ_y and μ_x denote the estimated means for Y and X, respectively. We can use the *t-test* to examine the following hypotheses:

$H_0 : \mu_Y = \mu_X$

$H_A : \mu_Y \neq \mu_X$

$$t = \frac{\overline{Y} - \overline{X}}{\sqrt{s_p^2 \left(\dfrac{n_2 + n_1}{n_1 n_2} \right)}}$$

(7-4)

Example 7.3→t-test. Let us use the spam-email data to conduct a t-test for the variable v55 (average length of capital run) by the response variable, v58 (which has a value of 1 for spam-email and 0 for non-spam email). From Section 5.4.2 we know that variable v55 is not distributed normally, so we transfer it by using the log transformation function before taking the t-test. Stata codes to conduct the t-test and the result of the test are shown in Displays 7.3 and 7.4, respectively. We found that the log-transferred means of the measurement of "average length of capital run" are statistically significantly different between the non-spam and spam-email groups; the non-spam group had a value of $\mu_Y = 0.67$ ($\sigma_Y = 0.51$) and the spam group had a value of $\mu_X = 1.38$ ($\sigma_X = 0.85$). The difference is at the significant level of 10^{-6}.

Display 7.3
Stata codes to conduct t-test for variable v55 by v58 of the spam data

```
#delimit;
use F:\Book\Chapter 7\spam.dta;
gen logv55=log(v55);
ttest log_v55,by(v58);
```

Display 7.4
Result of the t-test for variable v55 by v58 of the spam data

```
Two-sample t test with equal variances
------------------------------------------------------------------------------
  Group |     Obs        Mean    Std. Err.   Std. Dev.   [95% Conf. Interval]
--------+---------------------------------------------------------------------
      0 |    2788     .6743098   .0095829    .5059914     .6555196    .6931001
      1 |    1813    1.382272    .0200796    .8549759     1.34289    1.421654
--------+---------------------------------------------------------------------
combined|    4601     .9532786   .0110595    .7501766     .9315966    .9749607
--------+---------------------------------------------------------------------
   diff |             -.7079622  .0200845                 -.7473374   -.6685869
------------------------------------------------------------------------------
       diff = mean(0) - mean(1)                            t =  -35.2492
   Ho: diff = 0                             degrees of freedom =      4599

    Ha: diff < 0                 Ha: diff != 0                   Ha: diff > 0
 Pr(T < t) = 0.0000      Pr(|T| > |t|) = 0.0000           Pr(T > t) = 1.0000
```

LINEAR REGRESSION MODELING

Linear regression modeling analysis is applied when we have more than one predictor variable to be analyzed with the response variable at the same time. For example, we may want to examine that certain characteristics of traffic data, such as, source IP address, destination IP address, user' job functions, and protocol types (e.g., HTTP, UDP, TCP,) are associated with anomaly-free traffic. Multiple regression analysis provides a robust solution to ensure that all the important variables are pooled together to construct a final set of predictors for a given outcome.

Multiple Regression

The ordinary least squares (OLS) multiple linear regression method is the most popular modeling technique used in the research and business fields, and it usually is referred as "multiple regression," "OLS regression," or simply "OLS." We will use the term "OLS regression" throughout this book. OLS regression provides a method for studying the relationship between a single response variable Y and one or more predictor variables $X_1, X_2, ..., X_k$. We use OLS regression to acquire two major advantages: (1) to predict Y values by combining multi-contribution from $X_1, X_2, ..., X_k$, and (2) to understand how a particular predictor variable X_i affects the response variable, Y, while taking into account contributions from other variables. Let us consider a simple OLS regression model below

$$y_i = \beta_0 + \beta_1 x_{i1} + \beta_2 x_{i2} + \cdots + \beta_k x_{ik} + \varepsilon, \tag{7-5}$$

where β_0 and β_k are estimated parameters from the sample data, ε is an error term that are assumed to be normally distributed $\varepsilon \sim N(0, \sigma)$, and σ does not depend on $x_1, x_2, ..., x_k$. Equation (7-5) specifies a linear relationship between the response variable, Y, and $X_1, X_2, ..., X_k$, which explains a proportion of the variance in the response variable. The key assumptions for equation (7-5) include: (1) error terms are normally distributed, (2) there is a linear relationship between the response variable and its predictors, (3) variables are measured with high reliability, and (4) variance of errors is the same across all levels of each predictors, which is also known as "homogeneity of variance."

Though we fit OLS regression when the response variable is a continuous variable, it is reasonable to have a binary variable as a predictor as well. Note that OLS regression requires the latent term ε to be normally distributed. In practical, the predictor variables can have a different distribution, and when the response variable does not follow a normal distribution, we can employ one of the transformation methods examined in Chapter V to convert it to be normally distributed. When the sample size gets large, the restriction of normality to ε is going to be loose by the central limit theorem. Moreover, we can also fit the nonlinear relationship by taking a transformation of the response or predictor variables. For example, we can create a new variable, $z = x^2$, to represent the square of x.

The sample size also affects the number of allowable predictor variables in OLS regression. A 10 - 1 rule (that stands for 10 observations per predictor variable) has been used in practice. Thus, if we want to fit an OLS regression with 10 variables, the minimum sample size should be $n = 100$.

Example 7.4→Linear Regression. Let us fit a linear regression model using MIT-DAPRA data. We first convert the initial connection-level data to the site-level (IP address) data so that the response variable is the rate of anomaly-free connections, and the protector variables are also rates (e.g., rate of HTTP connections, rate of UDP connections) for each site. We can now fit a regression model with the continuous response variable. There is a total of 9008 individual IP addresses in the 7-week MIT-DAPRA data. The Stata codes to accomplish such a transformation and to fit a regression model are given in Display 7.5, and the results are described in Display 7.6.

Display 7.5
Stata codes for fitting a linear regression model

```
#delimit;
clear;
set mem 854566;
use F:\Book\Chapter 7\mit_list.dta, clear;
gen byte normal=(attack=="-");
drop v13 score;

do create_var.do ; /* see Appendix CH8 */
gen total=1;

collapse (sum)total normal t2 ll udp icmp samePort sameIP http smtp
         urp ecr eco snmp ftp port domain telnet finger,by(IP_s);
gen t2_rate=t2/total;
gen ll_rate=ll/total;
gen udp_rate=udp/total;
gen icmp_rate=icmp/total;
gen smPt_rate=samePort/total;
gen smIP_rate=sameIP/total;
gen http_rate=http/total;
gen smtp_rate=smtp/total;
gen urp_rate=urp/total;
gen ecr_rate=ecr/total;
gen eco_rate=eco/total;
gen snmp_rate=snmp/total;
gen ftp_rate=ftp/total;
gen port_rate=port/total;
gen dom_rate=domain/total;
gen tel_rate=telnet/total;

replace normal=1 if normal==0;
gen normal_rate=normal/total;
gen log_normal=log(normal_rate);

regress log_normal
t2_rate ll_rate udp_rate icmp_rate smPt_rate smIP_rate http_rate smtp_rate
urp_rate ecr_rate eco_rate snmp_rate ftp_rate port_rate dom_rate tel_rate;
```

Display 7.6
Results of the linear regression model from Stata

```
     Source |       SS          df        MS                  Number of obs =    9008
------------+------------------------------                  F( 16,  8991) = 3720.19
      Model |  13869.0392        16   866.814949              Prob > F      =  0.0000
   Residual |  2094.92672      8991   .233002638              R-squared     =  0.8688
------------+------------------------------                  Adj R-squared =  0.8685
      Total |  15963.9659      9007   1.77239546              Root MSE      =  .4827

-----------------------------------------------------------------------------------
 log_normal |    Coef.    Std. Err.      t     P>|t|      [95% Conf. Interval]
------------+----------------------------------------------------------------------
    t2_rate |  -.8912051   .2300322   -3.87    0.000    -1.342121   -.4402897
    l1_rate |  -.9891625   .2905418   -3.40    0.001    -1.558691   -.4196344
    udp_rate |  -4.093308   .3897894  -10.50    0.000    -4.857384   -3.329232
   icmp_rate |  -2.716454   .2906728   -9.35    0.000    -3.286239   -2.146669
   smPt_rate |   .7569575   .2566894    2.95    0.003     .2537878   1.260127
   smIP_rate |   1042.864   96.80233   10.77    0.000     853.1093   1232.619
   http_rate |   1.405031   .3501308    4.01    0.000     .7186946   2.091367
   smtp_rate |   2.792778   .4351287    6.42    0.000     1.939826   3.645729
    urp_rate |   3.711793   10.1912     0.36    0.716    -16.26528   23.68887
    ecr_rate |  -1.105747   .1809239   -6.11    0.000    -1.460399   -.7510945
    eco_rate |  -1.527449   .2505468   -6.10    0.000    -2.018578   -1.03632
   snmp_rate |   5.520481   .438151    12.60    0.000     4.661605   6.379357
    ftp_rate |  -1.805777   .2616315   -6.90    0.000    -2.318634   -1.29292
   port_rate |  -6.458482   .3720217  -17.36    0.000    -7.187729   -5.729235
    dom_rate |   6.001472   .3473438   17.28    0.000     5.320599   6.682345
    tel_rate |   .6092135   .3505493    1.74    0.082    -.077943    1.29637
       _cons |   .2380207   .30714      0.77    0.438    -.3640436   .8400851
-----------------------------------------------------------------------------------
```

The OLS model illustrates some interesting results. The adjusted R^2 (R-squared) value is 0.87, which indicates that the model has good predictive power. The R^2 value ranging from 0 to 1.0, represents the proportion of the variability in the response variable, Y, which is explained by the predictor variables in the linear regression (i.e., the changes in the response variable can be explained by changes in the predictor variables). A high R^2 value indicates the pattern of the response variable that can be predicted by the predictor variables. We will revisit the concept of R^2 in Chapter XII. The model suggests that the higher the rates of connections on HTTP, SMTP, SNMP, domain, same (source and destination) IP addresses and same ports, the more likely the site is to be anomaly-free.

Multiple Logistic Regression

When we have a dichotomous response variable we cannot fit it with an OLS regression because it violates the assumption of normality of the LOS regression, since a dichotomous variable does not follow a normal distribution. A logistic regression model (Rice, 1994; Kleinbaum, 1994; Dacid & Hosmer, 2000), also known as a "logit model," can be used for data in which the response variable is binary or dichotomous which is usually coded as 1 for the presence of an event, and 0 for the absence of an event. Logistic regression transforms the binary response variable into a logit format and applies the maximum likelihood estimation (MLE) method to estimate the probability of a certain event occurring at the log-odds scale. The use of multiple logistic regression has grown significantly during the past two decades. It has become the standard method for regression analysis of dichotomous data in many fields, including business, finance, criminology, engineering, and the life sciences. Recent interests in the use of this technique in network security have grown rapidly (Hastie, Tibshirani & Friedman, 2001; Maloof, 2006; dos Santos, de Mello & Yang, 2007).

Let y_i that has a 1 or 0 value be the response variable for the ith observation, ($i = 1,2,..,$ n), and p_i be the probability of $y_i = 1$ for k predictor variables $x_1, x_2, ..., x_k$. The multiple logistic regression model can be represented as:

$$y_i = \log\left[\frac{p_i}{1 - p_i}\right] = \beta_0 + \beta_1 x_{i1} + \beta_2 x_{i2} + \cdots + \beta_k x_{ik} \tag{7-6}$$

$$p_i = \frac{\exp(\beta_0 + \beta_1 x_{i1} + \beta_2 x_{i2} + \cdots + \beta_k x_{ik})}{1 + \exp(\beta_0 + \beta_1 x_{i1} + \beta_2 x_{i2} + \cdots + \beta_k x_{ik})}. \tag{7-7}$$

The expression on the left-hand side of Equation (7-6) is usually referred to as the logit or log-odds, and Equation (7-7) has the desired property that no matter what the values of β_k and x_{ik} are, p_i always has a range from 0 to 1. The parameter β_k is a logit coefficient that indicates the log-odds increase by β_k for every unit increase in the predictor variable x_k. That is,

$$e^{\beta_k} = \frac{e^{\beta_0 + \beta_1 x_1 + \beta_2 x_2 + \cdots + \beta_i (x_i + 1) + \cdots + \beta_k x_k}}{e^{\beta_0 + \beta_1 x_1 + \beta_2 x_2 + \cdots + \beta_i x_i + \cdots + \beta_k x_k}}.$$

This is similar to an OLS regression, where β_k measures the contribution of the kth predictor variable to effect the response variable. Exponentiating β_k yields an adjusted (adjusted for other variables) odds ratio (OR) that measures how much more likely (or unlikely) it is for the response variable to be present among those with $x_k = 1$ than among those with $x_k = 0$ for a binary predictor variable, or for every unit increase in which x_k is continuous. For example, assuming the response variable is an attack (yes = 1, no = 0), and if x_k denotes whether a connection is UDP, then the OR is 1.5, which estimates that an attack is 1.5 times as likely to occur among UDP connections than among non-UDP connections (assume p<0.05 for UDP).

In multiple logistic regression, the response variable can only take the value of 1 or 0. However, similar to OLS regression the predictor variables $x_1, x_2, ..., x_k$ can be continuous, binary, or ordinal. A categorical variable with G categories can be converted into $G - 1$ dummy variables. The sample size also affects the number of allowable predictor variables in logistic regression. Because the response variable can only take 1 or 0, the 10 - 1 rule is to count the minimum (either presence or absence) number of events of the response variable. If we want to fit a logistic regression model with 10 predictor variables and a presence response rate of 0.2, the minimum sample size is $n = 10 \times 10 / 0.2 = 500$. If the response variable has a high presence rate (e.g., 0.8), we use its reverse number, (i.e. 1-0.8=0.2) to calculate the sample size.

Unlike OLS regression, multiple logistic regression does not assume linearity in the relationship between the predictor variables and the response variable. Additionally, it does not require normally distributed variables, nor does not assume homoscedasticity, and in general it has less stringent requirements. Theoretically, multiple logistic regression requires that observations are independent and that the predictor variables are linearly related to the logit of the response variable.

Example 7.5→Logistic Regression. The spam-email dataset includes 4601 emails, of which 39.4% are labeled as spasm. The dataset has a binary response variable that has value 1 for spam emails and 0 for non-spam emails and 47 measurements on each email in the dataset. It is interesting to know which of the 47 measurements are associated with the spam email outcome. Thus, we fit the spam-email data to a multiple logistic regression model with the spam indicator as the response variable, and the 47 measurements as predictors. The R codes of this analysis and the results are shown in Displays 7.7 and 7.8, equally.

Display 7.7
R codes to fit a multiple logistic regression with spam-email data

```
require(Design)
# Read Ascii data to the data object spam
spam<-read.table("F:\\Book\\Chapter 7\\spam_r.txt",header=TRUE, sep=",")
#Fit the logistic model with v58 as the response variable
glmfit <-glm(formula=v58 ~
      v1+v2+v3+v4+v5+v6+v7+v8+v9+v10+v11+v12+v13+v14+v15+v16+v17+v18+v19+
      v20+v21+v22+v23+v24+v25+v26+v27+v28+v29+v30+v31+v32+v33+v34+v35+
      v36+v37+v38+v39+v40+v41+v42+v43+v44+v45+v46+v47+v48+v49+v50+v51+
      v52+v53+v54+v55+v56+v57,data=spam,binomial(link=logit),method="glm.fit"
'
      x=TRUE,y=TRUE)
Summary(glmfit)
```

Display 7.8
Results of spam-email multiple logistic regression model

```
> summary(glmfit)

Call:
glm(formula = v58 ~ v1 + v2 + v3 + v4 + v5 + v6 + v7 + v8 + v9 +
      v10 + v11 + v12 + v13 + v14 + v15 + v16 + v17 + v18 + v19 +
      v20 + v21 + v22 + v23 + v24 + v25 + v26 + v27 + v28 + v29 +
      v30 + v31 + v32 + v33 + v34 + v35 + v36 + v37 + v38 + v39 +
      v40 + v41 + v42 + v43 + v44 + v45 + v46 + v47 + v48 + v49 +
      v50 + v51 + v52 + v53 + v54 + v55 + v56 + v57, family = binomial(link =
logit), data = spam, method = "glm.fit", x = TRUE, y = TRUE)

Deviance Residuals:
      Min          1Q      Median          3Q         Max
-4.127e+00   -2.030e-01  -1.967e-06   1.140e-01   5.364e+00

Coefficients:
            Estimate Std. Error z value Pr(>|z|)
(Intercept) -1.569e+00  1.420e-01 -11.044  < 2e-16 ***
v1          -3.895e-01  2.315e-01  -1.683 0.092388 .
v2          -1.458e-01  6.928e-02  -2.104 0.035362 *
v3           1.141e-01  1.103e-01   1.035 0.300759
v4           2.252e+00  1.507e+00   1.494 0.135168
v5           5.624e-01  1.018e-01   5.524 3.31e-08 ***
v6           8.830e-01  2.498e-01   3.534 0.000409 ***
v7           2.279e+00  3.328e-01   6.846 7.57e-12 ***
v8           5.696e-01  1.682e-01   3.387 0.000707 ***
v9           7.343e-01  2.849e-01   2.577 0.009958 **
v10          1.275e-01  7.262e-02   1.755 0.079230 .
v11         -2.557e-01  2.979e-01  -0.858 0.390655
v12         -1.383e-01  7.405e-02  -1.868 0.061773 .
v13         -7.961e-02  2.303e-01  -0.346 0.729557
```

continued on following page

Display 7.8 continued

```
v14          1.447e-01  1.364e-01   1.061 0.288855
v15          1.236e+00  7.254e-01   1.704 0.088370 .
v16          1.039e+00  1.457e-01   7.128 1.01e-12 ***
v17          9.599e-01  2.251e-01   4.264 2.01e-05 ***
v18          1.203e-01  1.172e-01   1.027 0.304533
v19          8.131e-02  3.505e-02   2.320 0.020334 *
v20          1.047e+00  5.383e-01   1.946 0.051675 .
v21          2.419e-01  5.243e-02   4.615 3.94e-06 ***
v22          2.013e-01  1.627e-01   1.238 0.215838
v23          2.245e+00  4.714e-01   4.762 1.91e-06 ***
v24          4.264e-01  1.621e-01   2.630 0.008535 **
v25         -1.920e+00  3.128e-01  -6.139 8.31e-10 ***
v26         -1.040e+00  4.396e-01  -2.366 0.017966 *
v27         -1.177e+01  2.113e+00  -5.569 2.57e-08 ***
v28          4.454e-01  1.991e-01   2.237 0.025255 *
v29         -2.486e+00  1.502e+00  -1.656 0.097744 .
v30         -3.299e+00  3.137e-01  -1.052 0.292972
v31         -1.702e-01  4.815e-01  -0.353 0.723742
v32          2.549e+00  3.283e+00   0.776 0.437566
v33         -7.383e-01  3.117e-01  -2.366 0.017842 *
v34          6.679e-01  1.601e+00   0.417 0.676490
v35         -2.055e+00  7.883e-01  -2.607 0.009124 **
v36          9.237e-01  3.091e-01   2.989 0.002803 **
v37          4.651e-02  1.754e-01   0.265 0.790819
v38         -5.968e-01  4.232e-01  -1.410 0.158473
v39         -8.650e-01  3.828e-01  -2.260 0.023844 *
v40         -3.046e-01  3.636e-01  -0.838 0.402215
v41         -4.505e+01  2.660e+01  -1.694 0.090333 .
v42         -2.689e+00  8.384e-01  -3.207 0.001342 **
v43         -1.247e+00  8.064e-01  -1.547 0.121978
v44         -1.573e+00  5.292e-01  -2.973 0.002953 **
v45         -7.923e-01  1.556e-01  -5.091 3.56e-07 ***
v46         -1.459e+00  2.686e-01  -5.434 5.52e-08 ***
v47         -2.326e+00  1.659e+00  -1.402 0.160958
v48         -4.016e+00  1.611e+00  -2.493 0.012672 *
v49         -1.291e+00  4.422e-01  -2.920 0.003503 **
v50         -1.881e-01  2.494e-01  -0.754 0.450663
v51         -6.574e-01  8.383e-01  -0.784 0.432914
v52          3.472e-01  8.926e-02   3.890 0.000100 ***
v53          5.336e+00  7.064e-01   7.553 4.24e-14 ***
v54          2.403e+00  1.113e+00   2.159 0.030883 *
v55          1.199e-02  1.884e-02   0.636 0.524509
v56          9.118e-03  2.521e-03   3.618 0.000297 ***
v57          8.437e-04  2.251e-04   3.747 0.000179 ***
---
Signif. codes:  0 '***' 0.001 '**' 0.01 '*' 0.05 '.' 0.1 ' ' 1

(Dispersion parameter for binomial family taken to be 1)

    Null deviance: 6170.2  on 4600  degrees of freedom
Residual deviance: 1815.8  on 4543  degrees of freedom
AIC: 1931.8

Number of Fisher Scoring iterations: 13
```

We can use the Wald test to determine if a predictor variable is statistically significantly associated with the response variable. From Display 7.8 we can identify that many variables (e.g., v2, v5, v6, v7) are statistically significantly associated with the response variable at the significance level of $\alpha = 0.05$. Although the Wald test is known to have high type II errors and can be biased when there is insufficient data for each category or value of x_i, it is a widely used approach for scanning variables.

A multinomial logistic regression model is used for data in which the response variable is often unordered or polytomous, and predictor variables are binary, continuous or categorical predictors. This type of model is therefore measured on a nominal scale. It was introduced by McFadden in 1974 (McFadden, 1974), and since then, variants of multinomial logistic models occur frequently in many areas of application. In the healthcare field, it is also referred to as the polychotomous, or polytomous logistic regression model. We will use the term "multinomial" throughout in this book. Unlike the binary logistic model, in which a response variable has only a binary choice (e.g., presence/absence of a characteristic), the response variable in a multinomial logistic model can have more than two choices that are coded categorically. Even though the response variable can be coded as 0,1,2,..., n, the numerical values are arbitrary in the sense that outcomes coded with lower values (0, 1, etc.) are not necessarily less than those coded with higher values. Therefore, the values of the response variable are noted to be "unordered." One of the categories is considered the reference category; this is similar to when the 0 value coded category is usually the reference value in a binary logistic model.

Let Y be a response variable with 5 categories, $g = 0,1,2,3,4$ and let 0 be the reference. Also, let $\pi_i^{(g)}$ denote the probability of the ith observation being in category g; more specifically, $\pi_i^{(g)} = P(y_i = g)$. Then, for a multinomial logistic regression model with k predictor variables $x_1, x_2, ..., x_k$, the model with the logit link can be represented as:

$$\log\left(\frac{\pi_i^{(g)}}{\pi_i^{(0)}}\right) = \beta_0^{(g)} + \beta_1^{(g)} x_{i1} + \beta_{i2}^{(g)} + ... + \beta_{ik}^{(g)}. \tag{7-8}$$

In this model, the same variables appear in each of the g categories, and a separate intercept, $\beta_0^{(g)}$, and slope parameters, $\beta_1^{(g)}, \beta_2^{(g)}$, and $\beta_k^{(g)}$ are usually estimated for each contrast. The parameter, $\beta_k^{(g)}$, represents the additive effect of a 1-unit increase in the kth variable, x_k, on the log-odds of being in category g, rather than in the reference category. It may be more meaningful to interpret the value of $\exp \beta_k^{(g)}$, which is the multiplicative effect of a 1-unit increase on the odds of x_k being in category g, rather than the reference category. An alternative way to interpret the effect of the kth variable, x_k, is to use predicted probabilities $\pi_i^{(g)}$ for different values of x_k:

$$\pi_i^{(g)} = \frac{\exp(\beta_0^{(g)} + \beta_1^{(g)} x_{i1} + \beta_{i2}^{(g)} + ... + \beta_{ik}^{(g)})}{1 + \sum_{j=1}^{4} \exp(\beta_0^{(j)} + \beta_1^{(j)} x_{i1} + \beta_{i2}^{(j)} + ... \beta_{ik}^{(j)})} \tag{7-9}$$

The probability of being in the reference category 0 can then be calculated by subtraction:

$$\pi_i^{(0)} = 1 - \sum_{j=1}^{4} \pi_i^{(j)}$$

Example 7.6→Multinomial Logistic Regression. Let us use the KDD-cup 1999 data to fit a multinomial logistic regression model. The training sample of the KDD-cup 1999 data includes 24 attack types that can be grouped into 5 categories: 0 = anomaly-free, 1 = probe, 2 = DoS, 3 = U2R, and 4 = R2L (Table 7.6). The category of 0 is used as a reference.

Although the predictor variables included more than 40 variables as described in Example 7.1, let us use only eight variables: (1) count (number of connections to the same host as the current connection in the past two seconds), (2) srv_coun (number of connections to the same service as the current connection in the past two seconds), (3) dst_host (number of connections having the same destination host), (4) dst_hos1 (number of connections having the same destination host and using the same service), (5) ICMP (yes/no), (6) TCP (yes/no), (7) HTTP (yes/no), and (8) logged_i (log in successfully, yes/no), which are all statistically significantly associated with at least one category. We can use the SAS procedure PROC CATMOD or Stata's command mlogit to fit this multinomial logistic regression model and Display 7.9 shows the corresponding Stata codes. Note that in SAS, to make results more easily interpretable, we can include all predictor variables in the DIRECT statement. More detailed information about the use of the PROC CATMOD can be found from http://v8doc. sas.com/sashtml/stat/ chap22/sect17.htm, and Allison (1999). The output of the model is given in Display 7.10.

Display 7.9
Stata codes to fit a multinomial logistic regression model with KDD-cup 1999 training data

```
#delimit;
clear;
set mem 345454;
use "F:\Book\Chapter 7\KDD_TRAI.DTA", clear;
 mlogit outcomes count srv_coun dst_host dst_hos1 ICMP TCP HTTP logged_i
if training==1,basecategory(0) rrr;
```

Table 7.6 Frequency by category

Attack Types	Training dataset (N = 494,021)	
	#	%
Legitimate users (normal)	97,278	19.7
Surveillance and other probing (probe)	4,107	0.8
Denial of service (DoS)	391,458	79.2
Unauthorized access to local super user (root) privileges (U2R)	52	0.0
Unauthorized access from a remote machine (R2L)	1,126	0.2

Display 7.10
Results of the multinomial logistic regression model with KDD-cup 1999 training data

```
Multinomial logistic regression                    Number of obs   =     494021
                                                   LR chi2(32)     =  488163.18
                                                   Prob > chi2     =     0.0000
Log likelihood = -32086.671                        Pseudo R2       =     0.8838

--------------------------------------------------------------------------------
   outcomes |       RRR   Std. Err.       z    P>|z|     [95% Conf. Interval]
------------+-------------------------------------------------------------------
PROB        |
      count |  1.062956     .001135    57.18   0.000     1.060734    1.065183
   srv_coun |  .9125357    !0023177   -36.04   0.000     .9080043    .9170897
   dst_host |  .9856395    .0003421   -41.67   0.000     .9849692    .9863102
   dst_hos1 |   1.00642    .0004412    14.60   0.000     1.005555    1.007285
       ICMP |  32.27284    3.257968    34.42   0.000     26.47937    39.33387
        TCP |  3.701714    .4142716    11.69   0.000     2.972638    4.609606
       HTTP |  .0015436    .0005817   -17.18   0.000     .0007375    .0032309
   logged_i |   .003853    .0012685   -16.89   0.000      .002021    .0073456
------------+-------------------------------------------------------------------
DOS         |
      count |  1.051872    .0011049    48.14   0.000     1.049709     1.05404
   srv_coun |  .9770101    .0011246   -20.21   0.000     .9748083    .9792168
   dst_host |  1.013457    .0002421    55.96   0.000     1.012983    1.013932
   dst_hos1 |  .9849431    .0003162   -47.26   0.000     .9843235    .9855631
       ICMP |  15.88103    1.216468    36.10   0.000     13.66714    18.45354
        TCP |  24.78995    1.339717    59.41   0.000     22.29844    27.55986
       HTTP |  6.997173    .4807872    28.31   0.000     6.115545    8.005898
   logged_i |  .1389133    .0074404   -36.85   0.000     .1250697    .1542891
------------+-------------------------------------------------------------------
U2R         |
      count |  1.040297    .0080063     5.13   0.000     1.024723    1.056108
   srv_coun |  .6167332    .1411078    -2.11   0.035     .3938614    .9657199
   dst_host |  .9887794    .0023057    -4.84   0.000     .9842706    .9933089
   dst_hos1 |  .9285183    .0118448    -5.81   0.000     .9055909    .9520263
       ICMP |  1.65e-13    7.42e-07    -0.00   1.000            0          .
        TCP |  1.646619     1.42739     0.58   0.565     .3011057    9.004653
       HTTP |  1.64e-14    4.12e-08    -0.00   1.000            0          .
   logged_i |  12.11133    7.757096     3.89   0.000     3.451534     42.4983
------------+-------------------------------------------------------------------
R2L         |
      count |  .7164863    .0252549    -9.46   0.000     .6686587    .7677349
   srv_coun |  1.025978    .0062322     4.22   0.000     1.013836    1.038266
   dst_host |  .9960471    .0004119    -9.58   0.000     .9952402    .9968546
   dst_hos1 |  .9764022    .0007629   -30.56   0.000      .974908    .9778987
       ICMP |  1.23e-06    2.503707    -0.00   1.000            0          .
        TCP |  8.91e+08           .        .       .            .          .
       HTTP |  .0143022    .0072138    -8.42   0.000      .005322    .0384355
   logged_i |  5.111496    .6338568    13.16   0.000      4.00861    6.517818
--------------------------------------------------------------------------------
(outcomes==normal is the base outcome)
```

Display 7.10 illustrates the associations between predictors and the response variable's categories: prob (surveillance and other probing), DoS (denial of service), U2R (unauthorized access to local super user [root] privileges), and R2L (unauthorized access from a remote machine) with normal as the reference. The model shows that the association between a predictor and the response variable varies by the type of attacks that the response variable represented. For example, presence of HTTP is statistically significantly associated with increasing the odds of DoS, but it is also statistically significantly associated with decreasing the risk of R2L and prob, and has no effect on U2R.

Model Time to Event

So far our discussions have been restricted to time-independent associations between the response variable and the predictor variables, $Y \sim X_i (i = 1, 2, \ldots, k)$. When the outcome variable of interest becomes time dependent, $Y(t)$, meaning the outcome is timed until an event occurs, we cannot use the above methods to examine the association. Instead, we have to employ the time to event analysis approach, which is also known as "survival analysis" in the healthcare, medicine and life science fields, "failure analysis" in mechanical systems, "reliability analysis" in engineering, and "duration analysis" in economics. Let us use the term "survival analysis" in this book because we use this approach to measure our network being free from an attack event (e.g., attack, system crash, malicious codes) as shown in Figure 7.3.

Depending on the measurement and tasks, we may use a second, minute, hour, or day as a unit of time. Although more than one event could occur at the same time (or sequentially within a given time period), in this book we will focus on the phenomenon of only one event. Readers who are interested in more than one event may refer to the book, *Computing Risk* by Pintilie (2006). When the response variable becomes time-dependent, each observation in the dataset is linked with its survival time. We may have some information about individual user's or site's survival time, but we do not know the exact time, in such a case, we have the so-called censoring analytical problem. Mainly there are two causes for censoring to occur during a monitoring period: (1) users may withdraw due to jobs changes (e.g., employment terminated, position changed); sites can be lost due to be removed from the network, or (2) users or sites may not experience the event before the monitoring period ends (event-free during the entire period).

Let us assume that we monitor a network system with a 10-day window for four users or sites with the response variable as attack (yes/no). Figure 7.4 illustrates the concept of censoring graphically for this example. User A is followed from the start of the monitoring period until day 3, when his/her information is lost due to retirement; this user is censored with a censored time duration of 3 days. User B is followed from the start of the time until he/she is attacked at day 8; his/her survival time is 8 and is not censored. User C enters the monitoring period on the 7th day and is followed until the end of the monitoring period without having an event. This user's censored time is 4 days. User D enters the period on the 2nd day and is followed until the 6th day when he/she has the event. There is no censoring here, and the survival time for User D is 5 days.

In Table 7.8 Users A and C are censored because we do not know their exact information on the right side of the monitoring period, occurring when a user withdraws or at the end of the monitoring period. In survival analysis, this phenomenon is referred to as "right-censored." Since the majority of survival data are right-censored as in the case of network traffic data, we will focus on right-censored data only.

Survival analysis involves two functions, (1) the survivor function $S(t)$, which gives the probability that an individual survives longer than some specified time t, and (2) the hazard function $h(t)$, which gives the instantaneous potential per unit time for the event to occur, given that the individual has survived up to time t. Figure 7.5 shows a particular survivor function $\hat{S}(t)$ represented by the Kaplan-Meier survival curve.

We use the Cox proportional hazards model, a modeling procedure used to adjust for censoring, and may include numeric predictors, one or more of which may be time-dependent, and require no assumption about the distribution of event times. The inverse of the time to event occurrence is called the hazard—if an event is expected to occur in 10 months (assuming the unit of time is months), the hazard is 1/10 (event per month). One concern when using the Cox proportional hazards model is the way in which the hazard changes over time. The hazard of some events might be likely to increase significantly with the passage of time, such as the system crash due to some particular types of attacks, for instance, an attack of denial-of-service. Other types of events, however, might become less frequent over longer periods of time. For example, user behavior could be greatly impacted in the weeks immediately following a new security-related application or policy initialized, and then the likelihood of behavior changes might decrease as time passes. Still other types of events might be subject to fluctuating risks, both increasing and decreasing, over time.

Let t be time, and X_i ($i = 1,2,..., k$) be the predictor variables on the event times. The Cox proportional hazards model can be presented as

$$h(t) = \lambda(t)e^{(\beta_0+\beta_1x_1+\beta_2x_2+\cdots+\beta_kx_k)} \qquad (7\text{-}10)$$

where $h(t)$ represents the hazard function and $\lambda(t)$ represents an unspecified initial hazard function.

Example 7.7→ Survival Analysis for Network Behavior Changes. Let us use the MIT-DAPRA data to demonstrate how survival analysis can be used to track changes in network system behavior. As we mentioned that the first two weeks of the MIT-DAPRA data are all anomaly-free traffic so any anomalous traffic starts from the 3rd week to the 7th week. Thus, the aim of our survival analysis is to examine the user behavior changes over a 5-week period that counts for a total of 25 days (Monday to Friday for each week). Let us use the IP address to represent a particular site or group and count the volume of anomaly-free and anomalous traffics for each site and each day. For instance, let us use a binary classification rule that $c_i = 1$ for denoting the ith site changes its behavior pattern from anomaly-free to anomaly and $c_i = o$ for otherwise. We use the ratio of the total anomalous traffic, v_i, over total traffic, V_i, to indicate any behavior pattern changes as showing below:

$$c_i = \begin{cases} 1, & \dfrac{v_i}{V_i} < 0.5 \\[2mm] 0, & \dfrac{v_i}{V_i} \geq 0.5 \end{cases} .$$

Moreover, although a site may switch its behavior pattern multi-time within the 25-day or 5-week period, for example, the ith site may change from anomaly-free ($c_i = 0$) to anomalous ($c_i = 1$) on the 10th day and back to anomaly-free on the 15th and being an anomalous pattern again on the 20th, and the jth site may change from the anomaly-free pattern to an anomalous pattern on the 20th and continues to be anomalous until the end of monitoring period. In either of these cases we only count the first event of a pattern change; once a site has a pattern change occurred we would stop following it. Thus, a pattern change occurred for the ith site is on the 10th and for the jth site is on the 20th. Finally we create a simple behavior score for fitting the survival model. The score is constructed based on four anomaly-free associated binary variables: (1) UDP, (2) HTTP, (3) SMTP, and (4) same port of source and destination (samePort). We average the site-specific daily traffic volumes contributed by

Figure 7.3 Time to event

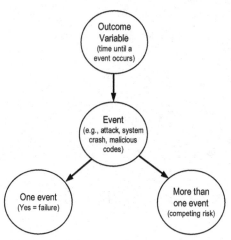

Figure 7.4 Right censoring data

	\multicolumn{11}{c}{Days}
	1	2	3	4	5	6	7	8	9	10	End
A	x	x	x	Withdrawn							
B	x	x	x	x	x	x	x	x	Attacked		
C							x	x	x	x	
D		x	x	x	x	x	Attacked				

Table 7.8 Example of censoring data

User or group	Survival time (day)	Failed (yes/no)	Censored (yes/no)
A	3	No	Yes
B	8	Yes	No
C	4	No	Yes
D	5	Yes	No

Figure 7.5 An example of the Kaplan-Meier survival curve

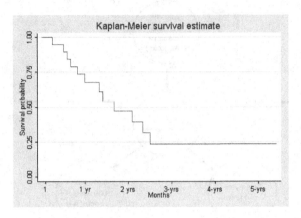

each of these four variables. Our hypothesis is that a site with a high score seems to be more likely to be anomaly-free. The Stata codes to prepare data for conducting survival analysis and fit a Cox proportional hazards model are given in Display 7.11 showing below.

Display 7.11
Stata codes to fit a Cox proportional hazards model with MIT-DARPA data

```
#delimit;
capture log close;
clear;
*set matsize 1410;
set mem 560000k;
set more 1;
use "F:\Book\Chapter 7\MIT_list",replace;
/*------------------------------------------------
 Baseline: normal patterns (41 IP_s sites retrieved)
------------------------------------------------*/;
gen byte Total=1;
replace index=lower(index);
keep if substr(index,1,6)=="week-1" |substr(index,1,6)=="week-2";
```

continued on following page

Display 7.11 continued

```
gen byte udp=(substr(service,length(trim(service))-1,1)=="/" &
substr(service,length(trim(service)),1)=="u");
gen byte samePort=(port_s==port_d);
gen byte sameIP=(IP_s==IP_d);
gen byte http=(trim(service)=="http");
gen byte smtp=(trim(service)=="smtp");
collapse (sum) Total (mean) udp samePort http smtp,by(IP_s);
keep if Total>10;
sort IP_s;
save temp_1,replace;
/*------------------------------------------------
 Monitor period (only 39 IP_s sites to be monitored)
-----------------------------------------------*/;
use "F:\Book\Chapter 7\MIT_list",replace;
gen byte Total=1;
gen byte Normal=(attack=="-");
drop if substr(index,1,6)=="week-1" |substr(index,1,6)=="week-2";
gen byte udp=(substr(service,length(trim(service))-1,1)=="/" &
substr(service,length(trim(service)),1)=="u");
gen byte samePort=(port_s==port_d);
gen byte sameIP=(IP_s==IP_d);
gen byte http=(trim(service)=="http");
gen byte smtp=(trim(service)=="smtp");
collapse (sum) Total Normal (mean) udp samePort http smtp,by(index IP_s);
keep if Total>10;
sort IP_s;
merge IP_s using temp_1;
keep if _m==3;
drop _m;
replace index=lower(index);
do time_7.do; / Appendix CH7 */;
gen rate=Normal/Total;
sort time IP_s;
gen byte Anomaly=(rate<0.5);
sort IP_s;
gen str6 week=substr(index,1,6);
encode week,gen(iweek);
save temp_2,replace;
keep if Anomaly==0;
collapse (max)time (mean) udp samePort http smtp,by(IP_s);
sort IP_s;
save temp_3,replace;
use temp_2,replace;
keep if Anomaly==1;
collapse (min)time (mean) udp samePort http smtp,by(IP_s);
append using temp_3;
sort IP_s time;
gen aa=(IP_s==IP_s[_n-1]);
drop if aa==1;
drop aa;
gen score=(udp +samePort+ http +smtp);
gen byte Anomaly=(time<25);
stset time,failure(Anomaly);
```

```
* Kaplan-Meier survival estimates, by week;
sts graph,xtitle(Days) ytitle(Probability of anomaly-free);

* Smoothed hazard estimates;
sts graph, hazard kernel(gauss) width(5 7)xtitle(Days) ytitle(Smoothed hazard
function);

* Fit the Cox model;
stcox score,hr robust;
gen str10 group="Anomaly" if Anomaly==1;
replace  group="Anomaly-free" if Anomaly==0;
gr box score,by(group);
```

There were a total of 2,992,261 observations across 9008 individual sites represented by IP addresses, of which 1262 sites have at least 10 observations from the entire MIT-DAPRA data within the 7-week period, and only 39 sites have at least 10 observations daily from week one to week seven. Display 7.12 shows the list of these 39 sites, the score for being anomaly-free, the final behavior pattern (group), and the time (day) when the pattern was changed (note, initially all sites were anomaly-free). There are a total of 12 sites that have changed their behavior patterns from anomaly-free to anomalous.

Display 7.12
List of sites used for survival analysis

```
         IP_s       time    score        group |
|----------------------------------------------|
| 135.008.060.182    25    .942467   Anomaly-free |
| 135.013.216.191    18    .4917266       Anomaly |
| 172.016.112.020    25   1.596048   Anomaly-free |
| 172.016.112.050     6    .201938       Anomaly |
| 172.016.112.149    25    .9618024  Anomaly-free |
|----------------------------------------------|
| 172.016.112.194    25    .9583151  Anomaly-free |
| 172.016.112.207    25    .9635356  Anomaly-free |
| 172.016.113.050     7    .952381       Anomaly |
| 172.016.113.084    25    .9517432  Anomaly-free |
| 172.016.113.105    25    .964501   Anomaly-free |
|----------------------------------------------|
| 172.016.113.204    25    .9513945  Anomaly-free |
| 172.016.114.050    20    .9988209       Anomaly |
| 172.016.114.148    25    .4076966  Anomaly-free |
| 172.016.114.168    25    .9083219  Anomaly-free |
| 172.016.114.169    25    .968396   Anomaly-free |
|----------------------------------------------|
| 172.016.114.207    25    .9583608  Anomaly-free |
| 172.016.115.005    25    .9727479  Anomaly-free |
| 172.016.115.087    25    .9784692  Anomaly-free |
| 172.016.115.234    25    .9815342  Anomaly-free |
| 172.016.116.044    25    .9939337  Anomaly-free |
|----------------------------------------------|
| 172.016.116.194    25    .9810044  Anomaly-free |
| 172.016.116.201    25    .9832515  Anomaly-free |
| 172.016.117.052    25    .9834497  Anomaly-free |
| 172.016.117.103    25    .9844607  Anomaly-free |
| 172.016.117.111    25    .9831676  Anomaly-free |
|----------------------------------------------|
| 172.016.117.132    25    .9755785  Anomaly-free |
| 192.168.001.001    25          1   Anomaly-free |
| 192.168.001.005    25          1   Anomaly-free |
| 192.168.001.010     7    .3724526       Anomaly |
| 192.168.001.020    25    .8599985  Anomaly-free |
|----------------------------------------------|
| 192.168.001.090    24   1.75811        Anomaly |
| 194.007.248.153     9    .0894454      Anomaly |
| 194.027.251.021     8    .3091476      Anomaly |
| 195.073.151.050    25    .9337767  Anomaly-free |
| 195.115.218.108    19    .1308353      Anomaly |
|----------------------------------------------|
| 196.037.075.158    12    .9812468      Anomaly |
| 196.227.033.189    14    .3776979      Anomaly |
| 197.182.091.233     8    .9809446      Anomaly |
| 197.218.177.069    25    .2488828  Anomaly-free |
+----------------------------------------------+
```

Figure 7.6 Distribution of hazard risk being anomalous by hours and weeks

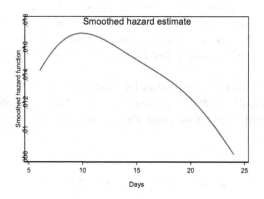

Figure 7.7 Survival curve by days

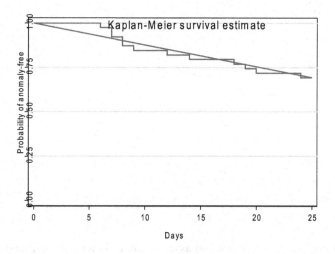

Figure 7.8 Distribution of the behavior score by anomaly-free and anomalous site groups

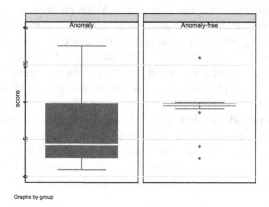

Figures 7.6 and 7.7 show the distributions of hazard risk being anomalous by days, and the Kaplan-Meier survival curves by days, respectively. We can find from Figure 7.6 that the hazard was increased on the 10th day that is the median day of pattern changes for all 12 sites. Figure 7.7 also illustrates that there were almost no anomaly events during the first five days for all of the 39 sites but started to change on the 6th day, and the probability of randomly pick up a site to be anomaly-free is about 0.69 at the end of monitoring period.

Display 7.13 shows the fitted Cox proportional hazards model with the behavior score as a predictor. The model suggests that the behavior score is statistically significantly associated with the behavior pattern; a site with a high score is more likely to have an anomaly-free pattern (Figure 7.8).

Display 7.13
Results of the fitted Cox proportional hazards model with MIT-DARPA data

```
* Fit the Cox model;
. stcox score,hr robust;

        failure _d:  Anomaly
  analysis time _t:  time

Iteration 0:    log pseudolikelihood = -42.129061
Iteration 1:    log pseudolikelihood = -38.332558
Iteration 2:    log pseudolikelihood = -38.206206
Iteration 3:    log pseudolikelihood = -38.206203
Refining estimates:
Iteration 0:    log pseudolikelihood = -38.206203

Cox regression -- Breslow method for ties

No. of subjects     =        39          Number of obs   =         39
No. of failures     =        12
Time at risk        =       827
                                          Wald chi2(1)    =       6.74
Log pseudolikelihood =  -38.206203        Prob > chi2     =     0.0094

------------------------------------------------------------------------
            |              Robust
         _t | Haz. Ratio  Std. Err.      z    P>|z|     [95% Conf. Interval]
------------+-----------------------------------------------------------
      score |  .0976185   .0874766    -2.60   0.009     .0168564    .5653263
------------+-----------------------------------------------------------
```

Figure 7.9 graphically examines and assesses the violations of the proportional-hazards assumption based on the log-log plot. We divided the behavior score to two groups: greater than the mean and lower than the mean. Although the use of such a graphical method to examine the validity of the assumption could be subjective, this method also provides a quick and easy approach to understand if a single baseline survivor function is good enough. That is, if the plotted lines are reasonably parallel, the proportional-hazards assumption has not been violated so we can fit all sites with different scores together with a single baseline survivor function. Note that the lines in Figure 7.9 can be considered approximately parallel.

Survival analysis provides a robust approach to measure both system and user behavior when such behavior is time-dependent. However, survival analysis has not been employed widely in network security and fundamental studies are desired. For readers who are interested in obtaining a more comprehensive understanding on survival analysis, Kleinbaum (1996) provides a good step-by-step self-learning textbook, entitled Survival Analysis:

Figure 7.9 Use log-log plot to assess the proportional-hazards assumption

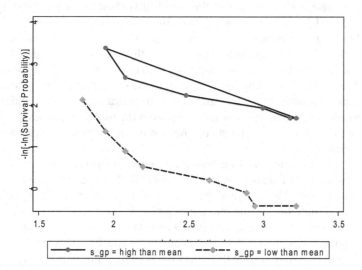

A Self-learning Text. Additional materials also can be found from Lee (1992), Klein & Moeschberger (1997), and Hosmer & Lemeshow (1999).

ROBUSTNESS ASSOCIATION

A regression model provides point estimates and interval estimates for the association between predictor variables and the response variable. Because a point estimate is just a single value of the statistic used to approximate the true parameter, we usually ask two questions: (1) how accurate is the point estimate, and (2) how robust is the association? The interval estimates of a point estimate provide a solution to the first question, which gives a range of the true parameter with a predetermined threshold (e.g., a confidence interval at a significance level of 0.05). We will discuss the interval estimate methods in Chapter XI. In this section we will address this second question regarding the robustness of the association. The question asks that if we fit the model with different samples drawn from the same population, does the association still hold, and if so, what is the probability that the association will hold?

Stepwise Regression Analysis

Model selection is a fundamental task in statistical analysis, and it is widely recognized as a central element to good inference. When a large set of predictor variables is available, we want to select a subset of them that are robust enough to construct a good and reliable model. This is the process of model selection. Usually, in a multiple regression modeling process, we only need to keep variables that are statistically significantly associated with the response variable in the final model. We can identify these variables by fitting all the variables into a model and then removing insignificant variables according to a predetermined threshold (e.g., a significance level of 0.10, 0.05, 0.01, etc.). We can also accomplish this task automatically by using the forward (start with the null model and add variables one at a time in the order that are best to associate with the response variable) or backward (start with all variables and delete one at a time, in the order that are worst to associate with the response variable) stepwise regression method that utilizes the likelihood ratio test to determine which variables to add or drop from the model. Although the stepwise procedure has a risk of overfitting the model, but it is useful only for exporting and selecting variables initially.

Example 7.8→Variable Selection Based on Stepwise Procedure. Let us now fit a backward stepwise logistic regression with the 1999 KDD-cup training data. The initial number of predictor variables is 46 and the response variable is anomalous (yes/no): only 44 variables are eligible for loading into the stepwise produce after restricting variables with low frequency values. An insignificance threshold of 0.05 for removing variables is used to select potential predictors detecting anomaly-free traffics. This threshold ensures that a variable will be removed from the model if it is statistically significantly associated with the response variable at the significance level of 0.05 or higher. The Stata codes used to accomplish the model and Stata output are shown below.

Display 7.14
Stata codes used to fit a backward stepwise logistic regression model based on KDD-cup 1999 data with a significance level of 0.05 for removing variables

```
#delimit;
clear;
set mem 345454;
use "F:\Book\Chapter 7\KDD_TRAI.DTA", clear;
/*-------------------------------------------------------------
Backward selection with remove at significant level of 0.05
---------------------------------------------------------*/;
stepwise, pr(0.05):
logistic normal
duration src_byte dst_byte land wrong_fr urgent hot num_fail logged_i
num_comp root_she su_attem num_root num_file num_shel num_acce is_guest
count srv_coun serror_r srv_serr rerror_r srv_rerr same_srv diff_srv
srv_diff dst_host dst_hos1 dst_hos2 dst_hos3 dst_hos4 dst_hos5 dst_hos6
dst_hos7 dst_hos8 dst_hos9 rej s0 sf rst icmp udp http hot_0 ;
```

Display 7.15
Results of the fitted a backward stepwise logistic regression model

```
                        begin with full model
p = 0.6792 >= 0.0500  removing srv_diff
p = 0.4695 >= 0.0500  removing rej
p = 0.3535 >= 0.0500  removing num_shel
p = 0.2852 >= 0.0500  removing serror_r
p = 0.2675 >= 0.0500  removing rerror_r
p = 0.0546 >= 0.0500  removing urgent
p = 0.7138 >= 0.0500  removing num_root
p = 0.6901 >= 0.0500  removing dst_hos9
p = 0.9443 >= 0.0500  removing su_attem
p = 0.8990 >= 0.0500  removing num_comp
p = 0.0670 >= 0.0500  removing num_acce


Logistic regression                        Number of obs   =     494021
                                           LR chi2(32)     = 477660.66
                                           Prob > chi2     =     0.0000
Log likelihood = -6248.4233                Pseudo R2       =     0.9745
```

normal	Odds Ratio	Std. Err.	z	P>|z|	[95% Conf. Interval]	
duration	1.00019	.0000147	12.94	0.000	1.000162	1.000219
src_byte	.9999992	2.33e-07	-3.65	0.000	.9999987	.9999996
dst_byte	.9999991	1.28e-07	-6.96	0.000	.9999989	.9999994
land	1958.824	2707.092	5.48	0.000	130.5078	29400.49
sf	.1219192	.0623801	-4.11	0.000	.0447253	.3323458
hot	.8272297	.0115088	-13.63	0.000	.8049776	.8500969
num_fail	4.153833	1.703069	3.47	0.001	1.859759	9.277719
logged_i	.176206	.0325227	-9.41	0.000	.1227192	.2530049
dst_hos8	.0001281	.0000316	-36.30	0.000	.0000789	.0002078
root_she	11.54408	5.973395	4.73	0.000	4.187085	31.82783
http	351409.3	114992.5	39.02	0.000	185043	667350.3
s0	.0001107	.0000532	-18.93	0.000	.0000431	.0002842
num_file	3.309616	.2775701	14.27	0.000	2.807949	3.900911
udp	.1071626	.0204002	-11.73	0.000	.0737908	.1556266
dst_hos7	.0115627	.0073107	-7.05	0.000	.0033487	.0399251
is_guest	5.69e+08	2.64e+08	43.48	0.000	2.30e+08	1.41e+09
count	.9699031	.0018383	-16.12	0.000	.9663068	.9735129
srv_coun	1.009742	.0019314	5.07	0.000	1.005964	1.013535
icmp	.0678118	.0129418	-14.10	0.000	.0466504	.0985725
srv_serr	.029071	.0237932	-4.32	0.000	.0058451	.1445861
rst	.1514539	.0521555	-5.48	0.000	.077118	.2974438
srv_rerr	.0075447	.0040418	-9.12	0.000	.0026402	.0215599
same_srv	2.032858	.5195758	2.78	0.006	1.231826	3.354785
diff_srv	5.240146	1.328486	6.53	0.000	3.188205	8.612727
hot_0	7.90e+08	2.94e+08	55.02	0.000	3.81e+08	1.64e+09
dst_host	.99014	.0005119	-19.17	0.000	.9891372	.9911438
dst_hos1	1.012634	.0005599	22.71	0.000	1.011537	1.013732
dst_hos2	1.483245	.2340759	2.50	0.012	1.088634	2.020896
dst_hos3	623.5556	120.7218	33.24	0.000	426.6587	911.3175
dst_hos4	.0134376	.0014337	-40.39	0.000	.0109019	.016563
dst_hos5	9.83e-06	2.91e-06	-38.98	0.000	5.51e-06	.0000176
dst_hos6	.0164352	.0052622	-12.83	0.000	.0087749	.0307829

The stepwise logistic regression modeling process identified 33 variables as variables that were statistically significantly associated with the response variable. The model had a ROC area value of 0.98 with a χ^2 value of 477,660. Its predictive ability ranged from the 0.00 in the lowest deciles to 1.00 in the highest deciles, which is indicative that the model may be capable of having good discrimination.

Stepwise procedures have been criticized since it can yield a biologically implausible model (Greenland, 1989) and can select irrelevant, or noise variables (Flack & Chang, 1987; Griffiths & Pope, 1987). Shtatland, Cain, and Barton, (2000) used SAS PROC LO-GISTIC as an example to demonstrate that the use of a significance level of 0.05 for entry variables may be unreasonable, and could also be dangerous because the model could be either over fitted or under fitted. They believe that if we blindly rely on stepwise logistic regression, we will most likely get a poor choice for the purposes of interpretation and prediction. The problem is not that we cannot obtain a good model by using the stepwise procedure, but rather, that we may face the risk that we will fail to carefully scrutinize the resulting model, and report such results as the final or best model incorrectly (Hosmer and Lemeshow, 2000). Thus, the stepwise results illustrated in Example 7.8 may include some noises, which could mean that the 33 variables may not be robust; in other words, we do not know if these variables are still statistically significant if we fit the model with a different sample that is drown from the same population. To answer this question we can employ the bootstrap resampling method (Efron & Tibshirani, 1994) to fit the model n times and calculate the probability of a variable being statistically significant in the n models. We have briefly mentioned the bootstrap resampling method in Chapter VI and will revisit this topic in the next section.

Bootstrapping Approach

A fundamental challenge in the network intrusion detection area is to make probability-based inferences about a set of population characteristics (e.g., θ and σ which represent the "true" user behavior pattern based on the complete network traffic from the full life circle of a particular network system) based on a set of estimators (e.g., $\hat{\theta}$ and $\hat{\sigma}$ which represent an observed user behavior pattern) using a sample acquired from the population. The bootstrap method, a nonparametric statistical resampling approach, can be used to address this challenge. Bootstrapping aims to make better statistical inferences and addresses the sample variability issue. The bootstrap method has been widely used in statistics and quantitative social science fields since Bradley Efron published his first article on this method in 1979 (Efron, 1979). Bootstrapping differs from the traditional parametric approach for making an inference in that it involves "resampling" the original data with replacement numerous times in order to generate an empirical estimate of the entire sampling distribution of an estimator rather than having strong distributional assumptions and analytic formulas (Efron & Tibshirani, 1986; Mooney & Duval, 1993). This unique attribute allows us to make inferences in cases where such analytic solutions are unavailable and where such assumptions are untenable in anomaly detection. During bootstrapping, a new sample is generated by drawing n observations with replacement from the original data, and a new estimate is calculated. The resulting empirical distribution based on bootstrap analysis approximates the "true" user behavior pattern, which provides an approach to obtain an approximation of the estimate pattern in the absence of prior information about the true distribution of the estimate or the original data—common situation of retrieving information in anomaly detection.

The bootstrap simulation procedure can be employed in conjunction with the stepwise multiple logistic regression technique to identify robust predictors. We can carry out a large numbers of simulations, usually $B \geq 1,000$ iterations, during which each iteration generates a new sample by drawing n observations with replacement from the original data. Within each of the iteration, we can then fit the stepwise logistic model to yield a set of variables that are statistically significantly associated with the response variable. Thus, B iterations of the simulation will yield B sets of predictors meeting the predefined significance level (e.g., $\alpha = 0.05$). We can select variables based on their probability of meeting the predefined significance level that is included in B iterations. Using a binary classification rule, if $c_i = 1$ then we select the ith variable and $c_i = 0$ for otherwise,

$$c_i = \begin{cases} 1, & \dfrac{b_i}{B} \geq \rho \\ 0, & \dfrac{b_i}{B} < \rho \end{cases},$$

where b_i is the total number of occurrences where the ith variable met the predefined significance level and ρ is the probability threshold that determines the strength of the association between the index variable and the response variable.

Example 7.9→Robust Predictors for Intrusion Detection. With non-parametric bootstrapping and a total of bootstrap iterations of $B = 3000$, we fit 3,000 multiple stepwise logistic regression models based on random sampling with replacements from the original KDD-cup 1999 training data. These models yielded a mean ROC area value of 0.999 (95% of confidence interval: $0.99 - 1.00$) and a mean χ^2 value of 516,490. Using a probability of $\rho = 0.85$ as a threshold, 16 variables that are statistically significantly associated with the response variable, having a Wald χ^2 absolute value of 10 or higher, were identified as robust predictors (Figure 7.10) to detect intrusion. Among these variables, the probability ranged from 0.85 (rate of connections to different services) to 1.00 (TCP, HTTP, RST, "guest login," "connections to the same host as the current connection," "connections having the same destination host," "connections having the same destination host and using the same service," "rate of connections to the current host having the same source port," and "rate of connections to the same service coming from different hosts"). Overall, these variables demonstrated strong associations with the response variable. Table 7.8 shows the odds ratio and standardized estimate of each variable yielded by the final model. A variable with a standardized estimate less than 0 or an odds ratio less than 1 indicates that the variable has a negative association with the response variable, and a connection with this characteristic was unlikely to be an anomaly. Compared to Figure 7.10, which shows the likelihood of each predictor's being statistically significantly associated with the response variable, Table 7.8 shows the strength of each predictor associated with the response variable. The areas under the ROC curve were 1.00, with an $R^2 = 0.96$ and a goodness-of-fit value of 0.06 for the final model with 16 variables (we will review the concept of the goodness-of-fit in Chapter XII). Predictive ability ranged from the 0.00 in the lowest deciles to 1.00 in the highest deciles, indicative that the model had good discrimination.

Analysis of Clustering Data

As we mentioned in Chapters I and III, one situation in network security to consider is that network traffics are clustered by groups. When data have clustering, the observations within a group may not be treated as independent, but the groups themselves are independent. In practice, network traffic always comes from different groups that can be, for example, users, sites, sub-network systems, departments, organizations, and even regions, and each group may have its own characteristics in its network system or policy (e.g., a group can install a group-specific application for intrusion prevention). This situation indicates that the traffic may be independent across groups, but may not necessary be independent within groups; such a condition affects the estimated standard errors and variance-covariance matrix of the estimators. One of the risks of such a situation is that we may identify variables as being statistically significantly associated with the response variable, but they do not hold such association essentially.

There are several approaches that can be used to address the issue of observations clustering within groups. One is the Huber-White sandwich estimator of variance method (Huber, 1967; White, 1980) and the other is the hierarchical modeling method. We will use an example to explain the Huber-White sandwich method in this section and will discuss the hierarchical modeling method in Chapter VIII.

Example 7.10→ Model Clustered Data. The Huber-White sandwich method has been implemented by many software applications. Let us use the Stata software and the MIT-DARPA data to illustrate how the clustering situation may impact our estimates, and how to adjust the clustering using the cluster() option provided by Stata. The corresponding codes to employ the cluster() option are presented in Display 7.16, and the results are showed in Display 7.17. There are 9008 groups in the data and the first part of the results shows a model that is not adjusted for clustering across the groups. The second part of Display 7.17 shows the model adjusted by groups. We can see that after being adjusted for clustering, five variables (l1, udp, icmp, eco, and telnet) do not become statistically significant in the model.

Figure 7.10 Probability of predictor variables significantly associated with anomaly-free traffic

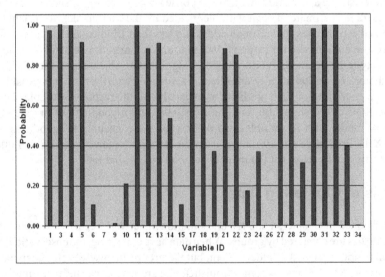

Table 7.8 Variables significantly associated with the response variable

ID	Predictor Variables	Odds Ratio	95% Confidence Interval	P value	Standardized Estimate
1	Length (number of seconds) of the connection	0.90	0.88 - 0.91	<0.001	-0.0611
2	ICMP (reference)	1.00			
3	TCP	0.69	0.60 -0.79	<0.001	-0.1001
4	UDP	0.08	0.07 -0.09	<0.001	-0.2799
5	HTTP	1.63	1.47 -1.81	<0.001	0.0907
8	REJ (reference)	1.00			
11	RST	108.61	81.16 -145.34	<0.001	0.1419
12	Login successfully	0.71	0.64 -0.78	<0.001	-0.0684
13	Number of compromised	1.03	1.01 -1.05	<0.001	0.0159
17	Guest login	8.65	7.26 -10.32	<0.001	0.0443
18	Connections to the same host as the current connection in the past two seconds	87.48	73.69 -103.84	<0.001	2.4652
21	Rate of connections to the same service	0.13	0.12 -0.14	<0.001	-1.1455
22	Rate of connections to different services	0.73	0.71 -0.74	<0.001	-0.1763
27	Connections having the same destination host	2.17	2.10 -2.23	<0.001	0.4264
28	Connections having the same destination host and using the same service	0.29	0.27 -0.30	<0.001	-0.6852
30	Rate of different services on the current host	0.75	0.73 -0.77	<0.001	-0.1588
31	Rate of connections to the current host having the same source port	3.36	3.18 -3.56	<0.001	0.6686
32	Rate of connections to the same service coming from different hosts	1.36	1.35 -1.38	<0.001	0.1712

Display 7.16
Stata codes to fit logistic models without and with adjusted standard error for clustering within sites

```
/*-----------------------------------------------------------------
Model without adjusted the standard error for clustering within sites
------------------------------------------------------------*/;
logistic normal
  t2 l1 udp icmp samePort sameIP http smtp urp ecr eco snmp ftp port domain
telnet finger;

/*-----------------------------------------------------------
 Model adjusted the standard error for clustering within sites
------------------------------------------------------*/;
logistic normal
t2 l1 udp icmp samePort sameIP http smtp urp ecr eco snmp ftp port domain
telnet finger, cluster(IP_s);
```

Display 7.17
Results of fitted logistic models without and with adjusted standard error for clustering within sites

```
/*-----------------------------------------------------------
Model without adjusted the standard error for clustering within sites
------------------------------------------------------------*/;

Logistic regression                        Number of obs   =    3013860
                                           LR chi2(17)     = 3741600.93
                                           Prob > chi2     =     0.0000
Log likelihood = -136285.09                Pseudo R2       =     0.9321

------------------------------------------------------------------------------
     normal | Odds Ratio   Std. Err.      z    P>|z|     [95% Conf. Interval]
------------+-----------------------------------------------------------------
         t2 |  .1051994    .0025275    -93.73   0.000     .1003604    .1102718
         l1 |  .3189943    .0075564    -48.23   0.000     .3045226    .3341538
        udp |  .7752408    .0235177     -8.39   0.000     .7304904    .8227326
       icmp |  .1915067    .0061975    -51.07   0.000      .179737    .2040471
   samePort |  10.63872    .3231717     77.84   0.000     10.0238    11.29136
     sameIP |  .0047241    .0021685    -11.67   0.000     .0019213    .0116159
       http |   1429.63    33.4197     310.79   0.000     1365.606    1496.655
       smtp |  386.3628    11.91467    193.16   0.000     363.7022     410.4352
        urp |  6930.101    6934.191      8.84   0.000     975.0695    49254.23
        ecr |  .0262402    .0007955   -120.08   0.000     .0247265    .0278466
        eco |  .7804815    .0235569     -8.21   0.000     .7356499    .8280453
       snmp |  1527.044    56.95703    196.55   0.000     1419.393     1642.86
        ftp |  76.09021    1.733625    190.13   0.000     72.76712    79.56506
       port |  .0103673    .0003192   -148.38   0.000     .0097601    .0110123
     domain |  304.3127    11.30613    153.91   0.000     282.9407    327.2991
     telnet |  4.165461    .1408742     42.19   0.000     3.898305    4.450926
     finger |  21.04113    .6462998     99.18   0.000     19.81178    22.34676
------------------------------------------------------------------------------

/*-----------------------------------------------------------
 Model adjusted the standard error for clustering within sites
------------------------------------------------------------*/;

Logistic regression                        Number of obs   =    3013860
                                           Wald chi2(17)   =    1435.38
                                           Prob > chi2     =     0.0000
Log pseudolikelihood = -136285.09          Pseudo R2       =     0.9321

                       (Std. Err. adjusted for 9008 clusters in IP_s)
```

continued on following page

Display 7.17 continued

normal	Odds Ratio	Robust Std. Err.	z	P>|z|	[95% Conf. Interval]	
t2	.1051994	.0998284	-2.37	0.018	.0163783	.6757041
l1	.3189943	.2710989	-1.34	0.179	.0603094	1.687256
udp	.7752408	.7897027	-0.25	0.803	.1052825	5.708435
icmp	.1915067	.2343157	-1.35	0.177	.0174063	2.106983
samePort	10.63872	9.046559	2.78	0.005	2.009443	56.32519
sameIP	.0047241	.0045995	-5.50	0.000	.0007008	.0318475
http	1429.63	1153.542	9.00	0.000	294.0387	6950.927
smtp	386.3628	248.1785	9.27	0.000	109.7058	1360.696
urp	6930.101	10494.26	5.84	0.000	356.2572	134807.9
ecr	.0262402	.0373678	-2.56	0.011	.0016099	.4276956
eco	.7804815	1.061354	-0.18	0.855	.0543049	11.21725
snmp	1527.044	1732.712	6.46	0.000	165.1991	14115.48
ftp	76.09021	69.33794	4.75	0.000	12.75449	453.9358
port	.0103673	.0073234	-6.47	0.000	.0025965	.0413952
domain	304.3127	310.5103	5.60	0.000	41.18919	2248.314
telnet	4.165461	3.31191	1.79	0.073	.8767634	19.7899
finger	21.04113	14.20556	4.51	0.000	5.602668	79.02115

SUMMARY

In this chapter we discussed essential techniques for modeling associations between the response variable and the predictor variables. We discussed various approaches for examining such associations, including bivariate analysis, statistical tests, multiple modeling techniques, and bootstrapping. Generally, we may have two situations in the measuring association between and among variables in network security. In one situation, we know individual variable distribution from the descriptive analysis but we do not know how these variables are associated with each other. In other words, we have no pre-designed patterns in mind but like to have the data tell us. This situation fits the multivariate analysis and we have discussed it in Chapter V. Another situation is that we have a targeted variable (i.e., a response variable) and we like to know how the other variables are related to it. This situation fits the bivariate and regression analyses that we discussed this chapter.

The advantage of using statistical methods in network security is that they offer a wide availability of approaches, ranging from simple significance tests to complex analyses, which include bivariate analysis, multiple regression, and multivariate analysis. Although the field of network security is still in its junior status and many difficult topics for research need to be addressed, given the rapid advancement in computer and network technology, as well as increased information and national security threats, the demand for adopting robust statistical methods in intrusion detection and prevention has intensified significantly. Regardless, this demand presents many challenges and numerous fundamental questions need to be studied.

REFERENCES

Agresti, A. (1996). *An introduction to categorical data analysis.* New York: John Wiley.

Agresti, A. (2002). *Categorical data analysis.* New York: Wiley-Interscience.

Allison, P. D. (1999). *Multiple regression: A primer.* CA: Pine Forge Press.

Berry, W. D., & Feldman, S. (1985). *Multiple regression in practice.* Sage University Newbury Park, CA: Sage.

Bozdogan, H. (2003). *Statistical data mining and knowledge discovery.* Florida: Taylor & Francis CRC Press, pp. 373-383.

Burnham, K, P., and Anderson, D. R. (1998). *Model selection and inference: A practical information-theoretic approach.* New York: Springer-Verlag.

Cohen, J., & Cohen, P. (1983). *Applied multiple regression/correlation analysis for the behavioral sciences.* Hillsdale, New Jersey: Lawrence Erlbaum Associates, Inc.

Cox, D. R. & Snell, E. J. (1989). *Analysis of binary data* (2nd edition). London: Chapman & Hall.

Dacid W. & Hosmer, S.L. (2000). *Applied logistic regression,* 2nd Edition. New York: John Wiley & Sons, Inc.

dos Santos, M.L., de Mello, R.F. & Yang, L.T. (2007). Extraction and classification of user behavior. *Lecture notes in Computer Science,*4808, pp. 493-506. New York: Springer.

Efron, B. (1979). Bootstrap methods: Another look at the jackknife. *Annals of Statistics, 7,* 1-26.

Efron, B. & Tibshirani, E. R. (1986). Bootstrap methods for standard errors, confidence intervals, and other measures of statistical accuracy. *Statistical Science,1*(1), 57-77.

Efron, B. & Tibshirani, E. R. (1994). *An introduction to the bootstrap.* London: Chapman & Hall.

Goonatilake, R., Herath, A., Herath, S., & Herath, J. (2007). Intrusion detection using the chi-square goodness-of-fit test for information assurance, network, forensics and software security. *J. Comput. Small Coll. 23*(1), 255-263.

Greenland, S. and Pope, P. J. (1987). Small sample properties of probit models. *Journal of the American Statistical Association. 82,* 929-937.

Greenland, S. (1989). Modeling variable selection in epidemiologic analysis. *American Journal of Public Health, 79*(3), 340-349.

Griffiths, W.E. and Pope, P.T. (1987). Small sample properties of probit models. *J. Am. Stat. Assoc. 82,* 929-937.

Hastie, T. Tibshirani, R. Friedman, J. (2001). *The elements of statistical learning: Data mining, inference, and prediction.* New York: Springer-Verlag.

Hosmer, D. W. & Lemeshow, S. (1999). *Applied survival analysis: regression modeling of time to event data.* New York: John Wiley & Sons, Inc.

Hosmer, D.W. and Lemeshow, S. (2000). *Applied logistics regression,* second Ed., New York: John Wiley & Sons, Inc.

Huber, P. J. (1967). The behavior of maximum likelihood estimates under nonstandard conditions. In *Proceedings of the Fifth Berkeley Symposium on Mathematical Statistics and Probability.* Berkeley, CA: University of California Press, 1, pp. 221-223.

Kayacik, G. H. & Zincir-Heywood, A. N. (2005). Selecting features for intrusion detection: a feature relevance analysis on KDD 99 benchmark, in *Proceedings of the Third Annual Conference on Privacy, Security and Trust.*

KDD-Cup, (1999). *KDD data available on the web.* Retrieved January 21, 2004 from http://kdd.ics.uci.edu/databases/kddcup99/kddcup99.html.

Klein, J. P. & Moeschberger, M. L. (1997). *Survival analysis: techniques for censored and truncated data.* New York: Springer-Verlag.

Kleinbaum, D. G. (1994). *Logistic regression: A self-learning text.* New York: Springer-Verlag.

Kleinbaum, D. G. (1996). *Survival analysis: A self-learning text.* New York: Springer-Verlag.

Lee, E. T. (1992). *Statistical methods for survival data analysis,* 2nd Edition. New York: Wiley-Interscience.

Long, J. S. (1997). *Regression models for categorical and limited dependent variables.* Thousand Oaks, CA: Sage Publications.

Masum, S., Ye, E.M., Chen, Q., & Noh, K. (2000). Chi-square statistical profiling for anomaly detection. In *Proceedings of the 2000 IEEE Workshop on Information Assurance and Security.*

McFadden, D. (1974). Conditional logit analysis of qualitative choice behavior. In P. Zarembka (ed.), *Frontiers in econometrics.* New York: Academic Press. pp. 105-142.

Maloof, M. A. (2006). *Machine learning and data mining for computer security.* New York: Springer-Verlag.

Mandel, J. (1964). *The statistical analysis of experimental data.* New York: Dover Publications, Inc.

McCullagh, P. & Nelder, J. A. (1989). *Generalized linear models.* 2nd Edition. New York: Chapman & Hall/CRC.

Menard, S (2002). *Applied logistic regression analysis,* 2nd Edition. CA: Sage Publications. Series.

Mooney, C. Z. & Duval, R. D. (1993). *Bootstrapping: a nonparametric approach to statistical inference.* New York: SAGE Publications.

Myers, R. H., Montgomery, D. C. & Vining, G. G. (2002). *Generalized linear models with applications in engineering and the sciences.* New York: Wiley-Interscience.

O'Connell, A. A. (2006). *Logistic regression models for ordinal response variables.* Thousand Oaks, CA: Sage Publications.

Pampel, F. C. (2000). *Logistic regression: A primer.* CA: Sage Publications. pp. 35-38.

Pearson, K. (1896). Mathematical contributions to the theory of evolution—III. Regression, heredity, and panmixia. *Philosophical Transactions of the Royal Society of London, A, 187,* 253-318.

Pearson, K. & Filon, L.N.G. (1898). Mathematical contributions to the theory of evolution—IV. On the probable errors of frequency constants and on the influence of random selection on variation and correlation. *Philosophical Transactions of the Royal Society of London, A, 191,* 229-311.

Pintilie, M (2006). *Computing risks: A practical perspective.* New York: Wiley & Sons.

Press, S. J. & Wilson, S. (1978). Choosing between logistic regression and discriminant analysis. *Journal of the American Statistical Association, 73,* 699-705.

Rice, J. C. (1994). Logistic regression: An introduction. *Advances in social science methodology, 3,* 191-245.

Ryan, T. P. (1997). *Modern regression methods.* New York: Wiley-Interscience.

Shtatland, E. S., Cain, E. and Barton, M. B. (2000). *The perils of stepwise logistic regression and how to escape them using information criteria and the output delivery system.* Retrieved September 9, 2007 from http://www2.sas.com/proceedings/sugi26/p222-26.pdf

Stata (2006). *Stata reference.* TX: Stata Press

Stolfo, J., Fan, W., Lee, W., Prodromidis, A., Chan, P. K. (2000). Cost-based modeling and evaluation for data mining with application to fraud and intrusion detection. In *Proceedings of the DARPA Information Survivability Conference.*

Tabachnick, B. G., Fidell, L. S. (2001). *Using multivariate statistics*, fourth edition. Needham Heights, Massachusetts: Allyn and Bacon.

Vapnik, V. N. (1998). *Statistical learning theory.* New York: Wiley-Interscience.

Vapnik, V. N. (1999). An overview of statistical learning theory, *IEEE Trans. Neural Netw. 10,* 988-999.

White, H. (1980). A heteroskedasticity-consistent covariance matrix estimator and a direct test for heteroskedasticity. *Econometrica, 48,* 817-830.

APPENDIX

Time_7.do (Stata codes)

```
gen  byte time=0 if substr(index,1,6)=="week-1" | substr(index,1,6)=="week-2";

replace  time=1 if substr(index,1,6)=="week-3" & substr(index, 8,3)=="mon";
replace  time=2 if substr(index,1,6)=="week-3" & substr(index, 8,3)=="tue";
replace  time=3 if substr(index,1,6)=="week-3" & substr(index, 8,3)=="wed";
replace  time=4 if substr(index,1,6)=="week-3" & substr(index, 8,3)=="thr";
replace  time=5 if substr(index,1,6)=="week-3" & substr(index, 8,3)=="fri";

replace  time=6 if substr(index,1,6)=="week-4" & substr(index, 8,3)=="mon";
replace  time=7 if substr(index,1,6)=="week-4" & substr(index, 8,3)=="tue";
replace  time=8 if substr(index,1,6)=="week-4" & substr(index, 8,3)=="wed";
replace  time=9 if substr(index,1,6)=="week-4" & substr(index, 8,3)=="thr";
replace  time=10 if substr(index,1,6)=="week-4" & substr(index, 8,3)=="fri";

replace  time=11 if substr(index,1,6)=="week-5" & substr(index, 8,3)=="mon";
replace  time=12 if substr(index,1,6)=="week-5" & substr(index, 8,3)=="tue";
replace  time=13 if substr(index,1,6)=="week-5" & substr(index, 8,3)=="wed";
replace  time=14 if substr(index,1,6)=="week-5" & substr(index, 8,3)=="thr";
replace  time=15 if substr(index,1,6)=="week-5" & substr(index, 8,3)=="fri";

replace  time=16 if substr(index,1,6)=="week-6" & substr(index, 8,3)=="mon";
replace  time=17 if substr(index,1,6)=="week-6" & substr(index, 8,3)=="tue";
replace  time=18 if substr(index,1,6)=="week-6" & substr(index, 8,3)=="wed";
replace  time=19 if substr(index,1,6)=="week-6" & substr(index, 8,3)=="thr";
replace  time=20 if substr(index,1,6)=="week-6" & substr(index, 8,3)=="fri";

replace  time=21 if substr(index,1,6)=="week-7" & substr(index, 8,3)=="mon";
replace  time=22 if substr(index,1,6)=="week-7" & substr(index, 8,3)=="tue";
replace  time=23 if substr(index,1,6)=="week-7" & substr(index, 8,3)=="wed";
replace  time=24 if substr(index,1,6)=="week-7" & substr(index, 8,3)=="thr";
replace  time=25 if substr(index,1,6)=="week-7" & substr(index, 8,3)=="fri";
```

Chapter VIII
Measuring User Behavior

You are alive. Do something. The directive in life, the moral imperative was so uncompli-
cated. It could be expressed in single words, not complete sentences. It sounded like this:
Look. Listen. Choose. Act.

- Barbara Hall

INTRODUCTION

Measurement plays a fundamental role in our modern world, and the measurement theory
uses statistical tools to measure and to analyze data. In this chapter, we will examine several
statistical techniques for measuring user behavior. We will first discuss the fundamental
characteristics of user behavior, and then we will describe the scoring and profiling approaches to measure user behavior. The fundamental idea of measurement theory is that
measurements are not the same as the outcome being measured. Hence, if we want to draw
conclusions about the outcome, we must take into account the nature of the correspondence
between the outcome and the measurements. Our goal for measuring user behavior is to
understand the behavior patterns so we can further profile users or groups correctly. Readers
who are interested in basic measurement theory should refer to Krantz, Luce, Suppes &
Tversky (1971), Suppes, Krantz, Luce & Tversky (1989), Luce, Krantz, Suppes & Tversky
(1991), Hand (2004), and Shultz & Whitney (2005).

Any measurement could involve two types of errors, systematic errors and random
errors. A systematic error remains the same direction throughout a set of measurement

processes, and can have all positive or all negative (or both) values consistently. Generally, a systematic error is difficult to identify and account for. System errors generally originate in one of two ways: (1) error of calibration, and (2) error of use. Error due to calibration occurs, for example, if network data is collected incorrectly. More specifically, if an allowable value for one variable should have a range from 1 to 1000 but we incorrectly limit the range to a maximum of 100, then all the collected traffic data corresponding to this variable will be affected in the same way, giving rise to a systematic error. Errors of use occur, for example, if the data is collected correctly but was somehow transferred incorrectly. If we define a "byte" as a data type for a variable with a maximum range greater than 256, we expect incorrect results on observations with values greater than 256 for this variable.

A random error varies from a process to process and is equally likely to be randomly selected as positive or negative. Random errors arise because of either uncontrolled variables or specimen variations. In any case, the idea is to control all variables that can influence the result of the measurement and to control them closely enough that the resulting random errors are no longer objectionable. Random errors can be addressed with statistical methods. In most measurements, only random errors will contribute to estimates of probable error. One of the common random errors in measuring user behavior is the variance. A robust profiling measurement has to be able to take into account the variances in profiling patterns on (1) the network system side, such as variances in network groups or domains, traffic volume, and operating systems, (2) the user side, such as job responsibilities, working schedules, department categorization, security privileges, and computer skills must also be considered. The profiling measurement must be able to separate such variances from the system and user sides. Hence, revolutionizing network infrastructure or altering employment would have less of an impact on the overall profiling system. Recently, the hierarchical generalized linear model has been increasingly used to address such variances; we will further discuss this modern technique later in this chapter.

USER BEHAVIOR PATTERN

An essential task in network security is to monitor and analyze network traffic for profiling user behavior. A robust intrusion detection system has to hold parameters representing both normal and abnormal user behavior patterns, and such parameters require to be recalibrated consistently to adjust for changes in network and user behavior over time. Thus, measuring user behavior is an essential step leading to the development of a robust anomaly detection system. Even after 30 years, Denning's six main components: (1) subjects, (2) objects, (3) audit records, (4) profiles, (5) anomaly records, and (6) activity rules (1987) still remain true today and have also become individual research topics for modern intrusion detection systems (Marchette, 1999; Oh & Lee, 2003; Anderson, Selby & Ramsey, 2007; Bae, Lee & Lee, 2007; Mazhelis & Puuronen, 2007; Isohara, Takemori & Sasase, 2008).

Structures and Attributes

User behavior is a widely used term that is loosely defined—it could have different meanings and be measured differently depending on the research areas. For example, in the human-computer interaction (HCI) field, user behavior means accommodation of human diversity, which in the social science and computer design field may have more value on human engineering.

HCI uses one of three approaches to gather user behavior information: (1) videotaping of user activities, (2) recording user activities via logging data from a particular application, and (3) using an unobtrusive application that exists in the background across all the applications installed on the index machine, to record user behavior with timestamps throughout the index machine with timestamps (Westerman et al., 1996). If we want to adapt any HIC methods, it is clear that these approaches are not always feasible for network security, specifically for intrusion detection and prevention. This is because not every user can be located physically and each user may access information using multiple machines. Network system-level traffic data are the key source to measure user behavior, and additional data can provide useful information as well. Nevertheless, the research produced from HCI is valuable for network security. For example, the idea of using keystroke data as a potential data source for profiling users was obtained from the early HCI research. More information on HCI can be found from Nielsen and Mack (1994), Shneiderman (1998), and Peeece, Rogers & Sharp (2002). They provide excellent fundamental introductions to both theories and practical guidelines for capturing and measuring user behavior from HCI perspectives.

In general, we can think of user behavior connecting with at least three types of characteristics: (1) system-specific, (2) work-specific, and (3) person-specific. System-specific characteristics associate with the network system and the computer environment that a particular user who belongs to. We can have more freedom to choose an operating system for our own workstation(s) at home. However, in many circumstances, we do not have the privilege of choosing our favorable network system in the work place and is most likely decided by the IT department of an organization, company or institution. Thus, system-specific characteristics will be similar for users or user groups connecting within a network system. Work-specific characteristics are most likely related to job responsibilities, working schedules, and type of works to which a particular user is assigned. Person-specific characteristics include computer skills, predilections for particular software applications, and interests. The skill difference associated with computing, such as typing, will result in different keystroke patterns, while a difference in personal interests could result in different patterns of web browsing. For example, the web visit sequence patterns will differ between users who visit news sites first thing in the morning versus users who have interest to know the weather condition in the morning.

Usually there are two aspects in user behavior that need to be considered: the within-group and between-group variances. The within-group variance represents the changes that occur at the individual user, site, or group level. For example, if a user changes his/her working schedule, his/her login time zone will subsequently be changed; such a change could impact his/her profiling parameters but should not affect his/her profiling status. That is, if he/she belongs to a low risk pattern, he/she should still be with the same pattern. The between-group variance represents the difference between users, sites, or groups. The parameters used to describe a low risk pattern do not necessary have to be the same between two low risk users or among a group of low risk users. All these parameters should, however, be within a range in which the low risk pattern fills.

At the individual user-level, Garg, et, al. (2006) conducted a simulation to measure user behavior based on mouse movement and keyboard activity. Kukreja, Stevenson, and Ritter (2006) developed an approach to automate the generation of user data by parameterizing user behavior in terms of user intention (malicious/normal), user skills, types of applications installed on a machine, and mouse movement and keyboard activities. The user behavior parameters are used to generate templates, which can be further customized. This framework is called Usim, and it can achieve rapid generation of user behavior data based on the templates for GUI based systems. The data can be used to rapidly train and test intrusion detection algorithms and can provide useful insights to improve the detection precision.

At the system-level, Wang and Cannady (2005) proposed a risk score approach that included 14 predictors to measure user behavior. The score is constructed by taking into account the effect size of each variable associated with the response variable, attack (yes/no). They developed the score with a training sample drawn from the KDD-cup 1999 data and validated the score by a testing sample that includes new attacks that were not present in the training sample. They reported that the predictive performance of the score between the training and the testing samples is comparable in sensitivity, specificity, and the misclassification rate.

In an ideal world, we can measure all information in three areas: system-specific, work-specific, and person-specific. We assume that we can use k binary variables to represent the results of each measurement for each area, and then the unique combination of such binary variables may represent user behavior in a corresponding area. With two binary variables, the possible combinations are 00, 11, 01, and 10. Thus, let N be the total number of observations, k be the total number of binary variables, and J be the total number of covariate patterns that are the combination of k variables among the N observations in a dataset, where $J \leq N$. We have

$$J \leq 2^k. \tag{8-1}$$

If we assume that each covariate pattern represents an individual user pattern, Equation (8-1) suggests that the number of such patterns has an exponential relation with the number of binary variables (Figure 8.1). The good news is that in many situations the actual number of covariate patterns is significantly less that the theoretically maximum number, 2^k.

Example 8.1→ Covariate Patterns. A covariate pattern is a combination of a set of variables in which each variable is possibly associated with the response variable of interest. Using 10% of the KDD-cup 1999 training data and assigning 6 variables: TCP (yes/no), UDP (yes/no), HTTP (yes/no), RST (yes/no), login-successfully (yes/no) and guest-login (yes/no), yielded nine patterns as shown in Table 8.1. Note that these represent the possible patterns at the system-level. Patterns "000000", "100000", "and "100100" are associated with having a high risk of being anomalous and patterns "010000", "100010", "101000", and "101010" are associated with having low risk connections. The associations for patterns "100011" and "101110" are unclear.

Analysis of Variance

Assume we have TCP/IP data from four different departments within a company: D1 (Research and Development), D2 (Human Resource), D3 (Finance), and D4 (Customer Relationship). Let us randomly draw samples from these departments from 8:30am to 9:00am for four randomly selected users, User-1, User-2, User-3, and User-4. We measure their network traffic in four dimensions, denoted by M1 (total number of connections), M2

Figure 8.1 Relationship between the number of covariate patterns with the number of variables

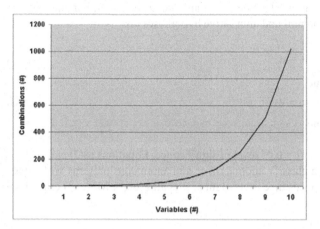

Table 8.1 Covariate patterns and outcome

Pattern	Connection		Anomaly (%)
	Total (#)	Rate (%)	
000000	28,360	57.41	99.50
010000	2,035	4.12	5.31
100000	10,993	22.25	98.67
100010	1,380	2.79	6.52
100011	68	0.14	51.47
100100	133	0.27	97.74
101000	557	1.13	3.23
101010	5,860	11.86	3.81
101110	13	0.03	69.23

(average number of connections having the same destination host), M3 (average number of connections having the same destination host and using the same service), and M4 (average number of connections to the same service as the current connection in the past two seconds). Table 8.2 shows the results of these measurements.

The within-group (user) variance for each measure is displayed in the rows, and the columns display the between-group (department) variations. It is clear that for measures M1 and M2, users from the same department share similar statistics and have a great between-group variance. For measure M3, both between- and within-group variances are large and for measure M4, the within-group variance is much larger than the between-group variance. To determine the actual variance we need to identify the sources of such variances for each measurement, and separate the total variability into components that are associated with each source.

Assume that we have m groups and the ith group ($i = 1, 2, \ldots, m$) has a sample size of n_i. The total number of observations of m groups is:

$$\sum_{i=1}^{m} n_i .$$

Even though the between-group variance in behavior could be small and insignificant, it may still have a value that is greater than zero. Let μ represent a measure of anomaly-free behavior and ν represent a measure of anomalous behavior. For anomaly-free and anomalous behavior, the null and alternative hypotheses are:

$$H_0 : \mu_1 = \mu_2 = \cdots = \mu_i = \mu \qquad (8\text{-}2)$$

H_a: H_0 is not true,

$$H_0 : \mu_1 = \mu_2 = \cdots = \mu_i = \nu \qquad (8\text{-}3)$$

H_a: H_0 is not true,

respectively, at an $\alpha = 0.05$ level of significance. Equations (8-2) and (8-3) establish a conceptual model to classify anomaly-free and anomalous patterns with an assumption that the within-group variance is constant across all groups. More specifically, we have

$$\sigma_1^2 = \sigma_2^2 = \cdots \sigma_i^2 = \sigma^2,$$

where σ_i^2 is the variance of the ith group and can be estimated as

$$\sigma_i^2 = \frac{\sum_{j=1}^{n_i}(\mu_{ij} - \mu_i)^2}{n_i - 1}, \qquad (8\text{-}4)$$

where μ_{ij} denotes the jth observation within the ith group. With Equation (8-4) we can estimate the total variance of m groups by taking a weighted average of the individual variance as shown below:

Table 8.2 Example of within-group and between-group variances

	Measure	D1	D2	D3	D4
M1	User-1	4,000	2,000	800	10,000
	User-2	4,100	2,000	890	12,000
	User-3	3,900	1,990	900	11,000
	User-4	4,000	2,010	850	30,000
M2	User-1	120	50	150	200
	User-2	130	55	160	210
	User-3	200	60	155	205
	User-4	150	45	145	220
M3	User-1	190	500	300	50
	User-2	95	210	610	250
	User-3	1000	400	305	160
	User-4	80	230	280	45
M4	User-1	400	410	350	420
	User-2	30	8	16	20
	User-3	9	10	15	12
	User-4	100	90	100	80

$$\sigma^2 = \frac{\sum_{i=1}^{m}(n_i - 1)\cdot \sigma_i^2}{\sum_{i=1}^{m} n_i - m}. \tag{8-5}$$

Moreover, the between-group variability can be measured by squaring the deviation of the mean observation in each group from the overall mean, μ:

$$\frac{\sum_{i=1}^{m}(\mu_i - \mu)^2}{m-1}. \tag{8-6}$$

The ratio of equations (8-5) to (8-6) provides an F test statistic to make a decision on accepting or rejecting the null hypotheses for equations (8-2) and (8-3)

$$F = \frac{\dfrac{\sum_{i=1}^{m}(\mu_i - \mu)^2}{m-1}}{\dfrac{\sum (n_i - 1)\cdot \sigma_i^2}{\sum_{i=1}^{m} n_i - m}} \tag{8-7}$$

If $F > F_{N-m}^{m-1}(\alpha)$ at an $\alpha = 0.05$ level of significance, we reject H_0.

The assumption of that within-group variance is constant across all groups is only true in an ideal world. Essentially that assumption cannot be satisfied and the total variance, σ_t^2 is composed by the between-group, σ_b^2, and within-group variances, σ_w^2,

$$\sigma_t^2 = \sigma_b^2 + \sigma_w^2. \tag{8-8}$$

If the response variable is binary we have $\sigma_w^2 = \pi^2/3$. In general, σ_b^2 and σ_w^2 can be obtained by using the hierarchical generalized linear modeling approach that will be examined detailed in Section Hierarchical Generalized Linear Model.

Changes in Behavior Patterns

User behavior is not stationary but may change over time due to two fundamental causes: system-specific and user-specific factors. At the system-specific level, when the entire network system is upgraded, for instance, expanding the bandwidth from 100 Mbps to 10 Gbps, as a result of users taking advantage of the fast network connection speed; their behavior patterns may change correspondingly. Moreover, a new security-related network policy or regulation may also impact user behavior patterns. Many factors may cause changes to user behavior at the user-specific level, such as job reasonability, working schedules, interests and improved computer skills over time.

Given various circumstances it is understandable that change in user behavior is an ongoing process and requires consecutive measurement. Statistical parameters representing a pattern at the time t may need to be reestimated and evaluated at the time $t + i$ ($i = 1, 2, \cdots, k$). Accordingly, to track behavior changes at both the system and user levels, we have to employ statistical methods for the analysis of repeated measurements and model such data repeatedly and measure it longitudinally. The materials presented in previous chapters did not address the repeated and longitudinal modeling techniques but we will discuss it in this section.

In general, the term "repeated measurements" refers to observing a subject (e.g., user, group or site) on multiple occasions. Depending on the design of a project, the unit of an occasion could be time, for example, second, hour, day, month or year, or the order of a serial process. For instance, a web browsing process could be considered a repeated measurement process in which a user is repeatedly measured for his/her interests by the websites he/she visits, in which case, the browsing sequence represents the occasions of such a repeated measurement process. Display 8.1 shows a list of 11 users denoted by "user_id", the websites visited are denoted by "code", and the sequence of the visits is denoted by "time." For example, user 10001 visited three sites, denoted by 1000, 1001, and 1002, but user 10010 visited six websites, 1010, 1000, 1011, 1012, 1013, and 1014. Appendix A in Chapter III provides detailed labels of these websites.

Display 8.1
First 25 observations from the raw web sequence data from www.microsoft.com

```
          user_id    code    time|
     |---------------------------|
 1.  |   10001      1000      1  |
 2.  |   10001      1001      2  |
 3.  |   10001      1002      3  |
 4.  |   10002      1001      1  |
 5.  |   10002     ·1003      2  |
     |---------------------------|
 6.  |   10003      1001      1  |
 7.  |   10003      1003      2  |
 8.  |   10003      1004      3  |
 9.  |   10004      1005      1  |
10.  |   10005      1006      1  |
     |---------------------------|
11.  |   10006      1003      1  |
12.  |   10006      1004      2  |
13.  |   10007      1007      1  |
14.  |   10008      1004      1  |
15.  |   10009      1008      1  |
     |---------------------------|
16.  |   10009      1009      2  |
17.  |   10010      1010      1  |
18.  |   10010      1000      2  |
19.  |   10010      1011      3  |
20.  |   10010      1012      4  |
     |---------------------------|
21.  |   10010      1013      5  |
22.  |   10010      1014      6  |
23.  |   10011      1015      1  |
24.  |   10011      1016      2  |
25.  |   10011      1017      3  |
     +---------------------------+
```

From Display 8.1 we can see that the repeated measurement and longitudinal data are clustered and nested, in which multiple observations (visits) over time are nested within a user to be measured. With this particular data structure, the standard assumption of independent observations could be or is more likely to be violated because of the lack of independence among observations within the same subject (e.g., site, user, or group). Analyzing this

Figure 8.2 Subject-specific logistic regression (dot-lines) versus marginal logistic regression (bold line)

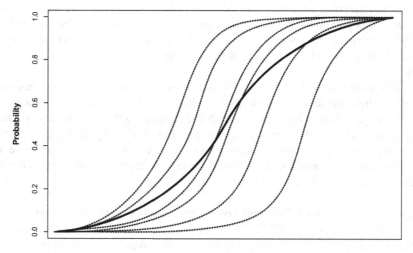

type of data demands that we take into account the between-observation variance and the between-subject variance. Accordingly, there have been remarkable advances in methods for analyzing clustered and nested data in recent years, especially in the healthcare and life science areas. Rich literature on analyzing and modeling repeated measures and longitudinal data are available (Little, Schnabel & Baumert, 2000; Davis, 2002; Diggle, Heagerty, Liang & Zeger, 2002; Fitzmaurice, Laird & Ware, 2004; Frees, 2004; Rabe-Hesketh & Skrondal, 2005); although many of them used medical and healthcare data as examples, the principles remain helpful and can be applied to the network security area.

The response variable to be modeled with repeated measurement data can be either continuous or binary. In the case of tracking changes in user behavior patterns, we are interested in a binary variable that indicates if a pattern is changed or unchanged. Let y_{ij} denote a binary response variable (e.g. anomaly-free or anomaly) for the ith subject (e.g., a user or a site) on the jth occasion, and let us assume there are n_i repeated measurements on the ith subject and each y_{ij} is observed at time t_{ij}. We can extend the logistic regression model presented in Chapter VII for such longitudinal and repeated measurements data as follows:

$$y_{ij} = \log\left[\frac{p_{ij}}{1 - p_{ij}}\right] = \beta_0 + \beta_1 t_{ij} + \beta_2 x_{ij1} + \beta_3 x_{ij2} + \cdots + \beta_k x_{ijk}, \qquad \text{and} \qquad (8\text{-}8)$$

$$y_{ij} = \log\left[\frac{p_{ij}}{1 - p_{ij}}\right] = \beta_{0i} + \beta_1 t_{ij} + \beta_2 x_{ij1} + \beta_3 x_{ij2} + \cdots + \beta_k x_{ijk}, \qquad (8\text{-}9)$$

where x_{ij} can be time-independent (e.g., user's gender) or time-dependent (e.g., connections within a given time window). If x_{ij} is time-independent, we have $x_{ij} \to x_i$.

Equation (8-8) is reflected as a marginal model or population-averaged model that aims to make inferences about population averages, and models the overall population-averaged probabilities (i.e., how does the whole system change its behavior over time). This is what is modeled in a cross-sectional data. The marginal approach leads to modeling separately the means and the covariance matrix of the observations. It is appropriate when our focus is on about the population-average. For example, in a security-related intervention the average difference between groups with new security applications (e.g., hardware, software or policies) and groups without these applications is most important, not the difference for any one individual.

Equation (8-9) is reflected as a subject-specific model or more generally, a random effect model, which includes a random effect term, $b_i = \beta_i - \beta_0$ for each individual subject. It models the individual, subject-specific probabilities and allows us to express how much a subject's trajectory can be translated as compared to what is expected according to its characteristics. It is appropriate when we want to focus on an individual's response. Figure 8.2 illustrates an example of a possible difference in regression coefficients between subject-specific and marginal logistic regression models.

Example 8.1→ Model User Behavior Over Time. Let us fit both marginal and subject-specific models using the MIT-DAPRA data. Similar to Example 7.7 we use the IP address to represent a particular site or group and measure the proportion of daily anomaly-free traffic volume out of the total traffic volume as a classifier for behavior changes with the same rule used in the Example 7.7:

$$c_i = \begin{cases} 1, & \dfrac{v_i}{V_i} < 0.5 \\[2mm] 0, & \dfrac{v_i}{V_i} \geq 0.5 \end{cases},$$

where $c_i = 1$ for denoting the ith site changes its behavior pattern and $c_i = 0$ for otherwise; v_i denotes daily total volume of anomaly-free traffic, and V_i denotes daily total volume of traffic. Note, in this example the subject is site therefore the term "subject-specific" means "site-specific."

We use the day as the unit of occasions to measure the change in patterns, combine the first two weeks data as a baseline for each site, and follow them over the remaining five weeks to see if there are any behavior pattern changes (Figure 8.3). Since each week of the MIT-DAPRA data include 5 days, Monday to Friday, hence the 7-weeks of data contribute to a maximum of total 30 individual occasions for a site. That is, days 1 to 5 are corresponding to week-1 and week-2, days 6-10 are corresponding to week-3 days and days 25 to 30 are corresponding to the 7th week. Moreover, to establish a stable behavior pattern for each site, we restrict sites to having at least 100 observations in the first 2-week baseline period and also at least 100 at any subsequent week in the measurement period. This restriction results in a total of 39 sites in the final sample, and not all sites have 30 occasions, some sites may only have a minimum of 10 occasions.

As shown in Figure 8.3, within the 30-day monitoring period, a site may switch its behavior pattern multiple times. For example, the ith site may change from anomaly-free

Figure 8.3 Possible changes in behavior pattern

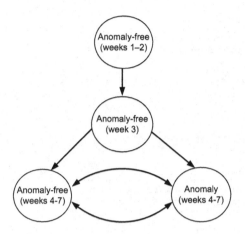

to anomalous on the 11th day and back to anomaly-free on the 15th and begin an anomalous pattern again on the 20th. Similarly, the jth site may change from the anomaly-free pattern to an anomalous pattern on the 20th and continue to be anomalous until to the end of monitoring period. In Example 7.7, however, we only counted the first occurrence of a change—once a site had a change, we stopped following it. With repeated measurement data, we count all the changes during the monitoring period.

The response variable, y_{ij}, of the analysis is the observed behavior patterns (yes/no) and the time variable is the individual day as mentioned previously. The predictor variables associated with behavior pattern include 4 binary variables that represent the "type of service or protocol": (1) HTTP (yes/no); (2) SNMP (yes/no); 3) Domain (yes/no), and 4) Telnet (yes/no). The Stata codes to prepare MIT-DARPA data for conducting this example are listed in Display 8.2.

Display 8.2
Stata codes for preparing the repeated measurement data and conducting the longitudinal analysis

```
#delimit;
capture log close;
clear;
*set matsize 1410;
set mem 560000k;
set more 1;
use "F:\Book\Chapter 8\MIT_list",replace;
/*-------------------------------------------------
  Baseline: normal patterns (39 sites retrieved)
-----------------------------------------------*/;
```

continued on following page

Display 8.2 continued

```
gen byte Total=1;
replace index=lower(index);
keep if substr(index,1,6)=="week-1" |substr(index,1,6)=="week-2";
replace index="week-1&2-"+substr(index, 8,3);
do create_var; /* this do program is listed in Appendix CH8 */;

collapse (sum) Total (mean)
lonin len_1 udp icmp samePort sameIP http smtp snmp ftp domain frag telnet
finger ,by(index IP_s);
keep if Total>100;
sort IP_s index;
gen Normal=Total;
save temp_0,replace;
collapse (sum) Normal,by(IP_s);
keep IP_s;
sort IP_s;
save temp_1,replace;
/*-----------------------------------------------
 Monitor period (only 39 sites to be monitored)
-----------------------------------------------*/;
use "F:\Book\Chapter 8\MIT_list",replace;
gen byte Total=1;
gen byte Normal=(attack=="-");
drop if substr(index,1,6)=="week-1" |substr(index,1,6)=="week-2";
do create_var; /* this do program is listed in Appendix CH8 */;

collapse (sum) Total Normal (mean)
lonin len_1 udp icmp samePort sameIP http smtp snmp ftp domain frag telnet
finger ,by(index IP_s);
keep if Total>100;
sort IP_s;
merge IP_s using temp_1;
keep if _m==3;
drop _m;
append using temp_0;
replace index=lower(index);

do time; /* full codes are listed in Appendix CH8 */;
gen rate=Normal/Total;
sort time IP_s;
gen byte Anomaly=(rate<0.5);
sort IP_s;
gen str8 week=substr(index,1,8) if substr(index,1,8)=="week-1&2";
replace week=substr(index,1,6) if week=="";
encode IP_s,gen(iIP_s);
encode week,gen(iweek);

graph bar (mean) Anomaly, over(week)
ytitle(Probability of changing in behavior patterns)
ylabel(0 0.02 0.04 0.06 0.08 0.1);
graph bar (mean) Anomaly, over( time)
ytitle(Probability of changing in behavior patterns)
 ylabel(0 0.05  0.10 0.15 );
```

Figure 8.4 shows the probability of changes in behavior patterns among the 39 sites over the measurement period. As we can see, there were no pattern changes within the initial 10 days of which the first five days are baseline and the rest of five days belong to the beginning week (week-3) of the monitoring period. Display 8.3 shows a section of the final longitudinal dataset, where two sites are identified as had pattern changes. The site 195.115.218.108 has changed its pattern from anomaly-free to anomaly on day 19th (the 826th observation), and changed back to anomaly-free status on the next day. The site 196.037.075.158 had pattern changes occur on the 12th day (the 844th observation) and were back to anomaly-free on the 14th (the 846th observation) and changed again on the 19th day (the 851th observation), and finally back to anomaly-free status on the next day, the 20th.

Figure 8.4 Rate of changes in behavior patterns (anomaly-free to anomaly)

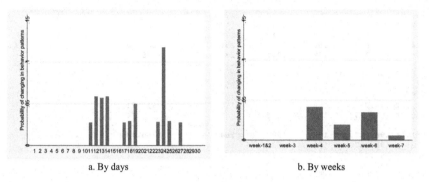

a. By days	b. By weeks

Display 8.3
Change in behavior patterns for two sites over the 5-week of monitoring period

OBS	IP_s	Total	Normal	Time (day)	Rate	Anomaly
808.	195.115.218.108	519	519	1	1	0
809.	195.115.218.108	275	275	2	1	0
810.	195.115.218.108	399	399	3	1	0
811.	195.115.218.108	406	406	4	1	0
812.	195.115.218.108	215	215	5	1	0
813.	195.115.218.108	773	773	6	1	0
814.	195.115.218.108	317	317	7	1	0
815.	195.115.218.108	178	178	8	1	0
816.	195.115.218.108	165	165	9	1	0
817.	195.115.218.108	136	136	10	1	0
818.	195.115.218.108	132	132	11	1	0
819.	195.115.218.108	197	196	12	.9949238	0
820.	195.115.218.108	225	225	13	1	0
821.	195.115.218.108	116	116	14	1	0
822.	195.115.218.108	280	280	15	1	0
823.	195.115.218.108	162	162	16	1	0
824.	195.115.218.108	449	449	17	1	0
825.	195.115.218.108	285	285	18	1	0
826.	**195.115.218.108**	**11289**	**372**	**19**	**.0329524**	**1**
827.	195.115.218.108	243	243	20	1	0
828.	195.115.218.108	391	391	21	1	0
829.	195.115.218.108	349	349	22	1	0
830.	195.115.218.108	241	241	23	1	0
831.	195.115.218.108	191	191	24	1	0
832.	195.115.218.108	387	387	25	1	0
838.	196.037.075.158	440	440	6	1	0
839.	196.037.075.158	387	387	7	1	0
840.	196.037.075.158	190	190	8	1	0

continued on following page

Display 8.3 continued

```
841. | 196.037.075.158      170      170     9          1          0 |
842. | 196.037.075.158      140      140    10          1          0 |
843. | 196.037.075.158      210      210    11          1          0 |
844. | 196.037.075.158     1017      255    12    .2507375          1 |
845. | 196.037.075.158     2011      233    13    .1158628          1 |
     |-----------------------------------------------------------------|
846. | 196.037.075.158      116      116    14          1          0 |
847. | 196.037.075.158      558      558    15          1          0 |
848. | 196.037.075.158      195      195    16          1          0 |
849. | 196.037.075.158      171      170    17    .9941521          0 |
850. | 196.037.075.158      656      656    18          1          0 |
     |-----------------------------------------------------------------|
851. | 196.037.075.158      927      164    19    .1769148          1 |
852. | 196.037.075.158      323      323    20          1          0 |
853. | 196.037.075.158      455      455    21          1          0 |
854. | 196.037.075.158      252      252    22          1          0 |
855. | 196.037.075.158      338      338    23          1          0 |
     |-----------------------------------------------------------------|
856. | 196.037.075.158      233      233    24          1          0 |
857. | 196.037.075.158      485      485    25          1          0 |
```

The Stata codes used to fit the marginal model and subject-specific model are shown in Display 8.4. As we discussed in the marginal model that aims to make inferences about population averages, the marginal expectation is the average response over the subpopulation that shares a common value of the predictor variables. The subject-specific model, however, aims on an individual site's response.

Display 8.4
Stata codes used to fit the marginal and subject-specific models

```
#delimit;
iis iIP_s;
tis time;
xtdes, i(iIP_s) t(time);
/*-------------------------------------------------
 Population-averaged logit model
---------------------------------------------------*/;
xtlogit Anomaly http smtp domain telnet,i(iIP_s) pa robust nolog;
predict phat_pa,mu;
/*-------------------------------------------------
 Group-specific logit model
---------------------------------------------------*/;
xtlogit Anomaly http smtp domain telnet,i(iIP_s) nolog;
predict phat_re,xb;
```

Displays 8.5 and 8.6 illustrate the outputs of the fitted marginal model and the subject-specific model. The marginal model shows that the three types of service or protocol: HTTP, SNMP and Domain are statistically significantly associated with the anomaly-free pattern, and Telnet is statistically significantly associated with the anomaly pattern.

Display 8.5
Fitted marginal model

```
GEE population-averaged model                    Number of obs      =      1029
Group variable:                      iIP_s       Number of groups   =        40
Link:                                logit       Obs per group: min =         1
Family:                           binomial                      avg =      25.7
Correlation:                   exchangeable                     max =        30
                                                 Wald chi2(4)       =     21.88
Scale parameter:                        1        Prob > chi2        =    0.0002

                                 (Std. Err. adjusted for clustering on iIP_s)
-----------------------------------------------------------------------------
             |             Semi-robust
   Anomaly   |    Coef.    Std. Err.      z     P>|z|    [95% Conf. Interval]
-------------+---------------------------------------------------------------
      http   | -3.73646    1.110458    -3.36    0.001   -5.912919   -1.560002
      smtp   | -4.742358   1.574674    -3.01    0.003   -7.828662   -1.656053
    domain   | -3.897671   1.194887    -3.26    0.001   -6.239607   -1.555735
    telnet   | 10.17783    4.522082     2.25    0.024    1.314708   19.04094
     _cons   | .6110879    .6034779     1.01    0.311   -.5717071   1.793883
-----------------------------------------------------------------------------
```

Display 8.6
Fitted subject-specific model

```
Random-effects logistic regression              Number of obs      =      1029
Group variable (i): iIP_s                        Number of groups   =        40

Random effects u_i ~ Gaussian                   Obs per group: min =         1
                                                               avg =      25.7
                                                               max =        30

                                                 Wald chi2(4)       =     30.93
Log likelihood  =  -40.73285                     Prob > chi2        =    0.0000

-----------------------------------------------------------------------------
   Anomaly   |    Coef.     Std. Err.     z     P>|z|    [95% Conf. Interval]
-------------+---------------------------------------------------------------
      http   | -12.58522   3.669474    -3.43    0.001   -19.77725   -5.393179
      smtp   | -10.98127   2.412241    -4.55    0.000   -15.70918   -6.253369
    domain   | -14.26096   10.89823    -1.31    0.191   -35.6211    7.099175
    telnet   | 16.3055     17.78073     0.92    0.359   -18.54409   51.1551
     _cons   | -.3346997   .9697104    -0.35    0.730   -2.235297   1.565898
-------------+---------------------------------------------------------------
   /lnsig2u  | 2.340812    .424837                       1.508146   3.173477
-------------+---------------------------------------------------------------
    sigma_u  | 3.2233      .6846886                       2.12564   4.887781
       rho   | .7595043    .0775997                      .5786658   .8789612
-----------------------------------------------------------------------------
Likelihood-ratio test of rho=0: chibar2(01) =    37.39 Prob >= chibar2 = 0.000
```

The output of subject-specific model includes an additional subject-level variance component, σ_b^2, and its standard deviation, σ_b (labeled *sigma_u*). The variance component is parameterized as the log of variance, $\ln(\sigma_b^2)$, in Display 8.6 (labeled *lnsig2u*). The ρ (labeled *rho*) in the output measures the importance of σ_b^2 and is defined as

$$\rho = \frac{\sigma_b^2}{\sigma_b^2 + \sigma_w^2},$$

which also knows as intra-subject correlation and represents the proportion of the total variance contributed by the subject-level variance component and and the within-subject variance, σ_w^2 ($\sigma_w^2 = \frac{\pi^2}{3}$ for fitting a logistic model). When $\rho = 0$, the subject-level variance component is unimportant, and the subject-specific estimator is no different from the population-averaged estimators. Stata software includes a likelihood-ratio test for $\rho = 0$ at the bottom of the output (Stata, 2005). In Display 8.6, the significance level of the likelihood-ratio test is $P < 0.0001$, so that we can reject the null hypothesis that subject-level variance component is not important ($\rho = 0$) at least at the 0.0001 level. The concept of the intra-subject correlation is also useful to assess the reliability of profile; we will reexamine this correlation in Chapter XII.

SCORING METHODS

The process of obtaining a measurement includes assigning values or memberships of a category to the observations being measured; these values or memberships must be assigned in a logical way such that their associations reflect the relationship of the attributes of the observations being measured. *Scoring* of a measurement is a particular method to be used in the assigning process. A statistical scoring model for intrusion detection can be constructed by identifying variables that are robust and associated with network traffics and represent user or group behavior. Depending on the purpose of scoring and the available data sources, a scoring model can be fitted either at the system-level or user-level in which different information is required to estimate a score. Technically, we may have three approaches to assign a score for each observation: (1) scoring based on regression while a labeled response variable is available, (2) scoring based on preexisting knowledge, and (3) scoring based on some test measurement theory, such as item response theory, which evaluates the relationship between the difficulty of testing items and the testers ability. We will discuss these methods in the following sections.

Score Based on Regression Models

If a labeled response variable is available, we can use the logistic regression discussed in Chapter VII to score each observation on the probability of being abnormal or anomaly-free. The simplest approach is to use the equation (7-7) to assign a predicted probability for each observation in the data. Almost all statistical packages provide a function to retrieve predictive values after fitting to a model. Displays 8.7 and 8.8 are SAS and Stata codes to obtain the predictive values for each observation in the MIT-DAPRA data based on a logistic regression model. Because the response variable is coded as anomaly-free (yes/no), we are scoring for anomaly-free status. The higher the score, the more likely the observation will be anomaly-free. The overall anomaly-free rate is 38.4% for the full data with 3013860 observations.

Display 8.7
SAS codes to obtain a predicted value from a logistic regression model

```
/*-----------------------------------------------------------------
   SAS codes
-------------------------------------------------------------*/;
 libname temp 'F:\Book\Chapter 8\';
 proc logistic data=temp. var_16_trai descending;
 model normal=
 Duration TCP UDP HTTP RST logged_I Num_comp is_guest Count Same_srv
 Diff_srv Dst_host Dst_hos1 Dst_hos3 Dst_hos4 Dst_hos5/lackfit rsq stb;
 /* ------------------------------------------------
 The result file contains two new variables:
 Phat holds predictive values, and
 pr_residual holds residual values
 -----------------------------------------------------*/;
 output out=Result_file
 (keep=normal phat pr_residual) p=phat reschi=pr;
 run;
```

Display 8.8
Stata codes to obtain a predicted value from a logistic regression model

```
#delimit;
clear;
set mem 854566;
use F:\Book\Chapter 8\temp.dta, clear;
gen byte normal=(attack=="-");
drop v13 score;
do create_var; /* Appendix CH8  */;
logistic normal
t2 len_1 udp icmp samePort sameIP http smtp urp ecr eco snmp ftp port domain
telnet finger;
predict score;

set seed 232434;
gen ran=invnormal(uniform());
sort ran;
list IP_s attack normal score in 1/24;
```

Table 8.3 shows a randomly selected 24 observations with their scores based on the logistic modeling approach. We can see that the 7th observation is underscored by the model.

Score by Pre-Existing Knowledge

There may be some situations that we cannot assign or do not want to assign a score directly from a regression model. One situation is when a labeled response variable is not available from the training data or is insufficient, and as a result, we cannot fit a regression model to obtain the predictive values. Another situation could be that the model does not fit well, so the predictive values may include a bias. Other situations could arise from the available data not being large enough to divide data to training and testing datasets. In any of such situations, we can construct a score model based on our preexisting knowledge.

Table 8.3 Observations scored based on a logistic model

ID	IP address	Anomaly	Anomaly-free	Score
1	172.016.116.044	-	1	0.9927816
2	230.001.010.020	neptune	0	0.0009964
3	010.020.030.040	neptune	0	0.0009964
4	010.020.030.040	neptune	0	0.0009964
5	230.001.010.020	neptune	0	0.0009964
6	172.016.115.087	-	1	0.9927816
7	192.168.001.020	-	1	0.0877603
8	172.016.112.020	-	1	0.9577984
9	010.020.030.040	neptune	0	0.0009964
10	010.020.030.040	neptune	0	0.0009964
11	230.001.010.020	neptune	0	0.0009964
12	209.030.070.029	smurf	0	0.0051168
13	172.016.114.168	-	1	0.9927816
14	010.020.030.040	neptune	0	0.0009964
15	230.001.010.020	neptune	0	0.0009964
16	010.020.030.040	neptune	0	0.0009964
17	230.001.010.020	neptune	0	0.0009964
18	010.020.030.040	neptune	0	0.0009964
19	230.001.010.020	neptune	0	0.0009964
20	199.174.194.008	smurf	0	0.0051168
21	230.001.010.020	neptune	0	0.0009964
22	172.016.115.005	-	1	0.9927816
23	135.013.216.191	neptune	0	0.0009964
24	010.020.030.040	neptune	0	0.0009964

Let us consider the first situation of the labeled response variable not being available in our data. Let D be an anomaly-free sample of the network traffic with k variables, and n sites (or users) of which each group has m observations. Let i denote a site ($i = 1, 2, \cdots, n$), j denote a network connection within the ith site ($j = 1, 2, ..., m$), and let x_k denote the kth binary variable ($k = 1, 2, ..., K$) that has value of 1 to associate with an anomaly-free connection or 0 for an abnormal connection. We can score site activities as

$$\hat{s}_{ij} = \frac{1}{K} \sum_{k=1}^{K} w_k x_{kij}, \tag{8-10}$$

where w_k is a weight for the kth variable, K is the total number of variables, and $\hat{s}_{ij}$ is an observed score of the jth connection at the ith site. Because x_k is associated as anomaly-free, Equation (8-10) measures the likelihood of an individual network traffic being anomaly-free, whereby a connection with a high score is more likely to be anomaly-free. Different weighing approaches could be used to calculate the score. For example, the frequency of a variable could be used to weigh each variable and regression coefficients could also be used as weights. Equation (8-10) represents an anomaly-free score. We also can model the score in the opposite direction of Equation (8-10) as

$$\hat{s}_{ij} = \frac{1}{K} \sum_{k=1}^{K} v_k (1 - x_{kij}) \tag{8-11}$$

where v_k is a weight corresponding to the kth variable. Equation (8-11) represents an anomaly score.

If we have a labeled response variable but we want to assign a score based on the fitted regression coefficients, the simple way to do this is to use the regression coefficient as a weight in Equations (8-10) or (8-11). A regression coefficient provides information on the association between the predictor variable and the response variable. To take into account the effect size of such an association, we can calculate the standardized coefficients for each variable. The standardized coefficient is designed to measure the relative importance of the predictor variable in a regression model, since ordinary coefficients cannot generally be compared among different variables. This is due to the fact that coefficients depend directly on the metrics in which the variables are measured. Thus, we can use the standardized coefficients as the weight term in our scoring model as

$$w_k = \tau_k \Big/ \sum_{k=1}^{K} \tau_k \tag{8-12}$$

where τ_k is the standardized coefficient for the kth variable. We can further standardize the raw score through the standard z-score transformation by using Equation (5-12) as discussed in Chapter V, to obtain a standardized distribution of the score.

Example 8.2→Risk Score. Wang and Cannady (2005) developed an anomaly behavior score model for intrusion detection based on the KDD-cup 1999 data. The score demonstrates a high sensitivity, specificity and a low misclassification in detecting network attacks (0.90, 0.94, and 0.08, respectively). They used 10% of the training data to develop the score and the full testing data to evaluate the score. Bivariate analysis and stepwise logistic regression modeling with a significance threshold of 0.01 for added variables and an insignificance threshold of 0.05 for removed variables were used to select potential variables that associate with the response variable (anomaly, yes/no). Variables with a frequency >0.1% and also demonstrated a significant association with the response variable in the bivariate analysis were eligible for loading into the stepwise process for further analysis. Continuous variables with uneven distributions were normalized through the standardized z-score transformation. Fourteen variables (Table 8.4) were selected by the stepwise process and were used for constructing the score model by using Equations (8-11) and (8-12). A variable with a standardized estimate less than 0, or an odds ratio less than 1, indicates that the variable had a negative association with the response variable. Moreover, an observation with this characteristic was unlikely to be an anomaly.

Based on Table 8.4, Wang and Cannady generated two scores for both the training and the testing samples. The training sample-based score had a mean of 1.57 with a standard deviation of 0.46 and a range of 0.00 to 2.25; the testing sample-based score had a mean of 1.80 with a standard deviation of 0.49 and ranged from 0.00 to 2.40. The correlation coefficient between the two scores was 0.96. Figure 8.5 shows the distribution of the score and the association between the score and the likelihood of being an anomaly based on these unique connections. Note that the relationship between the score and probability of being intrusion is not linear, but exponential. This figure clearly demonstrates how a score model could be used to distinguish the anomaly-free and anomaly groups – nearly all of the anomaly-free connections (99.80%) had a score value less than 1.25, and 98.00% of anomalous connections had a score of 1.25 and up.

Semi-Item Response Model

Item response theory (IRT) is a modern test measurement theory used to evaluate the relationship between the difficulty of testing items and the testers ability. IRT refers to a group of statistical models that represent, in probabilistic terms, the association between a person's response to a typical item (e.g., test question) and his/her ability to have a correct response to the item. Such ability is represented using a latent variable or trait that is postulated to exist, but cannot be directly observed or measured. IRT addresses the difference between items, and presents this difference in terms of the item's difficulty. The first IRT model was developed by Lord (1952) as an alternative approach to classical test theory. Since then, IRT and its corresponding models have been recognized as a modern measurement theory, and the tools have been widely used in many research areas, such as psychology, education, healthcare, economy, and life science. For more detailed fundamental materials on IRT and its applications, see Andrich (1988), Embretson & Reise (2000), and Boeck & Wilson (2004).

All IRT models contain one or more parameters describing the item and one or more parameters describing the person. The most commonly used IRT models are the one- or two-parameter logistic models. The one-parameter model predicts the probability that a person gives a correct response to a certain item, and the two-parameters model also estimates an item's discrimination power, which shows how well the item differentiates between persons at higher and lower ability levels.

We can view the system-level's measurement as a filter that scans network traffic through a set of variables known to be associated with anomaly-free observations and the combination pattern of such variables. If we treat such a filter process as a "test"—anomaly-free, pass or fail, and we have enough data to make a rational statistical inference, we should be able to estimate an expected "test" score that represents a likelihood of being anomaly-free for each network traffic. This is the basic idea of attaining a score based on IRT. This score could be further used to measure user behavior at the system-level. The advantage of constructing a score model based on IRT is that the approach allows us to separate user characteristics with profiling characteristics and ensure that the estimated "test" score will only depend on the system-level variables.

Let us fit a one-parameter IRT model. To fit the IRT framework for intrusion detection, we replace the term "person" with the term *user*, "item" with *variable*, "trait-level" with *ability-level*, and *association* to replace the term "difficulty." Let β_k denote the association of the kth variable with an anomaly-free pattern (that is, if an observation with the kth variable is present, the observation is more likely to be anomaly-free) and let θ_i represent the ability-level (of being anomaly-free) for the ith user. A one-parameter logistic IRT model for testing network traffic (anomaly-free or abnormal) can be presented as

$$\log\left[\frac{P_{ki}}{1+P_{ki}}\right] = \beta_k + \theta_i, \qquad (8\text{-}13)$$

Table 8.4. Variables associated with the response variable based on the training sample

Variables	Odds Ratio	95% Confidence Interval	P value	Standardized Estimate
Length (number of seconds) of the connection	0.89	0.88 - 0.90	<0.001	-0.0599
ICMP (reference)	1.00			
TCP	0.72	0.62 -0.83	<0.001	-0.1111
UDP	0.08	0.07 -0.09	<0.001	-0.2879
HTTP	1.56	1.48 -1.82	<0.001	0.1001
REJ (reference)	1.00			
RST	105.72	80.32 -140.41	<0.001	0.1310
Guest login	8.76	7.31 -10.02	<0.001	0.0462
Connections to the same host as the current connection in the past two seconds	88.02	73.43 -102.98	<0.001	2.5002
Rate of connections to the same service	0.12	0.11 -0.14	<0.001	-1.1505
Rate of connections to different services	0.72	0.70 -0.73	<0.001	-0.1693
Connections having the same destination host	2.18	2.09 -2.22	<0.001	0.4154
Connections having the same destination host and using the same service	0.28	0.26 -0.30	<0.001	-0.6798
Rate of different services on the current host	0.74	0.72 -0.76	<0.001	-0.1699
Rate of connections to the current host having the same source port	3.35	3.17 -3.60	<0.001	0.6590
Rate of connections to the same service coming from different hosts	1.37	1.35 -1.38	<0.001	0.1800

Figure 8.5 Distribution of network connections (bars) and the risk score (curves)

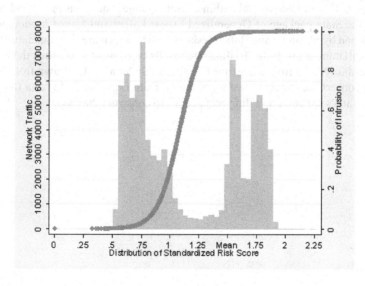

the item characteristic function is

$$P_{ki}(\theta_i,\beta_k) = \frac{\exp(\theta_i - \beta_k)}{1 + \exp(\theta_i - \beta_k)},\ x_1 \leq \theta_i \leq x_2 .$$ (8-14)

Given an ability-level of θ_i, the test response function that predicts the expected test score of being anomaly-free for the test as a whole is

$$S(\theta_i) = \frac{1}{n} \sum_{k=1}^{m} P_{ki}(\theta_i,\beta_k).$$ (8-15)

We can use Equation (8-14) to draw an item characteristic curve (ICC) for each variable to display the relationship between the ability-level and the probability of a variable being present. An ICC reflects the true relationship among the unobservable variables and observable variables. A set of ICCs could therefore represent a pattern of user behavior. We hypothesize that anomaly-free and abnormal network traffics will have different ICCs, and such a difference can be quantitatively measured through Equation (8-15) within a restricted range of the ability-level.

IRT models have two main fundamental assumptions: data are unidimensional, and have local independence. Data that is unidimensional has items that link to a single ability. Local independence means that the probability of responding to a typical item is unrelated to the probability of responding to any other item; that is, after taking a person's abilities into account, no relationship exists between a person's responses to different items. Nevertheless, these assumptions usually cannot be strictly met in practice (Hambleton, Swaminathan, & Rogers, 1991).

Example 8.3→Measure Behavior Patterns Using IRT. Let us use the MIT-DARPA data to fit a semi-IRT model for profiling users. The "semi" means that we modality Equation (8-14) by restricting its ability-level within a limited range. Equations (8-13) and (8-14) are fitted with the Stata package of Generalized Linear Latent and Mixed Modeling framework developed by Skrondal and Rabe-Hesketh (2004), which are downloadable from the http://www.gllamm.org website. To illustrate results conveniently, we shift the minimum value of the ability-level from a negative to a zero value for all ICCs drawn from Equation (8-14), and convert the expected test score drawn from Equation (8-15) to a 0-100 scale. Display 8.9 shows the corresponding Stata codes to construct the model.

Display 8.9 Stata codes for fitting the semi-item response model

```
#delimit;
capture log close;
clear;
set mem 500000k;
set more 1;
use "F:\book\Chapter 8\temp",replace;
gen byte Normal=(attack=="-");
drop v13 score attack;
/*------------------------------------------------------------------
  Training sample week 1 and 2 and have at least 10 connections
------------------------------------------------------------------*/;
keep if Normal==1;
keep if substr(index,1,6)=="week-1" || substr(index,1,6)=="week-2";
gen byte n=1;
egen total=sum(n),by(IP_s);
keep if total>9;
sort IP_s;
gen byte training=1;
save week_1_2,replace;
keep IP_s;
save sites,replace;
/*------------------------------------------------------------------
  Testing sample weeks 3-7 and have at least 10 connections and 10% sample
------------------------------------------------------------------*/;
use "F:\book\Chapter 8\temp",replace;
drop if substr(index,1,6)=="week-1" || substr(index,1,6)=="week-2";
gen byte n=1;
egen total=sum(n),by(IP_s);
keep if total>9;
sort IP_s;
merge IP_s using sites;
keep if _m==3;
drop _m;
gen byte Normal=(attack=="-");
gen byte  training=0;
append using week_1_2;
tab training Normal,col row chi;
set seed 12335465;
sample 10, by(IP_s training);
drop n total ;
gen n=1;
egen total=sum(n),by(IP_s);
drop if total<10;
/*----------------------------------------------------------
  Create distributions for stating time and duration
----------------------------------------------------*/;
do create_var; /*Appendix CH8  */
gen str4 pattern=string(samePort)+string(Service)+string(l1_n)+ string(t2_n);
sort pattern;
save IRT_all_100,replace;
/*----------------------------------------------------------
  Anomaly-free only
-------------------------------------------------------*/;
use IRT_all_100,replace;
keep if Normal==1;
save IRT_normal,replace;
gen n=1;
collapse (sum) wt2=n,by(pattern);
merge pattern using IRT_normal;
keep if _m==3;
** Fit IRT (anomaly-free);
do fit_irt.do; /* Appendix CH8  */;
```

continued on following page

Display 8.9 continued

```
/*------------------------------------------------------------------
 Training only
-----------------------------------------------------------------*/;
use IRT_all_100,replace;
keep if training==1;
save IRT_normal,replace;
gen n=1;
collapse (sum) wt2=n,by(pattern);
merge pattern using IRT_normal;
keep if _m==3;
** Fit IRT (anomaly-free);
do fit_irt.do; /* Appendix CH8  */;
/*-----------------------------------------------------
    Test (normal)
---------------------------------------------------*/;
use IRT_all_100,replace;
keep if Normal==1 & training==0;
save IRT_attack,replace;
gen n=1;
collapse (sum) wt2=n,by(pattern);
merge pattern using IRT_attack;
keep if _m==3;
** Fit IRT (anomaly-free);
do fit.irt.do  /* Appendix CH8  */;
/*--------------------------------------------------
    Test (attack)
-----------------------------------------------*/;
use IRT_all_100,replace;
keep if Normal==0 & training==0;
save IRT_attack,replace;
gen n=1;
collapse (sum) wt2=n,by(pattern);
merge pattern using IRT_attack;
keep if _m==3;
** Fit IRT (anomaly-free);
do fit.irt.do  /* Appendix CH8  */;
```

Table 8.5 shows the estimated results acquired from the IRT models based on different samples, in which the coefficient, " $-\beta_k$ ", represents the association between the ith predictor and an anomaly-free pattern. For that pattern, the service type in HTTP, SMTP, FTP, UDP, or SNMP is the most likely factor to be presented. The level of an association is -4.0 for the training sample and –3.7 for the testing with only anomaly-free connections subset. Conversely, "duration of a session greater than one" seems to be the most unlikely factor for the abnormal pattern; the estimated difficulty parameter is 5.4. These estimated parameters are further used to calculate the expected test score using Equation (8-15), and all variables were statistically important to be included for the score calculation.

Figure 8.6 graphically displays the ICCs of the four variables conforming to the IRT models. Each of the four ICCs predicts the probability that a user with a given ability-level will actually have the corresponding variable presented. Corresponding with Table 8.4, the position and order of the individual ICC do not change remarkably for all anomaly-free network traffic between the training and testing samples (upper left and middle), but they do change significantly between the abnormal and anomaly-free traffic data (lower left). When restricting the trait-level to a range of 10-15, the pattern difference is more clear (Figure 8.6 right). This finding suggests that ICCs as a whole provide great information about user behavior and could be used to distinguish different patterns.

Table 8.5. Results from the item response model

Model	Estimated Coefficient (β)	Standard Error	95% Confidential Interval
Training sample (anomaly-free connections)			
Source port is same as the destination port	-3.8746	0.0370	-3.95 to -3.80
Service (HTTP, FTP, UDP, SMTP, or SNMP)	4.0363	0.0400	3.96 to 4.11
Duration of the session more than one	-3.2044	0.0270	-3.25 to -3.15
Not fall within 2 SD of the mean (mean + SD)	-2.8133	0.0226	-2.86 to -2.77
Testing sample (anomaly-free connections)			
Source port is same as the destination port	-3.7435	0.0236	-3.79 to -3.70
Service (HTTP, FTP, UDP, SMTP, or SNMP)	3.6675	0.0227	3.62 to 3.71
Duration of the session more than one	-2.1444	0.0116	-2.17 to -2.12
Not fall within 2 SD of the mean (mean + SD)	-1.8041	0.0102	-1.82 to -1.78
Testing sample (abnormal connections)			
Source port is same as the destination port	-1.7911	0.0290	-1.85 to -1.73
Service (HTTP, FTP, UDP, SMTP, or SNMP)	-3.7216	0.0506	-3.82 to -3.62
Duration of the session more than one	-5.4403	0.0918	-5.62 to -5.26
Not fall within 2 SD of the mean (mean + SD)	-4.4030	0.0622	-4.52 to -4.28

The expected test score for three particular ability-levels, 10, 12.5, and 15 show remarkable differences between anomaly-free and anomaly patterns (Table 8.5). At the low ability-level, the anomaly-free pattern has an approximate score of 29.3 while the anomaly pattern has a score of 4.4—a difference in range of 25 in a 0 to 100 scale. When the ability-level increases to 15, the absolute difference in the score between patterns is approximately 21. Although the true relationship between the expected test score and the ability-level is not linear but exponential, such a relationship can be considered as linear when restricting the ability-level to a range of 10 to 15 (Figure 8.7).

The IRT based score modeling approach, however, has limitations that warrant discussion. First, because IRT is a test-oriented measurement theory, Example 8.3 treats all users, regardless of whether they are normal or abnormal, as test "takers": the difference between the two patterns, anomaly-free and anomaly, is measured by the "test" scores at individually given an ability-level. This assumption implies that in theory, an abnormal user can also get a high score of being normal if the ability-level becomes high (e.g., as shown in Figure 8.4, if the x-axis value becomes infinite, then all users will reach the top score.). Although such an assumption is accurate in test measurement, it is controvertible in network security. To avoid this contravention it is important to set up a pre-determined positive range, $x_1 \leq \theta \leq x_2$, for the ability-level, which will limit all users to be measured within this range. This approach has been presented in Equation (8-14), and therefore we use the term of "Semi-Item Response Model" to distinguish the traditional IRT without such a restriction. In Example 8.3, we used $x_1 = 10$ and $x_2 = 15$, which were selected based on the training data. The test score is approximately linear when associated with the ability-level. Although this range fit well with the training sample, such a range has not been

Figure 8.6 Patterns difference in ICCs

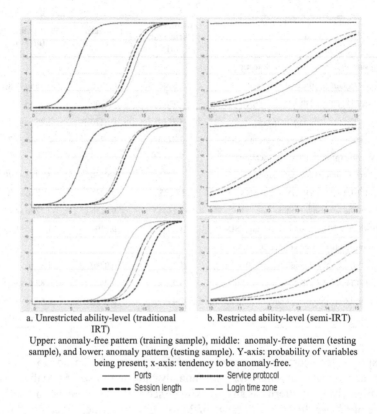

a. Unrestricted ability-level (traditional IRT)　　b. Restricted ability-level (semi-IRT)

Upper: anomaly-free pattern (training sample), middle: anomaly-free pattern (testing sample), and lower: anomaly pattern (testing sample). Y-axis: probability of variables being present; x-axis: tendency to be anomaly-free.

——— Ports　　••••••••• Service protocol
━━━• Session length　— — — Login time zone

validated and additional studies are necessary to assess the reliability and feasibility of the range. In addition to this limitation, the presented four variable-based IRT model should be viewed as a pilot study due to restriction of data availability, to demonstrate the feasibility and achievability of applying IRT in network security. The one-parameter model presented in Example 8.3 provides limited information about predictor variables; when a large numbers of potential predictor variables are available, a two-parameter IRT model is worth attempting, which may provide the discriminatory power between normal and abnormal users for each variable.

PROFILING MODELS

Although one of the ultimate goals of network security is to detect intrusion and anomaly activities in real time, profiling user behavior is a fundamental step leading toward success of this goal. With increasing threats in information and computer network security, the demand for the development of new methods and algorithms in profiling user behavior has

Table 8.6. Expected test score to be normal

Ability-level	Anomaly-free		Anomaly
	Training	Testing	Testing
$\theta = 10$	27.5	31.1	4.4
$\theta = 12.5$	48.8	61.9	26.2
$\theta = 15$	87.7	92.1	68.7

Figure 8.7. Differences in expected score between anomaly-free and anomaly patterns

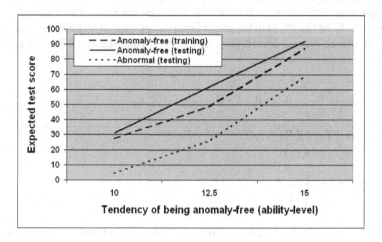

been significantly increased. In this section we will introduce basic profiling methods and modeling approaches. Specifically, we will illustrate two methods, hierarchical generalized linear modeling and probability procedures.

Hierarchical Generalized Linear Model

In practice, data used for profiling user behavior is structured on multilevel. Individuals can be in various types of groups with the lower-level observations nested within higher level(s). There are variables describing individuals, and variables describing groups. While various hierarchical infrastructures for intrusion detection have been suggested (Zhang, Li, Manikopoulos, Jorgenson and Ucles, 2001; d'Auriol and Surapaneni, 2005; Rice and Danieles, 2005; Wang and Cannady, 2005), the desired profiling measurement could also be constructed hierarchically. Let us assume that the unit of network traffic is connections—for a particular system as we mentioned in previous chapters, we will have at least three levels of data: (1) the networks characteristics (which include sub-network systems, software and hardware configurations for each of such sub-systems), daily traffic volume, and number of users, (2) the group-level data that describes user characteristics such as user gender, job responsibility, working schedule, department, and user-specific behavior pattern-related statistics, and (3) individual connections. Such a type of hierarchical data structure is very common in network security. Figure 8.8 graphically illustrates a three level hierarchical data structure where we can see that connections are nested within groups and groups are nested within the sub-network systems. We have to take into account such multilevel data structure for our profiling models.

The hierarchical generalized linear model (HGLM) is a modeling technique dedicated to analyzing data with multilevel structures (Snijders & Bosker, 2000; Raudenbush & Bryk, 2002). It accounts for the within-group correlation of the predictor variables and the response variable, and separates the within-group variation from the between-group variation. It treats the between-group variance as a random effect and assumes such effects are normally distributed with a mean of zero. Let us consider using the indices i, j and l to denote groups, connections, and sub-networks. Let x_k be the kth predictor variable at the connection-level, η_t be the tth variable at the group-level, and let v_z be the zth variable at the sub-network-level. A three-level hierarchical generalized logistic model with a random intercept can be simply presented as

$$\text{Level-1: } y_{ijl} = \log\left[\frac{p_{ijl}}{1 - p_{ijl}}\right] = \beta_{0il} + \beta_1 x_{ijl1} + \beta_2 x_{ijl2} + \cdots + \beta_k x_{ijlk} \quad (8\text{-}16)$$

$$\text{Level 2: } \beta_{0il} = \gamma_0 + \gamma_{0l} + \gamma_1 \eta_{i1} + \gamma_2 \eta_{i2} + \cdots + \lambda_t \eta_{it} + \omega_{il} \quad (8\text{-}17)$$
$$\omega_{il} \sim N\left(0, \tau_l^2\right)$$

$$\text{Level 3: } \gamma_{0l} = \xi_0 + \xi_1 v_{l1} + \xi_2 v_{l2} + \cdots + \zeta_z v_{lz} + \delta_l \quad (8\text{-}18)$$
$$\delta_l \sim N\left(0, \psi^2\right)$$

Equations (8-16) to (8-18) represent a particular hierarchical random intercept logistic model, which can be used for profiling analysis.

Although a task of profiling user behavior is different from a task of classification individual network traffic, profiling analysis does utilize the results from classification analysis. Since we cannot develop a classification system that is free of false alarm rates, we most likely conduct a profiling analysis acknowledging the fact that the profiling results may not reflect the "true" user behavior. Such a deviation could be caused by the initial task of classification; for example, the classification algorithm could generate false rates that are too high, the profiling algorithm may not take into account the within-group and between-group variances well, or both. Nevertheless, one of the profiling aims is to examine if a stream of traffic from a particular user, site, or group is extremely different from the overall groups, and if so, detect that user, site, or group.

Let us assume that data are structured only on two levels: connection and group. Let $y_{ij} = 1$ if the jth observation in the ith group is anomaly-free and 0 otherwise. We can simply present Equations (8-16) to (8-18) as

Level-1: $y_{ij} = \log\left[\dfrac{p_{ij}}{1-p_{ij}}\right] = \beta_{0i} + \beta_1 x_{ij1} + \beta_2 x_{ij2} + \cdots + \beta_k x_{ijk}$ \hfill (8-19)

Level 2: $\beta_{0i} = \gamma_0 + \gamma_1 \eta_{1i} + \gamma_2 \eta_{2i} + \cdots + \lambda_{ti} \eta_{ti} + \omega_i$ \hfill (8-20)

$$\omega_i \sim N(0, \tau^2)$$

where η_t denotes the tth variable at the group-level (e.g., user working schedule). We can calculate the group-specific standardized anomaly-free rate for the ith group as

$$\hat{s}_i(X) = \frac{\sum_{j=1}^{n_i} \hat{y}_{ij}}{\sum_{j=1}^{n_i} \hat{e}_{ij}} \times \overline{y},$$ \hfill (8-21)

where $\hat{s}_i$ is the ith group standardized anomaly-free ratio, $\overline{y}$ is the overall anomaly-free rate for all the groups, and $\hat{y}_{ij}$ and $\hat{e}_{ij}$ are the predicted group-specific probability of anomaly-free and the expected probability of being anomaly-free for the jth connection, respectively (Normand, Wang, & Krumholz, 2007). $\hat{y}_{ij}$ and $\hat{e}_{ij}$ are defined mathematically below:

$$\hat{y}_{ij} = \frac{\exp(\beta_{0i} + \sum_{k=1}^{K} \beta_k x_{kj})}{1 + \exp(\beta_{0i} + \sum_{k=1}^{K} \beta_k x_{kj})}, \text{ and}$$ \hfill (8-22)

$$\hat{e}_{ij} = \frac{\exp(\beta_0 + \sum_{k=1}^{K} \beta_k x_{kj})}{1 + \exp(\beta_0 + \sum_{k=1}^{K} \beta_k x_{kj})}.$$ \hfill (8-23)

Figure 8.8 Three levels hierarchical data structure

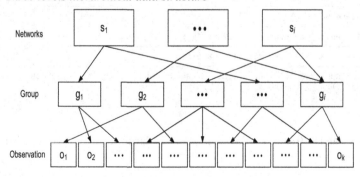

Note $\hat{e}_{ij}$ only counts the overall intercept without considering the different intercept at the individual group-level, but $\hat{y}_{ij}$ does.

Using Equations (8-21), (8-22) and (8-23) we can estimate a group-specific standardized anomaly-free rate for each group included in the system and then rank groups based on these rates. For example, we can classify groups into three mutually exclusive categories with approximately 10% in the "low" (anomaly-free), 10% in the "high", and 80% in the middle based on the percentile method. We may pay more attention to the 10% of groups that are classified as "low" and monitor those classified as middle to see if any group is toward the "low" category. We will revisit these approaches in Chapter XI.

Example 8.4→Risk-standardized Anomaly-free Rate. The MIT-DARPA data include IP address and individual connection levels information. Let us assume that the IP addresses represent individual sites and construct a two-level hierarchical random intercept logistic model of the training dataset with a total of 39 individual sites. The response variable for this model is anomaly-free (yes/no) and the predictor variables are the variables identified from Chapter VII. SAS provides a *GLIMMIX* macro that can be used to fit this model. We need to download the *GLIMMIX* macro from SAS in case it has not been installed. The SAS program used to conduct this model and the resulting output are given in Display 8.10 below.

Display 8.10
SAS codes to fit a two-level hierarchical random intercept logistic regression model

```
Libname HGLM "F:\book\Chapter 8\";
%include "F:\Book\Chapter 8\glimmix.sas";
%include "F:\Book\Chapter 8\profile_macro.sas"; /* Appendix CH8 */;
data temp;
set HGLM.final_SAS;
run;
%let var=udp icmp samePort sameIP http smtp ecr eco snmp ftp domain
telnet finger;
%Random_effect(temp,normal, IP_s,,&var, profile);
%Soln_2(profile);
%let outvar=;
data pred_6;
set _pred;
Random_phat_6=exp(pred)/(1+exp(pred));
run;
data Fix_6;
set _soln;
run;
%IDS_Get_xbate(Fix_6);
%let Fix_6=&outvar;
/*------------------------------------------------------------------
 Calculate phat
-------------------------------------------------------------------*/
%IDS_Get_Phat(pred_6,pred_6,&Fix_6,Fix_phat_6);
/*------------------------------------------------------------------
 Calculate SMR Standard Mortality Ratio
-------------------------------------------------------------------*/
%IDS_Get_SMR(pred_6,SMR_6,IP_s,normal,Random_phat_6,Fix_Phat_6,SMR_OBS_6,
SMR_Phat_6);
```

Figures 8.9 and 8.10 show the distribution of standardized anomaly-free ratio by sites. A

Figure 8.9 Distribution of standardized anomaly-free ratio by sites

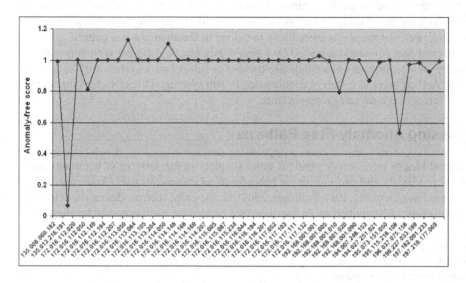

Figure 8.10 Radar plot of the standardized anomaly-free ratio

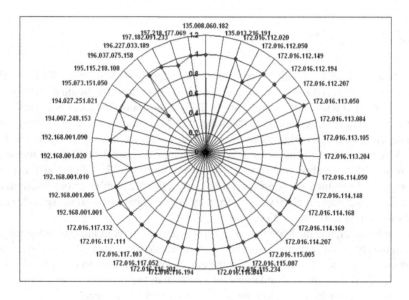

sites with a standardized anomaly-free ratio < 1 indicates that site is more likely to belong the abnormal pattern and should be monitored closely. A site with the ratio close to 1 indicates that the site's predicted value is same as the expected value, and a site with the ratio greater than 1 indicates that the site is more likely to belong to the anomaly-free pattern.

It is clear that connections issued by a single user can be different with connections issued by others, and users at a single department or sub-network system are likely to be more alike than users at different departments or sub systems. One of factors that cause such differences is between-group variance.

Assessing Anomaly-Free Patterns

The initial idea of intrusion detection is quite simple; use the patterns of legitimate user behavior to identify and distinguish the behavior of an anomalous user (Anderson, 1972; Anderson, 1980; Denning, 1987; Stallings, 2003). Statistically, such an idea can be achieved by establishing a distribution of an anomaly-free pattern for each group or for the entire network system. If we have sufficient data, than using the central limit law, we can construct such patterns to follow a normal distribution; that is, *pattern* ~ $N(\mu, \sigma)$. With such a pattern, we can classify incoming network traffics based on its probability of failing in the pre-established normal pattern.

Several approaches can be used to assess a normal pattern and to estimate the parameters, μ and σ. Let us use the anomaly-free score described in Equation (8-9)

$$\hat{s}_{ij} = \frac{1}{K} \sum_{k=1}^{K} w_k x_{kij}$$

to illustrate a potential approach to constructing an anomaly-free pattern. We know that $\hat{s}_{ij}$ represents the observed likelihood of an individual network traffic being anomaly-free, since an observation with a high score is more likely to be anomaly-free. Theoretically we can represent group or site behavior by the mean, $\mu_i = E(s_{ij})$, and variance, $\sigma_i^2 = E(s_{ij} - \mu_i)^2$, of its true score, s_{ij}. But in reality we do not know the true score of each group that is to be profiled. What we have is the observed score from sampled network traffics, but we do not know how accurate the observed mean $\hat{\mu}_i = E(\hat{s}_{ij})$ and variance, $\hat{\sigma}_i^2 = E(\hat{s}_{ij} - \hat{\mu}_i)^2$ is to the true mean, μ_i, and variance, σ_i^2. Moreover, when only a limited number of observations are available for each group, an observed pattern may not be stable and a group-specific score may not follow a normal distribution.

We can however, use the bootstrapping approach to infer about the user behavior patterns from the observed patterns. Let b_s be the bth resample from D ($b = 1, 2, ..., B$), s_{ij}^b be a corresponding score, and $\hat{\mu}_{1b}^*, \hat{\mu}_{2b}^*, \cdots, \hat{\mu}_{ib}^*$ be the corresponding means to n groups ($i = 1, 2, ..., n$). When a large volume of simulations are conducted, the simulated mean scores tend to follow a normal distribution and are more likely to represent the "true" behavior pattern. Thus, for the jth observation within the ith group, we can expect its score to follow

$$\hat{s}_{ij} \sim N(\mu_i^*, \sigma_i^{*2}), \tag{8-24}$$

where μ_i^* denotes the mean of the simulated scores for the ith group, and the variance of μ_i^* is given by

$$\sigma_i^{*2} = \frac{1}{B-1}\sum_{b=1}^{B}[\hat{\mu}_{ib}^* - \mu_i^*]^2 \qquad (8\text{-}25)$$

(Efron, 1982). As a result, although the underlying "true" anomaly-free user behavior pattern is unknown for each site, the properties of such a pattern could be inferred.

Example 8.5→Normal Pattern. Let us use the first two weeks of the MIT-DAPRA list files that do not include any abnormal TCP/IP connections to establish an anomaly-free behavior pattern for each site in the data. To ensure having enough observations to establish a stable distribution for each site, we restrict to using only those sites that have at least 100 observations and must also have at least 5 observations in the 3rd through 7th weeks

Table 8.7 Variables used for constructing the anomaly-free score

Variables	First two weeks	
	Sample size (#)	Estimator
Connection		
Start time zone in hour (mean, SD)	366,545	13.2 (3.7)
Fall within 2 SD of the mean (mean + SD)	345,561	94.28
Duration of the session in minutes (mean, SD)	366,545	4.1 (197.9)
Fall within 2 SD of the mean (mean + SD)	352,122	96.07
Service		
UDP (%)	11,381	3.10
FTP (%)	8,220	2.24
HTTP (%)	317,040	86.49
SMTP (%)	23,797	6.49
URP (%)	10	0.00
ECR (%)x	0	0.00
ECO (%)	1,616	0.44
SNMP (%)	0	0.00
Port (%)x	1	0.00
Port		
Source port is same as the destination port (%)	7,480	2.04
IP address		
Source IP address is same as the destination address (%)	0	0.00

Table 8.8 Parameters estimated from bootstrapping

Site (IP address)	Bootstrap parameters*				
	Sample size (#)	Mean	SD	1th percentile	99th percentile
135.008.060.182	2,185	0.3055	0.0629	0.2999	0.3121
135.013.216.191	3,073	0.3080	0.0592	0.3043	0.3116
172.016.112.020	5,563	0.3168	0.0721	0.3126	0.3199
172.016.112.050	1,124	0.2960	0.0627	0.2889	0.3002
172.016.112.149	16,564	0.2826	0.0542	0.2769	0.2865
172.016.112.194	19,127	0.2872	0.0541	0.2820	0.2910
172.016.112.207	20,848	0.2830	0.0518	0.2785	0.2865
172.016.113.050	377	0.2924	0.0772	0.2862	0.2980
172.016.113.084	15,368	0.2854	0.0541	0.2801	0.2883
172.016.113.105	9,964	0.2854	0.0552	0.2810	0.2887
172.016.113.204	14,551	0.2837	0.0540	0.2786	0.2878
172.016.114.050	1,612	0.2689	0.0791	0.2639	0.2733
172.016.114.148	22,715	0.2846	0.0538	0.2805	0.2880
172.016.114.168	12,804	0.2826	0.0565	0.2796	0.2854
172.016.114.169	18,885	0.2793	0.0503	0.2755	0.2827
172.016.114.207	17,975	0.2819	0.0543	0.2782	0.2863
172.016.115.005	14,953	0.3207	0.0600	0.3136	0.3226
172.016.115.087	16,215	0.3199	0.0578	0.3165	0.3207
172.016.115.234	15,315	0.3093	0.0552	0.3074	0.3105
172.016.116.044	14,802	0.3099	0.0544	0.3051	0.3105
172.016.116.194	16,468	0.3091	0.0529	0.3048	0.3183
172.016.116.201	17,125	0.3058	0.0590	0.3036	0.3110
172.016.117.052	17,310	0.3178	0.0573	0.3127	0.3226
172.016.117.103	13,001	0.3248	0.0620	0.3202	0.3315
172.016.117.111	18,740	0.3145	0.0570	0.3114	0.3185
172.016.117.132	12,532	0.2947	0.0462	0.2928	0.2951
192.168.001.001	2,395	0.3568	0.0642	0.3541	0.3585
192.168.001.005	788	0.4561	0.0440	0.4561	0.4561
192.168.001.010	737	0.3796	0.0624	0.3782	0.3806
192.168.001.020	5,177	0.3737	0.0422	0.3737	0.3737
192.168.001.090	1,044	0.3501	0.0565	0.3484	0.3522
194.007.248.153	2,717	0.2954	0.0608	0.2918	0.2985
194.027.251.021	2,306	0.3047	0.0614	0.2993	0.3094
195.073.151.050	2,142	0.3069	0.0611	0.3021	0.3113
195.115.218.108	1,976	0.3114	0.0608	0.3049	0.3161
196.037.075.158	1,929	0.3003	0.0619	0.2959	0.3059
196.227.033.189	1,841	0.3028	0.0607	0.2985	0.3081
197.182.091.233	2,521	0.3069	0.0625	0.3011	0.3110
197.218.177.069	1,776	0.2940	0.0601	0.2895	0.2982

* Unique connections

Figure 8.11. Box plots of observed and bootstrapped anomaly-free scores (group-I: all observations, group-II: without repeated observations, and group-III: bootstrap results)

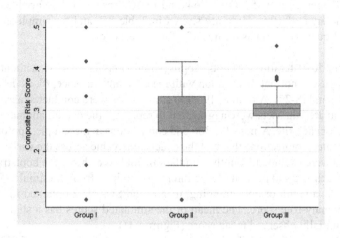

Figure 8.12 Patterns of four randomly selected IP addresses

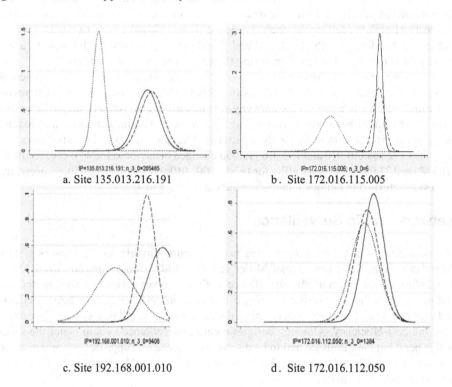

a. Site 135.013.216.191

b. Site 172.016.115.005

c. Site 192.168.001.010

d. Site 172.016.112.050

for evaluation. There are a total of 39 sites that meet these criteria. Among these 39 sites the number of observations per site ranged from 377 to 22,715, with a mean of 9,399, and 25th, 50th, and 75th percentiles of 1,976, 9,964, and 16,468, respectively. Variables used for constructing the anomaly-free score are shown in Table 8.7, and for simplification, the weight term in Equation (8-9) has a value of 1 for all variables.

Let us conduct 5000 iterations of bootstrapping simulations for each site, without repeated observations to yield a normal distribution with mean, μ, and variance, σ^2, as described in Equations (8-24) and (8-25). A total of 195,000 simulations were conducted across the 39 sites. These simulated datasets were aggregated to represent the overall anomaly-free behavior patterns for each site. Among the 366,545 connections in the sample, approximately 91.7% were repeated connections that had the exact same value across the variables listed in Table 8.8 and were excluded from the simulation. Table 8.8 shows the bootstrap-based parameters for each site and the confidence intervals obtained from the simulations based on the sample. As a result of bootstrapping, means and SDs were obtained for each site based on its anomaly-free score. The mean of the simulated scores has a slightly higher value than the initially observed mean score (Figure 8.11).

Figure 8.12 shows the distributions of risk scores of four sites: 135.013.216.191, 172.016.115.005, 192.168.001.010 and 172.016.112.050. In each plot, the left side distribution (dotted line) is the normalized baseline anomaly-free pattern established by using the bootstrapping simulation with the training data, and the right side distributions represent the normalized pattern in the testing data with two sub-testing samples (denoted by solid and dashed lines). We can see that there is a clear difference in patterns between the training and testing data for sites 135.013.216.191 and 172.016.115.005; 95.6% and 100.0% of traffics in the testing data are anomaly-free during the entire 5-week testing period.

The difference in patterns on IP address site 192.168.001.010 is not clear, and there is almost no discriminate power for site 172.016.112.050. This could be caused by weaknesses of the method used to establish the anomaly-free pattern. It also could be an indicator that these sites had multi-behavior changes during the 5-week monitoring period and may require using weekly traffic data to assess their patterns. The raw MIT-DARPA data shows that both sites 192.168.001.010 and 172.016.112.050 changed behavior in the 4th week, resulting in 65.4% and 73.0% abnormal traffics for 192.168.001.010 and 172.016.112.050, respectively. Both sites returned to being anomaly-free during weeks 5 to 7.

Network Traffic Surveillance

Monitoring network traffic is an ongoing task to ensure a highly secure network system (Marchette, 2003; Robertson, Siegel, Miller, & Stolfo, 2003; Wang, Papageorgiou & Messmer, 2006). Developing a useful surveillance method involves various measuring, scoring and profiling methods on traffic volume, communication efficiency, intervention effects and user behavior. The key characteristics of a successful surveillance system are usefulness and cost-efficiency. Although design an entire surveillance system is not the focus of this book but the discussed and to be discussed methods and approaches are important towards to establish such a system. Below we emphasize several basic goals that a successful surveillance system desires to reach.

First, a system should reveal important trends in the traffic volume and user behavior across the whole network system in a timely manner, and also be robust enough to inform future security-related improvement efforts, including both policy changes and equipment updates. A system should help signal whether security-related measures, initiatives and practice patterns are affecting user behavior and the preference of network system. For example, it should help assess whether a new Internet policy is leading improved network traffic and/or lowering anomalous events.

Second, a system needs to control for secular changes over time in the traffic populations that are monitored, to focus on priority areas that may change dynamically, and to make optimal use of established measures that may also vary dynamically. A desired surveillance system should form a dashboard of indicators that can track progress toward company's ultimately secure goals.

Third, a desired system should make use of the full range of data collected the network system and other available security-related data from different sources. With utilizing rich data sources the surveillance system can leverage and enhance network security as a whole.

Finally, a good surveillance system also supports ad hoc analysis upon request. To achieve this goal, the system needs to be equipped with a number of basic data analysis functions and to have user-friendly data display capability.

SUMMARY

In this chapter we discussed the characteristics and attributes of user behavior, and the methods could be used to measure and analyze them. We also illustrated examples of scoring user activities and profiling user behavior based on the scores. As we know, user behavior is not a static concept, but rather, may change over time and the statistical parameters representing such patterns have to be re-estimated regularly to match with such changes. Accordingly, to analyze such repeatedly measured data, longitudinal statistical modeling techniques that are able to take into account the changes in user behavior should be considered as an important aspect in measuring user behavior. Measurement errors are unavoidable. Because of them, some uncertainty will always surround any measurement result. The challenge is to develop methods for marking a better estimate of the "true value" of a measured quantity. We will discuss the uncertainty issue again at Chapter XI.

REFERENCES

Anderson, P. J. (1972). *Computer security technology planning study, Volume II, ESD-TR-73-51,* Vol. II, Electronic Systems Division. Air Force Systems Command, Hanscom Field, Bedford, MA.

Anderson, P. J. (1980). *Computer security threat monitoring and surveillance.* Fort Washington, PA: James P. Anderson Co.

Anderson, G. F., Selby, D. A., & Ramsey, M. (2007). Insider attack and real-time data mining of user behavior. *IBM Journal of Research & Development, 51*(3/4), 465-467.

Andrich, D. (1988). *Rasch models for measurement.* Beverly Hills: Sage Publications.

Bae, I. H., Lee, H. J., & Lee, K.S. (2007). Design and evaluation of a dynamic anomaly detection scheme using the age of user profiles, (pp. 136-140). In *Proceedings of the Fourth International Conference on Fuzzy Systems and Knowledge Discovery* (FSKD 2007), 3.

Boeck, P. D. & Wilson, M. (2004). *Explanatory item response models, a generalized linear and nonlinear approach.* New York: Springer-Verlag.

d'Auriol, B. J. & Surapaneni, K. (2005). A computation-communication sequencing model for intrusion detection systems, (pp. 140-143). In *Proceedings of 2005 International Conference on Security and Management* (SAM'05).

Davis, C. S. (2002). *Statistical methods for the analysis of repeated measurements.* New York: Springer-Verlag.

Denning, D. (1987). An Intrusion-detection model. *IEEE Transaction on Software Engineering, 2*(13), 222-232.

Diggle, P.J., Heagerty, P., Liang, KY, & Zeger, S.L. (2002). *Analysis of longitudinal data, 2nd Ed.* London: Oxford University Press.

Efron, B. (1982). *The jackknife, the bootstrap, and other resampling plans.* Philadelphia: SIAM.

Embretson, S. E. & Reise, S. P. (2000). *Item response theory for psychologists.* New Jersey: Lawrence Erlbaum Associates, Publishers.

Fitzmaurice, G. M., Laird, N. M., & Ware, J. H. (2004). *Applied longitudinal analysis.* New Jersey: Wiley-Interscience.

Frees, E. (2004). *Longitudinal and panel data.* London: Cambridge University Press.

Garg, A., Vidyaraman, S., Upadhyaya, S., Kwiat, S. (2006) USim: A user behavior simulation framework for training and testing IDSes in GUI based systems, anss, (pp. 196-203). In *Proceedings of 39th Annual Simulation Symposium (ANSS'06).*

Hand, D.J. (2004). *Measurement theory and practice: The world through quantification.* New York: Arnold.

Hambleton, R. K., Swaminathan, H. & Rogers, H. J. (1991). *Fundamentals of item response theory.* Newbury Park, California: Sage Publications.

Isohara, T., Takemori, K. & Sasase, I. (2008). Anomaly detection on mobile phone based operational behavior. *IPSJ Digital Courier, 4*, pp. 9-17.

Krantz, D. H., Luce, R. D., Suppes, P., and Tversky, A. (1971), *Foundations of measurement, Vol. I: Additive and polynomial representations.* New York: Academic Press.

Kukreja, U., Stevenson, W. E. and Ritter, F. E. (2006). RUI—recording user input from interfaces under Windows and Mac OS X. *Behavior Research Methods, 38*(4), 656-659.

Little, T. D., Schnabel, K. U. & Baumert, J. (2000). *Modeling longitudinal and multilevel data: practical issues, applied approaches, and specific examples.* New Jersey: Lawrence Erlbaum Associates Publishers.

Luce, R. D., Krantz, D. H., Suppes, P., and Tversky, A. (1990). *Foundations of measurement, Vol. III: Representation, axiomatization, and invariance.* New York: Academic Press.

Lord, F. M. (1952). *A theory of test scores (Psychometric Monograph No.7).* Iowa City, IA: Psychometric Society.

Marchette, D. J. (1999). A statistical method for profiling network traffic, (pp. 119-128). In *Proceedings of the Workshop on Intrusion Detection and Network Monitoring.*

Marchette, D. J. (2003). Statistical opportunities in network security. In *Proceedings of the 35th Symposium on the Interface of Computing Science and Statistics, Computing Science and Statistics, 35*, 28-38.

Mazhelis, O. & Puuronen, S. (2007). A framework for behavior-based detection of user substitution in a mobile context. *Computers & Security, 26*(2), 154-157.

Nielsen, J., & Mack, R. L. (eds.) (1994). *Usability inspection methods.* New York: John Wiley & Sons.

Normand, S.L.T., Wang, Y., and Krumholz, H. M. (2007). Assessing surrogacy of data sources for institutional comparisons. *Health Service Outcomes Research Method, 7*(1-2), 79-96.

Oh, H. S. & Lee, S. W (2003). An anomaly intrusion detection method by clustering normal user behavior. *Computers & Security, 22*(7), 596-612.

Peeece, J., Rogers, Y., & Sharp, H. (2002). *Interaction design: Beyond human-computer interaction.* New York: John Wiley & Sons.

Rabe-Hesketh, S. & Skrondal, A. (2005). *Multilevel and longitudinal modeling using Stata.* Texas: A Stata Press Publication.

Raudenbush, S. W. & Bryk, A. S. (2002). *Hierarchical linear models: Applications and data analysis methods, 2nd Edition.* London: SAGE Publications.

Rice, G. W. & Danieles, T. E. (2005). A hierarchical approach for detecting system intrusions through event correlation, (pp. 499-804). *Proceeding of Communication, Network, and Information Security.*

Robertson, S., Siegel, E. V., Miller, M., & Stolfo, S. J. (2003). Surveillance detection in high bandwidth environments, (pp. 130-138). In *Proceedings of the 2003 DARPA DISCEX III Conference.*

Shneiderman, B. (1998). *Designing the user interface: Strategies for effective human-computer interaction (3rd Edition).* MA: Addison-Wesley.

Shultz, K.S. & Whitney, D.J (2005). *Measurement theory in action: Case studies and exercises.* California: Sage Publications Inc

Skrondal, A & Rabe-Hesketh, S. (2004). *Generalized latent variable modeling: Multilevel, longitudinal and structural equation models.* Boca Raton, FL: Chapman & Hall/CRC.

Snijders, A.B. T. & Bosker, R. J. (2000*). Multilevel analysis: An introduction to basic and advanced multilevel modeling.* London: SAGE Publications.

Stallings, W. (2003). *Network security essentials, applications and standards. 2nd Ed.* New Jersey: Pearson Education.

Stata (2005). *Longitudinal/panel data.* Stata Corporation, TX: College Station.

Suppes, P., Krantz, D. H., Luce, R. D., and Tversky, A. (1989). *Foundations of measurement, Vol. II: Geometrical, threshold, and probabilistic representations.* New York: Academic Press.

Wang, Y. & Cannady, J. (2005). Develop a composite risk score to detect anomaly intrusion, (pp. 445-449). In *Proceedings of the IEEE SoutheastCon 2005.*

Wang, Y., Papageorgiou, M. & Messmer, A. (2006). A real-time freeway network traffic surveillance tool. *IEEE Transactions on Control Systems Technology,14*(1), 18-32.

Westerman, S. J., Hambly, S., Alder, C., Wyatt-Millington, C. W., Shrayane, N. M., Crawshaw, C. M., & Hockey, G. R. J. (1996). Investigating the human-computer interface using the Datalogger. *Behavior Research Methods, Instruments, & Computers, 28*(4), 603-606.

Zhang, Z., Li, J., Manikopoulos, C. N., Jorgenson, J., & Ucles, J. (2001). HIDE: A hierarchical network intrusion detection system using statistical preprocessing and neural network classification, (pp. 85-90). In *Proceedings of the 2001 IEEE Workshop Information Assurance and Security.*

APPENDIX

Create_var.do (Stata codes to create binary variables for the MIT-DAPRA data)

```
#delimit;
gen timeZone=real(substr(time_b,1,2))+real(substr(time_b,4,2))/60+
real(substr(time_b,7,2))/3600;
sum timeZone,d;
gen byte t2=(timeZone > (_result(3)-2*sqrt(_result(4))) & timeZone <
(_result(3)+2*sqrt(_result(4))));
gen lonin=(timeZone>=8 & timeZone<=17);
gen length=real(substr(duration,1,2))* 3600+real(substr(duration,4,2))*60+
real(substr(duration,7,2));
gen byte len_1=(length==1);
gen byte udp=(substr(service,length(trim(service))-1,1)=="/" &
substr(service,length(trim(service)),1)=="u");
gen byte icmp=(substr(service,length(trim(service))-1,1)=="/" &
substr(service,length(trim(service)),1)=="i");
gen byte samePort=(port_s==port_d);
gen byte sameIP=(IP_s==IP_d);
gen byte http=(trim(service)=="http");
gen byte smtp=(trim(service)=="smtp");
gen byte urp=(substr(trim(service),1,3)=="urp");
gen byte ecr=(substr(trim(service),1,3)=="ecr");
gen byte eco=(substr(trim(service),1,3)=="eco");
gen byte snmp=(substr(trim(service),1,4)=="snmp");
gen byte ftp=(substr(trim(service),1,3)=="ftp");
gen byte domain=(substr(trim(service),1,6)=="domain");
gen byte frag=(substr(trim(service),1,4)=="frag");
gen byte telnet=(substr(trim(service),1,6)=="telnet");
gen byte finger=(substr(trim(service),1,6)=="finger");

gen byte Service=(http==1 | smtp==1 | ftp==1 | udp==1 | snmp==1);
gen byte t2=(timeZone >_result(3)-2*sqrt(_result(4))) & timeZone<
    (_result(3)+2*sqrt(_result(4))));
gen byte l1_n=(length~=1);
gen byte t2_n=(t2==0);
```

Time.do (Stata codes)

```
gen byte time=1 if substr(index,1,8)=="week-1&2" & substr(index, 10,3)=="mon";
replace  time=2 if substr(index,1,8)=="week-1&2" & substr(index, 10,3)=="tue";
replace  time=3 if substr(index,1,8)=="week-1&2" & substr(index, 10,3)=="wed";
replace  time=4 if substr(index,1,8)=="week-1&2" & substr(index, 10,3)=="thr";
replace  time=5 if substr(index,1,8)=="week-1&2" & substr(index, 10,3)=="fri";
replace  time=6 if substr(index,1,6)=="week-3" & substr(index, 8,3)=="mon";
replace  time=7 if substr(index,1,6)=="week-3" & substr(index, 8,3)=="tue";
replace  time=8 if substr(index,1,6)=="week-3" & substr(index, 8,3)=="wed";
replace  time=9 if substr(index,1,6)=="week-3" & substr(index, 8,3)=="thr";
replace  time=10 if substr(index,1,6)=="week-3" & substr(index, 8,3)=="fri";
replace  time=11 if substr(index,1,6)=="week-4" & substr(index, 8,3)=="mon";
replace  time=12 if substr(index,1,6)=="week-4" & substr(index, 8,3)=="tue";
replace  time=13 if substr(index,1,6)=="week-4" & substr(index, 8,3)=="wed";
replace  time=14 if substr(index,1,6)=="week-4" & substr(index, 8,3)=="thr";
replace  time=15 if substr(index,1,6)=="week-4" & substr(index, 8,3)=="fri";
replace  time=16 if substr(index,1,6)=="week-5" & substr(index, 8,3)=="mon";
replace  time=17 if substr(index,1,6)=="week-5" & substr(index, 8,3)=="tue";
replace  time=18 if substr(index,1,6)=="week-5" & substr(index, 8,3)=="wed";
replace  time=19 if substr(index,1,6)=="week-5" & substr(index, 8,3)=="thr";
replace  time=20 if substr(index,1,6)=="week-5" & substr(index, 8,3)=="fri";
replace  time=21 if substr(index,1,6)=="week-6" & substr(index, 8,3)=="mon";
replace  time=22 if substr(index,1,6)=="week-6" & substr(index, 8,3)=="tue";
replace  time=23 if substr(index,1,6)=="week-6" & substr(index, 8,3)=="wed";
replace  time=24 if substr(index,1,6)=="week-6" & substr(index, 8,3)=="thr";
replace  time=25 if substr(index,1,6)=="week-6" & substr(index, 8,3)=="fri";
replace  time=26 if substr(index,1,6)=="week-7" & substr(index, 8,3)=="mon";
replace  time=27 if substr(index,1,6)=="week-7" & substr(index, 8,3)=="tue";
replace  time=28 if substr(index,1,6)=="week-7" & substr(index, 8,3)=="wed";
replace  time=29 if substr(index,1,6)=="week-7" & substr(index, 8,3)=="thr";
replace  time=30 if substr(index,1,6)=="week-7" & substr(index, 8,3)=="fri";
```

Fit_irt.do (Stata codes to fit one-parameter logistic IRT model)

```
sort pattern;
gen a=(pattern==pattern[_n+1]);
keep if a==0;
drop _m Normal training IP_s a;

rename samePort y1;
rename Service y2;
rename l1_n y3;
rename t2_n y4;
gen patt=_n;
reshape long y, i(patt) j(var);
tab var,gen(d);

rename y ab;
rename patt type;

** One-parameter logistic model;
gllamm ab d1-d4, i(type) family(bin) link(logit) nrf(1)  weight(wt) nocons
adapt ;

matrix list e(b);
twoway (function y=1/(1+exp(-[ab]d1 -x)),range(0 5)pstyle(p0))
(function y=1/(1+exp(-[ab]d2 -x)),range(0 5) clpatt(dot) clwidth(thick)
pstyle(p0)) (function y=1/(1+exp(-[ab]d3 -x)),range(0 5) clpatt(dash)
clwidth(thick) pstyle(p0)) (function y=1/(1+exp(-[ab]d4 -x)),range(0 5)
clpatt(longdash) clwidth() pstyle(p0)),
legend( label(1 "Ports")label(2 "Service protocol") label(3 "Session length")
label(4 "Login time zone")) xtitle("") ytitle("") saving(test_attack,replace);
```

Profile_macro.sas (SAS codes to fit mixed model)

```
%Macro profile_macro;
%Macro IDS_Get_Mu(Infile);
data xx (keep=coef_var);
set &Infile;
coef_var= trim(estimate);
ID=1;
k=_N_;
if _N_=1;
PROC SQL NOPRINT;
    SELECT coef_var INTO:mu separated by ' ' FROM xx  ;
QUIT;
%let outMu=&mu;
run;
%mend;

%Macro IDS_Get_Phat(Infile, OutFile, InVar, OutVar);
data &Outfile (drop =temp_phat intercept);
set &Infile;
intercept=1;
temp_phat=&InVar;
&OutVar=exp(temp_phat)/(1+exp(temp_phat));
run;
%Mend;
```

continued on following page

```
%macro IDS_Get_SMR(Infile, Outfile, Groupc, Outcome,
Phat_n,Phat_D,SMR_OBS,SMR_Phat);
proc sql noprint;
create table &outfile as select &Groupc,
count(*) as total, sum(normal) as total_normal, avg(&outcome) as &Outcome,
avg(&Phat_n) as &Phat_n, avg(&Phat_D) as &phat_D, std(&Phat_n) as SD_n,
std(&Phat_D) as SD_D from &Infile where &outcome~=. & &Phat_n~=. & &Phat_D~=.
group by &Groupc;
create table &outfile as select &Groupc,
total, total_normal, &Outcome, &Phat_n, &phat_D, &outcome/&phat_n as &SMR_OBS,
&phat_n/&Phat_D as &SMR_Phat, SD_n/SD_D as STD_SMR,
(SD_n/SD_D)/sqrt(total) as SE_SMR from &Outfile;
quit;
%Mend;

%Macro IDS_Get_Tau(Infile);
data xx (keep=coef_var);
set &Infile;
coef_var= trim(estimate);
ID=1;
k=_N_;
if _N_=1;
PROC SQL NOPRINT;
    SELECT coef_var INTO:tau separated by ' ' FROM xx  ;
QUIT;
%let outTau=&tau;
run;
%mend;

%Macro IDS_Get_xbate(Infile);
data xx (keep=coef_var);
set &Infile;
coef_var=trim(effect) || '*' || '(' || trim(estimate) ||')' || '+';
ID=1;
k=_N_;
PROC SQL NOPRINT;
    SELECT coef_var INTO:xbate separated by ' ' FROM xx;
QUIT;
%let zero=0;
%let outvar=&xbate &zero;
run;
%mend;

%Macro IDS_Get_xbate_wo_Intercept(Infile);
data xx (keep=coef_var);
set &Infile;
coef_var=trim(effect) || '*' || '(' || trim(estimate) ||')' || '+';
ID=1;
k=_N_;
if _N_>1;
PROC SQL NOPRINT;
    SELECT coef_var INTO:xbate separated by ' ' FROM xx;
QUIT;
```

```
%let zero=0;
%let outvar_w=&xbate &zero;
run;
%mend;

%Macro Random_effect (infile, outcome, sub, Beta2, InVar, outRandomfile,
title_text);
%glimmix (data=&Infile,
        PROCOPT=METHOD=REML COVTEST,
        stmts=%str(class &sub;
        model &outcome=&InVar /solution;
  random  intercept &Beta2/solution subject=&sub type=un;
 ods output solutionr=&outRandomfile;),
  error=binomial, link=logit);
  Title &title_text;
run;
%Mend;

%Macro Soln_2(outfile);
data &Outfile;
set _soln;
L_95=exp(Estimate-1.96*stderr);
H_95=exp(Estimate+1.96*stderr);
OR=exp(Estimate);
CI_95=compress(round(L_95,0.01)) || "-" || compress(round(H_95,0.01));
p_value=Probt;
run;
%mend;
%mend;
```

Section III
Classifications, Profiles, and Making Better Decisions

Chapter IX
Classification Based on Supervised Learning

Whatever you are by nature, keep to it; never desert your line of talent. Be what nature intended you for and you will succeed.

- Sydney Smith

INTRODUCTION

Classification plays an important role in network security. It classifies network traffic into different categories based on the characteristics of the traffic and aims to prevent network attacks by detecting intrusion as early as possible. If a labeled response variable is available then the classification belongs to the statistically supervised learning theme. The term "supervised learning" comes from the Artificial Intelligence field where research is focused on machine learning (Nilsson, 1996). In general, a supervised learning task can be described by giving a training sample with known patterns, φ, represented by predictors, X, and a labeled response variable, Y, to select $y = (y_1, y_2, \cdots, y_g) \in Y$ values for new $x = (x_1, x_2 \ldots, x_k) \in X$ values. $Y(y_1, y_2, \ldots y_g)$ may be either a binary class, or multilevel classes, $(g > 2)$. As we discussed previously, these classes cannot be determined absolutely and they are based on the degree of our belief, which is expressed in terms of probability (Woodworth, 2004). In this chapter, we will focus mainly on the binary classification task and we will discuss several modeling approaches, including both parametric and nonparametric methods. Readers who are interested in obtaining fundamental information on supervised learning and machine learning algorithms should refer to Lane & Brodley (1997), Vapnik

(1998, 1999), Hosmer & Lemeshow (2000), Duda, Hart & Stork (2001), Hastie, Tibshirani & Friedman (2001), Müller Mika, Rätsch, Tsuda & Schölkopf (2001), Herbrich (2002), Vittinghoff, Glidden, Alpaydin (2004), Shiboski & McCulloch (2005), Maloof (2006), Neuhaus & Bunke (2007), and Diederich (2008).

GENERALIZED LINEAR METHODS

Given a sample of traffic with a known and labeled response variable, Y, and a set of predictors, $(X_1, X_2, \cdots X_k)$ a relationship of $Y = f(X, \theta)$, such as the regression function shown in Figure 9.1, can be established. Such a regression function, regardless of being linear or nonlinear, assumes that the response variable meets the assumption of following a normal distribution. When such an assumption cannot be approximately satisfied, for example, the response variable is binary or counts, or the response variable is continuous but the assumption of normality is completed unrealistic (e.g., the response variable is the failure time of a network system under a particular attack), we can use the generalized linear modeling approach. A generalized linear model (GLM) allows us to fit regression models while the response variable can follow a variety of distributions (e.g., normal, binomial, Poisson, exponential). Generally, a GLM has three components: (1) a response variable and its distribution, (2) a set of predictors, and (3) a link function that links the predictors to the response variable. In this section we will review the three important members of the family of the GLM: logistic, Poisson, and Probit regressions; each of which can be employed as powerful supervised learning procedures. For comprehensive introductions to GLM, please refer to McCullagh & Nelder (1989) and Myers, Montgomery & Vining (2002).

Logistic Regression

We discussed the multiple logistic regression models in Chapter VII, where we used them for modeling associations between the response variable and the predictor variables. Such a modeling technique can also be used for classification and has been widely used for classification in many disciplines. More specifically, we use logistic regression for binary classification and multinomial logistic regression for g-class classification ($g > 2$). Let us

Figure 9.1 Statistically supervised learning

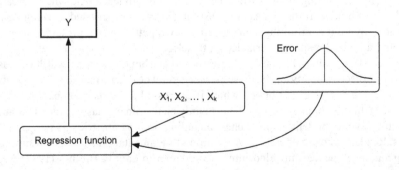

consider the binary classification task first. Recall Equations (7-6) and (7-7) of the logistic regression model described in ChapterVII:

$$\log\left[\frac{p_i}{1-p_i}\right] = \beta_0 + \beta_1 x_{i1} + \beta_2 x_{i2} + \cdots + \beta_k x_{ik}$$

$$p_i = \frac{\exp(\beta_0 + \beta_1 x_{i1} + \beta_2 x_{i2} + \cdots + \beta_k x_{ik})}{1 + \exp(\beta_0 + \beta_1 x_{i1} + \beta_2 x_{i2} + \cdots + \beta_k x_{ik})},$$

where we focused on the logit coefficient β_i ($i = 1, 2, \ldots, k$), which provides an association of each predictor variable x_i with the response variable. When we fit a logistic regression model for classification, we focus on predicting the value, p_i, generated by the predictor variables, $x_1, x_2 \ldots, x_k$, and their corresponding coefficients, $\beta_1, \beta_2 \ldots, \beta_k$, for the probability of the response variable being present for each observation. Specifically, we are interested in estimating the parameters based on a training dataset and obtaining the predictive probability having a positive response for another dataset in which the response data is unknown.

Example 9.1→Classification based on a Logistic Model. Let us use the KDD-cup training data to fit a logistic model with a labeled response variable, anomaly-free (yes/no), and the 16 variables discussed in Chapter VII. We now want to predict the membership, anomaly-free (yes/no) for all observations in the testing data. Because the predicted membership is presented by the probability of being anomaly-free and it is a continuous variable we will use a threshold of 0.5 as a classification rule. Observations with a probability of anomaly–free greater than this threshold will be classified as anomaly-free:

$$c_i = \begin{cases} 1, & p_i > 0.5 \\ 0, & p_i \le 0.5, \end{cases}$$

where c_i denotes the classification result for the ith observation, 1 for anomaly-free and 0 otherwise. The Stata codes used to conduct this classification example along with 25 randomly selected observations are shown in Displays 9.1 and 9.2. Please note that this example is similar to the data presented in Table 8.3.

Display 9.1
Stata codes for classification based logistic regression model

```
#delimit;
clear;
set mem 343434;
use F:\Book\Chapter 9\var-16-all,replace;

gen byte anomaly_free=(attack==0);
logistic anomaly_free
logged_i is_guest RST TCP UDP HTTP Duration Num_comp Count Same_srv Diff_srv
Dst_host Dst_hos1 Dst_hos3 Dst_hos4 Dst_hos5 if training==1;
predict phat;

gen byte Anomaly_free=(phat>0.5);
gen byte Matched=(anomaly_free==Anomaly_free);
set seed 14454;
gen random=invnormal(uniform());
sort training random ;
list anomaly_free phat Anomaly_free Matched if training==0 in 1/25;
```

Display 9.2
25 randomly selected observations from the testing data

	Observed	phat	Classified (phat>0.5)	Matched
1.	0	8.37e-06	0	1
2.	0	5.66e-06	0	1
3.	0	.9753929	1	0
4.	0	.0000891	0	1
5.	0	8.25e-06	0	1
6.	0	8.95e-06	0	1
7.	0	8.25e-06	0	1
8.	0	8.25e-06	0	1
9.	0	.8654925	1	0
10.	0	8.25e-06	0	1
11.	0	8.25e-06	0	1
12.	0	8.25e-06	0	1
13.	0	8.59e-06	0	1
14.	0	8.25e-06	0	1
15.	0	.0000616	0	1
16.	1	.9794738	1	1
17.	0	8.25e-06	0	1
18.	0	.9032891	1	0
19.	1	.9756885	1	1
20.	0	8.25e-06	0	1
21.	0	8.25e-06	0	1
22.	1	.9743692	1	1
23.	1	.9146771	1	1
24.	0	.8259395	1	0
25.	0	8.25e-06	0	1

In Display 9.2, columns "Observed", "phat", "Classified", and "Matched" represent the observed anomalous status (1 for anomaly-free and 0 for others), predicted probability of anomaly-free, classified group (1 for anomaly-free and 0 for others), and the agreement between observed and classified results.

Now let us extend the binary classification to a *g*-class classification ($g > 2$). Recall Equations (7-8) and (7-9) from Chapter VII, we have a multinomial logistic regression model with k predictor variables, $x_1, x_2 \ldots, x_k$, and g classes

$$\log\left(\frac{\pi_i^{(g)}}{\pi_i^{(0)}}\right) = \beta_0^{(g)} + \beta_1^{(g)} x_{i1} + \beta_{i2}^{(g)} + \ldots + \beta_{ik}^{(g)},$$

where $g = 0, 1, 2, \ldots, j$. We can obtain the predicted probabilities from each class membership as

$$\pi_i^{(g)} = \frac{\exp(\beta_0^{(g)} + \beta_1^{(g)} x_{i1} + \beta_{i2}^{(g)} + \ldots + \beta_{ik}^{(g)})}{1 + \sum_{j=1}^{g} \exp(\beta_0^{(j)} + \beta_1^{(j)} x_{i1} + \beta_{i2}^{(j)} + \ldots \beta_{ik}^{(j)})}$$

The probability of being in the reference class 0 is

$$\pi_i^{(0)} = 1 - \sum_{j=1}^{g} \pi_i^{(j)}$$

Example 9.2→Classification based on Multinomial Logistic Model. We have briefly fitted a multinomial logistic regression model based on 10% of the KDD-cup 1999 training data in Example 7.6 of Chapter VII. Now let us refit this model to estimate the parameters and then use these parameters to classify observations in the testing data into five classes: normal = 0, *probe* (surveillance and other probing) = 1, *DoS* (denial of service) = 2, *U2R* (unauthorized access to local super user [root] privileges) = 3, and *R2L* (unauthorized access from a remote machine) = 4. We will take the following steps to construct the actual classification approach.

First, for each observation in the training and testing data, we calculate the predicted probability of being in each of the response classes, g, π_i^g (g = *normal, probe, DoS, U2R,* and *R2L*). Then we assign the membership based on which class an observation belongs to by calculating the aggregated mean and its SD for each attack type, which is based on the probability of an individual observation in the training sample. Since each observation has five different predicted probabilities that correspond to five classes, in general, a predicted probability that directly links to the index choice should have the highest aggregated mean. That is, for g = normal, the mean probability of $\pi^{(normal)}$ should be higher than $\pi^{(probe)}$, $\pi^{(DoS)}$, $\pi^{(U2R)}$, and $\pi^{(R2L)}$. Therefore, in the third step we calculate a threshold that allows us to convert the predicted probability into a binary flag for each attack type in the training sample. The threshold is determined based on the average value of the predicted means, excluding the mean linked with the index attack type. For example, assuming that the index attack type is *probe* and that the predicted means of probability are 0.01, 0.40, 0.02, 0.01 and 0.02 for being a *normal, probe, DoS, U2R,* and *R2L* attack, respectively, the threshold is calculated as (0.01+0.02+0.01+0.02)/4 = 0.02. Any observation in the testing sample that has a predicted probability greater than 0.02, will be considered as a potential *probe* attack.

Table 9.1 shows the means and SDs of the predicted probability of being classified as a certain attack type by the training and testing samples. Overall, *normal, probe,* and *DoS* showed similar mean values between the training and testing samples, but *U2R* and *R2L* were 10 times greater in the training sample than in the testing sample because of new attacks that were included in the testing sample. Figure 9.2 shows the distribution of predicted means graphically. The thresholds were 0.28, 0.01, 0.13, and 0.001 for *normal, probe, DoS,* and *U2R* respectively. Since the predicted mean probability for *R2L* was 0.26, which is lower than *U2R*'s 0.45, the threshold for *R2L* was calculated based on the means of *normal, probe,* and *DoS* without *U2R*.

Poisson Regression

Sometimes we may classify traffic data based on incidence and frequency (Stallings, 2003; Zhou & Lang, 2003). We may want to know how frequently an abnormal event occurred within a given time period, for example, we may want to estimate the incidence rate of an *R2L* attack daily within an organization and also take into account the system characteristics. Using such incidence information, we can conduct risk assessment on the network system. Poisson regression provides such a method for us to model the count and incidence rate. Moreover, when we only have the aggregated data, such as the total number of connections, or the number of connections that are anomalous, at the system, group, site, or user level, we cannot fit the logistic regression model with the aggregated data but we may be able to fit the data through a Poisson model.

Poisson regression models the number of occurrences of an event by using the maximum-likelihood regression approach. The response variable of a Poisson regression model is a nonnegative count variable and the predictor variables can be categorical, binary or continuous. There are two essential concepts related to the Poisson models: the exposure size, E, and incidence rate, ρ. The exposure size is the total number of observations at risk (of being anomalous); it can be divided into k subintervals, where $E_1 + E_2 + \cdots + E_k = E$. The incidence rate is the rate at which events occur, and can be multiplied by the exposure size to obtain the expected number of observed events, for example, 10 *DoS* attacks per day, 10 spam every 1000 emails, etc. An incidence rate of 10 *DoS* attacks per day multiplied by an exposure time of a week equals 70 *DoS* attacks per week.

Let us assume that over very small exposures, ε, the probability of finding more than one event is small compared to ε, and the non-overlapping exposures are mutually independent. The incidence rate, ρ_i, for the ith observation within the jth subinterval and the expected number of events, c_j, can be estimated form a Poisson regression model as

$$\rho_i = e^{\beta_0 + \beta_1 x_{1i} + \beta_2 x_{2i} + \cdots + \beta_k x_{ki}}, \text{ and} \tag{9-1}$$

$$c_i = E_i e^{\beta_0 + \beta_1 x_{1i} + \beta_2 x_{2i} + \cdots + \beta_k x_{ki}}, \tag{9-2}$$

respectively.

Table 9.1. Predicted mean values based on the multinomial logistic regression model

Attack Types	Training		Testing	
	Mean	SD	Mean	SD
Predicted probability for normal				
Legitimate users (normal)	**0.97**	**0.10**	0.97	0.13
Surveillance and other probing (probe)	0.22	0.27	0.21	0.32
Denial of service (DoS)	0.00	0.05	0.06	0.17
Unauthorized access to local super user (root) privileges (U2R)	0.38	0.41	0.57	0.30
Unauthorized access from a remote machine (R2L)	0.52	0.35	0.95	0.18
Predicted probability for probe				
Legitimate users (normal)	0.01	0.05	0.01	0.04
Surveillance and other probing (probe)	**0.50**	**0.28**	0.43	0.32
Denial of service (DoS)	0.00	0.04	0.02	0.07
Unauthorized access to local super user (root) privileges (U2R)	0.02	0.13	0.01	0.05
Unauthorized access from a remote machine (R2L)	0.01	0.05	0.01	0.04
Predicted probability for DoS				
Legitimate users (normal)	0.02	0.07	0.02	0.12
Surveillance and other probing (probe)	0.27	0.26	0.34	0.26
Denial of service (DoS)	**0.99**	**0.06**	0.92	0.19
Unauthorized access to local super user (root) privileges (U2R)	0.03	0.12	0.28	0.22
Unauthorized access from a remote machine (R2L)	0.21	0.31	0.23	0.11
Predicted probability for U2R				
Legitimate users (normal)	0.00	0.00	0.00	0.00
Surveillance and other probing (probe)	0.00	0.00	0.00	0.00
Denial of service (DoS)	0.00	0.00	0.00	0.00
Unauthorized access to local super user (root) privileges (U2R)	**0.11**	**0.14**	0.01	0.04
Unauthorized access from a remote machine (R2L)	0.01	0.02	0.00	0.01
Predicted probability for R2L				
Legitimate users (normal)	0.01	0.05	0.00	0.03
Surveillance and other probing (probe)	0.01	0.02	0.02	0.07
Denial of service (DoS)	0.00	0.00	0.00	0.00
Unauthorized access to local super user (root) privileges (U2R)	0.45	0.34	0.12	0.25
Unauthorized access from a remote machine (R2L)	**0.26**	**0.20**	0.02	0.09

SD denotes standard deviation

Figure 9.2. Mean predicted probabilities of anomaly by attack types and samples

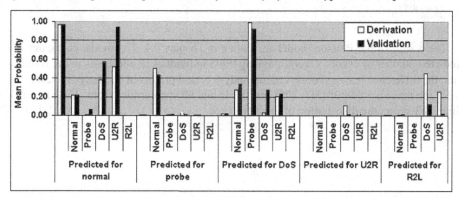

Example 9.3→Classification based on Poisson Model. Let us use the MIT-DARPA data to fit a Poisson regression model that aims to estimate the incidence rate of anomalous events at the user-level, taking into account the site-level characteristics. The following Stata codes given in Display 9.3 first convert the data from the unit of individual connection to the site-level, and then fit the Poisson model and conduct classification based on the Poisson model.

Display 9.3
Stata codes to fit a Poisson regression model

```
#delimit;
clear;
set mem 854566;
use F:\Book\Chapter 9\temp.dta, clear;
gen byte normal=(attack=="-");
drop v13 score;

do create_var.do; /* Appendix CH8 */;
gen total=1;

/*--------------------------------------------------------
 Converts data to site (IP address) level
-------------------------------------------------*/;
collapse (sum) total normal t2 l1 udp icmp samePort sameIP http smtp
urp ecr eco snmp ftp port domain telnet finger,by(IP_s);

gen t2_rate=t2/total;
gen l1_rate=l1/total;
gen udp_rate=udp/total;
gen icmp_rate=icmp/total;
gen smPt_rate=samePort/total;
gen smIP_rate=sameIP/total;
gen http_rate=http/total;
gen smtp_rate=smtp/total;
gen urp_rate=urp/total;
gen ecr_rate=ecr/total;
gen eco_rate=eco/total;
gen snmp_rate=snmp/total;
gen ftp_rate=ftp/total;
gen port_rate=port/total;
gen dom_rate=domain/total;
gen tel_rate=telnet/total;

poisson normal
t2_rate l1_rate udp_rate icmp_rate smPt_rate smIP_rate http_rate smtp_rate
urp_rate ecr_rate eco_rate snmp_rate ftp_rate port_rate dom_rate tel_rate
,exposure(total) irr;
predict hat;
gen diff=normal-hat;
sum diff,d;
```

The results of the Poisson model are shown in Display 9.4. The model calculates the predicted number of events. Overall, among 9008 individual IP addresses in the training data, the difference between observed anomaly-free and predicted anomaly-free events is small, the mean is <0.0001 (SD=205) and the 1st and 99th percentiles from -11.6 to -0.003. Figure 9.3 shows the distribution of the difference.

Display 9.4
Results of the fitted Poisson regression model

```
Iteration 0:   log likelihood = -9643642.1
Iteration 1:   log likelihood = -652260.12
Iteration 2:   log likelihood = -240587.36
Iteration 3:   log likelihood = -60207.695
Iteration 4:   log likelihood = -47774.751
Iteration 5:   log likelihood = -47396.67
Iteration 6:   log likelihood = -47395.032
Iteration 7:   log likelihood = -47395.027
Iteration 8:   log likelihood = -47395.027

Poisson regression                        Number of obs   =       9008
                                          LR chi2(16)     = 1977088.08
                                          Prob > chi2     =     0.0000
Log likelihood = -47395.027               Pseudo R2       =     0.9542

------------------------------------------------------------------------------
    normal |       IRR   Std. Err.      z    P>|z|     [95% Conf. Interval]
-----------+------------------------------------------------------------------
   t2_rate |   1.70016   .0266979    33.80   0.000     1.64863      1.7533
   l1_rate |  .3241466    .019412   -18.81   0.000    .2882478    .3645164
  udp_rate |  216.7056   24.46017    47.65   0.000    173.6971    270.3632
 icmp_rate |  13.85629   1.465235    24.86   0.000    11.26254    17.04737
  smPt_rate |  .5179785   .0123033   -27.69   0.000    .4944172    .5426627
 smIP_rate |   2.5e+240   1.6e+241    87.58   0.000    1.0e+235    6.0e+245
 http_rate |  362.9657   40.51093    52.81   0.000    291.6502    451.7196
 smtp_rate |  319.1102   37.31813    49.30   0.000     253.745    401.3136
   urp_rate |  .0000178   7.80e-06   -24.99   0.000    7.56e-06    .000042
   ecr_rate |  .7144712   .0525877    -4.57   0.000    .6184908    .8253464
   eco_rate |  14.11164   1.037182    36.01   0.000    12.21844    16.29819
  snmp_rate |  2.552457   .0696585    34.34   0.000    2.419516    2.692702
   ftp_rate |  329.4349   36.67029    52.08   0.000    264.8623    409.7502
  port_rate |  3.883038   .4431289    11.89   0.000    3.104797     4.85635
   dom_rate |  3.569159   .1069739    42.45   0.000    3.365533    3.785105
   tel_rate |  52.11694   7.515369    27.42   0.000    39.28565    69.13913
     total |  (exposure)
------------------------------------------------------------------------------
```

```
                                diff
-------------------------------------------------------------------
      Percentiles      Smallest
 1%    -11.62056      -8601.926
 5%    -.9983751      -5248.102
10%    -.9668419      -3981.455     Obs                  9008
25%    -.0091963      -2243.316     Sum of Wgt.          9008

50%    -.0091963                    Mean             9.47e-08
                       Largest      Std. Dev.        205.0052
75%    -.0091963       4478.735
90%    -.0030654       4795.094     Variance         42027.14
95%    -.0030654       6970.871     Skewness         7.527439
99%    -.0030654       9520.645     Kurtosis         1155.876
```

Probit Regression

Probit regression, proposed by Bliss in 1935, is another widely used method for modeling binary response data. Probit regression and logistic regression are similar to each other; probit uses the cumulative normal probability distribution and logistic uses log odds that an observation falls into one category of Y versus another. Similar to the logistic model, the response variable for a probit model has to be binary and the predictor variables can be binary, ordinal or continuous. Let y_i, which has a value of 1 or 0, be the response variable for the ith observation ($i = 1, 2, ..., n$), and p_i be the probability that $y_i = 1$, for k predictor

Figure 9.3 Distribution of difference between observed and predicted anomaly-free events

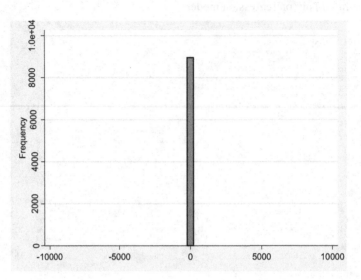

variables $x_1, x_2, \ldots, x_k$ represented by X. A probit model is defined as

$$\Pr(y_i \neq 0 \mid X) = \Phi(\beta_0 + \beta_1 x_1 + \beta_2 x_2 + \cdots + \beta_k x_k), \qquad (9\text{-}3)$$

where Φ is the cumulative distribution function of the standard normal distribution. We estimate the coefficients with the maximum likelihood method. By comparing equations (9-3) and (7-6), we know that the difference between the probit and logistic models is the distribution of errors. The probit model assumes a normal distribution of errors, while the logit model assumes a logistic distribution of errors.

Example 9.4→Classification based on Probit Model. Let us use the KDD-cup 1999 data with the 16-variable identified from Chapter VII to fit both logit and probit models, and compare the classification results yielded by the two models. We first use the training dataset to estimate the parameters for each model and then use them to calculate the predicted probabilities of being an anomaly for each observation in the testing dataset. Because we have two sets of parameters representing two models, each observation has two predicted probabilities, *bitphat* and *logphat*, denoted as the probit and logistic models, respectively. The Stata codes to accomplish this task and the Stata output are shown in Displays 9.5 and 9.6, separately.

Display 9.5
Stata codes to fit probit and logistic regression models

```
/*-------------------------------------------------
Probit model
-----------------------------------------------*/;
probit attack logged_i is_guest RST TCP UDP HTTP Duration Num_comp Count
Same_srv Diff_srv Dst_host Dst_hos1 Dst_hos3 Dst_hos4 Dst_hos5 if training==1;
predict bitphat;

/*----------------------------------------------------
 Logit model
---------------------------------------------------*/;
logistic attack logged_i is_guest RST TCP UDP HTTP Duration Num_comp Count
Same_srv Diff_srv Dst_host Dst_hos1 Dst_hos3 Dst_hos4 Dst_hos5 if training==1;
predict logphat;
```

Display 9.6
Results of probit and logistic regression models

```
/*-------------------------------------------------------
 Probit model
-----------------------------------------------------*/;

Probit regression                          Number of obs   =     494021
                                           LR chi2(16)     =  453656.41
                                           Prob > chi2     =     0.0000
Log likelihood = -18250.546                Pseudo R2       =     0.9255

--------------------------------------------------------------------------
    attack |    Coef.    Std. Err.      z     P>|z|    [95% Conf. Interval]
-----------+--------------------------------------------------------------
  logged_i | -.2299707   .0248003    -9.27   0.000    -.2785784   -.1813631
  is_guest |  1.174585   .0533955    22.00   0.000     1.069932    1.279238
       RST |  2.608887   .0777201    33.57   0.000     2.456559    2.761216
       TCP | -.3782921   .036563    -10.35   0.000    -.4499543    -.30663
       UDP | -1.419548   .0370179   -38.35   0.000    -1.492102   -1.346994
      HTTP |  .3122213   .0258095    12.10   0.000     .2616355    .3628071
  Duration | -.0643548   .003265    -19.71   0.000    -.0707541   -.0579555
  Num_comp |  .0113948   .0015724     7.25   0.000     .0083131    .0144766
     Count |  1.996691   .0450813    44.29   0.000     1.908333    2.085048
  Same_srv | -1.092921   .0208121   -52.51   0.000    -1.133712    -1.05213
  Diff_srv | -.1684544   .0048552   -34.70   0.000    -.1779705   -.1589383
  Dst_host |  .3769351   .0070957    53.12   0.000     .3630278    .3908423
  Dst_hos1 | -.6639935   .0129183   -51.40   0.000    -.6893129   -.6386741
  Dst_hos3 | -.1359976   .0052953   -25.68   0.000    -.1463763    -.125619
  Dst_hos4 |  .537476    .0143442    37.47   0.000     .5093618    .5655902
  Dst_hos5 |  .1522685   .0034806    43.75   0.000     .1454467    .1590904
      _cons |  3.162269   .0666186    47.47   0.000     3.031699    3.292839
--------------------------------------------------------------------------

. predict bitphat;
(option p assumed; Pr(attack))

/*----------------------------------------------------------
 Logit model
--------------------------------------------------------*/;

Logistic regression                        Number of obs   =     494021
                                           LR chi2(16)     =  453454.54
                                           Prob > chi2     =     0.0000
Log likelihood = -18351.483                Pseudo R2       =     0.9251
```

continued on following page

Display 9.6 continued

```
----------------------------------------------------------------------
   attack | Odds Ratio  Std. Err.      z    P>|z|    [95% Conf. Interval]
----------+-----------------------------------------------------------
 logged_i |  .7052227    .0337212    -7.30   0.000    .6421328    .7745111
 is guest |  8.65386     .7765311    24.05   0.000    7.25821    10.31787
      RST |  108.6071   16.14184     31.54   0.000    81.16108   145.3346
      TCP |  .6884878    .0463639    -5.54   0.000    .6033579    .785629
      UDP |  .0777619    .0055668   -35.68   0.000    .0675821    .0894751
     HTTP |  1.630797    .0855891     9.32   0.000    1.471385    1.80748
 Duration |  .8950696    .0056617   -17.53   0.000    .8840414    .9062354
 Num comp |  1.029267    .0079397     3.74   0.000    1.013823    1.044947
    Count |  87.48874    7.656162    51.10   0.000    73.69929   103.8583
 Same_srv |  .1252268    .0054335   -47.88   0.000    .1150177    .1363422
 Diff_srv |  .7263038    .0072585   -32.00   0.000    .7122158    .7406705
 Dst_host |  2.167089    .0336008    49.88   0.000    2.102223    2.233956
 Dst_hos1 |  .2885484    .0076743   -46.73   0.000    .2738923    .3039886
 Dst_hos3 |  .7497863    .0085298   -25.31   0.000    .7332531    .7666921
 Dst_hos4 |  3.362365    .0966901    42.17   0.000    3.178098    3.557316
 Dst_hos5 |  1.364228    .0096948    43.71   0.000    1.345359    1.383363
----------------------------------------------------------------------

. predict logphat;
(option p assumed; Pr(attack))
```

The comparisons of the results are shown in Table 9.2. We used the sensitivity, specificity, and correctly classified rate to evaluate the classification results obtained from two models. These measurements are standard measurements for assessing the goodness of classification (Pepe, 2002). We will examine them in greater detail in Chapter XII.

NONPARAMETRIC METHODS

In this section, we are going to discuss three nonparametric classification techniques, k-nearest neighbor (KNN), Naïve Bayesian approach, and classification regression trees. KNN uses the majority vote in similarity to decide a classification result. The general principle of KNN is to find the k data points in the training sample to determine the k-nearest neighbors based on a distance measure. Naïve Bayesian approach, also called Naïve Bayes Classifier, is a simple probability-based classification algorithm using Bayes' theorem. Tree methods are nonparametric and nonlinear. The key element of a tree algorithm is a set of logical conditions that determine and split the tree, and there is no need for any assumptions on the underlying relationships between the predictor variables and the response variable. Detailed mathematical and methodological contexts about these nonparametric classification techniques are beyond the scope of this book, but, we have provided references for readers who are interested in obtaining more detailed information about these methods and

Table 9.2 Compared classification results yielded from probit and logistic models varied by different thresholds

Measure of classification	Threshold=0.4		Threshold=0.5		Threshold=0.6	
	Logistic	Probit	Logistic	Probit	Logistic	Probit
Sensitivity	0.9148	0.9139	0.9133	0.9122	0.9120	0.9087
Specificity	0.9455	0.9515	0.9529	0.9598	0.9600	0.9668
Correctly classified rate	0.9208	0.9212	0.9212	0.9215	0.9213	0.9200

Figure 9.4 Classification results between logistic and probit models

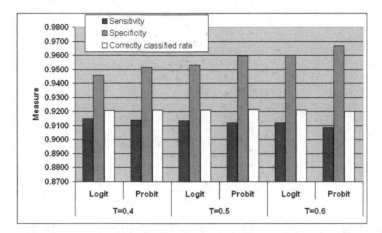

their applications: Shakhnarovish, Darrell & Indyk (2005) for KNN, McCallum & Nigam (1998), DuMouchel (1999), Rish (2001), Barbard, Wu & Jajodia (2001), Congdon (2002), Mozina, Demsar, Kattan & Zupan (2004), for Naïve Bayesian, and Breiman, Friedman, Olshen & Stone (1983), Li & Ye (2003), Amor, Benferhat & Elouedi (2004) for the decision tree method. In the following sections, we will examine how to apply these methods for classifying network traffic.

k-Nearest Neighbor Classification

The K-nearest neighbor classification algorithm aims to assign a membership to an observation based on the simple idea that similar observations belong in similar categories. Unlike the logistic regression, which classifies observations by estimating the probabilities of being in each category based on the training data, KNN uses training data to classify observations directly without estimating any probabilistic structure. Other classification algorithms, such as, linear discriminant functions, support vector machines, neural networks, and decision trees, also use this approach.

Let $p_i (i = 1, 2, \ldots n)$ denote the ith observation with k variables, $p_i = (x_1, x_2, \ldots x_k)$, and let $D = \{p_1, p_2, \cdots, p_n\}$ denote an k-dimensional space. In the procedure of KNN classification, we first position each observation in the training data to be a data point in the D space based on the values of its k variables. Because we know the membership that each observation belongs to, we can label each point with its class. Thus, each observation in the training data has two attributes: its position in D and the membership of its class. For a new observation, $q = (x_1^q, x_2^q, \ldots x_k^q)$, with a unknown membership, we first position it into the D space so we have, $D = \{q, p_1, p_2, \ldots p_n\}$. We then measure the distance

$$d_j \sim (p_i, q), \ j = 1, 2, \ldots m$$

Figure 9.5 Two new data points (circle) with their K-nearest neighborhood regions

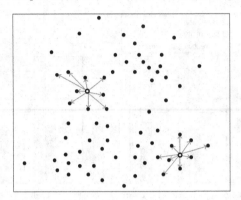

between q and the ith pre-existing point, p_i, which is within the K nearest neighborhood region, $D_K = \{q, p_1, p_2, \ldots p_K\}$. Since we know the memberships of each of the K nearest pre-existing points, $p_1, p_2, \ldots, p_k$, we can assign a membership to q based on the majority memberships of $p_1, p_2, \ldots, p_k$ (Figure 9.5). If there is no majority existing, q is considered inconclusive. The determination of K can be challenging—it is sensitive to the accuracy of classification, and should be a small, odd value in order to reduce the misclassification rate.

We define the term "nearest neighbor," based on distance functions. The most widely used distance function is the Euclidean distance:

$$d(p_i, q_j) = \sqrt{\sum_{c=1}^{k} (x_{ci} - x_{cj})^2} \tag{9-4}$$

where k represents the number of variables for each point. Other measures include the absolute distance or City-block

$$d(p_i, q_j) = \sum_{c=1}^{k} |x_{ci} - x_{cj}|, \tag{9-5}$$

the squared Euclidean distance

$$d(p_i, q_j) = \sum_{c=1}^{k} (x_{ci} - y_{cj})^2, \tag{9-6}$$

and the maximum-value distance or Chebychev

$$d(p_i, q_j) = \max_{c=1,2,\cdots,k} |x_{ci} - x_{cj}|. \tag{9-7}$$

Any points within the neighborhood region, $D_K = \{q, p_1, p_2, \ldots p_K\}$, have four basic properties: (1) $d(p,q) \geq 0$, meaning the distance is always greater than or equal to zero, (2) $d(p,q) = 0$ if and only if $p = q$, (3) $d(p,q) = d(q,p)$, q and p are exchangeable, and (4) $d(p,q) + d(q,p) \geq d(p,Z)$, representative of a triangle inequality.

The KNN classification is based on the intuitive assumption that observations close to each other are more similar, and that a new observation is most likely to belong to the pre-existing point that satisfies the condition, $\min(d_1, d_2 \ldots d_K)$. Thus, we can assign a weight, w_j, in the process of membership assessments:

$$w_j = \frac{\dfrac{1}{e^{d_j}}}{\displaystyle\sum_{j=1}^{K} \dfrac{1}{e^{d_j}}}. \tag{9-8}$$

Equation (9-8) weighs the contributions of the neighbors based on their relative close-ness to q, therefore the nearer neihhbors contribute more to the membership of q than the more distant ones.

Example 9.4→k-Nearest Neighbor Classification. Let us use the spam-email data to fit a KNN model with the SAS procedure, *PROC DISCRIM,* which replaces the old version of *PROC NEIGHBOR.* We first randomly divide the spam-email data into two subsets, a training sample and a testing sample. We then use the training data to fit the KNN model using *PROC DISCRIM* with *METHOD = MPAR* and *K =* options, where the choice *K* is specified. As we mentioned earlier, *K* should be a small odd number. We will show the association of different *K* values with the accuracy of classification. The following SAS codes are given in Display 9.7 complete the analysis, and the corresponding results are shown in Display 9.8.

Display 9.7
SAS codes for k-nearest neighbor analysis

```
/*-------------------------------------------------------------------
Nonparametric discrimination: k-Nearest-Neighbor Method
-----------------------------------------------------------*/;
libname KNN 'F:\Book\Chapter 9\';
data spam;
set knn.spam;
training=( UNIFORM(12345)>0.5);
run;

data training testing;
set spam;
if training=1 then output training;
else output testing;
run;
proc freq data=spam;
table v58*training;
run;

proc discrim data =training method=npar k=3 pool=yes metric=full testdata=testing
testout=result;
class v58;
var v1-v57;
run;

proc freq data=result;
table _into_*v58;
run;
```

Display 9.8
SAS output of the for k-nearest neighbor analysis

```
            The SAS System         20:51 Tuesday, July 24, 2007  30

                   The FREQ Procedure

                Table of v58 by training

            v58        training

            Frequency,
            Percent  ,
            Row Pct  ,
            Col Pct  ,      0,      1,  Total
            ƒƒƒƒƒƒƒƒƒˆƒƒƒƒƒƒƒƒˆƒƒƒƒƒƒƒƒˆ
               0 ,   1398 ,   1390 ,   2788
                 ,  30.38 ,  30.21 ,  60.60
                 ,  50.14 ,  49.86 ,
                 ,  60.47 ,  60.73 ,
            ƒƒƒƒƒƒƒƒƒˆƒƒƒƒƒƒƒƒˆƒƒƒƒƒƒƒƒˆ
               1 ,    914 ,    899 ,   1813
                 ,  19.87 ,  19.54 ,  39.40
                 ,  50.41 ,  49.59 ,
                 ,  39.53 ,  39.27 ,
            ƒƒƒƒƒƒƒƒƒˆƒƒƒƒƒƒƒƒˆƒƒƒƒƒƒƒƒˆ
            Total     2312     2289     4601
                      50.25    49.75   100.00

            The SAS System         20:51 Tuesday, July 24, 2007  31

                  The DISCRIM Procedure

        Observations   2289      DF Total            2288
        Variables        57      DF Within Classes   2287
        Classes           2      DF Between Classes     1


                  Class Level Information

              Variable                                       Prior
     v58      Name     Frequency     Weight   Proportion  Probability

      0      _0          1390         1390     0.607252    0.500000
      1      _1           899      899.0000    0.392748    0.500000

            The SAS System         20:51 Tuesday, July 24, 2007  32

                   The DISCRIM Procedure
     Classification Summary for Calibration Data: WORK.TRAINING
        Resubstitution Summary using 3 Nearest Neighbors

                  Squared Distance Function

               2                    -1
              D (X,Y) = (X-Y)' COV   (X-Y)

       Posterior Probability of Membership in Each v58
```

continued on following page

Display 9.8 continued

```
        m (X) = Proportion of obs in group k in 3
         k        nearest neighbors of X

       Pr(j|X) = m (X) PRIOR  / SUM ( m (X) PRIOR  )
                  j       j   k    k         k

   Number of Observations and Percent Classified into v58

      From v58            0              1          Total

           0           1332             58           1390
                      95.83           4.17         100.00

           1             81            818            899
                       9.01          90.99         100.00

       Total           1413            876           2289
                      61.73          38.27         100.00

      Priors            0.5            0.5


              Error Count Estimates for v58

                         0              1          Total

      Rate            0.0417         0.0901         0.0659
      Priors          0.5000         0.5000

            The SAS System        20:51 Tuesday, July 24, 2007   33

                    The DISCRIM Procedure
      Classification Summary for Test Data: WORK.TESTING
      Classification Summary using 3 Nearest Neighbors

                  Squared Distance Function

                    2                  -1
              D (X,Y) = (X-Y)' COV  (X-Y)

      Posterior Probability of Membership in Each v58

        m (X) = Proportion of obs in group k in 3
         k        nearest neighbors of X

       Pr(j|X) = m (X) PRIOR  / SUM ( m (X) PRIOR  )
                  j       j   k    k         k

   Number of Observations and Percent Classified into v58

      From v58            0              1          Total

           0           1288            110           1398
                      92.13           7.87         100.00

           1            160            754            914
                      17.51          82.49         100.00

       Total           1448            864           2312
                      62.63          37.37         100.00

      Priors            0.5            0.5
```

continued on following page

Display 9.8 continued

```
              Error Count Estimates for v58

                        0           1        Total

     Rate             0.0787      0.1751     0.1269
     Priors           0.5000      0.5000


         The SAS System        20:51 Tuesday, July 24, 2007   34

                  The FREQ Procedure

             Table of _INTO_ by v58

                _INTO_     v58
        Frequency,
        Percent  ,
        Row Pct  ,
        Col Pct  ,       0,        1,   Total
                 fffffffff'ffffffff'ffffffff'
               0 ,    1288 ,     160 ,    1448
                 ,   55.71 ,    6.92 ,   62.63
                 ,   88.95 ,   11.05 ,
                 ,   92.13 ,   17.51 ,
                 fffffffff'ffffffff'ffffffff'
               1 ,     110 ,     754 ,     864
                 ,    4.76 ,   32.61 ,   37.37
                 ,   12.73 ,   87.27 ,
                 ,    7.87 ,   82.49 ,
                 fffffffff'ffffffff'ffffffff'
           Total      1398       914      2312
                     60.47     39.53    100.00
```

The randomly selected training dataset includes 2289 emails (49.8% of the total), of which 39.3% (n=899) are spam-email, and the testing dataset has 2312 e-mails (50.2% of the total), of which 39.5% (n=914) are spam-emails. The *DISCRIM* procedure with *K* - 3 classifies 818 of 899 spam-emails and 1332 of 1390 non-spam emails correctly. The observed misclassification rate for the training data is (81 + 58) / 2289 = 0.0607, or 6.1%. Using the parameters obtained from the training data to assign a membership to the 2312 data points in the testing data, we obtain 82.5% (754 of 914) accuracy in spam-emails and 92.1% (1288 of 1398) accuracy in non-spam emails. The overall misclassification rate for the testing data is 11.7%, a substantial increase of 5.6% from the training data. Table 9.2 shows that the classification results vary by different *K* values and Figure 9.6 displays the results graphically. It seems that *K* - 3 shows the highest correctly classified rate but also provides an unbalance of sensitivity and specificity. As we mentioned previously we will examine sensitivity and specificity in greater detail in Chapter XII.

The KNN algorithm has several good attributes. It is simple to implement and use, easy to explain its predictions, and robust for noisy data by averaging k-nearest neighbors. On the other hand, the algorithm also has several disadvantages. For example, it does demand a large memory space to store all the sample data, and it takes more time to classify a new data point than in a regression model. This is because it needs to calculate and compare the distance from the data point to all other existing points within the neighbor range.

Naïve Bayesian Classifier

The Naïve Bayesian Classifier (NBC) aims to predict the probability of class membership for each observation based on Bayes' Theorem. We use the term conditional probability as an event, Y, occurring when it is known that an event, X, has occurred. We denote this phenomenon as $P(Y \mid X)$ and read it as probability of, Y, given X,

$$P(Y/X) = \frac{P(X \cap Y)}{P(X)} \quad \text{if } P(X) > 0, \tag{9-9}$$

where $X \cap Y$ is the intersection of the two events, X and Y, (Figure 9.7). Equation (9-9) indicates that if the events, Y, and X, can both occur, then the probability of such an occurrence is equal to the probability of the X occurrence multiplied by the probability of Y, given that X occurs,

$$P(X \cap Y) = P(X)P(Y/X). \tag{9-10}$$

Let $\{Y_1, Y_2, \ldots, Y_k\}$ be a set of events forming a partition of the sample space D, where $P(Y_i) \neq 0$ for $i = 1, 2, \ldots, k$, and X be any event in D such that $P(X) \neq 0$. Then, for $j = 1, 2, \ldots, k$, the Bayes rule is

$$P(Y_j \mid X) = \frac{P(Y_j \cap X)}{\sum\limits_{i=1}^{k} P(Y_i \cap X)} = \frac{P(Y_j)P(X \mid Y_j)}{\sum\limits_{i=1}^{k} P(Y_i)P(X \mid Y_i)}. \tag{9-11}$$

Readers who would like to gain more background in Bayes' Theorem should refer to textbooks on general probability theory, such as, Mendenhall & Beaver (1991), Ash, (1993), Stirzaker (1999), Ross (2002), and Ghahramani (2005).

Example 9.6→Naïve Bayesian Classifier for Spam-email. The Bayes rule enables the calculation of the likelihood of event Y given that X has happened. We can use this attribute in text classification to determine the probability of an email being classified as spam by looking at the frequencies of some specific words in that email. Overton (2004) demonstrates the use of NBC for detecting email malware (e.g., viruses, trojans, worms). He reported that an NBC-based text filtering could accurately identify worms and viruses, such as W32.Bagle, and that it is able to spot even mutated versions of the worms without giving the classifier any special knowledge of viruses.

Example 9.7→Naïve Bayesian Classifier for Network Traffic. R has an NBC function, *naiveBayes*, developed by David Meyer, which allows us to fit a Naïve Bayesian model that computes the conditional posterior probabilities of a categorical response variable given independent predictor variables using the Bayes rule. Let us use the KDD-cup training data to illustrate how we can fit such a model. Because the *naiveBayes* function is included in the *e1071* package, we have to install and load this package before we can fit the model.

Table 9.2 Association of change in K with the accuracy of classification

Measure of classification	k=3	k=5	k=7	k=9
Sensitivity	0.8249	0.9004	0.8818	0.8589
Specificity	0.9213	0.8512	0.8805	0.8956
Correctly classified rate	0.8832	0.8707	0.8811	0.8811

Figure 9.6 Sensitivity, specificity and correctly classified rate by different k values

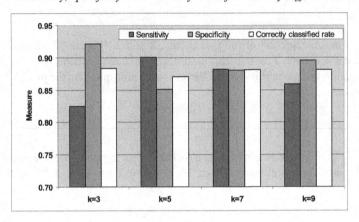

Figure 9.7 Intersection of two events, X and Y

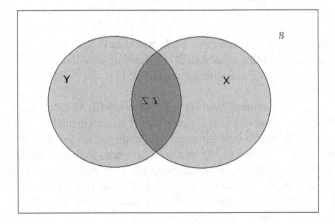

Display 9.9 lists the R codes to fit the model. Note that we only use six binary variables: logged_i, is_guest, RST, TCP, UDP, and HTTP, as the predictor variables. The response variable is attack (yes/no).

Display 9.9
R codes for fitting a Naïve Bayesian model

```
install.packages('e1071')
library('e1071')
library(kernlab)
KDD<-read.table("F:\\book\\Chapter 9\\KDD_16_val_r.txt",header=TRUE,sep = ",")
data(KDD)
## Keep the first 6 variables and the response variable
KDD_6<-KDD[,c(1,2,3,4,5,6,17)]
## create training and testing datasets
set.seed(1234)
index <- sample(1:dim(KDD_6)[1])
KDDtrain <-KDD_6[index[1:floor(2*dim(KDD_6)[1]/3)],]
KDDtest <-KDD_6[index[((2*ceiling(dim(KDD_6)[1]/3))+1):dim(KDD_6)[1]],]
#Fit the Naive Bayes model
NBC <- naiveBayes(attack ~ ., data=KDDtrain)
predict(NBC, KDDtrain[,-7])
#Classification based on the training data
traing <- predict(NBC, KDDtrain[,-7])
table(train, KDDtrain$attack)
#Classification based on the testing data
test <- predict(NBC, KDDtest[,-7])
```

Display 9.10 illustrates the classification results. The training data includes 207352 observations of which 92.7% ((153151+39061)/207352) were correctly classified by the NBC, and the testing data includes 103675 observations of which 92.7% ((76521+19565)/103675) were correctly classified. The misclassification rates for both training and testing samples are the same, 0.073 or 7.3%.

Display 9.10
Results of the Naïve Bayesian model

```
train      Anomaly  Normal
   Anomaly  153151    1321
   Normal    13819   39061

Test       Anomaly  Normal
   Anomaly   76521     645
   Normal     6944   19565
```

The NBC has a strong independent assumption, which states that the values of the attributes of an example are independent given the class of the example. This assumption is difficult to meet in practice, therefore such an independent assumption is a key weakness of the Naïve Bayesian approach. However, NBC also has several strengths, including high performance—it has comparable performance with decision tree and selected neural network classifiers. It also has a self-learning capability—each training example can incrementally increase or decrease the probability that a hypothesis is correct, meaning prior knowledge can be combined with observed data.

Regression Trees

The tree-based classification is a child of the computer age. Classification based on trees has been increasingly employed in network security (Hossain, 2002; Li & Ye, 2003; Abbes, Bouhoula & Rusinowitch, 2004; Chen, Abraham & Yang, 2007; Minaei-Bidgoli, Analoui, Shahhoseini & Rezvani, 2007). In this section, we will examine the regression tree method that classifies subjects through a process known as binary recursive partitioning, where the data is split into partitions and then split again on each of the branches. In the early 1960s, Morgan and Sonquist (1963) first began using regression trees at the University of Michigan. A decade later, Breiman and Friedman independently began to use the tree methods in classification; Olshen and Stone joined and contributed, and the Classification and Regression Trees (CART) method was created (Breiman, Friedman, Olshen & Stone, 1983).

CART is a binary tree analysis that belongs to the family of nonparametric regression methods and is based on the recursive partitioning method. It constructs a binary tree that is free of distributional assumptions and works with both continuous and categorical variables. Each node of the tree is split into two children nodes, in which the original node is labeled as a parent node. The term "recursive" refers to the fact that the binary partitioning process is applied repeatedly to reach a given number of splits. In general, we start with full data and split the data into groups. We repeat the process until data in all groups are no longer to be split, that is, the terminal nodes are too small or too few to be split. There is no further pruning or amalgamation of small groups is possible. Finally, we display the results, the tree, graphically. Any numeric predictive variables are divided into $X \leq a$ and $X > a$; where a is a threshold value used to split the data. The maximum level that a tree can grow to is $2^{(m-1)} - 1$, where m is the number of groups. Figure 9.8 shows a popular example of CART that has been used widely to illustrate the concept of how the classification and regression tree model works. In that figure, the response variable is "Species" (the species of Iris) that has three classes, Setosa, Versicolor, and Virginica. We can see from the tree that if the value of the predictor variable "Petal length" is less than or equal to 2.45, the species is classified as "Setosa". If the petal length is greater than 2.45, then additional splits are required to classify the species further.

In general, let D be a sample of network traffic with a size of n observations and a set of variables, $X = (x_1, x_2, ..., x_k)$. Assume observations can be classified into g groups, where $n_1 + n_2 + \cdots + n_g = n$, and let C be the set of groups, $C = (c_1, c_2, ..., c_g)$. A systematic way of predicting a class membership is to find a classification rule that assigns the class membership in C for every variable, x, in X. Our goal is to find a tree that has terminal nodes that are relatively "pure" (i.e., the tree contains observations that almost all belong to the same class). For regression tree problems, node purity is usually defined in terms of the sums-of-squares deviation within each node. Using the tree shown in Figure 9.8 as an example, there are three tasks to keep in mind when constructing a regression tree: (1) the selection of the splits, (2) the decisions of when to declare a node as being terminal or to continue splitting the node, and (3) the assignment of each terminal node to a class. Breiman, Friedman, Olshen and Stone (1983) indicated that the third task is simple, and the challenges are in finding good splits and in knowing when to stop splitting. They suggest using a training dataset with the Bayes rule to accomplish these tasks.

Figure 9.8 An example of IRIS data

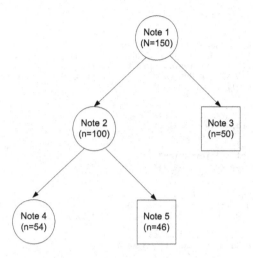

(Note 1: entire group, Species=Setosa, misclassification=0.67; Note 2: petal length > 2.45, Species=Versicolor, misclassification=0.50; Note 3: petal length ≤2.45, Species=Setoca, misclassification=0.00; Note 4: petal width ≤1.75, Species=Versicolor, misclassification=0.09; and Note 5: petal width >1.75, Species=Virginica, misclassification=0.02)

Example 9.8→Classification based on Regression Trees. SAS provides a classification and regression tree macro called *treedisc.sas*. Let us use this macro to construct a classification and regression tree with the 10% KDD-cup 1999 training data as a training data. For simplicity, let us only include six binary predictor variables: (1) logged_I, (2) is_guest, (3) RST, (4) TCP, (5) UDP, and (6) HTTP in the model. The codes to conduct this example are given in Display 9.11.

Display 9.11
SAS codes to fit classification and regression trees

```
libname KDD 'F:\book\Chapter 9\risk_score\';
%Include 'F:\Book\Chapter 9\xmacro.sas';
%Include 'F:\Book\Chapter 9\treedisc.sas';

data trining;
set  kdd.var_16_trin;
run;
data testing;
set  kdd.var_16_val;
run;
Proc Format;
    Value AttackF
        1='Yes'
        0='No';
Run;
```

continued on following page

Display 9.11 continued

```
proc contents data=testing;
run;
Options PS=90 LS=80;
Title2 "Discrimination/Separation Information";
%TreeDisc(data=trining, depvar=attack, ordinal=logged_i is_guest RST TCP UDP
          HTTP,NOMINAL=Duration Count Diff_srv Dst_hos1 Dst_hos3 Dst_hos4
          Dst_hos5 Dst_host Num_comp Same_srv, outtree=trd, options=noformat,
          trace=none);

Options PS=55 LS=80;
*** draw the tree diagram in graphics mode;
%TreeDisc(intree=trd, draw=graphics);

Options PS=90 LS=80;
Title2 "Classification Information";
*** Generate DATA step code to classify observations;
%TreeDisc(intree=trd, code=print);

Options PS=55 LS=80;
*** Save the classification rules learned from training data to classifer.sas;
%TreeDisc(intree=trd, code='F:\Book\Chapter 9\classifer.sas');

Title2 "Classification of Original Data";
*** Classify the data using the code generated above;
Data Classified;
   Set trining;
   %Inc 'F:\Book\Chapter 9\classifer.sas';
   Into=Put(into_,AttackF.);
run;

*** Cross-tabulate actual species with the predicted species (INTO_);
Proc Freq Data=Classified;
 Tables attack*Into_;
 Format attack Into_ AttackF.;
title Classification on Training data;
Run;

/*-----------------------------------------
 Classification test data
-----------------------------------------*/;
*** Classify these artificial data;
Data test;
   Set testing;
   %Inc 'F:\ Book\Chapter 9\classifer.sas';
run;
Proc Freq Data=test;
 Tables attack_val*Into_;
 Format attack_val Into_ AttackF.;
Title "Classification on testing data";
run;
```

The binary tree is constructed by partitioning the dataset into two or more subsets of observations based on the categories of one of the predictor variables. After the dataset is partitioned according to the chosen predictor variable, each subset is considered for further partitioning using the same algorithm that was applied to the entire dataset. Additionally, each subset is partitioned without regard to any other subset. This process is repeated for each subset until a stopping criterion is met. Thus, this recursive partitioning forms a tree structure, and the root of the tree is the entire dataset, and the subsets and sub-subsets form the branches of the tree. Subsets that meet a stopping criterion and thus are not partitioned are leaves. Any subset in the tree, including the root or leaves, is a node.

The predictor variable used to form a partition is chosen to be the variable that is most significantly associated with the response variable according to a χ^2 test of independence in a contingency table. The main stopping criterion used by the *treedisc.sas* macro is the p value from the χ^2 test. A small p value indicates that the observed association between the predictor and the response variables is unlikely to have occurred solely as the result of sampling variability. If a predictor has more than two categories, then there may be a large number of potential ways to partition the data based on the categories. In this case, a combinatorial search algorithm can be used to find a partition that has a p small value of the χ^2 test. The p value for each χ^2 test is adjusted for the multiplicity of partitions. Predictor variables can be nominal, ordinal, or ordinal with a floating category. For a nominal variable, the categories are not ordered and therefore can be combined in any way to form a partition. For an ordinal variable, the categories are ordered, and only categories that are adjacent in the order can be combined when forming a partition.

The classification rules learned from the training data are used to assign memberships to the testing data. The SAS program shown in Display 9.11 saves these rules to a SAS file named classifer.sas (Display 9.12). Applying these rules to the testing data, the misclassification rate is 5.5%, 5% higher than the misclassification rate in the training data. Figure 9.9 shows the actual tree for the KDD-cup 1999 data.

Display 9.12
Classification rules learned from the training data

```
*** TREEDISC Decision Tree Code ***;
 * DV counts: 97278   396743 ;
 node_ = 1;
 into_ = 1;
 tie_ = 0;
 post_ = 0.8030893424;
 if -1e38 <= HTTP <= 0.5 then do;
    * DV counts: 35392   394336 ;
    node_ = 2;
    into_ = 1;
    tie_ = 0;
    post_ = 0.9176409264;
    if -1e38 <= UDP <= 0.5 then do;
       * DV counts: 16215   393159 ;
       node_ = 4;
       into_ = 1;
       tie_ = 0;
       post_ = 0.9603907429;
```

continued on following page

Display 9.12 continued

```
if -1e38 <= TCP <= 0.5 then do;
   * DV counts: 1288  282314 ;
   node_ = 6;
   into_ = 1;
   tie_ = 0;
   post_ = 0.9954584241;
end;
else
if 0.5 <= TCP then do;
   * DV counts: 14927  110845 ;
   node_ = 7;
   into_ = 1;
   tie_ = 0;
   post_ = 0.8813169863;
   if -1e38 <= LOGGED_I <= 0.5 then do;
      * DV counts: 1504  109756 ;
      node_ = 8;
      into_ = 1;
      tie_ = 0;
      post_ = 0.986482114;
      if -1e38 <= RST <= 0.5 then do;
         * DV counts: 1472  108459 ;
         node_ = 10;
         into_ = 1;
         tie_ = 0;
         post_ = 0.9866097825;
      end;
      else
      if 0.5 <= RST then do;
         * DV counts: 32  1297 ;
         node_ = 11;
         into_ = 1;
         tie_ = 0;
         post_ = 0.9759217457;
      end;
   end;
   else
   if 0.5 <= LOGGED_I then do;
      * DV counts: 13423  1089 ;
      node_ = 9;
      into_ = 0;
      tie_ = 0;
      post_ = 0.9249586549;
      if -1e38 <= IS_GUEST <= 0.5 then do;
         * DV counts: 13052  775 ;
         node_ = 12;
         into_ = 0;
         tie_ = 0;
         post_ = 0.9439502423;
         if -1e38 <= RST <= 0.5 then do;
            * DV counts: 13025  771 ;
            node_ = 14;
            into_ = 0;
            tie_ = 0;
            post_ = 0.944114236;
         end;
         else
```

continued on following page

Display 9.12 continued

```
                              if 0.5 <= RST then do;
                    * DV counts: 27   4 ;
                    node_ = 15;
                    into_ = 0;
                    tie_ = 0;
                    post_ = 0.8709677419;
                end;
            end;
            else
            if 0.5 <= IS_GUEST then do;
                * DV counts: 371   314 ;
                node_ = 13;
                into_ = 0;
                tie_ = 0;
                post_ = 0.5416058394;
            end;
        end;
    end;
    end;
    else
    if 0.5 <= UDP then do;
        * DV counts: 19177  1177 ;
        node_ = 5;
        into_ = 0;
        tie_ = 0;
        post_ = 0.9421735285;
    end;
end;
else
if 0.5 <= HTTP then do;
    * DV counts: 61886  2407 ;
    node_ = 3;
    into_ = 0;
    tie_ = 0;
    post_ = 0.9625620207;
    if -1e38 <= RST <= 0.5 then do;
        * DV counts: 61847  2314 ;
        node_ = 16;
        into_ = 0;
        tie_ = 0;
        post_ = 0.9639344773;
    end;
    else
    if 0.5 <= RST then do;
        * DV counts: 39  93 ;
        node_ = 17;
        into_ = 1;
        tie_ = 0;
        post_ = 0.7045454545;
    end;
end;
```

In addition to SAS, several tree packages are also available in R. For example, Ripley (1996) contributes an R package to fit a CART model in R. The tree is grown by binary recursive partitioning using the response in the specified formula and choosing splits from the terms of the right-hand-side. The detailed usage and arguments of the function are available at http://pbil.univ-lyon1.fr/library/tree/html/tree.html. The example codes are shown in Display 9.13.

Display 9.13

R codes to fit a classification or regression tree

```
library(MASS)
data(training)
cpus.ltr <- tree(attack ~ syct+mmin+mmax+cach+chmin+chmax, cpus)
cpus.ltr
summary(cpus.ltr)
plot(cpus.ltr);   text(cpus.ltr)

data(iris)
ir.tr <- tree(Species ~., iris)
ir.tr
summary(ir.tr)
```

There are other tree-based methods that are available to implement. These methods include the Quick, Unbiased, Efficient Statistical Trees (QUEST) algorithm and Chi-squared Automatic Interaction Detector (CHAID). QUEST was developed by Loh and Shih (1997), and is a binary-split decision tree algorithm for classification and data mining. Although QUEST shares a similar objective with CART, it has some unique attributes, for instance, it uses an unbiased variable selection approach; it uses an imputation algorithm instead of surrogate splits to handle missing values, and it is compatible with categorical predictor variables that can have many categories. QUEST also can use the CART algorithm to produce a tree with univariate splits when data contains no missing values. The CHAID initially designed by Kass in 1980, is a descendent of works from Morgan and Messenger (1973). Unlike the CART algorithm that constructs binary trees, CHAID constructs non-binary trees that can have more than two branches attach to a single root or node. With

Figure 9.9 Classification regression tree based on the KDD-cup 1999 data

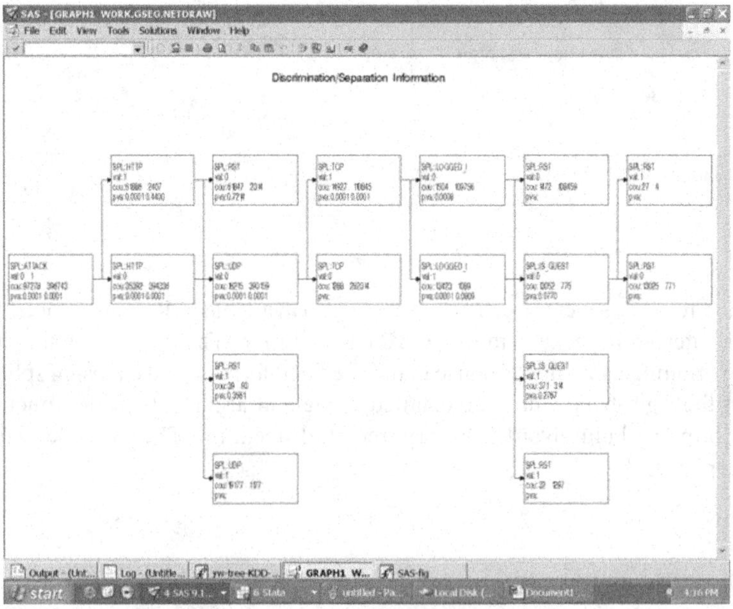

this attribute, CHAID is able to classify a categorical response variable that has more than two categories.

OTHER LINEAR AND NONLINEAR METHODS

In this section we will briefly examine three useful supervised learning approaches that have been employed in network security: the linear discriminant analysis (LDA), the support vector machines (SVM), and the random forests[1] (RF) classification algorithm. Similarly to KNN, if we have two datasets, a training sample that includes observations that have been categorized into g known classes, and a testing sample that contains observations for which the class membership is unknown, we can then use LDA to assign the membership for each observation in the testing dataset based on the knowledge learned from the training dataset. We can do so by using SVM or RF.

Rich literature is available on these approaches. Readers should refer to Press & Wilson (1978), Hand (1981, 1983, and 1998), Huberty, Wisenbaker, Smith & Smith (1986), and Langbehn & Woolson (1997) for more detailed information on LDA and its applications. For readers who would like to obtain tutorials on SVM should refer to Burges (1998), Schölkopf, Burges & Smola, (1999), Schölkopf, Smola, Williamson & Bartlett (2000), Shawe-Taylor & Cristianini (2000), Suykens (2001), Sanchez (2003), Smola & Schölkopf (2004), and Chen, Lin & Schölkopf (2005). Fundamental information of RF can be found from Ho (1995, 1998, 2002), Pavlov (2000), and Breiman (2001).

Linear Discriminant Analysis

LDA belongs to the multivariate analysis family and aims to describe the relationships of grouping variables and then assigns a membership for each observation to a class by identifying boundaries between classes of observations. Classification based on LDA is carried out by discriminant functions, in which the number of functions depends on the level of classes of the response variable in the training data. For a binary classification only one discriminant function is required, and for a multi-class classification, there can be at most $g-1$ discriminant functions, where g is the number of classes of the response variable. The most popular classification task is the binary response variable for LDA. Figure 9.10 illustrates an example of such a classification. An ideal discriminant function should not be parallel with others; rather, it should be orthogonal.

Several methods for LDA have been proposed over time, and the most popular methods include the Fisher discriminant function (for binary classification), and the multivariate analysis of variance method (for classification with more than two classes). Accordingly, we will focus on the Fisher discriminant function for binary classification in this book, but detailed information on other methods can be found from Hand's (1981) comprehensive review.

Assume that we have a sample of n network traffic observations with two classes identified by a response variable y that has a value of 1 to indicate anomaly-free traffic, and 0 to indicate abnormal traffic. Also, the sample data includes a set of variables, $x_1, x_2,$ ..., x_k. The discriminant function to assign an observation to one of the two classes can be represented by the Fisher linear discriminant function:

Figure 9.10 Linear discriminant function for binary classification

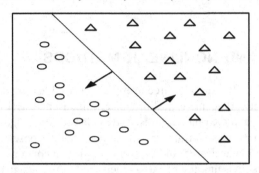

$$L = a_1x_1 + a_2x_2 + \cdots + a_kx_k \qquad\qquad\qquad (9\text{-}12)$$

where $x_1, x_2, ..., x_k$ are the variables associated with the membership of the known classes g, $a_1, a_2, ..., a_k$ are the corresponding coefficients of the variables, and L aims to maximize the ratio of its between-group variance to its within-group variance. We use the F–test to assess if the discriminant model is significant.

Example 9.8→Classification Based on LDA Let us use the full spam-email data to fit a binary linear discriminant model with the following R codes described in Display 9.14, and results are shown Figure 9.11 graphically.

Display 9.14
R codes to fit a binary linear discriminant model with spam-email data

```
library(MASS)
spam<-read.table("F:\\Book\\Chapter 9\\spam_r.txt",header = TRUE, sep = ",")
data(spam)
## create training and testing datasets
set.seed(2323)
index <- sample(1:dim(spam)[1])
spamtrain <- spam[index[1:floor(2 * dim(spam)[1]/3)],]
spamtest <- spam[index[((2 * ceiling(dim(spam)[1]/3)) + 1):dim(spam)[1]],]
#Fit the LDA model
LDA<-lda(v58~v1+v2+v3+v4+v5+v6+v7+v8+v9+v10+v11+v12+v13+v14+v15+v16+v17+v18+
v19+v20+v21+v22+v23+v24+v25+v26+v27+v28+v29+v30+v31+v32+v33+v34+v35+v36+v37+
v38+v39+v40+v41+v42+v43+v44+v45+v46+v47+v48+v49+v50+v51+v52+v53+v54+v55+v56+
v57,data=spamtrain,prior=c(0.5,0.5))
#Display results graphically
plot(LDA, dimen=2,type="both",cex=2,col="grey", ylim=c(0,0.6),xlim=c(-4,6))
# Assessing the performance of the discriminant function
class<-predict(LDA,method="plug-in")$class
table(class,spamtrain$v58)
# predict mail type on the test dataset
mailtype <-predict(LDA,spamtest)$class
## check results
table(mailtype,spamtest$v58)
```

Display 9.15 shows the result of the classification derived from the binary linear discriminant model. The misclassification rates are 0.093 ((183 + 102)/3068), or 9.3%, for the

Figure 9.11 Probability distributions of being spam-emils based on linear discriminant analysis

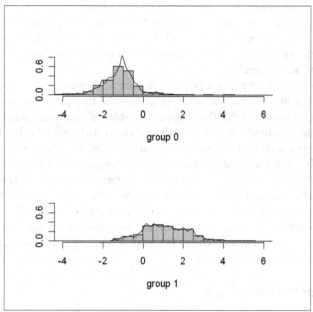

training data and 0.099 ((62+90)/1533), or 9.9%, for the testing data, respectively. We can see that the misclassification rates are high for both training and testing datasets, which indicate that the model does not have good performance. However, this technique has the advantage of being extremely simple (Everitt, 2005).

Display 9.15
Assessing performance of the discriminant model

```
                table(class,spamtrain$v58)

            class      0    1
                0  1750  183
                1   102 1033

           table(mailtype,spamtest$v58)

         mailtype      0    1
                0   874   90
                1    62  507
```

As we found in Example 9.8, although discriminant analysis is extremely simple, it also could generate a high misclassification rate. Hand (1998) suggests several approaches to reduce the misclassification rate on discriminant analysis, whereby the key is to improve the estimate on coefficients on Equation (9-12). One approach is to use the bootstrapping resampling method. The other common approach known as the "leaving-one-out" method that uses $n-1$ observations as a training sample and use the remaining observation to test the algorithm. Then, a new training sample of $n-1$ observations will be generated and the algorithm is tested with a new remaining observation. This process will be repeated n times, so that each observation in the sample is tested (Hand, 1998). It is clear that because the "leaving-one-out" method desires numerous computing resources, it is only feasible when the sample size is small.

We need to keep in mind that LDA has the same assumptions to the data as the linear regression method does, such as normality, independence, linearity and homoscedastic relationships. LDA also assumes that the response variable is a dichotomy that all observations have to belong to a particular class (and only one class), and each class has to be mutually exclusive. Having a sufficient sample size is also important for getting better performance in LDA. Usually we recommend at least 10 observations per class for the response variable and 10 observations for each predictor variable. Moreover, the class sizes of the response variable should be balanced, and the maximum ratio of the large class over the small class for a response variable with two classes should be no greater than 9. Thus, if we have a training dataset with 10% of the observations are belonging to the class A and the remaining data belonging to the class B, we can fit this data with logistic regression, but may not with the linear discriminant function.

Support Vector Machines

The SVM method, developed by Cortes and Vapnik (1995), is a new machine learning approach derived from advances in statistical learning theory developed during the 1960s. It can be used to fit with both linear and nonlinear data for binary classification and regression estimation. Recently, SVM have become one of the common algorithms for machine learning and data mining. While SVM based applications have been widely used in many areas from economics, life science, and computer science to political decision-support, this method has also been increasingly employed for network security (Mukkamala, Janoski & Sung, 2002; Kim & Park, 2003; Peddabachigari, Abraham & Thomas, 2004; Xu & Wang, 2005; Chen & Chen, 2007; Khan, Awad & Thuraisingham, 2007).

SVM uses a nonlinear mapping to transform the original training data into a higher dimensional space, where it searches for the linear optimal separating hyperplane called a decision boundary. With an appropriate nonlinear mapping to a sufficiently high dimensional space, data from two groups can always be separated by a hyperplane. It first finds an optimal separating hyperplane to split the groups in the training sample, and then assigns the membership of data from the testing sample based on their position corresponding to the hyperplane.

Assume that our training data has two labeled binary classes, g_1 and g_2, where each data point is represented by a k-dimensional vector. The fundamental goal of SVM is to find an optimal separating hyperplane to split the g_1 and the g_2 classes in a data space by maximizing the margin between the closest points of the groups. Theoretically, there are infinite hyperplanes that can be found to separate the two classes, but our goal is to find the one that minimizes the classification error. We can achieve this goal by searching the hyperplane with the largest margin between the closest points of g_1 and g_2 as shown in Figure 9.12. The data points lying on the boundaries are defined as support vectors, and the middle of the margin is our optimal separating hyperplane.

Because we want to get as large of a margin as possible, we are interested in obtaining the hyperplanes, that are parallel to the middle optimal separating hyperplane, that are closest to these support vectors in either class. Thus, we can have

$$W \cdot X - b = 1, \text{ and} \tag{9-13}$$

$$W \cdot X - b = -1, \tag{9-14}$$

where W is a vector perpendicular to the separating hyperplane, X is a k-dimensional vector, and b is an offset that allows us to increase the margin. Ideally, there should not be any data points between the hyperplanes defined by Equations (9-13) and (9-14). Thus, for any data point q_i, we want to have

$$w \cdot x_i - b \geq 1, \text{ or} \tag{9-15}$$
$$w \cdot x_i - b \leq -1. \tag{9-16}$$

If the training data is linearly separable, we should be able to find such hyperplanes that satisfy Equations (9-15) and (9-16). Because the distance between the hyperplanes is

$$\frac{2}{|w|},$$

we have to minimize $|w|$ subject to the constraints in Equations (9-15) and (9-16) to maximize the margin. This is a quadratic programming optimization problem (Wikipedia, 2006) and we can write it as:

$$\text{min} \, imize\left(\frac{1}{2}\right)\|w\|^2, \text{ subject to } c_i(w \cdot x_i - b) \geq 1, \ 1 \leq i \leq n. \tag{9-17}$$

Although we cannot find a linear separating function for nonlinear binary classification, we can map data points to a higher-dimensional space where a linear classification can be conducted, as shown in Figure 9.13 (Heasrt, Shholkops, Dumais, Osuna, and Platt, 1998, Meyer, 2006).

Example 9.9→Classification based on SVM. R has the package *svm* and *ksvm* (see R documentation on support vector machines http://rss.acs.unt.edu/Rdoc/library/kernlab/html/ksvm.html). The following R codes fit an SVM model using the spam-email data with the *ksvm* command. For more information on using R to fit SVM, refer to Karatzoglou, Meyer & Hornik (2006).

Figure 9.12 Margins and support vectors

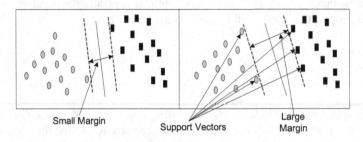

Figure 9.13 Transfer nonlinear separable data from input space to feature space for linear classification

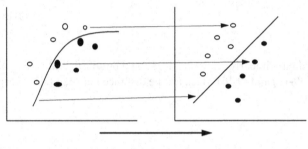

Map from input to feature space

Figure 9.14 Classification results based on support vector machines

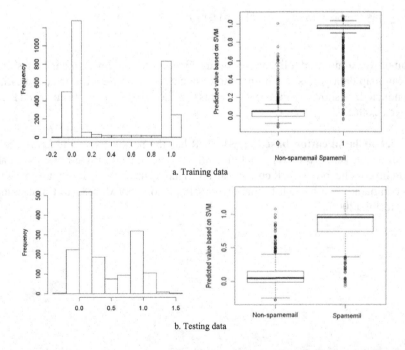

Display 9.16
R codes to fit a support vector machines model

```
library('e1071')
library(kernlab)
spam<-read.table("F:\\Book\\Chapter 9\\spam_r.txt",header = TRUE, sep = ",")
attach(spam)
## create training and testing datasets
set.seed(2323)
index <- sample(1:dim(spam)[1])
spamtrain <- spam[index[1:floor(2*dim(spam)[1]/3)],]
spamtest <- spam[index[((2*ceiling(dim(spam)[1]/3))+1):dim(spam)[1]],]
## train a support vector machine
SVM <-ksvm(v58~.,data=spamtrain,kernel="rbfdot",kpar=list(sigma=0.05),
C=5,cross=3)
group<-predict(SVM,spamtrain[,-58])
boxplot(group~spamtrain[,58],,xlab="Non-spamemail Spamemil",
ylab="Predicted value based on SVM")
hist(group)
##use 0.5 as a cutoff point
spamtrain$spam <-(group[,1]>0.5)
table(spamtrain$spam,spamtrain$v58)
## predict mail type on the test data
mailtype <-predict(SVM,spamtest[,-58])
## Check results
table(mailtype,spamtest$v58)
summary(mailtype)
hist(mailtype)
boxplot(mailtype~spamtest[,58],xlab="Non-spamemail Spamemil",
ylab="Predicted value based on SVM")
#use 0.5 as a cutoff point
spamtest$spam <-(mailtype[,1]>0.5)
table(spamtest$spam,spamtest$v58)
```

The randomly selected training and testing datasets include 3068 observations for the training data, of which 38.9% (n = 1193) are spam-email, and 1533 observations for the testing data, of which 40.4% (n = 620) are spam-email. Figure 9.14 shows the histogram and box-plot figures of the classification results on the training and testing samples. Using a probability of 0.5 as a threshold of being a spam-email, the SVM classifies 1132 of 1193 spam-emails and 1860 of 1875 non-spam emails correctly in the training data. The observed misclassification rate for the training data is (15+61)/3068=0.025, or 2.5%. Using the parameters obtained from the training data to assign a membership to 1533 data points in the testing data, we obtain 83.9% (520 of 620) accuracy in spam-emails and 96.9% (885 of 913) accuracy in non-spam emails. The overall misclassification rate for the testing data is 8.3%, an increase of absolute 5.8% from the training data. Nevertheless, this misclassification rate is still low than the LDA-based misclassification rate (8.3% vs. 9.9%).

Random Forest

RF is a classification algorithm that uses multi-decision trees developed by Leo Breiman and Adele Cutler (Breiman, 2001). Random forest constructs trees based on revised samples acquired from the original training data using the bootstrapping method. After the forest is constructed, new data points are assigned a class membership by each tree, and a final classification is conducted based on the majority votes of the trees within the forest. This is similar to the KNN algorithm. Although the random forest method is relative new, studies have illustrated the potential advantages of applying this method in network security (Zhang & Zulkernine, 2006; Gharibian & Ghorbani, 2007).

Let D be a sample space for the training data with a size of n observations and k predictor variables, $X = (x_1, x_2, \ldots, x_k)$. Let us assume that observations can be classified into g groups, where $n_1 + n_2 + \cdots + n_g = n$, and C represents the set of groups, $C = (c_1, c_2, \ldots, c_g)$. The RF algorithm will generates numerous classification trees (Figure 9.15) and each tree grows using the following steps outlined by Breiman and Cutler (2002): (1) randomly draw a sample of size n observations *with replacements* from the original training data, D. This sample will be the training data used to construct the tree, T_i; (2) randomly select j variables from the k predictor variables $(j < k)$. The best split on these j variables will be used to split the node. The value of j is held constant during forest growth, and (3) each tree is grown to the fullest extent possible; there is no pruning.

After the forest is constructed, new data points can be classified by adding them to each of the trees in the forest. Each tree assigns a class membership to the new data, known as the tree "vote" for that class. Therefore, the forest chooses the classification that has the most votes across all the trees in the forest:

$$C = \max_c \sum f(x_{ij}, T_i).$$

Example 9.10→Using Random Forests to Predict Spam-email. Let us construct an RF model with the package *randomForest* from R. Display 9.17 lists the R codes used to fit an RF model using the spam-email data with the *randomForest* command. For more information on using R to construct random forests, refer to R documentation on Classification and Regression with Random Forest (http://rweb.stat.umn.edu/R/library/randomForest/html/randomForest.html).

Figure 9.15 Trees in the random forest

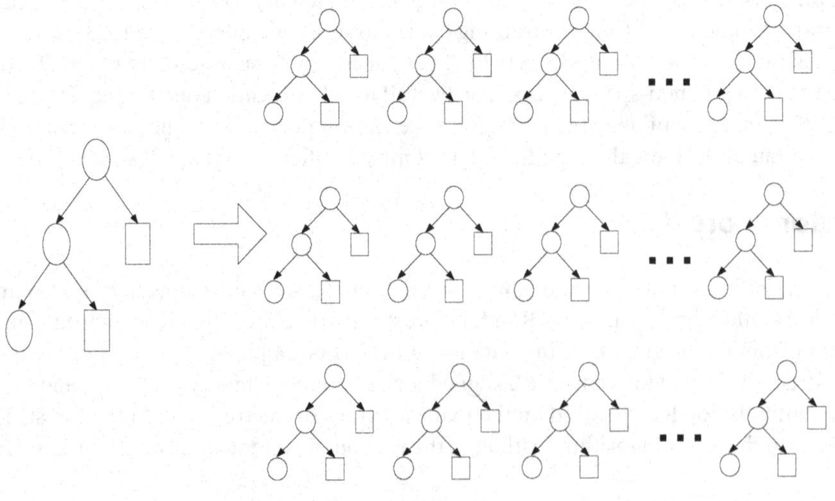

Display 9.17
R codes to construct random forests

```
library (randomForest)
## Classification:
spam<-read.table("f:\\book\\Chapter 9\\spam_r.txt",header=TRUE,sep=",")
attach(spam)
## create training and testing datasets
set.seed(2323)
index <- sample(1:dim(spam)[1])
spamtrain <- spam[index[1:floor(2*dim(spam)[1]/3)],]
spamtest <- spam[index[((2*ceiling(dim(spam)[1]/3))+1):dim(spam)[1]],]
##Fit random forest model
RF <- randomForest(v58 ~., data=spamtrain, importance=TRUE,proximity=TRUE)
## Look at variable importance:
print(RF)
round(importance(RF), 2)
varImpPlot(RF)
##class' membership on test data
pred <- predict(RF, spamtest)
summary(pred)
## use 0.2 as a threshold
spamtest$spam <-(pred>0.2)
spamtest$v58[spamtest$v58==0]<-"non-spam"
spamtest$v58[spamtest$v58==1]<-"spam"
spamtest$spam[spamtest$spam==0]<-"non-spam"
spamtest$spam[spamtest$spam==1]<-"spam"
table(observed = spamtest$v58, predicted = spamtest$spam)
```

Display 9.18 shows selected outputs from the fitted RF model. A regression RF model was fitted and can be used to explain about 82% of the variance. The numbers of variables tried at each split was 19. The testing sample includes 1533 observations of which 621 are spam-email and 912 are non spam-email. Using a value of 0.2 as the threshold for classification, 608 of 621 (97.9%) spam-emails and 784 of 812 (86.0%) non spam-emails were correctly classified. The overall misclassification rate is 0.092 ((13+128)/1533), or 9.2%. Figure 9.16 shows the importance of variables in the RF model.

Display 9.18
Results of the random forests model

```
Call:
randomForest(formula = v58 ~ .,data=spamtrain,importance=TRUE,proximity=TRUE)
               Type of random forest: regression
                     Number of trees: 500
No. of variables tried at each split: 19

          Mean of squared residuals: 0.04392359
                    % Var explained: 81.51
                summary(pred)
   Min. 1st Qu.  Median    Mean 3rd Qu.     Max.
0.00000 0.01889 0.16930 0.40840 0.92410 1.00000

                    predicted
            observed    non-spam spam
                non-spam     784  128
                    spam      13  608
```

Figure 9.16 Importance of variables (right: the mean increase in accuracy; left: the mean increases the mean squared error (MSE))

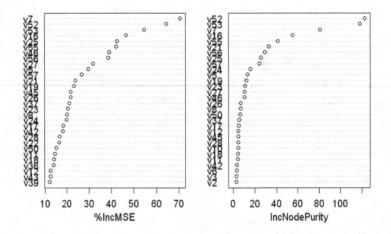

SUMMARY

Traffic data can be classified into a binary class (i.e. anomaly-free and all others) or multilevel classes (e.g., anomaly-free, likely to be anomaly-free, anomaly, likely to be anomaly, and unable to determined). In this chapter, however, we mainly focused on the common statistically supervised learning algorithms and methods for binary classification. In the real world, it is possible that a data point belongs to more than one class or has similar attributes for multi-membership. This is a complex situation. In short, the multilevel classification situation can be addressed by using multi-classification algorithms and then making decisions based on the membership functions acquired from the algorithm.

Generally, the logistic, Poisson, and probit models discussed in this chapter have many advantages over OLS regression because they are more statistically robust and easier to use in practice. Also, the assumptions for these models are relatively relaxed. We do not require the assumption of a linear relation between the response and predictor variables, or the assumption of homoscedasticity, nor do we require that the response variable be normally distributed. Because of these advantages, logistic and multinomial logistic regressions have been used an increasing amount in place of the linear discriminant analysis.

Over the past decade, statistical methods for profiling user behavior and classifying network traffic have been studied and have grown substantially, but the fundamental question still remains: how good is the performance of classification? When addressing this question, many obstacles have arisen, such as challenges in the measures of similarity and dissimilarity, challenges in defining a "gold-standard" classification model, and challenges in creating the training and testing data.

Moreover, sometimes the training data includes a labeled response variable for each observation, but other times, such labeled information is not available. If we do not have labeled response data or the data is too small to provide sufficient information, unsupervised methods must be applied; these methods will be reviewed in Chapter X.

REFERENCES

Abbes, T., Bouhoula, A. & Rusinowitch, M. (2004). Protocol analysis in intrusion detection using decision tree, In *Proceedings of Information Technology: Coding and Computing (ITCC 2004)*, pp. 404-408.

Alpaydin, E. (2004). *Introduction to machine learning*, MA: MIT Press.

Amor, N. B., Benferhat, S. & Elouedi, Z. (2004). Naive Bayes vs decision trees in intrusion detection systems. In *Proceedings of the 2004 ACM Symposium on Applied Computing* (SAC '04). pp. 420-424.

Androutsopoulos, I., Paliouras, G., Karkaletsis, V., Sakkis, G., Spyropoulos, C. and Stamatopoulos, P. (2000). Learning to filter spam email: A comparison of a naive bayesian and a memorybased approach. *In Proceedings of Workshop on Machine Learning and Textual Information Access, 4.*

Ash, C. (1993). *The probability tutoring book: an intuitive course for engineers and scientists (and everyone else!)*. New York: IEEE Press Marking.Barbard, D., Wu, N. & Jajodia, S. (2001) Detecting novel network intrusions using Bayes estimators. *Proceedings of the 1st SIAM International Conference on Data Mining.* pp.24-29.

Bliss, C.I. (1935). The calculation of the dosage-mortality curve. *Annals of Applied Biology* (22), 134-167.

Breiman, L. (2001). Random forests. *Machine Learning, 45*(1), 5-32.

Breiman, L. & Cutler, A. (2002). Random forests Leo Breiman and Adele Cutler, retrieved on April 14, 2008 from http://oz.berkeley.edu/~breiman/RandomForests/cc_home.htm.Breiman, L., Friedman, J.H., Olshen, R. A., and Stone, C. J. (1983). *Classification and regression trees.* CA: Wadsworth & Brooks.

Burges, C. J. C. (1998). A Tutorial on support vector machines for pattern recognition, *Data Mining and Knowledge Discovery, 2*, 121-167.

Chen, Y., Abraham, A., & Yang, B. (2007). Hybrid flexible neural-tree-based intrusion detection systems: Research Articles. *International Journal of Intelligent System, 22*(4), 337-352.

Chen, R. & Chen, S. (2007). An intrusion dsetection based on support vector machines with a voting weight schema, *Lecture Notes in Computer Science*, 4570, pp. 1148-1157.

Chen, P. H., Lin, C. J. and Schölkopf, B. (2005). A tutorial on v-support vector machines, *Applied Stochastic Models in Business and Industry*, 21(2), pp. 111-136.

Congdon, P. (2002). *Bayesian statistical modeling*, New York: John Wiley & Sons, Ltd.

Cortes, C. & Vapnik, V. (1995). Support-vector network. *Machine Learning, 20*, 1-25.

Cristianini, N., Shawe-Taylor, J.(2000). *An introduction to support vector machines*. London: Cambridge University Press.

Diederich, J. (2008). *Rule extraction from support vector machines.* New York: Springer-Verlag.

Duda, R. O., Hart, P. E. & Stork, D. G. (2001). *Pattern classification 2nd Edition.* New York: Wiley-Interscience.

DuMouchel, W. (1999).Computer intrusion detection based on Bayes factors for comparing command transition probabilities, *Technical Report 91, National Institute of Statistical Sciences,* Accessed October 30, 2007 from http://www.niss.org/downloadabletechreports.html.

Everitt, B. (2005). *An R and S-Plus companion to multivariate analysis.* New York: Springer-Verlag.

Gharibian, F. & Ghorbani, A.A. (2007). Comparative study of supervised machine learning techniques for intrusion detection, In *Proceedings of the Fifth Annual Conference on Communication Networks and Services Research*, pp. 350-358.

Ghahramani, S. (2005). *Fundamentals of probability with stochastic processes, 3rd edition*, New Jersey: Pearson Education, Inc.

Hand. D. J. (1981) *Discrimination and classification.* New York: John Wiley and Sons.

Hand, D. J. (1983). A comparison of two methods of diacriminant analysis applied to binary data. *Biometrics, 39*, 683-694.

Hand, D.J. (1998). Discriminant analysis, linear. In P Armitage and T Colton (eds.), *Encyclopedia of Biostatistics*. New York: John Wiley & Sons, Inc.

Hastie, T. Tibshirani, R. & Friedman, J. (2001). *The elements of statistical learning: Data mining, inference, and prediction.* New York: Springer-Verlag.

Heasrt, M. A., Shholkops, B., Dumais, S., Osuna, E., and Platt, J. (1998). Trends and controversies—support vector machines. *IEEE Intelligent Systems, 13*(4), 18-28.

Herbrich, R. (2002). *Learning kernel classifiers theory and algorithms.* Massachusetts: The MIT Press.

Ho, T. K. (1995). Random decision forest. In *Precedings. of the 3rd International Conference on Document Analysis and Recognition*, pp. 278-282.

Ho, T. K. (1998). The random subspace method for constructing decision forests. *IEEE Trans. on Pattern Analysis and Machine Intelligence 20*(8), 832-844.

Ho, T. K. (2002). A data complexity analysis of comparative advantages of decision forest constructors. *Pattern Analysis and Applications 5*, pp. 102-112.

Hosmer, D. W. & Lemeshow, S. (2000). *Applied logistic regression, 2nd ed.* New York: John Wiley & Sons, Inc.

Hossain, M. (2002). Integrating association rule mining and decision tree learning for network intrusion detection: A preliminary investigation, In *Proceedings of the 2002 International Conference on Information Systems, Analysis and Synthesis*, pp.65-70.

Huberty, C. J., Wisenbaker, J. M., Smith, J. D., & Smith, J. C. (1986). Using categorical variables in discriminant analysis, *Multivariate Behavioral Research. 21*, 479-496.

Karatzoglou, A., Meyer, D., and Hornik, K. (2006). Support vector machines in R. *Journal of Statistical Software, 15*(9). Accessed October 30, 2007 from http://www.jstatsoft.org/v15/i09/v15i09.pdf

Khan, L. Awad, M. & Thuraisingham, B. (2007). A new intrusion detection system using support vector machines and hierarchical clustering, *International Journal on Very Large Data Bases, 16*(4), 507-521

Kim, D.S. & Park, J.S. (2003). Network-based intrusion detection with support vector machines, *Lecture Notes in Computer Science, 2662*, 747-756.

Lane, T., & Brodley, C. E. (1997). *Detecting the abnormal: Machine learning in computer security.* Technical Report TR-ECE 97-1. Purdue University, School of Electrical and Computer Engineering, West Lafayette, IN.

Langbehn, D. R. & Woolson, R. F. (1997). Discriminant analysis using the unweighted sum of binary variables: a comparison of model selection methods. *Statistics in Medicine, 16*, 2679-2700.

Li, X. & Ye, N. (2003). Decision tree classifiers for computer intrusion detection. In B. Tjaden and L. R. Welch, (Eds.), *Real-time system security*. Commack, NY: Nova Science Publishers.

Loh, W-Y. and Shih, Y-S. (1997), Split selection methods for classification trees, *Statistica Sinica, 7*, 815-840.

Maloof, M. A. (2006). *Machine learning and data mining for computer security*. New York: Springer-Verlag.

McCallum, A. and Nigam K. (1998). A comparison of event models for Naive Bayes text classification. *In AAAI/ICML-98 Workshop on Learning for Text Categorization*, Technical Report WS-98-05, AAAI Press, pp. 41-48.

McCullagh, P. & Nelder, J. A. (1989). *Generalized linear models, 2nd edition*. New York: Chapman & Hall/CRC.

Mendenhall, W. & Beaver, R. J. (1991). *Intrduction to probability and statistics, 6th edition*. Massachusetts: Pws-Kent publishing company.

Meyer, D. (2006). *Support vector machines: The interface to libsvm in package 31071*. Retrieved September 06, 2007 from http://cran.r-project.org/doc/vignettes/e1071/svmdoc.pdf

Minaei-Bidgoli, B., Analoui, M., Shahhoseini, H.S. & Rezvani, M. H. (2007). Performance analysis of decision tree for intrusion detection with reduced DARPA offline feature sets. *In Proceedings of the 2007 International Multi-conference of Engineers and Computer Scientists (IMECS'07)*, Hong Kong.

Morgan, J. N. and Sonquist, J. A. (1963) Problems in the analysis of survey data, and a proposal. *Journal of the American Statistical Association, 58*, 415-435.

Morgan, J. N. and Messenger, R. C. (1973). *THAID: A sequential analysis program for the analysis of nominal scale dependent variables*. Technical report, Institute for Social Research, University of Michigan, Ann Arbor.

Mozina M, Demsar J, Kattan M, & Zupan B. (2004). Nomograms for Visualization of Naive Bayesian Classifier. In *Proc. of PKDD-2004*, pp. 337-348.

Mukkamala, S. Janoski, G. & Sung, A. (2002). Intrusion detection using neural network and support vector machines. In *Proceedings of the IEEE 2002 International Joint Conference on Neural Networks, 1702-1707*.

Müller, K. R., Mika, S., Rätsch, G., Tsuda, K. and Schölkopf, B. (2001). An introduction to kernel-based learning algorithms. *IEEE Transaction. Neural Network. 12*, 181-201.

Myers, R. H., Montgomery, D. C. & Vining, G. G. (2002). *Generalized linear models with applications in engineering and the sciences*. New York: Wiley-Interscience.

Neuhaus, M., & Bunke, H. (2007). *Bridging the gap between graph edit distance and kernel machines. Series in machine perception and artificial intelligence, v. 68*. Singapore: World Scientific.

Nilsson, N. J. (1996). *Introduction to machine learning* Accessed May 26, 2007 from http://robotics. stanford.edu/people/nilsson/MLDraftBook/MLBOOK.pdf

Peddabachigari, S., Abraham, A. & Thomas, J. (2004). Intrusion detection systems using Decision trees and support vector machines, *International Journal of Applied Science and Computations, 11*(3), 118-134.

Pepe, M. S. (2002). *The statistical evaluation of medical tests for classification and prediction.* London: Oxford University Press.

Pavlov, Y. L. (2000). *Random forests.* Utrecht: VSP.

Press, S. J., & Wilson, S. (1978). Choosing between logistic regression and discriminant analysis. *Journal of the American Statistical Association, 73,* 699-705.

Ripley, B. D. (1996) *Pattern recognition and neural networks.* Cambridge, London: Cambridge University Press.

Rish, I. (2001). An empirical study of the naive Bayes classifier. *In Proceedings of IJCAI 2001 Workshop on Empirical Methods in Artificial Intelligence.*

Ross, M. S. (2002). *A first course in probability 6th edition.* New Jersey: Prentice Hall.

Sanchez, V. D. (2003). Advanced support vector machines and kernel methods, *Neurocomputing, 55,* 5-20.

Sch"olkopf, B., Smola, A., Williamson, R. C., & Bartlett, P. (2000). New support vector algorithms. *Neural Computation, 12,* 1207-1245.

Schölkopf, S., Burges, C. J. C., Smola, A. J.(1999). *Advances in kernel methods: support vector learning.* Cambridge, MA: MIT Press.

Shakhnarovish, Darrell, and Indyk (2005). *Nearest-neighbor methods in learning and vision.* MA: The MIT Press.

Shawe-Taylor, J. & Cristianini, N. (2000). *Support vector machines and other kernel-based learning methods.* London: Cambridge University Press.

Smola, A. J. & Schölkopf, B. (2004). A tutorial on support vector regression, *Statistics & Computing, 14,* 199-222.

Stallings, W. (2003). *Network security essentials, applications and standards. 2nd Ed.* New Jersey: Pearson Education.

Stirzaker, D. (1999). *Probability and random variables: A beginner's guide.* London: Cambridge University Press

Suykens, J. A. K. (2001). Support vector machines: A nonlinear modeling and control perspective, *European Journal Control, 7,* pp. 311-327.

Vapnik, V. N. (1998). *Statistical learning theory.* New York: Wiley-Interscience.

Vapnik, V. N. (1999). An overview of statistical learning theory, *IEEE Trans. Neural Netw. 10,* pp. 988-999.

Vittinghoff, E., Glidden, D. V., Shiboski, S. C. & McCulloch, C. E. (2005). *Regression models in biostatistics: Linear, logistic, survival, and repeated measures models.* New York: Springer.

Xu, X. & Wang, X. (2005). An adaptive network intrusion detection method based on PCA and support vector machines. *Lecture Notes in Computer Science, 3584.*pp.696-703.

WikipediA, (2006). *The free encyclopedia.* http://www.wikipedia.org/

Woodworth, G. G. (2004) *Biostatistics a Bayesian introduction*. New Jersey: John Wiley & Sons, Inc.

Zhang, J. & Zulkernine, M. (2006). A hybrid network intrusion detection technique using random forests. In *Proceedings of the First International Conference on Availability, Reliability and Security (ARES'06)*, pp. 262-269.

Zhou, M. & Lang, S. D. (2003). Mining frequency content of network traffic for intrusion detection. In *Proceedings of the IASTED International Conference on Communication, Network, and Information Security*, 101-107.

ENDNOTE

[1]   Random Forests™ is a trademark of Leo Breiman and Adele Cutler and is licensed exclusively to Salford Systems for the commercial release of the software. Additionally, the trademarks also include RF™, RandomForests™, RandomForest™and Random Forest™.

Chapter X
Classification Based on Unsupervised Learning

Truth and love are the only things worth living for and the only things worth dying for.
                                                            - Rebecca Ann Talcott

INTRODUCTION

The requirement for having a labeled response variable in training data from the supervised learning technique may not be satisfied in some situations: particularly, in dynamic, short-term, and ad-hoc wireless network access environments. Being able to conduct classification without a labeled response variable is an essential challenge to modern network security and intrusion detection. In this chapter we will discuss some unsupervised learning techniques including probability, similarity, and multidimensional models that can be applied in network security. These methods also provide a different angle to analyze network traffic data. For comprehensive knowledge on unsupervised learning techniques please refer to the machine learning references listed in the previous chapter; for their applications in network security see Carmines, Edward & McIver (1981), Lane & Brodley (1997), Herrero, Corchado, Gastaldo, Leoncini, Picasso & Zunino (2007), and Dhanalakshmi & Babu (2008).

Unlike in supervised learning, where for each vector $X = (x_1, x_2, ..., x_n)$ we have a corresponding observed response, Y, in unsupervised learning we only have X, and Y is not available either because we could not observe it or its frequency is too low to be fitted with a supervised learning approach. Unsupervised learning has great meanings in practice because in many circumstances, available network traffic data may not include any anomalous events or known anomalous events (e.g., traffics collected from a newly constructed network system). While high-speed mobile wireless and ad-hoc network systems have become popular, the importance and need to develop new unsupervised learning methods that allow the modeling of network traffic data to use anomaly-free training data have significantly increased.

PROBABILITY MODELS

In this section, we discuss three probabilistic classification modeling approaches: a density estimation-based model, a latent class model, and a hidden Markov model. All these models do not require a labeled variable in the training data and can be considered as unsupervised learning approaches.

Density Estimation

As we mentioned that the initial idea of intrusion detection is quite simple: use normal patterns of legitimate user behavior to identify and distinguish the behavior of an anomalous user (Anderson, 1972; Anderson, 1980; Denning, 1987; Stallings, 2003). Statistically, such an idea can be achieved by establishing the distribution of anomaly-free pattern. If we have sufficient data we can construct such a pattern and classify network traffics based on the probability of the traffic failing in the pattern:

$$c_i = \begin{cases} 1 & P(a < X < b) > T \\ 0 & P(a < X < b) \leq T \end{cases},$$

where a and b are the pre-determined range of the pattern and T is the threshold to categorize the traffic. Several approaches can be used to develop an anomaly-free pattern. Let us use the preexisting knowledge-based anomaly-free score developed in Chapter VIII and the bootstrap results described in Example 8.5 to demonstrate a simple probability density-based unsupervised learning classification model. For each site, $i = 1, 2, \cdots$ included in the sample D, we can establish an anomaly-free pattern, $N(\mu_i^*, \sigma_i^{*2})$ based on Equations (8-9), (8-25) and (8-26):

$$\hat{s}_{ij} = \frac{1}{K} \sum_{k=1}^{K} w_k x_{kj},$$
$$\hat{s}_{ij} \sim N(\mu_i^*, \sigma_i^{*2}), \text{ and}$$

$$\sigma_i^{*2} = \frac{1}{B-1} \sum_{b=1}^{B} [\hat{\mu}_{ib}^* - \mu_i^*]^2$$

The probability of the jth observation being anomaly-free at the ith site, $\hat{p}_{ij}$, can be estimated through the normal probability density function,

$$\hat{P}_{ij}\{\hat{s}_{ij} \in A\} = \int_A \frac{\hat{s}_{ij}}{\sqrt{2\pi}\sigma_i^*} e^{-\frac{1}{2}(\frac{\hat{s}_{ij}-\mu_i^*}{\sigma_i^*})^2} d\hat{s}_{ij}, \qquad (10\text{-}1)$$

where A is the range of the anomaly-free pattern. Furthermore, the proportion of anomaly-free observations at each site, $\hat{\theta}_i$, can be calculated with the Maximum Likelihood Estimation (MLE) method

$$\hat{\theta}_i = \frac{1}{n_i}\sum_{j=1}^{n_i}\hat{y}_{ij},$$

where

$$\hat{y}_{ij} = \begin{cases} 1 & if \ \hat{p}_{ij}(\hat{s}_{ij} \in A) > T \\ 0 & if \ \hat{p}_{ij}(\hat{s}_{ij} \in A) \le T \end{cases} \qquad (10\text{-}2)$$

We can use training data to determine the threshold of the probability being anomaly-free, T.

Example 10.1→Anomaly-free Pattern. Let us continue Example 8.5, which carried out 5000 iterations of bootstrapping simulations to yield a normal distribution for all 39 sites in both training and testing samples. The number of observations per site in the training sample ranged from 377 to 22,715, with a mean of 9,399, and 25th, 50th, and 75th percentiles of 1,976, 9,964, and 16,468, respectively. The testing sample had a mean of 27,279 observations per site with a SD of 40,831. The 25th, 50th, and 75th percentiles were 10.998, 16,703, and 19,975 respectively.

Using the normal probability density function, we can calculate the probability of being anomaly-free for each observation in the training sample based on Equation (10-1) with the site-specific parameters, μ_i^* and σ_i^*, obtained from the bootstrapping simulations. The

Figure 10.1. Mean probability of being anomaly-free by deciles

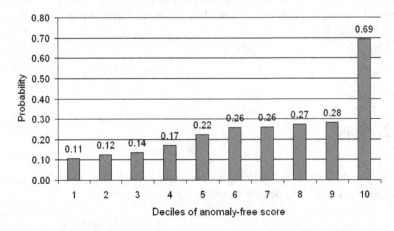

probability ranged from 0.00 to 1.00 with a mean value of 0.24 and a SD of 0.16. The 25th and 75th percentiles were 0.13 and 0.27, respectively. The 95th percentile was 0.67 and the 5th percentile was 0.11. Figure 10.1 shows the probability range by deciles. Theoretically, since all observations in the training sample are anomaly-free, such observations should have high values in probability of being anomaly-free and, therefore, observations with low probability decrease sensitivity and contribute noise to the classification. The determination of a probability threshold, T, described by Equation (10-2) has to take into account the impact on sensitivity. Based on the distribution of probability described above, we can set the threshold to be $T = 0.10$, which corresponds to the lowest decile and a sensitivity of 0.90. This assumes that less than 10% of connections could be misclassified.

Next we can conduct the classification for each observation from the testing sample based on the threshold value of $T = 0.10$. The probability of any connection being anomaly-free can be calculated using the normally probability density function for each network traffic in the testing sample across 39 sites. The mean probabilities ranged from 0.0000 to 0.9969 (25th, 50th, and 75th percentiles were 0.1694, 0.2741, and 0.6793, respectively) for anomaly-free traffics and 0.0000 to 0.9728 (25th, 50th, and 75th percentiles were 0.0000, 0.0000, and 0.0000, respectively) for abnormal traffics included in the testing sample. With $T = 0.10$ as a probability threshold in Equation (10-2), all 1,063,883 connections in the testing data are classified as either anomaly-free ($P(x \in A) > 0.10$) or abnormal ($P(x \notin A) \geq 0.90$) based on their score described in Equation (8-9). The proportion of observed anomaly-free traffics ranged from 4.4% to 100.0%, and the proportion of correctly classified connections ranged from 27.9% to 100.0% across 39 sites. The largest volume site (135.013.216.191) included 214,972 connections, of which 9,487 were observed as anomaly-free traffics. 98.4% of these are correctly classified, yielding a sensitivity value of 0.9837, a specificity value of 0.9887, a ROC value of 0.9862, and a correctly closefisted rate of 0.9885. In comparison with the largest volume site, the median volume site (172.016.114.148), which included 36,657 connections also has satisfying classification results of 0.9968, 1.000, and 0.9968 for sensitivity, specificity, and correctly closefisted rate, respectively. Correspondingly, the smallest volume site (192.168.001.090) has all anomaly-free connections (n = 954); roughly 82.2% of traffics are correctly classified. It is the 6th site with the lowest correctly classified rate. The remaining five sites have the lowest correctly classified rates ranging from 0.1119 to 0.6887, totaling 50,338 traffics (4.7% of all traffics). Figure 10.2 displays the theoretical user behavior patterns represented by the scores from all sites together in the training and testing samples and illustrates that the probability model is able to separate the anomalous pattern from the anomaly-free pattern. Figure 10.3 shows the probability distributions to be anomaly-free for the first two sites (135.008.060.182 and 135.013.216.091) that were in Table 8.8 of Example 8.5, for which the correctly classified rates were 0.9698 and 0.9885, respectively.

This preliminary example has room for further explorations. For example, different weighing approaches could be used to calculate the score, which was discussed in Chapter VIII. Moreover, an adaptive self-learning function and algorithm could be developed to adjust parameters based on learned information. As illustrated in Figure 10.2, the two normal user behavior patterns have different means, $\mu_{training} - \mu_{testing} \neq 0$, and the probability model could be improved by taking into account this difference in order to improve the model's performance.

Figure 10.2. Theoretically overall site behavior patterns

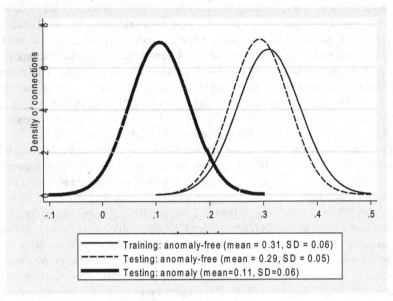

Figure 10.3. Distributions of the probability to be anomaly-free by first two sites in Table 8.8

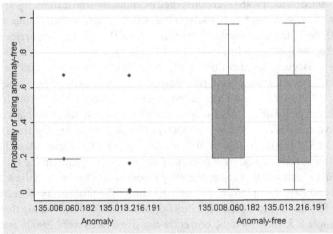

Latent Class Models

A latent class model is a parametric model that uses observed data to estimate parameter values for the model. It finds subtypes of related observations (latent classes) from multivariate categorical data. The "latent class" indicates that the categorical membership of a given observation is not directly observed, but rather, its probability of being assigned a given class is assumed to depend on which latent class the observation belongs to. A latent class

Figure 10.4 Structure of a latent class model with i manifest binary variables, 2^i patterns and two classes

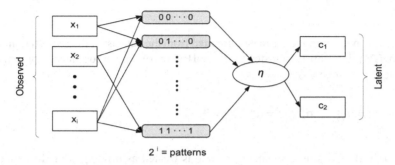

2^i = patterns

model includes two types of variables: manifest and latent variables. We call a variable a manifest variable if it can be measured directly, and we call a variable a latent variable if it cannot be observed or measured directly (Figure 10.4). The assumption of a latent class model is that the interaction between a set of manifest variables, $M_1, M_2 ..., M_i$, can be explained by $j < i$ latent class variables, with $C_1, C_2, ..., C_j$ classes (Goodman, 1974). A latent class model also assumes latent conditional independence, which is conditionally based on the level of the latent variables and the fact that the manifest variables are independent. Comprehensive background on latent class models can be found in Bartholomew (1987), Fornell & Yi (1992), Loehlin (1992), and Harenaars & McCutcheon (2002).

Let us assume that there are three manifest variables, X_1, X_2, X_3 which have j different covariate patterns (combinations) of their respondent values (e.g., $000, 010, ..., 111$). Let Z denote a latent variable with two latent classes, anomaly-free: $c = 1$ and anomaly: $c = 2$. Let π_c represent the proportion of traffics in the population in class c, where, $\pi_1 + \pi_2 = 1$. Each network connection is a member of one of these two classes, as well as a member of j covariate patterns, which means we do not know which class it belongs to, but we do know which pattern it belongs to. The standard latent class model assumes that X_1, X_2, X_3 are conditionally independent given Z, which can be written as follows:

$$P(X_1 = x_1, X_2 = x_2, X_3 = x_3) = \sum_z \pi_z^Z \pi_{x_1|z}^{X_1|Z} \pi_{x_2|z}^{X_2|Z} \pi_{x_3|z}^{X_3|Z}, \qquad (10\text{-}3)$$

where

$$\pi_{x_1|z}^{X_1|Z} = P(X_1 = x_1 \mid Z = z),$$

$$\pi_{x_2|z}^{X_2|Z} = P(X_2 = x_2 \mid Z = z), and$$

$$\pi_{x_3|z}^{X_3|Z} = P(X_3 = x_3 \mid Z = z).$$

The joint distribution of X_1, X_2, X_3, and Z under the latent model has the following log-linear representation:

$$\log(P(X_1 = x_1, X_2 = x_2, X_3 = x_3, Z = z)) =$$
$$\alpha + \alpha_z^Z + \alpha_{x_1}^{X_1} + \alpha_{x_2}^{X_2} + \alpha_{x_3}^{X_3} + \alpha_{zx_1}^{ZX_1} + \alpha_{zx_2}^{ZX_2} + \alpha_{zx_3}^{ZX_3} \qquad (10\text{-}4)$$

where α's are model parameters to be estimated from the data using the Expectation Maximization (EM) algorithm (Dempster, Laird, and Rubin, 1977). The log-linear representation of the latent class model is shown as

$$\alpha_{x_1 x_2}^{X_1 X_2} = \alpha_{x_1 x_3}^{X_1 X_3} = \alpha_{x_2 x_3}^{X_2 X_3} = \alpha_{x_1 x_2 x_3}^{X_1 X_2 X_3} = \alpha_{x_1 x_2 x_3 y}^{X_1 X_2 X_3 Y} = 0.$$

For the EM algorithm, the latent variable is treated as missing data. To handle the missing data, we calculated the probability of assigning a network connection to class c using Bayes rule, and the positive and negative predictive values can correspondingly be obtained using the following Equations (Skrondal and Rabe-Hesketh, 2004):

$$P(c=1 \mid y_j) = \frac{\pi_1 \prod_{i=1}^{3} P(y_{ij} \mid c=1)}{\sum_c \pi_c \prod_{i=1}^{3} P(y_{ij} \mid c)} \quad \text{and} \qquad (10\text{-}5)$$

$$P(c=2 \mid y_j) = \frac{\pi_2 \prod_{i=1}^{3} P(y_{ij} \mid c=2)}{\sum_c \pi_c \prod_{i=1}^{3} P(y_{ij} \mid c)}. \qquad (10\text{-}6)$$

Example 10.2→Classification based on Latent Class Model. We will conduct this example in three sequential steps: (1) prepare data; (2) fit the latent class model; and (3) evaluate results. We first step creates training and testing samples and categorizes all network traffics in the training sample into different patterns based on the combination of each connection's features, which are represented by a set of binary predictor variables. Next, we develop a latent class model with two classes (anomaly-free or anomaly) and fitted the model with the testing sample. The model estimated parameters for each predictor variable and calculates conditional probabilities of belonging to anomaly-free and anomaly latent classes for each covariate pattern in the training sample. The pattern-specific probabilities are further used to classify traffic to either an anomaly-free or anomalous class.

Finally, we will compare the unsupervised learning latent class model-based classification results with the conventionally supervised learning logistic regression model-based results. The evaluation is conducted through three approaches. First, we assess the stability of the patterns identified from the training sample through the testing sample. Then, we assign the pattern-specific probabilities estimated from the training sample to the patterns in the testing sample. If a pattern of traffic in the testing sample is the same as the pattern in the training sample, the traffic will have the same probability of belonging to a corresponding latent class as it has in the training sample. The actual labeled response variable included in the training and testing samples is used as a "gold-standard" to compare latent class model-based classification results. Finally, we fit data with a logistic regression model and compare the performance of classification results between the two models.

We will use the KDD-cup data to draw the training and testing samples. To save the computing times, we randomly select 10% of data from the full KDD-cup training dataset as the subtraining sample. The labeled response variable is not used to develop the latent model but is used as a "gold-standard" to evaluate the classification results from the latent model. The predictor variables that served as manifest variables in the latent model are binary variables with a value of 1 for present and a value of 0 for absent. These variables are selected based on previous studies (Mukkamala, Tadiparthi, Tummala, and Janoski, 2003; Wang and Seidman, 2006), which include three "types of the service or protocol" dummy variables: TCP, HTTP and UDP, two login status indication variables: login-successfully and guest-login, and one "normal or error status of the connection" variable—RST. All these variables have demonstrated (Wang and Seidman, 2006) that they have at least a probability of 0.85 to be statistically significantly associated with abnormal network traffics.

Bivariate and descriptive analyses are conducted to compare the frequency of characteristics for each predictor variable between the training and testing samples, as well as the Frequency of different predictor variables' combination patterns. A pattern with less than 10 traffics is excluded to ensure that the latent model will be fitted with stable patterns. Equations (10-3) to (10-6) are calculated using the Generalized Linear Latent and Mixed Models developed by Skrondal and Rabe-Hesketh (Skrondal and Rabe-Hesketh, 2004). A probability of 0.5 is used as a threshold to classify connections into the anomaly-free or abnormal class for both the latent class and logistic regression models. Sensitivity, specificity, the area under the ROC curve, and the correctly classified rate are calculated for evaluating the classification results yielded by the latent and by the logistic models. The Stata codes used to conduct this example are shown in Display 10.1.

Display 10.1 Stata codes to fit the latent class model

```
#delimit;
clear;
set mem 500000k;
use F:\Book\Chapter 10\kdd_trai,replace;
gen byte attack=(NORMAL==0);
/*------------------------------------------------------
  Create 10% sample for training data
------------------------------------------------------*/;
keep attack TCP UDP HTTP RST logged_I is_guest;
gen str6 pattern=string(TCP)+string(UDP)+string(HTTP)+string(RST) +
string(logged_i)+string( is_guest);
gen n=1;
set seed 12335465;
sample 10,by(pattern);
sort pattern;
gen byte sample_10=1;
save pattern_temp,replace;
collapse (sum) wt2=n,by(pattern);
drop if wt2<=10;
```

continued on following page

Display 10.1 continued

```
merge pattern using pattern_temp;
keep if _m==3;
sort pattern;
gen a=(pattern==pattern[_n+1]);
keep if a==0;
drop _m n a;
/*------------------------------------------------
 Fit latent class model                    (
------------------------------------------------*/;
do latent_model.do; /* Codes are listed in Appendix */;
/*------------------------------------------------
 Pattern of manifest variables training sample
------------------------------------------------*/
tab attack if patt~=patt[_n+1] [w=wt2],sum(prob2);
tab attack if patt~=patt[_n+1] [w=wt2],sum(prob1);
list pattern wt2 prob2 prob1  patt attack if patt~=patt[_n+1];
keep pattern prob*;
sort pattern;
save xx,replace;
/*------------------------------------------------
 Testing data
------------------------------------------------*/;
use kdd_val,replace;
gen byte attack=(NORMAL==0);
keep attack TCP UDP HTTP RST logged_i is_guest;
gen str6 pattern=string(TCP)+string(UDP)+string(HTTP)+string(RST) +
string(logged_i)+string( is_guest);
gen n=1;

append using pattern_temp;
sort pattern;
merge pattern using xx;
keep if _m==3;
drop _m;
save xx_v,replace;
gen n=1;
collapse (sum) wt2=n (mean) attack, by(pattern sample_10);
/*------------------------------------------------
 Pattern of manifest variables in testing sample
------------------------------------------------*/
list if sample_10==1;
list if sample_10==0;
use xx_v,replace;
```

continued on following page

Display 10.1 continued

```
Classification results
------------------------------------------------------------------*/;
logistic attack TCP UDP HTTP RST logged_i is_guest if sample_10==1;
lroc;
predict phat;
tab attack if sample_10==0,sum(phat);
gen byte Latent=(prob1>0.5);
gen Logistic=(phat>0.5);
tab attack Latent if sample_10==0,col row;
tab attack Logistic if sample_10==0,col row;
tab attack Latent if sample_10==1,col row;
tab attack Logistic if sample_10==1,col row;
logistic attack Latent if sample_10==1;
lroc;
lstat;
logistic attack Latent if sample_10==0;
lroc;
lstat;
logistic attack Logistic if sample_10==1;
lroc;
lstat;
logistic attack Logistic if sample_10==0;
lroc;
lstat;
```

Table 10.1 illustrates the frequency and rate of the predictor variables based on the training and testing samples. Overall, there is no difference between the initial training data and the final 10% sample, and no remarkable difference between the final training and testing samples.

Table 10.2 shows the parameters estimated from the latent class model. The posterior probability is 0.84 with a SD of 0.37 for classifying traffic as anomaly, while there are 79.9% of observed anomalous traffics in the training sample.

For a set of k binary variables, there are 2^k different patterns of combinations that can be potentially observed, and the combinations of the six selected predictor variables, arranged as TCP (yes/no), UDP (yes/no), HTTP (yes/no), RST (yes/no), login-successfully (yes/no) and guest-login (yes/no), only yielded nine covariate patterns. They are an important concept in logistic regression analysis. We will revisit this topic again in Chapter XII.

Probabilities of being an anomaly-free and being an anomalous traffic are estimated by the latent class model for all traffics included in the testing sample. Because the traffics represent a two-second window, most observations in both the training and the testing samples had exactly the same values of the predictor variables longitudinally, which resulted in an unbalanced distribution of the data frequency across the nine patterns. More than 50% of the traffics have a value of "no", presented as "000000" for all the predictor variables in both the training and testing samples. The second highest volume pattern is "100000", which represents traffics of TCP being "yes" and all others being "no." It included 22.3% and 20.5% of traffics in the training and testing samples, respectively. The lowest volume pattern is different between the two samples, from "101110" (0.03%) in the training to "101000" (0.13%) in the testing samples. Overall, the top three high volume patterns

Table 10.1. Descriptive analysis on data characteristics

Variables	Training				Testing	
	Initial data		Final 10% sample		(N = 310,786)	
	(N = 494,021)		(N = 49,399)			
	#	%	#	%	#	%
Type of protocol						
Transmission control protocol (TCP)	190,065	38.47	19,007	38.47	119,111	38.33
User datagram protocol (UDP)	20,354	4.12	2,035	4.12	26,703	8.59
Hyper text transfer protocol (HTTP)	64,293	13.01	6,430	13.02	41,237	13.26
Network service on the destination						
RSTO or RSTOS0 or RSTR (RST)	1,493	0.30	149	0.30	2,627	0.73
Content features within a connection suggested by domain knowledge						
Login-successfully	73,237	14.82	7,324	14.83	53,645	17.25
Guest-login	685	0.14	68	0.14	754	0.24
Outcome						
Anomaly-free traffic	97,278	19.69	9,725	19.69	60,593	19.50

Table 10.2. Estimate based on the training sample

Variables	Class c = 1 (anomaly-free)		Class c = 2 (anomaly)	
	Estimate	SE	Estimate	SE
Transmission control protocol (TCP)	-708.02	0.4809	-6,055.00	2.2556
User datagram protocol (UDP)	-2.58	0.0224	-405.9300	0.2694
Hyper text transfer protocol (HTTP)	-280.69	0.1949	-0.4714	0.0149
RSTO or RSTOS0 or RSTR (RST)	-8.04	0.3194	-14858.0000	58.6519
Login-successfully	-191.42	0.2249	-817.7900	0.0365
Guest-login	-7.80	0.2834	-120.0200	
Intercept	0.67	0.0095	-	-
SE denotes standard error				

included approximate 91.5% of traffics for the training sample and 86.5% of traffics for the testing sample (Table 10.3).

The pattern-level mean probability of being anomalous based on the "gold-standard", the observed outcome, ranges from 0.0323 ("101000") to 0.9950 ("000000") and 0.0262 ("101010") to 0.9977 ("000000") for the training and testing samples, correspondingly. Using a probability of 0.5 as a classifying threshold, six patterns in the training and four from the testing samples are correctly matched with the "gold-standard" results. All the top three high volume patterns are correctly matched. Thus, although the matched rates at the pattern-level do not seem high, they were remarkably high at the traffic-level, in which approximately 92.9% and 86.5% traffics in training and testing samples could be correctly matched.

Based on the estimated parameters, probabilities of being abnormal and anomaly-free at the traffic-level are calculated for both training and testing samples. The probability of being anomalous ranges from 0.00 to 1.00 with a mean value of 0.9517 (SD = 0.2067) and

Table 10.3. Probabilities of being anomaly-free and anomaly by patterns

Covariate Pattern*	Training (n = 49,399)					Testing (n =310,786)		
	Frequency		Probability to be**		Observed (anomaly, %)	Frequency		Observed (anomaly, %)
	Total (#)	Rate (%)	Anomaly-free	Anomaly		Total (#)	Rate (%)	
000000	28,360	57.41	0.0000	0.9999	0.9950	164,969	53.08	0.9977
010000	2,035	4.12	0.0000	1.0000	0.0531	26,703	8.59	0.3972
100000	10,993	22.25	0.0130	0.9869	0.9867	63,649	20.48	0.9781
100010	1,380	2.79	1.0000	0.0000	0.0652	12,017	3.87	0.7268
100011	68	0.14	1.0000	0.0000	0.5147	653	0.21	0.8224
100100	133	0.27	0.0070	0.9928	0.9774	1,559	0.50	0.9513
101000	557	1.13	1.0000	0.0000	0.0323	402	0.13	0.9179
101010	5,860	11.86	1.0000	0.0000	0.0381	40,268	12.96	0.0262
101110	13	0.03	1.0000	0.0000	0.6923	566	0.18	1.0000

* Order of predictive variables: TCP (yes/no), UDP (yes/no), HTTP (yes/no), RST (yes/no), login-successfully (yes/no) and guest-login (yes/no)

** The testing sample has the same probabilities of being anomaly-free and anomaly as the training sample.

the 25th to 75th percentiles are 0.9869 and 1.0000 respectively for all abnormal traffics. The probability of being anomaly-free ranged from 0.00 to 1.00 with a mean of 0.7041 (SD = 0.4561), and 25th and 75th percentiles were 0.00 to 1.00 for all anomaly-free traffics in the training sample. The testing sample had the same patterns of probability distribution; the means were 0.9869 (SD = 0.0966) and 0.7720 (SD = 0.4194), and the 25th to 75th were 0.9869 to 1.0000 and 0.9999 to 1.0000, for abnormal and anomaly-free traffics, respectively.

Using the same threshold of 0.5 to classify traffics, Table 10.4 compares the classification results obtained from the latent class model and the logistic regression model for the two samples. The logistic model achieves higher performance in all six measurements than the latent model but the differences between these two models are not remarkable. The correctly classified rates are 94.8% vs. 98.4% in the training sample and 90.6% vs. 92.5% in the testing sample. The largest difference is the specificity that measures the probability that traffic be classified as anomaly-free for true anomaly-free traffic (Figure 10.5). Theoretically, the supervised learning logistic regression model is expected to have better performance because its classifications are derived from a clear relationship of observed response-predictors, while the unsupervised learning latent class model's classifications are based on the predictive variables only.

Hidden Markov Model

Hidden Markov Models (HMMs) have been thought as one of the most successful modeling ideas in the last 5 decades (Cappe, Moulines & Ryden, 2005). The basic idea of an HMM is to determine the observed sequence by the underlying unobservable process. It has been found to be the greatest useful in problems that have an inherent temporality, for example, states at time *t* that are directly impacted by the states at *t* - 1 (Duda, Hart & Stork, 2001). An HMM has three attributes: (1) the states are not observable,(2) observations are probabilistic of state, and (3) state transitions are probabilistic.

Table 10.4. Evaluation of classification results

Measure of classification	Latent class model		Logistic regression model	
	Training	Testing	Training	Testing
ROC	0.8812	0.8294	0.9831	0.9779
Sensitivity	0.9905	0.9550	0.9887	0.9148
Specificity	0.7718	0.7038	0.9666	0.9676
Positive predictive value	0.9466	0.9301	0.9918	0.9915
Negative predictive value	0.9524	0.7911	0.9545	0.7332
Correctly classified	0.9475	0.9060	0.9844	0.925

Because the assumption of the regular Markov processes, which says the next state depends only on the current state and the past and future are independent, is too restrictive to be applicable to many realistic applications (Rabiner, 1989), so the concept of Markov models has been extended to include the case where the observation is a probabilistic function of the state. Thus, an HMM can be considered as a typical regular Markov process with a set of observed sequential outcomes and unobserved (hidden) sequential states, which are linked by parameters. In a regular Markov model, because the states are directly observable so the state transition probabilities are the only parameters to be estimated. In an HMM the states are not directly observable but the variables influenced by the hidden states are visible and the observation is a probabilistic function of a hidden state. For a useful introduction to HMM refer to *A Tutorial on Hidden Markov Models and Selected Applications in Speech Recognition* by Rabiner(1989).

In short, a simple first-order (the first-order means that the states at time t only depend on the states at time $t - 1$,), discrete state and discrete time HMM consists of five basic elements: (1) a set of states, (2) a set of observable outcomes (of which the set of states is associated with), (3) a probability distribution for each of the observable outcomes at each state, (4) an initial state distribution, and (5) a state transition probability distribution matrix. As we mentioned, we cannot observe the current state, but we can produce an output with a certain probability distribution. Let us consider the first-order discrete state and discrete time HMM. Let N be the number of states, $S = \{S_1, S_2, \cdots, S_N\}$ be individual states, and q_t be a particular state at time t. Let M be the number of observable outcomes, each individual be $V = \{v_1, v_2, \cdots, v_M\}$, and A be a transition probability matrix,

$$A = \begin{vmatrix} a_{11} & a_{12} & \cdots & a_{1N} \\ a_{21} & a_{22} & \cdots & a_{2N} \\ \vdots & \vdots & \vdots & \vdots \\ a_{N1} & a_{N2} & \cdots & a_{NN} \end{vmatrix}$$

where

Figure 10.5. Performance differences between the latent class and logistic regression models

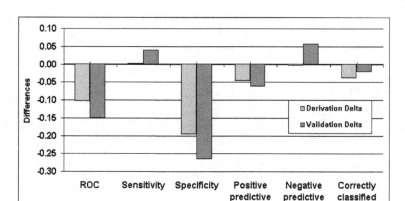

$$a_{ij} = p(q_{t+1} = S_j \mid q_t = S_i), \ 1 \leq i, j \leq N, \tag{10-7}$$

$$a_{ij} \geq 0 \quad \text{and} \quad \sum_{j=1}^{N} a_{ij} = 1.$$

Let $\pi_i = \{\pi_i\}$ be initial state distribution, where

$$\pi_i = p(q_1 = S_i), 1 \leq i \leq N, \tag{10-8}$$

and $B = \{b_j(k)\}$ be the observed outcome probability distribution in state S_j, where

$$b_j(k) = p(v_k = t \mid q_t = S_j), 1 \leq j \leq N \text{ and } 1 \leq k \leq M. \tag{10-9}$$

With the model parameters N and M and Equations (10-7) to (10-9) we can use the HMM to generate an observation sequence

$$O = \{O_1, O_2 \cdots, O_T\}, \tag{10-10}$$

where T is the total number of observations in the sequence and O_t is one of the observable outcome in v_t (Rabiner, 1989). W can graphically illustrate an HMM with five states as shown in Figure 10.6. Note that a state can be revisited at any different steps, not every state need to be visited and a particular state may be visited sequentially.

There are 3 basic problems for an HMM: (1) given observation $O = \{O_1, O_2, \ldots O_T\}$ and model $\lambda = (A, B, \pi)$, estimate $p(O \mid \lambda)$, (2) given observation $O = \{O_1, O_2, \ldots O_T\}$ and model $\lambda = (A, B, \pi)$, find the optimal state sequence $q = (q_1, q_2, \ldots, q_T)$, (3) given observation $O = \{O_1, O_2, \ldots O_T\}$, estimate model parameters $\lambda = (A, B, \pi)$ that maximize $p(O \mid \lambda)$ (Rabiner, 1989).

Figure 10.6 A 5-state Hidden Markov Model

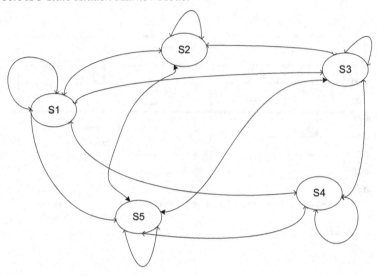

Example 10.3→HMM-based Intrusion Detection. Wright, Monrose, and Masson (2004) presented A HMM application to profile network applications using the packet-level information that remains intact and observable after encryption; namely, packet size and arrival time. They demonstrate classification accuracy close to that of other recent techniques, and show success in classifying a variety of common network applications as observed from real Internet traffic traces. Additional information on the use of HMM in network security can be found from Gao, Ma & Yang (2002), Cho & Park (2003), Ourston, Matzner, Stump, & Hopkins (2003), and Qian & Xin (2007).

Example 10.4→Three-state HMM in Continuous Time. As examined previously, the MIT-DARPA data can be converted into a longitudinal format for monitoring site behavior over time. Let us use this longitudinal data to fit a three-state HMM that allows a site to move through the three states continuously through time. We first use the full 7-week data to create the longitudinal data with the date as a time variable. We require that each site (denoted by an IP address) has to have at least 50 observations and has to be repeated at least 30 times (i.e., at least to be measured 30 days) in the converted longitudinal dataset. We then categorize the sites into three groups based on their daily traffics:

$$g = \begin{cases} 1 & \rho = 0 \\ 2 & 0 < \rho < 0.5, \\ 3 & \rho > 0.5 \end{cases}$$

where ρ is the daily anomalous rate. These three groups correspond to three states: anomaly-free, mild anomaly, and severe anomaly, for each site on each day. A site can move from one state to another in any direction. Display 10.2 shows the Stata codes used to conduct this data conversion.

Display 10.2
Stata codes used to create the longitudinal dataset for fitting the HMM

```
#delimit;
clear;
set mem 654566;
use g:\Book\Data\MIT_list.DTA, replace;
gen MD=substr(date,1,2)+"/"+substr(date,4,2);
gen n=1;
collapse (sum) n,by(IP_s MD);
keep if n>50;
gen q=1;
collapse (sum) q,by(IP_s);
keep if q>=30;
keep IP_s;
sort IP_s;
save HMM,replace;
use g:\Book\Data\MIT_list.DTA, replace;
gen byte Attack=(attack~="-");
drop v13 score;
sort IP_s;
merge IP_s using HMM;
keep if _m==3;
gen MD=substr(date,1,2)+"/"+substr(date,4,2);
gen n=1;
collapse (sum) n Attack,by(IP_s MD);
gen rate=Attack/n;
sort IP_s MD;
keep if n>50;
encode MD,gen(md);
gen stage=1 if rate==0;
replace stage=2 if rate>0 & rate<0.5;
replace stage=3 if rate>=0.5;
sort IP_s MD
gen first=(md==1 & IP_s==IP_s[_n+1]);
outsheet IP_s md stage first using HMM.txt, c replace nol;
list IP_s md stage first in 1/20;
```

The final longitudinal dataset includes a total of 1202 individual days across 29 sites. Display 10.3 lists the first 20 observations of the converted longitudinal data for site 135.008.060.182. Site 135.008.060.182 had moved six times across the three states. More specifically, it moved from state 2 (mild anomaly) to state 1 (anomaly-free) on the 3rd day, and moved from state 1 to state 3 (severe anomaly) on the 10th day, etc.

Display 10.3
First 20 observations of the converted longitudinal data for site 135.008.060.182

```
+----------------------------------------+
|           IP_s      Day    state   first |
|----------------------------------------|
 1. | 135.008.060.182   06/01       2       1 |
 2. | 135.008.060.182   06/02       2       0 |
 3. | 135.008.060.182   06/03       1       0 |
 4. | 135.008.060.182   06/04       2       0 |
 5. | 135.008.060.182   06/05       1       0 |
|----------------------------------------|
 6. | 135.008.060.182   06/08       1       0 |
 7. | 135.008.060.182   06/09       1       0 |
 8. | 135.008.060.182   06/10       1       0 |
 9. | 135.008.060.182   06/11       1       0 |
10. | 135.008.060.182   06/12       3       0 |
|----------------------------------------|
11. | 135.008.060.182   06/15       1       0 |
12. | 135.008.060.182   06/16       1       0 |
13. | 135.008.060.182   06/17       1       0 |
14. | 135.008.060.182   06/18       1       0 |
15. | 135.008.060.182   06/19       1       0 |
|----------------------------------------|
16. | 135.008.060.182   06/22       1       0 |
17. | 135.008.060.182   06/23       1       0 |
18. | 135.008.060.182   06/24       1       0 |
19. | 135.008.060.182   06/25       1       0 |
20. | 135.008.060.182   06/26       2       0 |
+----------------------------------------+
```

For this type of longitudinal dataset, we can use the *msm* package from R to fit a three-state HMM in continuous time (day). Display 10.4 lists the R codes used to construct the model. Note that the transition probability matrix defined in Display 10.4 is solely for illustrating purpose and can be revised based on additional observed data.

Display 10.4
R codes used to fit the three-state HMM

```
## Multi-state HMM
require("msm")
HMM<-read.table("g:\\Book\\2007\\Chapter 10\\hmm.txt",header=TRUE,sep = ",")
statetable.msm(stage, IP_s, data=HMM)
twoway3.q <-rbind(c(0.5,0.25,0.25),c(0.15,0.15,0.15),c(0.1,0.1,0.1))
crudeinits.msm(state ~ day, IP_s, data=HMM, qmatrix=twoway3.q)
HMM.msm <-msm( state ~ day, subject=IP_s,data=HMM,qmatrix=twoway3.q,
               exacttimes=TRUE, control=list( trace=2,REPORT=1))
HMM.msm
prevalence.msm(HMM.msm, times=seq(0, 40, 1))
plot.prevalence.msm(HMM.msm,mintime=0,maxtime=40)
```

Using the function *statetable.msm*, we can summarize the multi-state data as a frequency table of paired consecutive states as shown:

		To		
		1	2	3
From	1	910	93	11
	2	93	30	5
	3	12	4	9.

Figure 10.7 Observed prevalence (solid line) vs. expected prevalence (dashed line).

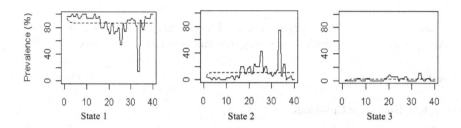

For example, we can see that 910 observations stayed with state 1, while 93 moved from state 1 to state 2, 11 from state 1 to state 3, 12 from state 3 to state 1, etc. Figure 10.7 compares the observed and expected numbers of individuals occupying a state at a series of times by each state. We can see that the model does not fit well in states 1 and 2, but the predicted and observed anomalous events are relatively similar in state 3.

SIMILARITY MODELS

Similarity analysis focuses on measuring the similarity and dissimilarity between observation groups based on a similarity-matrix. Using the data cube concept described in Chapter IV, similarity analysis focuses on the observations' dimension and aims to partition observations into relatively homogeneus groups based on the intra-observation similarities. Thus, for a set of observations, the goal of similiarity analysis is to form smaller subgroups of similar observations so that in each subgroup, observations are similaer to each other, but the subgroups themseleves are dissimilar from to each other. The most popular methods to measure similarity include hierarchical cluster analysis, k-mean clustering, and a self-organizing map (SOM). We will briefly discuss each of these methods in the following sections. Readers who are interested in gaining more information should refer to Hartigan (1975) and Everitt (2001) for cluster analysis, Hartigan & Wong (1979) for k-mean clustering, and Kaski (1997) for SOM.

Measuring Similarity

Great volumes of measurements have been developed for measuring the similarity between data points. Figure 10.8 graphically illustrates an example of measuring similarity with observations.

Let $p_i (i = 1, 2, \ldots n)$ and $q_j (j = 1, 2, \ldots n)$ denote the ith observation and j^{th} observation with k variables $p_i = (x_{1i}, x_{2i}, \ldots x_{ki})$ and $q_j = (x_{1j}, x_{2j}, \ldots x_{kj})$ in a k-dimensional space, $D = \{p_1, p_2, \cdots p_i, \cdots q_j, \cdots p_n\}$. The basic idea of measuring similarity and dissimilarity between p_i and q_j is to measure the distance between p_i and q_j

$$d \sim (p_i, q_j).$$

For continuous variables, as we discussed in Chapter IX, the Euclidean distance

$$d(p_i, q_j) = \sqrt{\sum_{c=1}^{k} (x_{ci} - x_{cj})^2}$$

(10-11)

is a widely used method. In addition, several of its extended formulas can also provide similar measurement information, including the squared Euclidean distance:

$$d(p_i, q_j) = \sum_{c=1}^{k} (x_{ci} - x_{cj})^2,$$

(10-12)

the absolute distance or City-block

$$d(p_i, q_j) = \sum_{c=1}^{k} |x_{ci} - x_{cj}|,$$

(10-13)

and the maximum-value distance

$$d(p_i, q_j) = \max_{c=1,2,\cdots,k} |x_{ci} - x_{cj}|, \text{ and}$$

(10-14)

the correlation coefficient similarity measure

$$d(p_i, q_j) = \frac{\sum_{c=1}^{k} (x_{ci} - \bar{x}_i)(x_{cj} - \bar{x}_j)}{\sqrt{\sum_{c=1}^{k} (x_{ci} - \bar{x}_i)^2 \sum_{c=1}^{k} (x_{cj} - \bar{x}_j)^2}},$$

(10-15)

Figure 10.8 Intra-observation similarity (the bold lines between squares measure distance between group centers and the thin lines measure distance from a group center to a group member)

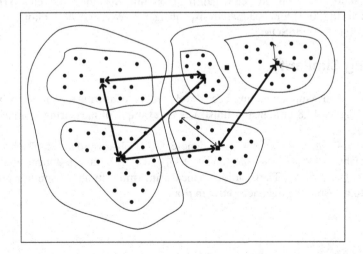

where k represents the number of variables for each observation, and $\bar{x}_i$ and $\bar{x}_j$ are the means for the ith and j^{th} observations over the k variables.

When X represents a set of binary variables, the distance-based measurements may not be appropriate but we can measure the degree of matching based on a contingency table. Lets consider a simple 2×2 cross-table, and let k_1 be the total number of variables that p_i and q_j are both present. Let k_2 be the total number of variables that p_i is present and q_j is absent, k_3 be the total number of variables that p_i is absent and q_j is present, and k_4 be the total number of variables that p_i and q_j are both absent (Table 10.5).

Sokal and Michener (1958) proposed to measure the match or agreement rate between p_i and q_j by

$$r = \frac{k_1 + k_2}{k_1 + k_2 + k_3 + k_4}. \tag{10-16}$$

We can measure the similarity based on the agreement on present for both p_i and q_j by the Jaccard coefficient (1908)

$$r = \frac{k_1}{k_1 + k_2 + k_3}. \tag{10-17}$$

Similarly, we can measure the agreement on the present rate by using the Russell coefficient (1940)

$$r = \frac{k_1}{k_1 + k_2 + k_3 + k_4}. \tag{10-18}$$

In addition, there are many coefficients used for measuring the similarity through measuring the agreement between p_i and q_j across their variables. For example, the Pearson matching coefficient

$$r = \frac{k_1 k_4 - k_3 k_4}{\sqrt{k_1 + k_2)(k_1 + k_3)(k_2 + k_4)(k_3 + k_4)}} \tag{10-19}$$

has a measuring range from -1 to 1.

Table 10.5 Measure similarity with binary variables

p_i	q_j		Total
	Present	Absent	
Present	k_1	k_2	$k_1 + k_2$
Absent	k_3	k_4	$k_3 + k_4$
Total	$k_1 + k_3$	$k_2 + k_4$	$k_1 + k_2 + k_3 + k_4$

Although equations (10-11) to (10-19) all measure similarity, we can obtain the dissimilarity d_{ij} between the ith and j^{th} observations, using

$$d_{ij} = 1 - s_{ij}, \text{ or} \qquad\qquad\qquad (10\text{-}20)$$

$$d_{ij} = \sqrt{s_{ii} + s_{jj} - 2s_{ij}}, \qquad\qquad\qquad (10\text{-}21)$$

where s_{ij} is the similarity between the ith and j^{th} observations. This is similar to the KNN algorithm that we have discussed in Chapter IX.

Example 10.5→Measure Similarity. Let us use the Euclidean distance (Equation 10-11) to measure the similarity of variables, *v1* to *v57*, for the first 8 observations of the spam-email data. We create a matrix called ED to hold the Euclidean distance between all the observations for variables *v1* to *v57*. The Stata codes used to create the ED matrix and the results are shown in Display 10.5.

Display 10.5
Stata codes to measure similarity and the results of first 8 observations in the spam-email data

```
. matrix dissimilarity ED =v1-v57  in 1/8,Euclidean
. matrix list ED

symmetric ED[8,8]
           obs1        obs2        obs3        obs4        obs5        obs6        obs7      obs8
obs1          0
obs2  751.07127           0
obs3  2025.8779    1289.516           0
obs4  89.533956    839.2237   2115.3484           0
obs5  89.533967    839.2237   2115.3484    .00282841          0
obs6  228.70643   977.80383   2254.5474    139.3143    139.3143           0
obs7  175.55623   921.13195   2200.2389   86.863617   86.863616   59.240845           0
obs8  234.42902   983.14402    2252.275    144.98452   144.98452   6.4268646   63.572175      0
```

We found that the observations #4 and #5 are the most similar pair with an Euclidean distance of <0.003 and observations #3 and #6 are the most dissimilar pair with an Euclidean distance of >2254. Display 10.6 shows the actual data of observations #3 to #6.

Display 10.6
List of pairs observations #3 vs. #6 and $4 vs. #5

Variable	Value (observation #3)	Value (observation #6)	Value (observation #4)	Value (observation #5)
v1	0.06	0	0	0
v2	0	0	0	0
v3	0.71	0	0	0
v4	0	0	0	0
v5	1.23	1.85	0.63	0.63
v6	0.19	0	0	0
v7	0.19	0	0.31	0.31
v8	0.12	1.85	0.63	0.63
v9	0.64	0	0.31	0.31
v10	0.25	0	0.63	0.63
v11	0.38	0	0.31	0.31
v12	0.45	0	0.31	0.31
v13	0.12	0	0.31	0.31
v14	0	0	0	0
v15	1.75	0	0	0
v16	0.06	0	0.31	0.31
v17	0.06	0	0	0
v18	1.03	0	0	0
v19	1.36	0	3.18	3.18
v20	0.32	0	0	0
v21	0.51	0	0.31	0.31
v22	0	0	0	0
v23	1.16	0	0	0
v24	0.06	0	0	0
v25	0	0	0	0
v26	0	0	0	0
v27	0	0	0	0
v28	0	0	0	0
v29	0	0	0	0
v30	0	0	0	0
v31	0	0	0	0
v32	0	0	0	0
v33	0	0	0	0
v34	0	0	0	0
v35	0	0	0	0
v36	0	0	0	0

continued on following page

Display 10.6 continued

v37	0	0	0	0
v38	0	0	0	0
v39	0	0	0	0
v40	0.06	0	0	0
v41	0	0	0	0
v42	0	0	0	0
v43	0.12	0	0	0
v44	0	0	0	0
v45	0.06	0	0	0
v46	0.06	0	0	0
v47	0	0	0	0
v48	0	0	0	0
v49	0.01	0	0	0
v50	0.143	0.223	0.137	0.135
v51	0	0	0	0
v52	0.276	0	0.137	0.135
v53	0.184	0	0	0
v54	0.01	0	0	0
v55	9.821	3	3.537	3.537
v56	485	15	40	40
v57	2259	54	191	191

Hierarchical Cluster Analysis

Cluster analysis, belonging to the multivariate analysis family, was proposed initially by Tryon (1939). It aims to group observations in such a way that maximizes the degree of similarity between two observations if they belong to the same cluster (class) and minimizes otherwise. With cluster analysis we can discover the data structures in the dimension of observations without any prior hypotheses. However, the analysis does not provide informa-tion on why such structures exist. A detailed review of this topic can be found from Everitt (2001). Clustering analysis is similar to the KNN algorithm that we discussed in Chapter IX. The major difference between these two approaches is that with cluster analysis, we do not need any prior hypotheses on the clustering , while in KNN we classify observations based on a prior trained sample.

Because various approaches of measuring similarity are available, great ranges of cluster analysis methods are available, which may give different results depending which approach we choose. However, there are generally two hierarchical clustering algorithms: agglomerative hierarchical cluster and divisive clustering. The agglomerative hierarchi-cal clustering algorithm is a bottom-to-top method that starts from the largest number of clusters within each cluster to the smallest size—that is, the initial number of clusters G is equivalent to the number of observations N , where each cluster g_j includes only one member. Next, the algorithm combines the closest two clusters based on their similarity. As a result of the 2nd step, the number of clusters is reduced to G - 1, one cluster g_j has 2

Table 10.6 Popular linkage methods for comparing cluster groups

Clustering method	Parameters			
	α_i	α_j	β	λ
Single linkage or nearest neighbor approach	$\dfrac{1}{2}$	$\dfrac{1}{2}$	0	$-\dfrac{1}{2}$
Complete linkage	$\dfrac{1}{2}$	$\dfrac{1}{2}$	0	$\dfrac{1}{2}$
Weighted-average linkage	$\dfrac{1}{2}$	$\dfrac{1}{2}$	0	0
Centroid linkage	$\dfrac{n_i}{n_i+n_j}$	$\dfrac{n_i}{n_i+n_j}$	$-\alpha_i\alpha_j$	0
Median linkage	$\dfrac{1}{2}$	$\dfrac{1}{2}$	$-\dfrac{1}{4}$	0
Ward' linkage	$\dfrac{n_i+n_k}{n_i+n_j+n_k}$	$\dfrac{n_j+n_k}{n_i+n_j+n_k}$	$\dfrac{-n_k}{n_i+n_j+n_k}$	0
Average linkage	$\dfrac{n_i}{n_i+n_j}$	$\dfrac{n_j}{n_i+n_j}$	0	0

members and the rest of the clusters still have only one member. This step will be repeated until all observations belong to the same cluster.

The divisive hierarchical clustering algorithm is a top-to-bottom method that begins with one cluster with all observations as its members. Next this cluster is divided into two sub-clusters based on the similarity across all observations. Next, one of the two clusters is split into two so there are now three clusters. We repeat this step until all the observations are in their own classes. Note that our goal in the 2nd step is to divide the observations into the best possible split clusters, which could lead to having a total of $2^{(N-1)} - 1$ possible splits to be considered.

In agglomerative hierarchical cluster analysis, besides to measuring similarity to compare observations, we also need to compare between clusters, and the method used to make such comparisons is called linkage. There are a variety of linkages that are available and the most commonly used are shown in Table 10.6. The notations are based on the Lance and Williams recurrence Equation below

$$d_{k(i,j)} = \alpha_i d_{ki} + \alpha_j d_{kj} + \beta d_{ij} + \lambda |d_{ki} - d_{kj}|, \tag{10-22}$$

where d_{ij} is the distance between cluster i and cluster j, $d_{k(i,j)}$ is the distance between cluster k and the new cluster formed by joining clusters i and j, and α_i, α_j, β, and λ are parameters that are based on the particular hierarchical cluster analysis method shown in Table 10.6. n_i, n_j and n_k are the number of observations in clusters i, j and k.

Example 10.6→Cluster Analysis-based Classification. Both SAS and Stata provide procedures and commands for agglomerative hierarchical cluster analysis. SAS also has a procedure for divisive clustering analysis. Let us use 1% of the spam-email data that includes continuous variables of v1 to v57 to fit the agglomerative hierarchical cluster model using the SAS *PROC CLUSTER* procedure that hierarchically clusters observations in classes using one of eleven linkage methods that SAS provided. The SAS codes for conducting the analysis are given in Display 10.7 and the cluster result is shown in Figure 10.9.

Display 10.7
SAS codes to fit a hierarchical cluster model (1% of spam-email data)

```
/*------------------------------------------------------------
   Hierarchical Clustering Methods
-----------------------------------------------------------*/;
libname Cluster 'F:\Book\Chapter 10\';
options ls=64 ps=45 nodate nonumber;
data spam; set cluster.spam; if ( UNIFORM(12345)>0.99); qid=_N_; run;
proc cluster data = spam method=centroid nonorm out=tree;
id qid; var v1-v57; run;
proc tree data=tree out=cluster_out nclusters=5;
id qid; run;
/*------------------------------------------------
Compare to the response variable v58
---------------------------------------------*/;
proc sql noprint;
create table classification as select v58, spam.qid, cluster, CLUSNAME
from spam innor join cluster_out on spam.qid=cluster_out.qid; quit;
proc freq data=classification; table CLUSNAME*v58; run;
```

In general, the data for cluster analysis using SAS can be either coordinates or distances—if the data are coordinates, *PROC CLUSTER* computes (possibly squared) Euclidean distances. If we want to perform a cluster analysis on non-Euclidean distance data, we can do so by using the SAS *%Distance* macro, which can compute many kinds of distance matrices. This macro can be downloaded from the SAS website, http://support.sas.com/ctx/samples/index.jsp?sid=475&tab=downloads. For a good introduction on using the *PROC CLUSTER* producer, refer to *Multivariate Data Reduction and Discrimination with SAS Software* by Khattree and Naik (2000).

Because cluster analysis requires great resource use of the CPU, the *PROC CLUSTER* procedure is not practical for very large datasets. SAS also has another procedure called *PROC FASTCLUS*, which requires that the time is proportional to the number of observations. SAS recommends that for clustering large data hierarchically, use the *PROC FASTCLUS*

Figure 10.9 Dendrogram based on 1% of spam-email data (qid denotes individual email)

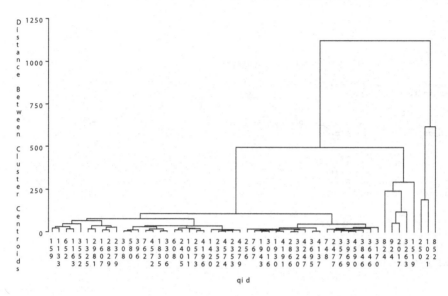

The 1% sample of spam-email data includes 54 observations that are distributed across five clusters: cluster #5 (qid=852), cluster #4 (qid=1519), cluster #3 (qid=250 and 1021), cluster #2 (qid=824, 924, 2017 and 3263), and cluster #1 includes the remainder (n=46)."

procedure to obtain a preliminary cluster analysis producing a large number of clusters, and then use *PROC CLUSTER* to cluster the preliminary clusters hierarchically.

We need to keep in mind that, like principal component analysis and factor analysis, the results from cluster analysis are subjective and depend on our interpretation. The procedures are simply descriptive and should be considered from an exploratory point of view rather than an inferential one.

Example 10.7→Cluster Analysis with Binary Data. Next, let us use the MIT-DARPA data with the 16-variables identified in Chapter VIII, to fit a binary hierarchical cluster model with Stata. Because the 16 variables are binary, we have to use one of the matching coefficients to measure similarity. We will use the Sokal and Michener's simple matching method shown in Equation (10-16). We will also use Ward's linkage method as the hierarchical clustering approach. The goal of this example is the same as in Example 10.5: to evaluate whether or not we can use the cluster analysis to categorize network traffics. Because the cluster analysis requires great computing resources and memory, we will randomly select 1% of the sample to fit the cluster model. Since 1% of traffics still incorporates too many observations for displaying in cluster tree, we can use the *cutnumber()* options to limit the number of branches of the tree, which we will limit in this example to 20, 10, 5 and 3. Stata codes to conduct this example are shown in Display 10.8.

Display 10.8
Stata codes to fit a binary hierarchical cluster model (based on 1% of data)

```
#delimit;
clear;
set mem 654566;
use F:\Book\Chapter 10\MIT_list.DTA, replace;
keep
normal t2 l1 udp icmp samePort sameIP http smtp urp ecr eco snmp ftp port
domain telnet finger;

cluster ward
t2 l1 udp icmp samePort sameIP http smtp urp ecr eco ftp port domain telnet
finger, match name(ward);

cluster list ward;
cluster tree,cutnumber(20);
cluster tree,cutnumber(10);
cluster tree,cutnumber(5);
cluster tree,cutnumber(3);

cluster gen gp_5=group(5);
cluster gen gp_3=group(3);
cluster gen gp_2=group(2);
tab gp_5 normal,col row;
tab gp_3 normal,col row;
tab gp_2 normal,col row;
```

Figure 10.10 Dendrograms based on 1% of MIT-DAPRA data

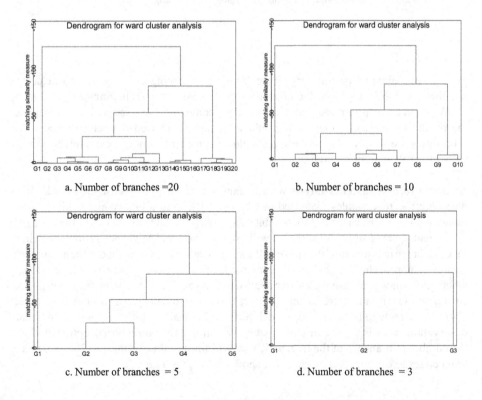

a. Number of branches =20

b. Number of branches = 10

c. Number of branches = 5

d. Number of branches = 3

Figure 10.10 shows dendrograms from Ward clustering. Subfigures a and b suggest the presence of 5 groups (clusters), and c and d suggest 2 groups among the 1% sample of the full MIT-DARPA data. Since the ultimate goal of fitting the cluster model is to classify all traffics into a binary class, anomaly-free and anomaly, we can do so after the model is fitted via Stata. The classification result based on the two groups is shown in Display 10.9. We see that 99.8% of traffics in *G1* are anomaly and 77.9% of traffics in *G2* are anomaly-free, and the overall misclassification rate is 11.1%, indicating that the cluster model given in Display 10.8 achieves a reasonable performance.

Display 10.9
Stata outputs of the fitted binary hierarchical cluster model

```
           |        normal
    gp_2 |       No        Yes |     Total
-----------+----------------------+-----------
      G1 |     1,504          3 |     1,507
         |     99.80       0.20 |    100.00
         |     81.92       0.26 |     50.03
-----------+----------------------+-----------
      G2 |       332      1,173 |     1,505
         |     22.06      77.94 |    100.00
         |     18.08      99.74 |     49.97
-----------+----------------------+-----------
   Total |     1,836      1,176 |     3,012
         |     60.96      39.04 |    100.00
         |    100.00     100.00 |    100.00
```

Table 10.7 illustrates the impact of different linkage methods on the performance of classification by comparing the results of classification across different linkage methods described in Table 10.6. It suggests that the Ward's method provides the best classification results.

Example 10.8→Web Visit Patterns. Modeling user behavior on the web has attracted much attention recently (Frías-Martínez and Karamcheti, 2002). Many of the web sequence data related studies have been focused on predicting the next requested webpage (Srikant, Yang, 2001; Mobasher and Cooley, 2000; Spiliopoulou, Pohle, and Faulstich, 1999; VanderMeer, Dutta, and Datta, 2000; Yang, Tian-Yi and Zhang, 2000; Yang, Zhang, Li and Lu, 2001). The goal of being able to predict such requests from users is to improve web intelligent services to benefit a variety of web-based businesses; such benefits include, for example,

Table 10.7 Comparison of classification results by different linkage methods

Measure of classification	Complete linkage	Weighted-average	Centroid linkage	Average linkage	Ward' linkage	Median linkage
Sensitivity	0.6767	0.6767	0.6098	0.6098	0.9980	0.6094
Specificity	0.9419	0.9419	1.000	1.000	0.7794	0.000
Correctly classified rate	0.7055	0.7055	0.6099	0.6099	0.8888	0.6092

improving websites, directing e-commerce services, and developing efficient web search algorithms.

User behavior on the web is also an important aspect associated to network security. As mentioned in Chapter III, when we are on the Internet, it is possible to become a victim of malicious programs from drive-by download sites that automatically install malicious codes unbeknownst to the user. Conversely, by analyzing the web visit sequence data, we may be able to track these sources of such malicious codes. For example, if we identified certain of security risks or threats caused by malicious codes for a group of users, we can analyze these users web patterns, and alarm them for the risk of being attacked by malicious codes, and also alarm others who have the same patterns about these potential security threats.

Clustering analysis and Markov chain analysis have been the techniques used mainly for analyzing web sequence data. In this example, let us conduct a pilot clustering analysis of the web sequence data examined in Chapter III. As discussed in Chapter VI, one of the goals of analyzing web sequence data is to categorize websites together based on their similarity. The result of such a categorization can be future used to group users based on their interests. This goal also can be achieved by cluster analysis. Using the SAS codes given in Display 3.8 to reshape the web sequence data from the initial row-based format to the column-based format and restricting the websites to have a frequency of visits at least 1% or high, we reduce the total number of websites from 294 to 47. Consequently, there are 47 websites can be clustered to several groups and the SAS codes to accomplish this analysis are given in Display 10.10.

Display 10.10
SAS codes to cluster websites on the web visit sequence data

```
Libname web "F:\book\Chapter 10\";
%include "F:\book\Chapter 10\polychor.sas" ;
%include Freq_cutoff.sas;  /* Codes are listed in Appendix CH10  */;
data tempz;
set web.visit_final;
run;
/*-----------------------------------------------
 The most visited websites:
   0.01=47 websites
   0.1 = 7 websites
-----------------------------------------------*/;
%let OutVar;
%FREQ_Cutoff(TEMPz,  vcode1000-vcode1295,0.01)
proc means data=tempz;
var &outvar;
run;
```

continued on following page

Display 10.10 continued

```
data tempz1 (
keep=user_ID
vcode1000-vcode1004 vcode1007-vcode1010 vcode1014 vcode1017 vcode1018 vcode1020
vcode1021 vcode1024-vcode1027 vcode1030-vcode1032 vcode1034-vcode1041 vcode1045
vcode1046 vcode1049 vcode1052-vcode1054 vcode1058 vcode1060 vcode1067 vcode1070
vcode1074-vcode1076 vcode1078 vcode1119 vcode1123 vcode1130 vcode1295);
set tempz;
run;
/*------------------------------------------------------------
  Cluster analysis
----------------------------------------------------------*/;
%polychor(data=tempz1,var=_numeric_,type=distance,id=web_id,out=dist,maxiter=10
0);
proc print noobs;
run;
proc cluster data=dist method=ward outtree=tree noprint;
id web_id;
run;
proc tree data=tree horizontal;
id web_id;
run;
proc tree data=tree ;
id web_id;
run;
```

Figure 10.11 shows the dendrograms of clustering results for 47 websites. By choosing different values of semi-partial r-squared, we can group these websites in a variety of combinations. For instance, using a semi-partial r-squared of 0.03, sites 1025 (Web Site Builder's Gallery), 1026 (Internet Site Construction for Developers), 1038 (SiteBuilder Network Membership), 1053 (Jakarta), 1027 (Internet Development), 1041 (Developer Workshop), and 1070 (ActiveX Technology Development) can go together as a Developer-specific group. Sites 1024 (Internet Information Server), 1030 (Windows NT Server), 1078 (NT Server Support), 1074 (Windows NT Workstation), and 1076(NT Workstation Support) can be clustered together as a system-specific group.

K-Means Clustering

The k-means clustering seeks to classify n individual observations into g predetermined non-overlapping groups in which the within-group sum of squares is minimized. The k-means clustering is a popular classification procedure that has been applied in many areas. Unlike the hierarchical cluster analysis where we do not decide the number of groups initially, the k-means clustering analysis requires to pre-specify the number of groups to be grouped. Although the idea of k-means is simple, to consider all the potential partitions of the n observations in to g groups, where $n_1 + n_2 + \cdots + n_g = n$, and select the lowest within-group sum of squares. In practice, it will involve a great deal of computing resources. The maximum number of possible combinations of groups to be tested with the g pre-determined groups could be

$$C_n^{n_1,n_2,\cdots,n_k} = \frac{n!}{n_1!n_2!\cdots n_g!}.$$

K-means clustering is an iterative procedure to assign observations to the desired g groups. We start the procedure with g randomly initial group centers and assign observa-

Figure 10.11 Dendrograms of web visits sequence data with at least of 1% of frequency of visits

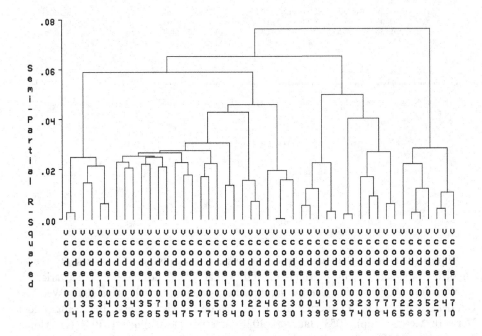

Table 10.8 Results of K-means cluster with different measurements

Measure of classification	Euclidean	Squared	City-block	Maximum	Correlation
Sensitivity	0.8946	0.8946	0.0954	0.8858	0.6939
Specificity	0.019	0.019	0.9853	0.0237	0.2141
Correctly classified rate	0.3641	0.3641	0.6346	0.3634	0.4032

tions to a group with the closest center. We then compute the mean distances of observations assigned to each of the groups, and replace the process again. These steps continue until all observations remain in the same group from the previous iteration. An observation will only be resigned to a different group if it is closer to the other group center than its current group center.

Example 10.9→Classification of Spam-email Based on K-means Clustering. Let us use the spam-email data to fit k-means clustering models with difference measurements of similarity functions. Because this is a binary classification, spam-email: yes or no, the k-means cluster number is 2. We compare the cluster results with the true response variable *v58* to see: (1) if the k-means cluster analysis can be used for real network security data, and (2) which measurements of similarity provide the best accuracy of classification. The Stata codes to complete this example are given in Display 10.11.

Display 10.11

Stata codes used to fit k-means clustering models with different measurements of similarity

```
#delimit;
use F:\Book\Chapter 10\spam.dta,replace;
log using kmeans,replace;
cluster kmeans v1-v57,k(2)name(euclidean) euclidean;
tab v58 euclidean,col row;
cluster kmeans v1-v57,k(2)name(squared) L2squared;
tab v58 squared,col row;
cluster kmeans v1-v57,k(2)name(cityblock) cityblock;
tab v58 cityblock,col row;
cluster kmeans v1-v57,k(2)name(maximum) maximum;
tab v58 maximum,col row;
cluster kmeans v1-v57,k(2)name(correlation) correlation;
tab v58 correlation,col row;
log close;
```

Table 10.8 shows the classification results from k-means clustering analysis with different measure functions. Euclidean/Squared, and Maximum measurements provide high sensitivity, but City-block shows a high specificity. It is clear that using k-means clustering alone can result in high false positive or false negative rates.

MULTIDIMENSIONAL MODELS

The multidimensional modeling technique is a branch of the multivariate analysis family models and aims to reduce the variable dimensions of the original data space. It is different with the previous discussions on dimension-reduction techniques, since we do not know how many dimensions to reduce before we conduct the analysis. In multidimensional

Figure 10.12 Plots of component loadings and scores

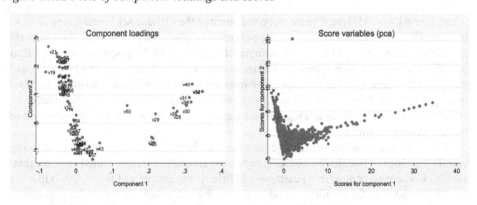

a. Component 1 vs. component 2　　　　b. Component scores

analysis we have an idea of the desired number of dimensions, which should be equal to the categorical number of the response variable. Although we do not have the actually labeled response variable in the unsupervised learning environment, we do have a rough idea of the potential categories of what the response variable could have. For example, in the spam-email situation, we may only want to have two dimensions: one that represents all of the spam emails and the other that represents non-spam emails. In this section we will introduce several linear and nonlinear dimension-reduction techniques: (1) principal components analysis, (2) multidimensional scaling, and (3) artificial neural network based self-organizing maps. Principal components analysis is a linear dimensionality reduction method, whereas multidimensional scaling and self-organizing maps are nonlinear dimensionality reduction methods. For additional information on principal components analysis refer to Snook & Gorsuch (1989), Shyu, Chen, Sarinnapakorn & Chang (2003); for multidimensional scaling refer to Schiffman, Reynolds, & Young (1981), Coxon & Anthony (1982), Cox & Cox (2001), Young & Hamer (1994), Bronstein, Bronstein & Kimmel (2006), and Abdi (2007), and for SOM refer to Obermayer & Sejnowski (2001), Kohonen (2001) and Samarasinghe (2007).

Principal Components Analysis

We have discussed the principal components analysis in Chapter VI as a linear tool for dimensionality reduction where we do not pre-specify the maximum number of uncorrelated principal components to be retained. Let X be a set of k observed variables, $X = (x_1, x_2, ..., x_k)$, and let Y be a set of uncorrelated variables $Y = (y_1, y_2, ... y_k)$, each of which is a linear combination of the k variables. Recall Equation (6-2)

$$y_1 = b_{11}x_1 + b_{12}x_2 + \cdots + b_{1k}x_k$$

$$y_2 = b_{21}x_1 + b_{22}x_2 + \cdots + b_{2k}x_k$$

......

$$y_k = b_{k1}x_1 + b_{k2}x_2 + \cdots + b_{kk}x_k,$$

where $y_j (j = 1, 2, ..., k)$ is the jth principal component of the variable set X, and $b_{ij} (i = 1, 2, ..., k)$ is the coefficient for x_i. When we use principal component analysis for classification we want to limit the components to the same number of categories of the response variable. That is, if the response variable is binary, we aim to have a model where the first two principal components, y_1 and y_2, contain most of the information of the original variables. The first principal component, y_1, carries a maximal overall variance, and the 2nd component, y_2, carries a maximal variance among all unit linear combinations that are uncorrelated to the first principal component.

The challenge of using principal component analysis as a classification tool is being certain that the pre-specified number of components is adequately represented in the original variables. There are a number of methods (Jolliffe, 1986; Everitt and Dunn, 1991) that are available to address this challenge, and here are a few rules that may be useful in practice: (1) set the minimal threshold of acceptable variance which we wish to account for, typically the value range is between 70% to 95%; (2) fit a principal component model without restricting the maximal number of principal components, (3) use the scree-plot to check the eigenvalues to see if the first g components (equivalent to the number of categories of the response variable) count the cumulative percentage of variance explained by reaching the minimal percentage of acceptable variance. Jolliff (1972) conducted a simulation study and suggests excluding components extracted from the correlation matrix whose associated eigenvalues are less than 0.7.

An issue in interpreting the scree-plot is that no guidance is given with respect to its stability under sampling. How different could the plot be with different samples? The approximate variance of an eigenvalue, $\hat{\lambda}$, of a covariance matrix for multivariate normal distributed data is $2\lambda^2 / n$. From this we can derive confidence intervals for the eigenvalues. These scree-plot confidence intervals aid in the selection of important components (Stata, 2007). We can also conduct simulations to address this issue.

Example 10.10→Classification based on PCA. Let us use the spam-email data to conduct principal component analysis with Stata. Because the response variable, v58, in spam-email data is a binary variable, we want to retain only two principal components. With these two components we can calculate a score for each component and assign such a score to each observation. Our hypothesis is that there should be a significantly different in mean scores by the two categories of the response variable. The Stata codes used to conduct this example are shown in Display 10.12.

Display 10.12
Stata codes used for classification based on principal components analysis

```
#delimit;
Use F:\book\Chapter 10\spam,replace;
gen V58="Non-spam" if v58==0;
replace  V58="Spam" if v58==1;

pca v1-v57, comp(2);
loadingplot;
scoreplot;
predict pc1 pc2;
corr pc1 pc2;
tab V58,sum(pc1);
ranksum(pc1),by(V58);
tab V58,sum(pc2);
ranksum(pc2),by(V58);
scatter  pc1 pc2,by(V58);
```

Figure 10.12 illustrates component loadings and their corresponding scores. As we described in Chapter VI, the second component (pc2) is designed to be uncorrelated with the first component (pc1). To examine if this condition is satisfied, we can calculate the correlation coefficient between the scores drawn from two components and we found that such a correlation coefficient is 0, as shown in Display 10.13.

Display 10.13
Correlation and difference in scores between components one and two

```
Corr pc1 pc2
(obs=4601)

             |     pc1       pc2
-------------+------------------
        pc1 |  1.0000
        pc2 |  0.0000   1.0000


. tab V58,sum(pc1)

             |  Summary of Scores for component 1
        V58 |      Mean   Std. Dev.       Freq.
-------------+------------------------------------
   Non-spam |  .60746447  3.1259423        2788
       Spam | -.93414833   .51403296        1813
-------------+------------------------------------
      Total |  1.674e-09  2.5674759        4601

. ranksum pc1,by(V58)

Two-sample Wilcoxon rank-sum (Mann-Whitney) test

        V58 |      obs    rank sum    expected
-------------+---------------------------------
   Non-spam |     2788   8449627.5     6415188
       Spam |     1813   2137273.5     4171713
-------------+---------------------------------
   combined |     4601  10586901    10586901

unadjusted variance    1.938e+09
adjustment for ties   -7668.2059
                      ----------
adjusted variance      1.938e+09

Ho: pc1(V58==Non-spam) = pc1(V58==Spam)
            z =  46.208
    Prob > |z| =   0.0000

. tab V58,sum(pc2)

             |  Summary of Scores for component 2
        V58 |      Mean   Std. Dev.       Freq.
-------------+------------------------------------
   Non-spam | -.88962222  1.1553244        2788
       Spam |  1.3680456  1.7752467        1813
-------------+------------------------------------
      Total | -1.370e-09  1.807602         4601

. ranksum pc2,by(V58)
```

continued on following page

Display 10.13 continued

```
Two-sample Wilcoxon rank-sum (Mann-Whitney) test

       V58 |      obs      rank sum     expected
------------+-----------------------------------
  Non-spam |     2788     4400854.5      6415188
      Spam |     1813     6186046.5      4171713
------------+-----------------------------------
  combined |     4601     10586901     10586901

unadjusted variance     1.938e+09
adjustment for ties    -7668.2059
                       ----------
adjusted variance       1.938e+09

Ho: pc2(V58==Non-spam)  = pc2(V58==Spam)
             z = -45.751
     Prob > |z| =   0.0000
```

Moreover, Display 10.13 also shows that the mean scores drawn from the first component are 0.61 and –0.93 for non-spam and spam emails, respectively. Similarly, mean scores drawn from the second component are –0.89 and 1.37 for non-spam and spam emails, respectively (Figure 10.13). Using the two-sample Wilcoxon rank-sum (Mann-Whitney) test, we found that these differences in scores are statistically significant, which suggests that principle components analysis could be employed as an unsupervised learning tool to filter spam emails.

Let s_{ij} be a score of the ith observation and the jth component ($j = 1$ for first component and $j = 2$ for second component), and E_j be a categorical variable that has a value a for spam email, b for non-spam, and c for unable to determined. We can construct the following classification rule to scan each incoming email:

$$\begin{cases} E_1 = a & s_{i1} < 0 & and & s_{i2} \geq 0 \\ E_2 = b & s_{i1} \geq 0 & and & s_{i2} < 0 \\ E_3 = c & otherwise. \end{cases}$$

Using the spam-email data we have the classification results as shown in Table 10.9, where we can see that the two principal component-based algorithm captured 77.1% (1398/1813) of the spam emails correctly, which is equal to a sensitivity value of 0.7711. Although there are a large number of emails labeled as pending, if we are only interested in detecting spam emails, we can combine the pending category into non-spam so that we have a binary response variable instead of a three-level response variable. In this case, we have a correctly classified rate of 86.4%, a specificity value of 0.9247, and a sensitivity value of 0.7711.

Multidimensional Scaling

Multidimensional scaling attempts to identify underlying factors called dimensions that represent the pattern of proximities, similarities or distances, among a set of observations and variables. Unlike factor analysis, which measures similarities between variables through the correlation matrix, a multidimensional scaling model supports any kind of similarity or dissimilarity matrix in addition to correlation matrices. Also, unlike the cluster analysis, multidimensional scaling constructs approximations for dissimilarities, not for similarities. The dissimilarities can be calculated from observations in the space D, or can be pre-determined. The basic idea of multidimensional scaling analysis is to find a low-dimensional space (e.g., two dimensions) that approximately represents the dissimilarities between observations in the originally full-dimensional space. There are many methods of multidimensional scaling that are available, including classical multidimensional scaling, non-metric multidimensional scaling, unidimensional scaling, procrustes analysis, biplots, unfolding, individual differences scaling, etc. Discussing all of these methods is beyond the scope of this book, and we will only discuss classical multidimensional scaling analysis. Detailed information about other methods can be found in the book, *The Analysis of Proximity Data,* authored by Everitt and Rabe-Hesketh (1977), and a more complete introduction to multidimensional scaling can be obtained from *Multidimensional Scaling* by Kruskal and Wish (1977).

Generally, multidimensional scaling employs Euclidean distance to measure the dissimi-larity. Let $p_i (i = 1, 2, \ldots n)$ and $q_j (j = 1, 2, \ldots n)$ denote the ith and j^{th} observations with k variables $p_i = (x_{1i}, x_{2i}, \ldots x_{ki})$ and $q_j = (x_{1j}, x_{2j}, \ldots x_{kj})$ in an k-dimensional space $D = \{p_1, p_2, \cdots p_i, \cdots q_j, \cdots p_n\}$. We first create a $n \times n$ dissimilarity matrix, M,

$$
M = \begin{vmatrix} d_{11} & d_{12} & \cdots & d_{1n} \\ d_{2j} & d_{22} & \cdots & d_{2n} \\ \vdots & \vdots & d_{ij} & \\ d_{n1} & d_{n2} & \cdots & d_{nn} \end{vmatrix}
$$

from the n observations and k variables, and then construct a low-dimensional matrix, M_L, that is approximated from M, with the Euclidean distances in a matching configuration, Z, of n points in a g-dimensional space for all i, j:

$$
dissimilarty(x_i, x_j) \approx E(z_i, z_j) \tag{10-22}
$$

Usually, we have $g = 2$ or $g = 3$.

Multidimensional scaling analysis involves a sequence of steps that can be briefly sum-marized: (1) assign points to arbitrary coordinates in the k-dimensional space, (2) compute Euclidean distances among all pairs of points to generate a M_L matrix, (3) compare the M_L matrix with the initial input M matrix by evaluating the stress function. The smaller the value, the greater the correspondence between the two matrices, (4) adjust coordinates of each point in the direction that best maximizes stress, and (5) repeat steps 2 through 4 to minimize the stress function.

Figure 10.13 Histograms of component scores

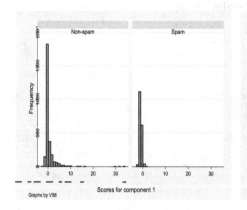

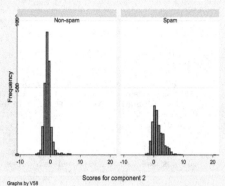

a. Component 1   b. Component 2

Table 10.9 Classifications of spam emails based on principal components

Predicted	Observed		Total
	Spam	Non-spam	
	Total (#)	Total (#)	
Spam	1398	210	1608
Non-spam	47	858	905
Pending	368	1720	2088
Total	1813	2788	4601

Example 10.11→Classification based on MDS. Let us use the spam-email data to fit a classical multidimensional scaling model that is known as Torgerson scaling or Torgerson-Gower scaling (Borg Groenen, 1997). It takes an input matrix giving dissimilarities between pairs of variables and outputs a coordinate matrix whose configuration minimizes a loss function. We want to retrieve data from the 57-dimensional space to a two-dimensional space and assess the performance of two-dimensional classification results using the SAS *MDS* procedure and the Stata *mds* command. The SAS and Stata codes to conduct the analysis are shown in Displays 10.14 and 10.15, respectively.

Display 10.14
SAS codes to fit a classical multidimensional scaling model

```
Libname MDS 'F:\Book\Chapter 10\';
Data spam;
Set mds.spam;
Qid=_N_;
Run;
Title2 "Multidimensional Scaling (Absolute Distances)";
Proc MDS Data=spam.spam Level=Absolute Out=MDSout
        Dimension=2 PData PConfig PFinal;
 Var v1-v57;
 Id qid;
Run;

Title2 "Multidimensional Scaling (Non-metric Scaling)";
Proc MDS Data=spam Level=Ordinal Out=MDSout
        Dimension=2 PConfig PFinal;
 Var v1-v57;
 Id qid;
Run;
```

Display 10.15
Stata codes to fit a classical multidimensional scaling model

```
#delimit;
set matsize 5000;
use F:\Book\Chapter 10\spam,replace;
gen qid=_n;
sort qid;
gen V58="Non-spam" if v58==0;
replace  V58="Spam" if v58==1;

mds v1-v57,id(qid)std(v1-v57)dimension(2);
mdsconfig, autoaspect;
mdsshepard;
save temp,replace;

predict dm1 dm2,config;
merge qid using temp;
drop _m;
corr dm1 dm2;
tab V58,sum(dm1);
ranksum(dm1),by(V58);
tab V58,sum(dm2);
ranksum(dm2),by(V58);
scatter  dm1 dm2,by(V58);
```

The fitted classical multidimensional scaling model is shown in Display 10.16. There are a few notes that warrant discussion: first, unlike cluster analysis and principal component analysis, multidimensional scaling analysis takes a great deal of computing resources. This is because its algorithm involves multi-iteration steps, which were described previously. Second, similar to principal component analysis, the quality of a two-dimensional approximation is unsatisfactory based on the spam-email data, which we can see since the first two dimensions do not carry a great eigenvalue. The squared cumulative eigenvalue only carries about 53% of the total variations and even if we expend the dimensions from two to ten we still have about 71% of squared cumulative eigenvalues. This can be improved by collecting more robust predictive variables in the data. But, in practice we may not have enough prior knowledge on such variables. Finding such variables is an ongoing challenge in the network security field.

Display 10.16
Stata output of the fitted classical multidimensional scaling model

```
. mds v1-v57,id(qid)std(v1-v57)dimension(2)

Classical metric multidimensional scaling
    dissimilarity: L2, computed on 57 variables
                                        Number of obs        =        4601
    Eigenvalues > 0       =        57    Mardia fit measure 1 =      0.1730
    Retained dimensions   =         2    Mardia fit measure 2 =      0.5283

    -------------------------------------------------------------------------
                 |                       abs(eigenvalue)         (eigenvalue)^2
    Dimension    | Eigenvalue      Percent    Cumul.       Percent    Cumul.
    -------------+-----------------------------------------------------------
             1   |   30322.89        11.56     11.56        42.41     42.41
             2   |   15030.154        5.73     17.30        10.42     52.83
    -------------+-----------------------------------------------------------
             3   |   9214.4988        3.51     20.81         3.92     56.75
             4   |   7420.5334        2.83     23.64         2.54     59.29
             5   |   7112.5561        2.71     26.35         2.33     61.62
             6   |   6727.683         2.57     28.92         2.09     63.71
             7   |   6504.321         2.48     31.40         1.95     65.66
             8   |   6324.6266        2.41     33.81         1.85     67.51
             9   |   5958.313         2.27     36.09         1.64     69.15
            10   |   5873.9415        2.24     38.33         1.59     70.74
    -------------------------------------------------------------------------
```

Third, Display 10.17 shows that the distribution of scores obtained from multidimensional scaling analysis is almost identical with the scores from principal component analysis. This is because the classical metric of multidimensional scaling analysis with Euclidean distance is equivalent to principal component analysis and the multidimensional scaling configuration coordinates are comparable to the principal components (Figure 10.13). Keep in mind, however, that multidimensional scaling supports nonlinear dimensionality reduction, while principal component analysis is a linear procedure.

Display 10.17
Wilcoxon rank-sum test of difference in coordinates of the approximating configuration by variable v58 (spam and non-spam)

```
. tab V58,sum(dm1)

             |        Summary of MDS dimension 1
        V58  |        Mean      Std. Dev.        Freq.
    ---------+-----------------------------------------
    Non-spam |    .60746447      3.1259423         2788
        Spam |   -.93414833       .51403295        1813
    ---------+-----------------------------------------
       Total |    2.279e-09      2.5674759         4601

. ranksum dm1,by(V58)
```

continued on following page

Display 10.17 continued

```
Two-sample Wilcoxon rank-sum (Mann-Whitney) test

        V58 |      obs     rank sum      expected
------------+-----------------------------------
   Non-spam |     2788    8449627.5       6415188
       Spam |     1813    2137273.5       4171713
------------+-----------------------------------
   combined |     4601     10586901      10586901

unadjusted variance    1.938e+09
adjustment for ties    -7668.2059
                       ----------
adjusted variance      1.938e+09

Ho: dm1(V58==Non-spam) = dm1(V58==Spam)
            z =   46.208
    Prob > |z| =   0.0000

. tab V58,sum(dm2)

            |     Summary of MDS dimension 2
        V58 |      Mean    Std. Dev.         Freq.
------------+-----------------------------------
   Non-spam |  -.88962222   1.1553244          2788
       Spam |   1.3680456   1.7752467          1813
------------+-----------------------------------
      Total |  -4.018e-10    1.807602          4601

. ranksum dm2,by(V58)

Two-sample Wilcoxon rank-sum (Mann-Whitney) test

        V58 |      obs     rank sum      expected
------------+-----------------------------------
   Non-spam |     2788    4400854.5       6415188
       Spam |     1813    6186046.5       4171713
------------+-----------------------------------
   combined |     4601     10586901      10586901

unadjusted variance    1.938e+09
adjustment for ties    -7668.2059
                       ----------
adjusted variance      1.938e+09

Ho: dm2(V58==Non-spam) = dm2(V58==Spam)
            z =  -45.751
    Prob > |z| =   0.0000
```

Self-Organizing Maps

A SOM, also known as a Kohonen network, is a nonlinear dimension-reduction method used to map high-dimensional data onto a low-dimensional grid (usually the grid is in a two dimensional space). The grid arranges data in such a way that observations that are close to each other in the high-dimensional space are also close together in the low-dimensional grid. Thus, a SOM aims to accomplish two tasks: (1) reducing dimensions, and (2) displaying similarities (Germano, 1999) graphically. This approach is similar to multidimensional scaling except a SOM uses a grid to map data to a low-dimensional space. As discussed earlier, because multidimensional scaling requires numerous computing resources, when

Figure 10.14 Configuration plot with two dimensions from multidimensional scaling analysis

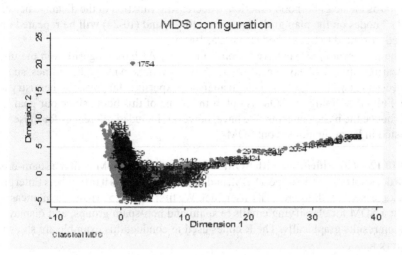

the data size is large the computing burden is significant. In this case, a self-organizing mapping approach can be adapted.

A SOM is composed by two levels of nodes (or two layers of neurons from the AI perspective): an input level and a competition level (Figure 10.15). The coefficients that connect the individual node between the input and the competition levels are called model (reference) vectors in the input space. Therefore a SOM represents a set of model vectors in the input space in which one vector corresponds to each node in the competition level. The number of model vectors to represent all available observations should be optimally limited.

The SOM algorithm can be briefly summarized as a sequence of steps. First, we randomly assign an initial value to each model vector, m_i $(i = 1, 2, \cdots, n)$, as in Figure 10.15. Next, we determine the similarity between the input vector and the node in the competition map based on the Euclidean distance measure:

$$\|x - m_c\| = \min_i \|x - m_i\| \tag{10-23}$$

where the node m_c is the one that produces the smallest distance. Third, we update all the model vectors that belong to nodes centered around the node $m_c = m_c(x)$ as

$$m_i(t+1) = \begin{cases} m_i(t) + \alpha(t)[x(t) - m_i(t)], & i \in \lambda_c(t) \\ m_i(t), & i \notin \lambda_c(t) \end{cases} \tag{10-24}$$

where t denotes the iteration of the learning process, and $\alpha(t)$ is the learning scalar to control the magnitude of the learning step. It ranges from 1 to 0 and decreases during the learning process. $\lambda_c(t)$ is the neighborhood function, a decreasing function of the distance between the ith and c^{th} nodes on the map grid. Equations (10-23) and (10-24) will be repeated until the required threshold to be reached (Honkela, 1998).

Over the last decade, SOMs have become a popular AI-based algorithm in the unsupervised learning area, and have been adopted by researchers in many disciplines, such as signal processing, control theory, financial analysis, experimental physics, chemistry and medicine. Fully describing the SOM is out of the scope of this book, since our goal is to briefly introduce the basic concepts. We have, however, included references for those who are interested in learning more about SOMs.

Example 10.12→Classification with SOM. Let us construct a SOM with the spam-email data. Stata does not currently support SOM, and SAS only supports it through its Enterprise Miner package, so we will use R to fit this model. We first use the 57 spam-email measurements to fit a SOM for classifying emails to spam and non-spam groups, and display the classification results graphically. The R codes used to conduct this example are shown in Display 10.18 below.

Display 10.18
R codes to fit a Self-organizing map model

```
#install.packages('klaR')
#library(klaR)
require("klaR")
install.packages('som')
library(som)
spam<-read.table("F:\\Book\\Chapter 10\\spam_r.txt",header=TRUE,sep = ",")
#Fit SOM with 57 spam-email related measurements
spamsom <-som(spam[,1:57],xdim=50,ydim=50)
spam$v59[spam$v58==0]<-"non-spam"
spam$v59[spam$v58==1]<-"spam"
shardsplot(spamsom, data.or = spam, vertices = FALSE)
opar <- par(xpd = NA)
legend(25,52,col=rainbow(2),xjust=0.5,yjust=0,legend=(spam$v59),pch = 16,
horiz = TRUE)
```

Figure 10.16, also known as shardsplot, displays the corresponding SOM for the spam-email data, and was proposed by Cottrell & de Bodt (1996). We can see that the fitted SOM model arranges the emails to spam and non-spam groups reasonably.

SUMMARY

In this chapter we discussed several fundamental unsupervised learning statistical approaches for classifying network traffic when a labeled response variable is not available in the data. Over time, network traffic data have been primarily analyzed in a framework of modeling for associations, one of which is the spervised learning method, which requires both anomaly-free and abnormal events included in the training data. However, in many

Figure 10.15 Grid of self-organization map

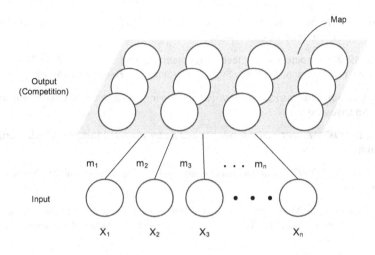

Figure 10.16 Spam data represented by self-organization map

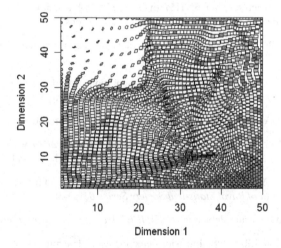

real world scenarios, available network traffic data either may not include any anomalous events or such events are inadequate to fit a conventional regression model or a supervised learning algorithm. For example, initial audit data are more likely to have all anomaly-free events in newly constructed network systems and, therefore, only unsupervised learning model can be activated initially before a certain percent of abnormal events is acquired. While high-speed mobile wireless and ad-hoc network systems have became more and more popular, the importance and need to develop new unsupersied learning algorithms have significantly increased. Being able to train intrusion detection systems with anomaly-free data has become an essential challenge in modern network security.

REFERENCES

Abdi, H. (2007). Metric multidimensional scaling. In N.J. Salkind (Ed.), *Encyclopedia of Measurement and Statistics*. Thousand Oaks, CA: Sage.

Anderson, P. J. (1972). Computer security technology planning study, Volume II. *ESD-TR-73-51, Vol. II*, Electronic Systems Division, Air Force Systems Command,   Hanscom Field, Bedford, MA.

Anderson, P. J. (1980). *Computer security threat monitoring and surveillance*. Fort Washington, PA: James P. Anderson Co.

Bartholomew, D. (1987). *Latent variable models and factor analysis*. London: Charles Griffin & Company Limited.

Borg, I. and Groenen, P.(1997). *Modern multidimensional scaling: Theory and applications*. New York: Springer-Verlag.

Bronstein, A. M, Bronstein, M.M, and Kimmel, R. (2006). Generalized multidimensional scaling: a framework for isometry-invariant partial surface matching. In *Proc. National Academy of Sciences (PNAS)*, *103*(5), 1168-1172.

Cappe, O. Moulines, E., Ryden, T. (2005). *Inference in hidden Markov models*. New York: Springer-Verlag.

Carmines, B., Edward, G. & McIver, J. P. (1981). Analyzing models with unobserved variables: Analysis of covariance structures, (pp. 65-115). In George W. Bohmstedt and Edward F. Borgatta, (Eds.), *Social Measurement*. Thousand Oaks, CA: Sage Publications.

Cho, S. B. & Park, H. J. (2003) Efficient anomaly detection by modeling privilege flows using hidden Markov model. *Computer and Security, 22*(1), 45-55.

Cottrell, M., & de Bodt, E. (1996). A Kohonen map representation to avoid misleading interpretations, (pp. 103–110). In *Proc. of the European Symposium on Atrificial Neural Networks*, D-Facto.

Cox, M.F., & Cox, M.A.A. (2001). *Multidimensional scaling*. Chapman and Hall.

Coxon, & Anthony P.M. (1982). *The user's guide to multidimensional scaling, with special reference to the MDS(X) library of computer programs*. London: Heinemann Educational Books.

Dempster, A.P., Laird, N.M., & Rubin, D.B. (1977). Maximum likelihood from incomplete data via the EM algorithm. *Journal of Royal Statistical Society Series B*39, 1-38.

Denning, D. (1987). An intrusion-detection model. *IEEE Trans. on Software Eng, 13*(2), 222-232.

Dhanalakshmi, Y. & Babu, I.R. (2008). Intrusion detection using data mining along fuzzy logic and genetic algorithms, *International Journal of Computer Science and Network Security, 8*(2), 27-30.

Duda, R. O., Hart, P. E. & Stork, D. G. (2001). *Pattern classification, 2nd Ed*. NY: Wiley-Interscience.

Everitt, B.S. and Dunn, G. (1991). *Applied multivariate data analysis*, London: Edward Arnold.

Everitt, B.S. and Rabe-Hesketh, S. (1977). *The analysis of proximity data*. London: Arnold.

Everitt, B.S. (2001). *Cluster analysis*. London: Arnold.

Fornell, C., & Yi, Y. (1992). Assumptions of the two-step approach to latent variable modeling. *Sociological Methods & Research, 20*(1), 291-320.

Frías-Martínez, E. and Karamcheti, V. (2002). *A Customizable Behavior Model for Temporal Prediction of Web User Sequences*. WEBKDD 2002: pp. 66-85

Gao, B, Ma, H. & Yang, Y. (2002). HMMS (hidden markov models) based on anomaly intrusion detection method, (pp. 381-385). In *Proceedings of the First International Conference on Machine Learning and Cybernetics.*

Germano, T. (1999). *Self organizing maps.* Retrieved September 12, 2007, from http://davis.wpi.edu/~matt/courses/soms/

Goodman, L. (1974). Exploratory latent structure analysis using both identifiable and unidentifiable models, *Biometrika, 61*, 215-231.

Harenaars, J.A. & McCutcheon, A. L. (2002). *Applied latent class analysis.* Cambridge, London: Cambridge University Press.

Hartigan, J.A. (1975). *Clustering algorithms.* New York: John Wiley & Sons, Inc.

Hartigan, J.A. & Wong, M.A. (1979). A K-means clustering algorithm: Algorithm AS 136. *Applied Statistics, 28*, 126-130.

Herrero, A., Corchado, E., Gastaldo, P., Leoncini, D., Picasso, F. & Zunino, R. (2007). Intrusion detection at packet level by unsupervised architectures. *Lecture Notes in Comp Science, 4881*, 718-727.

Honkela, T. (1998). Description of Kohonen's self-organizing map. Retrieved September 21, 2007, from http://mlab.uiah.fi/~timo/som/thesis-som.html

Jaccard, P. (1908). Nouvelles recherches sur la distribution florale. *Bulletin de la Societe Vaudoise des Sciences Natureical 44*, 223-270.

Jolliffe, I.T. (1972). Discarding variables in a principal components analysis 1: artificial data, *Applied Statistics, 21*, 160-31.

Jolliffe, I.T. (1986). *Principal components analysis.* New York: Springer.

Kaski, S. (1997). Data exploration using self-organizing maps. *Acta Polytechnica Scandinavica, Mathematics, Computing and Management in Engineering Series, 82*(57), 100-110.

Khattree, R. and Naik, D. N. (2000). *Multivariate data reduction and discrimination with SAS software.* North Carolina: SAS Institute Inc.

Kohonen, T. (2001). *Self-organizing maps.* Springer series in information sciences, 30. Berlin: Springer.

Kruskal, J. B., and Wish. M. (1977). *Multidimensional scaling.* Sage Publications.

Lane, T. & Brodley, C. E. (1997). Detecting the abnormal: machine learning in computer security. *Technical Report TR-ECE 97-1*, Purdue University, School of Elect and Computer Eng, West Lafayette, IN.

Loehlin, J. C. (1992). *Latent variable models: An introduction to factor, path, and structural analysis, 2nd Edition.* Hillsdale, New Jersey: Lawrence Erlbaum.

Mobasher, B., Cooley, R.(2000). Automatic personalization based on Web usage mining. *Communications of the ACM, 43*(8), 142-151.

Mukkamala, S., Tadiparthi, G. R., Tummala, N., & Janoski, G. (2003). Audit data reduction for intrusion detection, (pp. 456-460). In *Proc of the IEEE 2003 Int Joint Conference on Neural Networks.*

Obermayer, K., & Sejnowski, T. J. (2001). *Self-organizing map formation: Foundations of neural computation.* Computational neuroscience. Cambridge, Mass: MIT Press.

Ourston, D., Matzner, S., Stump, W., & Hopkins, B. (2003). Applications of hidden Markov models to detecting multistage network attacks. In *Proc of the 36th Annual Hawaii Int Conf on System Sciences, 6*(9), 10-15.

Rabiner, L.R. (1989). A tutorial on hidden Markov models and selected applications in speech recognition. In *Proceeding of the IEEE, 77*(2), 257-288.

Russell, P. F. and Rao, T. R. (1940). On habitat and association of species of anopheline larvae in south-eastern Madras. *Journal of the Malaria Institute of India, 3,* 153-178.

Qian Q. & Xin, M. (2007). Research on hidden Markov model for system call anomaly detection, *Intelligence and Security Informatics* (PAISI' 2007), *4430,* 152-159

Samarasinghe, S. (2007). *Neural networks for applied sciences and engineering from fundamentals to complex pattern recognition.* Boca Raton, FL: Auerbach.

Schiffman, S. S. Reynolds, M. L., & Young, F. W. (1981). *Introduction to multidimensional scaling.* New York: Academic Press.

Shyu, M., Chen, S., Sarinnapakorn, K., & Chang, L. (2003). A novel anomaly detection scheme based on principal component classifier. In *Proc of the IEEE Foundations and New Directions of Data Mining Workshop, in conjunction with the 3rd IEEE Int Conference on Data Mining (ICDM).*

Skrondal, A. Rabe-Hesketh, S. (2004). *Generalized latent variable modeling: multilevel, longitudinal and structural equation models.* Boca Raton, FL: Chapman &Hall/CRC.

Snook, S.C., & Gorsuch, R.L. (1989). Principal component analysis versus common factor analysis: A Monte Carlo study. *Psychological Bulletin, 106,* 148-154.

Sokal, R. R. and Michener, C. D. (1958). A statistical method for evaluating systematic relationships. *University of Kansas Science Bulletin 38,* 1409-1438.

Spiliopoulou, M., Pohle, C., Faulstich, L.(1999). Improving the effectiveness of a Web site with Web usage mining, (pp. 142-162). In *Proceedings of WEBKDD99.*

Srikant, R., Yang, Y. (2001). Mining Web logs to improve website organization, (pp.430-437). In *Proceedings of WWW10.* Hong Kong.

Stallings, W. (2003). *Network security essentials, applications and standards, 2nd Ed.* NJ: Pearson Edu.

Stata (2007). *Stata reference.* TX: Stata Press

Tryon, R. C. (1939). *Cluster analysis.* Edwards Brothers.

VanderMeer, D., Dutta, K., Datta, A. (2000). Enabling scalable online personalization on the Web, (pp.185-196). In *Proceedings of EC'00.*

Wang, Y. & Seidman, L. (2006). Risk factors to retrieve anomaly intrusion information and profile user behavior. *International Journal of Business Data Communications and Networking, 2*(1), 41-57.

Wright, C., Monrose, F., and Masson, G. M. (2004, October 29-29). HMM profiles for network traffic classification. In *Proceedings of the 2004 ACM Workshop on Visualization and Data Mining For Computer Security,* (pp. 9-15). (Washington DC). New York: ACM.

Yang, Q., Tian-Yi, I., Zhang, H. (2001). Minin high-queality cases for hypertext prediction and perfecting, (pp. 744-755). In D.W. Aha and I. Watson (Eds.), *ICCBR 2002, LNAI 2080.* Berlin, Heidelberg: Springer-Verlag.

Yang, Q., Zhang, H., Li, I., Lu, Y.(2001). *Mining Web logs to improve Web caching and prefetching,* (pp. 483-492). In N. Zhong et al., (Eds.) New York: Springer-Verlag; Berlin: Heindelberg.

Young. F. W. and Hamer. R. M. (1994). *Theory and applications of multidimensional Scaling.* Hillsdale, NJ: Eribaum Associates.

APPENDIX

SAS Macro Freq_Cutoff

```
%MACRO FREQ_Cutoff(INFILE, INVAR, CUTOFF,Condition);
  PROC SUMMARY DATA=&INFILE;
    VAR &INVAR;
      &condition;
    OUTPUT OUT=TEMP_1 MEAN=;
  PROC TRANSPOSE DATA=TEMP_1(DROP=_TYPE_ _FREQ_) OUT=TEMP_1(DROP=_LABEL_)
    NAME=VARN PREFIX=VARM;
  DATA TEMP_1;
    SET TEMP_1;
    IF VARM1>=&CUTOFF;
  PROC IML;
    USE TEMP_1;
    READ ALL VAR _CHAR_ INTO X;
    N=NROW(X);
    CLOSE;
    VARK="";
    VARKN=0;
    DO I=1 TO N;
      VARKN=VARKN+1;
      VARK=VARK + ' ' + X[I];
    END;
    NAMES={VARK};
    CREATE TEMP_1 FROM VARK[C=NAMES];
    APPEND FROM VARK;
    CLOSE;
    NAMES={VARKN};
    CREATE TEMP_2 FROM VARKN[C=NAMES];
    APPEND FROM VARKN;
    CLOSE;
  PROC SQL NOPRINT;
    SELECT VARK INTO:VARK
    FROM TEMP_1;
    SELECT VARKN INTO:VARKN
    FROM TEMP_2;
  QUIT;
    %let outvar=&vark;
      %put The total number of variables is &VARKN;
      %put variables is &outvar;
  RUN;
%MEND;
```

Latent_model.do (Stata codes to fit a latent model)

```
/*-----------------------------------------------------------------
  Latent_model.do
-------------------------------------------------------------*/;
#delimit;
rename TCP y1; rename UDP y2; rename HTTP y3; rename RST y4;
rename logged_i y5; rename is_guest y6;
gen patt=_n; reshape long y, i(patt) j(var); tab var,gen(d);
list patt var y d1 d2 d3 d4 d5 d6 attack wt2 if patt==1, clean;
eq d1: d1; eq d2: d2; eq d3: d3; eq d4: d4; eq d5: d5; eq d6: d6;

gllamm y,i(patt) ip(fn) nip(2) nrf(6) eqs(d1 d2 d3 d4 d5 d6) weight(wt)
l(logit) f(binom) nocons;
gllamm,allc;
eq load: d1 d2 d3 d4 d5 d6;
gllamm y d1 d2 d3 d4 d5 d6, i(patt) eqs(load) ip(f) nip(2) weight(wt)
 l(logit) f(binom) nocons;
gllamm,allc;
** Conditional response probabilities;
 * Predictions based on two-class one-factor model;
matrix m=e(zlc2); gen u01 = m[1,1]; gen u11 = m[1,2];
gllapred mu0, mu us(u0); gllapred mu1, mu us(u1);
** Posterior probabilities using gllapred;
gllapred prob, p;
```

Chapter XI
Decision Analysis in Network Security

Laughter gives us distance. It allows us to step back from an event, deal with it and then move on.

-Bob Newhard

INTRODUCTION

Decision analysis, a derivative of game theory, was introduced by Von Neumann in the early 1920s and was adopted in Economics in the late 1940s (Von Neumann and Morgenstern, 1947). It is a systematically quantitative approach for assessing the relative value of one or more different decision options based on existing and new information and knowledge. Figure 11.1 shows a general decision-marking process graphically.

Network security relates both offline and online decision-making processes. The offline decision-making process involves fundamental security issues, such as determining the thresholds of classification, selecting sampling methods and sampling sizes for collecting network traffic, and deciding baseline patterns for profiling. Offline decisions usually require more statistical analyses and take more time to reach a not just reasonable, good or better, but the "best" solution. The online decision-making process, however, usually requires a response quickly, which could make it more difficult to achieve a good solution. For instance, when an alarm emerging, an immediate action is needed to decide if this alarm is an indication for a real attack or it is a false alarm? In such a circumstance, we do not have much time to conduct a complex analysis but we have to take an action on that alarm

Figure 11.1 A general decision-marking process

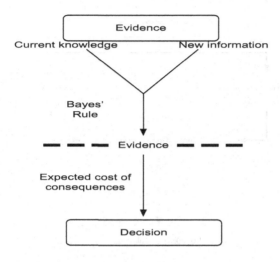

instantaneously. Many online decisions could be analyzed complexly and be involved a sequence of compositely interrelated decisions that we may not be able to encompass quickly. As a result, the aim of online decision-making is more likely to focus on a reasonable, a good or a better solution rather than the best solution. In particular, given the uncertainty in decision-making processes, we may never be able to reach the best solution for either offline or online decision-marking processes in many circumstances of network security. Decision-making also associates with network management that is about knowledge—if we know what our network and servers are doing, making decisions could be easier.

The primary challenge in the decision-making process is uncertainty. To address this issue of uncertainty, we need to assess risks—risk assessment that utilizes the theory of probability is a fundamental element of decision analysis (Figure 11.2). There is no doubt that risk and uncertainty are important concepts to address for supporting decision-making in many situations. Our goals for decision analysis are the ability to define what may happen in the future and to choose the "best" (or at least a good or better) solution form among alternatives.

Under the primary challenge of uncertainty, decision analysis has several tasks, including how to describe and assess risks, how to measure uncertainties, how to model them and how to communicate with them. All these tasks are not easy to accomplish due to the task themselves, which cannot be clearly defined. For example, even though we have a general idea of what risk means, if we were asked to measure it, we would find little consensus on the definition. Nevertheless, decision analysis provides a tool for us to find a solution in confusing and uncertain territory. It gives us a technique for finding a robust and better solution from many alternatives. In this chapter, we will introduce some methods on decision analysis including analyzing uncertainty, statistical control charts and statistical ranking methods, but we will not discuss the decision tree, a classical decision analysis technique, in this chapter. Readers who are interested in obtaining essential decision analysis information

Figure 11.2 A flowchart of risk assessment

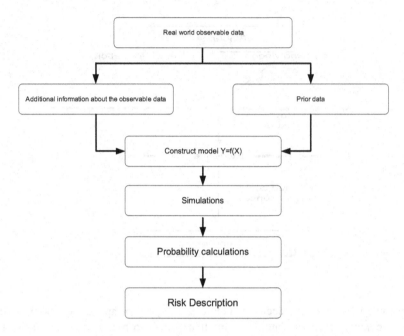

(e.g., decision tree) should refer to Raiffa (1968), Hattis & Burmaster (1994), Zheng & Frey (2004), Gelman, Carlin, Stern & Rubin (2004), Aven (2005), and Lindley (2006).

ANALYSIS OF UNCERTAINTY

Uncertainty results from a lack of knowledge regarding the true values of certain aspects of the real world. Sometimes those aspects involve an object, a situation, a process, or a quantity. In network security, sensitivity, specificity, and misclassification rates are common measures used to specify the uncertainty of classification. Aven (2005) suggested dividing uncertainty into two categories: (1) stochastic uncertainty, and (2) knowledge-related uncertainty. Stochastic uncertainty occurs during sampling and is represented by random variables. Knowledge-related uncertainty characterizes the locking of information about the object being studied.

Uncertainty impacts both classification and profiling results in network security. Statistical theory provides various approaches to measure and address uncertainty. One of the most frequently used approaches is to establish an interval estimate for a given point estimate. While there are advantages in computer hardware and software, large-scale simulations have become a popular method to improve the accuracy of estimates and reduce the uncertainty. Also, difference testing methods (e.g., parametric and non-parametric) may also impact uncertainty. We will discuss each of these in the following sections. Readers who would like to have a more comprehensive background on analysis of uncertainty should refer to Lindley (2006).

Interval Estimates

The key statistical tool to measure uncertainty is probability. Although uncertainty can be addressed by gathering additional and better data and by developing robust models, probability is the fundamental instrument to assess uncertainty. As discussed in previous chapters, data can be improved by linking additional data sources resulting in better and more extensive measurements. The essential technique to better model uncertainty is to correctly establish a probability distribution function for the object to be measured. Let X be an unknown continuous variable from a sample; the true value of X can be presented in probability form:

$$P(a < X \le b) = \int_a^b f(x)dx, \tag{11-1}$$

where $f(x)$ is a probability density function for X, and a and b are the interval values for the true X value. Thus, instead of presenting X by a single value, Equation (11-1) provides an interval range that X will likely lie in. We reflect a and b as the interval estimate of X. Interval estimates provide a great tool for addressing variability and uncertainty and plays an important rule in profiling user behavior. For instance, we can use the point estimate and its corresponding interval estimate to describe the traffic patterns for sites, groups or users.

A confidence interval is an interval estimate of a population parameter. If we let θ be a population parameter, and let $\hat{\theta}_l = (X_1, X_2, \cdots, X_n)$ and $\hat{\theta}_u = (X_1, X_2, \cdots, X_n)$ be functions of the sample data $\hat{X}_1, \hat{X}_2, \cdots, \hat{X}_n$, then the confidence interval of θ is

$$P_\theta \{\hat{\theta}_l \le \theta \le \hat{\theta}_u\} = \gamma, \tag{11-2}$$

where γ is the certainty level ($\gamma = 1 - \alpha$) and $\hat{\theta}_l$ and $\hat{\theta}_u$ are the lower and upper confidence intervals for θ, respectively. The theory of confidence intervals treats the population parameter, θ, as fixed but its interval as random because it is based on a random sample (Ruppert, 2004). Thus, although we do not know the true θ (this is the uncertainty), we do know its possible range in which it most likely to fall (this is the certainty). Generally, if all possible samples of a given size are selected from a given population and all possible values of a given estimator are then calculated, a confidence interval that is of a given width can then be constructed around each of these values. The percentage of resulting intervals that will contain the true population parameter is referred to as the confidence level of the interval (Kohler, 1988).

As we repeatedly take samples from our population and construct a confidence interval for each possible sample, we expect the true value of the population parameter θ to be included in the range of $\hat{\theta}_l$ to $\hat{\theta}_u$. Depending on the question being asked and the size of the sample, we could use different certainty levels, such as $\gamma = 80\%$, 90%, 95% and 99% as the confidence levels of the interval. The low uncertainty level leads to increased width of the confidence interval as shown in Figure 11.3.

In practice, for a random sample of size n drawn from a population with a unknown mean, μ, and a known standard deviation, σ, we can calculate the confidence interval as

Figure 11.3 Relationship between the level of uncert-inty and the confidence interval

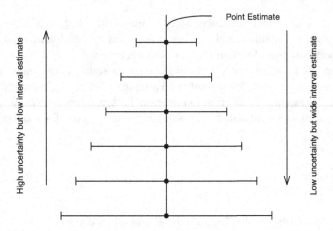

Table 11.1 z^* values

Confidence level (γ)	$\alpha/2$	z^*
80%	0.100	1.283
90%	0.050	1.645
95%	0.025	1.960
99%	0.005	2.576

$$\hat{\mu} - z^* \frac{\sigma}{\sqrt{n}} < \mu < \hat{\mu} + z^* \frac{\sigma}{\sqrt{n}} \qquad\qquad (11\text{-}3)$$

where $\hat{\mu}$ is the sample mean and z^* is the factor associated with γ to determine the confidence level. z^* values are listing In Table 11.1.

Equation (11-3) calculates the confidence interval for a normally distributed continuous variable. If we draw a random sample of size n from a large population with an unknown proportion, ρ, of successes, we can approximately calculate the confidence interval for ρ as:

$$\hat{\rho} - z^* \sqrt{\frac{\hat{\rho}(1-\hat{\rho})}{n}} < \rho < \hat{\rho} + z^* \sqrt{\frac{\hat{\rho}(1-\hat{\rho})}{n}}, \qquad\qquad (11\text{-}4)$$

where $\hat{\rho}$ is the estimate of sample proportion. Equation (11-4) calculates the confidence interval for a variable following the binomial distribution when the sample size is large (i.e., $n > 30$). In the long run, for the 95% confidence interval, 95% of all samples from the same population will give an interval that covers the mean.

Figure 11.4 Sample size and width of confidence interval

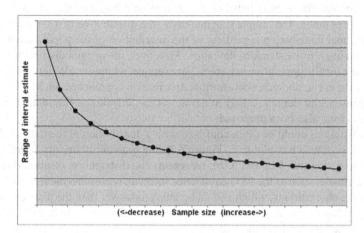

Equaltions (11-3) and (11-4) indicate that the sample size *n* also associates with the uncertainty in addition to the z^* value. To reduce the uncertainty without increasing the confidence interval, we can increase the sample size *n*. Figure 11.4 shows the relationship between the sample size and the width of the confidence interval.

Example 11.1→95% Confidence Interval. The MIT-DARPA data include a total of 3,013,860 observations with a proportion of point estimate on anomaly-free rate as 38.4% and the interval estimate at the 95% confidence interval level ranges from 38.3% to 38.5%. This is a very narrow interval estimate, so we may consider the point estimate to be the "true" rate. However, a randomly drawn sample of size 301 has a point estimate of anomaly-free rate of 40.2% with a wide confidence interval, ranging from 34.6% to 46.0%, an absolute range of 11.4%, to cover the "true" rate of the initial data (Display 11.1).

Display 11.1
Relationship between the sample size and confidence interval

```
. ci normal

    Variable |        Obs        Mean    Std. Err.      [95% Conf. Interval]
-------------+---------------------------------------------------------------
      normal |    3013860    .3839226    .0002801       .3833735    .3844717

sample 0.01
(3013559 observations deleted)

. ci normal

    Variable |        Obs        Mean    Std. Err.      [95% Conf. Interval]
-------------+---------------------------------------------------------------
      normal |        301    .4019934    .0283075       .3462869    .4576998
```

We need to keep in mind that although we may model our data in many different ways, the uncertainty with the normal distribution assumption is based on the central limit theorem, which states that as the sample size increases, the distribution of a sample mean gets closer to a normal distribution regardless of the distribution of the population as long as the population has a finite standard deviation. Moreover, the normal distributions are not suitable models for all quantitative variables. For example, we may use Weibull distributions to model time to event, and other non-normal distribution approaches, such as fuzzy-logic (Smith, Parkinson, and Bement, 2002), and time-series (Shlyakhter, Kammen, Broido, and Wilson, 1994) have also been proposed.

Interval estimates could be often confused with a distribution of the data. A data distribution plot, such as a box-plot (e.g., Figure 5.3) or a probability density function-based normal plot (e.g., Figures 5.1a and 5.1b), represents the distribution of observations, but an interval estimate, such as the 95% confidence interval, represents the possible range of the mean of the observations, which should be much narrower than the distribution of the observations. This different is due to an analogy on the difference between a SD, σ, (which denotes the spread of the data) and a SE,

$$\frac{\sigma}{\sqrt{n}},$$

(which denotes the error associated with an estimate of the mean of the distribution as we discussed in Chapter VI). The data distribution associates with the SD, but the interval estimate associates with the SE.

Interval estimates can be utilized for profiling behavior. In the real world, a live network system as a whole may not be anomaly-free absolutely; that is, its anomaly-free rate cannot be 100% at the system level, but we can have a threshold value for an acceptable anomaly-free rate. Let T denote such a pre-specified threshold, and let $\hat{\rho}_i$ denote an anomaly-free rate for the ith site, a_i and b_i denote the lower and upper interval estimates of the $\hat{\rho}_i$ for that site, respectively. We can identifiy sites that have significantly higher or lower anomaly-free rates than the threshold using the following defination:

$$c_i = \begin{cases} 1 & T \leq a_i \\ 0 & a_i < T < b_i \\ -1 & b_i \leq T \end{cases}, \tag{11-5}$$

where c_i functions as a simply rule for classification: (1) $c_i = 1$ indicates that the ith site has a significantly high anomaly-free rate, (2) $c_i = -1$ indicates that the ith site has a significantly low anomaly-free rate, and (3) $c_i = 0$ indicates that the ith site's anomaly-free rate is no different from the acceptable rate.

Figure 11.6 graphically illustrates Equation (11-5). The horizontal line shows the predetermined acceptable threshold of the anomaly-free rate, which is 0.6, from a given time period. The dots denote the point estimates for each selected site, and the vertical lines around each of these estimated rates show the interval estimates, which indicate how much variation in anomaly-free rates might be due to chance. If an interval estimate crosses the horizontal line, it indicates that we cannot be certain at the given interval range that the

Figure 11.5 Distribution and interval estimate. Samples from the same population gave these 95% confidence intervals (The idea of this figure is credited to Moore & McCabe's book (1998), Introduction to the Practice of Statistics).

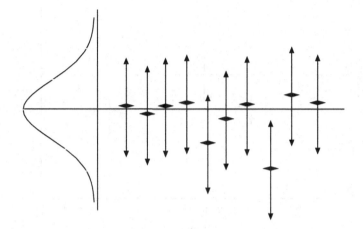

site's anomaly-free rate is any different than the pre-determined threshold. Even if its point estimate (the dot) appears to be lower or higher than the threshold. However, if the interval estimate falls entirely above or below the horizontal line, then we can say that the difference between the site's rate and the threshold for anomaly-free is statistically significant: (1) if it is below the line, then the site's rate significantly lower (worse) than the acceptable rate, and (2) if it is above the line, then it is significantly higher (better) than the acceptable rate. In Figure 11.6, site #1 is significantly higher than the acceptable rate, and sites #7 and #16 are significantly lower than the acceptable rate.

Simulation

As discussed previously, sample variability contributes to uncertainty. An alternative and perhaps more robust approach to take into account sample variability is to use a simulation techniques, of which there are two groups of fairly new methods: one is known as the Markov Chain Monte Carlo (MCMC) method and the other is bootstrap. MCMC could, for example, take account of the site sharing some common source of uncertainty, such as the true extent to which anomalous rates should be adjusted for other factors (e.g., departments, job responsibilities). When using MCMC methods we are not interested in finding simple point estimates. Instead, we make a large number of randomly drawn samples based on the joint posterior distribution of all the parameters, and use random samples to obtain the "true" distribution of the population. Modern computer power has made using the MCMC method feasible for increasingly large problems and is starting to have a dramatic effect on the practice of statistics in difficult contexts. The WinBUGs software reviewed in Chapter II is an ideal software application to conduct MCMC simulations, although similar analyses can be carried out with other statistical packages and possibly even with

Figure 11.6. Interval estimates as a profiling tool

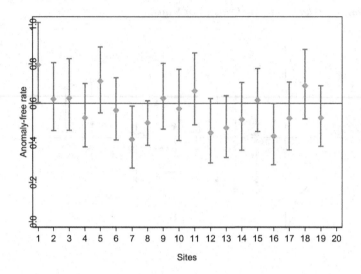

more advanced spreadsheet programs. Theoretically, MCMC, which uses the Metropolis, Metropolis-Hastings, and Metropolis-Hastings-Green algorithms and the Gibbs sampler, allows us to simulate any distribution on a finite-dimensional state space specified by any unnormalized density. More detailed fundamental materials on MCMC can be found from Congdon (2002), Andrieu, Freitas, Doucet & Jordan (2003), Robert & Casella (2005), Gamerman & Lopes (2006). More technical discussions and applications of MCMC can be found in *Markov Chain Monte Carlo in practice* by Gilks, Richardson & Spiegelhalter (1996), and *SAS for Monte Carlo Studies: A Guide for Quantitative Researchers* by Fan, Felsovalyi, Sivo & Keenan (2002).

Let us use synthetic data to illustrate how we can use the MCMC simulation method to address uncertainty. Let us assume that we have three groups, labeled Group I, Group II, and Group III, respectively, each have anomalous rates of 3.0% (95% confidence interval, 2.0 to 4.1), 5.1% (95% confidence interval, 3.1 to 6.9), and 6.2 (95% confidence interval, 2.9 to 9.8) over a period of one month. Our goal is to rank these groups for the risk of anomalous traffics. The relative probability of the underlying true rate for each group is represented by an appropriate normal distribution as shown in Figure 11.7 from left to right for groups I to III. The distribution for Group I, for example, has a mean of 3.0 and an SD of 0.5. These distributions could be given a Bayesian interpretation, although no subjective judgment has gone into their calculation.

For each group, a random "true" rate can be successively drawn from the distribution of that group. That is, the chance of drawing a value of, say, 3.0 for Group I is proportional to the height of the distribution for Group I at rate = 3.0. The first drawings are shown in Table 11.2 in which values of 3.12, 5.71, and 5.82 were obtained for three groups, Group I, Group II and Group III, respectively. These random drawings can then be ranked, as shown in the right side of Table 11.2 for each group. This process is known as an iteration and is then repeated. The next set of simulated anomalous rates show that Group I is ranked "low", Group II is ranked "Middle", and Group III is ranked "High". Such reversals are to be expected given the clear overlap of the distributions. The simulation should be run sufficiently long enough to ensure adequate accuracy of the conclusions, for example, 10,000 iterations with the final iteration producing values of 3.01, 5.02, and 6.81. For each group we then have 10,000 simulated ranks. For example, Group I was ranked "Low" on 7372 (73.7%) iterations, "Middle" on 1727 (17.3%) iterations, and "High" on 901 (9.0%). The distribution of these simulated ranks is shown in Figure 11.8. The "true" rank of Group II is even more uncertain than that of Group I as it ranked as the "Middle" on only 55.2% occasions. Thus we can conclude that there is a 9.0% of probability that the high anomalous group is Group I, a 21% of probability it is Group II, and a 70% probability it is Group III.

We also can obtain an interval estimate from the simulations. For example, with carrying out 10,000 iterations for each group, we can sort them in seceding order and then identify the 95% confidence interval by using positions 250 and 9,750.

Bootstrap, which as we briefly discussed in Chapter VII, is another popular simulation method in addition to MCMC. Because of the large size of network traffic data we may not be able to fit a MCMC model with WinBUGS. However we can conduct MCMC-like simulations based on the bootstrap procedure using SAS. Bootstrapping is a computer-based non-parametric simulation statistics method and aims to create better statistical inferences. It also addresses the sample variability issue, and has been widely used in statistics and quantitative social science since 1979 when Bradley Efron first published his article on this method (Efron, 1979). Additional fundamental background materials on bootstrapping can be found from Efron (1982), and Efron & Tibshirani (1994).

Example 11.2→Bootstrap to Obtain Interval Estimates. In Chapter VIII we discussed the use of hierarchical generalized linear modeling to profile group, site or user behavior. However, we only reported the point estimate (Figure 8.8) without the interval estimate for each group due to the statistic described in Equation (8-24), which is a complex function of parameter estimates where the theoretically-based standard errors are not easily derived. Conversely, we can use the bootstrapping resampling technique to empirically construct the sampling distribution for each group-specific anomaly-free measure to avoid making

Figure 11.7 Distributions of three groups

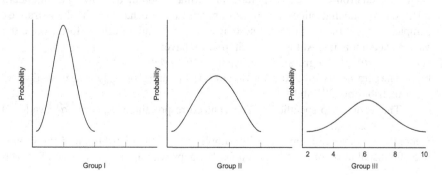

Table 11.2 Sample of simulations

Iteration	Group I		Group II		Group III	
	Simulated Rate	Simulated Rank	Simulated Rate	Simulated Rank	Simulated Rate	Simulated Rank
1	3.12	middle	5.71	high	5.81	high
2	2.89	low	4.65	middle	4.32	middle
3	2.99	low	5.11	high	7.89	high
...						
...						
10,000	3.01	low	5.02	middle	6.81	high

Figure 11.8 Possible true ranks of three groups based on simulations (In each group, the ranks are low [light gray], middle [gray] and high [dark gray] from the left bar to the right bar)

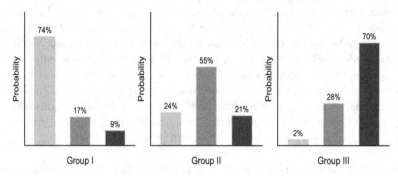

unnecessary assumptions. We can adopt the algorithm for conducting such simulations developed by Normand (2007) for profiling hospital performance as described below.

Let I denote the total number of groups in the sample and let B denote for samples drawn from bootstrap. We repeat steps $1-4$ for $b = 1, 2, \cdots, B$ times:

1. Sample I groups with replacement.
2. Fit the model described in Equations (8-22) and (8-23) using all observations within each sampled group. We use the parameter estimates obtained by fitting the model to all the data as starting values. If some groups appear more than once in a bootstrapped sample, we treat them as distinct so that we have I random effects to estimate the variance components. At the end of Step 2, we have:
   a. The estimated regression coefficients of the predictors, $\hat{\beta}^{(b)}$.
   b. The parameters governing the random effects, and group adjusted anomaly-free distribution, $\hat{\mu}^{(b)}$ and $\hat{\tau}^{2(b)}$.
   c. The set of group-specific intercepts and corresponding variances, $\{\hat{\alpha}_i^{(b)}, \text{vâr}(\hat{\alpha}_i^{(b)}) ; i = 1, 2, ..., I\}$.
3. Generate a group's random effect by sampling from the distribution of the group-specific distribution obtained in Step 2c. We approximate the distribution for each

random effect by a normal distribution. Thus, we draw $\alpha_i^{(b*)} \sim N\,(\hat{\alpha}_i^{(b)}, \text{vâr}(\hat{\alpha}_i^{(b)}))$ for the unique set of group indices obtained from Step 1.

4. Within each unique group, i, sampled in Step 1, and for each observation, j, in that group, calculate $\hat{y}_{ij}^{(b)}$, $\hat{e}_{ij}^{(b)}$, and $\hat{s}_i\,(z)^{(b)}$ where $\hat{\beta}^{(b)}$ and $\hat{\mu}^{(b)}$ are obtained from Step 2 and $\hat{\alpha}_i^{(b*)}$ is obtained from Step 3.

Now we can have an interval estimate from the sorted B standardized estimates. For example, we can have the 95% confidence interval by identifying the 2.5^{th} and 97.5^{th} percentiles of the B standardized estimates. For each group, we compute the probability of good performance in anomaly-free distribution by the relative frequency of the B standardized estimates that are less than the specified threshold. For example, we may be interested in identifying only groups with an 80% or greater probability of having a standardized anomaly-free rate less than a pre-determined threshold. This approach addresses the relative degree of confidence for profiling results based on the different samples sizes for each group. We estimate this probability using the bootstrap method. The SAS codes for conducting the simulation are given in Display 11.2 and Appendix.

Display 11.2
SAS codes to conduct MCMC-like bootstrap simulations

```
data temp;
set your data;
run;
%IDS_Random(temp,attack,group,&outvar6,site_6)  /* full codes are listed in */
                                                  /* Appendix CH11  */;
data pred_6;
set _pred;
Random_phat_6=exp(pred)/(1+exp(pred));
run;

data Fix_6;
set _soln;
run;
%IDS_Get_xbate(Fix_6);
%let Fix_6=&outvar;

%IDS_Get_Phat(pred_6,pred_6,&Fix_6,Fix_phat_6);
%IDS_Get_SMR(pred_6, SMR_6, group, attack,Random_phat_6,Fix_Phat_6,SMR_OBS_6,
SMR_Phat_6);

/*-----------------------------------------------------------------
 Create a sample at site level
 ---------------------------------------------------------------*/;
proc sql noprint;
create table site_smple as select IPs,count(*) as total from temp group by
group;
quit;
/*-----------------------------------------------------------------
Bootstrap 1,000 times to get interval estimates
 ---------------------------------------------------------------*/
%New_Bootstrap30(temp,Site_Smple, sim_data, 1, 1000);
```

Figure 11.9 shows the distribution of the standardized anomaly-free rate calculated based on Normand's standardized risk-adjusted equation (8-24) with the MIT-DAPRA data. A total of 1382 groups with at least 5 observations were included in the figure. Among these groups, the mean of the standardized anomaly-free rate is 37.2% (SD =14.4%) which ranged

Figure 11.9 Distribution of standardized anomaly-free rate

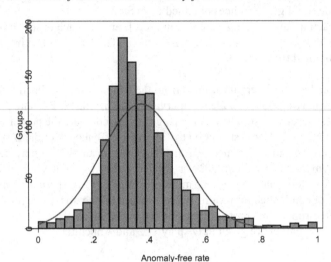

from 0.03% to 99.8%. The 25th and 75th percentiles of the rate are 28.5% and 43.4%%, respectively. The 95th percentile is 64.1% and the 5th percentile is 18.2%. We can see that the model provides a good platform for future discrimination among groups.

Parametric and Non-Parametric Methods

Parametric methods require a parametric assumption (e.g., normality) while non-parametric methods do not rely on such an assumption. Therefore in a circumstance where we are not able to normalize data we can use non-parametric methods to conduct an analysis. Let us assume that we have developed an anomaly-free score to profile user behavior patterns based on 100 individuals, each of whom contributed at least 500 connections. Let us also assume that the score ranges from 0.25 to 2.25 with a mean of 1.25 (SD = 0.75). If we want to know what percentage of users have a score of 2.00 and high, the parametric approach would make an assumption about the distribution of the data, which assumes that the data is normally distributed, and calculates the probability to have the value 2.00 from the distribution

$$N(1.25, 0.75^2), \ P(x \geq 2.0) = p(Z > \frac{2 - 1.25}{0.75}) = 0.1587.$$

The non-parametric approach, on the other hand, would directly calculate the percentage of scores that are above 2.00 from the 100 individuals, regardless of the distribution.

Similarly, when we conduct a hypothesis test, we usually employ parametric methods that include the t-test and the F-test. When we cannot be sure that the data meet the normalized assumption, and when we do not want to use a transformation function to match the assumption (or when the transformation does not work well), a non-parametric test can be adopted to protect against such violations of assumptions. For example, the t-test requires three assumptions: normality, equal variances, and independence. The non-parametric alternative, the Mann-Whitney-Wilcoxon test, does not rely on the normality assumption, although it still requires the equal variances and independence assumptions.

Example 11.3→ Non-parametric Test. The v57 variable that measures the number of capital letters (capital_run_length_total) in the spam-email data is designed to be associated with the outcome of a spam email. Let us test if it is statistically significantly associated with the response variable v58 (spam yes/no). Because this variable does not follow a normal distribution, we use the non-parametric test. The Stata code and the test results are shown in Display 11.3 below.

Display 11.3
An example of Wilcoxon rank-sum test

```
Use F:\Book\Chapter 11\spam.dta

. sum v57,d
                                 v57
-----------------------------------------------------------------
          Percentiles      Smallest
  1%            3               1
  5%            6               1
 10%           10               1         Obs                4601
 25%           35               1         Sum of Wgt.        4601

 50%           95                         Mean           283.2893
                             Largest      Std. Dev.      606.3479
 75%          266            9090
 90%          725            9163         Variance        367657.7
 95%         1223           10062         Skewness        8.707011
 99%         3027           15841         Kurtosis        148.6701

. ranksum v57,by(v58)

Two-sample Wilcoxon rank-sum (Mann-Whitney) test

        v58 |      obs    rank sum    expected
------------+-----------------------------------
          0 |     2788   5089455.5     6415188
          1 |     1813   5497445.5     4171713
------------+-----------------------------------
   combined |     4601   10586901    10586901

unadjusted variance    1.938e+09
adjustment for ties    -73183.266
                       ----------
adjusted variance      1.938e+09

Ho: v57(v58==0) = v57(v58==1)
             z = -30.112
    Prob > |z| =   0.0000
```

The results indicate that we cannot reject the null hypothesis that there is no difference in medians of v57 between spam and non-spam emails. Rather, they are statistically significantly different.

The confidence intervals examined with Equaltions (11-3) and (11-4) are parametric but we can also attain a confidence interval based on a non-parametric approach. For example we can use bootstrap to draw B samples with replacements and then calculate a rate from each sample. Thus, at the end of bootstrapping simulations we will have B total number of rates and if we sort them from low to high we will have the interval estimate. Let us use the spam-email data and Stata's command, *bootstrap*, to show an example of using the bootstrapping approach to acquire the 95% confidence interval on the variable v58 (spam or non-spam). Displays 11.4 and 11.5 show the Stata codes and results, respectively.

Display 11.4
Stata code to conduct bootstrap estimates for the binary variable (spam vs. non-spam)

```
#delimit;
 use F:\Book\Chapter 11\spam.dta;
 set seed 1234;

bs "summarize v58" "_result(3)",reps(1000) saving(BP_spam);
use bp_spam, replace;
sum _bs_1,d;
histogram _bs_1;
```

Display 11.5
Results of bootstrapping estimates for the binary variable (spam vs. non-spam)

```
Bootstrap statistics                    Number of obs    =     4601
                                        Replications     =     1000

------------------------------------------------------------------------
Variable   |  Reps  Observed     Bias  Std. Err. [95% Conf. Interval]
-----------+------------------------------------------------------------
    _bs_1  |  1000  .3940448 -.0002573  .0072331    .379851  .4082386  (N)
           |                                        .3794827 .4081721  (P)
           |                                        .3805694 .4090415  (BC)
------------------------------------------------------------------------
Note:  N  = normal
       P  = percentile
      BC  = bias-corrected

                            _result(3)
--------------------------------------------------------------------
      Percentiles     Smallest
 1%     .3764399      .3688329
 5%     .3818735      .370789
10%     .3849163      .3738318    Obs              1000
25%     .3890459      .3738318    Sum of Wgt.      1000

50%     .3936101                  Mean         .3937874
                 Largest          Std. Dev.    .0072331
75%     .398609       .4142578
90%     .4030646      .4142578    Variance     .0000523
95%     .4059987      .4149098    Skewness     .0196406
99%     .4111063      .4175179    Kurtosis     3.132318
```

Figure 11.10 shows the distribution of the spam rate based on 1000 iterations from which we can see that the "true" rate of spam-email base don the spam-email data fills in a range of 0.369 to 0.418. We can draw the interval information by sorting the rates ascending and take data points at the 25th and 975th as the lower and higher bounds of the 95% confidence interval, which they are 0.379 and 0.408, respectively. The point estimate of the spam-email rate, however, is 0.394.

STATISTICAL CONTROL CHART

Variation exists throughout network communications. Different hardware, software, operating systems, users, and data collection methods together contribute combined and mixed variation to the traffic. Although such variation can be considered randomly distributed, it could impact user behavior and the corresponding behavior pattern even if the pattern itself remains unchanged. Under such circumstances, individual traffic stream, which could be a result of chance rather than a real deviation from the actual pattern, provides insufficient information to support decision-making. Consequently measuring on a series of streams within a given time period provide a more stable and statistically robust approach to recognize and predict any real pattern changes.

Statistical control charts have the capability to meet such a need and are a powerful tool that supports decision-making. Control charts monitor a process and alert people when the process has been disturbed to the point of being out of control. Figure 11.11 shows an example of control charts. Shewhart (1931) was the first person to use the control chart at the Bell Telephone Laboratories in 1924. Control charts allow us to set a range for the max and min thresholds of system or user behavior and to determine whether or not any anomalies have occurred during the course of network traffic monitoring.

In general, if a new data point on the chart has a higher value than the previous one, but both points are within the control limits, then the chart reflects natural variation within a stable process. If this increase were to be acted upon as if the process had fundamentally changed, the analysis and subsequent action taken could be wrong (as the process probably remains unchanged). The probability of measurement points occurring outside control limits within an unchanged process varies by the range of the upper and lower limits. A wide range of limits prevents too many false alarms, but may also conceal significant trends, as too few true alarms may be missed. A special cause is most often intermittent, and will show up as a spike on the chart. However, a trend in the data streams may indicate that a special cause is making the process unstable. A quality improvement initiative may result in such a trend. There is a separate set of rules that apply for instability within limits, including rules for trends.

Upper and Lower Control Bounds

Several statistical approaches can be used to define the upper and lower control bounds, or the control limits of control charts. We can have static control bounds where the values do not change over a period of a monitoring process, or we can use dynamic control bounds where the values of upper and lower will change over time. Let $\hat{\mu}$ be the mean anomaly-free score of a pattern as described in Chapter VIII, let $\hat{\sigma}$ be the standard derivation of the pattern, and let $t_i (i = 1, 2, ..., j)$ be the time series of a period to be monitored. We can then create a simple control chart by drawing a horizontal center line, y_c, based on $\hat{\mu}$, and drawing horizontal control limits based on $\hat{\sigma}$:

$$y_c = \hat{\mu}, \tag{11-6}$$

$$y_u = \hat{\mu} + \frac{k\hat{\sigma}}{\sqrt{n}}, \text{ and} \tag{11-7}$$

Figure 11.10 Distribution of spam rate based on bootstrap analysis

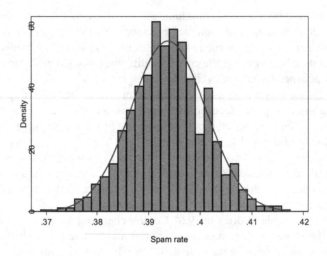

Figure 11.11 An example of a control chart

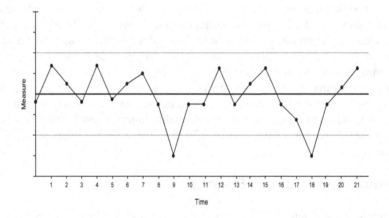

$$y_l = \hat{\mu} - \frac{k\hat{\sigma}}{\sqrt{n}}, \qquad\qquad (11\text{-}8)$$

where n is the sample size and k is a constant to control the interval range of the control limits. Figure 11.12 shows a series of mean anomaly-free scores, $\hat{\mu}_i$ for a site over a week period with $k = 3$ (so the control limits are approximately equivalent to 99% confidence interval). Any $\hat{\mu}_i$ that does not fall in the control limits is evidence of a possible abnormality.

Moreover, by modifying Equations (11-6) to (11-8), we can construct dynamic control limits that vary based on the time, $t_i\,(i = 1, 2, \ldots, j)$, and $\hat{\mu}_i$.

Figure 11.12 A site's anomaly-free score within a week period (IP address: 172.016.113.084)

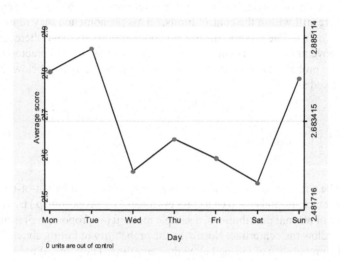

Control Charts for Proportion

Let us assume that we want to evaluate a threshold-based simple binary intrusion detection algorithm that classifies a connection being abnormal if an observed value is above the threshold, and being anomaly-free if the observed value is below the pre-specified threshold. Note that we may have two types of uncertainties: algorithm-specific uncertainty measured by the probability of a missing classification that is contributed by the pre-selected threshold and network-specific uncertainty that is contributed by mixed variations from a particular network system.

Let $\hat{p}$ be the allowed proportion of the rate of false alarms per minute. We want to monitor the false alarm rate over 24 hours with the given threshold, and because we know that $\hat{p}$ from a sample of size n ($n = 24 \times 60 = 1{,}440$) has an approximately normal distribution of $N(p, \sqrt{p(1-p)/n})$, we can construct a control chart using Equations (11-9 to 11-11) to monitor false alarm rate changes over the course of the monitoring period. If we find that the rate falls out of the control limits too frequently, we can adjust the threshold of the evaluation algorithm and repeat the monitoring process again.

$$y_c = \hat{p} ,\tag{11-6}$$

$$y_u = \hat{p} + k\sqrt{\hat{p}(1-\hat{p})/n} \text{ , and}\tag{11-7}$$

$$y_u = \hat{p} - k\sqrt{\hat{p}(1-\hat{p})/n}.\tag{11-8}$$

Out-of-Control Signal

Sometimes a series of values will lie consecutively above or below the centerline even though they are still within the control limits. This phenomenon may represent a signal that is out-of-control. The 9-point rule is a method that suggests that if there are 9 consecutive points above or below the centerline, the process tends to be characterized by a lack of control. The probability of a run of 9 consecutive points above or below the centerline can be calculated as

$$p(x) = \prod_{i=1}^{9} \frac{1}{2} = \left(\frac{1}{2}\right)^9 = 0.001953,$$

which could be a strong signal to indicate that the system could be out-of-control. This is based on the centerline and how true its process mean μ (or proportion ρ) is. By the natural characteristic of normal distributions, a sample mean $\hat{\mu}$ (or proportion $\hat{\rho}$) is more likely to fall above or below the centerline. Normally, the probability of falling above the centerline is same to the probability of falling below the centerline. Therefore, if points fall one side consecutively, the probability will be low and it seems likely to indicate an out-of-control in the monitoring period (Figure 11.13).

In summary, the control chart can be used to measure whether the network traffic is stable within a monitoring period and to determine if its variance is due to special causes. This determines if valid comparisons can be made and indicates the correct approach to improve the process. It also can be used to measure whether or not a quality improvement initiative, such as a new network secure policy being enforced, a new secure hardware or software being installed, has been effective. However, the control chart provides little by itself about quality. As a process control tool, it can be stable with minimal natural varia-

Figure 11.13 The 9-point rule

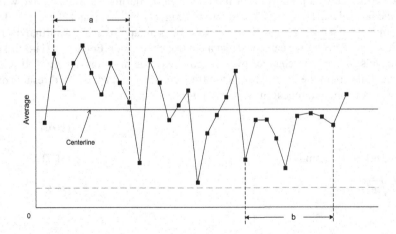

tion and still reflect poor quality if the frequency of a quality associated adverse event is too high.

RANKING

Ranking is a non-parametric statistical procedure. With scoring observations within each user, we can group the observations in an ordinal scale order. This process is called ranking. For example, if we sort student test scores in descending order and group students into 3 groups defined by high scores (top 25%), low scores (bottom 25%) and middle scores (between top 25% and bottom 25%), we ranked the students based on their test scores. In general, ranking would provide a simple and efficient approach to use a sequence of ordinal numbers to reduce unnecessarily detailed measures, and makes it possible to evaluate complex information based on simple criteria.

We mentioned in Chapter I that the reality of intrusion detection and prevention in network security is that we are unlikely to have a pure anomaly-free environment; rather, we are more likely to have to retain some level of anomalies, which could be true anomalous events, true anomaly-free events but misclassified as "anomalies", and a mix of the true and false anomalies. The challenge for us is how to monitor the system behavior with these existing noises. Moreover, while there is a great variability on behavior across groups, sites, and users, questions on how we can decide and select reasonable threshold(s) for ranking them and for identifying outliers for the monitor arise.

In this section we will discuss several ranking approaches that could be useful for proofing user or system behavior. These approaches include: (1) identifying groups that are below a threshold with varying degrees of uncertainty, and (2) identifying groups that are better and worse than the varying thresholds with a constant degree of uncertainty. Approaches to discrete categories include (1) using interval estimates with varying degrees of uncertainty to define ranking groups, and (2) analyzing the relationship between probability and interval estimate methods.

Percentiles

The most widely used ranking methods to identify groups are based on the percentile that is the value below a certain percent of observations, including decile, quantile, and quartile. The relationship between percentile and decile, quantile and quartile is shown below in Table 11.3. The difference between the first and third quartiles (Q1 to Q3) is also known as the inter-quartile range (IQR) and is a more stable measure for the min to max range.

If the 10th percentile corresponds to a score of 20, then 10% of observations in the sample have their values below 20. Simliarly, a score in the 99th percentile means that 99% of observations have their values below the index score whatever of the 99th is represented. The difference between percentile and percentage is that a percentile is a reflection on the whole observation in the sample, and a percentage is a reflection on the baseline of the denominator. For example, in a test that contains a total of 100 questions and we correctly answer 75 of them, the precentage of correct answers is obviously 75%. However, if the test is so difficult that only 10% of test-takers correctly answered 75% of the test, a test-taker with a score of 75% is in the 90th percentile.

Let x_p be the pth percentile, and x_i be the value of a score X in ascending order for $i = 1, 2,...,n$. The pth percentile can be calculated as (Stata, 1997):

$$x_p = (1-h)x_i + hx_{i+1}, \tag{11-12}$$

where i is the largest integer $i \le (n+1)p/100$, and $h = (n+1)p/100 - i$. Both SAS and Stata have procedures to create percentile, decile, quantile, and quartile. In SAS we can use *PROC UNIVERSAL* to get statistics for percentile, quantile and quartile, use *PROC MEANS* for any non-standard percentile (e.g., 98th), and use *PROC RANK* for decile grouping. Correspondingly, Stata has the *pctile* command to create a variable containing percentiles, and *xtile* command to create a variable to group observations based on percentiles.

Example 11.4→Ranking based on Percentile. In the Wang and Cannady (2005) risk score study, a percentile-ranking method was used to assess the stability and goodness of a score across the training and testing samples. They created 5 risk groups based on the percentile of each score in the following manner: Group I $< 5^{th}$ percentile $\le$ Group II $< 25^{th}$ $\le$ Group III $< 75^{th} \le$ Group IV $< 95^{th} \le$ Group V. These groups were created to classify each observation in both the training and testing samples, and used sensitivity, specificity,

Table 11.3 Relationships between percentile, decile quantile, and quartile

Percentile	Decile	Quantile	Quartile
P10	D1		
P20	D2	q1	
P25			Q1
P30	D3		
P40	D4	q2	
P50	D5		Q2
P60	D6	q3	
P70	D7		
P75			Q3
P80	D8	q4	
P90	D9		
P100	D10	q5	Q4

Table 11.4. Comparison of the goodness and stability of score using percentile method

Risk Groups	Anomaly (%)	
	Training	Testing
I [0 – 0.60)	0.2	0.0
II [0.60 – 0.73)	0.3	2.0
III [0.73 – 1.61)	49.8	57.1
IV [1.61 – 1.84)	100.0	92.6
V [≥1.84)	100.0	99.6

and misclassification rate to measure the score performance in classification across the 5 groups. Using these groups, they evaluated the stability of the score by comparing the performances of score-based classification results between the training and the testing samples (Table 11.4). With the percentile ranking method, they illustrated that no remarkable difference existed between the two samples although the thresholds used to construct risk groups were determined by the training sample. Overall, the risk score demonstrated great stability for classification.

Example 11.5→ Sampling Network Traffic on Quantile of the Anomalous Risk Score. Let us assume that we are going to develop a sampling plan for network traffic surveillance. To acquire as much information as possible about the system behavior with limited resources, we decide to take a dynamic sampling approach that collects traffic data from sites and sub-systems based on their risk of being anomalous. That is, we will sample less traffic for sites with low risk and take more data from high risk sites. For this sampling plan we have two tasks to be accomplished: (1) assess the risk of being anomalous for each site, and (2) categorize sites based their risk. Although various methods and approaches are available, let us use the scoring models introduced in Chapter VIII for task 1 and the quantile method for task 2.

Let us use the MIT-DARPA data to simulate this plan. To simplify the analysis we randomly draw 10% of data from the raw MIT-DARPA data and assign an anomalous score to each observation in the 10% sample based on Equation (8-11) with $v_k = 1$ for all k. We then collapse the risk score from the observation-level to the site-level, and keep these sites that have at least 100 observations. Finally, we rank sites by quantile based on their risk score. The Stata codes to conduct this example and the distribution of the risk score by quantile are shown in Display 11.6.

Figure 11.14 Distributions of site-level anomalous score

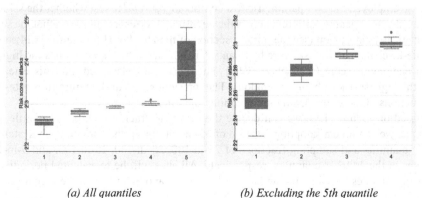

(a) All quantiles   (b) Excluding the 5th quantile

Display 11.6
Stata codes and results for Example 11.5

```
#delimit;
use "F:\Book\Chapter 11\temp.dta", clear;
gen byte Attack=(attack~="-");
drop v13 score;
set seed 12566;
sample 10,by(IP_s);
do create_var.do;  /* Appendix CH11 */;
gen score=t2+l1+udp+(samePort==0)+(http==0)+(smtp==0)+ecr+eco+(snmp==0)
+port+(ftp==0)+(urp==0)+(domain==0)+frag+(finger==0)+(telnet==0);
gen week=substr(index,6,1);
gen n=1;
collapse (sum) n Attack (mean) score,by(IP_s week);
gen rate=Attack/n;
keep if n>100;
gen log_score=log(score);
xtile gp_5 =log_score,nq(5) altdef ;
nptrend log_score , by(gp_5);
tab gp_5,sum(log_score);

. tab gp_5,sum(log_score)

5 quantiles |          Summary of log_score
    of log  |       Mean    Std. Dev.        Freq.
------------+-----------------------------------------
          1 |  2.2560622    .01018606           45
          2 |  2.2796878    .00574845           44
          3 |  2.2924481    .00242118           45
          4 |  2.3009245    .00322061           44
          5 |  2.3944087    .05776143           44
------------+-----------------------------------------
      Total |  2.3044319    .05404866          222

nptrend log_score , by(GP_5)
     GP_5       score        obs       sum of ranks
        1           1         45           1035
        2           2         44           2970
        3           3         45           5040
        4           4         44           6886
        5           5         44           8822

         z  = 14.57
Prob > |z| = 0.000
```

Because the distribution of the anomalous score may not follow a normal distribution, we used the *log()* command to transform the score to the log scale (Equation 5.10) and also employed the non-parametric test command, *nptrend* to test whether the score is statistically significantly different across the quantiles. The test result shows that the score is statistically significant (see the bottom section of the Display 11.6). Figure 11.14 shows the site-level anomalous risk score by quantile, in which the fifth quantile has the highest mean anomalous score ($\hat{\mu} = 2.39$, $\hat{\sigma} = 0.06$). Therefore, sites classified into this category have the highest risk of being anomalous. The top right graph of the figure illustrates the distributions of the scores from the remaining quantiles.

Based on Figure 11.14, we can decide the sampling fractions for each quantile. For example, we take a sampling fraction of 35-in-100 for all the sites and sub-system in the 5th quantile, and sampling fractions of 25-in-100, 20-in-100, 15-in-100, and 5-in-100 for sites in the 4th to 1st quantiles, respectively. All sites will be reevaluated periodically for their quantiles based on the updated risk of being anomalous from the recent sample data. Therefore, a site may be sampled by different sampling fractions during different time periods.

Probability and Interval Estimate

As we discussed, interval estimates provide a great tool for evaluating variability and uncertainty when profiling user or system behavior, and has been widely used in ranking procedures. Assume that we want to identify a surveillance list of sub-network systems that may have a high risk of being attacked. We can create such a list with the interval estimation method. For example, we can list all the sites with their 95% confidence intervals that fill out a pre-determined threshold of anomaly-free rate as

$$\begin{cases} s_i = 1 & b < \hat{\rho} \\ s_i = 0 & a < \hat{\rho} < b \end{cases}$$

where s_i is a classifier that has a value 1 to indicate the ith site to be in the surveillance list and 0 for otherwise. a and b are the lower and upper bounds of the 95% confidence interval of point estimate of the anomaly-free rate. $\hat{\rho}$ is the pre-determined threshold value that can be the mean of the top 25th percentile sites' anomaly-free rates or a particular number we selected. We also can identity sites with low risk of be anomalous by setting $s_i = 1$ if $a > \hat{\rho}$.

Table 11.5 Fixed threshold ($\hat{\rho} = 0.3719$) and varying interval estimates

Interval Estimate	Sites Identified	
Total site =1382	(#)	(%)
95% confidence interval	4	0.29
90% confidence interval	7	0.51
80% confidence interval	12	0.87
70% confidence interval	16	1.16

Table 11.6 Fixed interval (95% confidence interval) but varying thresholds

Threshold	Sites Identified	
Total site =1382	(#)	(%)
$\hat{\rho} = 0.5171 (\hat{\mu} + \hat{\sigma})$	8	0.58
$\hat{\rho} = 0.2284 (\hat{\mu} - \hat{\sigma})$	1	0.07
$\hat{\rho} = 0.40$ (arbitrary threshold)	4	0.29
$\rho = 0.10$ (arbitrary threshold)	0	0.00

Table 11.7 Fixed threshold as aggregated mean and varying probability

Threshold	Sites Identified	
Total site =1382	(#)	(%)
$P(x < 0.3719) > 0.95$	0	0.00
$P(x < 0.3719) > 0.90$	1	0.07
$P(x < 0.3719) > 0.80$	4	0.29

Example 11.6→Rank based on Confidence Intervals. Let us use the simulation results from Example 11.2 to identity sites based on their interval estimates, and let $\hat{\rho} = 0.3719$ be the mean of the aggregated standardized anomaly-free rate. Let us also assume that the threshold is held as a constant and vary the certainty by using any of the following confidence intervals: 95%, 90%, 80%, and 70%. Table 11.5 shows the number of sites identified by different interval estimates.

Alternatively, we can fix the interval estimate but vary the threshold. For example, with a fixed 95% of confidence interval and varying thresholds, we identify different sites to be monitored (Table 11.6).

In addition to interval estimates, we can identify these groups or sub-systems to be monitored use a probability approach and identify different groups to be monitored based on different probability values. For example, we can list all the groups with the probability of their point estimate of anomaly-free rate being less than a pre-determined threshold greater than a given probability, T:

$$\begin{cases} s_i = 1 & P(x < \hat{\rho}) > T \\ s_i = 0 & 0 \leq P(x < \hat{\rho}) \leq T \end{cases}$$

where T could be 0.8 or any particular number that is reasonable in practice. We can hold the threshold constant and vary the certainty by calculating the probability of the standardized anomaly-free rate to be lower than the threshold. Using the aggregated rate as a fixed threshold, we can identify different groups to be monitored based on different probability values. Table 11.7 shows an example of such an approach using three different probability values. Conversely, we can vary the threshold and obtain different corresponding probability values. Table 11.8 shows number of groups being identified with different thresholds and probabilities.

As we can see from the above Tables, both interval estimate and probability provide us a tool to profile and identify outlier groups many improvements in standardized anomaly-free rate would lead to important network security gains. For example, if we could increase the anomaly-free rate at the system-level to the 75th percentile, we would prevent a great number of possible alarms.

Figure 11.14 Probability of standardized anomaly-free rate above system average

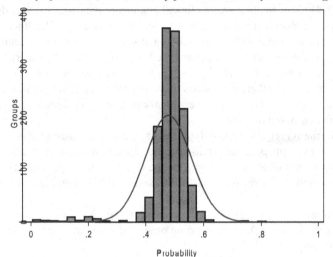

Table 11.8 Fixed probability as T = 0.8 and varying threshold

Thresholds	Sites Identified	
Total site =1382	(#)	(%)
1.1 times greater than the mean	1	0.07
1.2 times greater than the mean	1	0.07
1.1 times lower than the mean	24	1.74
1.2 times lower than the mean	16	1.16

Achievable Benchmark of Performance

Policy choices determine thresholds and acceptable levels of uncertainty, but data should inform policy choices. To properly prevent both intentional and unintentional network attacks, we need to reach multi-goals. For example, we may want to control the anomaly rate to be below a particular threshold such as, for example, 10 alarms per hour. We choose this threshold based on our knowledge regarding network system infrastructure, our experience on historical data, or through arbitrary means. Nevertheless, once we determine a threshold, it actually becomes the benchmark and it may have a great impact on secure policies, procedures, and regulations. It is important to have a statistically robust and evidence-based approach to determine a benchmark. The achievable benchmark of performance (ABP) approach that we propose in this book is designed to provide a statistical method for determining a reasonable benchmark. The concept of our ABP germinated in healthcare research where researchers then called it the Achievable Benchmark of Care (ABC) method (Kiefe, Allison, Williams, Person, Weaver, Weissman, 2001; Weissmann, Allison, Kiefe, Farmer, Weaver, Williams, Child, Pemberton, Brown, Baker, 1999; Kiefe, Weissman, Allison, Farmer, Weaver, Williams, 1998; Mohr, Mahoney, Nelson, Batalden, Plume, 1996; Berkey, 1994). This method was a clinical healthcare measure that was developed at the University of Alabama at Birmingham to improve the quality of healthcare.

Similar to the ABC method, the ABP is a tool to facilitate network security and protect attacks and anomalous events. It derives the benchmark from the security and protection practices already being achieved by "best practice" systems or groups. It is not a measure of direct outcome. Rather, it provides a statistically sound and data-driven approach to help us select a good and achievable benchmark that already achieves "best practice" rather than experience-based opinions.

Let $\hat{\rho}$ be the aggregated adjusted standardized anomaly-free rate of the entire user group of the network system, $\hat{\rho}_i$ be the group-specific adjusted standardized anomaly-free rate for the ith group with n_i observation, and x_p be the threshold of pth percentile ($p = 1, 2, \cdots, 10$) of the group-specific rates $\hat{\rho}_1, \hat{\rho}_2, \cdots, \hat{\rho}_m$. To create an ABP, we complete the following steps:

1.   Calculate $\hat{\rho}_i$ for each group in the system, $\hat{\rho} \sim (\hat{\rho}_1, \hat{\rho}_2, \cdots, \hat{\rho}_m)$,
2.   Rank the $\hat{\rho}_1, \hat{\rho}_2, \cdots, \hat{\rho}_m$ in descending order and cumulate the observations carried by each group,
3.   Define 'superior performance' to be the anomaly-free rate above or equal to x_p, also in addition to a set number of observations. For example, we can define superior performance as $\hat{\rho} \geq x_{90}$, the 90th percentile, and also include 10% of total observations. We can then calculate x_p by using Equation (11-9):

$$x_p = (1 - h)x_i + hx_{i+1}.$$

SUMMARY

Decision analysis encompasses the use of analytic techniques by information technology professionals to make better evidence-based decisions in practice. In this chapter we have discussed topics mainly related to decision analysis in network security. We discussed the methods used to address uncertainty that include interval estimates and simulations, methods to monitor network traffic at system and sites or user groups levels, and ranking and profiling methods for system surveillance. Overall many of these methods and approaches have been widely used in a vast range of areas such as healthcare, decision-supporting, decision-making, and quality control in engineering and manufacturing processes. Moreover, with rapid advance in computer hardware and software, allows us to conduct uncertainty analyses through large-scale simulations such as the MCMC simulation. Although in some situations, we may find that the MCMC is not always practical for extremely large problems since we may still have an issue with the computer speed, the MCMC continues to gain popularity and is a robust tool used to assess uncertainty. Great care must be taken to ensure that the simulation methods have been run for long enough to give accurate results. Statistics can be reviewed as a universal guide to the unknown (Kohler, 1988). By developing and utilizing techniques for the careful collection, effective presentation, and proper analysis of numerical information, statistics facilitates wiser decision making in the face of uncertainty.

REFERENCES

Andrieu, C., Freitas, N. de., Doucet, A., & Jordan, M. I., (2003).An introduction to MCMC for machine learning, *Machine Learning,* 50, pp. 5-43.

Aven, T. (2005) *Foundations of risk analysis: a knowledge and decision-oriented prespective,*John Wiley & Sons, Ltd

Berkey, T (1994). Benchmarking in health care: Turning challenges into success. *Jt Comm J Quality Improvement,* 20: pp. 277-284.

Chernick, M. R. (1999). *Bootstrap methods: a practitioner's guide.* New Jersey: Wiley-Interscience.

Congdon, P. (2002). *Bayesian statistical modeling.* New York: John Wiley & Sons, Ltd.

Efron, B. (1982). *The jackknife, the bootstrap, and other resampling plans.* Philadelphia: SIAM.

Efron, B. & Tibshirani, E. R. (1994) *An introduction to the bootstrap.* London: Chapman & Hall.

Fan, X. Felsovalyi, A., Sivo, S. A., Keenan, S. C. (2002). *SAS for Monte Carlo studies: a guide for quantitative researchers.* North Carolina: SAS Institute Inc.

Gelman, A. Carlin, J. B. Stern, H. S. & Rubin, D. B. (2004). *Bayesian data analysis 2nd Edition.* New York: Chapman & Hall/CRC.

Gamerman, D. & Lopes, H. F. (2006). *Markov Chain Monte Carlo: stochastic simulation for Bayesian inference, 2nd Ed (Texts in Statistical Science Series),* New York: Chapman & Hall/CRC.

Gilks, W. R., Richardson, S., & Spiegelhalter, D. J. (1996). *Markov Chain Monte Carlo in practice.* London: Chapman & Hall.

Hattis, D. & Burmaster, D. E. (1994) Assessment of variability and uncertainty distributions for practical risk analyses. *Risk Analysis, 14*(5), pp.713–730.

Kiefe, C. I, Allison, J. J, Williams, O. D, Person, S. D, Weaver, M. T, Weissman, N. W. (2001). Improving quality improvement using achievable benchmarks for physician feedback: A randomized controlled trial. *JAMA*; *285*(22), 2871-2879.

Kiefe, C. I., Weissman, N.W., Allison, J.J., Farmer, RM., Weaver, M. & Williams, O. D. (1998). Methodolgy matters-XII. identifying achievable benchmarks of care: concepts and methodology. *International Journal for Quality in Health Care*; *10*(5), 443-7.

Kohler, H. (1988). *Statistics for business and economics.* London: Scott, Foresman and Company.

Lindley, D. S. (2006). *Understanding uncertainty.* New York: John Wiley & Sons, Ltd.

Mohr, J. J., Mahoney, C. C., Nelson, E. C. Batalden, P. B. and Plume, S. K. (1996). Improving health care, part 3: Clinical benchmarking for best patient care. *Journal of Quality Improvement, 22,* 599-616.

Mooney, C. Z. & Duval, R. D. (1993). *Bootstrapping: A nonparametric approach to statistical inference.* New York: SAGE Publications.

Moore, D. S. & McCabe, G. P. (1998). *Introduction to the practice of statistics. 3rd ed.* NY: W. H. Freeman and Company.

Neumann, V. J, Morgenstern, O. (1947). *Theory of games and economic theory.* New York: Wiley.

Normand, S. L. T, Wang, Y, and Krumholz, H. M. (2007). Assessing surrogacy of data sources for institutional comparisons. *Health Serv Outcomes Res Method, 7*(1-2):79-96.

Raiffa, H. (1968). *Decision analysis.* Massachusetts: Addison-Wesley.

Robert, C. P. & Casella, G. (2005). *Monte Carlo statistical methods.* New York: Springer-Verlag.

Ruppert, D. (2004). *Statistics and finance: An introduction.* New York: Springer-Verlag.

Shewhart, W. A. (1931). *Economic control of quality of manufactured product.* New York: D. Van Nostrand Company.

Shlyakhter, A. I., Kammen, D. M., Broido, C. L. and Wilson, R. (1994) Quantifying the credibility of energy projections from trends in past data: the US energy sector, *Energy Policy, 22*(2), 119-130.

Smith, R. E. Parkinson, W. J. and Bement, T. R. (2002). Uncertainty distributions using fuzzy logic. In *Fuzzy logic and probability applications: Bridging the gap.* New York: SIAM.

Wang, Y. & Cannady, J. (2005). Develop a composite risk score to detect anomaly intrusion. In *Proceedings of the IEEE SoutheastCon 2005,* pp. 445-449.

Weissmann, N.W., Allison, J. J, Kiefe, C. I, Farmer, R. M, Weaver, M. T, Williams, O. D, Child, I. G, Pemberton, J. H, Brown, K. C, Baker, C. S. (1999). Achievable benchmarks of care: The ABC™s of benchmarking. *Journal of Evaluation in Clinical Practice; 5*(3), 269-81.

Zheng, J. & Frey, H. C. (2004). Quantification of variability and uncertainty using mixture distributions: Evaluation of sample size, mixing weights, and separation between components *Risk Analysis, 24*(3), 553-571.

APPENDIX

SAS Macro to Conduct MCMC-Like Bootstrap Simulations

```
/* ------------------------------------------
MACRO TO DRAW 1000 BOOTSTRAP SAMPLES
----------------------------------------------*/;
%MACRO Bootstrap(Infile_raw,infile_hp, outdata, startpoint, endpoint);
proc sort data=&inFile_hp;
by prov_num;
run;
%do jj=&startpoint %to &endpoint;
    proc surveyselect data=&inFile_hp method=urs samprate=1
        out=BSP_hp ;
    run;
    data bsp_hp;
    set bsp_hp;
        do i=1 to numberhits;
            output;
        end;
        drop i;
    run;
    data bsp_hp;
    set bsp_hp;
    Site_ID=_N_;
    run;
    proc sql noprint;
    create table BSP as select Site_ID, &Infile_raw..* from &infile_raw innor
    join bsp_hp on bsp_hp.group=&infile_raw..group;
    quit;
    %IDS_Random(BSP,attack, Site_ID,&outvar6, prov_num_6);
    %let OutTau=;
    %IDS_Get_Tau(_cov);
        %let tau_6=&outTau;
    %put &tau_6;
        %let OutMu=;
        %IDS_Get_Mu(_soln);
        %let mu_6=&outMu;
    %put &mu_6;

    %let OutVar_w=;
    %IDS_Get_xbate_WO_Intercept(_soln);
    %let Fix_6_w=&outvar_w;
    %put &Fix_6_w;

    data solnr;
    set _solnr;
    mu_i=&mu_6+estimate;
    run;
    proc sql noprint;
    create table uniq as select group,estimate,mu_i,stderrpred,solnr.Site_ID
    from bsp_hp innor join solnr on solnr.Site_ID=bsp_hp.Site_ID;
    quit;
```

continued on following page

```
   data uniq;
   set uniq;
   inv=normal(34456+&jj);
   run;

   proc sort data=uniq;
   by group inv;
   run;

  data step_2c (drop=inv);
  set uniq;
     by group;
  if first.group then output;
  run;
  data step_2c;
  set step_2c;
  beta_zero=mu_i + (stderrpred)*rannor(34456+&jj);
  run;

  %Let ran_6_w=beta_zero+&Fix_6_w;
  %put &ran_6_w;
  proc sql noprint;
  create table pred_6 as select group,beta_zero, _pred.* from _pred innor
  join step_2c on step_2c.Site_ID=_pred.Site_ID;
  quit;
  data pred_6;
  set  pred_6;
  pred_6=exp(pred)/(1+exp(pred));
  run;

  %IDS_Get_Phat(pred_6,pred_6,&ran_6_w,Random_phat_6);
  data Fix_6;
  set _soln;
  run;

  %IDS_Get_xbate(Fix_6);
  %let Fix_6=&outvar;
  %IDS_Get_Phat(pred_6,pred_6,&Fix_6,Fix_phat_6);
  %IDS_Get_SMR(pred_6,sim_6_xx,group,attack,Random_phat_6,
   Fix_Phat_6,SMR_OBS_6,  SMR_Phat_6);

   data sim_BSP_&JJ;
   set sim_6_xx;
   iteration=&jj;
   run;
   proc append base=&outdata data=sim_BSP_&JJ;
   run;
   dm 'log; clear';
   dm 'output; clear';
 %end;
%MEND;

%include "F:\book\Chapter 11\IDS-random.sas";
%include "F:\book\Chapter 11\IDS-get-phat.sas";
%include "F:\book\Chapter 11\Prog\IDS-get-smr.sas";
%include "F:\book\Chapter 11\IDS-get-xbate.sas";
%include "F:\book\Chapter 11\IDS-get-xbate-WO-Intercept.sas";
%include "F:\book\Chapter 11\IDS-get-Tau.sas";
%include "F:\book\Chapter 11\IDS-get-mu.sas";
%include "F:\book\Chapter 11\New_bootstrap30.sas";
```

Chapter XII
Evaluation

I have always been delighted at the prospect of a new day, a fresh try, one more start, with perhaps a bit of magic waiting somewhere behind the morning.

- J.B. Priestly

INTRODUCTION

Increasing the accuracy of classification has been a constant challenge in the network security area. While expansively increasing in the volume of network traffic and advantage in network bandwidth, many classification algorithms used for intrusion detection and prevention face high false positive and false negative rates. A stream of network traffic data with many positive predictors might not necessary represent a true attack, and a seemingly anomaly-free stream could represent a novel attack. Depending on the infrastructure of a network system, traffic data can become very large. As a result of such large volumes of data, a very low misclassification rate can yield a large number of alarms; for example, a system with 22 million hourly traffics with a 1% misclassification rate could have approximately 75 alarms within a second (excluding repeated connections). Validating every such case for review is not practical. To address this challenge we can improve the data collection process and develop more robust algorithms. Unlike other research areas, such as the life sciences, healthcare, or economics, where an analysis can be achieved based on a single statistical approach, a robust intrusion detection scheme need to be constructed hierarchically with multiple algorithms. For example, profiling and classifying user behavior hierarchically, using hybrid algorithms (e.g., combining statistics and AI). On the other hand, we can improve the precision of classification by carefully evaluating the results. There are several key elements that are important for statistical evaluation in classification and prediction, such as reliability, sensitivity, specificity, misclassification, and goodness-of-fit. We also need to evaluate the goodness of the data (consistency and repeatability), goodness of the classification, and goodness of the model. We will discuss these topics in this chapter.

DATA RELIABILITY, VALIDITY, AND QUALITY

Data reliability and validity play essential roles in network security. Reliability refers to whether or not data can be replicated from either one observer to another (inter-observer reliability) or by the same observer on more than one occasion (intra-observer reliability). Reliability also means that for any data elements used, the results are reasonably complete and accurate, meet our intended purposes, and are not subject to inappropriate alteration (e.g., variables agreement from two sources). Data reliability analysis addresses the uncertainty brought by data and can be considered as a special type of risk analysis (Aven, 2005). Reliable data has basic requirements, including completeness, accuracy and consistency. Completeness reflects that the data contains all of the variables and observations required for a task; accuracy reflects that the data is collected from the correct sources and is recorded correctly; consistency refers to the need to obtain and use data that is clear and well defined enough to yield similar results in similar analyses. For example, if certain data is collected at multiple network systems, inconsistent interpretation of the data rules can lead to data that is unreliable when aggregated them as a whole. Assessments of reliability should be made in the broader context of the particular characteristics of the engagement and the risk associated with the possibility of using data of insufficient reliability.

In addition to reliability, other data quality considerations are also important. In particular, we should consider the validity of data. Data validity refers to whether the data actually represent what we think is being measured. That is, a network protocol variable should only contain information about the protocol in use, and not any other information. Assessments of both data reliability and validity can provide important information about the quality of the network traffic collected. For a comprehensive introduction to data reliability and validity refer to *Reliability and Validity in Qualitative Research* by Kirk & Miller (1987). Data quality assessment is an important aspect in network security. When the quality of data is unknown, using such data would very likely lead to an incorrect or unintentional message and the results based on such data will have a significant amount of limitations. Although the levels of data quality are affected by many factors, such as sampling methods, sampling time zone, type of network systems, and software used to collect the data, the importance of this topic has been overlooked, and only a few published studies have reported on this topic in network security. We will outline some of the attributes for assessing data quality.

Reliability Test

Data reliability test, intra-observer and inter-observer reliability analyses have to be conducted repeatedly during a data collection process. The essential measurement to examine reliability is the kappa statistic, which measures the agreement between two unique observers and two (or more) ratings. It is scaled to be 0 when the amount of agreement is what would be expected when observed by chance, and 1 when there is perfect agreement. A value of 0.81 or higher is considered an almost perfect matched as shown in Table 12.1 (Landis & Koch, 1977).

Let assume that we want to sample individual packets from a particular network by randomly selecting one out of m packets within a time window and let X be a vector of k observed random variables, $X(x_1, x_2, \ldots x_k)$, in the sample. To be sure that the sampled packets are consistent and can be repeated, we can create two samples, S_1 and S_2, with the same sampling approach but with a different seeding number of randomness. Note that we now have two sets of variables (assume all variables are binary), $X_{s1}(x_{s11}, x_{s12}, \ldots x_{s1k})$ and $X_{s2}(x_{s21}, x_{s22}, \ldots x_{s2k})$, and the agreement of each pair (x_{s1i}, x_{s2i}) for the ith variable can be calculated using Equation (12-1):

$$\rho_e = (170/300 \times 110/300 + 190/300 \times 130/300) = 0.482 \qquad (12\text{-}1)$$

where ρ_0 is the observed proportion of agreement, and ρ_e is the expected proportion of agreement (or the chance agreement). Table 12.2 and Equations (12-2) and (12-3) illustrate the calculations for ρ_0 and ρ_e.

$$\rho_0 = \frac{a+d}{a+b+c+d} \qquad (12\text{-}2)$$

$$\rho_e = \frac{a+b}{a+b+c+d} \cdot \frac{a+c}{a+b+c+d} + \frac{b+d}{a+b+c+d} \cdot \frac{c+d}{a+b+c+d}. \qquad (12\text{-}3)$$

Table 12.1 Kappa statistic

Kappa-statistic	Agreement
Below 0.00	Poor
0.00 - 0.20	Slight
0.21 - 0.40	Fair
0.41 - 0.60	Moderate
0.61 - 0.80	Substantial
0.81 - 1.00	Almost perfect

Table 12.2 Agreement for a pair of variables

Sample one	Sample two		Total
	Present	Absent	
Present	a	b	$a+b$
Absent	c	d	$c+d$
Total	$a+c$	$b+d$	$a+b+c+d$

Table 12.3 Kappa-statistic for a pair of variables

Sample one	Sample two		Total
	Yes	No	
Yes	100	70	170
No	10	120	130
Total	110	190	300

We need to keep in mind that with rare events the percent agreement can be very high just due to chance.

Example 12.1→Kappa Statistic. Let two samples, S_1 and S_2, with a pair of variables (x_{s1i}, x_{s2i}) have the data shown in Table 12.3. The observed agreement, $P_o = (100 + 120) / 300 = 0.733$, the expected agreement, $P_e = (170 / 300 \times 110 / 300 + 190 / 300 \times 130 / 300)\ 0.482$, and the Kappa statistic,

$$\hat{k} = \frac{0.733 - 0.482}{1 - 0.482} = 0.485,$$

indicate a moderate agreement between the two variables.

The Stata codes used for this calculation are given in Display 12.1 following:

Display 12.1
Stata codes to calculate the Kappa-statistic

```
tabi 100 70 \10 120,col row replace

  Sample |       Sample two
     One |    Present     Absent|      Total
---------+----------------------+----------
 Present |       100         70 |        170
         |     58.82      41.18 |     100.00
         |     90.91      36.84 |      56.67
---------+----------------------+----------
  Absent |        10        120 |        130
         |      7.69      92.31 |     100.00
         |      9.09      63.16 |      43.33
---------+----------------------+----------
   Total |       110        190 |        300
         |     36.67      63.33 |     100.00
         |    100.00     100.00 |     100.00

kap row col [freq=pop]

               Expected
Agreement     Agreement      Kappa    Std. Err.         Z      Prob>Z
-------------------------------------------------------------------------
   73.33%        48.22%      0.4850      0.0533       9.11      0.0000
```

The results show that if we believe that the pair variables (x_{s1i}, x_{s2i}) from two samples are by chance to measure the same phenomenon, we would expect to have an agreement of 48.2%. In fact, the observed agreement is 73.3%, or 48.2% of the way between chance-agreement and perfect-agreement. The Z-score indicates that we can reject the hypothesis of these two variables that agree randomly. If we repeat the Kappa test n times for each pair (x_{s1i}, x_{s2i}) and if:

$$\min(\hat{k}_i, i = 1, 2, \ldots, k) \geq c,$$

where c is the desired threshold of agreement, we can be sure that our sampling approach and process are good and the collecting data are consistency and repeatability.

Reliability also impacts the profile. One aspect in measuring the quality of a profile is consistency—the probability of the profiling results being the same if the profiling analysis is repeated. More specifically, given a time period and a sampling method, we can acquire many different traffic samples from a network system. If a site is profiled to be in a class based on one of such possible samples, what is the probability that it will be classified in the same class based on a different sample acquired from the same network system within the same time period? This measurement of reliability is associated with two key variables: intra-site correlation and the number of observations within each site. Let n denote the number of observations within a site and ρ denote the intra-site correlation. The reliability, R can be calculated as

$$R = \frac{n\rho}{1 - \rho + n\rho}, \tag{12-4}$$

where ρ is the proportion of total variation in response variable due to site, and it is defined as

$$\rho = \frac{\sigma_b^2}{\sigma_b^2 + \sigma_w^2},$$

σ_b^2 is the between-site variance, and σ_w^2 is the within-site variance. These variance values can be estimated by using the hierarchical generalized linear modeling approach, which we discussed in Chapter VIII. Figure 12.1 shows the relationship between R, ρ, and n graphically. Sample size, n, plays an important role in the reliability of a profile. If we present Equation (12-4) using n

$$n = \frac{R}{\rho(1 - R)} - \frac{R}{1 - R}, \tag{12-5}$$

we can see that when $\rho \to 0$ we will have $n \to \infty$, and when $R \to 1$ we will also have $n \to \infty$ (Figure 12.1). Therefore, either high reliability or less between-site variance will require a large sample size for each site to be classified reliably.

Validity Check

The data validity test focuses on checking the range of values and identifying outliers and missing or incorrect values by examining the distribution, frequency, attribute and prop-

Figure 12.1 Relations between intra-site correlation, sample size, and reliability

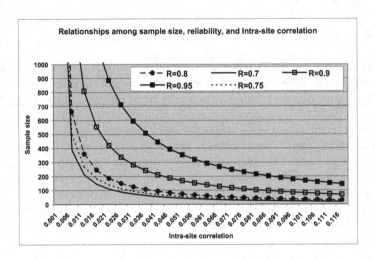

erty for each variable in a dataset. The goal of data validity testing is to identify variables with potential data validity issues. Although many approaches can be used to detect an outlier, the methods discussed on Chapters IV and V should be enough to conduct a quick data validity test. For example, we can either plot the data or run descriptive analysis on the variables of interest. The following example (Display 12.2) shows a distribution of the variable v57 (capital_run_length_total) in the spam-email data. Using the *sum* command in Stata, we can see that there are four largest values, 9090, 9163, 10062, and 15841 falling out of the pattern in which the 99th percentile is 3027.

Display 12.2
Data validity test through variable distribution examination

```
Sum v57,d
                                    v57
-----------------------------------------------------------------
       Percentiles       Smallest
  1%          3                1
  5%          6                1
 10%         10                1         Obs                   4601
 25%         35                1         Sum of Wgt.           4601
 50%         95                          Mean             283.2893
                            Largest      Std. Dev.        606.3479
 75%        266             9090
 90%        725             9163         Variance         367657.7
 95%       1223            10062         Skewness         8.707011
 99%       3027            15841         Kurtosis         148.6701
```

It is our responsibility to understand these data points and decide how these data points should be treated. They can be considered outliers because they are at least three times larger than the 99th percentile value. However, if the attribute of the variable does not have an upper limit then they may not be considered as outliners. There is no absolute correct or incorrect solution in terms of whether or not the data points are outliers, and the answer depends on many factors, including allowable data ranges, previous experiences, or network system-specific infrastructures. Our potential actions to these data points include, but are not limited to, replacing them by the value of the 99th percentile value, replacing them by the mean, setting them to be missing, or leaving them without action. There is no a gold-standard approach to follow-up, except if we are absolutely sure that these values are invalid.

Data cleaning is also an important step related to having a final reliable and valid set of data. We need to ask several fundamental questions about data quality, such as, do we have all of the data that we expected to have? Do the data elements make sense? Do the size and volume of the data make sense? Many data problems can be avoided or minimized with a properly designed data collection tool that will alert us when unusual values occur and will not record any impossible values. If the suspected data is found and we have access to the original source, then the data should be verified.

The association of missing values is also vital for data validity check. A variable with a large proportion of missing values may not be used in further analyses if the missing value is unexpected and is caused during the data collection process, or the actual values are removed because they are invalid. If the variable is binary, for example, present or absent, we can simply assign the missing value to be absent and create a dummy variable that has value 1 for indicating the missing and 0 otherwise. In the analysis we will have two variables, the original binary variable that is coded 1 for present and 0 for either missing or absent, and the dummy variable that is coded 1 for missing and 0 otherwise. We can adapt the same approach for continuous variables in that we can replace the missing value with the overall mean and use a dummy variable to denote the observations with missing values.

Data Quality

Assessing data quality is a fundamental task in any research area. One of the ultimate goals for conducting data reliability and validity analyses is to understand the data better and evaluate its quality. There are many known and unknown factors that contribute to the quality of data. In practice, it could be difficult to answer a simple question, such as, how good is the data? We may not be able to find a dataset to be really "good" or "high" in quality. As guidelines, here are some common attributes that can be used to measure the quality of data:

1. **Significance of data:** Data should be significant in addressing and answering the underlying research questions. This is the basic measurement in assessing data quality. If a dataset can only address 5% of the questions of interest, it could still potentially be useful, but may need additional data collection efforts.
2. **Source of data:** Data needs to be collected from dependable and reliable source(s).
3. **Sampling of data:** Given the natural characteristic of network traffic, data needs to be collected through a statistically sound sampling approach.
4. **Size of data:** Sample size needs to be determined to achieve the requirements of sensitivity and specificity and avoid either over sampling or under sampling the data.

5. **Cost of data:** Increasing the quality of data could increase the costs of collecting data. However, high costs do not always result in high quality data.

6. **Time of data:** Data for real time intrusion detection and protection has to be collected in real time and all parameters drawn from models should be updated frequently. The unit for updating can be hourly, daily, weekly or monthly depending on the attributes of the system.

7. **Complexity of data:** Complex data is more likely to decrease data quality. Data should not be designed to be complex beyond the capacity of a detection system or beyond the requirements of the system.

8. **Structure of data:** Quality data has a clear and detectable data structure and avoids unnecessary complications in data structure. Primary and foreign keys should be available for linking datasets acquired from different sources.

9. **Reliability and validity of data:** Data has to satisfy the requirements of reliability and validity tests. Assessing data reliability and validity provide a directional intervention during the data collecting process if any issues on reliability and validity assessments arise.

Figure 12.2 displays these attributes graphically. In general, these attributes help us make better judgments in evaluating and assessing a particular dataset. High quality data does not mean that we require the data to be error-free. Although we desire error-free data, given the fact that network traffic data is usually represented with large volumes, the reality is that we may not be able to confirm every piece of the data to be error-free. Accordingly, measuring errors in network traffic may be considered acceptable under certain circumstances, but we have to assess the associated risk and make sure that any error is not able to statistically significantly impact the classification and profiling results, and address these concerns with the appropriate statistical treatments.

Figure 12.2 Attributes associated with data quality

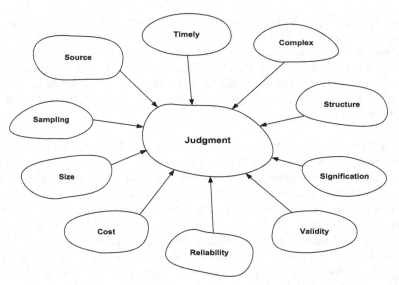

GOODNESS OF CLASSIFICATION

In general, we have two basic questions of classification: (1) how accurate is the classification, and (2) how good is it? To answer the first question, we need to measure the sensitivity, specificity, positive predictive value (PPV), negative predictive value (NPV), and misclassification rate. And to answer the second question, we evaluate the classification results using the receiver operating characteristic (ROC) area, or the area under ROC curve.

Sensitivity measures the probability that a statistical test is positive for a true positive statistic, and specificity measures the probability that a statistical test is negative for a true negative statistic. In intrusion detection, a model with a sensitivity value of 0.95 means that 95% of the abnormal events have been correctly recognized as anomalous, and a specificity value of 0.95 means that 95% of the anomaly-free events have not been classified as anomalous. The relationship between the values of sensitivity and specificity tends to be nonlinear and inversely proportional (i.e., increasing one value will systematically decrease the other). The PPV is the ratio of true positives to all classified positive results, and measures how likely a positive result will indeed be true. The NPV is defined as the ratio of true negatives to all classified negative results, and measures how likely a negative result will be true. The misclassification rate measures the proportion of events that are anomaly-free but are incorrectly identified as anomalous, and the proportion of events

Table 12.4 Classification crosswalk results between the true and predicted

Classification	$Y = 1$	$Y = 0$
$\hat{Y} = 1$	a(true positive)	b(false positive)
$\hat{Y} = 0$	c(false negative)	d (true negative)

Figure 12.3 Relationship of sensitivity and specificity

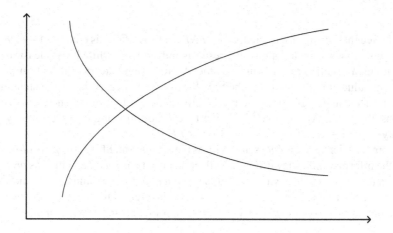

that are anomalous but are incorrectly classified as anomaly-free. It is 0 when all of the observed anomaly-free and abnormal events are correctly classified, and 1 when there is 100% misclassification. The area under the ROC curve measures the discriminating power of a model fitted by the predicted probability. It ranges from 0.5 to 1.0. A model with no predictive power has a value of 0.5, and a perfect model has a value of 1.0.

Sensitivity and Specificity

Sensitivity and specificity refer to the accuracy for binary classification data. The related measures include false positive fraction (FPF) and false negative fraction (FNF) inaddition to PPV and NPV. Let Y denote the true status of a stream of network traffic where 1 indicates anomalous and 0 indicates anomaly-free traffics. Also let $\hat{Y}$ denote a classification result that has value 1 for positive and 0 for negative for anomalous traffic based on a classification algorithm. We can illustrate the results of $Y \sim \hat{Y}$ in a 2×2 table (Table 12.4).

Sensitivity and specificity can be calculated as:

$$Sensitivity = \frac{a}{a+c}, \text{ and} \tag{12-6}$$

$$Specificity = \frac{d}{b+d}, \tag{12-7}$$

respectively. FNF, FPF, PPV, and NPV are definted as follows:

$$FNF = \frac{c}{a+c} \tag{12-8}$$

$$FPF = \frac{b}{b+d} \cdot \tag{12-9}$$

$$PPV = \frac{a}{a+b}, \text{ and} \tag{12-10}$$

$$NPV = \frac{d}{c+d}. \tag{12-11}$$

We can see that sensitivity is equal to $1 - FNF$, and specificity is equal to $1 - FPF$. PPV measures how likely it is that a positive result is indeed true, while NPV measures how likely is it that a negative result is indeed true. An intrusion detection algorithm that has a sensitivity value of 0.80 and a specificity value of 0.85 indicates that the system misses 20% of true abnormal traffic data and incorrectly identifies 15% of the anomaly-free traffic data as abnormal. An ideal classification meets the following criteria: sensitivity=1, specificity=1, $PPV = 1$, $NPV = 1$, $FNF = 0$, and $FPF = 0$.

In computer science, we reflect sensitivity as the *hit rate* and FPF as the *false alarm rate*. Also, in the information retrieval area we reflect sensitivity as *recall* and PPV as *precision*. In statistical science, sensitivity is referred to *statistical power* (β), and FNF is known as a Type II error (β). FPF is known as Type I error and is referred to as the *significance level* (α); therefore, specificity is equal to $1 - \alpha$. Although the ultimate goal of a classification task is to reach both a sensitivity value of 1.0 and a specificity value of 1.0, the realistic relationship between values of sensitivity and specificity tend to be nonlinear and inversely proportional, as shown in Figure 12.3 (Jizba, 2000; Zhang, & Lu, 2002).

Between sensitivity and specificity, which is more important? The answer depends on the goal of classification, the available resources, and the importance of the system(s) to be protected. If the system requires to be protected at all costs, then sensitivity should take the highest priority regardless of any limitations on resources. Increasing specificity should be considered when there is a need to increase the efficiency. Although we may theoretically have both the PPV and the NPV to reach 1.0 if $b = 0$ and $c = 0$, we may never be able to achieve this point since the true anomaly-free rate usually cannot be pre-determined.

Example 12.2→Measure Performance of Classification based on Logistic Model. Let us fit a logistic model with attack (1/0) as the response variable Y, and use the 16 predictor variables discussed in Chapter VII with the 1999 KDD-cup training data, and then use this model to predict the $\hat{Y}$ value for the testing data. The binary classification is conducted with a therohld of $\hat{Y} > 0.5$ (yes/no). Stata codes used to fit the model and to predict the $\hat{Y}$, are shown in Display 12.3 below in addition to the correspinnding results.

Display 12.3
Classification based on logistic regression model with a therohld of $\hat{Y} > 0.5$

```
Use var-16-all,replace
tab training

   training |      Freq.    Percent       Cum.
------------+-----------------------------------
        0 |    311,029      38.63      38.63
        1 |    494,021      61.37     100.00
------------+-----------------------------------
     Total |    805,050     100.00

logistic attack logged i is guest RST TCP UDP HTTP Duration Num comp Count Same srv
Diff_srv Dst_host Dst_hos1 Dst_hos3 Dst_hos4 Dst_hos5 if training==1;

Logistic regression                              Number of obs   =      494021
                                                 LR chi2(16)     =   453454.54
                                                 Prob  chi2      =      0.0000
Log likelihood = -18351.483                      Pseudo R2       =      0.9251
----------------------------------------------------------------------------------
     attack | Odds Ratio   Std. Err.      z     P|z|    [95% Conf. Interval]
------------+---------------------------------------------------------------------
   logged_i |  .7052227    .0337212    -7.30   0.000    .6421328    .7745111
   is_guest |  8.65386     .7765311    24.05   0.000    7.25821    10.31787
        RST |  108.6071   16.14184     31.54   0.000    81.16108   145.3346
        TCP |  .6884878    .0463639    -5.54   0.000    .6033579    .785629
        UDP |  .0777619    .0055668   -35.68   0.000    .0675821    .0894751
       HTTP |  1.630797    .0855891     9.32   0.000    1.471385    1.80748
   Duration |  .8950696    .0056617   -17.53   0.000    .8840414    .9062354
   Num comp |  1.029267    .0079397     3.74   0.000    1.013823    1.044947
      Count |  87.48874   7.656162     51.10   0.000    73.69929   103.8583
   Same_srv |  .1252268    .0054335   -47.88   0.000    .1150177    .1363422
   Diff_srv |  .7263038    .0072585   -32.00   0.000    .7122158    .7406705
   Dst_host |  2.167089    .0336008    49.88   0.000    2.102223    2.233956
   Dst_hos1 |  .2885484    .0076743   -46.73   0.000    .2738923    .3039886
   Dst_hos3 |  .7497863    .0085298   -25.31   0.000    .7332531    .7666921
   Dst_hos4 |  3.362365    .0966901    42.17   0.000    3.178098    3.557316
   Dst_hos5 |  1.364228    .0096948    43.71   0.000    1.345359    1.383363
----------------------------------------------------------------------------------
```

continued on following page

Display 12.3 continued

```
Note: 0 failures and 1 success completely determined.

predict prob if training==0;
(option p assumed; Pr(attack))
(494021 missing values generated)

gen byte Yhat=(prob0.5);
tab Yhat attack if training==0;

              |       attack
     Yhat |         0          1 |     Total
-----------+----------------------+----------
        0 |    57,802     21,706 |    79,508
        1 |     2,791    228,730 |   231,521
-----------+----------------------+----------
    Total |    60,593    250,436 |   311,029
```

Table 12.5 displays the classification results in a format similar to the Table 12.4 and Table 12.6 shows the classification results of which both sensitivity and specificity seem reasonable.

Example 12.3→Evaluation of Risk Score. In the study of the risk score model conducted by Wang and Cannady (2005) discussed in Chapter VIII, they also compared the performance of classification results between the training and the testing samples, and found that no remarkable difference in key classification measurements between the training and testing samples. The testing sample-based score showed comparable ROC (0.96 vs. 1.00), specificity (0.94 vs. 0.99), slightly low sensitivity (0.90 vs. 0.98), and a high but acceptable misclassification rate (0.08 vs. 0.02) with the training sample, respectively (Table 12.7). We will discuss the ROC in this next section and the misclassification in the next section.

Example 12.4→Measure Performance of Classification based on Multinomial Logistic Model. Let us examine the goodness of classification from the multinomial logistic regres-

Table 12.5 Classification crosswalk results based on testing data

Classification	$Y = 1$	$Y = 0$
$\hat{Y} = 1$	a=228730	b=2791
$\hat{Y} = 0$	c=21706	d=57802

Table 12.6 Measures drived from the testing data

Measure	Value	Source
Sensitivity	0.9133	228730 / 250436
Specificity	0.9539	57802 / 60593
PPV	0.9879	228730 / 231521
NPV	0.727	57802 / 79508

sion discussed in Example 9.1 of Chapter IX by comparing the classification results between the multinomial logistic model and the KDD-cup 1999 winning entry (Elkan, 2000) using the testing sample. Table 12.8 shows the comparison results where each observation is classified into one of five response categories based on the highest probability of being a typical attack and the corresponding threshold determined from the training sample. The multinomial model-based classification yielded a slightly lower ROC area than the KDD-cup 1999 winning results that were based on a decision tree algorithm. Overall, the sensitivities of the multinomial logistic model-based classification results were comparable with the KDD-cup 1999 winning results, and the specificities were slightly lower than the winning results in *anomaly-free, probe,* and *DoS.* For *U2R* and *R2L,* the model-based results showed higher sensitivities than the winning results (25.9% vs. 13.2%, and 11.2% vs. 8.4%), with similar specificity values. Although the winning results achieved a low misclassification rate of 0.5% in *anomaly-free,* the model had a lower average misclassification rate than the winning results (18.9% vs. 35.7%). It significantly reduced the misclassification rates in *probe* and *U2R* (2.2% and 0.4%, respectively), where 12.3% of *probe* attacks and 73.7% of *U2R* attacks had been misclassified as *anomaly-free* by the KDD-cup winning results.

Receiver Operating Characteristic Curve

The ROC curve method was initially used in the signal detection theory during the World War II for analysizing radar signals, and is now widely used in computer science, menching learning, biomedical science, and healthcare research areas (Bamber, 1975; Hanley & McNeil, 1982; DeLong, DeLong & Clarke-Pearson, 1988). Using a threshed *T*, we define a binary test from the predicted probability $\hat{p}$ as

$$\hat{Y} = \begin{cases} 1 & \hat{p} \geq T \\ 0 & \hat{p} < T \end{cases}.$$

An ROC curve plots the sensitivity (1-FNF) at the y-axis and the 1-specificity (FPF) at the x-axis for binary classification data. Each point on the ROC plot represents a sensitivity

Table 12.7. Classification results

Measure of Classification	Score	
	Training	Testing
ROC	0.9956	0.9554
Sensitivity	0.9791	0.9010
Specificity	0.9903	0.9434
Misclassification rate	0.0174	0.0802

Table 12.8. Comparisons of classification results with the KDD-cup 1999 winning entry

Measure	Attack Types									
	Multinomial logistic regression model					KDD-cup 1999 winning entry				
	Anomaly-free	Probe	DoS	U2R	R2L	Anomaly-free	Probe	DoS	U2R	R2L
ROC	0.967	0.935	0.978	0.665	0.859	0.996	0.917	0.986	0.566	0.542
Sensitivity (%)	98.3	85.6	97.2	25.9	11.2	99.5	83.3	97.1	13.2	8.4
Specificity (%)	86.5	75.9	93.7	99.2	98.5	91.9	99.4	99.7	99.9	99.9
Misclassification (%)	2.6	2.2	2.3	0.4	87.1	0.5	12.3	2.3	73.7	89.7

Figure 12.4 ROC curve

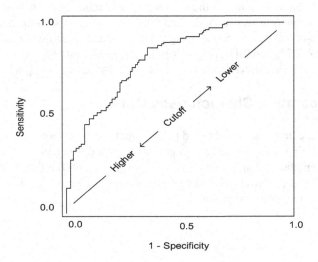

and 1-specificity pair corresponding to the threshold, T, that varies at each point, with 1 at the starting point of the curve to 0 at the end of the curve (Figure 12.4). The area under the ROC curve measures the discriminating power of classification probabilities fitted by the predicted probability, which ranges from 0.5 to 1.0. The greater the discriminating power, the more bowed the curve will be. A random classification with no discriminating power has a value of 0.5 (the ROC curve will coincide with the diagonal), and a perfect classification has a value of 1.0. An ideal classification has both false positives and false negatives as zero. That is, $c = 0$ and $b = 0$, as seen in Table 12.4.

ROC analysis is a useful tool for seeking possibly optimal models. The area under ROC curve can be calculated by the ROC using the trapezoidal rule on the ROC to find an approximate value for a definite integral. In SAS the *PROC LOGISTIC* procedure automatically calculates the value for us, known as c-statistic. In Stata we can use the *lroc* command after the model is fitted to get an ROC value of the fitted model. Stata also has a *roctab* command that reports the area of ROC, its standard error, and its confidence interval for given results on classification.

Figure 12.5 ROC curve for the 16-variable model based on KDD-cup training data

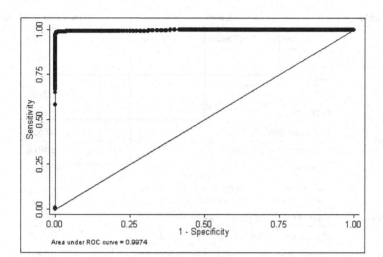

Example 12.5→ROC Curve. Let us use the data and the model from the previous section, the 16-variable model with a training dataset yielded an area under ROC curve of 0.9974 under ROC curve (Figure 12.5). Table 12.9 shows the area under the ROC curves generated by each of the 16 variables individually. We can see that three variables, *count, HTTP* and *logged_i,* have the area under ROC curve greater than 0.80, and these three variables together yeiedied an area under ROC curve of 0.9925.

Because the ROC curve is the function of a cutoff point that assigns data to the binary group, it is worth directly plotting sensitivity and specificity versus the cutoff point to seek the best threshold for classification. Use the spam-email data with the variable *v58* (spam=1, non-spam=0) as a response variable and *v1 to v57* as predictor variables, Figure 12.6 illustrates the changes in sensitivity and specificity while the probability threshold value varies. It suggests that a threshold of 0.37 provides a balance in both sensitivity and specificity.

Misclassification

Misclassification measures the probability of disagreement between the true and predicted binary statues by dividing the number or paired observations in the disagreement cells by the total number of paired observations. For the convenience of discussion, let us repeat Table 12.4 below, and define the misclassification rate as

$$m = \frac{c+b}{a+b+c+d},$$
(12-12)

Table 12.9 Area under ROC curve for individual variable

Variable	Label	Area under ROC curve
Duration	Length (number of seconds) of the connection	0.5593
TCP	TCP	0.7521
UDP	UDP	0.5971
HTTP	HTTP	0.8151
RST	RST	0.5013
logged_i	Login successfully	0.8553
Num_comp	Number of compromised	0.4976
is_guest	Guest login	0.5015
Count	Connections to the same host as the current connection in the past two seconds	0.9879
Same_srv	Rate of connections to the same service	0.6270
Diff_srv	Rate of connections to different services	0.6196
Dst_host	Connections having the same destination host	0.7891
Dst_hos1	Connections having the same destination host and using the same service	0.4677
Dst_hos3	Rate of different services on the current host	0.5190
Dst_hos4	Connections having the same destination host and using the same service	0.7482
Dst_hos5	Rate of connections to the same service coming from different hosts	0.7528

Figure 12.6 Changes in sensitivity and specificity by probability threshold value

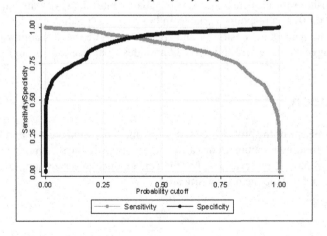

where a, b, c and d. are defined in Table 12.4 and recall below.

	$Y = 1$	$Y = 0$
$\hat{Y} = 1$	a(true positive)	b(false positive)
$\hat{Y} = 0$	c(false negative)	d (true negative)

Similarly, the correct classification rate can be calculated as

$$c = \frac{a+d}{a+b+c+d}.$$ (12-13)

Because the predictive values (PPV and NPV) depend not only on the performance of the classification algorithm but also on the prevalence of true positive events, sensitivity and specificity, they are considered more relevant to the classification task and should be reported to describe the accuracy (Pepe, 2003). Thus, using Equations (12-6) and (12-7), we can write the probability of misclassification as the function of sensitivity, specificity and overall prevalence of the true positive events:

$$\Pr(\hat{Y} \neq Y) = \rho(1 - sensitivity) + (1 - \rho)(1 - specificity)$$ (12-14)

$$\rho = \frac{a+c}{a+b+c+d},$$

where ρ is the population prevalence of the true positive response. Equation (12-14) is useful when we only know sensitivity, specificity and the rate of the true positive events.

Example 12.6→Misclassification. We can calculate the probability of misclassification for data shown in Table 12.5 using $\rho = 0.8052$:

$$P(\hat{Y} \neq Y) = 0.8052(1 - 0.9133) + (1 - 0.8052)(1 - 0.9539) = 0.0772.$$

Example 12.7→Evaluation of a New Algorithm for Scoring Spam-email. Suppose that we want to evaluate the performance of scoring for a new algorithm, and suppose that we have a baseline for scoring results, which could be derived from a well-developed algorithm or from a manual reviewing method. We use this baseline as a "gold-standard" for the evaluation. The score is a continuous variable that is defined as the probability of receiving at least one spam-email per hour. Using this score we can create two binary classification variables, Class I denotes 5 or more spam-emails per hour, and Class II denotes 15 or more spam-emails per hour. Our aim is to compare the results based on the new algorithm with the "gold-standard" results and answer the question regarding whether the new algorithm

Table 12.10 First 25 observations on a study of spam-email derived from the new algorithm and the "gold-standard"

Observation	New Algorithm			"Gold-standard"		
	Score	Class I	Class II	Score	Class I	Class II
1	0.005	0	0	0.025	0	0
2	0.458	1	1	0.460	1	1
3	0.336	1	1	0.247	1	1
4	0.104	1	0	0.212	1	1
5	0.004	0	0	0.003	0	0
6	0.000	0	0	0.001	0	0
7	0.706	0	0	0.065	1	0
8	0.652	1	1	0.596	1	1
9	0.000	0	0	0.000	0	0
10	0.009	0	0	0.002	0	0
11	0.317	1	1	0.315	1	1
12	0.059	1	0	0.064	1	0
13	0.090	1	0	0.072	1	0
14	0.003	0	0	0.014	0	0
15	0.005	0	0	0.007	0	0
16	0.005	0	0	0.078	1	0
17	0.001	0	0	0.006	0	0
18	0.029	0	0	0.095	1	0
19	0.055	1	0	0.293	1	1
20	0.145	1	0	0.142	1	0
21	0.402	1	1	0.411	1	1
22	0.023	0	0	0.018	0	0
23	0.258	1	1	0.276	1	1
24	0.000	0	0	0.000	0	0
25	0.064	1	0	0.063	1	0

scoring is satisfactory compared to the "gold standard" scoring. Table 12.10 illustrates the first 25 of the total 96 observations in the data, which includes both scores and classification groups derived from the new algorithm and the "gold-standard."

We can use several approaches to evaluate the performance of the new algorithm when comparing with the "gold-standard," for example: (1) assessing the correlation coefficient, (2) calculating the Kappa statistic, (3) calculating ROC curve, and (4) computing sensitivity, specificity and the misclassification rate. The Stata program to accomplish the above evaluation approaches is showed in Display 12.4, and the corresponding output is given in Display 12.5.

Display 12.4
Stata program to compare the performance of the new algorithm and the "gold-standard"

```
#delimit;
use F:\book\Chapter 12\"example 12-7",replace;
/*------------------------------------------------------------
   1. Compare correlation coefficients
-----------------------------------------------------------*/;
corr score_new score_baseline;
/*------------------------------------------------------------
   2.  Calculate Kappa statistics
-----------------------------------------------------------*/;
 kap class_5_new class_5_baseline;
 kap class__15_new class_15_baseline;
/*------------------------------------------------------------
 3.  Calculate ROC area
-----------------------------------------------------------*/;
 roctab class_5_new class_5_baseline,table graph summary;
 roctab class__15_new class_15_baseline,table graph summary;
/*------------------------------------------------------------
 4.  Calculate sensitivity, specificity and misclassification
-----------------------------------------------------------*/;
 tab class_5_new class_5_baseline,col row;
 tab class__15_new class_15_baseline,col row;
```

Display 12.5

```
Results of evaluation of the new algorithm of scoring spam-email
/*------------------------------------------------------------
   1. Compare correlation coefficients
-----------------------------------------------------------*/;
. corr score_new score_baseline;
(obs=96)

               | score_new score_baseline
---------------+------------------
    score_new |   1.0000
score_baseline |   0.8973    1.0000

/*------------------------------------------------------------
   2.  Calculate Kappa statistics
-----------------------------------------------------------*/;
.  kap class_5_new class_5_baseline;
```

continued on following page

Display 12.5 continued

```
                Expected
Agreement      Agreement    Kappa   Std. Err.          Z    Prob>Z
-------------------------------------------------------------------
   82.29%        49.35%     0.6504    0.0983         6.61    0.0000

. kap class__15_new class_15_baseline;

                Expected
Agreement      Agreement    Kappa   Std. Err.          Z    Prob>Z
-------------------------------------------------------------------
   92.71%        70.18%     0.7555    0.1020         7.41    0.0000

/*----------------------------------------------------------------
   3.  Calculate ROC area
   ------------------------------------------------------------*/;
. roctab class_5_new class_5_baseline,table graph summary;

class_5_new|   class_5_baseline
           |         0         1 |     Total
-----------+----------------------+----------
         0 |        43        15 |        58
         1 |         2        36 |        38
-----------+----------------------+----------
     Total |        45        51 |        96


                      ROC                   -Asymptotic Normal--
            Obs       Area    Std. Err.     [95% Conf. Interval]
          -----------------------------------------------------
             96     0.8444       0.0343      0.77711    0.91164

. roctab class_15_new class_15_baseline,table graph summary;

class_15_new |   class_15_baseline
             |         0         1 |     Total
-------------+----------------------+----------
           0 |        75         4 |        79
           1 |         3        14 |        17
-------------+----------------------+----------
       Total |        78        18 |        96


                      ROC                   -Asymptotic Normal--
            Obs       Area    Std. Err.     [95% Conf. Interval]
          -----------------------------------------------------
             96     0.8864       0.0492      0.78993    0.98296

/*----------------------------------------------------------------
```

continued on following page

Display 12.5 continued

```
4.  Calculate sensitivity and specificity
---------------------------------------------------------------*/;
.  tab class_5_new class_5_baseline,col row;


class_5_new|   class_5_baseline
           |         0          1 |     Total
-----------+----------------------+----------
        0 |        43         15 |        58
           |     74.14      25.86 |    100.00
           |     95.56      29.41 |     60.42
-----------+----------------------+----------
        1 |         2         36 |        38
           |      5.26      94.74 |    100.00
           |      4.44      70.59 |     39.58
-----------+----------------------+----------
    Total |        45         51 |        96
           |     46.88      53.13 |    100.00
           |    100.00     100.00 |    100.00


.  tab class_15_new class_15_baseline,col row;


class_15_new |   class_15_baseline
             |         0          1 |     Total
-------------+----------------------+----------
          0 |        75          4 |        79
             |     94.94       5.06 |    100.00
             |     96.15      22.22 |     82.29
-------------+----------------------+----------
          1 |         3         14 |        17
             |     17.65      82.35 |    100.00
             |      3.85      77.78 |     17.71
-------------+----------------------+----------
      Total |        78         18 |        96
             |     81.25      18.75 |    100.00
             |    100.00     100.00 |    100.00
```

Display 12.5 shows that when compared with the "gold-standard," the new scoring algorithm yielded ROCs of 0.84 (95% CI 0.78-0.91) and 0.89 (95% CI 0.79-0.98), sensitivity values of 0.71 (36/51) and 0.78 (14/18), specificity values of 0.96 (43/45) and 0.96 (75/78) for Class II, and I respectively. Using Equation (12-12), the misclassification rates are 0.178 and 0.073 for Classes I and II, respectively.

ASSESS MODEL PERFORMANCE

We can assess model performance through three fundamental aspects: (1), goodness-of-fit, (2) predictive power, and (3) residual analysis. These measures may not align together. A well-fitted model may have low predictive power, and a good predictable model may show a poor fit as judged by any of goodness-of-fit statistics. We will discuss each of these aspects in the following sections. Because the scope of work on evaluating model performance involves a grate amount of topics, we will mainly restrict our discussion to the logistic regression model. Readers who are interested in gaining more detailed information on models other than the logistic model should refer to O'Connel (2006).

Goodness-of-Fit

Let Y be the vector for observed sample values of a response variable, $Y = (y_1, y_2, \ldots, y_n)$, and let $\hat{Y}$ be the vector for the predicted values of the response variable, $\hat{Y} = (\hat{y}_1, \hat{y}_2, \ldots, \hat{y}_n)$. Hosmer and Lemeshow (2000) suggest that if the summary measure of the distance between Y and $\hat{Y}$ are small, and the contribution of each pair, $(y_i, \hat{y}_i)$, to these summary measures is not systematic and is small relative to the error structure of the model, then the model is said to have been fitted. In general, the assessment on goodness-of-fit involves three tasks, (1) computation and evaluation of the overall measure of fit, (2) examination of the individual components of the summary statistics, and (3) examination of other measures of the difference between the components of Y and $\hat{Y}$. In logistic regression, the summary measures that are directly based on the distance between the observed and fitted values include Person χ^2 test, the deviance residual test, and the Hosmer-Lemeshow test.

Let N be the total number of observations, k be the total number of predictor variables, J be the total number of covariate patterns that are the combination of k variables among the N observations in a dataset, where $J \leq N$, and let m_j, $j = 1, 2, \ldots, J$, be the total number of observations having covariate pattern j, where $\sum m_j = N$, and y_j and p_j are the total number of positive responses of the response variable and the predicted probability of a positive response with the jth covariate pattern, j, respectively. The Pearson χ^2 goodness-of-fit statistic is

$$\chi^2 = \sum_j^J \frac{(y_j - m_j p_j)^2}{m_j p_j (1 - p_j)} \tag{12-15}$$

with approximately $J - k$ degrees of freedom for the estimation dataset. Equation (12-15) suggests that if the number of covariate patterns is small, the Pearson χ^2 goodness-of-fit statistic will also be small, so the model is more likely to be fitted. The concept of covariate patterns is important in logistic regression. The latent class modeling approach examined in Chapter X assigns the membership of the latent class based on covariate patterns. Because two observations that have identical predictor variables are in the same pattern, we can use covariate patterns to represent key statistical information in a sample. Such information includes, for example, the number of covariate patterns, the number of observation with each of the patterns, and the number of positive responses with each of the patterns.

The deviance residual is defined as follows:

$$d_j = \pm \sqrt{2 \left[y_j \ln\left(\frac{y_j}{m_j p_j} \right) + (m_j - y_j) \ln\left(\frac{m_j - y_j}{m_j (1 - p_j)} \right) \right]} \tag{12-16}$$

and the summary statistic based on the deviance residual is the deviance of d_j

$$D = \sum_{j=1}^J d_j^2. \tag{12-17}$$

We can obtain the Pearson χ^2 of goodness-of-fit and deviance statistics from SAS *PROC LOGISTIC* where which we can specify the *AGGREGATE* and *SCALE=PEARSON* as showing in Displays 12.6 and 12.7.

Display 12.6
SAS codes to obtain Pearson χ^2 of goodness-of-fit and deviance statistics

```
libname KDD 'F:\book\Chapter 12\';
proc logistic data=KDD.var_16_trin descending;
model attack= Duration TCP UDP HTTP RST logged_I Num_comp is_guest Count
Same_srv Diff_srv Dst_host Dst_hos1 Dst_hos3 Dst_hos4 Dst_hos5/aggregate
scale=Pearson lackfit RSQ;
run;
```

Display 12.7
Pearson χ^2 of goodness-of-fit and deviance residual statistics from SAS

	Deviance and Pearson Goodness-of-Fit Statistics			
Criterion	Value	DF	Value/DF	Pr > ChiSq
Deviance	36383.5474	91E3	0.3983	1.0000
Pearson	3000759.40	91E3	32.8465	<.0001

Association of Predicted Probabilities and Observed Responses			
Percent Concordant	99.7	Somers' D	0.995
Percent Discordant	0.3	Gamma	0.995
Percent Tied	0.0	Tau-a	0.315
Pairs	38594365554	c	0.997

We must acknowledge that the model does not fit well because the Pearson χ^2 statistic is highly significant ($p < 0.0001$). This is likely due to particular attributes of the network data as well as the large size of the data. In practice, a model with many variables and a large sample tends to less likely to be fitted. The lack of fitting also could be due to over-dispersion that typically occurs when the observations are correlated or are collected from clusters or groups. As we discussed in Chapter VIII, data clustering or grouping introduce heterogeneity. When over-dispersion occurred, the standard errors of parameter estimates are likely to be too small, causing Wald tests to be large and leading to biased inferences. To address the potential over-dispersion issue, we can use the *SCALE =* options in SAS *PROC LOGISTIC*, which provides three options that can be used to accommodate over-dispersion: *SCALE = WILLIAMS, SCALE = DEVIANCE,* and *SCALE = PEARSON*. The Williams option requires the response variable to be in success/trial format (binomial distribution), and both *DEVIANCE* and *PEARSON* can be used for binary response vari-able. *SCALE = DEVIANCE,* and *SCALE = PEARSON* multiply the covariance matrix by the corresponding dispersion parameter reported under Value/DF in SAS output showed in Display 12.7. We can identify possible areas of over-dispersion by simply checking the dispersion parameter of the deviance. If the value is not greater than 1, then we can ignore the evidence of over-dispersion. Because the above SAS output shows that the deviance has a value of *Value/DF* of 0.3983, we know that the model seems good for over-dispersion, Moreover, we also know the model has a good discrimination with an area of 0.997 under the ROC curve.

The Hosmer-Lemeshow test divides the predicted probabilities into g groups based on percentile ranks (e.g., $g = 10$ to correspond deciles) and then computes a Pearson χ^2 from the $2 \times g$ table of observed and predicted frequencies. Let $\hat{C}$ be the Hosmer-Lemeshow goodness-of-fit statistic, n_k be the total number of observations in the kth, $k = 1, 2, ..., g$ group, c_k be the number of covariate patterns in the kth group, o_k be the total number of positive responses among the c_k covariate patterns, and $\bar{p}_k$ be the mean predicted portability of positive responses of the response variable. The Hosmer-Lemeshow goodness-of-fit statistic is

$$\hat{C} = \sum_{k=1}^{g} \frac{\left(\sum_{j=1}^{c_k} y_j - n_k \sum_{j=1}^{c_k} m_j p_j\right)^2}{n_k \sum_{j=1}^{c_k} m_j p_j \left(1 - \sum_{j=1}^{c_k} m_j p_j\right)}. \tag{12-18}$$

We can use the *LACKFIT* option in the SAS *PROC LOGISTIC* MODEL statement to obtain the Hosmer-Lemeshow goodness-of-fit statistic (Display 12.6). For Stata we can use the *left, group(10)* after the model is constructed. The following SAS output shows the Hosmer-Lemeshow goodness-of-fit statistic for the 16-variable model obtained from SAS based on the KDD-cup training data. Note that the Hosmer-Lemeshow goodness-of-fit statistic is also statistically significant in which it indicates that the model does not fit well (Display 12.8).

Display 12.8
SAS output of Hosmer-Lemeshow goodness-of-fit statistic

```
            Partition for the Hosmer and Lemeshow Test
    Group      Total    Observed     Expected    Observed    Expected

       1       49402         140       388.01       49262    49013.99
       2       49402        3885      3575.56       45517    45826.44
       3       49402       46914     46984.74        2488     2417.26
       4       49525       49516     49515.45           9        9.55
       5       38597       38597     38594.97           0        2.03
       6       27233       27233     27232.04           0        0.96
       7      230460      230458     230452.1           2        7.88

         Hosmer and Lemeshow Goodness-of-Fit Test

            Chi-Square        DF     Pr > ChiSq
             198.2361          5        <.0001


                 Model Fit Statistics

                                          Intercept
                             Intercept          and
            Criterion             Only    Covariates

            AIC             14924.662       1151.408
            SC              14935.773       1340.284
            -2 Log L        14922.662       1117.408


       R-Square    0.0276    Max-rescaled R-Square    0.9262
```

In addition to Person χ^2 test, deviance residual test, and the Hosmer-Lemeshow test, the Akaike information criterion (AIC) is also a goodness-of-fit measure that can be used to compare one model to another. A model with a lower value in the AIC indicates a more desirable model (*Akaike, 1974*). In Display 12.8 the AIC value for the intercept is only 14925 and is further reduced to 1151. An absolute reduction of 13774 is obtained after including 16 predictor variables to the model.

Predictive Ability

The predicative ability focuses on a model's classification discrimination. It is measured by a set of statistics, mainly including the area under the ROC curve, coefficient of determination, calibration, and the range of the predicted probability between the lowest predicted decile to the highest predicted decile. We have discussed the ROC curve previously, and now we will discuss the other three measures.

We refer the coefficient of determination as R^2 (R-squared). In OLS regression models, R^2 is defined as the ratio of the sum of squares explained by a regression model and the total sum of squares around the mean. It is referred to as the proportion of variance explained by the model. However, we have to keep in mind that in logistic regression there is no true R^2 value as there is in OLS regression. Let $L(0)$ denote the likelihood of a null logistic model that includes only the intercept, and let $L(\beta)$ be the likelihood of a logistic model with the intercept and other predictor variables, Cox and Snell (1989) proposed a R^2 for logistic regression:

$$R^2 = 1 - \left[\frac{L(0)}{L(\beta)}\right]^{\frac{2}{n}} \tag{12-19}$$

where n is the sample size. Since Equation (12-19) only can achieve a maximum of less than 1 for logistic models, Nagelkerke (1991) provides an adjusted R^2 that can reach the maximum value of 1:

$$R_{adj}^2 = \frac{R^2}{1 - [L(0)]^{\frac{2}{n}}}. \tag{12-20}$$

We can obtain both R^2 and R_{adj}^2 by including the *RSQ* option in the SAS *PORC LOGISTIC* model statement as the codes shown in Display 12.6. The corresponding results are given in the bottom of Display 12.8, and the R^2 and R_{adj}^2 are 0.0276 and 0.9262, respectively.

Calibration reverses the process to regression. It evaluates the degree of correspondence between the predicted probabilities of the positive responses produced by a model and the actual positive responses observed. The predictive range assesses the distribution of predicted probability. A common approach is to divide the predicted values in decile group and then compare the observed and predicted values within each decile, as well as compare observed values that fall between the lowest and highest decile. SAS codes to accomplish this table are given in Display 12.9.

Display 12.9
SAS codes to create predictive range by deciles

```
/*-----------------------------------------------------------------
   Fit the logistic model with the KDD-cup training data and output the
predicted probability of being anomalous for each observation
-----------------------------------------------------------------*/
proc logistic data=training descending;
model attack=Duration TCP UDP HTTP RST logged_I Num_comp is_guest Count
Same_srv Diff_srv Dst_host Dst_hos1 Dst_hos3 Dst_hos4 Dst_hos5/rsq lackfit
scale=none aggregate;
output out=phat(keep= attack  xb  phat  pr) p=phat xbeta=xb reschi=pr;
run;
/*-----------------------------------------------------------------
   Ranking the predicted probability of being anomalous to decile
   group and compare the means for observed and predicted by each group
-----------------------------------------------------------------*/
proc rank data=phat out=phat (keep=attack phat group) group=10;
   var phat;
   ranks group;
run;
proc means data=phat mean;
   class group;
   var attack phat;
run;
```

Table 12.11 Predictive range by deciles

Decile group	Total (#)	Observed (Y)	Predicted ($\hat{Y}$)
Lowest	80505	0.12086	0.01403
2nd	80505	0.17375	0.08230
3rd	80504	0.75256	0.79219
4th	80505	0.99407	0.99946
5th	93594	0.99821	0.99994
6th	563	1.00000	0.99997
7th	226997	1.00000	0.99997
8th	864	1.00000	0.99997
9th	48387	0.99988	0.99999
Highest	112623	0.99993	0.99999

Table 12.11 shows the predictive range from the 16-variable model with the KDD-cup training data. As we can see the model has a good predictive ability that ranges from 12.09% to 99.99% for the observed outcome. However, the model does not perform well in the lowest and the 2nd deciles. This could be that the some of the mixed attack types in the KDD-cup 1999 data were not be captured by the 16-variable model.

Residual Analysis

Residual analysis is another key component for evaluating a model performance. Usually, a high R^2 value does not guarantee that the model fits the data well. A residual is the difference between the observed response and predicted response, which can be plotted to visually detect outliers, and observations with extremely large residuals. Residual analysis may lead to the development of separate models for different types of conditions. For logistic regression, it is typical to use the standardized difference between the observed and expected probabilities. Let us consider a simple linear regression model

$$Y_i = \beta_0 + \beta_1 x_{i1} + \beta_2 x_{i2} + \cdots + \beta_k x_{ik} + \varepsilon_i$$

where β_0 and β_k are parameters to be estimated from the sample data, y_i is the observed response, and ε_i contains deviations that are assumed to be independent and normally distributed $\varepsilon_i \sim N(0,\sigma)$. Let $\hat{\beta}_0$ and $\hat{\beta}_k$ be the estimated parameters so the estimated regression line is given by:

$$\hat{Y}_i = \hat{\beta}_0 + \hat{\beta}_1 x_{i1} + \hat{\beta}_2 x_{i2} + \cdots + \hat{\beta}_k x_{ik},$$

and as the residuals are given by:

$$e_i = Y_i - (\hat{\beta}_0 + \hat{\beta}_1 x_{i1} + \hat{\beta}_2 x_{i2} + \cdots + \hat{\beta}_k x_{ik}). \tag{12-21}$$

The e_i come from the data and correspond to the model deviations ε_i that come from the population. We assume that e_i has the following attributes: (1) normally distributed with mean 0, and $e_i \sim N(0, \sigma)$, and (2) the variance σ is constant, and independent. Thus, for OLS regression, we can simply plot the residuals to check the performance of a model.

However, residuals in logistic regression are different with the OLS that we assume the variance of e_i is a constant and does not depend on the conditional mean. In logistic regression, with the binary response variable, e_i follow a binomial distribution and the variance depends on the conditional mean rather than a constant.

Let N be the total number of observations, and let k be the total number of predictor variables. Also, let J be the total number of covariate patterns from the combination of k variables among the N observations in a dataset, where $J \leq N$, and let m_j, $j = 1, 2, \ldots, J$, be the total number of observations having covariate pattern j, where

$$\sum m_j = N.$$

Finally, let y_j and $\hat{y}_j$ be total number of positive responses of the observed response variable and the predicted probability of a positive response with covariate pattern j, respectively. The Pearson residual for logistic regression is defined as follows

$$r(y_j, \hat{y}_j) = \frac{y_j - m_j \hat{y}_j}{\sqrt{m_j \hat{y}_j (1 - \hat{y}_j)}}. \qquad (12\text{-}22)$$

Figure 12.7 Distribution of Pearson residuals (excluded outliners) in Example 12.8

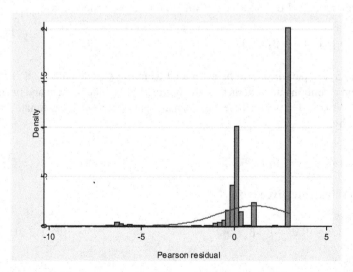

The Pearson residuals represent the contribution of each observation to the Pearson χ^2. In practice the standardized Pearson residuals that have a standard deviation of 1 is often used. Residuals may be plotted to detect outliers visually.

Example 12.8→Residual Analysis in Logistic Regression. Let us use Stata to illustrate the residual analysis. After we fit the 16-variable model with the KDD-cup training sample as shown in section of Sensitivity and Specificity, we can use the *predict* command to obtain the Pearson residual and check its distribution (Display 12.10). We can also obtain the standardized Pearson residuals by using the *rstandard* option.

Display 12.10
Residual analysis using Stata

```
. predict r,residuals
. (1 missing value generated)
. sum r,d

                           Pearson residual
-----------------------------------------------------------------
        Percentiles      Smallest
  1%     -6.363614       -1682.812
  5%      -.9559199      -216.1205
 10%      -.2690839       -64.12703    Obs             494020
 25%       .0194335       -61.84486    Sum of Wgt.     494020

 50%       .960283                     Mean           1.363862
                         Largest       Std. Dev.      5.304467
 75%      2.788038        96.5078
 90%      2.788038        96.5078      Variance       28.13737
 95%      2.788038        96.5078      Skewness      -54.90261
 99%      2.788038        96.5078      Kurtosis       20739.18
```

As we can see from the results above, there are a number of outliers in the data. When we exclude the outliers, for example, restricting the residual values within the 1st and 99th percentiles, the distribution pattern does not undergo substantial change; the mean and SD are 1.11 and 1.92, respectively. Figure 12.7 shows the distribution graphically.

An ideally fitted logistic model will have a mean approximately equal to 0 and a variance value around 1 for both the Pearson residuals and deviance residuals (Hosmer & Lemeshow, 2000). It is not surprising that the above model does not fit well because we may never be able to fit a perfect model with TCP/IP data alone.

SUMMARY

In this chapter we have discussed the procedures and methods to evaluate data and classification results. We discussed reliability and validity tests for assessing the goodness of data. We do not consider the data to be sufficiently reliable if we find that the data is incomplete, inaccurate or inconsistent based on the kappa statistic measurement and data agreement between two datasets. If the data is not reliable, using such data would most likely lead to an incorrect or unintentional message, and the results based on such data will have a significant amount of limitations. Similarly, we may not be able to use the collected data if the variables in the data are not sufficiently valid. Finally, we should not consider the data to be good quality if we find that the data does not satisfy the basic attributes described in Section Data Reliability, Validity, and Quality.

We also examined the use of sensitivity, specificity, positive predictive value, negative predictive value, and misclassification for assessing classification, and the use of ROC, Person χ^2 test of goodness-of-fit and other measures for assessing model performances. Sensitivity needs to be given first priority for a highly secure system and specificity should be considered for a highly efficient system or when there are limitations on resources. In general, fitting data to a regression model runs a basic risk of over-fitting the model. Strategies are available for avoiding this risk including, for example, using random samples in training and testing, using more than one testing sample, and restricting the number of predictor variables. While the demand for improving the performances of intrusion detection and intrusion prevention systems has increased significantly, the topics discussed in this chapter are vital to the development of robust intrusion detection and prevention systems.

REFERENCES

Akaike, H. (1974). *A new look at the statistical model identification. IEEE Transactions on Automatic Control 19(6), 716–723.*

Aven, T. (2005). *Foundations of risk analysis: A knowledge and decision-oriented perspective,* New York: Wiley.

Bamber, D. (1975). The area above the ordinal dominance graph and the area below the receiver operating characteristic graph. *Journal of Mathematical Psychology, 12,* 387-415.

Cox, D.R. and E. J. Snell (1989). *Analysis of binary data (2nd edition).* London: Chapman & Hall.

DeLong, E. R., DeLong, D. M. and Clarke-Pearson, D. L. (1988). Comparing the areas under two or more correlated receiver operating curves: A nonparametric approach. *Biometrics, 44,* 837-845.

Elkan, C. (2000). Results of the KDD'99 classifier learning contest. *ACM Transactions on Information and System Security, 3(4),* 262-294.

Hanley, J. A., and McNeil, B. J. (1982). The meaning and use of the area under a receiver operating characteristic (ROC) curve. *Radiology, 143,* 839-843.

Hosmer, D.W. & Lemeshow, S. (2000). *Applied logistic regression (2nd Edition).* New York: Wiley.

Kirk, J. and Miller, M.L. (1987). *Reliability and validity in qualitative research.* Sage Publications Inc.

Jizba, R. (2000). Measuring search effectiveness. Retrieved November 2, 2006, from http://www. hsl.creighton.edu/hsl/Searching/Recall-Precision.html

Nagelkerke, N. J. D. (1991). A note on a general definition of the coefficient of determination. *Biometrika, 78(3),* 691-692.

O'Connel, A.A. (2006). *Logistic regression models for ordinal response variables.* Thousand Oaks: Sage.

Pepe, M. S. (2003). *The statistical evaluation of medical tests for classification and prediction.* London: Oxford University Press.

Wang, Y. & Cannady, J. (2005). Develop a composite risk score to detect anomaly intrusion. In *Proceedings of the IEEE SoutheastCon 2005,* (pp.445-449).

Zhang, D., & Lu, G. (2002). Improving retrieval performance of Zernike moment descriptor on affined shapes. Retrieved December 23, 2004, from http://personal.gscit.monash.edu.au/~dengs/resource/papers/icme02a.pdf

About the Author

Yun Wang, PhD, is a senior biostatistician and information specialist at the Center for Outcomes Research and Evaluation, Yale University and Yale-New Haven Health System, and a consultant at Qualidigm. He has degrees in mathematics, computer science, information system, and criminal law with concentration in criminal statistics. His research interests include developing large complex information systems and applying statistical modeling techniques for information analyses, information security, and patient private protection.

Index

Symbols

1999 KDD-cup data 70

A

achievable benchmark of performance 421
analysis of variance 264
anomaly-free patterns, assessing 292
assessing for normality 145
assess model performance 447

B

Bayesian methods 36
behavior pattern data 69
behavior patterns, changes in 267
bivariate analysis 221
bivariate association, measure of 221
bootstrapping approach 252

C

categorical variables, fitting and graphing 139
clustering data, analysis of 253
cluster sampling 197
computer network traffic 60
control charts for proportion 413
correlation analysis 223
cross-sectional data 117

D

data, centering 153
data contents 125
data explanatory analysis 124
data normalizing 146
data reliability 428
data structure detection 173
data transformation 144
Defense Advanced Research Projects Agency (DARPA) 70
demographic data 68
density estimation 349
descriptive analysis 125
discrete and continuous variables, fitting and graphing 135
dispersion 133
distribution, binomial 112
distribution, normal 110
distribution, poisson 114

F

factor analysis 173

G

generalized linear methods 306
goodness of classification 435

H

Hidden Markov Model 359
hierarchical cluster analysis 370
Hierarchical Generalized Linear Model
    287

I

inear discriminant analysis (LDA) 333
interval estimates 399
intrusion, detection and prevention 9
intrusion detection 172
item response theory (IRT) 280

K

k-means clustering 377
k-nearest neighbor (KNN) 316
k-nearest neighbor classification 317
Kerberos logs 60

L

latent class model 352
linear discriminant analysis 333
linear regression modeling analysis 232
logistic regression 306
longitudinal data 119

M

masquerading user data 90
MATLAB 55
mean and frequency 128
measuring similarity 365
misclassification 441
MIT-DARPA 70
modeling methods, linear and nonlinear 14
model time to event 240
multidimensional modeling 379
multidimensional scaling 383
multiple linear regression method 232
multiple logistic regression 234

N

naïve Bayesian classifier 323
network data 104

network data modules 116
network security, brief history of 3
network traffic surveillance 296
non-parametric methods 408
nonparametric methods 316

O

ordinary least squares (OLS) 232
outliers 133

P

packet, flow and session 61
panel data 120
parametric methods 408
percentiles 415
poisson regression 310
predicative ability 451
principal component analysis 183
principal components analysis 380
probability, and interval estimate 419
probability models 349
probit regression 313
profiling models 286
publicly available data 70

Q

qualitative variables 106
quantitative variables 106

R

R 48
R, attributes 53
R, running 52
random forest 339
random forests (RF) classification 333
random variables 105
ranking 415
receiver operating characteristic (ROC)
    curve 439
regression trees 326
reliability test 428
residual analysis 453
robustness association 249

S

S-Plus 54
sample, what and how to 189
sample size 199
sample size, estimating 201
sample size, simulation on 203
sampling bias 199
sampling network traffic 188
sampling variability 199
SAS, running 41
SAS system 37
SAS system, attributions 44
score, based on regression models 276
score, by pre-existing knowledge 277
scoring methods 276
self-organizing maps 388
Semi-Item Response Model 280
sensitivity 436
sequence data, fitting and graphing 142
similarity models 365
simple network management protocol
    (SNMP) 60
simple random sampling (SRS) 190
simulation 403
SPAM-email data 77
specificity 436
Stata 45
Stata, attributes 47
Stata, running 46
statistical approaches, in practice 14
statistical control chart 411
statistical packages 54

statistical test of an association 228
stratified sampling 194
support vector machines (SVM) 333, 336
system-specific data 60

T

TCP/IP data 62
transmission control protocol/Internet
    protocol (TCP/IP) 60

U

uncertainty, analysis of 398
upper and lower control bounds 411
user-specific data 65
user interface, R 49
user interface, SAS 37
user interface, Stata 45

V

validity 428
validity check 431
variable distributions 109
variables 104
variables, response, predictor and latent
    107
visualizing analysis 134

W

Web sequence data 65, 78
WinBUGS 56